DATE DUE			

From Locke to Saussure
*Essays on the Study of Language
and Intellectual History*

Princeton University and the McKnight Foundation have provided partial support for the publication of this book. The University of Minnesota Press gratefully acknowledges this assistance.

From Locke to Saussure

Essays on the Study of Language and Intellectual History

Hans Aarsleff

University of Minnesota Press □ Minneapolis

Copyright © 1982 by the University of Minnesota.
All rights reserved.
Published by the University of Minnesota Press,
2037 University Avenue Southeast, Minneapolis, MN 55414
Printed in the United States of America.
Second printing, 1983

Library of Congress Cataloging in Publication Data

Aarsleff, Hans.
   From Locke to Saussure.

   Includes index.
   1. Languages—Philosophy—History—Addresses,
essays, lectures. 2. Linguistics—History—Addresses,
essays, lectures. I. Title.
P106.A2 1981   401   81-10428
ISBN 0-8166-0964-0   AACR2
ISBN 0-8166-0967-5 (pbk.)

The University of Minnesota
is an equal-opportunity
educator and employer.

To the memory of
Richard P. Blackmur

Die grossen Worte aus den Zeiten, da
Geschehn noch sichtbar war, sind nicht für uns.
Wer spricht von Siegen? Überstehn ist alles.

Preface

This volume contains fourteen essays on the study of language and intellectual history, from the rise of science in the seventeenth century to the publication of Saussure's *Cours de linguistique générale* early in this century. The first essays were written when the history of linguistics was barely known, let alone understood and recognized; but by the time I wrote the recent essays, two journals had come into existence to meet the new demand. It is exciting to have had a share in this development from the start. Today there can be no doubt that the history of the study of language makes both a legitimate subject in its own right and a contribution to our understanding of intellectual history. In this respect it resembles the history of science, which has given a strong impulse to my own work.

The essays are linked by an overall plan which I have had in mind from the beginning. This, as well as my main themes and arguments, is set forth in the Introduction, and I hope that those interested in the full scope of the book will begin with the Introduction before turning to the individual essays. In the original versions all quotations from Latin, French, and German texts were given in those languages. They have here been replaced by English translations, which are mine except where otherwise noted. All translations from Swedish and Danish are my own.

Since Leibniz figures prominently in some of these essays, readers may wish to know that there is now a good English text of the *New Essays on Human Understanding,* translated and edited with useful notes by Peter Remnant and Jonathan Bennett.

I wish to thank my friends Jonathan Arac, David Bromwich, Craig Christy, Anthony Grafton, Eugene Hill, and Michael Seidel for giving helpful advice on the Introduction. I am also grateful to the publishers and editors of the journals and volumes in which the essays appeared for permission to reprint them here. The original place of publication is noted on the opening page of each essay.

This volume would not have appeared without the initiative and encouragement of the University of Minnesota Press. It makes me especially happy that the volume is published by the Press of the great university where I spent my formative years in this country in the 1950s.

Hans Aarsleff
October 1981

Contents

Introduction 3

Leibniz on Locke on Language 42

The Study and Use of Etymology in Leibniz 84

The History of Linguistics and Professor Chomsky 101

Locke's Reputation in Nineteenth-Century England 120

The Tradition of Condillac: The Problem
 of the Origin of Language in the Eighteenth Century
 and the Debate in the Berlin Academy before Herder 146

Condillac's Speechless Statue 210

Thomas Sprat 225

John Wilkins 239

An Outline of Language-Origins Theory since the Renaissance 278

Bréal vs. Schleicher: Reorientation in Linguistics
 during the Latter Half of the Nineteenth Century 293

Wilhelm von Humboldt and the
 Linguistic Thought of the French *Idéologues* 335

Taine and Saussure 356

Wordsworth, Language, and Romanticism 372

Bréal, "la sémantique," and Saussure 382

Index 401

From Locke to Saussure
Essays on the Study of Language
and Intellectual History

Introduction

The essays in this collection are devoted to what is commonly called the history of linguistics. They were published over the last twenty years in books and journals, which, though not obscure, have made access difficult. They are now for the first time brought together in response both to the recent sharp rise of interest in the subject and to the wish of many to have these essays in a single volume that makes them readily available. A glance at their titles in the table of contents will show that they deal with topics that cover the last three centuries, from Locke and his century to Saussure in ours. Though they may seem to present a bewildering variety of subjects, they are in fact linked by a single plan and by common themes that constitute the historical framework of the modern study of language. Agreeing with Condillac and Saussure that language is the first human and social institution, I wish to restore the study of language to its rightful place in intellectual history. This reorientation opens the way for something that has not hitherto been possible: we can begin to understand the role that the study of language has played in literature, criticism, religious and social thought, science, pedagogy, political ideologies, and philosophy; and to see those interrelations as something more than a scattering of local encounters to be met in ad-hoc fashion where they seem to occur. Intellectual history is lame without the study of language. Since my essays make a contribution to interdisciplinary study, they should prove useful for students in a number of fields, including comparative literature.

It is the aim of this introduction to explain the plan and argument that tie the essays together to form a whole. I shall first tell how they came to be written, and make some remarks on method and procedure.

I shall then give an account of the central theme, from Locke and Condillac to Saussure. I shall close with a section on the interrelations of language and science in the early part of the nineteenth century, with attention also to some of Balzac's novels.

I

Let me start by considering two fairly simple questions about my approach to the study of language. 'History of linguistics' has come to be the accepted term for the subject of most of these essays. The term is now so widely current and comprehensive that there is no need to abandon it. But one could on good grounds argue that 'history of linguistics' be reserved for the study of what linguists actually do with language in their detailed work, with sound changes, morphology, etymology, syntax, and the like. This is the craft of linguistics, and it has been the object of many useful publications. I doubt, however, that a coherent history of this craft can be pushed back behind the creation of comparative and historical philology as academic disciplines in the early decades of the nineteenth century. Though an interesting subject, this history is not my concern, for reasons that I think will be clear to the reader. One could call my subject 'reflections on language' or 'the philosophy of language,' but these terms have an air of pretension, suggesting among other things that the study of language is several separate modes of study. I do not think that is the case. There is no need to quarrel over terms. Whatever we call it, I am committed to the view that the study of language is unitary. No coherent history of the study of language is possible unless we see it that way.

The second question is this. I pay little attention to *grammaire générale*, universal grammar, and 'Cartesian linguistics.' Whatever the history of that subject, it has not until recently been a serious matter for contention, though it may for periods have been forgotten or ignored. There is ample proof that the Port-Royal grammar and logic were accepted by Locke, who quoted them often with approval. Leibniz certainly was in a good position to know the grammar, but he paid only the slightest attention to it. And around 1900, Antoine Meillet remarked that the child in the acquisition of language creates the entire grammar without the least assistance. I am concerned with the acquired part of language, for it is this part that has caused widely divergent interpretations and in the process has changed literary theory as well as the conception of man's nature, of the right procedure in science, and much else. It is the study of the acquired part of language that has had a history of change with significant consequences.

My interest in the subject goes back to the late 1950s when I was working on a dissertation for the English Department at the University of Minnesota. In those days there was no interest in the history of linguistics. It was generally agreed that this history had been definitively settled by the works of four great scholars—Rudolf von Raumer, Theodor Benfey, Holger Pedersen, and Vilhelm Thomsen—and it was their history that went into the textbook-preface accounts in general works on the study of language. Scholarly, comprehensive, and packed with information, their four books agreed in two fundamental respects: the modern study of language was created in the second decade of the nineteenth century by such figures as Bopp, Rask, and Grimm; its archetype was comparative and historical Indo-European philology; and all language study before that date was irrelevant or prescientific, to be treated, if at all, only in annalistic fashion as a series of fumbling anticipations of what progress had at last brought into the light of day. Second, all four scholars agreed that Germany was the home and source of language study; thus the history of the discipline became also the history of its academic institutionalization.

There was no room for the philosophy of language. The only work that mattered was technical, detailed, and academic. With the method settled once and for all, speculation on major issues was both harmful and irrelevant. In 1902 Thomsen mentioned Herder's prize-essay on the origin of language and Horne Tooke's *Diversions of Purley* as typical examples of the eighteenth-century mode. He granted that they might have some importance in the history of ideas, but he also firmly believed that they had little to do with the study of language and that they had not, either directly or indirectly, moved it one inch forward. Being subjective speculations, they were bound to miscarry for lack of any concept of philological empiricism, of historical principles, and of the life of language in general. A few years later Holger Pedersen wrote a review of the early parts of Adolf Noreen's innovative *Vårt Språk*, which paid much attention to theoretical questions, chiefly in the opening chapter of the general introduction to this very large work. On this chapter Pedersen remarked: "Incidentally, a chapter on the classification of linguistic science seems to me out of place in a grammar. Let us develop the science, then its natural organization will automatically become obvious." With this faith in 'natural organization' theory and method were unnecessary; they were not the observer's problem.

In its own terms this history remains useful, but only as an account of the achievements of a particular period, which in fact was quite short. Even on its own terms I felt some doubt that it could be maintained. Wilhelm von Humboldt, for instance, wrote to Bopp that he had reason to believe that Bopp's *Conjugationssystem* (1816) owed something to the universal grammatical principles of Silvestre de Sacy, who had been Bopp's teacher in Paris. And in 1960 Paul Diderichsen showed that the early formation of Rask's thought owed much to the eighteenth-century orientation of his teachers and that Rask in fact remained unimpressed by Romantic thought. But in the substantial monograph of 1960 Diderichsen paid no attention whatever to Turgot, though his article on etymology in the French *Encyclopédie* is given prominence by Rask. I pointed this out in correspondence, and four years later Diderichsen wrote an article on Rask in which citation from Turgot occupied several pages, with the observation that Turgot in many ways had a better grasp of the subject than Rask. It would seem likely that Diderichsen overlooked Rask's emphasis on Turgot because the familiar and settled history had no room for him. That history began after 1800, and it had nothing to do with French thought.

Arens's great anthology of texts in the history of linguistics did much to change this view, but chiefly because of its wide chronological coverage rather than any radical revision. German scholarship still formed the core, previous work was still only a prelude, and eighteenth-century philosophy—typically in the treatment of Condillac—was still misrepresented in familiar fashion. Turgot had no place in the first edition in 1955; he was still absent in the second edition published in 1969.

I have more recently seen that the standard history has had an equally confining effect at the other end of the nineteenth century. If the linguistic thought of Saussure's *Cours* is to be accommodated, then its origins must be found in the Bopp-Schleicher tradition that Saussure knew so well, and more particularly in the early *Mémoire* on the Indo-European vowel system, which gave Saussure the highest credentials within that mode of study. This has been argued and is in fact the accepted view. But in the recent essays on Schleicher, Bréal, Taine, and Saussure, I have tried to show why this view is unconvincing. Saussure owes a very great deal to Bréal and Taine, who were both proponents of that revival of eighteenth-century thought which is the central feature of the late nineteenth-century reaction against the Romantic tradition in European thought, and not least in language study. Taine of course had no place in the history at all since he was not a linguist, and Bréal has remained unread or misunderstood, for reasons I have suggested in the essay on "Bréal, 'la sémantique,' and Saussure."

Thus, even on its own terms, the standard history does not work. It works only for the closely controlled academic procedures in the period it was designed to cover. It is the internal history of an institutionalized professorial craft.

This was my problem as I was trying to find my bearings in the late 1950s. It seemed to me that something that could be called a history of the study of language would need to have room for much more, both in previous centuries and within the nineteenth century. Perhaps because I was working with English materials, I was in a position to become especially aware of this. Horne Tooke, for instance, working in the late decades before 1800, became very influential in England. He was taken up by the Utilitarians, and for James Mill's *Analysis of the Phenomena of the Human Mind* (1829) Tooke supplied the foundation of the Utilitarian philosophy of mind, which was a psychology. His materialist etymological philosophy was also the lexicographical basis of Charles Richardson's *New Dictionary of the English Language*. It was the desire to counter the ideology of this successful dictionary that during the 1850s gave the impetus to the preparation of a new English dictionary, the work that eventually became the *Oxford English Dictionary*. It was in fact a characteristic move against what was considered the deplorable and shallow philosophy of the eighteenth century.

This reaction, incidentally, is a reminder that the quarrel between the nineteenth century and its predecessor was waged on philosophical and ideological grounds, with Locke, the *philosophes*, and the Utilitarians pitted against the Victorian or rather the European sage. The rejection of eighteenth-century linguistic thought is only one aspect of this confrontation. The enormous popularity of comparative-historical philology no doubt owes much to the fact that it became the arsenal of the sage. I have dealt with this confrontation in the essay on Locke's reputation in the nineteenth century, and I shall say more about it in the last section of this introduction. A viable history of the study of language ought to be able to accommodate such events: they are part of history.

The title of my dissertation was "The Study of Language in England 1780-1860," completed in the spring of 1960 and later, substantially changed, published under that title. It forms a complement to these essays, with which it shares a method I have found reasons to elaborate but not to alter. In the introduction to the book I explained what I had in mind: "The task of gaining the proper depth of historical perspective within a given period can only be satisfied by seeking to recapture all relevant contemporary knowledge without reference to or misguidance by the later accumulation of scholarly opinion and assignment of influences, which are far too often and too easily accorded the status of unquestioned doctrine. My work is an essay in the application of that method. . . . I have deliberately avoided any attempt to force the subject matter into the molds of current doctrine and terminology. Similarly, the history of Paracelsism cannot be written in current medical terminology, and the history of medieval mechanics would be of little use if written according to the canons of quantum mechanics." While working on the dissertation, my own thoughts were developing along parallel lines with those that were being traced in the history of science, revealed with éclat in Thomas Kuhn's *Structure of Scientific Revolutions*. Both in science and in language study there was a need to revise nineteenth-century positivist history. I have since kept in touch with both the history of science and the sociology of science, the latter concern showing most readily perhaps in the essay on Bréal and Schleicher. I have published nine entries in the *Dictionary of Scientific Biography*, of which the two longest, on Thomas Sprat and John Wilkins, are reprinted here. Science and language have always kept close relations.

In the introduction to the book I also cited two authorities with whom I still agree: Paul Oskar Kristeller and Alexandre Koyré. Kristeller wrote: "The historian of science will do well to recognize that the positive scientific discoveries of the past were never unrelated to the theoretical and philosophical assumptions of the investigating scientist, whether they were true or false from our point of view, whether consciously expressed or tacitly accepted by him." And Koyré made this wonderfully succinct statement about a common practice: "The mania of the search for 'forerunners' has often falsified the history of philosophy beyond remedy." If there is any freshness and innovation in my work, it stems in large measure from the effort to follow the principles I developed in the late 1950s.

Since Horne Tooke claimed to be rewriting Locke's philosophy in purely linguistic terms, the dissertation explored "the seventeenth and eighteenth-century background" in a long opening chapter with subheadings on "language and the new learning," "philosophical language," "words," and "the origin of language." It was the preparation of this chapter that gave me the knowledge of arguments and figures that became my subjects in the next years. It alerted me to the importance of such men as John Wilkins, Boyle, Locke, Leibniz, Berkeley,

Hume, Condillac, du Marsais, de Brosses, James Harris, Lord Monboddo, Thomas Reid, Adam Smith, Dugald Stewart, Herder, and many others, as well as to the prominent roles of the Royal Society and the French *Encyclopédie* in these matters. In the book this chapter was much shorter, with concentration on Condillac's *Essai sur l'origine des connaissances humaines* (1746), which was here for the first time placed in its central position in the history of language study. The *Essai* is the first statement and source of the philosophy that Condillac argued in subsequent works, especially in the *Course of Study for the Prince of Parma* under such titles as "Grammar," "The Art of Writing," "The Art of Reasoning," and "The Art of Speaking," all of which clearly enough reveal their linguistic relevance while the title of the *Essai*, characteristically, was not thought to do so. With the late publication date of the *Course of Study* in 1775, inattention to the *Essai* has had the odd effect of making Condillac appear much less original than he was. For in the meantime Diderot, Rousseau, Turgot, and others had in publication advanced arguments which they found in Condillac but which came to be credited to them instead of him, though both Rousseau and Diderot made a point of acknowledging their debt to Condillac, who in fact remarked that he was being plagiarized. Thus placing the *Essai* in its proper context also has significant consequences for intellectual history.

In "Leibniz on Locke on Language" I tried to identify the positions of the two philosophers, to locate them in the seventeenth-century background, and on this basis to explain the reasons for disagreement. The effort taught me a great deal about the seventeenth century, about the Adamic language, and about the relevance of language to science and epistemology at large. It became clear to me that Locke in behalf of the new science was directing his argument against the theory of knowledge and the nature of man contained in the Adamic language doctrine. Previously missing—with some odd consequences for the history of philosophy—this background, once identified, cast new light on our understanding of the *Essay*. It is in the Adamic doctrine, for instance, that we find the doctrine of innate notions, rather than in Descartes. The writing of this essay also made me see clearly that the pedagogically convenient and ideologically loaded separate-box distinction between rationalism and empiricism is unfounded, as Leibniz in facing Locke also realized—and Leibniz in fact argued more strongly against Descartes than against Locke. If anything, Locke is a rationalist empiricist, to cite the term Durkheim used approvingly to indicate Taine's importance for his generation. The essay on Locke's reputation in the nineteenth century analyzes why and how this distinction came to be made and accepted. In 1968 I dealt with a debated question in Locke's political philosophy in "The State of Nature and the Nature of Man in Locke," an essay that also has a linguistic dimension.

I returned to the background of the essay on Locke and Leibniz in five lectures given in the spring of 1964 for the Program in the History and Philosophy of Science at Princeton, under the title "Language, Man, and Knowledge in the Sixteenth and Seventeenth Centuries." There is a copy in the Library of the Warburg Institute. They especially explored neo-Platonic and cabbalistic linguistic thought, some aspects of seventeenth-century German poetry and mysticism, the philosophical language and efforts to "repair the ruins of Babel," and the reaction of the Royal Society. They laid the foundations for seven entries in the *Dictionary of Scientific Biography* on Andreae, Bisterfeld, Boehme, Comenius, Sebastian Franck, Theodore Haak, and Valentin Weigel. With the exception of Haak, each of these was in his own way committed to linguistic mysticism and the universalist or encyclopedic arguments that form part of the microcosm-macrocosm doctrine and its Adamicism. Here an important concept is that of etymology, the study and use of which I explored with reference to Leibniz in an essay written in 1966. This subject is especially open to misunderstanding since later canons of etymology have made error and nonsense of what the seventeenth century was trying to do. It is a good example of how views that became accepted much later can completely block our understanding of what in this case was chiefly a philosophical problem about man's nature and the origin of language. Seventeenth-century discussions of etymology were not stupid, but different.

The next essay was "The Tradition of Condillac." It may be the best known of these essays, no doubt because it addresses itself to problems that were already familiar, especially in the history of German thought and literature. It argued that German interest in the origin and philosophy of language, as it unfolded in Herder's prize-essay, was not a native product but stemmed from the efforts of Maupertuis, then the newly appointed president of the Berlin Academy, to enliven philosophy in Germany by giving it a basis in Condillac's thought. Maupertuis's own essays were followed by others, which via Michaëlis' prize-essay *On the Influence of Opinions on Language and of Language on Opinions* led directly to Herder's essay. In addition to exploring the main features of Condillac's linguistic thought, my essay established a connection between French and German philosophy. This essay also had a natural place for a section on "Locke, Condillac, and Professor Chomsky," which was soon developed in the article on

"The History of Linguistics and Professor Chomsky" in the days when 'Cartesian linguistics' was the rage. This is the only example of significant overlap among these essays, but since the section in the Condillac essay forms an integral part of its subject, I thought the section should be retained. I explored the matter again in an essay on "'Cartesian Linguistics': History or Fantasy?" which also details Locke's uses of Port-Royal.

There would now seem to be a general agreement that 'Cartesian linguistics' was "a memorable error," but it did immeasurably more for the history of linguistics than any other publication. The book could hardly have been written without doctrinaire acceptance of the nineteenth-century distinction between rationalism and empiricism, by now conventional but without foundation in the texts at issue. It was to explore how this opinion ever came to be held that I wrote the essay on Locke's reputation, though I deliberately made no mention of that motive. I have already suggested how much I gained from that essay in my understanding of the conflict between the century of Condillac and the century of, say, Joseph de Maistre, Victor Cousin, and Max Müller. Here is yet another example that intellectual history and political ideology are indispensable for an understanding of language study. This conviction was confirmed when some years later I turned to linguistics in the latter part of the nineteenth century, a period in which eighteenth-century thought was being revived, in language study as in other subjects, as part of the reaction against depreciation of Locke, Condillac, and their followers. For somewhat similar reasons Kant was at the same time being revived in German neo-Kantianism, but owing to Kant's well-known indifference to any philosophy of language, this revival could not have the same effect as the one that occurred in France.

With the benefit of this insight I returned to Condillac in 1972 in the essay on his speechless statue. That statue, from the *Traité des sensations*, has always been the *pièce de résistance* in the denigration of Condillac as a shallow, materialist philosopher who wished to reduce Locke's reflection to mere sensation. Objections to that interpretation have often been raised, even in the nineteenth century, but could never prevail against the ideological attraction of so easy and splendid a target as the materialist Condillac. The statue, it was argued, proved that the senses alone were "enough to account for the richest intellectual and emotional experiences of man." Since Condillac made language the condition for human knowledge and intellectual development, I wished to show that the mute statue could not possibly sustain the argument it was made to support, and that it proved, on the contrary, how man's fundamental reason and reflection alone make speech and language possible.

During the next years I wrote the two interrelated essays on Thomas Sprat and John Wilkins. Though biographically oriented, they belong to intellectual history in their effort to gain a better understanding of the philosophy of the Royal Society and the new science. In the Sprat essay I tried to show how the *History of the Royal Society* came to be written as an ideological defense designed to ensure the reputation and English patronage of the young society. It did so chiefly by ignoring the embarrassing background of the society in the early London meetings in the mid-1640s and by angrily rejecting any imputation of French influence. Here Bacon was for the first time made the patron saint of English science. Sprat's famous work pertains to the sociology of science and learning rather than to history. In fact it is a mistake to read it as a history in our sense, for that term in the title had the contemporary and more original meaning that is also illustrated when Boyle writes of "the history of cold" and "the history of the spring of air"—that is, investigation and description.

To ensure the right effect, Sprat's *History* was carefully directed by the society, chiefly by Wilkins who knew so much about what it was useful to say and not to say. Since Wilkins was the key figure in the formation of the society, his biography also becomes the story of its background, orientation, and the secret debts it incurred. He was the successful proponent and defender of Copernican astronomy and of Kepler and Galileo, a position that was incompatible with Bacon's rejection of Copernicus. The Baconianism of the new science is not argued by Wilkins in his influential books, which cite Bacon only rarely and merely in ceremonial and general fashion. For Wilkins, Marin Mersenne was the important figure. He kept closely informed about Mersenne's writings, and I try to show how this influence was mediated. One result of these findings is that recent arguments about the Rosicrucian origins of English science cannot be maintained. In the generation before the Royal Society Mersenne had become the powerful critic of mysticism and linguistic Adamicism owing to their incompatibility with the method of science. Here he was also arguing against Bacon's belief that we would eventually be able to "look into the natures of things." In the context of the new science Mersenne was the first to formulate the linguistic arguments that Wilkins shared and which later took form in Locke's *Essay*. Already in 1625 Mersenne had said in *La Vérité des sciences*:

> But whatever phenomena we study in philosophy, it is pointless to think
> that we could penetrate the nature of bodies or whatever occurs inside

them, for our senses, without which we cannot know anything, see only what is exterior, and no matter what we do, we shall never arrive at the point of making our intellect equal to the nature of things; that is why I think Bacon's design is impossible, and that his teaching will lead to nothing more than new experiences, which one can easily explain by ordinary philosophy.

This is a rejection of essentialism, and it looks forward to Locke's concept of nominal essence. Wilkins fully shared these principles, but late in life, oddly, produced his largest work, the *Essay towards a Real Character and a Philosophical Language*, in an effort to "repair the ruins of Babel" in ways that conflicted with his earlier and influential writings. His *Essay* is therefore an anomaly, and the scientists were unimpressed. Locke for his part rejected the philosophical language as a chimera.

Shortly before I wrote the essay on Wilkins I did a long review-article that concentrated on "the survival of eighteenth-century French philosophy before Saussure." This was the first time that I dealt with Bréal, Taine, and Saussure and with the reaction against what Bréal saw as the fifty years of language study that had been dominated by Germany. Faced with a period of revival for eighteenth-century thought, and having myself carried the history up to Condillac, Herder, and the late years of the century, I was eager to see what this revival meant for Saussure's generation. This article was an introduction to the subjects of my most recent essays. If Saussure's *Cours* was innovative by the same token that it was a reaction, it would be interesting to see what the background was, if indeed there were any. I had at no point been convinced by attempts to find the source of Saussure's thought in the Bopp-Schleicher tradition.

In "Bréal vs. Schleicher" I tried to show that Bréal's critique was directed against Schleicher's organicism and its claim that since language is an autonomous phenomenon, linguistics must also be a natural science without reference to man, mind, and society. Bréal said that the reading of Bopp and Schleicher could make one believe "that one was in fact reading a geological treatise of the world or witnessing a series of crystallizations of speech." He continued with a statement that contains the radical innovation he was advancing: "But is it possible to believe that the science we study consists only in this exterior observation of the forms of language? We do not think so. In the description of human language we must not forget man, who is at the same time both the foundation and the end, for in language everything proceeds from him and addresses itself to him." Bréal was reintroducing mentalism into linguistics, the study of function as well as of form. The history of language follows a principle that is not its own; "it always keeps in step, if not with political history, at least with the intellectual and social history of the people." Bréal had a strong social conscience. Though I don't think he ever used the phrase, language was for him a 'social institution.' He was an excellent student of the history of linguistics, which plays a prominent role in his theory. He was especially impressed by Condillac and the *idéologues*; he reacted strongly against the incipient racism of Schleicher and dismissed the idea that language history has been a process of decay from a state of perfection. He was committed to the principle of uniformitarianism, a feature that Anatole France rightly noted as a characteristic quality of Bréal's thought. For that reason Bréal stressed the need to study contemporary language, including dialects and slang, not merely the dead forms of the past. Here Bréal was perhaps, with many of his contemporaries, influenced by Claude Bernard's recent arguments for the priority of physiology over the old comparative anatomy and the mere study of bones and fossils.

In the same essay I also deal with Madvig's writings in linguistic theory, which from their start in the 1830s had argued consistently that comparative philology was only a particular mode of language study that had no right to the claim of exclusive legitimacy. For Madvig language is the work of man designed to serve the social needs of communication, it forms a system, and the linguistic sign is arbitrary; he ridiculed the doctrine of the decline and decadence of language. Bréal certainly knew of Madvig, but whether he owed him anything I have not been able to determine. Madvig did, however, think that there was a disturbing similarity between his own work and what he later read in Whitney. In any event, the closer study of Schleicher, Madvig, and Bréal supported my belief that the great tradition of comparative-historical philology is a closed episode in the history of linguistics, which of course does not mean that it has not continued to bear fruit in later years.

Bréal and some of his contemporaries, for instance Otto Jespersen, occasionally cite certain statements by Wilhelm von Humboldt with approval. I was puzzled by this since Bréal's anti-Romantic and pro-Enlightenment stance might have been expected to preclude such approval. I therefore returned to some papers I had given in the early 1970s, and the result was the essay on Humboldt and the French *idéologues*. According to all the literature, Humboldt was of the purest German water, indebted, it was said, especially to Herder and the "German movement," which it was further said was the source of the philosophy of language. The evidence does not support that view. There is nothing in the material to show that Humboldt paid any attention to Herder's prize-essay; in fact it would seem that he held a low opinion of Herder as a philosopher. But there is plenty of evidence that Humboldt during his years in Paris in the late 1790s stayed closely in touch with the *idéologues* and their linguistic thought, and it would seem beyond question that he is deeply indebted to French philosophy and the problems that were then being debated in Paris, for example about the status of Basque, linguistic anthropology, the principle of linguistic relativism, the crucial role of language in culture, and the place of language in knowledge and education.

Since the *idéologues* were followers of Condillac, the argument for Humboldt's debt to them confirmed my view of Condillac's continuing importance. Thus it was not surprising that Bréal could find statements in Humboldt that served his arguments about the omission of man in German philology. Here again the history of the study of language caused a revision of intellectual history. It also suggests that what is called Romanticism in the larger sense is not a total rejection of the Enlightenment, that we owe this belief rather to eagerness for dissociation from the philosophy that had been made responsible for the French Revolution. The division is not actual but a product of nineteenth-century ideology.

My awareness of the relations between Taine and Saussure came about almost by accident. I had begun, for other reasons, to read Taine intensely. I was soon struck by his use of Condillac, the centrality of signs in his philosophy, the analysis of the double nature of the sign with the telling illustration of the sheet of paper so unusual and never before identified outside Saussure, the concept of value, the all-important insistence on structure, and the distinction between successivity and simultaneity in historical study. With so many things coming together in a closely structured context, I saw no possibility that Saussure could have been ignorant of Taine's principles. The conceptual and terminological similarities can in fact be carried beyond what I had space to say in that essay. And given Taine's amply attested importance in the intellectual life of Paris in the 1880s when Saussure lived and worked there, there was no reason to be surprised by the similarity.

In the essay on "Bréal, 'la sémantique,' and Saussure," I returned to Bréal since I knew enough to suspect that his work was important. This even the plain facts suggested. He held the chair in comparative grammar at the Collège de France for forty years, was lifetime secretary of the Société de linguistique de Paris, the teacher and patron of linguists who did significant work, prominent in the intellectual life of Paris, on intimate terms with Renan and Taine, active on many important committees on education and educational reform on all levels, and greatly admired for his personal charm, incisive mind, and the clarity of his style. When Bréal died in 1915, Meillet said that Bréal and Saussure were the two masters who shaped the French school of linguistics, and Vendryes has written that Saussure's legendary seminars in Paris during the 1880s had a decisive effect on French linguistics, "which has re-enforced that of Michel Bréal." In a letter to Meillet, Saussure called Bréal "notre maître excellent." When not ignored, Bréal has been misrepresented. His *sémantique* has been described as a mere repetition of what a German scholar in the 1820s had called semasiology. His linguistic principles have been read only in the *Essai de sémantique*, published in 1897, though he had expounded them in teaching and publication already in the late 1860s as well as in many articles over the next thirty years, a fact that is made clear in the *Essai*. As early as 1879 Bréal wrote to an Italian correspondent, "I am also preparing a book on the intellectual laws of language, on which I have been working for some years: it is what one could call 'la sémantique.'" It was his life's work to lay new foundations in linguistics on grounds other than the study of mere exterior dead forms, of what he with Saussure and many of his contemporaries called 'la phonétique.' Bréal created the term *sémantique* to point out the contrast.

My argument is this: Bréal's *sémantique* is not a particular and minor branch of linguistics; it is a *linguistique générale*. It was the answer to his never-ceasing critique of the Bopp-Schleicher tradition, the tenor of which he summed up by citing the words of Schleicher: "Languages are natural organisms which, outside the human will and subject to fixed laws, are born, grow, develop, age and die; thus they also illustrate the series of phenomena that are usually comprehended under the term life. Consequently, the science of language is a natural science." For Bréal this was meaningless talk, made possible by submission to metaphor. Bréal stated his own view in this passage:

> Language has its seat in the intellect; it cannot be conceived otherwise. If it precedes and survives us, it is because it exists in the intellect of our co-citizens as well as in ours, because it has existed before us in our parents and because we in turn transmit it to our children. It is made by the agreement of many intellects, by the consent of many wills, some living and acting, others long since vanished and dead. It does not diminish the importance of language to grant it only this ideal existence. It is, on the contrary, to place it among the number of things that occupy the first rank and exercise the most influence in the world, for it is ideal existences—religions, laws, traditions, customs—that give form to human life.

The Saussurean implications of those words are obvious. On this basis Bréal built a linguistic theory and principles that later emerged in Saussure's *Cours*. Some of these principles appear in Bréal's terminology (such as *langue, parole,* and *valeur*), whereas others are given equally distinct roles in the conceptual framework though they rarely figure in the terminology (such as structure, linearity, binary opposition, syntagmatics, and the distinction between diachrony and synchrony). Bréal obviously held that language is a social institution and that the linguistic sign is arbitrary. It is also clear that Bréal was familiar with Taine's philosophy. Saussure could without facing any conflict incur a debt to both in the preparation of the *Cours*, the great summa that gave linguistics a new beginning. Bréal anticipated much that later appeared in the thought of the neogrammarians, but he still found that they remained too closely committed to the naturalistic fallacy, for instance in the familiar doctrine of exceptionless soundlaws.

With the essay on Bréal and Saussure I arrived at the completion of my argument for the coherent tradition that reaches from the seventeenth century to the great figure who early in the present century again made the study of language relevant to all other forms of intellectual life.

Except for the unpublished manuscript on "Language, Man, and Knowledge," none of my essays had discussed the importance of language study for literary theory and practice. I had long been aware, however, that there is a close connection between these disciplines which has rarely been treated in more than desultory and conventional fashion, based on ill-founded generalization drawn at second-hand from trusted intellectual history. In "Wordsworth, Language, and Romanticism" I have tried to give an example of what can be done. The accepted view is this: in his theory of poetic diction Wordsworth rejected the poetic practice of the eighteenth century at the same time as he rejected that century's philosophy, which, it is claimed, was responsible for the practice. The corollary is that Wordsworth in some mysterious fashion was parallelling or drawing on ideas that at the same time were given expression in German Romantic thought, and that these ideas found expression chiefly in his poetry, which would then somehow, paradoxically, be at variance with his own theory. My argument is that he rejected the practice and the theory that went with it, but built his own critical theory on the innovative eighteenth-century philosophy that had given language a central role in our understanding of the ways of knowing, communication, and the potentialities of expression. This was the philosophy of Condillac and the *idéologues*, to which Wordsworth would have had access while in France and which quickly made its way into English as well. This philosophy had bared "the sad incompetence of human speech," the difficulty of ever gaining assurance that two speakers fully understand each other, but it was also a philosophy that made the mind ever active in perception and in the neverending creation and 'rectification' of language. Here lies the foundation of the expressive theory of Romantic aesthetics. It is a false nineteenth-century doctrine that Condillac had made the mind passive and inert, a mere recording device.

When Wordsworth sought escape from empty, conventional speech in the language really spoken by men, he was consistently following the principles he built on. For him true communal expression and sincerity, free from "falsehood and affectation," were paradigmatically illustrated in country epitaphs. It is a facile though popular and pedagogically convenient mistake to believe that Wordsworth was arguing for the introduction of colloquial speech into poetry and that, since his diction is often far from colloquial, he did not manage to hold things together. My argument makes it unnecessary to attribute a good deal of confusion to Wordsworth.

At the same time my argument combats the unexamined doctrine, prevalent in English studies, that Romantic thought and aesthetics have everything to do with German thought and nothing with French philosophy, a view that must be doubted on general grounds unless we are prepared to deny that French culture in the eighteenth century held the first position in Europe. We again run into difficulty owing to the estimation of the eighteenth century we have inherited from the nineteenth. Itself largely academic, this view has proved irresistibly attractive to academics and academia ever since. The nineteenth century created the divisions among disciplines and periods that are followed, with seats—on thrones and stools—for experts who rule within each box, ready to challenge all threats to the order they keep in their stalls. The divisions are treated as if they reflect the natural organization of what is there to study and know, when they were in fact introduced to serve administrative ends and the demands of personal ambition. Characteristically, during the eighteenth century when the universities counted for little, the organization of knowledge was less restrictive and thus more open to fruitful innovation. The current popularity of interdisciplinary study has inadvertently shown how difficult it is to get out of the old boxes, yet how unsatisfactory they are to their livelier occupants.

The case of Wordsworth is only an example. Several studies have, for instance, shown a close connection between the Adamic doctrine and poetic practice in the seventeenth century. Since particular speech

sounds were held to have expressive semantic content, poets structured their poems with regard to deliberate selection of words with
vowels, consonants, and combinations that suited the subject.

The poetry sought to imitate or recapture the natural perfection
of Adam's language, on the assumption that elements of that language
were still present in the poet's own language. There are excellent
studies of this practice in Swedish and German literature, but in English the subject is only beginning to gain attention. It would also
seem promising to explore the relations between Bréal's linguistic
thought and contemporary poetry, both French and English. The
relevant linguistic theory cannot simply be read out of the literary
texts or intuited from them. It is amply evident that many seventeenth-century poets studied language intensely as preparation for
the poetry they wrote, obvious in the case both of the German
'Sprachgesellschaften" and in Swedish and Danish poetry.

II

I have explained how my essays are held together by a single plan
that is designed to reveal the foundations of language study during the
last three centuries. This plan is reflected in the order of writing—and
usually also publication—which has followed the historical sequence
of the subjects. Each essay led to the next as I tried to throw light on
major themes and figures. The reader may ask if anything has been
omitted that might shatter the coherence and continuity I have tried
to establish, whether another selection of themes and figures would
not show a different pattern with equal or better right to constitute
the main tradition. I do not believe so. My conviction has two main
supports. There is first the coherence that has emerged; it could not
have been foreseen, but has all along gained often unexpected confirmation as new pieces fell into place. Thus there was nothing in the
conventional accounts that suggested Humboldt's debt to French
thought, which links him to the tradition of Condillac. And the significant revival of eighteenth-century thought in Saussure's generation
came to my attention only by extensive reading in the period. The
other support comes from my reading in the literature of the entire
period—primary, secondary, and (when possible) unpublished—undertaken to test and shape my argument and which I pursued far beyond
the canonical texts. If the sociology of science has demonstrated the
role of chance and serendipity in achievement, it is only natural to
assume that the same factors also apply in other areas of significant
innovation. The historian must seek to take those factors into account.

He must abandon the boxes and ignore the vertical columns that define traditional disciplines. Though Taine had no place in the vertical linguistic column, he all the same made a vital contribution to linguistic thought in his time.

Like Claude Bernard I believe that chance plays a role and that method or procedure arises in response to the problems and pressures of the material, to what happens in the laboratory and thinking about it. It is much like good style and clear exposition, which come about by a myriad of little decisions made along the way. "I think," said Bernard, "that blind faith in the fact that claims to silence reason is as dangerous for the experimental sciences as articles of faith based on sentiment or belief that likewise impose silence on reason. In a word, in the experimental method and elsewhere, *the only criterion is reason.*" On these grounds he argued, like Justus Liebig, against the prescriptions of Baconian method and for the need for hypotheses. The "natural organization" of the material does not come of itself, as Holger Pedersen argued against Noreen.

I have said that my work is based on wide reading also outside the canonical literature. Let me briefly explain some aspects of what this means. I have first of all tried to make myself familiar with all the writings I could possibly encompass by all the major figures, without prior assumptions about the safe selection of a few texts. I have sought to grasp the overall structure of arguments and conceptualization, even in the absence of terminological expression. Thus Locke and Condillac certainly held that language is a social institution, but they never used the term. Similarly, Bréal's argument and conceptualization prefigure Saussure's largely without the nearly compulsive terminology Saussure created—Saussure admitted the compulsion and offered a typical example when he cast about for the term that ultimately became 'sémiologie.' Among those he tried was 'signologie,' which, however, he found sounded just like 'sinologie,' unless one changed the former term to be spoken with a hard 'g,' but since that would have clouded the intended connection with 'signe,' he gave it up. Terminology is useful but also risky, for it does not always indicate what it is often hastily assumed to say. It must be tested against conceptualization. Etymology was altogether different in the seventeenth century from what it became in the nineteenth. Terminology is most useful when several terms appear together in similar contexts, as between Taine, Bréal, and Saussure. Clearly, unusual metaphors, like Taine's sheet of paper illustrating the double nature of the linguistic sign, are especially helpful.

The citation of indebtedness is to be treated with similar caution.

Condillac's debt to Locke would be obvious even if he had not acknowledged it, and so would Destutt de Tracy's to Condillac. But what Humboldt learned from the *idéologues* in Paris is never suggested by name or citation in his better-known writings. To support the argument I had to use biography, correspondence, diaries, and notebooks, which had long been ignored though in the public domain for years. Here such material was unusually important and uncommonly abundant, but I have also sought it with equal effort for other figures. Saussure never mentions Taine, rarely Bréal, but several times he gives some prominence to Gaston Paris. It has therefore been argued that Paris is much more important for Saussure than Bréal. But Paris is cited only on particular points that could not possibly have generated what was already laid out in Taine and Bréal—apart from the fact that Paris's points, on closer inspection, would seem to come from Bréal. Here the overall assessment of plausibilities—what Bernard called reason—must take precedence over the philological detail of citation. The sociology of science—in the work of Robert K. Merton, among others—has shown that mere citation is a very unreliable guide, subject to personal habits, flattery, forgetfulness, repression, or the desire for exclusion. In late nineteenth-century France, extended general treatment of the work of scholars still living and active seems even to have been avoided as a breach of good manners. Thus it has been argued that James Darmesteter's omission of Renan from his *Essais orientaux* (1893) implies a low opinion of Renan's scholarship. But as soon as Renan died, Darmesteter in the same year the essays were published wrote a glowing and no doubt sincere tribute to Renan in a long obituary in the *Journal Asiatique*. Scholars are most likely to cite the safe names, and least likely to mention those that do not fit the boxes and the vertical columns that define the integrity of the discipline. By the same token most historians are more comfortable with the philological evidence of citation than with the more telling testimony of conceptualization.

Whenever possible I have also made a point of reading widely in the contemporary periodicals without limiting myself to the professional journals. Often ignored or restricted to what by prior decision is alone assumed to be relevant, this literature is indispensable for an understanding of the intellectual quality of periods for which it is available. It reveals rising interest, emphases, controversies, changing views, methods, allegiances, and groupings, and it helps identify leading and innovative figures and ideas. For the intellectual history of France in the decades before 1900 it is immensely fruitful to read in *La Revue des Deux Mondes*, the *Revue philosophique*, the *Revue de métaphysique et morale, Mind*, the sociological journals, and many others. Such reading also shows the opposition between, on the one hand, Bréal and la Société de linguistique de Paris and its orientation, and on the other, the pugnacious assertion of traditional principles by the *Revue de linguistique*, guided by Hovelacque and Jules Vinson. Both views were heard, but the *Revue de linguistique* eventually ceased publication.

The testimony of the primary literature has throughout been my first concern. Though I have read it, I have paid much less attention to the secondary literature. I have already explained why I find the standard histories inadequate. The deeper problem is that their authority has tended to control intellectual history with regard to language. Thus it is said, for instance, that Locke did not know enough about etymology and failed to take account of onomatopeia, that Condillac lacked the benefit of Max Müller, that the German tradition owed nothing to French thought, and the like.

Readers will readily see why I cannot on most points agree with Foucault's *Les Mots et les Choses*, even granting that his orientation and interests are altogether different from mine. I agree that academic history, having made a fetish of continuities, has usually established only quasi-continuities. But I do not think continuity on the level of ideas and themes is only a surface effect so that no other course remains but to define systems of simultaneity in the manner of archeological description. Bad history is no reason for giving up history altogether. I do not agree that the history of science, intellectual history, and the history of language study cannot be more than matters of opinion.

But even taking Foucault on his own terms, I have doubts. He makes resemblance the épistémè of the sixteenth century, and replaces it with representation in the *âge classique* of the seventeenth and eighteenth centuries. I would see Adamicism as a more fundamental quality, of which resemblance is only the expression, and I find its greatest period in the seventeenth century so that the new épistémè is not in place until soon before 1700 at the earliest. Bacon may well, with Foucault, be said to have offered a critique of resemblance early in his century, but he still did not satisfy Mersenne, Wilkins, and Locke on the point that was crucial for science and the pivot of the new épistémè. Representation is a good term for one consequence of Locke's philosophy of signs, but like resemblance in Adamicism, it is a symptom rather than the real thing. Foucault makes Bopp one of the central figures in the new épistémè that came about early in the nineteenth century, carrying with it "this historical a priori which since the nineteenth century has been the nearly evident soil of our thinking." I would locate this a priori in Condillac, whose philosophy of language made time and progress the foundations of the human sciences. Foucault's archeology has no room for overlap; it is all or nothing in the period of each épistémè. I would not give the same importance to Bopp as Foucault—quite apart from the fact that Bopp's own work was comparative and typological, not historical— and I do not find that whatever happened soon after 1800 created the modern period. The re-emergence of the eighteenth century after 1850 is much too powerful to ignore. For these reasons I also find Foucault's periodizations conventional, that is, even on his terms I would structure the geological layers differently. I am also surprised that such major events as the French Revolution have no place in the scheme.

There is, incidentally, one aspect of Foucault's conceptualization that has not been noted, namely the degree to which its orientation is French, with the effect that his results cannot be so readily transferred abroad as seems generally to be assumed. This orientation shows in his choice of representative texts, but it is especially evident in his theoretical framework, which has much in common with that of Hippolyte Taine. Taine also treated periods as epochs with particular structures that made everything possible. Similar conceptualization in Taine and Foucault has caused frequent identity of terminology. The similarity is especially striking if one compares Foucault's method with Taine's analysis of the eighteenth century in *The Origins of Contemporary France*, the great work in which Taine, after 1871, without abandoning the conceptual tools he had long used, turned critic of the eighteenth century. The Revolution had been made possible, Taine argued, by the 'esprit classique,' which for all Frenchmen was like "the structure of their interior eye, the fixed form of intellect they carried with them without knowing or willing it." Taine was describing the épistémè that made everything else possible, and for him as for Foucault this mold was first of all formed by language, by what Taine in fact also called 'le discours.'

My arguments have met with some resistance, and from this I have taken heart. For many it is still hard to accept that Herder owes much to Condillac, that Humboldt is not the follower of Herder, and that the formation of Saussure's thought was not a spontaneous act of creation or a product of the Bopp-Schleicher tradition in philology. But my aim has not been to write textbook-preface history or to provide scholars with the comfort of seeing the integrity and innovative capacity of their disciplines confirmed once more. Here my work finds itself in the same situation as much recent publication in the history of science. Toward the end of "Bréal vs. Schleicher" I have said something about the heroic theory of science and the discovery fixation. I can add a passage by Hippolyte Delehaye, who foresaw that his *Légendes hagiographiques* would cause discomfort: "Recent progress in the study of hagiography has caused more than one misunderstanding. By its application to the lives of the saints, historical criticism offers nothing particularly surprising for those who are familiar with the study of texts and their interpretation; but the results have all the same not failed to upset the cherished beliefs of a great many people." I did not set out to upset beliefs, but have pursued my interest in the subject in order to see what would happen to our understanding of the history of language study.

III

In retrospect I can now trace the theme that holds my essays together to an observation that occurs in Locke's *Essay*. Locke said that speakers habitually believe that words are as good as things, "as if the name carried with it the knowledge of the species or the essence of it," thus assuming that language is a safe and simple nomenclature to the inventory of the world. This belief is a serious mistake, however. Words are about ideas, not about things; but the mistake is tenacious, "for without this *double conformity* of their *ideas*, they find they should both think amiss of things themselves, and talk of them unintelligibly to others." Locke's rejection of the double conformity gathers the basic features of his philosophy of language, which forms an integral part of the epistemological argument of the *Essay*. Locke offered a theory of knowledge for the new science of nature then taking shape in the work and aspirations of "the Royal Society of London for the Promotion of Natural Knowledge." Already in the first draft of the *Essay*, in 1671, Locke had noted the double-conformity problem, followed by these words: "And therefore in the discourse I have here made concerning humane intellect I could not avoid saying a great deal concerning words because so apt and usual to be mistaken for things." The problem was the "cheat of words," to cite a common contemporary phrase. The answer was a critique that laid the foundation of the modern study of language.

Here Locke stood on the line between past and future. Let me first look to the future and then return to the past. In the *Cours de linguistique générale* Saussure opened his discussion of "General Principles" with the famous chapter on the "Nature of the Linguistic Sign." It begins:

When reduced to its essential principles, language is for some people a nomenclature, that is a list of terms that correspond to as many things. This
conception is open to criticism in several respects. It assumes that ready-
made ideas exist before words; it does not tell us if the nature of the name
is vocal or mental . . . and it suggests that the link that unites a name to
a thing is a very simple operation, which is far from being true. This sim-
plistic view can, however, guide us to the truth, by showing that the linguistic unity is double, made by bringing two terms together.

Locke's double conformity was also crucial for Saussure. And midway in time between the two, Wilhelm von Humboldt had made a
similar observation that has often been cited as a characteristic formulation of his basic view: "The entire manner of the subjective perception of objects is necessarily carried over into the formation and use
of language. For the word originates precisely in this perception, it is
not a copy of the object itself, but of the image it creates in the mind.
. . . With objects man lives mainly according to the manner in
which language brings them to him." We need not assume that Humboldt had read Locke, though that is possible, or that Saussure had
read Locke and Humboldt, which would seem unlikely. But the obvious similarity of the three statements and the crucial position of each
in the writer's thought cannot be dismissed as merely fortuitous. We
are forced to assume that there is a demonstrable connection, a course
of coherence that links Locke, Humboldt, and Saussure. Locke's
double conformity is the theme which in one way or another informs
all the essays in this collection.

   Looking toward the past, Locke's argument was aimed at the most
widely held seventeenth-century view of the nature of language, a
doctrine that can best be called by the umbrella term the Adamic
language. Also an epistemological doctrine, it held that languages
even now, in spite of their multiplicity and seeming chaos, contain
elements of the original perfect language created by Adam when he
named the animals in his prelapsarian state. In the Adamic doctrine
the relation between signifier and signified is not arbitrary; the linguistic sign is not double but unitary. Still retaining the divine nature
of their common origin, languages were in fundamental accord with
nature, indeed they were themselves part of creation and nature. They
were divine and natural, not human and conventional. Even after the
Fall, Adam was the greatest philosopher, etymologist, and naturalist
who ever lived on earth. The authority of scriptural revelation ensured
that languages held a nomenclature, that words did name species and
essences. This was an essentialist and innatist doctrine, and it agreed
with the double-conformity expectation of ordinary speakers. Languages were a better avenue to the true knowledge of nature than the

mere self-help of man's deceiving senses and imperfect reason. Of course this precious inheritance did not lie open in the light of day; it was an esoteric doctrine. But with the stakes so high and the authority unrivaled, it is no wonder that mystics, scholars, and etymologists went to work to recapture the hidden truth and the living powers of words. Thus men were seen to be not merely, like Molière's M. Jourdain, speaking prose without knowing it: they were little Adams and spoke much greater truth than they knew. I shall soon show that something like this doctrine arose again in the early nineteenth century and then caused problems very similar to those the seventeenth century had faced in the relations between language and knowledge.

I am convinced that Locke's argument about the cheat of words was aimed not so much against the common thing-word habit, which all of us tend to follow in a pragmatic way, but against its much more serious embodiment in the Adamic language doctrine. If there were any truth in it, the word for gold, for instance, might by suitable means be made to reveal the nature and essence of gold, whereas for Locke it was impossible to know more than what he defiantly called the 'nominal essence.' By placing the imperfection in language rather than in our capacity for knowledge, Locke turned the entire question around, in the faith that God had willed man to possess sufficient powers to learn and know what was necessary for this life. In his critique of the Adamic doctrine Locke agreed with many of his great contemporaries, e.g., Mersenne, Robert Boyle, and John Wilkins. The grounds were theological and had a universal aim. If the reading of Scriptures had not brought about agreement, peace and safe conduct in this world, then the study of the Book of Creation, open to all, might do so. It was therefore crucial to ensure the independence of this study from the uncertain and diverse interpretations of the plan hidden in Scriptures. The universal testimony of manifest revelation would be lost if it borrowed doctrines from scriptural revelation regarding the study of nature. As in his political philosophy Locke insisted on Adam's ordinary humanity also in regard to language: "The same necessity of conforming his ideas of substances to things without him, as to *archetypes* made by nature, that *Adam* was under, if he would not willfully impose upon himself, the same are all men ever since under, too. The same liberty also that *Adam* had of affixing any new name to any *idea*, the same has anyone still."

It was in this context that Locke's *Essay* and its philosophy of language arose. If my argument is correct, it helps to identify a background that gives us a better understanding of what Locke was doing. To mention just one important point, it would seem evident that Locke's rejection of 'innate notions' was a move against the proponents of the Adamic doctrine with their radical commitment to innatism, rather than against Descartes, who did, however, seem to share the 'fixisme' and essentialism inherent in that doctrine. But for our purposes the important consequence is especially that with Locke's *Essay* laying the foundations of the modern study of language, the origins of this study become tightly intertwined with the major intellectual event in our centuries, the rise of the new science in the seventeenth century. This fact permits language study to gain its rightful place in intellectual history. We are no longer bound by the dicta of the standard history, which made language study before 1800 a miserable story of error and delusion, barely deserving to be remembered.

For Locke language was not divine and natural, but made by man and conventional, created by "ignorant and illiterate people, who sorted and denominated things by those sensible qualities they found in them." It was made according to need for the convenience of communication with "ease and dispatch." It is a social institution that reflects the world of its speakers, hence Locke's insistence on linguistic relativism long before this idea was attributed to Humboldt as a "genuine discovery." The relation between signifier and signified is arbitrary, contrary to the central assertion of the Adamic doctrine. Owing to the impenetrable subjectivity of ideas to which words are tied, each individual has a radically private language that virtually precludes all hope of perfect communication, a principle that was to reverberate through Condillac, Herder, Turgot, Destutt de Tracy, and Humboldt and that also became Wordsworth's problem. Goethe made the same observation in *Dichtung und Wahrheit*, in a passage that was written in 1813: "For that no one understands another, that the same words do not arouse the same thought in one man as in another, that a dialogue or a text causes different trains of thought in different individuals, was something I had long realized all too clearly." Locke rejected the possibility of a viable philosophical language on the same grounds that Michaëlis, Bréal, and Saussure did later. Locke's analyses identified the supreme importance of signs, and in the final chapter of the *Essay* he suggested a three-fold division of knowledge into natural philosophy, ethics—"the skill of rightly applying our own powers and actions for the attainment of things good and useful"—and "thirdly, the ways and means whereby the knowledge of both the one and the other of these is attained and communicated." This last he called 'semeiōtiké,' "the business whereof is to consider the nature of signs the mind makes use of for the understanding of things, or conveying its knowledge to others. For, since the things the mind contemplates are none of them, besides itself, present to the understanding, it is necessary that something else, as a sign or representation of the thing it considers, should be present to it; and these are *ideas*." Locke was seeing the need for semiotics, which have had such a successful career after Saussure. Locke's view of language was entirely functional.

Locke had presented his critique of language within a theory of knowledge which still assumed that the recalcitrance of words could be put to the test and overcome, even though it took the analytical penetration of a philosopher to do so. He had argued that words are indispensable both for memory and communication, and that we in fact habitually think in terms of words, which are like knots tying together bundles of ideas that would not have existed without this tagging of bundles. In a few pregnant and much-quoted remarks, he had also suggested that closer attention to language might tell us something about what had been in the minds of the first speakers, about their reasons and motives for sorting, bundling, and naming as they did. He had gone a long way toward saying that all knowledge is about signs, but he never took the final step of asserting the global role of language. That step was taken by Condillac in 1746 in his *Essai sur l'orgine des connaissances humaines*, which in the English translation ten years later was called "a supplement to Mr. Locke's *Essay*."

Condillac made all knowledge a function of signs and words. He presented his argument about the nature of language in terms of a hypothesis of the origin of language, thus suggesting the time perspective already latent in Locke. He was using the procedure of seeking the state of nature which had proved so useful in political philosophy, a procedure Dugald Stewart later called "theoretical or conjectural history." "The word principle," said Condillac, "is the synonym of beginning." At the beginning the linguistic and epistemological states of nature collapse into one.

Condillac posited three things. On the authority of the Bible he accepted, like Locke, that man is by nature a social creature and further that man is endowed with reason and the capacity for its exercise in reflection. He also postulated that all men are uniformly by nature endowed with the same gestural expression of mental states, such as pain, joy, fright, and surprise. The expression of pain in one individual will naturally elicit another individual's awareness of it. This is also true of gestures that are vocal, the 'cries of nature' or the 'language of action.' These three—sociability, reason, and the harmony of gestural expression—create a rudimentary epistemological state. They give Condillac's theory a uniformitarian cast, and he therefore, like his followers, believed that the creativity of language-making is constantly going on. The mind is not passive. His theory of language was an extrapolation from currently observable phenomena.

But though gestures form a basic, involuntary mode of communication, this 'language' is natural and has no origin. He sought the origin of the artificial language that begins when reason and reflection, taking their cue from vocal gestures, step in to suggest the deliberate creation of arbitrary, conventional signs made according to need in the common interest of self-preservation. In this context Condillac made much of the guiding role of pleasure and pain, like Locke in the political philosophy. It is impossible for knowledge to exist and expand without arbitrary, manmade signs which, when attached to the ideas initially suggested by communal need, put mind in control of knowledge. The signs become both a memory bank and a retrieval system, serving equally the needs of private thinking and the ends of communication. This firm linkage between signifier and signified is called the 'connection of ideas'—'la liaison des idées'—which, being an expresion of reason and reflection, is also controlled by them in the ever-widening expansion of the repertory of signs and of ratiocinative possibilities. The connection of ideas is a principle also occasionally used by Locke, and it is altogether different from the irrational chance association of ideas, which for Locke was "a kind of madness." Condillac also distinguished strictly between the two, though it is still widely believed, in the wake of nineteenth-century opinion, that Condillac and even Locke made all thinking and knowledge a function of association, thus sustaining a materialist theory of knowledge that reduced the mind to being a mere passive recording device. When Condillac in the *Essai*—in the first edition even on the title page—said that he reduced all that pertains to the understanding to a single principle, he meant the connection of ideas. He did not claim to reduce Locke's reflection to sensation, as a false interpretation of the statue has it.

From the slow beginnings of artificial signs—or words and speech—man's control of the world steadily grew as reflection was offered new material to work on. The fruitfulness of language and reflection worked for the reciprocal benefit of each to produce the 'origin and progress of language.' This process opened the way for the history of thought, as Locke had intimated. "It appears," wrote Lord Monboddo, "that, from the study of language, if it be properly conducted, the history of the human mind is best learned." Etymology gained new importance in a manner that Dugald Stewart aptly called "etymological metaphysics"—a term that with a curious twist could be applied just as well to the later philological arguments of Max Müller. For a long time the signs of language retained elements of gestural expression in a mixture of song and poetry that was to play a large role in Romantic esthetics. But this union was gradually resolved as language was refined to meet the practical demands of knowledge and control over things. Music moved into its own sphere, and the poet was left to make the best of a language that was largely foreign to his purposes. I have discussed this matter in the essay on Wordsworth.

The refinement of language was made both possible and necessary by the inescapable linearity of speech. It was one of Condillac's favorite pedagogical and epistemological devices to place his young Prince of Parma before a window with shutters that for a brief moment were opened to give him a view of the landscape. In remembering and talking about this landscape, the young man was forced to analyze the instantaneous unitary tableau he had seen into the elements he recalled as single units—trees, shrubbery, bushes, fences, groves, and the like. He was forced to think sequentially because discourse is linear. It was on this basis that Condillac in his later writings developed the principle that good science is a language well made. In the beginning words were also unitary much like the view from the window, before reflection increased the stock of signs. The progress of knowledge is advanced by the linearity of discourse.

It was Locke's aim to determine the certainty and extent of human knowledge, and to this end he found it necessary to analyze "the doubtful and uncertain use of words or (which is the same) *indetermined ideas*, which they are made to stand for." His discussion of language did not go beyond what for Wordsworth was the language of science. For Condillac, taking a global view of language, there could be no such limitation. Language was the first social institution and played a role in all human affairs, from the simplest everyday events to the most exalted creations of man. He treated the language of poetry as well as the place of language in culture at large. In a chapter in the *Essai* on the genius of languages he wrote: "Everything confirms that each language expresses the character of the people who speak it. . . . Of all writers, it is in the poets that the genius of languages finds most vivid expression. . . . For anyone who knows languages well, they become like a portrait of the character and genius of each people. He will see how the imagination has combined ideas according to opinions and the passions." The agreement of these statements with central doctrines in Romantic thought is obvious. Condillac provided the philosophical foundation of the concept of the *Volksgeist* with its emphasis on the culture-bound quality of national languages. It involves the principle of linguistic relativity, with its fruitful consequences for anthropology, and is on the national level a repetition of the principle that each individual has a private language, a point Condillac made in that chapter: "It is enough to study an individual for a little while to learn his language; I say *his* language, for each has his own according to his passions."

Condillac's philosophy of language shared one quality with the Adamic language doctrine: both were global. But whereas the Adamicists sought to recapture lost perfection and divine authority, Condillac pointed toward increasing states of perfection to be achieved by man in the future. There can be no doubt that Condillac more than anyone else gave life to the progress doctrine, with the concomitant temporalization of the history of thought and knowledge. His philosophy offered a pedagogical program for the perfectibility of man. The completion of this program was what the *idéologues* set out to attain in their *idéologie*, so called because it was a science of ideas based on language and words. But their efforts were soon foiled by Napoleon, who reorganized the Institut National to deprive them of their platform. Marx found the word 'idcology' in one of Napoleon's contemptuous remarks about the school he had come to see as a threat to his ambitions. The philosophy of the eighteenth century was forced into a sort of underground existence over the next fifty years, during the Empire, the Bourbon Restoration, and the July Monarchy, until it was revived by the renewal that began in the 1850s. This revival was initiated by Taine's critique of Cousin's eclective philosophy and spiritualism, which was a sort of wobbly version of German Romantic philosophy and *Naturphilosophie*—though as Heine gleefully noted in his book on the Romantic school in Germany, Cousin had very little German. I shall conclude the introduction with an effort to show what happened to the interrelations of language and knowledge in the nineteenth century.

IV

I have argued that the study of language holds a central position in the actual process of intellectual history during the last three centuries, indeed that our understanding of this history gains coherence and fruitfulness when centered on the first human and social institution, language. In this context the early part of the nineteenth century has a quality so extraordinary that it demands an explanation. Among all the modes of study and knowledge in the nineteenth century, there can be no doubt that the newly created comparative-historical philology offered the most dramatic refutation of eighteenth-century delusion and error. It quickly and completely usurped the entire territory, supported by rapid academic institutionalization—largely owing to Humboldt's program of education—and the enormous prestige that accompanies success. It became the model humanistic discipline. Factual, descriptive, classificatory, empirical, and comparative, the new philology appeared to satisfy every article of scientific—or rather academic—faith in objectivity and disengagement from ideology. It was also full of the excitement that new knowledge arouses, with the treasured benefit that, by opening the sacred books of the East, it gave Indo-European—or for some Indo-Germanic—mankind new sources of spirituality for troubled times. All this is beyond doubt. But something still more important happened. An alliance was effected between language study and science to sustain the argument for final causes and for assurance of the Creator's presence in Creation. Without this alliance it would not have been possible to revive the doctrine of species and essences which Locke had dismissed. Language again took a crucial position in the Great Argument.

In the early part of the century language and science assumed the same interrelationship that had caused problems for the new science in the seventeenth century and was creating trouble for Darwin now. It is typical that Max Müller was forced into polemics both with the linguist William Dwight Whitney and with the scientist Darwin. One could say that the Adamic doctrine was being revived in new terms. It is this argument that makes me see the great academic philological tradition as a closed period, as an aberration—which does not imply depreciation of its contributions to knowledge.

By 1800 the Revolution had already come to appear an apocalyptic event that threatened to annihilate the past, like a geological catastrophe. Fear of revolutionary thought and free-thinking—the danger of the 'libre examen' so often raised by clerics in Balzac's novels—led to repression, censorship, and tight central control over education, not to mention the more insidious forms of quiet academic submission to pressures and authority, masked by strident claims of dedication to pure objectivity and freedom of enquiry. In varying degrees, all these happened in most countries, not merely in France. Napoleon made it deliberate policy to favor the age of Louis XIV, just as suspicion of republican and democratic ideas caused virtual proscription of Greek studies, with Latin and the Roman Empire being raised to eminence instead. By 1830 scholars in Paris remarked that France had lost a generation of Greek scholarship. The study of the Middle Ages was actively favored for similar reasons. At the École normale, where he prepared a dissertation on Condillac, Taine was considered the most brilliant student in his class; but he was denied the *agrégation* by an examining committee whose report has never been found, though it was required that such reports be drawn up and deposited in the archives. Twenty years later, in the early 1870s, Georg Brandes in Copenhagen was not appointed to the chair for which he was the obvious and highly recommended candidate. Max Weber has detailed similar practices in Germany. Fear of revolutionary thought caused a constant sense of clear and present danger, which it took strong measures to meet.

That danger was identified in eighteenth-century philosophy, concentrated in the philosophy of language that contained its definition of man and the promise of his progress toward nearly perfect states of knowledge and society. It was this promise that the *idéologues* tried to fulfill in the closing years of the century before Napoleon began to manage the reaction, which others continued in the same spirit in the decades to come. Victor Cousin fought his crusade against Locke, Condillac, and the eighteenth century with the spiritualism he pieced together from German thought. In philosophy contempt for Locke became the beginning of wisdom. The nature of language was the ground where the battle was most intense. Here in particular language formed an alliance with science.

This alliance was made possible by Georges Cuvier. In December 1795 he gave the famous inaugural lecture that introduced the principles of his comparative anatomy. In 1800 his first volumes under that title appeared, and for the next decades he lectured on the subject at the Museum of Natural History to audiences so large, more than one thousand, that tickets of admission were hard to obtain. Comparative anatomy became the model science, and its principles were quickly adopted in language study and anthropology. Its popularity is widely attested in common locutions and metaphors, for instance Emerson's phrase describing language as "fossil poetry," a phrase soon quoted by Richard Chenevix Trench, who added "fossil ethics" and "fossil history." Cuvier himself regularly referred to language study as an illustration that supported his own findings. In his salon naturalists mixed with linguists, scholars, and philosophers.

Cuvier's anatomy is best known for the principle of the correlation of parts, or structure, which made it possible to reconstruct whole animals from sparse materials, a bone or a tooth, for instance. In Balzac's *Peau de Chagrin* the narrator muses ecstatically on this marvel as Raphaël, for a moment alone in the cabinet of antiquities, waits for the appearance of the antiquary. "Have you ever thrown yourself into the immensity of space and time by reading the geological works of Cuvier? . . . Fired by his retrospective gaze, we paltry human beings, born yesterday, can bridge the chaos, chant an endless hymn, and recreate the past of the universe in a sort of retrograde apocalypse." This "awe-inspiring resurrection" was the voice of a single man. If not a creator, Cuvier was a re-creator who inspired imagination.

But it was not the correlation of parts itself that cemented the alliance of science and language. Cuvier was firmly opposed to the idea of transformation that had been argued by Bonnet, among others, and that remained ever-present around him. When three-thousand-year-old mummies of cats, dogs, snakes, and birds were brought back from Egypt, Cuvier exulted: there, you see, no sign of change even over so many years. He insisted on the fixity of species by rejecting the sliding scale of the chain of being. There are discontinuities or jumps in the animal kingdom. He was what is nowadays called a saltationist. "Natural history," said Cuvier, "has a principle that is uniquely its own; it is that of the *conditions of existence*, popularly called *final causes*. As nothing can exist unless it unites the conditions that make its existence possible, the different parts of each being must be so coordinated as to make the entire being possible, not merely in itself, but in its relations with those that surround it." Species have forever been fixed since the moment of Creation. Indeed, to think otherwise would make natural history impossible. In a publication that appeared within a month of the inaugural lecture, Cuvier rejected the notion that climate could have played any role, "for that would mean to say that all quadrupeds derive only from a single species, that the differences they now present are only successive degenerations: in a word, it would reduce all natural history to nothing because its object would then be mere variable forms and fleeting types." It would make knowledge impossible. Observation, description, and classification are enough. Speculation is unnecessary; natural history pronounces what Cuvier called "sublime oracles." Speculation is dangerous, even impious. Cuvier's science had reintroduced essentialism along with final causes, the very idea that Mersenne and Locke had dismissed as incompatible with the aims and method of the study of nature.

William Whewell was a great admirer of Cuvier. Among the

"Aphorisms concerning Ideas" placed at the beginning of his *Philosophy of the Inductive Sciences* (1840), we find these:

> We take for granted that each kind of things has a special *character* which may be expressed by a Definition. The ground of our assumption is this: that reasoning must be possible.
>
> If (Scientific) Natural History were introduced into education, men might become familiar with the fixation of the signification of words by Types; and this agrees with the common processes by which words acquire their significations.
>
> The assumption of a Final Cause in the structure of each part of animals and plants is as inevitable as the assumption of an Efficient Cause for every event. The maxim that in organized bodies nothing is *in vain*, is as necessarily true as the maxim that nothing happens *by chance*.
>
> The Palaetiological Sciences point backwards with lines which are broken, but which all converge to the *same* invisible point: and this point is the Origin of the Moral and Spiritual, as well as of the natural world.

These aphorisms speak for themselves—they show, for instance, that Whewell reasserted the double conformity Locke had dismissed, and that Whewell like Cuvier felt that the fixity of types was a pre-condition for knowledge. Basing his philosophy on Cuvier, he yet more firmly linked science and language in a manner that revived the Adamic doctrine. Whewell's chief opponents were the Utilitarians, but his orientation shows perhaps most clearly in the little book *Indications of the Creator*, which he hastily put together from his own publications to counter Chambers's *Vestiges of Creation*. Both books gave language a central place in their arguments, Chambers in the familiar eighteenth-century fashion, Whewell in a manner he based on Cuvier and contemporary philology, a subject so dear to Whewell that Trinity College, Cambridge, during this mastership became the home of the linguistic turn against Locke and Condillac.

Max Müller was the untiring prophet of linguistic finalism, to give it a name. This occurred especially in his phenomenally popular *Science of Language*, first delivered as lectures at the Royal Institution in London in the early 1860s. The very title rang out his fundamental assertion. Nature, said Müller in the preface, may be defined so as to exclude the science of language, but "with the wider meaning assigned to nature in our days, I hold as strongly as ever that the study of human speech may claim not only admission to, but the highest place among the Physical Sciences." If we think this is a colossal instance of question-begging, the reason is that we do not share the assumption of final causes, which he held in common with Cuvier and Whewell. Language occupies the highest place precisely because it comes closest to proving the Great Argument. Establishing a firm boundary between man and brute, language "would seem to possess at the present moment peculiar claims on the attention of all who, while watching with sincere admiration the progress of comparative physiology, yet consider it their duty to enter their manly protest against a revival of the shallow theories of Lord Monboddo"—Müller's sarcastic euphemism for Darwin.

Müller admitted a difficulty, which once overcome enforces the transcendent importance of the science of language. In words quoted by Müller, Whewell had said that "natural history, when systematically treated, excludes all that is historical, for it classes objects by their permanent and universal properties, and has nothing to do with the narration of particular facts." Here Whewell agreed with Cuvier; we can know nothing about origins except our faith in the origin that lay just beyond the realm of natural history. Language and philology, however, take us from the synchronic dimension into the diachronic. Müller solved the problem posed for him by Whewell's statement by saying that, though there is continuous change in language, "it is not in the power of any man either to produce or change it." In other words, everything in language is natural, there is no *historical* change, and "language is independent of political history"—a key point in the ideology. Thus Müller agreed with Schleicher's organicism, which Bréal made it his first aim to dismiss.

It is, Müller believed, the great achievement of the science of language that it has collected, arranged, and classified the facts of language, thus illuminating not merely its nature and laws but also its origin by bringing us back to its ultimate constituents: roots or "phonetic cells"—Müller's rhetoric constantly reveals his argument, indeed makes it possible. Roots, he said, "stand like barriers between the chaos and kosmos of human speech." They are the names of full-fledged concepts, thus presupposing the prior formation of ideas. At this radical stage, then, we understand that language could not have come about gradually by human means. Like Cuvier, Müller never carried his science all the way to the first cause, he merely took us far enough to see no other possibility—as with Whewell's lines converging "to the *same* invisible point." Language is after all natural, like the Adamic language, and the "three branches of physical study, now generally spoken of as *Palaeontology, Embryology,* and *Comparative Anatomy*, have produced the same effect with regard to the problem of creation which our own linguistic studies have produced with regard to the problem of the origin of language and thought."

Science and language had thus joined forces to reassert essentialism. Locke and Condillac were shallow philosophers, and Darwin was vanquished with linguistic argument. Near the end of the *Science of Language* Müller quoted Cuvier on the error of figures of speech, of personifying Nature. "It is easy to see the puerility of those philosophers who have conferred on Nature a kind of individual existence, distinct from the Creator. . . . As our knowledge has advanced in astronomy, physics, and chemistry, those sciences have renounced the paralogisms which resulted from the application of figurative language to real phenomena. Physiologists only have still retained this habit, because, with the obscurity in which physiology is still enveloped, it was not possible for them to deceive themselves or others as to their profound ignorance of vital movements, except by attributing some kind of reality to the phantoms of their imagination." It made good sense for Cuvier to say this in 1819; much less, it may seem to us, for Max Müller in the 1860s, until we realize that he did not think he spoke figuratively when to us he appears evidently to do so. Müller encouraged the reader to look up the text he was citing. It was in fact a recent review of the *Origin of Species* by Pierre Flourens, Cuvier's protégé and successor at the Collège de France. In his reassertion of the fixity of species Flourens found that Darwin's argument was made possible at all only "because the author throughout uses figurative language without being aware of it and which deceives him as it has deceived all others who have used it."

I have explained why and how language and science came together to form an alliance against the linguistic philosophy that reigned before 1800. That argument became immensely popular with the sort of figure John Holloway has called the Victorian Sage. Though Holloway's book (1953) did not relate the sage to linguistic philosophy, he made some useful suggestions that assume a deeper meaning in our context. The sage had a distinct style; what gave his views "life and meaning lay in the actual words of the original, in the sage's own use of language, not in what can survive summarizings of their 'content.'" For Holloway the typical sage is Carlyle, who "does not wish to be thought of as explicitly allotting his own senses to these words, but as discovering what really they mean already, what their existing present use both depends upon, and perhaps conceals." In other words, Carlyle replaced ratiocinative discourse with the evocation of the true meaning of words, pointing to the meanings they hold deeper than their common significations, on the premise, of course, that this deeper meaning is somehow naturally available to all thoughtful readers. It is a style completely different from, say, John Stuart Mill's—not to mention Bentham's. This contrast defines their opposed philosophies, one of them committed to a moral view of language, the other to a functional view; one intimating divine and natural content, the other accepting only conventional and human origin.

The Victorian sage is also a European sage; his arsenal is philology, his instrument etymology. He is the prophet of words. The basic belief is affirmed by Trench. In one of his books he draws a lesson from the etymology of 'education.' It is not the process of "the filling of the child's mind, as a cistern is filled with waters brought in buckets from some other source." On the contrary, it is "the opening up of its own fountains," for "education must educe, being from 'educare,' which is but another form of 'educere'; and that is 'to draw out,' not 'to put in.'" This is in fact a Neo-Platonic topos, often cited at the time. It was a favorite with the mystics of the sixteenth and seventeenth centuries, though perhaps best known from Blake's epigram in *The Marriage of Heaven and Hell*: "The cistern contains: the fountain overflows." The point is of course the Platonic doctrine that to learn is to remember. This is only one among many details that show how congenial the Adamic doctrine was to the sage, by the same token that contempt for Locke was the beginning of wisdom.

The sage was a European and American figure. Among the type may be numbered Coleridge, Whewell, Adam Sedgwick, Trench, Julius Charles Hare, de Maistre, Renan, Max Müller, N. F. S. Grundtvig and H. L. Martensen in Denmark, Johann Erik Rydqvist and Erik Gustaf Geijer in Sweden, Henrik Steffens, Jacob Grimm, and in America Emerson and the transcendentalists. Many drew inspiration from Swedenborg, like Emerson who knew Guillaume Oegger's *La Vraie Messie, ou l'Ancien et le Nouveau Testaments examinés d'après les principes de la langue de la nature*, a work also known to Balzac. The intellectual lineaments of the anti-sage are suggested by the Utilitarians in England and at least one of their opponents, Hazlitt; by Stendhal, who was wholly committed to the philosophy of Destutt de Tracy; by Taine, Sainte-Beuve, Madvig, Heine, Alexander Herzen, Nietzsche, and Kierkegaard. Some of the men of the church whom Kierkegaard argued against were sages, and he would never qualify in any event, both because of the unequalled brilliance and irony of his style and because he treated Cuvier with levity. In the *Diary of the Seducer* we read: "I have already seen the little foot, and being myself a naturalist, I have therefrom been taught by Cuvier to draw conclusions that are certain."

The sage is brilliantly portrayed in Balzac's magnificent panorama of life. In the preface to the *Livre mystique*, which includes *Louis Lambert* and *Séraphîta*, he wrote that "the author has not thought it would be honorable for French literature to remain silent about a

poetry so grand as that of the mystics." Louis Lambert is the archetype of the young man who seeks all the knowledge that is open to
the sage, and his primary inspiration is language. Telling the narrator
about his reading, he says that he had

> often performed delightful voyages, embarked on a word into the abysses
> of the past, like an insect floating with the stream on a piece of grass. . . .
> What a beautiful book could be composed, telling the life and adventures
> of a word . . . there is enough to suggest an ocean of reflections. Is it not
> true that most words are dyed with the idea represented by their outward
> form. Imagine the genius that has made them! If it takes great intellect to
> create a word, how old is human speech? The bringing together of letters,
> their forms, the figure they give each word, trace precisely, according to
> the genius of each nation, unknown beings whose memory is in us. . . .
> The ancient picturing of human ideas represented by zoological forms,
> would it not have determined the first signs used in the Orient for the writ-
> ing of its languages? Would it not in the course of transmission have left
> some vestiges in our modern languages, which all share the debris of the
> primitive word of nations. . . . Is it to that ancient Spirit that we owe
> the mysteries hidden in human speech? Is there not in the word 'vrai' a
> sort of supernatural rectitude? Is there not in the terse sound it demands a
> vague image of chaste nudity, of the simplicity of the true in everything?
> . . . Does not every word tell the same story? All are stamped with a liv-
> ing power which they derive from the soul and which they pay back to it
> by the mysteries of action and the marvellous reaction that exist between
> speech and thought.

This passage reveals both the repertory and the manner of the sage.
Louis Lambert was making the same discovery that all children naturally make according to Trench, who, writing some fifteen years
after Balzac, observed: "There is a sense of reality about children
which makes them rejoice to discover that there is also a reality about
words, that they are not merely arbitrary signs, but living powers;
that, to reverse the words of one of England's false prophets, they
may be the fool's counters, but are the wise man's money." For
Lambert and Trench words are living powers that reveal the reality
that is naturally in them, open to all who have not been perverted by
listening to false prophets.

Louis Lambert is the story of a young man whose mind becomes
unhinged in the pursuit of deep knowledge. He perishes by the spirit.
The complement to Louis Lambert is Raphaël in *La Peau de Chagrin.*
Both face the perplexities that cast minds into turmoil during the
early decades of the nineteenth century and both are destroyed by
the lives they chose. Both seek fulfillment in intense study and
write a lost treatise on the will, mine the knowledge of their time,
find relief only when it is too late in the love for a girl called Pauline,

and both—like Faust—achieve after death a sort of apotheosis, thanks to the dedication of their Paulines.

La Peau de Chagrin is about the inefficacy of science for the conduct of life. When Raphaël seeks help from the scientists to stop the contractions of the skin and escape from the consequences, they have nothing but words to offer. One, "the great pontiff of zoology," tells him the skin is from the wild ass of Persia, "extremely rare, the onager of the ancients, *equus asinus*, the *koulan* of the Tatars, which Pallas has travelled to observe and given to science." But the Museum has no specimen of it, and all Raphaël gets out of the interview is that human science is "a nomenclature." The next scientist reduces all to motion, illustrated by a billard ball—"movement, locomotion, change of place? What immense vanity is hidden in words! A name, is it then a solution? Still, there is all of science." And the third scientist, a chemist, exclaims "by God, young man, that is true," in response to Raphaël's despairing words: "Since we cannot invent things, it seems that we are reduced to inventing names." Balzac had an uncanny grasp of the classificatory verbalism that reigned in the science of his time.

But this is not all. In *La Peau de Chagrin* Balzac also flays the sage. The grotesque and unnaturally old second-hand dealer from whom Raphaël gets the skin is a false sage; indeed, as we are reminded more than once, another Mephistopheles. Having, of course, made a deep study of languages, Raphaël easily translates the Arabic inscription and is immediately flattered by the old man, "ah, you read Sanskrit, perhaps you have travelled in Persia or Bengal?" To which Raphaël correctly replies no; he is neither reading Sanskrit nor has he travelled, as the old man soon claims he has himself, in the same breath as he claims to have learned all languages. He then engages in a bit of persuasive philosophizing and etymologizing to reveal the great mystery of human life. Willing and doing ("vouloir et pouvoir") are the ways of death, but "between these two terms of human action, there is another formula which the sages ("les sages") seize hold of, the source of my happiness and longevity. . . . Knowing ("savoir") leaves our feeble organization in a perpetual state of calm . . . no excess has worn down either my soul or my body." In the midst of his suicidal despair Raphaël finds assurance in the old man, who closes with an etymology, "doesn't the word 'sagesse' come from 'savoir'?" But later, when, in the Italian Theatre, he sees the old sage dressed up as an elegant young man escorting the "detestable Euphrasie," Raphaël has a vision of Goethe's Mephistopheles, "savoring all the pleasures of vengeance in the contemplation of the profound humiliation of this sublime wisdom ("cette sagesse sublime"), whose fall a short while ago had seemed impossible."

The meaning of the novel is in fact suggested by the title. The great pontiff of zoology tells Raphaël that the skin comes from the nearly mythical onager, "but there are differences of opinion about the origin of the name. Some say that it comes from the Turkish word *Chagri*, others that *Chagri* is the town where this zoological hide was subjected to the chemical preparation so well described by Pallas, which gives it the particular grain we admire; Mr. Martellens has written me that *Châagri* is a small stream." *La Peau de Chagrin* is a brilliant exploration of the pun contained in its title. The naturalist can only see one meaning, and Raphaël sees the other only when it is too late, overcome rather by the sage's etymologizing on 'savoir' and 'sagesse.' By an astonishing piece of irony the *Oxford English Dictionary*, on the authority of Littré, derives the meaning 'sorrow, affliction' from the Turkish "'çaghri' rump of a horse, hence the prepared skin of this part. The sense-development took place in French, where the word meaning rough and granular skin employed to rub, polish, file, became by metaphor the expression of gnawing trouble. In English the word in the original material sense is now written shagreen." This is exactly the kind of etymology at which the sage excelled. The etymology is no longer accepted, but *chagrin* for 'sorrow, affliction' in the French has still not given up the secret of its origin.

Near the end, when Raphaël gains insight into his state, he muses that "the key to all the sciences is without doubt in the question asked; we owe most of the great discoveries to: how? and wisdom ("la sagesse") in life consists perhaps in asking ourselves at every turn: why?" In the seventeenth century Robert Boyle had insisted that science is only concerned with the how, and Claude Bernard was to repeat this insistence after 1850. The alliance of language and science built the sage's arsenal and supplied the weapons for his crusade against Locke—against the eighteenth century, free-thinking, the immoral levity of revolutionary thought, and the arbitrariness of words. But this sage alliance had its liabilities. It destroyed Louis Lambert and Raphaël de Valentin. Michel Bréal put an end to this source of destruction, by acknowledging once again the dependence of language on its human use.

Leibniz on Locke
on Language

The subject of this paper is Locke's critique of language and Leibniz' reaction to that critique. The basic texts are Locke's *Essay* and Leibniz' discussion of its contents in the long dialogue which he gave the title *Nouveaux Essais sur l'Entendement*.[1] In spite of agreement on some points, their positions are fundamentally opposed. My purpose is to define the positions of each and to attempt to explain why Locke's analysis of "Words or Language in General"—as he phrased it in the title of III, i—proved unacceptable to Leibniz. My thesis is that their basic opposition turns on the question whether language is conventional or natural, and I shall try to show that Locke had deliberately taken his stand against the doctrines which Leibniz later advanced in his critique. Thus their disagreement can be defined within the history of the lively seventeenth-century debate about words and things, language and mind, and ultimately language and knowledge. Or, put differently: If the object of man's study is Nature, as to the Royal Society it certainly was, does language somehow find its place within Nature or does it exist only for man's convenience and entirely apart from Nature? If the former is the case, then one may expect that words can be made to yield some—and perhaps much—knowledge of reality; if the latter, none; and in either case, language may perhaps reveal something about the mind. My approach is historical, not philosophical; and I shall leave aside the aspects of Leibniz that have recently attracted the most attention, i.e., the logic, the calculus, the combinatorial characteristics and other related matters that have been treated by Russell, Couturat, and their followers.

Reprinted from *American Philosophical Quarterly* 1 (1964), 165-188.

The contrasted views of Locke and Leibniz form the final stage in the history of a subject that can most briefly be named Language and Natural Philosophy in the Seventeenth Century. It is a large subject, but here I shall include only as much of the background as is required to identify the origins of the opposition. This procedure will, I hope, also help to clarify and fix some fundamental aspects of Locke's doctrines and method in the *Essay*, which have been either poorly understood or have received interpretations that are too diverse for comfort and conviction. The *Essay* was literally epoch-making, and such works never fail to efface their own past; in fact, one can almost say that the *Essay* has no other history than that which was its own future, as if Locke merely wrote to give Berkeley and Hume something to write about. Unlike Locke, Leibniz often named his sources and gave citations, which may help to identify the *Essay*'s elusive background; and Leibniz' vast correspondence offers a further wealth of information.

For the sake of preliminary orientation, it may be useful to make a few remarks about language and philosophy, natural and otherwise, in the seventeenth century. It is familiar knowledge that many put upon language or words the burden of philosophical imperfection. Hence the success of philosophy must depend on overcoming the "cheat of words" as it was often phrased.[2] Two solutions offered themselves. On the one hand we find some men offering new signs modeled on the principle behind Arabic numerals, algebraic notation, and even hieroglyphics or Chinese characters, all of which are often mentioned in this context—Leibniz among others hoped that such signs might eventually become the only vehicle of philosophical knowledge. On the other hand we find an increasing concern with plain language and words. Here the solutions were more in doubt, but no less eagerly sought to overcome the stultifying consequences of the language of the schools—of scholasticism, its terms, and its nominalism—to take only the best-known instance. Here Locke's answer was certainly the most radical and has also proved the most lasting. Both were designed to insure that the reading of the book of nature be raised above confusion, uncertainty, and controversy for the sake of peace and order and the improvement of man's estate in this world. Religious devotion demanded no less. "Empty words" must be subdued to serve "real meaning." The other book of the Creator, Scriptures, required a similar answer to remove its reading beyond controversy and such subsequent disasters as the Thirty Years' War; thus all the great natural philosophers made a special point of knowing the sacred languages: Boyle, Newton, John Pell, Robert Hooke, and Locke, to mention only a few.[3]

The words of two men will illustrate two separate and typical doctrines. In the *Discours de la méthode* (1637), Descartes had said: "Those who have the strongest powers of reasoning and most skilfully manage their thoughts in order to make them clear and intelligible, always most readily gain assent for what they advance, even if they speak only the language of Lower Brittany and have never learned rhetoric." This was a defiant statement, and it did not fail to elicit a commensurate reaction; for men of good sense, plain words in whatever language or dialect, are enough.[4] To Locke the situation was somewhat different; he found that "the Extent and Certainty of our Knowledge . . . had so near a Connexion with Words, that unless their force and manner of Signification were first well observed, there could be very little said clearly and pertinently concerning Knowledge" (III, ix, 21). To Locke, unlike Descartes, the obstacle to good sense and knowledge was not merely a verbose enemy, not just some men's words, but words. The problem had become more acute since 1637 and pressed with special urgency on the experimenters in the Royal Society, who had to find good words and plain discourse to say the things they did. Leibniz would have agreed with Locke about the need for paying close attention to words, but he did not agree with Locke on the nature of language and words; hence "their force and manner of Signification" became a point at issue between the two philosophers.

I

It is familiar knowledge that the *Essay*, having been at least nearly 20 years in the making, made its first appearance in the world very early in 1690 and that Book III bears the title "Of Words." It is not so often remembered that both Book II and Book IV also have a good deal to say about words, especially the former. This is merely one example of the repetitiveness of the *Essay*, which Locke was aware of, but said he was "too lazie, or too busy" to remedy.[5] It is also familiar knowledge that Locke at the very end of Book II made the remark that he had not originally planned to devote a separate book to words but now found that it was "impossible to speak clearly and distinctly of our Knowledge, which all consists in Propositions, without considering, first, the Nature, Use, and Signification of Language." In III, ix, 21 he further confessed, "that when I first began this Discourse of the Understanding, and a good while after, I had not the least Thought, that any Consideration of Words was at all necessary to it."[6] The discussion of words had assumed crucial importance in his argument. In a letter to Molyneux of 20 Jan. 1692/3, he later admitted that "some parts of that third book . . . cost me more pains to express, than all the rest of my essay."

On the basis of the statements just quoted, we are sometimes told that Locke's close attention to words was an afterthought; perhaps it was in relation to the first inception of "this Discourse of the Understanding." But in that case the inception must by "a good while" have preceded the two 1671 drafts, for both of these grant words and their meanings a prominent place in the argument.[7] Thus, compared with the drafts, Book III marks a change in emphasis and strategy rather than in subject matter and argument. This circumstance suggests that Locke in the course of writing the *Essay* became more fully acquainted with the vast body of contemporary literature on language and its nature. This suggestion is clearly supported by the recently published accounts of Locke's reading during his years in France between 1675 and 1679, as well as by the list of books he sent home. They include, for instance, the Port-Royal Logic, the Port-Royal *Grammaire Générale et Raisonnée*, and Lancelot's grammars of Spanish, Italian, and French.[8] Furthermore, travel literature was one of Locke's special interests; it has been suggested that such reading seems a rather trivial occupation for a philosopher, but, of course, travel accounts were to him what the laboratory and experiments were to the men in the Royal Society. Travel accounts gave experimental knowledge of human nature and behavior, including language.[9] It is well to remember that the epigraph from Cicero's *De Natura Deorum*, which Locke originally placed on the title page of the *Essay*, occurs in a context that argues about the names of the gods and whether their existence has anything to do with their having names.[10] We may also relevantly recall the motto of the Royal Society: "Nullius in Verba,"—"in the words of no one," i.e., not bound by authority and tradition. It is drawn from this passage in Horace's *Epistles* I, i:

> Ac ne forte roges, quo me duce, quo lare tuter,
> Nullius addictus iurare in verba magistri,
> Quo me cumque rapit tempestas, deferor hospes.

II

Locke was fifty-six when the first publication appeared under his name while Leibniz' *Dissertatio de Arte Combinatoria* was in print in 1666 when its author was only twenty—and it was not his first publication. This interest in a philosophical language was one of the chief preoccupations of the century from its early decades and was by no means original with Leibniz, though he carried it beyond any stage reached by his predecessors. It bears an intimate relation both to his philosophy at large and to his life-time interest in other forms of language study.[11] This interest covered vernacular dialects both old and new, the German language, etymology, particular vocabularies of many sorts, and the nature of language itself. On these matters Leibniz was almost certainly more widely informed than Locke, though Locke undoubtedly knew much more than is immediately evident. Leibniz, however, had written a great deal on language before he came to the writing of his *Nouveaux Essais*, and his position is therefore easier to define.

In 1670 Leibniz edited a work by the Italian humanist Marius Nizolius, called *Anti-Barbarus seu de Veris Principiis et Vera Ratione Philosophandi contra Pseudophilosophos* (1553). For his edition Leibniz wrote a Preface on philosophical style, which is conventional for its time and not very different from many contemporary German works that dealt with the relationship between philosophy and knowledge on the one hand, language and words on the other. It presents some of the principles he also later adhered to:

> We may thus regard it as established that whatever cannot be explained in popular terms is nothing and should be exorcised from philosophy as if by an incantation, unless it can be known by immediate sense experience (like many classes of colors, odors, and tastes). (Leibniz, *Philosophical Papers and Letters*, a selection translated and edited, with an introduction, by Leroy E. Loemker. 2nd ed. Dordrecht: Reidel, 1966, p. 124.)[12]

This is the same basic tenet as Descartes voiced in his remark about the language of Lower Brittany. Leibniz continues that scholastic obscurity had been abandoned sooner in England and France than in Germany because the English and French have long been accustomed to cultivate philosophy in their own tongue; but with his German contemporaries and predecessors in these concerns, he is at the same time convinced that the German language has a philosophical mission, for it is especially rich in good, concrete terms pertaining to the "artes reales" and thus does not easily allow bad philosophy:

> But I venture to say that no European language is better suited than German for this testing and examination of philosophical doctrines by a living tongue. For German is very rich and complete in real terms, to the envy of all other languages. No people have for centuries more diligently cultivated the practical arts, among them especially the mechanical arts, so that even the Turks use German names for metals in the mines of Greece and Asia Minor. On the other hand, the German language is easily the poorest for expressing fictions, certainly far less fitted for this than French, Italian, and other languages derived from Latin. . . . Whoever wishes to retain or

to twist Latin terms into German will not be philosophizing in German but in Latin. . . . The reason why philosophy has only recently been dealt with here in the vernacular is that the German language is incompatible, not with philosophy, but with barbarous philosophy. And since this barbarous way of philosophizing has only lately been rejected it is not surprising that our language has been slow to come into philosophical use. (Loemker, p. 125.)[13]

Behind these words lies the conviction that a language that is un-mixed and original—that has, in other words, retained in its own stream the greatest number of root-woods ever since Babel and the Confusion—is somehow in closer accord with the Cosmos and Nature, with Creation and the Creator, with truth and reality. Consequently it is also better able than other languages to record the truths of natural philosophy, for it is itself "natural." German was as original as Hebrew and not inferior to Latin and Greek. Leibniz was devoted to Justus Georg Schottel's great epitome of the study of language, and especially of German, since the Reformation, the *Ausführliche Arbeit von der Teutschen Haubt-Sprache* (Braunschweig, 1663), which had said:

Let us pay attention to our German and note how the German language speaks with powerful short expression and pleasing sound at the bidding of the inner-most essence and without doubt is not on any level inferior to the Latin and Greek in setting-forth according to nature. . . . We hold therefore that the name of any object must first be studied and understood in terms of its nature and manner. "That language," says Bibliander [*De ratione omnium linguarum et literarum* (1548)], "is the most perfect whose words explain the natures of things. Such as that language is believed to have been, in which Adam imposed names on individual things."[14]

Clearly, this doctrine would lose its foundation if language were con-ventional rather than natural; further, the doctrine rested on the axiom concerning the ancient source of the German language and was sus-tained by historical study that attempted to reach back to the origin.

Many of the points that Leibniz had made in the Preface to Nizol-ius were repeated in a work from the early 1680s, his *Ermahnung an die Teutsche, ihren Verstand und Sprache besser zu üben*, whose title contains a characteristic linking of "Verstand" and "Sprache." But *Die Ermahnung* lay unpublished until 1846, unlike a later and better work, *Die Unvorgreiflichen Gedanken betreffend die Ausübung und Verbesserung der Teutschen Sprache*. It was in part written in the late 1690s, revised and expanded during the next ten years, and first published in 1717 in the *Collectanea Etymologica*, a collection of various pieces—by no means all by Leibniz—that was made by his for-mer secretary Johann Georg Eccard.[15] *Die Unvorgreiflichen Gedanken* exercised a steady and strong influence in Germany throughout the eighteenth century and beyond. But during his own lifetime the only public and international record of his interest in etymology and even in what we may more nearly call philology was the Latin treatise that stood at the head of the first volume of the *Miscellanea Berolinensia*, the memoirs of the Berlin Academy, whose founder Leibniz was. It appeared in 1710 and was the "Brevis designatio meditationum de originibus gentium, ductis potissimum ex indicio linguarum." In the eighteenth century it influenced a few German scholars—chiefly Johann Georg Wachter—but did not otherwise gain much attention until later, largely owing to that century's bias in favor of universal grammar and the philosophical question of the ultimate origin of language. It opened with a statement that has since become as famous as it was then prophetic:

> Since the distant origins of nations transcend history, languages take for us the place of old documents. The most ancient vestiges of languages remain in the names of rivers and forests, which very often survive the changes of populations. The most obvious are the appellations of places that have been established by men. Although many villages and towns are named after their founders, which is very common in Germany that is settled at a later period, other places, however, are named after their site, resources, and other qualities, and the etymology of those that have long existed is difficult. Furthermore, old personal names, of which no German nation retains more than the Frisians, lead us, so to speak, into the sanctuary of the ancient language. I therefore hold it as an axiom that *all the names that we call proper names were formerly appellatives*, otherwise they would not conform to any reason. Thus whenever we do not understand the name of a river, mountain, forest, nation, region, town, village, we must conclude that we have gone beyond the ancient language.[16]

The phrase "in sacraria veteris linguae" may stand as a motto for the outburst of philological activity that occurred round 1800.[17] This passage states the very important principle that proper names must at the outset have been appellatives, for otherwise they would exist without any reason, and Leibniz could not allow that sort of inconsistency in his philosophy.

III

But the work that more nearly concerns us was written some years before the publication of the "Brevis designatio." This work is Leibniz' critique of Locke's *Essay*, his *Nouveaux Essais sur l'Entendement*, which in its discussion of Book III had contained the same observations. The *Nouveaux Essais*, however, did not appear in print until 1765, when they were published by the notorious and fantastic Rudolf

Erich Raspe. This fact is of considerable historical importance, for thus Locke alone came to influence the lively concern with language among the French *philosophes*, spurred by Voltaire's dictum in the *Lettres Philosophiques*: "So many men of reason having made a romance of the soul, a sage has come who has modestly turned it into history [i.e., description]. Locke has revealed human reason in man, as an accomplished anatomist explains the springs of the human body." This goes for Condillac, Turgot, and many others as well as for a number of articles in the *Encyclopédie*, including Turgot's influential article on etymology.

In Germany the *Nouveaux Essais* gained a wide and rapid influence. Raspe's edition was noted in the *Göttingische Anzeigen* under 10 Jan. 1765, with special mention of Book III, ii as offering "a store of scholarly linguistic knowledge and of its application to the origin of nations, which surely only a philosopher such as Leibniz could offer. The fact that nearly all languages have common rootwords and other evident agreements seem for L. to prove a common origin of mankind, against which many consider the diversity of languages an objection." Having suggested a German translation of Monboddo's great work *Of the Origin and Progress of Language*, Herder wrote a Preface to the first volume, which came out at Riga in 1784. He rightly saw that the work was much more assured of success in Germany than in England and gave the revealing reason: "Locke now concerns us only in so far as he served truth, and we have already for a long time, owing to Leibniz, been accustomed also to find weaknesses in his philosophy."[18]

I shall not give a detailed account of Leibniz' fruitless effort to enter into direct correspondence with Locke; this history has been set forth in detail in the Introduction to the recent volume of the Leibniz *Akademie Ausgabe* that contains the *Nouveaux Essais* and related pieces. The *Essay* was brought to Leibniz' attention in Dec. 1690, but we have no proof that he became even somewhat acquainted with it until June 1695.[19] His first piece on the *Essay* was "Quelques remarques sur le livre de Mons. Lock intitulé Essay of Understanding," which he sent to Burnett in March 1696, who, however, did not communicate it to Locke until 24 March 1697, regretting that he could not "recover it sooner out of the hands of those that were more curious to see than willing to restore it. My own coppie was so much used to pieces that I have sent you a trew double of it."[20] Locke had then already with Cunningham "had a sight of it last summer, and he and I read it paragraph by paragraph over together, and he confessed to me, that some parts of it he did not understand; and I showed him in others, that Mr. L.——'s opinion would not hold, who was perfectly of my mind."[21] But before the arrival of the Burnett copy, Locke had received another, which he mentioned in a letter to Molyneux of 22 Feb. 1696/7; and early in April, he received a third copy via LeClerc, with the latter's comment on Leibniz: "I believe all the same that he doesn't understand you, and I doubt that he understands himself well, which I say entre nous."[22] These words closely resemble Locke's well-known and final judgment of Leibniz, expressed in the letter he wrote to Molyneux the next day:

> I must confess to you, that Mr. L——'s great name had raised in me an expectation which the sight of his paper did not answer, nor that discourse of his in the "Acta Eruditorum," which he quotes, and I have since read, and had just the same thought of it, when I read it, as I find you have. From whence I only draw this inference, that even great parts will not master any subject without great thinking, and even the largest minds have but narrow swallows.

Leibniz did not see these unkind words until after the publication of *Some Familiar Letters* in 1708, but he had heard nearly the same opinion from Burnett in a letter of 16 Dec. 1701:

> He is not eager to dispute with anybody about his writings; but I have also heard it said that he did not feel he understood what you had written well enough to answer you, which I tell you as a friend; but please do not cite me for this bit of information, since I have never been told to send you anything but his thanks and his esteem for you.[23]

Whether Locke was not up to controversy or criticism in 1701 is one thing; it is another that he strongly encouraged critical comments in his letter to Limborch of 29 Oct. 1697:

> I wish that my Essay were written in a language which these excellent men could understand, for by their careful and frank judgment of my work I could surely measure what there is in it that is true or false, and what there may be in it that is tolerable,

and he goes on to mention with regret that the third edition has not been doing as well as the first two.[24] Thus in spite of Leibniz' repeated attempts, in spite of Burnett's frequent assurances of Leibniz' profound and no doubt sincere respect for Locke, and in spite of Locke's own eagerness to receive criticism from others at the very same time, Leibniz never reached the man, whom of all his contemporaries he was most eager to engage in a philosophical exchange of ideas. A few years later, Leibniz found some comfort that he was indirectly reaching Locke through the correspondence with Lady Masham that began within a year of Locke's death—"It would seem that he has some share in it, at least regarding the opinion he undoubtedly held, and which he apparently did not hide in the company of that lady" were

Leibniz' words to Burnett in August 1704.[25] The consequence of Locke's silence was the extensive discussion of Locke's *Essay* that Leibniz presented in the *Nouveaux Essais*. The work was written between the summers of 1703 and 1705 and was made possible by the appearance of Coste's French translation of the *Essay* in the summer of 1700—Leibniz' English was not good enough to insure a correct reading of Locke's text, a matter on which Locke remarked in a letter to Molyneux on 22 Feb. 1696/7: "I suspect he has, in some places, a little mistaken my sense, which is easy for a stranger, who has (as I think) learned English out of England." Leibniz had planned to publish his discussion, but after Locke's death he decided not to do so because he did not wish to send abroad his arguments against a man who was no longer alive to defend himself.

Why Locke professed not to understand Leibniz is the philosophical question not of one century but of at least two. We cannot, perhaps, dismiss the possibility that Locke may have been influenced by the early rumblings of the undignified priority controversy over the calculus, which had already begun to take shape with Newton's cagey letter to Leibniz of 16 Oct. 1693, written to cushion some of the potential unpleasant consequences of the recent publication in John Wallis' *Opera* II of some of the letters from the 1670s that were supposed to show Leibniz' dependence on Newton in regard to the calculus.[26] But even without that unpleasant matter I am convinced that Locke had sufficient grounds for not responding to Leibniz. Their opposition was too fundamental.

To provide the fullest and fairest statement of Locke's doctrines, Leibniz wrote his *Nouveaux Essais* as a dialogue between a "lover of Truth" Philalethe and the "lover of God" Theophile; the latter is Leibniz while the former speaks for Locke and corresponds to Pierre Coste.[27] The procedure is simple. Philalethe presents Locke's views by direct quotation, paraphrase, summary, or a mixture of all three at such length as the matter may justify, often with omission of illustrations and examples; then Theophile answers. Sections may be telescoped into a single paragraph or entirely omitted; chapters may be severely shortened but none are completely left out. Departure from Locke's order occurs occasionally and shows that Leibniz took some care with the composition. For instance, most references to words and language in Book II are omitted and some of them transferred to Book III. A noteworthy example occurs in II, xi, 10-11, where Locke observes that animals "have not the faculty of abstracting, or making general *Ideas*, since they have no use of Words, or any other general Signs." Leibniz transposes most of this discussion to the opening

pages of Book III, where it is in fact more appropriate. Another sort
of significant change is found in the chapter "Of Enthusiasm," which
Locke in the fourth edition (1700) added as IV, xix. It deals with the
visions, perceptions, and language of mystics, but Locke gives no
names; Leibniz, however, adds the names that must almost certainly
have been in Locke's mind: Boehme, Quirinus Kuhlmann, Christine
Poniatowa, Drabitius, and their defender Comenius, all made infamous—and Comenius much maligned—by the recent publication of
Bayles's *Dictionnaire* (1697).[28] This is only one among many instances
of the light that the *Nouveaux Essais* may throw on the *Essay*. I have
only discovered one case in which Locke, or rather Philalethe, is
made to concede a point which he would hardly have granted. It occurs in the course of the discussion of the real and nominal essences
of substances and mixed modes, in III, x, 21 near the end of the long
analysis "Of the Abuse of Words." Here Philalethe is made to say: "I
now see that I would have made a mistake blaming this relation on
essences and internal constitutions, under the pretext that that would
be to make our words signs of nothing or something unknown." At
the end of the same chapter occurs one of several instances of humor
and good spirit; Locke has just delivered a diatribe against eloquence
as tending to insinuate false ideas, to excite the passions, and to se-
duce reason. Theophile answers that he admires the zeal for truth
and does not wholly despair of it "for it seems, Sir, that you oppose
eloquence with its own arms, and that you even have another kind of
eloquence, superior to the deceptive kind."

IV

The fundamental opposition between Locke and Leibniz is clearly
brought out by a statement Leibniz made in a letter to Burnett as
early as 22 Nov. 1695:

> It is not that this book is not more important and profound [than Locke's
> book on Education] and doesn't contain many good things, but that I am
> perhaps better placed than he is to get to the bottom in the search for
> truth, because I have myself perhaps had time and occasion to study more
> closely than he this matter of human understanding and the art of thinking
> and to join theory and practice by offering several discoveries that have
> appeared solid.[29]

This judgment Leibniz never found occasion to revise; he took the
Essay to be a "recherche de la vérité." Nearly all eighteenth-century
readers made the same mistake about the scope and intent of the
Essay, which perhaps would not have gained its supreme authority as
the arbiter of Truth if it had not been for this mistake. The readers

found a pattern they were familiar with and did not stop to think that they had been presented with something quite different. Epistles to the Reader are rarely read with care, nor, even if read, are they taken seriously. The *Essay* had a private origin. It was written "by incoherent Parcels" for "my own Information, and the Satisfaction of a few Friends"; but "those who advised me to publish it, advised me . . . to publish it as it is." Hence "I plainly tell all my Readers, except half a dozen, this Treatise was not at first intended for them; and therefore they need not be at the Trouble to be of that Number." Eustace Budgell said of Robert Boyle: "He has *animated* Philosophy; and put in *Action* what before was little better than a *speculative* Science."[30] Similarly, Locke put the mind and its philosophy in action. Both Boyle and Locke had the conviction that knowledge accumulates by a process that steadily may bring us closer to truth, but the Truth is never achieved; the process never ends. Boyle, Birch tells us, "wanted no capacity or abilities to have worked up a glorious system," but "he nobly despised this poor satisfaction and mean gratification, telling us plainly and expressly, that, notwithstanding all he had done, all the labour, pains, and expence bestowed in a life of natural inquiries, notwithstanding the vastly numerous and important observations and discoveries he made, he saw nothing but the first drawings of science."[31] Huygens and Leibniz, however, deplored the absence of what Birch saw as the greatest virtue; Huygens had hoped for "principles that would seem true," Leibniz for "sufficient application to push the consequences as far as they should be."[32] In this matter the opposition between the two Englishmen and the two Europeans was complete and explicit. Boyle said in 1666 that he had purposely forborne the perusal of Descartes' system of philosophy,[33] and 20 years later Locke wrote to Clarke that he did not think the works of nature could ever be reduced into a science:

> Natural philosophy, as a speculative science, I think, we have none, and perhaps I may think I have reason to say we never shall. . . . Not but that there are many things to be learnt in natural philosophy which abundantly reward the pains of the curious with delight and advantage. But these, I think, are rather to be found amongst such writers as have employed themselves in making rational experiments and observations, than writing speculative systems.

Among such writers Boyle was the best; but if the reader should have "a mind to launch further out into general speculations, I would recommend Descarte's principles, not as perfectly true or satisfactory to an inquisitive man, but yet perhaps the most intelligible and most consistent with itself of any yet to be met with."[34]

Thus one may say that the *Essay* has an esoteric background in the world of Boyle and the men of the Royal Society. It is not a meta-physical treatise, not a "recherche de la vérité." It does not pretend to offer a complete system of knowledge and truth, but to present a dis-cussion of the ways in which knowledge may be obtained and secured. Its nature is essentially practical, and for that reason it pays much attention to the ways in which we may wrongly come to believe we have certain knowledge when in fact we do not. It is to this problem that Book III "Of Words" is chiefly devoted.[35] It offers many instances of Leibniz' failure to understand Locke's limited scope and intent.

In III, v, 8, "Of the Names of Mixed Modes and Relations," Phila-lethe has presented Locke's doctrine of intranslatability among lan-guages: "Since men form arbitrarily different kinds of mixed modes, the result is that we find words in one language for which there are no corresponding words in another."[36] "This," Locke observed in words that Leibniz does not quote, "could not have happened, if these Species were the steady Workmanship of Nature; and not Col-lections made and abstracted by the Mind, in order to naming, and for the convenience of Communcation," which in the previous section he had called "the chief end of Language." Two sections later he reit-erates with one of his most telling and characteristic metaphors: "Though therefore it be the Mind that makes the Collection, 'tis the Name which is, as it were, the Knot, that ties them fast together."[37] But to III, v, 8, Leibniz answers: "The statement is true as regards names and the customs of men, but it changes nothing in the sciences and in the nature of things." A few lines later he concludes: "But in the science itself, apart from its history and actual existence, it is of no consequence whether people do or do not act in accordance with the dictates of reason." I am sure Locke would agree, but he was not talking about "la science" but about "l'histoire." He had stressed this point in I, i, 2, when he said: "I shall imagine I have not wholly mis-employ'd my self in the Thoughts I shall have on this Occasion, if, in this Historical, plain Method, I can give any Account of the Ways, whereby our Understandings come to attain those Notions of Things we have." On 26 June 1681 he had devoted a journal entry to this matter, beginning: "There are two sorts of knowledg in the world generall and particular founded upon two different principles i.e. true Ideas and matter of fact history." He repeated much of that entry in IV, xi, 13-14; Leibniz' long comment on those sections ends in this fashion:

These necessary truths, being anterior to the existence of contingent beings, must have their foundation in the existence of a necessary substance. It is there that I find the original of the ideas and truths that are engraved in our minds, not in the form of propositions, but as sources from which application and given occasions will cause actual affirmations to arise.[38]

It is no wonder that Locke did not understand Leibniz; his head would have reeled if he could have heard this sort of answer to his III, iii, 19: "I have already told you, Sir, that essences are perpetual, because here the questions concerns only the possible."

But then, how was Leibniz to know what Locke and his half dozen friends would have taken for granted, the "historical, plain method" of the natural philosophers in the Royal Society? The word "understanding" in the title is to be taken in its active sense as meaning something like "ways of getting to know something"—"mind" is no synonym for it. The *Essay* is about process, not about the still center and the possible. The aim of the *Essay* was much more limited than Leibniz saw; in I, i, 6 Locke had pointed out that "our Business here is not to know all Things, but those which concern our Conduct," i.e., conduct in regard to nature as the Royal Society would have understood it. The design of the *Essay* lay in a "little compass," as Locke wrote to Anthony Collins on 21 March 1703/4: "You have a comprehensive knowledg of it, & do not stick in the incidents, wch whether true or false make nothing to the main design of the *Essay*, wch lies in a little compass & yet I hope may be of great use to those who see & follow that plain & easy method of nature to carry them ye shortest & clearest way to knowledg."[39]

Locke shared the outlook of his fellow members in the Royal Society. His natural inclinations, his intellectual habits, and his methods were also theirs, though he modestly placed his own efforts below those of a Boyle, a Sydenham, a Huygens, or a Newton. For, as he explained in the "Epistle to the Reader," "'tis Ambition enough to be employed as an Under-Labourer in clearing the Ground a little, and removing some of the Rubbish that lies in the way of Knowledge." This rubbish he immediately proceeded to identify. "Philosophy, which is nothing but the true Knowledge of Things," had been impeded by the mistaken trust in language and words.

> Vague and insignificant Forms of Speech, and Abuse of Language, have so long passed for Mysteries of Science . . . that it will not be easie to perswade, either those who speak, or those who hear them, that they are but the Covers of Ignorance, and Hinderance of true Knowledge. To break in upon the Sanctuary of Vanity and Ignorance, will be, I suppose, some Service to Humane Understanding: Though so few are apt to think, they deceive or are deceived in the Use of Words; or that the Language of the Sect they are of, has any Faults in it, which ought to be examined or corrected, that I hope I shall be pardon'd, if I have in the third Book dwelt long on this Subject; and endeavoured to make it so plain, that neither the Inveterateness

of the Mischief, nor the Prevalency of the Fashion, shall be any Excuse for
those, who will not take Care about the Meaning of their own Words, and
will not suffer the Significancy of their Expressions to be enquired into.

This passage, so prominently placed, leaves no doubt about the great
importance that Locke attributed to Book III and its subject. It was
also a subject that Boyle—though he devoted no separate work to it—
constantly returned to, and naturally so, for what can a chemist
accomplish if he starts with a fixed notion of the real essence of gold.
Locke's journals and book lists show that he took care to own Boyle's
publications.[40] There can be no doubt that of all men, both living
and dead, Boyle was the one whose work and thought Locke knew
best and most admired, not least in regard to language and words.

In the *Origin and Forms of Qualities*, first published in 1666, Boyle
had said:

It was not at random that I spoke, when in the foregoing notes, about the
origin of qualities, I intimated that it was very much by a kind of tacit
agreement.that men had distinguished the species of bodies, and that those
distinctions were more arbitrary than we are wont to be aware of; for I
confess that I have not yet, either in *Aristotle* or any other writer, met
with any genuine and sufficient diagnostic and boundary for the discrim-
inating and limiting the species of things; or to speak more plainly, I have
not found that any naturalist has laid down a determinate number and sort
of qualities or other attributes, which is sufficient and necessary to constitute all portions of matter endowed with them, distinct kinds of natural
bodies: and therefore I observe that most commonly men look upon these
as distinct species of bodies that have had the luck to have distinct names
found out for them, though perhaps divers of them differ much less from
one another than other bodies, which (because they have been huddled up
under one name) have been looked upon as but one sort of bodies.[41]

The implications are sufficiently obvious to go without any other
comment than Locke's more general statement of the same principle
in III, ii, 5:

Because *Men* would not be thought to talk *barely* of their own Imaginations, but of Things as really they are; therefore they *often suppose their
Words to stand also for the reality of Things.*

But comforting as this supposition may be, it is false; words bear no
reliable relationship to things, being no better than "those *Ideas* we
have in our Minds," so that "it is a perverting the use of Words, and
brings unavoidable Obscurity and Confusion, whenever we make
them stand for anything" else. In the same work, Boyle suggests a
historical reason why words can have no authority in regard to things
and nature:

For my part that which I am solicitous about is, that what nature hath
made things to be in themselves, not what, logician or metaphysician will

call them in the terms of his art; it being much fitter in my judgment to alter words [by which he means not the phonetic form of the word but the bundle of ideas a word ties together], that they may better fit the nature of things, than to affix a wrong nature to things that they may be accommodated to forms or words that were probably devised, when the things themselves were not known or well understood, if at all thought on.[42]

This important doctrine is also maintained by Locke. In III, vi, 25, he says that even if "the *real Essences* of Substances were discoverable," we cannot "reasonably think, that the *ranking of things under general Names, was regulated by* those internal real Constitutions, or any thing else but *their obvious appearances.*" He continues:

> Since Languages, in all Countries, have been established long before Sciences. So that they have not been Philosophers, or Logicians, or such who have troubled themselves about *Forms* and *Essences*, that have made the general Names, that are in use amongst the several Nations of Men: But those, more or less comprehensive terms, have for the most part, in all Languages, received their Birth and Signification, from ignorant and illiterate People, who sorted and denominated Things, by those sensible Qualities they found in them.[43]

This, of course, explains the distinction between the real and nominal essence of a substance, of which only the latter can be known. Words are no better than men's attention to "obvious appearances" and "sensible qualities." And anyone who thinks otherwise will never become a chemist but remain an alchymist.[44]

V

Thus the *Essay* was, as it were, intended as a manual in the epistemology of the Royal Society, whose aim was the promotion of natural knowledge. The motive is clearly brought out in Oldenburg's words to Milton in 1656: "I propose to contemplate nature and its author more closely." The motto that appears on the title pages of Thomas Birch's editions of Boyle's *Works* says much the same: "To know the supreme cause from the causes of things."[45] Nature or Creation, "the unsealed book of God," revealed the Creator. To insure the success of this august enterprise nothing must be allowed to interpose itself between man and nature, neither innate notions nor words, for either would give man less than a clear view of his object. Locke stressed this objectivity in a familiar passage:

> I pretend not to teach, but to enquire. . . . For, methinks, the *Understanding* is not much unlike a Closet wholly shut from light, with only some little opening left, to let in external visible Resemblances, or *Ideas* of things without; would the Pictures coming into such a dark Room but stay there, and lie so orderly as to be found upon occasion, it would very much

> resemble the Understanding of a Man, in reference to all Objects of sight, and the *Ideas* of them.[46]

Knowledge grows by accumulation, and language is a tool to sort and denominate what comes to be compacted in that box—though often a blunt and inadequate tool. Thus when Theophile at one point says "all the same, ideas do not depend on names," he is missing the mark. Locke does not say that ideas depend on words, but that in practice they generally do; and that we need to realize to avoid error and to increase the order in the box.[47] The *Nouveaux Essais* do not take up the camera metaphor of the understanding, but in the Preface Leibniz uses another that holds a corresponding position in his conception of the mind. This is the equally familiar and in this case also traditional image of the block of marble whose veins outline a statue of Hercules; it is also, characteristically, a static image as any image that is designed to illustrate innateness is bound to be:

> Hercules would be as if innate in some sense, though it would require labor to discover these veins. In the same way ideas and truths are innate for us, as inclinations, dispositions, habits, and natural virtualities, and not as actions.

But to Locke, the work *is* the knowledge, not just the means of revelation. No pre-established harmony has traced veins in his understanding or insinuated words that would do the job of veins.

Here Leibniz seems to be involved in an inconsistency, for how can he insist on "this admirable pre-established harmony of mind and body," while at the same time maintaining that "ideas do not depend on names"? There must somehow be a connection, for language with its words must have its place within the great harmony. The resolution of this difficulty brings us to the fundamental difference between Leibniz and Locke on language, and it also defines their separate allegiances to existing doctrines concerning the nature of language. Strictly speaking, ideas may not depend on words, nor does the reverse hold. The answer is that they are interdependent, thus showing forth one aspect of the total harmony—as suggested in a phrase that occurs in Leibniz' long answer to III, ii, i: "There is something natural in the origin of words." This relationship may not be apparent from a synchronic view of speech forms such as Locke takes, but it will emerge from an historical and etymological consideration of many languages and dialects. A diachronic view will reveal that these seem to converge toward a common point as we trace them backward in time. Here Leibniz' wide philological knowledge of a great variety of early dialects came to his aid. His historical studies had made him very familiar with the increasing similarity of the German dialects and even of the Germanic languages as illustrated in the Middle Ages. It is this observation that supported his faith that there ultimately is a single radical and primitive language that underlies all the languages of mankind—and he believed this held for the entire earth, for the European languages and the Asian, African, Mexican, Chinese, and American all taken together. Thus if languages do not now reveal the harmony at mere inspection, it will be found to hold all the same.

In this perspective the doctrine of the Adamic language, which in its original purity was lost in the Fall, still retains some of its meaning, though Leibniz did not take that doctrine literally in the manner of, for instance, Paracelsus, Boehme, or Comenius. To Leibniz, as to Schottel and his predecessors, language in the process of time shows a descent from wisdom to a low point that occurred before the "discovery" of this relationship between language and creation, a discovery that in Germany had coincided with the Reformation. To Luther, the Gift of Tongues had given renewed assurance of the Truth contained in this relationship, and thus in his exegesis he replaced the allegorical mode of the Fathers with the Protestant study of the truth that lay concealed in the word, in languages.[48] Adam's naming of the animals was a creative act; it was both a striking manifestation of man's place in creation, of the harmony of the macrocosm and the microcosm, and at the same time a sign of man's control, for in the names he "knew" the creatures. Thus Adam was the greatest of philosophers even after the Fall, as Luther maintains in his lecture on Genesis 2:18-20.[49] Locke's old school-mate Robert South voiced the same doctrine in a sermon on Genesis 1:27, preached in St. Paul's on 9 Nov. 1662. Adam, he said,

> came into the world a philosopher, which sufficiently appeared by his writing the nature of things upon their names; he could view essences in themselves, and read forms without the comment of their respective properties. . . . An Aristotle was but the rubbish of an Adam, and Athens but the rudiments of Paradise.[50]

Further, since Adam's claim to being both the first and the greatest of philosophers rested on the act of naming, so he also was the first and the greatest of etymologists. In his "Discours sur la Science des Etymologies," first printed in the second edition (1694) of Gilles Ménages's *Dictionnaire Etymologique, ou Origines de la Language Françoise*, Besnier said: "One can say that the first man was also the first etymologist; and that this science was, so to speak, his first business." It was on these grounds that reformed man in languages and etymology found new guidelines to the reattainment of early knowledge and the wisdom that had been lost.

The mystics and visionaries of the seventeenth century were profoundly influenced by these doctrines, which in turn were strengthened by the mysticism of the Kabbala, which spread over Europe
after the expulsion of the Jews from Spain in 1492. The mystic's path
to knowledge was the same as Adam's, as Boehme explained in his
Aurora, oder Morgenröthe im Aufgang:

> For as Adam spoke for the first time, he gave names to all the creatures ac-
> cording to their qualities and inherent effects. And it is truly the language
> of all of nature, but not every man knows it, for it is a secret, a mystery,
> which by the grace of God has been granted to me by the spirit that has
> taken delight in me.[51]

Boehme's doctrines were widely known in England where all his
works appeared in translation between 1644 and 1663, many of
them before the publication of the German originals.[52] And in England they also received very forceful and complete, though compact,
statement in John Webster's *Academiarum Examen* from 1654,
which presented a severe critique of the universities, their learning,
and their teaching.

In this work Webster, like the men already active in the proto
Royal Society, cited Bacon with high admiration; advocated the wider
use of English and the mother tongue in order that "arts and sciences
may be taught in it, that thereby a more easie and short way may be
had to the attaining all sorts of knowledge";[53] and called "this *School
Philosophy* . . . altogether void of true and infallible demonstration,
observation, and experiment."[54] But unlike those natural philosophers, he also found truth in Plato, Descartes, Sir Kenelm Digby,
Robert Fludd, and the Rosicrucians; encouraged the active study of
astrology, alchemy, magic, and "Cabalistick Science";[55] and asserted
as fundamental doctrine that:

> . . . the mind receiveth but one single and simple image of every thing,
> which is expressed in all by the same motions of the spirits, and doubt-
> lessly in every creature hath radically, and naturally the same sympathy in
> voice, in sound, but men not understanding these immediate sounds of the
> soul, and the true *Schematism* of the internal notions impressed, and delin-
> eated in the several sounds, have instituted, and imposed others, that do
> not altogether concord, and agree to the innate notions, and so no care is
> taken for the recovery and restauration of the Catholique language in which
> lies hid all the rich treasury of natures admirable and excellent secrets.[56]

He further linked his adherence to this doctrine with profound respect for Boehme and the mystical belief in the reality of the language
of nature, for, as Webster said:

> I cannot (howsoever fabulous, impossible, or ridiculous it may be accounted
> of some) passe over with silence, or neglect that signal and wonderful secret

(so often mentioned by the mysterious and divinely-inspired *Teutonick* [who of course is Boehme] and in some manner acknowledged and owned by the highly-illuminated fraternity of the *Rosie Crosse*) of the language of nature: but out of profound and deep consideration, must adumbrate some of those reasons, which perswasively draw my judgment to credit the possibility thereof.[57]

Nowhere in the seventeenth century are we closer to what Locke was aiming at when in Book I he rejected what he in his own title of that book expressly called "innate notions." In terms that are highly reminiscent of Boehme, Webster subsequently argues that there must be a language of nature and that this was the language spoken by Adam when naming every living creature:

> I cannot but conceive that *Adam* did understand both their internal and external signatures, and that the imposition of their names was adaequately agreeing with their natures: otherwise it could not univocally and truely be said to be their names, whereby he distinguished them.[58]

Thus whatever agreement Webster might have gained among the natural philosophers, he forfeited entirely by his belief in the cognitive value of "innate notions" and by his closely related advocacy of the language of nature.[59] Webster's mysticism violated the objectivity that was the very foundation of natural philosophy, as the Royal Society saw it, and its successful pursuit of certain knowledge of Creation.

Boyle was fully aware of this problem; he therefore firmly rejected the doctrine of the language of nature, or, which is the same thing, the language of Adam. In the *Excellency of Theology*, written in 1665, he observed that considering the dim knowledge we are capable of in our present condition, the more reason we have to value religion, since it holds forth hope that we may attain a condition in which we shall gain "degrees and kinds of knowledge, to which we are here but strangers." He continued:

> In favour of which I will not urge the received opinion of divines, that before the fall (which yet is a less noble condition than is reserved for us in heaven), *Adam*'s knowledge was such, that he was able at first sight of them, to give each of the beasts a name expressive of its nature; because that, in spight of some skill (which my curiosity for divinity, not philosophy, gave me) in the holy tongue, I could never find, that the Hebrew names of animals, mentioned in the beginning of *Genesis*, argued a (much) clearer insight into their natures, than did the names of the same or some other animals in Greek, or other languages: wherefore, as I said, I will not urge *Adam*'s knowledge in paradise for that of the saints in heaven, though the notice he took of *Eve* at his first seeing her, (if it were not conveyed to him by secret revelation) may be far more probably urged, than his naming of the beasts.[60]

That passage may also serve as a reminder of the reason why Locke, Boyle, Newton, and other natural philosophers studied Hebrew and corresponded together about scriptural interpretation; it is only in a later and very ignorant perspective that this occupation has come to look as if it were the business of their idle hours. They had two books to read, Scripture and Nature. Boyle was assured that he might "safely compare several things in the books we call the scripture, to several other in that of nature" and averred that in the perusal of "true naturalists . . . I receive more pleasure and satisfaction, and am induced more to admire the works of nature, than by all their [the poets'] romantick and superficial narratives."[61] Boyle and his eminent friends did not depreciate poetry because they were illiterate and uncultured boors, for obviously if man can hope to gain real knowledge, poetry is of no consequence. The angels do not entertain *themselves* with poetry, though in the human perspective their entertainment is poetry and beautiful music; but for them it is enough to intuit directly. The order they contemplate demands no embellishments.[62]

With his clear awareness of the implications of the doctrine of natural language and "innate notions," we should not expect Locke to fail to make reference to Adam; and indeed he did. The last nine sections of III, vi, "Of the Names of Substances," are devoted to Adam's use of language. The details of the argument are too many to trace, but the "Conclusion" presents this succinct summary:

> What liberty *Adam* had at first to make any complex *Ideas* of mixed Modes, by no other Pattern, but by his own Thoughts, the same have all Men ever since had. And the same necessity of conforming his *Ideas* of Substances to Things without him, as to *Archetypes* made by Nature, that *Adam* was under, if he would not wilfully impose upon himself, the same are all Men ever since under too. The same Liberty also, that *Adam* had of affixing any new Name to any *Idea*; the same has any one still, (especially the beginners of Languages, if we can imagine any such,) but only with this difference, that in Places, where Men in Society have already established a Language amongst them, the signification of Words are very warily and sparingly to be alter'd. . . . But in Communication with others, it is necessary, that we conform the *Ideas* we make the Vulgar Words of any Language stand for, to their known proper Significations, (which I have explain'd at large already,) or else to make known that new Signification, we apply them to.

Few chapters in the entire *Essay* show greater and more evident and direct influence from Boyle than this one. Leibniz, however, does not comment on these sections.[63] Locke's long discussion of Adam's language also shows the close texture of his argument, and that its full meaning can only be recovered with some labor. Posterity lost the key to its understanding, but there can be no doubt that Locke's "half a dozen" friends did possess the key. Our understanding of the *Essay* depends, in turn, on our success in regaining their knowledge, chiefly from Boyle. But we can also indirectly add to it by an examination of Leibniz' responses to some fundamental aspects of Book III.

VI

Leibniz and Locke agree on several basic points. Book III opens with the well-known words: "God having designed Man for a sociable Creature, made him not only with an inclination, and under a necessity to have fellowship with those of his own kind; but furnished him also with Language, which was to be the great Instrument, and common Tye of Society." Having himself often stated the same conviction, Leibniz assents in typical fashion: "I am delighted to see that you are far from holding Mr. Hobbes's opinion." He also agrees that words have two functions: For the recording of our own thoughts as in memory and for the communication of our thoughts to others. This Leibniz had likewise said before, though in his answer he points to other kinds of useful signs, such as those of algebra, clearly intending to remind Locke of the combinatorial characteristics. They further agree on a practical matter, namely that language must work with "ease and dispatch" or "ease and quickness." But the agreement does not last beyond the first chapter.

At the very beginning of III, ii, Locke lays down the principle that is absolutely fundamental to his discussion of language, which had to open with a firm dismissal of any notion of natural language. He said:

> *Words* . . . come to be made use of by Men as *the Signs of* their *Ideas*; not by any natural connexion, that there is between particular articulate Sounds and certain *Ideas*, for then there would be but one Language amongst all Men; but by a voluntary Imposition, whereby such a Word is made arbitrarily the Mark of such an *Idea*. The use then of Words, is to be sensible Marks of *Ideas*; and the *Ideas* they stand for, are their proper and immediate Signification.

Language, then, is conventional, not natural; words bear no intrinsic relationship to things, but to ideas only—as we are often reminded by Locke's knot-and-bundle metaphor. The meaning of the word has nothing to do with its sound. Locke takes great care to be consistent in this matter and often restates his principle in passages that strike directly at the natural language doctrine. To take just one example, though a very important one, he realized that his argument against our being capable of gaining knowledge of the real essence of substances would collapse if language could in any manner be considered natural. Two passages will illustrate this point. Book III, iv, 11, says:

Simple Ideas . . . are only to be *got by* those *impressions*, Objects themselves make on our Minds, by the proper Inlets appointed to each sort. If
they are not received this way, all the *Words* in the World, *made use of to
explain, or define any of their Names, will never be able to produce in us
the* Idea *it stands for*. For Words being Sounds, can produce in us no other
simple *Ideas*, than of those very Sounds; nor excite any in us, but by that
voluntary connexion, which is known to be between them, and those simple *Ideas*, which common Use has made them Signs of. . . . In Light and
Colours, and all other simple *Ideas*, it is the same thing: for the signification of Sounds, is not natural, but only imposed and arbitrary.

Similarly, in III, ix, 4, Locke says:

Now since Sounds have no natural connexion with our *Ideas*, but have all
their signification from the arbitrary imposition of Men, the *doubtfulness*
and uncertainty *of their signification* . . . has its cause more in the *Ideas*
they stand for, than in any incapacity there is in one Sound, more than in
another, to signify any *Idea*: For in that regard, they are all equally perfect.

Not to have dismissed the last remnant of the doctrine of natural language would have allowed innateness to creep in by the back door.
Thus Book III repeats the argument of Book I, and it is reasonable to
surmise that Locke felt compelled to devote a separate book to words
owing to the increased knowledge of contemporary language doctrines that he gained during the 1670s and especially during the years
in France.[64]

Locke's statement of the conventionalist doctrine elicits the longest
single passage spoken by Theophile in the entire *Nouveaux Essais*, no
less than seven pages punctuated only twice by half-line interruptions
from Philalethe—one of which is "One more example would make it
easier to understand." The length of the answer was to be expected.
Locke's doctrine has brought both to the very center of their disagreement; Leibniz' long and detailed answer therefore offers an
especially fruitful opportunity for further exploration and identification of their positions.

Theophile's answer to III, ii, 1 opens:

I know that it is customary to say in the schools and elsewhere that the
significations of words are arbitrary (*ex instituto*), and it is true that they
are not determined by any natural necessity, but they are all the same
determined by reasons that are sometimes natural where chance has some
share, and sometimes moral where choice enters.

After mention of artificial language, Theophile makes this observation
concerning linguistic change: "As for languages that have existed for
a long time, there is hardly any that is not greatly changed today.
That is evident by comparing with ancient books and monuments that
remain." He supports his contention with copious citation of examples

from his wide knowledge of early documents, many of them legal. In this context he presents an essentially correct division of the Germanic languages and then finally arrives at this important conclusion:

> So that there is nothing in this to combat and not rather to favor the opinion of a common origin for all nations, and of an essentially basic and primitive language. If Hebrew or Arabic comes the nearest to it, it must be at least much changed, and it seems that the German has preserved more of the natural, and (to speak the language of Jacob Boehme) of the Adamic: for if we had the primitive language in its pure state, or well enough preserved to be recognizable, it would follow that the reasons of the connections would show in it, whether physical or of the nature of an arbitrary institution that is wise and worthy of the first author. But if we suppose that our languages are fundamentally derivative, they nevertheless have something primitive in themselves, which has arisen in them in relation to new root words, formed later within them by chance but for physical reasons.

He illustrates how this may occur by pointing out that man from the sounds made by frogs has both the Latin "coaxare" and the German "quaken." "For it seems that the noise of these animals is the primordial root of other words of the Germanic language. For since these animals make much noise, we apply it nowadays to chatterboxes and babblers, who are called *quakeler* in the diminutive." But these noises also give evidence of life, and "for that reason it has come about that *quek* in old German meant life or living, as may be observed in the earliest books, for *queksilber* is mercury, and *erquicken* is to strengthen, and, as it were, to bring to life or enliven after some infirmity or some great labor." He concludes: "Thus we may conclude that in regard to these words the Germanic language can be considered primitive, the ancients having had no need to borrow elsewhere a sound that is the imitation of that of frogs. . . . For it seems that the ancient Germans, Celts, and other peoples related to them, have by a natural instinct used the letter R to signify a violent movement and a noise like that of this letter."[65] But if "r" suggests violent movement, "l" suggests a gentler one. Thus a child who finds "r" too harsh will substitute "l," saying "mon levelend pele" for "mon reverend pere," the characteristic quality of "l" also being illustrated in "leben," "lind," "lentus," "lieben," "lauffen," etc. Again, this proves "that there is something natural in the origin of words that indicates a relation between things and the sounds and movements of the vocal organs."[66] Leibniz is here using the affective theory of the sound-thing connection, which has always played a major role in attempts to explain the origin of language. It was in fact in this manner that he believed Adam had found names for the animals: "But in languages formed little by little, words have come into being as occasion arose from the analogy of sound with the disposition [or 'affect'] of the mind that accompanied the perception of the thing. I am inclined to believe that Adam did not impose names in any other fashion."[67]

In this fashion Leibniz sought to rescue language—and the consistency of his own philosophy—from Locke's doctrine that words "*signify* only Mens peculiar *Ideas*, and that *by a perfectly arbitrary Imposition*" (III, ii, 8). Some of Leibniz' observations and many of his examples are not his own, Schottel's *Ausführliche Arbeit* being his most frequent source. But the total integration into his own philosophy is of course entirely original with him; and hence the very long answer to Locke's initial statement in III, ii is not a digression, but essential to the maintenance of Leibniz' over-all philosophy. In regard to the nature of language, however, Locke is certainly more radical and original than Leibniz; and there can, as we have seen, be no doubt whatever that Locke very well knew he was arguing against the sort of position that Leibniz later adopted in his critique. In general, Locke's saying that he did not feel he sufficiently understood Leibniz' early pieces on the *Essay*, may have been a polite—or circuitous—way of saying that he was surprised that Leibniz had understood so little.[68]

Toward the end of the answer to III, ii, 1, Leibniz, understandably, makes some remarks about etymology, a subject that Locke does not appear to have taken any interest in just as he never to my knowledge uses the word itself.

> Being the most ancient monuments of peoples, before writing and the arts, languages in general best indicate the cognations and migrations of peoples. That is why etymologies when well understood would be interesting and full of consequences. But we must be sure to bring together the languages of a number of peoples and not make too many leaps from one nation to another far away; here it is especially important to have the assurance of peoples that are located in between. And in general we should not trust etymologies without an abundance of concurring evidence.[69]

This warning against careless procedure in etymology is followed by this reference: "I remember that the late Clauberg, an excellent philosopher, has done a short essay on the origins of Germanic that makes one regret the loss of what he had promised on this subject." Clauberg was a well-known Dutch Cartesian, and the work to which Leibniz refers is his *Ars Etymologica Teutonum*, which he had first become acquainted with in the early months of 1699, though it had appeared in 1663.[70] In this work Clauberg had observed that words for the operations of the intellect originally had reference to sensible things and actions, noting for instance:

> From the Latin *capio* derive many words of the same meaning, thus *percipere, concipere, conceptus*," conception of sense." . . . Similarly German

nehmen is frequent in the same meaning, e.g., *abnehmen, in acht nehmen, wahrnehmen, rath nehmen, sich etwas fürnehmen, er lässet sich vernehmen.*[71]

On this basis he establishes one of his etymological rules: "Many words are transferred from sensible things to things that pertain to intellect"; for this principle he refers the reader to his *Logica Vetus et Nova* with these words: "In fact, properly speaking *capere* and *prehendere* are manual actions . . . but how words of that sort are transferred to the intellect I have explained elsewhere in the prolegomena to the Logic § 77."[72] This paragraph in the "Prolegomena" to the *Logica* reads:

> For whenever we wish to signify clearly something that is understood or can be understood by the mind, we use such modes of speaking by which in general the perceptions of corporal organs are properly designated (i.e., those which we attribute to them), or their sensible objects, e.g., from see- ing and visible things we transfer them to the intellect and intellectual things: it is evident, it evidently appears, I clearly see this, it shines forth, it is perspicuous, a sharp-sighted mind, even a blind man must see, clearer than the noonday sun, clear speech, etc; from touch: I hold, apprehend, comprehend, grasp, I have pinpointed it, I am getting close, I seize, it is palpable, etc.

This passage bears a striking resemblance to the well-known opening words of III, i, 5, which states the same principle and uses some of the same examples in the same order:

> It may also lead us a little towards the Original of all our Notions and Knowledge, if we remark, how great a Dependance our *Words* have on common sensible *Ideas*; and how those, which are made use of to stand for Actions and Notions quite removed from sense, *have their rise from thence, and from obvious sensible* Ideas *are transferred to more abstruse Significa- tions* . . . v.g. to *Imagine, Apprehend, Comprehend, Adhere, Conceive, Instill, Disgust, Disturbance, Tranquility,* &c. are all Words taken from the Operations of sensible Things, and applied to certain Modes of Thinking.

Locke may not have seen the *Ars Etymologica*, but the probability is very high that he knew the contents of the *Logica*, for it is men- tioned along with four other works by Clauberg in the five-page entry called "Methode pour bien etudier la doctrine de Mr de Cartes," which Locke entered in his Journal on 7 March 1678 while he was in Paris.[73] We further know that Locke bought a copy of the *Logica* round the same time, for on 30 June 1678, it figures in a list of "Books of mine put in the box marked C. B. No. 3." If, indeed, Locke's source is the *Logica*, then we gain valuable information not only about the com- position of the *Essay* and its chronology but also about his close knowledge of a particular work that commented on matters of lan- guage. We are, furthermore, again encouraged to assume that the years in France exposed Locke to much new material, which in turn influenced the *Essay* and helped determine the form it ultimately came to assume. The *Essay* itself gives few clues to Locke's reading and specific knowledge, but our right reading of it does in large measure depend on our success in recovering as much of that knowledge as we can.[74]

Leibniz gives a characteristic answer to the opening words of III, i, 5, to Locke's assurance, as stated later in the same section, that we shall "find, in all Languages, the Names, which stand for Things that fall not under our Senses to have had their first rise from sensible *Ideas*." Theophile says:

> The fact is that our needs have forced us to leave the natural order of ideas, for this order would be the same for angels and men and all intelligent beings in general, and we would have to follow it if we had no regard for our interests. So we have been forced into submission to what we are offered by the occasions and accidents to which our species is subject, and this order does not give the origin of notions, but, so to speak, the history of our discoveries.

The first part of this passage makes implied reference to man's banishment to the world of sense after the Fall. The concluding argument depends on the doctrine of harmony. The "origin of notions " implies, as Locke no doubt intended in his corresponding words, that the understanding alone has made those notions by the pattern "Nature . . . unawares suggested to Men," whereas "history of our discoveries" suggests that it is not a matter of making or inventing according to some more or less chance pattern, but of discovering what is already there, contained within the order of the pre-established harmony. But Locke would have been indifferent to Leibniz' distinction, and his practical—one might almost say pragmatic—insistence on objectivity forced him to dismiss the doctrine that some over-all harmony enveloped man and nature. Locke's method was the "historical, plain method," not the speculative method that could afford to operate with concepts of the possible and the contingent. Two of Locke's examples were that "angel" originally meant "messenger" and "spirit" meant "breath." Leibniz sensed dangerous impiety in those examples and implied a warning by telling of a certain Dutchman who had abused "this truth (that the terms of theology, ethics, and metaphysics are taken originally from gross things) in order to ridicule theology and the Christian faith in a little Flemish dictionary in which he provided the terms with definitions and explications not such as usage demands, but such as the original power of words seemed to carry, thus giving them a malicious turn." This impiety had cost its author a term in the workhouse. But with Locke the argument does not stick, for he was merely illustrating that we grasp the less familiar by the more familiar, the "Actions and Notions quite removed from sense" by those that are not. This view is not impious to men who shared the Royal Society's conviction that Nature was the great "unsealed book of God." In England piety could be exercised in a manner that on the Continent was considered downright materialism. Leibniz was shocked and disturbed, but Condillac and the French *philosophes*, who drew the same inference, were delighted half a century later. It is perhaps not untrue to say that one of the great reversals in modern European thought occurred by misunderstanding rather than by the more normal avenue of the consistent pursuit of ideas and their logical consequences.

In historical terms, we are left with the paradox that Locke's *Essay* throughout the eighteenth century exercised an influence on language study which I am sure was as foreign to his intentions as it would, with certain important qualifications, have been proper to those of Leibniz, who often voiced the opinion we find at the end of III, vii, 6:

> I truly believe that languages are the best mirror of the human mind, and
> that an exact analysis of the signification of words would give insight into
> the operations of the understanding better than any other means.

This bears much more resemblance than anything in Locke, to Turgot's conviction that etymology is "an interesting branch of experimental metaphysics," or to his optimistic battle cry that "those who study the march of the human mind must march at every moment with the torch of etymology in hand," in spite of Turgot's own claim "je parle d'après Locke."[75] But Leibniz' *Nouveaux Essais* lay unpublished in the library at Hanover until 1765, and by that time the *Essay* had been made to yield very nearly the same doctrines about etymology and the origin of language. To Locke language was only a tool, its discussion only incidental to his examination of our ways of lapsing into error and becoming diverted from certain knowledge. But to posterity words and language became, contrary to Locke's aims, Leibniz' mirror of the mind.[76]

Notes

1. Most frequently used texts with abbreviations:

Essay: John Locke, *An Essay Concerning Humane Understanding*, 5th ed. (London, 1706). This was the last edition to receive Locke's own revisions. This text is now available in *Everyman's Library*, nos. 332 & 984 (London, 1961), edited with an Introduction by John W. Yolton. This edition supersedes A. C. Fraser's edition. Fraser's edition is not reliable:

The text is inaccurate, the marginal section summaries do not follow Locke's own, and it often fails to give the textual information it purports to give.

Nouveaux Essais: Gottfried Wilhelm Leibniz, *Philosophische Schriften*, vol. VI (Berlin, Akademie-Verlag, 1962; *Sämtliche Schriften und Briefe*, hrsg. von der Deutschen Akademie der Wissenschaften zu Berlin; ser. 6). This is the latest volume in the Akademie Ausgabe of Leibniz, this volume edited by the Leibniz-Forschungsstelle der Universität Münster. This volume contains the *Nouveaux Essais* and related pieces, with an Introduction and apparatus. (See also *Gerhardt* below.) All references are given in the text by book, chapter, and section, a procedure that will facilitate easy cross-reference to other editions in case these texts are not available.

Locke, *Works*: *The Works of John Locke*, 9 vols. (London, 1794). The text of *Some Familiar Letters* is in vol. VIII, pp. 285-472 (correspondence with Molyneux) and in vol. IX, pp. 1-145 (correspondence with Limborch).

Aaron & Gibb: R. I. Aaron and Jocelyn Gibb, *An Early Draft of Locke's Essay*, together with Excerpts from his Journals (Oxford, 1936). Unless otherwise noted, quotation from the Journals refers to this edition.

King, *Life*: Peter King, *The Life of John Locke, with Extracts from his Correspondence, Journals and Commonplace Books* (London, Bohn's Standard Library, 1858).

Lough, "Locke's Reading": John Lough, "Locke's Reading during his Stay in France (1675-79)" in *The Library*, Fifth Series, vol. 8, no. 4 (December, 1953), pp. 229-258.

Coste: *Essai Philosophique concernant L'Entendement Humain* par M. Locke. Traduit de l'Anglois par M. [Pierre] Coste (Amsterdam, 1742).

Gerhardt: *Die Philosophischen Schriften von Gottfried Wilhelm Leibniz*, hrsg. von C. I. Gerhardt, 7 vols. (Berlin, 1875-1890). Vol. V contains the *Nouveaux Essais*, but both the Introduction and the text have been superseded by the Akademie Ausgabe listed above.

Boyle, *Works*: *The Works of the Honourable Robert Boyle* [ed. Thomas Birch], 6 vols. (London, 1772).

2. See, e.g., Locke to Molyneux, (26 Dec. 1692): "I can easily forgive those who have not been at the pains to read the third book of my essay, if they make use of expressions that, when examined, signify nothing at all, in defence of hypotheses, that have long possessed their minds . . . I find none so fit, nor so fair judges, as those whose minds the study of mathematics has opened, and dis-entangled from the cheat of words, which has too great an influence in all the other, which go for sciences: and I think (were it not for the doubtful and fallacious use that is made of those signs) might be made much more sciences than they are." Locke, *Works*, vol. VIII, pp. 300-301.

3. Cf. Thomas Birch, *The Life of the Honourable Robert Boyle* (London, 1744), pp. 98-99, quoting from "some loose sheets, intended as a part of his *Essay on the Scripture*," begun in 1652: "Those excellent sciences, the mathematics, having been the first I addicted myself to, and was fond of, and experimental philosophy with its key, chemistry, succeeding them in my esteem and applications; my propensity and value for real learning gave me so much aversion and contempt for the empty study of words, that not only I have visited divers countries, whose languages I could never vouchsafe to study, but I could never yet be induced to learn the native tongue of the kingdom I was born and for some years bred in." Cf. *ibid.*, p. 102, Boyle to John Mallet in Jan. 1652/3: "I [was] . . . very much delighted to find too, that you began to have a friendship for the Eastern tongues. For though to a person so used to the study, and replenished with the knowledge of things, as Mr. *Mallet*, the learning of words cannot but at first be very tedious; yet since to be a good grammarian is necessary to be a good divine; and he, that hath no skill in the original scripture himself, may be deluded by those, that translate it for him; you will find a rich compensation for the trouble of learning the holy tongue in the advantages of having learned it; and by the help of

that primitive language, wherein they were written, you may gain a free and safe access to those theological mysteries, which he, that is no linguist, must either totally ignore, or take upon trust."

4. In the *Principes*, in the "Lettre de l'auteur à celui qui a traduit le livre, laquelle peut ici servir de préface," Descartes made the same point in different terms: "We must conclude that those who have learned least about what has hitherto been called philosophy are most capable of apprehending the true philosophy."

5. See "Epistle to the Reader" in the paragraph that explains the consequences of "this discontinued way of writing." On several occasions, Locke himself referred to the repetitions and would have been happy to see them removed. Writing to John Wynne at Oxford, who had proposed to do an abridgment of the *Essay*, he said: "Let me add that several of those repetitions, which for reasons then I let it go with, may be omitted, and all the parts contracted into that form and bigness you propose." King, *Life*, p. 192. See also Locke to Molyneux, 26 April 1695, regarding the Latin translation then proposed: "One thing particularly you will oblige me and the world in, and that is, in paring off some of the superfluous repetitions, which I left in for the sake of illiterate men, and the softer sex, not used to abstract notions and reasonings. But much of this reasoning will be out of doors in a Latin translation." Locke, *Works*, vol. VIII, p. 356.

6. Cf. III, ix, 16.

7. See "Comparative Table of the *Essay* and Drafts" in Aaron & Gibb, p. 129. Thus in par. 4 (pp. 12-13), Locke says: "And therefor in the discourse I have here made concerning humane Intellect I could not avoid saying a great deale concerning words because soe apt and usuall to be mistaken for things." See also the rest of par. 4 and the concluding part of the long par. 27 (pp. 48-49), which went nearly *verbatim* into the *Essay* as IV, viii, 10. Locke likewise shows much interest in language in the entries on "Study" that he made in his Journal during the travels in Southern France between March and May 1677. See, e.g., King, *Life*, p. 105: "Words are, in their own nature, so doubtful and obscure . . . that if, in our meditations, our thoughts busy themselves about words, and stick at the names of things, it is odds but they are misled or confounded. This, perhaps, at first sight may seem but a useless nicety, and in the practice, perhaps, it will be found more difficult than one would imagine; but yet upon trial I dare say one's experience will tell him it was worth while to endeavour it." See also two journal entries on "Species" given in Aaron & Gibb, pp. 83-84 (19 Sept. 1676, written at Montpellier) and pp. 98-99 (19 Nov. 1677, written in Paris); the latter says: "The species of things are distinguished and made by chance in order to nameing and names imposed on those things which either the conveniencys of life or common observation brings into discourse." This is the subject that Locke deals with in III, v and especially in III, vi, 7ff, and the verbal similarities are striking; cf., e.g., III, vi, 36: "'Tis *Men*, who taking occasion from the Qualities they find united in them, and wherein, they observe often several individuals to agree, *range them into Sorts, in order to their naming*, for the convenience of comprehensive signs," and III, vi, 37: "So that we may truly say, such a manner of sorting of Things, is the Workmanship of Men."

8. See Lough, "Locke's Reading," *passim*. Some of these may have diverted Shaftesbury during his captivity in the Tower in 1677; on 16 Aug. 1677, Thomas Stringer wrote to Locke: "He apprehends there are some books both Latin and French, and other Janua linguarum or Colloquies, and also he desires to know what grammars. . . . Having your order, I opened the box of things, and have furnished him with those books you sent over. He has engaged to be very careful in restoring them; and in order thereunto, hath got a box to keep them in, apart from all other things." See King, *Life*, p. 39.

9. Most of the *Essay*'s infrequent references are to travel literature. Locke, *Works*, vol. IX, pp. 512-554, give "A Catalogue and Character of most Books of Voyages and Travels"

in Latin, Spanish, Italian, French, and English; there is some reason to believe that it was compiled by Locke himself. Shortly after his return from France, Locke wrote to Thoynard on 15 July 1679, thanking him for the books he had sent over and asking about their cost, "because I very much wish for an entirely open exchange of good books printed in your country (and especially of good travel accounts) and because I fear that our country produces too few to supply me with enough merchandise of this sort to maintain a proper exchange with you." Henry Ollion, ed., *Lettres inédites de John Locke* (La Haye, 1912), p. 28. In his letters to distant travelers, Locke never failed to include languages among his requests for information; see King, *Life*, p. 25, Locke to C. Cudworth, 27 April 1683, the young man having "got quite to the other side of the world." Locke wrote: "I should trouble you also with inquiries concerning their languages, learning, government, manners," where "languages" is inserted above the line (MS. Locke c. 24, fol. 35). Early in 1679 Locke was reading F. Geb. Sagard Theodat, *Histoire du Canada* (Paris, 1636) and on 3 March notes: "Letters. Hurons have no labials in their tongue." (MS. Locke c. 33, fol. 10). The same memoranda book contains these references: "Acta Eruditorum, Lipsiae 82, Rogue de l'origine de noms & de surnoms 12° Paris 81-85" (fol. 32v), and "Morhofius de Germanorum lingua & poesi 8° Kiel 82-271" (fol. 34). The Journal for 1683 under 17 May has this information drawn from "The English Atlas, vol I fol. Oxford 1680": "The Gronlanders call their king Cachico . . . and Casique being the name of their kings from thence quite to Chile one may imagine them all of one originall" (MS. Locke f. 7, p. 100).

10. The Cicero passage occurs in Book I, xxx (or paragraph 84) and is spoken by Cotta for the academics against the Epicurean doctrines expounded by Velleius in the early part of the book.

11. John Wilkins's *Essay Towards a Real Character and a Philosophical Language* (1668) was known to Leibniz when he wrote his first letter to Oldenburg on 13/23 July 1670: "From the excellent Hezenthaler I have obtained what your most celebrated Wilkins ponders on the creation of a perfect language for philsophical use." *Akademie Ausgabe*, 2nd ser., vol. I, p. 60. The English resident in Frankfurt, William Curtius, wrote to Leibniz on 13/23 Oct. 1670 that he was sending a copy (*ibid.*, p. 67), and on 29 April/9 May 1671, Leibniz wrote to Oldenburg that he had read it recently (*ibid.*, 104). Locke's emphatic rejection of the viability of a philosophical language (implicitly as an inescapable consequence of his analysis of words and language, explicitly in III, xi, 1-2) contrasts with Leibniz' belief in it. The problems I deal with in this paper are complementary to an understanding of this opposition in regard to the philosophical language. Some readers may later in this paper see intimations of my argument on that point.

12. Gerhardt, vol. IV, p. 143.

13. Gerhardt, vol. IV, p. 144. The same observations occur in Leibniz' *Unvorgreifliche Gedanken*, §9-11.

14. Schottel, pp. 60-61. Cf. p. 61: "Now, our generous universal mother, benevolent nature has also specially granted this to the Germans that they by means of lips, tongue, teeth and palate can speak an almost unlimited number of monosyllabic words, among them also the stems, as univocal indications of a single thing." And further P. 144: "While therefore in our German language the roots are nearly everywhere univocal, clear, bright, evident, perfect, yes their quality such that nature has performed its master stroke in them so that their secrets can be cultivated from the bottom; and also because our ages-old forefathers have not obtained them by begging from foreign nations and enemies, but rather have learned them at Babylon . . . why should we then be such thoughtless monsters toward our forefathers and attribute to them a tongue without language? Do we ourselves wish, against the course of common nature and against the bidding of truth owing to a shameful greediness for the outlandish, to turn our age-old stemwords—so rich in wonder, power, sap, and purity—

into bastards, patchwork, scraps, misformed words, monsters, and beggars' dregs?" For this subject and its history, the best exposition is Wolfgang Kayser's brilliant "Böhmes Natursprachenlehre und ihre Grundlagen," in *Euphorion*, vol. 31 (1930), pp. 521-562, as well as chap. 6 "Die Sprachtheorie als Grundlage für die Verwendung der Klangmalerei," in Kayser's *Die Klangmalerei bei Harsdörffer* (Leipzig, 1932), pp. 137-186. I cannot entirely agree with Kayser's polemic against Paul Hankamer's *Die Sprache, ihr Begriff und ihre Deutung im 16. und 17. Jahrhundert* (Bonn, 1927), to the effect that Böhme's "Natursprachenlehre" has nothing to do with "Klangmalerei" in German Baroque poetry; Kayser says little about Quirinus Kuhlmann, who is the crucial test. See also August Schmarsow, *Leibniz und Schottelius. Die Unvorgreiflichen Gedanken,* untersucht und herausgegeben (Trübner: Strassburg und London, 1877); it is vol. 23 in *Quellen und Forschungen zur Sprach- und Culturgeschichte der Germanischen Völkern.* And Friedrich Gundolf, "Justus Georg Schottel," in *Beiträge zur neueren Literaturgeschichte* vol. 16 (1930), pp. 70-86.

15. For the dating and the textual problems of *Die Ermahnung* and *Die Unvorg. Ged.*, see Paul Pietsch's edition in "Leibniz und die Deutsche Sprache" in *Wissenschaftliche Beihefte zur Zeitschrift des Allgemeinen Deutschen Sprachvereins*, Hefte 29 (July 1907) and 30 (April 1908), pp. 265-371, esp. pp. 290-291 and 313-327. For an English translation of the *Unvorg. Ged.*, see Ronald Callinger, *Gottfried Wilhelm Leibniz*, with an essay by Leibniz on the German Language, translated by Caryn and Bernhard Wunderlich (Troy, New York: Rensselaer Polytechnic Institute, 1976), pp. 66-84.

16. These points are clearly anticipated in Schottel's *Ausführliche Arbeit* in the Introduction to the long alphabetical register of German proper names given in "Libri V, Tractatus Secundus: De Nominibus Propriis veterum Teutonicorum seu Celticorum populorum." See esp. p. 1034: "It cannot be denied that the diverse names of towns, mountains, forests, regions, men, women, etc., often cause incomprehension and obscure understanding in the person who ponders them, which undoubtedly has its source in the fact that many old German words are no longer known in our current dialect, while a dictionary in which such words were listed and explained does not exist." The axiom that proper names derive from appellatives had been illustrated in the short piece called "Aliqvot nomina propria germanorvm ad priscam etymologiam restivta," which since 1554 had been ascribed to Luther and consequently exercised a considerable influence. Its first entry is typical: "*Rodolfus*, corrupted by the Latins, but in German it is called 'Rathulff,' that is 'counsel and aid,' for prosperity or aid is called 'Hulff,' 'Rat' counsel." Similar analysis had already been applied to the names that occur in the Old Testament. Though the work is not believed to be Luther's, it is printed in the Weimar edition of *Luthers Werke*, vol. L, pp. 135-159, with an introduction and notes.

17. See Sigrid von der Schulenburg's excellent monograph "Leibnizens Gedanken und Vorschläge zur Erforschung der Deutschen Mundarten," in *Abhandlungen der Preussischen Akademie der Wissenschaften*, Philologisch-historische Klass, Nr. 2 (1937), pp. 1-37. On his return from England in 1676, Leibniz brought a copy of John Ray's recent *Collection of English Words*, which he sent to Gerhard Meier in Bremen on 16 July 1694 with word that a new edition had just appeared. Later, in 1712, Leibniz sent a still unpublished "Epistolaris de Historia Etymologica Dissertatio" to Eckhart with advice, in the words of the monograph, that "as John Ray travelled over the counties of his native land collecting their particular words in addition to plants, so Eckhart will wander over the German regions to study the particular linguistic usage of each, and then also visit the other Germanic nations" (p. 5). These were the so-called "Landwörter," which in Germany received much attention during the eighteenth century. For additional evidence of Leibniz' preoccupation with language at the time when he was working with the *Essay*, see especially the letters to John Gabriel Sparwenfeld in J. F. Feller, *Otium Hanoveranum* (Leipzig, 1718), pp. 32-39; C. Kortholt, *Leibnitii Epistolae ad Diversos*, vol. III. (Leipzig, 1738), pp. 355-356; C. Vilh. Jacobowsky,

J. G. Sparwenfeld, Bidrag till en Biografi (Stockholm, 1932), *passim*. The letters in Feller and Kortholt contain much matter that also appears in the *Nouveaux Essais*, Bk. III, and in the "Brevis designatio." The best edition of this correspondence is Harald Wieselgren, "Leibniz' bref till Sparfvenfelt," in *Antiqvarisk Tidskrift för Sverige*, vol. 7, (1884-1885), No. 3, pp. 1-64. The ten letters reprinted here date between Dec. 1695 and Jan. 1700 and are of capital importance for an understanding of Leibniz' linguistic doctrines and knowledge; it is evident that Sparwenfeld supplied Leibniz with much information that was later included in the *Nouveaux Essais*.

18. B. Suphan, ed., *Herders Sämmtliche Werke*, vol. XV, p. 180.

19. Gerhardt, vol. III, p. 162, in letter to Burnett of 11/21 June 1695.

20. MS. Locke c. 4, fol. 197. In this as in other letters, Burnett is very clearly trying to lure Locke into answering and giving his opinion. He continues: "I am to wryte back to him againe within 10 or 12 days & iff you have any word to him, or any command for me I shall be glad of an opportunity to serve you both. . . . It is not possible to expresse in a letter the great character Monsieur Leibnitz hath of you as he lately so amplie and often declared Himself to [me] ."

21. Locke, *Works*, vol. VIII, p. 407, Locke to Molyneux 10 April 1697.

22. This copy of "Quelques remarques . . . " is found in MS. Locke c. 13, fol. 162-165, and it is endorsed in Locke's hand: "Leibnitz sent me by Mr le Clerc 9 Apr. 97." The text of Le Clerc's letter is printed in Gabriel Bonno, ed., *Lettres Inédites de Le Clerc à Locke* (Berkeley, 1959), pp. 98-99.

23. Gerhardt, vol. III, p. 281.

24. Locke, *Works*, vol. IX, p. 63; this part of the letter is written in French to make its contents easier to communicate to "ces excellens hommes," who did not read Latin, which is otherwise the language of the Locke-Limborch correspondence.

25. Gerhardt, vol. III, pp. 297-298. Cf. Lady Masham to Leibniz, 3 June 1704, on Locke's respect for Leibniz, in Gerhardt, vol. III, p. 351.

26. See H. W. Turnbull, ed., *The Correspondence of Isaac Newton*, vol. III (Cambridge, 1961), p. 285, and note the words: "For although I avoid philosophical and mathematical intercourse as much as possible, yet I was concerned that our friendship should not be diminished owing to silence." On the controversy, see J. E. Hofmann, *Geschichte der Mathematik*, vol. II and vol. III (Berlin, 1957), pp. 75-93 and pp. 4-24. Leibniz' first offense according to the English was his presumed failure to refer to Newton in his "Nova Methodus pro Maximis et Minimis" in the *Acta Eruditorum* for Oct. 1684 (pp. 467-473), which by 70 pages preceded his "Meditationes de Cognitione, Vertitate, et Ideis" from November of the same year; this was the item to which Leibniz referred in the piece on the *Essay* that Locke saw in Feb.-Mar. 1697 and of which he expressed his low opinion to Molyneux in the letter of 10 April 1697. It is worth noting that Locke owned the *Acta Eruditorum* and took care to keep up the series (MS. Locke fol. 29, p. 4: "*Acta Eruditorum* I have 82. 83. 84. 85. 86" and Wetstein's letters to Locke in MS. Locke c. 23, fol. 75 ff.). Oldenburg's supposed role in giving Leibniz access to Newton's material is well known; it is therefore interesting that Leibniz late in the 1690s still did not have the *Philosophical Transations* that had appeared since Oldenburg's death. MS. Locke c. 13, fol. 156a-156bv, contains a long list of items Leibniz hoped to acquire through Burnett, including "I wish to obtain from England all the philosophical transactions printed after those of the late Mr. Oldenburg or rather after the general index." In Feb. 1699, Leibniz again made the same request to his amanuensis in London, F. A. Hackman: "I ask you, Sir, also to remember for me the Transactions after the death of Mr. Oldenburg or after the general index." See Paul Ritter, "Neun Briefe von Leibniz an Friedrich August Hackman" in *Sitzungsberichte der Königlich Preussischen Akademie der Wissenschaften* (1915), p. 724.

27. Leibniz very carefully introduces the two participants in the dialogue at the beginning of Book I. It is clearly important to keep the two and their opinions apart and not take statements from Philalethe as if Leibniz subscribed to them; yet, surprisingly, this distinction has not always been observed. Gustav Konrad, at the beginning of his *Herders Sprachproblem im Zusammenhang der Geistesgeschichte* (Berlin, 1937), cites Philalethe's rendering of the opening paragraph of Book III on the social function of language as if this doctrine were Leibniz'; even if it is, the matter is not so simple. The historical consequences are of course bizarre, and Konrad does not escape them. The very same confusion occurs in Siegfried Korninger, "G. W. Leibnizens Sprachauffassung," in *Die Sprache, Zeitschrift für Sprachwissenschaft*, vol. 4 (1958), pp. 4-14. In general it may be said that German treatments of Leibniz on language are not what one would have hoped to find; they tend to be vitiated by a desire to make him a sort of Fichte on this subject, a notion that is not at all justified, least of all by *Die Unvorg. Ged.* which is most often cited in this connection. It is true that this work argues for the use of German words if they serve the purposes at hand, but Leibniz also argues for the free adoption of useful foreign terms that have no German counterparts; his attitude is by no means that of the mere purist (see, e.g., *Unvorg. Ged.* § 15-18).

28. The inception "Of Enthusiasm," however, preceded 1697, as appears from Locke to Molyneux 8 Mar. 1694/5 in Locke, *Works*, vol. VIII, pp. 350-351: "I have had some thoughts myself, that it would not be possibly amiss to add, in lib. iv. cap. 18, something about enthusiasm, or to make a chapter of it by itself." Returning from Holland late in 1697, John Wynne brought a copy of Bayle's *Dictionnaire*, which Locke, according to MS. Locke c. 23, fol. 129-132, had earlier commissioned him to buy. Locke was certainly familiar with two of the most notorious enthusiasts. His journal for 1678 contains under "Tuesd. Apr. 19" a brief shorthand entry marked "Drabicius Prophesie" in Locke's own hand; a transcription of this entry is printed in John Lough, *Locke's Travels in France* 1675-1679 (Cambridge, 1953), p. 190. All the information, the details, and the names of this entry are also contained in MS. Locke b. 4, fol. 40-48, which on fol. 47^v is endorsed in Locke's hand "Drabicius 25. Apr. 78." This document is a letter in French addressed to Louis XIV, setting forth the writer's own account of his first acquaintance with the prophecies, his initial doubt, and his final conversion to full conviction of their truth; the writer now exhorts the king to listen to the prophet's words and to conduct his policies in accordance with them for the ultimate purpose of securing peace in Europe. Both the autobiographical facts of the letter as well as its historical context make it virtually certain that it is a version of a letter written by the German poet, visionary, and enthusiast Quirinus Kuhlmann, who became so persuaded of the inspired truth in Drabitius' prophecies that he felt bound to carry their message to potentates both in the East and West—or as Bayle has it, "the reading of Drabicius compleated the ruin of Kuhlmann." He brought—or sought to bring—similar messages to Smyrna, Constantinople, and Moscow. Coming from London, he had passed through Paris shortly before the matter of Drabitius came to Locke's attention, arriving past the middle of March and departing on Palm Sunday, 2 Apr. (See Claus Victor Bock, *Quirinus Kuhlmann als Dichter* (Bern, 1957), p. 45.) It is of course obvious that Locke saw a very close connection between enthusiasm and the "association of ideas." The latter is a "sort of Madness," whose manifestation may be enthusiasm or mysticism, which in the tradition of Boehme depended chiefly on a certain readiness to take words—and especially the words and language of a particular party or sect—for reality. Locke's own words offer a good description of the result: "This gives Sense to *Jargon*, Demonstration to Absurdities, and Consistency to Nonsense" (II, xxxiii, 18).

29. Gerhardt, vol. III, p. 165.

30. *Memoirs of the Lives and Characters of the Illustrious Family of the Boyles*, 3rd ed. (London, 1737), p. 120.

31. Birch, *Life of Boyle*, pp. 317-318.

32. Gerhardt, ed., *Leibnizens Mathematische Schriften*, vol. II (Berlin, 1849), p. 128 (Huygens to Leibniz, 4 Feb. 1692), and p. 131 (Leibniz to Huygens 9/19 Feb. 1692). Note also Leibniz in the same letter p. 130: "It is correct, Sir, when you say that Descartes has spoken in decisive terms about the arrangement of the parts of matter, still it would be too bad if we did not have his system. Thus I am sorry that Mr. Boyle did not leave us his conjectures."

33. *Origin of Forms and Qualities* in Boyle, *Works*, vol. III, p. 11. See also Birch *Life of Boyle*, p. 111.

34. Benjamin Rand, ed., *The Correspondence of John Locke and Edward Clarke* (Oxford, 1927), p. 156. Similar statements occur in *Essay* IV, iii, 26 & 29, and IV, xii, 10.

35. In his *Diversions of Purley*, vol. I (2nd ed. 1798), p. 31, John Horne Tooke says that Locke's *Essay* has "merely on account of its title, reached to many thousands more than, I fear, it would have done, had he called it (what it is merely) A *Grammatical* Essay, or a Treatise on *Words*, or on *Language*." This view, which is Tooke's starting point, has often been considered plain absurd, but it actually makes better sense than has generally been allowed, for the intervening hundred years had shown a strong tendency to reduce Locke's philosophy to mere sensationalism. On this mistake, see R. I. Aaron, *John Locke*, 2nd ed. (Oxford, 1955), pp. 109-110.

36. These words are, with insignificant syntactical changes, taken from the Coste version, which is more explicit in its wording than the corresponding passage in the *Essay*. Cf. Locke to Thoynard 29 Nov. 1680: "I have just received Richelet's French dictionary and if I were to employ all the good words it contains, I still could not sufficiently express the sense of gratitude I feel for your friendship, of which I have proof at every moment. It came to me after I had written my letter and, though I have barely looked at it, it seems to me to have found the true secret of good dictionary-making, for the usual manner of rendering the words of one language by those of another is no more reasonable than sending to France for a receptacle for an English instrument that is unknown in France in regard both to form and use, for the words of different languages do not agree better than that." In *Lettres Inédites*, ed. Ollion, p. 83. This work by César-Pierre Richelet is a French-French dictionary with the characteristic title: *Dictionnaire françois, contenant les mots et les choses* (1st ed. Genève, 1680).

37. This image of the word as a knot that ties a bundle together is one that Locke uses often and with great emphasis; it calls attention both to the arbitrariness of the idea and to the active role performed by the word in preserving the idea as well as in fostering the opinion that it is not arbitrary, on the mistaken assumption that there is some sort of real—and hence not arbitrary—connection between word and object. The relevant passages are: II, xxxii, 6-8 (with the important concluding statement about the "double conformity" between thing-idea and idea-name); III, iii, 20; III, v, 4 & 10 & 13. With these should be taken II, xxii, 2-6, which without using the knot-and-bundle image makes the same point. It is characteristic that Leibniz either runs very lightly over or entirely omits these sections, and thus Locke's image nowhere occurs in his text. III, v, 13 in the Coste translation does not have the image, but the same point is made with equal force.

38. Cf. also *Nouveaux Essais* III, iii, 14 and IV, v, 2 where Theophile gives some very revealing and typical answers.

39. Brit. Mus. MS. Birch 4290, fol. 38v. This letter was first printed in [P. Des Maizeaux'] *Collection of Several Pieces of Mr. John Locke* (London, 1720). It is also in Locke, *Works*, vol. IX, p. 285. Locke offers an excellent gloss on his reasons for limiting his "business" within "a little compass" to those things "which concern our conduct." It is the long entry in the Journal for 8 Feb. 1677, reprinted in Aaron & Gibb, pp. 84-90, especially this passage on p. 88: "The businesse of men being to be happy in this world by the enjoyment of the things of nature subservient to life health ease and pleasure . . . we need noe other knowledg

for the atteinment of those ends but of the history and observation of the effects and operations of naturall bodys within our power, and of our dutys in the management of our owne
actions as far as they depend on our wills i.e. as far also as they are in our power." Therefore
"we have noe reason to complain if we meet with difficultys in other things which put our
reasons to a non plus confound our understandings and leave us perfectly in the darke under
the sense of our owne weaknesse, for those relateing not to our happynesse any way are noe
part of our businesse and therefor tis not to be wondered if we have not abilitys given us to
deale with things that are not to our purpose, nor conformeable to our state or end." This
entry echoes a large number of passages in Boyle, e.g., this one written ten years later: "It is
true, that to inquire to what purpose nature would have such or such effects produced, is a
curiosity worthy of a rational creature, upon the score of his being so: but this is not the
proper task of a naturalist, whose work, as he is such, is not so much to discover, why, as
how, particular effects are produced." *A Disquisition about the Final Causes of Natural
Things*, in Boyle, *Works*, vol. V, p. 443. On these grounds I do not find that the *Essay* and
the *Two Treatises* are disparate, though they are not, of course, systematically similar treatments of different subjects, but both deal with our "conduct." I have dealt with this problem in my essay on "The State of Nature and the Nature of Man," in *John Locke: Problems
and Perspectives, a Collection of New Essays*, ed. by John W. Yolton (Cambridge University
Press, 1969), pp. 99-136.

40. MS. Locke, fol. 16, pp. 39, 41, and 38, contain at least 37 items, many of them including several titles. Boyle's writings also frequently appear in the notes concerning books lent
and received back or left in boxes with friends and later returned. Locke saw Boyle often
during the years between his return from France and his departure for Holland. Locke's earlier
close association with Boyle during the Oxford years is a familiar matter.

41. Boyle, *Works*, vol. III, pp. 49-50. Cf. this passage from the *Sceptical Chymist*: "I might
tell you divers examples I have met with, of the contrariety of bodies, which according to
the chymists must be huddled up together under one denomination; I leave you to judge,
whether such a multitude of substances, as may agree in these slight qualities, and yet dis-
agree in others more considerable, are more worthy to be called by the names of a principle
(which ought to be pure and homogeneous) than to have appellations given them, that may
make them differ, in name too, from the bodies from which they so widely differ in nature."
Boyle, *Works*, vol. I. pp. 532-533. Some of the terms in the passage from the *Origin of Forms
and Qualities* are also used by Locke. Cf. "tacit agreement" and Locke in III, ii, 8: "'Tis
true, common use, by a tacit Consent, apropriates certain Sounds to certain *Ideas*." But
Boyle's plain-speaking use of "sort" and "kinds" as synonyms for "species" is especially
noteworthy, for this usage was also Locke's habit as early as Draft A: "The minde or the
man . . . ranks [a certaine number of those simple Ideas] togeather or else finds them
ranked togeather by others under one general name, which we call a species and if more
comprehensive a genus or in plaine English a sort or kinde." Aaron & Gibb, pp. 7-8. Cf. *Essay*
III, iii, 15: "The *Essence* of each *Genus*, or Sort, comes to be nothing but that abstract *Idea*,
which the General, or *Sortal* (if I may have leave so to call it from *Sort*, as I do *General* from
Genus,) Name stands for." In III, vi, 35 "sort" is used as a synonym for "species": "*Men
make sorts of Things*. For it being different Essences alone, that make different *Species*, 'tis
plain, that they who make those abstract *Ideas*, which are the nominal Essences, do thereby
make the *Species*, or Sort." Again III, vi, 37: "*The boundaries of the Species, whereby Men
sort them, are made by Men*. . . . So that we may truly say, such a manner of sorting of
Things, is the Workmanship of Men." The knot-and-bundle is Locke's metaphor for this sorting according to his repeated insistence that "the *making of* Species *and* Genera *is in order
to general Names*" (III, vi, 39). Further specific evidence of Locke's reading of Boyle may
also occur in his references to the Dasypodius clock in the Cathedral at Strassbourg in III, vi,

3 & 9; cf. Boyle, *Works*, vol. II, p. 39; vol. V, p. 163, and vol. V, p. 404. It is also mentioned in Evelyn's *Diary* for June 1645, and in Descartes' letter to Mersenne 8 Oct. 1629.

42. Boyle, *Works*, vol. III, p. 41.

43. This doctrine is also in Bacon, *Advancement of Learning* Bk. II: "Let us consider the false appearances that are imposed upon us by words, which are framed and applied according to the conceit and capacities of the vulgar sort." *Works*, eds. Spedding, Ellis, Heath, vol. III (London, 1870), p. 396.

44. See also Boyle, *Works*, vol. III, pp. 27-28 (in *Origin and Forms*). The same observations are made by Jacques Rohault in his *Traité de Physique*, 1st ed. (Paris, 1671), especially in § 2 of the Preface and in pt. I, chap. 4 "Avis touchant les mots." Locke took notes from the *Traité* on 4 March 1678, and late in June he packed it in a box to be sent back to England. Lough, "Locke's Reading," pp. 243 and 248. Cf. Aaron & Gibb, p. 108.

45. J. Milton French, ed. *The Life Records of John Milton*, vol. IV (New Brunswick, Rutgers University Press, 1956), p. 93. It is not clear whether Boyle himself used this motto; its first appearance in this context would seem to be in the title-page vignette executed by Bourguignon (1699-1773) and used for the Birch edition. (See R. E. W. Maddison, "The Portraiture of the Honourable Robert Boyle, F. R. S.," in *Annals of Science*, vol. 15 (1959), p. 158 and Plate VI.) But Boyle often made the same point, as for instance in his will when he wished the Royal Society "a happy success in their laudable attempts to discover the true nature of the works of God," and prayed "that they and all other searchers into physical truths, may cordially refer their attainments to the glory of the great Author of Nature, and to the comfort of mankind." Birch, *Life of Boyle*, p. 292.

46. II, xi, 17; cf. for the same image and the role of names I, ii, 15.

47. Leibniz' words are the answer to Locke's II, xxii, 4 on mixed modes.

48. See Peter Meinhold, *Luthers Sprachphilosophie* (Berlin, 1958), especially pp. 32-36 and 42-44. On Boehme and Comenius, see my entries in the *Dictionary of Scientific Biography*.

49. "What an ocean of knowledge and wisdom there was in this one man! And still concerning this knowledge, however much Adam lost in the Fall, nonetheless I believe that whatever until now is in the books of all wise men who wrote for so many centuries from the time when letters were born, it all could not equal that wisdom that even afterwards remained in Adam, but that has little by little become obscured in the descendants and almost extinguished." *Werke*, vol. XLII (Weimar, 1911), pp. 90-91.

50. *Sermons Preached on Several Occasions*, vol. I (Oxford, 1823), pp. 37-38.

51. *Aurora*, chap. 20, § 91 in *Sämtliche Schriften* (Faksimile-Neudruck der Ausgabe von 1730, ed. Will-Erich Peuckert), vol. I (Stuttgart, 1955), p. 296. The passage is immediately followed by a reference to Boehme's *Mysterium Magnum*, chap. 19, § 22, which reads: "Now, that Adam stood in the image of God and not that of the beasts is shown by the fact that he knew the property of all the creatures and gave names to all the creatures according to their essence, form, and property; he understood the language of nature as revealed and articulated word in all essence, for the name of each creature has its origin there." *Op. cit.*, vol. XVII, p. 130.

52. See M. L. Bailey, *Milton and Jakob Boehme: A Study of German Mysticism in Seventeenth-Century England* (New York, 1914), pp. 185-186 and Serge Hutin, *Les Disciples Anglais de Jacob Boehme* (Paris, 1960), pp. 37-42.

53. Webster, pp. 98-99.

54. *Ibid.*, p. 68.

55. *Ibid.*, p. 75.

56. *Ibid.*, p. 32.

57. *Ibid.*, p. 26.

58. *Ibid.*, p. 29.

59. It was precisely in these terms that Webster's attack was answered by John Wilkins (who wrote the Preface) and Seth Ward in their defense from the same year, *Vindiciae Academiarum*. Wilkins found that "above all, the man doth give me the freest prospect of his depth and braine, in that canting Discourse about the language of nature, wherein he doth assent unto the highly illuminated fraternity of the *Rosicrucians*. In his large encomiums upon *Jacob Behem*, in that reverence which he professes to judiciall Astrologie, which may sufficiently convince what a kind of credulous fanatick Reformer he is like to prove." Ward, in similar fashion, denied that "ever there was any such Language of Nature" (p. 22).

60. Boyle, *Works*, vol. IV, pp. 45-46. The naming of Eve is also advanced by Webster: "Now if it be denied that he understood by his intrinsick and innate light, what she was, and from whence she was taken (which I hold altogether untrue) and that God by extrinsick information told *Adam* from whence she was taken, yet did he immediately give unto her an adaequate name, suiting her original, which most significantly did manifest what was her nature, and from whence it came, and doubtless the name being exactly conformable, and configurate to the Idaea in his mind, the very prolation, and sound of the word, contained in it the vive expression of the thing, and so in verity was nothing else but that pure language of nature, which he then spake, and understood, and afterwards so miserably lost and defaced" (*Acad. Ex.*, p. 30). Boyle may well have had Webster in mind, for whereas the latter had cited the "Seraphical Apostle" from I Cor. 13:1 on "the tongues of men and Angels" in favor of his doctrine, Boyle cites I. Cor. 13:12 in favor of his: "For now we see through a glass darkly, but then face to face: now I know in part, but then shall I know even as also I am known." *Acad. Ex.*, p. 27 and Boyle, *Works*, Vol. IV, p. 46.

61. Boyle, *Works*, vol. IV, p. 18 (in the *Excellency of Theology*). Cf. *ibid.*, p. 47: "And as there is no doubt to be made, but that when *David* invented (as the scripture intimates, that he did) new instruments of musick, there was nothing in that invention that pleased him so much, as that they could assist him to praise God the more melodiously; so the pious student of nature finds nothing more welcome in the discoveries he makes of her wonders, than the rises and helps they may afford him, the more worthily to celebrate and glorify the divine attributes adumbrated in the creatures." Readers may wish to consult the beginning of Milton's *Of Education*, which in the big edition of the *Prose Works* is accompanied by an introduction and notes that show a grotesque, though not uncommon, miscomprehension of the problem.

62. Cf. the words that Locke intended to add to III, x, 13: "We cannot but think that angels of all kinds much exceed us in knowledge, and possibly we are apt sometimes to envy them that advantage, or at least to repine that we do not partake with them in a greater share of it. Whoever thinks of the elevation of their knowledge above ours, cannot imagine it lies in a playing with words, but in the contemplation of things, and having true notions about them, a perception of their habitudes and relations one to another. If this be so, methinks we should be ambitious to come, in this part, which is a great deal in our power, as near them as we can; we should cast off all the artifice and fallacy of words." King, *Life*, p. 362. The question of the language of the angels was commonplace during the seventeenth century. See, e.g., the opening of Samuel Tilly's letter to Locke on 11 Sept. 1655: "To be able to reveal their thoughts by only willing their discourse, is (they say) the privilidge of the Angels." In MS. Locke c. 20, fol. 175.

63. Examples of Locke's similarity to Boyle in this chapter have already been cited in the notes above. Two more points are worth noting. (1) In these sections, III, vi, 43-51, Locke argues against Adam's special authority in regard to language (and hence also in regard to wisdom) in a manner that closely parallels his arguments against Filmer's claims for Adam's parenthood and dominion in the first of the *Two Treatises of Government*. In both places

Locke asserts the principle of Adam's ordinary humanity—"and so *Adams* Sovereignty built on *property*, or as our A[uthor] calls it, *Private Dominion*, comes to nothing. Every Man had a right to the Creatures, by the same Title *Adam* had, viz. by the right every one had to take care of, and provide for their Subsistence: and thus Men had a right in common, *Adams* Children in common with him." Par. 87 in *Two Treatises*, ed. Peter Laslett (Cambridge, 1960), Locke several times supports his argument with close philological attention to the original Hebrew, e.g. paragraphs 25-27; and at least once, in par. 46, he presents an argument that clearly rejects the uniqueness of Adam's language: "When he [God] vouchsafes to speak to Men, I do not think, he speaks differently from them, in crossing the Rules of language in use amongst them. This would not be to condescend to their Capacities . . . but to lose his design in speaking, what thus spoken, they could not understand." Our knowledge of the chronology of composition of the parts of the two works in question makes it likely that Locke was working on both at the same or roughly the same time. (2) The rejection of the Adamic language was characteristic of Socinian doctrine. Wolfgang Kayser has observed: "So far as I can tell, at the time in question, only the Socinians refuse to draw conclusions from the act of namegiving to Adam's wisdom. They also deny that he should have possessed special powers of cognition." "Böhmes Natursprachenlehre und ihre Grundlagen," in *Euphorion*, vol. 31 (1930), p. 538. This argument is presented in Fausto Soccino's *De Statu Adami ante Lapsum*. Its full theological implications are presented in Soccino's [interpretation of John 1:1-15 in his *Explicatio primae partis primi capitis euangelistae Johannis*] : "*In the beginning was the word.* Those who in this place will have the word beginning designate the eternity of Christ stand convicted of the most obvious error from the mere fact that their opinion is supported by no authority whether in the New Law or the Old. And indeed you will nowhere in Scriptures find 'beginning' being used for eternity. Therefore we maintain that the word 'beginning' in this passage refers not to eternity, but to the order of those things which John is writing about Jesus Christ as the chosen son of God, in this matter imitating Moses who, writing his history, made this word 'beginning' also the very opening of Gen. 1:1. . . . Thus also, when John said 'in the beginning,' he meant those things by which he had organized the discourse, but not at all those that existed before." *Opera Omnia*, vol. I (Irenopoli [Amsterdam], post annum Domini 1656), pp. 77-78. This involves the characteristic Socinian rejection of the doctrine of the consubstantiality of the word.

64. In his *La Philosophie Générale de John Locke* (Paris, 1908), Henry Ollion, without further elaboration, remarks: "However that may be, Locke has certainly considered the doctrine of innateness as being based on the abuse of words" (p. 71). This, however, may merely refer to the observation that Locke frequently makes, as in III, ii, 5, that "because *Men* would not be thought to talk *barely* of their own Imaginations, but of Things as really they are; therefore they *often suppose their Words to stand also for the reality* of Things." But the passages quoted above can only refer to the abuse that arises from acceptance of the natural language doctrine. It should be remembered that Locke's own title for Book I, as evidenced by the first five editions, is simply "Of innate Notions" and not, as Fraser has it "Neither Principles nor Ideas are innate." "Notion" is no synonym for "idea," and much of Locke's argument, and its right understanding, depends on his introduction and use of the latter by contrast to the former. We have already seen that John Webster in his exposition of the Adamic language uses the terms "internal notions impressed" and "innate notions."

65. In England, George Dalgarno had made similar observations in his *Didascalocophus* (1680): "All languages guided by the instinct of nature, have more or less of Onomatopoeia in them, and I think our English as much as any. . . . Take for example, *wash, dash, plash, flash, clash, hash, lash, slash, trash, gash,* & c. So *grumble, tumble, crumble, jumble, fumble, stumble, bumble, mumble,* & c., of which kind of words, the learned, and my worthy friend Dr. Wallis has given a good account in his English Grammar. In all these and such like words

there is something symbolizing, and analogous to the notions of the things, which makes them both more emphatic and easy to the memory. But in words literally written, and of a meer arbitrary institution, there can be nothing symbolical." *Works of George Dalgarno* (Edinburgh: Maitland Club Reprint, 1839), p. 126. Leibniz was familiar with both Dalgarno's work and with John Wallis' *Grammatica Linguae Anglicanae*. Schottel's *Ausführliche Arbeit* presents a wealth of similar observations and examples.

66. This statement should be closely compared with John Webster's statement quoted above at footnote 56. Leibniz' examples are designed to demonstrate that the principles Webster attributes to the Adamic language can currently be seen to operate. Cf. this passage in a letter from Leibniz to Sparwenfeld written between April and August 1699: "It seems to me that *n, l, r, s, t,* have much in common in their formation. Those who might not know how to pronounce *r* well, change it to *l*, saying *mon levelend pele* instead of *mon reverend pere*, as the Florentines change *k* into *h*." See Harald Wieselgren, "Leibniz' bref till Sparfvenfelt," p. 53.

67. *Miscellanea Berolinensia* (Berlin, 1710), p. 2. The "Brevis designatio" was reprinted in L. Dutens, ed., *Leibnitii . . . Opera Omnia* (Genevae, 1768), vol. IV, pt. ii, pp. 186-198.

68. The reader may have noticed that Philalethe and Theophile often seem to argue at cross-purposes, the inevitable result of Theophile's occasional failure to understand Philalethe's position, or of disagreement so complete that no common ground is left. A notable case involving language occurs in IV, v, of the *Nouveaux Essais*, i.e. after Book III at a point where one might not have expected any misunderstanding. Philalethe has rendered Locke's statement in IV, v, 2 that "Truth properly belongs only to Propositions: whereof there are two Sorts, *viz.* Mental and Verbal; as there are two sorts of Signs commonly made Use of, *viz. Ideas* and Words." Theophile answers: "But what I find least to my taste in your definition of truth is that you seek the truth in words. Thus the same sense expressed in Latin, German, English, French will not be the same truth. And we shall have to say with Hobbes that truth depends on the good pleasure of men—which is to speak in a very strange manner." Leibniz is certainly not the only one to misunderstand Locke on this point, and Locke's lack of clarity is in part to blame. But Locke could at least in this case not have meant anything of the sort that Leibniz suggests, for what Locke does mean, though it is not clear from this passage alone, is of course not words as sounds, but words as knots that tie bundles of ideas together. In different languages the same number of ideas may be differently sorted into bundles, and some that are "bundled" in one may not be in another—hence the doctrine of intranslatability among languages. Locke's use of the word "language" rather than "the English language" or "English" has had very considerable consequences. I would very much doubt that Locke always meant to imply that he was talking about language in general every time he used the word "language"; but his usage made it possible for the eighteenth century to read parts of the *Essay* as a discussion of language at large in the manner of the Port-Royal *Logique* and the *Grammaire Générale et Raisonnée*. If Locke had been forced always to make the distinction between "langue" and "langage" as in French, the matter might have been different. Coste, in his translation, normally used "langage" for Locke's "language." The crossing of these two streams became immensely productive, and the eager eighteenth-century discussion of language, with wide use of Locke, cannot be imagined without it.

69. Cf. a very similar passage, which Leibniz may well have known, in le P. Besnier, *La Reunion des Langues* (Paris, 1674), p. 21: "Since the corruption of languages has occurred imperceptibly and little by little, we must take care, in order to discover it for certain, to rise only by little steps to the first source of their differences, taking good care not to make any wrong step that could take us a bit too far and make us go wrong so that we would have trouble getting back on the right track. That is the only means I have found to spread an air of plausibility on the entire matter, which has only as much probability as we give it by

proceeding so carefully that we never go from one extremity to the other without passing through the middle that was.like the link between the extremities. For it is on this enchainment of words and on this series of alterations that all the precision and the entire plausibility of the method depends." Leibniz had already heard of Besnier's *Reunion* in Paris shortly after it appeared. See letter to Sparwenfeld in Wieselgren, pp. 16-18, dated 29 Jan. 1697. The letter shows that Leibniz was also familiar with Besnier's "Discours sur la Science des Etymologies." In this letter, Leibniz takes a rather critical view of Besnier's work, an opinion shared by Sparwenfeld, who had known Besnier in Paris. The historical uses of etymology had been pointed out by Camden as quoted in Schottel's *Ausführliche Arbeit*, p. 127: "In language is to be found the most certain evidence of the origin of nations. For I do not believe that anybody will deny those who share a common language also to have been united in common origin. So that if all histories entirely perished, the community of languages themselves would easily prove it, indeed more easily than the authority of even the most eminent historians."

70. See Pietsch, p. 322.

71. See Eccard's *Collectanea Etymologica*, pt. I, pp. 193-194. On Clauberg's work, see N. Scheid, "Eine Philosophische Wortdeutungslehre aus dem Jahre 1663," in *Zeitschrift des Allgemeinen Deutschen Sprachvereins*, vol. 23 (1908), pp. 5-9.

72. Eccard, pp. 194-195. § 77 in the "Prolegomena" to Clauberg's *Logica* occurs only in the second and subsequent editions: Jon. Claubergii *Logica Vetus & Nova*, modum inveniendae ac tradendae veritatis, in genesi simul & analysi, facili methodo exhibens. Editio secunda mille locis emendata novisque Prolegomenis aucta. Amstelaedami, ex Officina Elzeviriana, 1658. In this edition, the "Prolegomena" occupy pp. 1-37 with a total of 103 paragraphs divided in five chapters. The first edition appeared in 1654, its "Prolegomena" had only 37 paragraphs, and total number of pages was 413 against 463 for the second edition.

73. Aaron & Gibb, pp. 105-111.

74. Peter Laslett has since kindly informed me that Clauberg's *Logica* appears on two occasions after Locke had purchased it in 1678; it was not in Locke's final library. It is item 736b in the forthcoming catalogue of Locke's library that is being prepared by Messrs. Laslett and J. R. Harrison. In his *Reunion des Langues*, Besnier makes an observation that is similar to Locke's and Clauberg's. He notes that "if we compare them to their first origin, most of our words are nothing but metaphors. . . . Thus when we say that the mind or the understanding applies itself to weigh, to conceive, to discourse, to explain, to untangle, to unravel matters, to discover truth; when we speak of trouble, aversions, agitation, and the consternation of the will in order to explain the actions of the most spiritual of worlds, we make use of images that are actually corporeal in their first origin, though most of them have lost their proper signification to assume another that is purely figurative" (pp. 38-39).

75. What is true of Turgot and the *philosophes* is also true of James Mill and the Utilitarian psychology he presents in his *Analysis*. See my article on "The Early History of the *Oxford English Dictionary*," in the *Bulletin of the New York Public Library*, vol. 66 (September, 1962), pp. 417-439.

76. It is a misunderstanding of the same sort to believe that Locke in the *Essay*—chiefly in Book III, but also elsewhere—proposed to give an exhaustive and systematic analysis of language. He was not dealing with language as a linguist or an etymologist, but as a philosopher who had certain practical concerns in mind, and they did not embrace all of language, and least of all in the manner we may nowadays conceive of such an enterprise. In his comment on III, ii, 1, R. I. Aaron says in his *John Locke*, pp. 208-209: "Unfortunately, Locke does not here examine those words which are obviously onomatopoeic, nor again words derived from an onomatopoeic source (as Leibniz did in discussing this passage). Indeed, he makes no attempt to examine the historical origins of language, though this would have been in

accordance with his own expressed method of procedure. It is true that etymology was in its infancy at the time, but Locke does not make use even of the limited information then available." I am sure that Locke was not at all interested in examining the "historical origins of language," and least of all as we understand that phrase. His unacknowledged disciples were, but Locke only used seemingly etymological observation in a simple, commonsense and practical fashion to support a point or make it plausible, but he never made an argument depend on it; he was interested in the origin of our notions but not in the origin of language. Onomatopoeia might have amused him, but I think he would also have found it rather trivial, a quirk rather than the source of a principle; after all, the question of the real or nominal essence of gold is not illuminated by onomatopoeic considerations. We have been told again and again that etymology at some point in time was in its infancy—it is the constant nineteenth-century phrase for the state of etymology in the eighteenth century (which is a gross injustice)—but I have never heard whether it has since been in its puberty or adolescence or is now in its senility. "Etymology" is one of the trickiest words of all, both philosophically and philologically, and nineteenth-century pride in its own accomplishments in that department should not deceive us.

The Study and Use
of Etymology in Leibniz

In this paper I propose to deal with Leibniz' study of etymology. In this context, the concept of etymology involves somewhat more than the sense the word has acquired during the last one hundred and fifty years. It is true that etymology to Leibniz meant the study of the history and origin of words, but it also included the more fundamental question of the nature of language itself. The study of etymology embraced such questions as the origin of language—was it to be found in the Hebrew, or was it perhaps, as Jakob Böhme believed, Adamic and natural? Or, in different terms, what is the relationship, if any, between a given word and the thing to which it refers? This question necessarily raises certain problems that pertain to the philosophy of language. Further, do all languages spring from a single source, and if it is assumed that they do, how is the present variety of languages to be explained? And finally, what practical lessons can be derived from the study of etymology? Leibniz sought answers to these questions, and I shall attempt to indicate what some of them were. I shall divide my paper in three parts. I shall begin with the history of Leibniz's interest in etymology. Secondly, I shall try to explain his philosophy of language in so far as it relates to etymology and discuss the relationship of this philosophy both to contemporary doctrines and to his own philosophical system. Thirdly, I shall deal with the methods and procedures he advocated. In the course of dealing with these questions, I shall also have occasion to refer to Leibniz' conception of the practical use and application of etymology, but time is too short for me to devote a separate part of the paper to this subject.[1]

Reprinted from *Studia Leibnitiana. Supplementa*, vol. III: *Erkenntnislehre, Logik, Sprach-philosophie, Editionsberichte* (Wiesbaden: Franz Steiner Verlag, 1969), 173-189. (Akten des Internationalen Leibniz-Kongresses, Hannover, 14-19 November 1966.)

I

In his *Ermahnung an die Teutsche ihren Verstand und Sprache besser zu üben*, Leibniz laid down two fundamental principles. First: "The bond of language, of social customs, and even of the common name unites individuals in a powerful though invisible manner and produces as it were a sort of affinity." And secondly: "Language is to be regarded as a bright mirror of the understanding."[2] Here in *Die Ermahnung*, these observations apply only to German, but Leibniz was soon to consider them to be true of language in general. It was to be some years, however, before he began to take a closer interest in language and etymology, and there can be no doubt that this interest developed in close connection with his historical studies. In 1685 he undertook the great task of writing the history of the House of Braunschweig-Lüneburg, a task that not only brought him face to face with early documents in a variety of languages and dialects, but also engaged him in correspondence that further stimulated his etymological studies. In the first letter to Hiob Ludolf in December of 1687, we see the beginning of this interest. He here suggests the desirability of having a dictionary of roots and primary words of many languages, for such a dictionary, "would also wonderfully illustrate the origins of nations."[3] A few years later in the spring of 1691, Leibniz gave a much more detailed account of the program he had in mind. Writing to Huldreich von Eyben about his eagerness to seek the earliest traces of man in history, he continued: "I must also in some measure consider the migrations of nations and the origins of languages. . . . I fully believe that the harmony of languages is the best means of determining the origin of nations, and virtually the only one that is left to us where historical accounts fail. It seems in fact that all languages from the Indus river to the Baltic Sea have a single origin."[4] Thus the study of languages and etymology becomes an auxiliary discipline to history, a principle that Leibniz was to state and restate again and again over the years. Within a year followed at least six letters that dealt extensively with the same subject—to Ludolf, La Loubère, and Tentzel. And now Leibniz was no longer merely seeking information from others, but also himself beginning to collect material. In April of 1692, he wrote to Ciampini: "I have become eager to collect something toward the harmony of languages. I am now looking into the languages of the interior of Scythia, and at the moment I hope to obtain something by the authority of the great king of Sarmatia."[5]

These passages are taken from the last published volume of the correspondence in the Akademie-Ausgabe. After this date the correspondence has been only very incompletely published, so that it becomes difficult to follow Leibniz' interest in language study, but there can be no doubt that it continued to grow steadily from now on. It is characteristic, for instance, that the correspondence with Gerhard Meier, begun in 1690, does not touch on etymology and dialects until December of 1693, though these subjects later became the chief business of that correspondence.[6] Leibniz continued this busy correspondence with Hiob Ludolf, and between 1695 and 1700 he wrote the ten long letters to Sparfvenfelt that are almost exclusively concerned with linguistic matters.[7] The correspondence with La Croze began in 1704, the year of Ludolf's death, and some of the very last letters Leibniz wrote, in October of 1716, were devoted to his linguistic studies, to La Croze on the 9th and to Kortholt as late as the 16th of October within a month of his death.[8] And, of course, Leibniz wrote on the same subject to an increasing number of other correspondents.

But the fruits of Leibniz' linguistic and etymological studies were not confined to the letters. In 1697 he published a short *Dissertatio de Origine Germanorum* and in 1715 another, *De Origine Francorum Disquisitio*.[9] Most important, however, was the program he laid down in the opening piece of the first volume of the Berlin Academy in 1710, the *Brief exposition of thoughts concerning the origins of nations, principally drawn from the evidence of languages*. This essay begins with a firm statement of his fundamental principle regarding the historical uses of etymology: "Since the distant origins of nations transcend history, languages take for us the place of old documents. The most ancient vestiges of languages remain in the names of rivers and forests, which very often survive the changes of populations."[10]

Some years earlier, round 1704, Leibniz had discussed the philosophy of language and the principles of etymology much more extensively in his commentary on Locke's *Essay*, entitled *Nouveaux essais sur l'entendement humain*, but these were not published until 1765.

During his last years, Leibniz planned the publication of parts of the vast collection of etymological material he had gathered over the years. Edited by Eckhart, it appeared in 1717 as *Leibnitii Collectanea Etymologica*, but apart from the *Unvorgreifflichen Gedancken, betreffend die Ausübung und Verbesserung der Teutschen Sprache*, some letters, and a few other pieces, most of the items in this volume were not by Leibniz, though practically all had been directly inspired by him. It did not include the most important item it had been planned to contain, namely Leibniz' own history of etymology. This is the

Epistolaris de Historia Etymologica Dissertatio, addressed to Eckhart, but never finished and never published. Designed as the introduction to the *Collectanea*, it is the final and by far the most comprehensive of Leibniz' writings on etymology. It incorporates much he had already said elsewhere, and it deals both with the philosophy of language and with historical etymology. It is in addition a very full bibliography of the vast body of etymological literature that was known to Leibniz. Here at one point, he admits that other work by which he could perhaps make a more important contribution to learning, had prevented him from devoting much time to etymology, and that he had instead tried to encourage others to pursue the study of etymology.[11]

II

The seventeenth century was intensely interested in the philosophy of language, perhaps especially in the Protestant countries which developed what has been called a "Sprachtheologie." With his habit of looking for whatever useful information he might find rather than concentrating on errors and aberrations, Leibniz found much material in works of this sort. But he rejected practically all the current doctrines and accepted none without considerable modification. One popular doctrine, based on Biblical authority, held that Hebrew was the original language of all mankind and the ultimate source of all languages. But Leibniz argued: "To say that Hebrew is the primal language is the same as saying that the stems of trees are primal, or that there is a region where stems are born instead of trees. Such things can be imagined, but they do not agree with the laws of nature and the harmony of things, that is with divine wisdom." To know Hebrew well, one would further have to study Syrian and Arabic, and also, if Hebrew was the Ursprache spoken still at the time of Moses, how was the contemporary existence of Egyptian to be explained?[12] Related to this doctrine was Jakob Böhme's belief that language had its origin in Adam's naming of the animals. When Adam in the Garden of Eden gave names to the animals, he named them appropriately according to their natures, and consequently this language was also, as Böhme said, a Natur-Sprache, and many mystics and fanatics—or as Leibniz occasionally called them "Platonici"—hoped to find the key to this language, in the tradition of Paracelsus, Caspar Schwenckfeld, Sebastian Frank, and Valentin Weigel. For if the key were found, then the relationship between words and the natures or essences of things would also be known. It seems that this at least was one doctrine against which Locke argued in the *Essay*, as summed up in his phrase that words gain meaning "by a perfectly arbitrary imposition." Leibniz dismissed the Natur-Sprache doctrine as utterly meaningless.[13] But he also rejected Locke's doctrine, though I shall not here deal with Leibniz' argument against Locke.[14]

To Leibniz the study of language was centered on words, on etymology: "The ground and soil of a language, so to speak, are the words, on which the idioms grow forth like fruit." It was further true "that words are signs not only of thoughts but also of things," and the connection of these three—word, thought, and thing—was not arbitrary, i.e. not without some underlying reason, for words were "not so arbitrary and accidental in origin as some suppose, for there is nothing accidental in the world except owing to our ignorance, when the causes are hidden from us."[15] There was after all, as he argued against Locke, "something natural in the origin of words that indicates a relation between things and the sounds and movements of the vocal organs."[16] Thus Leibniz returns to a modified form of the Platonic doctrine of the nature of language: "For languages have a certain natural origin, from the agreement of sounds with the dispositions of the mind [or 'affects'], which the appearances of things excite in the mind. And this origin I believe occurs not merely in the primal language, but also in languages that have grown up later in part from the primal language and in part from the new usage of men dispersed over the globe."[17]

Thus two laws of Leibniz' philosophical system also operate in languages: the law of sufficient reason because words are not arbitrary: there is a connection between words and things, even though we may rarely be able to find traces of it. And the law of continuity because there ultimately is a connection among all languages, which must all be assumed to have a common source.

As early as 1692, Leibniz had stated his conviction that practically all languages were merely variations of the same roots, though now often mixed and confused so that these roots cannot be recognized except by careful comparison of a large number of languages and dialects.[18] The first seeds of language, its origin, can be imagined to lie in simple interjections and particles, which express the agreement of sounds and the perceptions and affections which things arouse in man, a belief supported by the observation that particles often also are the root-words of language.[19] Even today, Leibniz observed, though we are widely separated from the original source of language, "if we suppose that our languages are fundamentally derivative, they nevertheless have something primitive in themselves, which has arisen in them in relation to new root words, formed later within them by chance but for physical reasons. Examples are offered by those that signify the sounds of animals or are based on them. Such, for example, is the Latin *coaxare* attributed to frogs, which bears some relation to *couaquen* or *quaken* in German."[20] This, of course, is an example of onomatopoeia, which Leibniz cites extensively in support of the natural connection between things and words. But onomatopoeia is only a particular case of many possible modes of connection. The word "nose," for instance, appropriately begins with N, this sound itself being pronounced through the nose.[21] Even specific letters—or as we would say sounds—may have particular effects: "As the letter R naturally signifies a violent movement, the letter L designates a gentler one. Accordingly we find that children and others for whom the R is too hard and too difficult to pronounce, substitute the letter L for it, as when they say, for example *mon levelend pele*. This gentle movement appears in *leben* (to live), *laben* (to comfort, invigorate), *lind, lenis, lentus* (slow), *lieben* (to love), *lauffen* (to move along quickly like flowing water) . . . *leien* (in Low-Saxon) to dissolve, to melt like snow, whence the name of the Hanoverian river *Leine*, which, arising in mountainous regions, swells greatly by the melted snow."[22] To us, these examples may at first seem merely amusing, but to Leibniz they are important because they lend support to the doctrine that all languages ultimately share in the universal harmony. We shall later, in considering Leibniz' method in etymology, see that he was very critical of the uses generally made of such "Lautphilosophie."

In these conceptions of the origin and nature of language, Leibniz may seem to come very close to Böhme's Adamic language, the Natur-Sprache, and it is true that he borrowed examples from contemporaries who held that doctrine, a fact that often makes him appear much more traditional than he is. As already remarked, he often insisted that he did not accept their doctrines and that his own was very different from theirs. He did not, for instance, ever believe that his observations pointed to facts, but only that they offered suggestions of some ultimate analogy. He also took a much wider view of languages than did his contemporaries. In space he ranged from Chinese and the languages of Asia in the East to Icelandic and Basque in the West, and he even sought information on the languages of sub-Sahara Africa, including that of the Hottentots. And as regards time, there is no indication that he ever accepted the traditional Old-Testament chronology, which was widely believed in his day and indeed also later. To Leibniz the changes from the original tongue had occurred over a much greater expanse of time.

Leibniz' *a priori* conviction that all languages shared in the universal harmony of things led him into a very curious conception in his philosophy of language and etymology, a conception that is, however, an inescapable consequence of his total view. This conception emerges in his letters to La Croze, with whom he corresponded on questions concerning Chinese. There had been speculation that it might be possible to find a key to the characters of Chinese writing, that they were, in other words, subject to a system and perhaps even a sort of philosophical language. For there must be some reason behind them, though the key may have been lost in the course of time: "Father Grimaldi did not believe that there is a key to the Chinese characters. But it is clear that there must have been some reason for making them, even though perhaps the passage of time has rendered the decipherment difficult and has caused irregularities to slip in."[23] Leibniz believed, therefore, that the study of Chinese was especially important, "This research seems to me so much more important, since, if we could discover the key to Chinese characters, we would find something that would aid the analysis of thoughts."[24] Some five years later, in 1712, La Croze suggested to Leibniz that Coptic might be a philosophical language, which in turn might offer insights into Chinese characters. Leibniz answered that even if this expectation could not be fulfilled, it was still very exciting that Coptic might be philosophical. "For hitherto" he continued, "we have not known of any such, although the reasons for the impositions of names sometimes become apparent within the ruins of ancient languages, particularly the Hebrew and Germanic."[25]

Here Leibniz is clearly assuming and hoping that a key to etymology may be found, similar to the hoped-for key to the system of Chinese characters. And if that etymological key were found, then we would have the philosophical foundation of the origin of language. In this sense it can be said that Leibniz' philosophy of language included the principle of Böhme's Natur-Sprache, but not as a matter of fact, but rather as a theoretical principle, which in turn was closely bound to the conviction, "that languages are the best mirror of the human mind, and that an exact analysis of the signification of words would give insight into the operations of the understanding better than any other means."[26] In practice, as opposed to theory, he believed that all mankind forms a single race, which has been modified according to the climates under which they lived, just as animals and plants assume different forms according to climatic conditions.[27]

Thus Leibniz' philosophy of language and etymology was based on the *a priori* assumption that the laws of sufficient reason and of continuity must also hold in regard to language. He postulated that all languages derived from a single source, and he believed that there was, ultimately, a non-arbitrary connection between words and things, based on analogy—"But in languages formed little by little, words have come into being as occasion arose from the analogy of sound with the disposition [or 'affect'] of the mind, that accompanied the perception of the thing. I am inclined to believe that Adam did not impose names in any other fashion."[28] These principles were in turn to determine his etymological method.

III

The seventeenth century did not use etymology to seek and perhaps gain information but rather to support—and as they thought prove—preconceived beliefs. As one seventeenth-century authority put it, in etymology it is entirely legitimate to add, subtract, transpose, and invert letters, for this procedure will seem reasonable when we consider that Hebrew writing goes from right to left, whereas in Greek and many other languages, it goes from left to right.[29] The typical etymologist also felt free to compare any two words in different languages, no matter how widely separated they were in time and place—Persian or ancient Hebrew with modern German, Greek with French, or Swedish with Hebrew. In this fashion it was possible to make etymology prove that the language spoken in the Garden of Eden was Swedish or—as someone else believed—Flemish. In other words, etymology was not subject to the method created by the nineteenth century. To this confident speculation, Leibniz answered that etymology is always, even at its best, highly uncertain. It works by conjecture rather than proof. To have any claim to validity at all, it must be the product of careful comparison of a wide number of forms, not only in different languages but also in different dialects. In 1698, he wrote to Ludolf: "Etymology deals with conjectures, not demonstrations; and I believe there are sometimes true origins that are not at all plausible: for in the mutations of languages chance rules as much as design."[30] All the same, he believed that etymology might ultimately be reduced to a science (and then it would become a branch of the science of meaning), but only as a result of careful and methodical analysis and comparison of a vast body of material, which would first have to be gathered. Its fulfilment would lie far in the future. He had no faith in the "Irrgarten der Lautphilosophie" into which he often found that his contemporaries and even friends wandered, including Gerhard Meier—"at times we have little disagreements, for etymologies are often problematical," Leibniz wrote to Sparfvenfelt in 1698.[31] Instead he encouraged his friend to engage in the empirical task of compiling a dictionary of the Saxon dialect, just as he stimulated many others to engage in similar work.

Leibniz devoted some sections of the *Epistolaris de Historia Etymologica Dissertatio* to these questions. He mentions that an Englishman had constructed a system of etymology by arranging primitive words according to certain classes of properties until they were reduced to the fewest possible categories. By this means the philosophy of words imitated that of things, an attempt that was commonly made in the seventeenth century by people who believed in Böhme's Natur-Sprache. But Leibniz continued that though one may wish to achieve this reduction, there is little hope of success. It was true, he admitted, that he himself had said a good deal about the force and natural signification of letters—as in onomatopoeia for instance—but he did not wish to suggest that these observations point to principles that can commonly or necessarily be seen to operate in languages today, for words have for many reasons changed far too much from their original significations for this to be possible.[32] Though the sound L, as earlier remarked, may indicate something soft and gentle, "it is wrong to maintain that this reason will stand out in every case, for the lion, the lynx, and the wolf are not at all gentle. . . . Owing to a variety of accidents and changes, most words are extremely altered and removed from their original pronunciation and signification."[33] Thus again, though Leibniz by his use of onomatopoeia and other forms of "Lautphilosophie" may seem to have much in common with his contemporaries, he is in fact far removed from sharing their conceptions.

In history Leibniz believed that the smallest causes, often unseen and unnoticed, were the true and profound causes of events, owing as he said to the "universal interconnection of things."[34] This of course also held in the changes of language, and hence the basic rule of all practical etymology, that it must observe the law of continuity. As early as 1692, he wrote to Tentzel that linguistic relationship was our only source of knowledge about the origin and cognation of early nations, but, he added, "the comparison would need to be conducted from one tribe to another, not even neglecting the dialects, for if distant nations are compared discontinuously, it is no wonder if the relations do not appear."[35] This was the rule that contemporary etymology had generally failed to observe. Leibniz repeated it again and again, for instance in the *Nouveaux essais*: "Being the most ancient monuments of peoples, before writing and the arts, languages in general best indicate the cognations and migrations of peoples. That is why etymologies when well understood would be interesting and full of consequences. But we must be sure to bring together the languages of a number of peoples and not make too many leaps from one nation to another far away; here it is especially important to have the assurance of peoples that are located in between."[36] Here again the continuity principle explains the importance of collecting and recording dialects as an indispensable prerequisite to ultimate demonstration of the relationship among nations. Already in 1687, in the first letter to Ludolf, Leibniz had said that in the future there would be scholars who made it their business to record spoken dialects because this material would be necessary to the completion of the harmony of languages.[37]

Apart from local Germanic dialects, Leibniz took special interest in Russian and the Slavic languages, partly of course for political reasons, but certainly also because there seemed to exist a discontinuous jump between the Germanic and Slavic languages, in spite of the fact that the two were now neighbors. In 1695 he wrote to Sparfvenfelt about his puzzlement that two contiguous languages could be so different, and he suggested that perhaps a now extinct people had previously lived between them and thus made the transition continuous.[38]

The Slavic languages, however, were not all. Leibniz also wished to gather as much information as possible about the languages spoken in the most distant eastern and south-eastern parts of the Czarist empire, again to satisfy the continuity principle, hoping that these distant languages might ultimately form a link to other Asian and perhaps to the still more distant American languages, though he admitted in 1691 that these languages, in the present state of our knowledge, seemed so different that one could believe they were the speech of a different race of men.[39] In order to gain the requisite information, he used the old device of trying to collect the Lord's Prayer in as many languages and dialects as at all possible—in the correspondence with his Russian connections he made at least a dozen such requests, apparently without much success, though the great compilation he had in mind was later made during the reign of Catherine the Great. In 1698, in a brief piece "Über die Sprachen der Tartarey," he wrote on this matter: "It would be useful if we could have the Lord's Prayer in those languages, with a word-for-word translation between the lines into a better-known language, in order better to be able to compare such languages with others for which we already have the Lord's Prayer." But even without whole versions of the Lord's Prayer, much could still be done by collecting the basic words of the vocabulary: "But when the Lord's

Prayer is not easy to obtain, we could still ask for words that are in it, such as: father, heaven, name, to come . . . earth, bread, give. . . . We could also ask for the names of other things, as, for instance, for some limbs of the human body and their use, such as: eyes, ears, to hear, to see, etc. And the same for relations and next of kin, as father, mother, daughter, brother, sister, man, woman, child, etc. The same for foods, drinks, clothes, arms: also for the names of some familiar animals, for the four elements and what pertains to them."[40]

To Leibniz theory and practice were never at variance. From theory he descended to an empirical program for the collection and analysis of a vast mass of linguistic material. The end would for ages lie beyond the horizon, but without the right method and the right beginning, without detailed, painstaking work and carefully organized cooperation, there would be no answers, no end at all.

IV

By his sharp departure from the practice and doctrines of his day, Leibniz hoped not only to gain historical information but also, ultimately and in a much longer perspective, perhaps to gain insight into the mind of man. He learnt much from the literature on language and etymology that was available to him, but he rejected the principles, though some of them still retained part of their meaning within his new system. Unfortunately his direct influence remained somewhat less than it might have been, and a number of etymological principles were later to be established independently, as it seems, of Leibniz. But he exercised a lasting and very important indirect influence through his encouragement to etymological study and the collection of material, of early texts, of dialects, of placenames, plantnames, family names, and other kinds of terms. He hoped it would ultimately become possible to find the Ariadne Thread to the labyrinth of languages, a seemingly impossible task, but no more impossible, in theory at least, than finding the formula that described a line traced through a number of scattered points. In the *Discours de métaphysique* he explained what he meant: "For in regard to the universal order, everything in it is in accord. This is so true that not only does nothing that is absolutely irregular occur in the world, but we could not even imagine anything of the sort. For let us suppose, for example, that someone put a number of points on a piece of paper in completely haphazard fashion, as is done by those who practice the ridiculous art of geomancy—I say that it is possible to determine a geometrical line of which the idea is constant and uniform according to a certain rule, so that this line will pass through all the points and in the same order in which the hand made them."[41] Applied to languages, this line is the analogue of the Ariadne Thread of which Leibniz wrote to Ludolf as early as 1687 when he first seriously began his linguistic and etymological studies.[42]

Leibniz would no doubt have been disappointed to know that during the eighteenth century Locke's influence on language study was greater than his own. But he could have found some consolation in the words of Herder, written some twenty years after the publication of the *Nouveaux essais*. With specific reference to the study of language, Herder wrote: "Locke now concerns us only in so far as he served truth, and we have already for long owing to Leibniz been accustomed also to find weaknesses in his philosophy."[43]

Notes

1. Most general works on Leibniz also deal with his study of language and etymology. More specific treatments will be found in: Landolin Neff, *Gottfried Wilhelm Leibniz als Sprachforscher und Etymologe* (Heidelberg, 1870-1871), 2 vols., 49 pp. and 53 pp. Louis Davillé, *Leibniz historien* (Paris, 1909), esp. pp. 319-324, 403-419, 502 ff., 690-692; this work has a wealth of valuable material and references. Sigrid von der Schulenburg, *Leibnizens Gedanken und Vorschläge zur Erforschung der deutschen Mundarten*. 1937. (= *Abhandlungen der Preussischen Akademie der Wissenschaften*, philologisch-historische Klasse, Nr. 2.) She had planned and in part completed articles on several aspects of Leibniz' study of language, including the subject of the present paper (see p. 9, n. 4; p. 20, n. 1; and p. 32, n. 4, and reference at end of note 4 below). Hans Arens, *Sprachwissenschaft* (Freiburg/München, 1955) devotes pp. 77-88 to Leibniz, in the form of long excerpts from the main texts, in German translation.

2. Pp. 292 and 305 in Paul Pietsch, *Leibniz und die deutsche Sprache*. In: *Wissenschaftliche Beihefte zur Zeitschrift des Allgemeinen Deutschen Sprachvereins*. R. 4, Heft 29 (Juli, 1907) and Heft 30 (April, 1908), pp. 265-371. *Die Ermahnung* will be found pp. 292-312, *Die Unvorgreifflichen Gedancken* pp. 327-356. *Die Ermahnung* is generally dated in the early 1680s, *Die Unvorgreifflichen Gedancken* after 1697. The metaphor of language as a mirror of the mind occurs several times in Leibniz; see e.g. reference to *Nouveaux essais* in fn. 26 below. For an English translation of *Die Unvorg. Ged.*, see "Leibniz on Locke on Language," note 15, above.

3. Akademie-Ausgabe, ser. I, vol. V, p. 31 [hereafter in short form: A I, v, 31] in Leibniz to Hiob Ludolf, 19 (?) Dec. 1687: "I would wish that, not by your labors but with your counsel, authority, and judgment, some little dictionaries be made by men skilled in languages, in which the roots and principal words of most known languages would be contained, with a little compendium of the grammar of each attached. . . . And then at last I believe we would come somewhat closer to what Skytte, Stiernhielm, and others have attempted in vain, namely the harmony of most languages and in most respects. Thereby the origins of nations would also be wonderfully elucidated, to say nothing of many other things that lie hidden in these arcane matters, which systematic collection would at the same time certainly reveal."

4. A I, vi, 442, in Leibniz to Huldreich von Eyben, Hann., 26 March/5 April, 1691. It remains true that Leibniz' study of natural language and linguistic affinity for the sake of historical knowledge was much advanced by his historical studies and especially by his travels (undertaken to further those studies) to the libraries, archives, and learned circles of Southern Germany, Austria, and Italy between November 1687 and June 1690. But it now seems clear to me that the impulse to that interest and the formulation of his aims had occurred earlier, based on the knowledge he had gained already in the 1670s of the Swedish doctrine that the Germanic nations had their original home in Sweden (or indeed all of mankind as was claimed by some) and from there had migrated to the Continent. This is the so-called Gothicism advocated by Georg Stiernhielm, Olof Verelius, and Olof Rudbeck. Leibniz made great efforts to keep informed about this work and was eager to refute the Swedish doctrine, which he thought lacked a sound foundation. In 1975 I concluded: "It is true that Leibniz' study of natural languages is linked to his work on the history of the ducal house he served; but it is the Swedish thesis that sets this study in motion, and the opportunity to gain knowledge of Asian languages that gives promise of ultimate success." See my review essay "Schulenburg's *Leibniz als Sprachforscher* [by Sigrid von der Schulenburg, Frankfurt am Main: Klostermann, 1973], with some observations on Leibniz and the study of language," *Studia Leibnitiana* 7 (1975), 122-134; see esp. pp. 125, 131-134.

5. A I, vii, 645, in Leibniz to Giov. Giusto Ciampini, Hann., 2 April, 1692. Other letters on linguistic and etymological matters from this period: to Grimaldi, A I, vi, 520 (Hann., 31 May/10 June, 1691). To La Loubère, A I, vii, 399 (Hann., 5/15 Oct., 1691), pp. 553-54 (Hann., 4 Feb., 1692); La Loubère to Leibniz, pp. 661-63 (Paris, 13 April, 1692). To Ludolf, A I, vii, 365-366 (Brschwg., 5/15 Sept., 1691), and Ludolf to Leibniz, pp. 557-61 (Frankf., 25 Jan./4 Feb., 1692); also Leibniz to Ludolf in *Ludolfi et Leibnitii Commercium Epistolicum*. Ed. A. B. Michaelis (Gottingae, 1755), p. 46 (Hann., 17 April, 1692) and p. 59 (Hann., 25 July, 1692). To Tentzel, A I, vii, 628-31 (Hann., 16/26 March, 1692).

6. Schulenburg, pp. 15-16.

7. "Leibniz' bref till Sparfvenfelt." Ed. Harald Wieselgren. In: *Antiqvarisk Tidsskrift för Sverige*, VII (1884-85), No. 3, pp. 1-64. This important correspondence is now in Stifts- och Landsbiblioteket, Linköping.

8. *Leibnitii Epistolae ad Diversos*. Ed. Christian Kortholt, I (Lipsiae, 1734), 452-54 (to La Croze) and 368-71 (to Sebastian Kortholt).

9. In addition to these two pieces see also the "Aufsatz von Leibniz über den Ursprung der Europäischen Völker" from 1712, in Waldemar Guerrier, *Leibniz in seinen Beziehungen zu Russland und Peter dem Grossen* (St. Petersburg und Leipzig, 1873), pp. 210-213.

10. "Brevis designatio meditationum de Originibus Gentium, ductis potissimum ex indicio linguarum." In: *Miscellanea Berolinensia* (Berlin, 1710), pp. 1-16 (Ravier, No. 305). Some time during the summer of 1716, Leibniz wrote to La Croze: "My conjectures on the origins of nations are briefly set forth in the Berlin Miscellanea, and I would be pleased to have your opinion in the matter, not merely to confirm and amplify my feelings, but also to correct them as needed." See Kortholt, I, 451.

11. For a brief description of the MS of the *Epistolaris*, see Schulenburg, p. 5, n. 3. The passage I refer to is in one of the earlier versions in Hannover, Nieders. Landesbibliothek, Ms. IV, 469, fol. 37r: "But distracted not only by other affairs and concerns, but also by consultations related to other kinds of study, in which it seems to myself and others possible to do something perhaps more worthwhile, I cannot hope to set these matters in order and to treat them with proper care; I strive to encourage others in their studies." Leibniz was quite aware that his historical and linguistic studies might seem to conflict with his other interests. On 25 July 1697, he wrote to Palmieri: "In regard to the diversity of nations I would strongly wish to be able to obtain samples of the languages of those countries, that is

to say those that are entirely different from the Russian, for example of that of the Chercassians, of the Czeremiss, of the Kalmucks, of the Siberians, etc., and perhaps we will by that means learn from what parts of Scythia the Huns and Hungarians have come. And since the jurisdiction of the Czar now extends to the borders of the Tartars of China, this will make a large part of the terrestrial globe better known, since the different races of nations cannot be better distinguished than by their languages and their harmony or cognation. I entreat you to suggest this in suitable fashion, and especially, if possible, without making too much noise. For there are many who do not care for these interesting things, which they take to be useless. You do not share their opinion, and neither do I." See Guerrier, pp. 10-11. At the end of 1698, Leibniz wrote in a similar vein to Sparfvenfelt, apologizing for having taken nearly a year to answer a letter and referring to all the demands that were being made on his time, "I am told that I am wrong to leave solid and eternal truths for researches in the changing and passing things contained in histories and laws." Wieselgren, p. 23.

12. Leibniz, *Otium Hanoveranum*. Ed. Joachim Friedrich Feller (Lipsiae, 1718), pp. 80-81 (Leibniz to Tentzel without date, but answer to letter of 17 June, 1697). Translation will be found in Neff, II, 28-29.

13. *Epistolaris*, Hannover, Ms. IV, 469, fol. 75r (§ 14): "Jacob Boehme, a cobbler turned philosopher and theologian, who created a wondrous philosophy and theology for himself from the reading of Tauler, Schwenkfeld, Sebastian Frank, Valentin Weigel, and similar German writers (chiefly mystics, enthusiasts, and alchemists), believed he could restore a certain natural language (Natur-Sprache), which he also called Adamic; so that he who found it would also know the secrets of nature and the properties of things. But no one doubts that this is certainly an illusion." See also Leibniz, *Die Philosophischen Schriften*. Ed. Gerhardt, VII, 198f., 204f.; Leibniz, *Opusculus et fragments inédits*. Ed. Couturat (Paris, 1903), p. 151; *Nouveaux essais*, III, ii, 1 (A VI, vi, 281); and Kortholt, III (Lipsiae, 1738), 350-54 (correspondence with Hermann von der Hardt from 1696 and 1699—these letters are incorrectly dated in Leibniz, *Opera omnia* Geneva, 1768. Ed. L. Dutens, VI, ii, 225-26).

14. On this subject, see "Leibniz on Locke on Language," reprinted above. On Boehme, Franck, and Weigel, see my entries in the *Dictionary of Scientific Biography*.

15. *Unvorgr. Ged.* § § 32, 5, and 50.

16. *Nouveaux essais*, II, ii, 1 (A VI, vi, 283).

17. Couturat, p. 151. This passage concludes: "And indeed onomatopeia often manifestly imitates nature, as when we assign quacking to frogs, when *st* for us means admonition to silence or quiet; and *r* running, when *hahaha* denotes laughing, *vae* affliction."

18. Dutens, VI, ii, 185 in "Conjecture de Monsr. Leibniz sur l'origine du mot BLASON," first published in *Journal des Sçavans*. XX (28 July, 1692), 513-515 (Ravier, No. 120): "For it seems in fact that nearly all languages are only variations, often much intermixed, of the same roots, but which it is difficult to identify without comparing many languages together, not neglecting dialects; with regard to them, it would be useful if scholars in each region would take pains to collect the characteristic words."

19. *Epistolaris*, fol. 75r (§ 15): "But now we treat languages accepted among the nations [i.e., ordinary languages]. For it is credible, in so far as the first men, or rather the nations who afterwards deviated from the language of the first man, formed particular words for themselves, for them to have adapted sounds to perceptions and affects, initially using interjections and short particles adapted to their affects, from which seeds, so to speak, languages gradually arose. Thus prepositions and other particles are often roots." The same point is made in "Brevis designatio" p. 2, and in several places in the letters.

20. *Nouveaux essais*, III, ii, 1 (A VI, vi, 281-82).

21. Wieselgren, p. 53 in letter to Sparfvenfelt (not dated but from the autumn of 1699): "In the letter *n* the tongue is more applied to the palate and the nose contributes to its

pronunciation, for by closing the nose our n is stopped so that it is a nasal letter, and there has been good reason to begin the word nose with this letter."

22. *Nouveaux essais*, III, ii, 1 (A VI, vi, 283).

23. Kortholt, I, 376 in letter to La Croze of 24 June, 1705.

24. Kortholt, I, 378 in letter to La Croze of 8 Oct., 1707. Cf. *ibid.*, p. 395 (letter to La Croze of 5 Nov., 1707).

25. Kortholt, I, 424 in letter to La Croze of 6 July, 1712.

26. *Nouveaux essais*, III, vii, 6 (A VI, vi, 333).

27. Wieselgren, pp. 16-17 in letter to Sparfvenfelt of 29 Jan., 1697: "In American there is also a wonderful difference between the Galibi or Carib Indians, who have much dignity and even spirit, and those of Paraguay, who appear to be children or pupils all their lives. This does not rule out that all human beings who inhabit the globe are all of the same race, having been altered by the different climates, just as we see that animals and plants change nature and become better or degenerate."

28. "Brevis designatio," p. 2.

29. Estienne Gvichart, *L'Harmonie etimologique des langues* (Paris, 1618) in the Preface: "In regard to the derivation of words by addition, subtraction, transposition and inversion of letters, it is certain this can and must happen if we intend to discover the etymologies. This is not difficult to understand if we bear in mind that the Hebrews write from right to left, and the Greeks and others from left to right. All scholars also admit such derivations to be necessary, and the truth of etymologies is the infallible proof."

30. Leibniz, *Collectanea Etymologica*. Ed. Johann Georg Eckhart (Hanoverae, 1717), II, 311 in letter to Ludolf of 12 Dec., 1698.

31. Wieselgren, p. 29 in letter to Sparfvenfelt of 27 Dec., 1698: "Gerhard Meyer, a theologian and preacher at Bremen, of the Reformed Church, works hard and untiringly on his Saxon Glossary. At times we have little disagreements. . . . "

32. *Epistolaris*, foll. 75v-76r (in § § 15-16): "Thus also R with Z indicates a rupture owing to a certain natural analogy between thing and sound. And it can be said that letters [sounds] that have a natural power in fact produce roots, others however being dependent in usage. Johan Clauberg perhaps intended to treat these or similar things in the work on the causes of the Germanic languages . . . and Gerhard Meier made reflections that are not inappropriate; . . . he thought the matter could be reduced to a kind of science, which I also believe. According to Thomas Hayne, this seems also to have been the opinion of Henry Jacob, a fellow of Merton College in Oxford, who, it would appear, had made a kind of system of the art of etymology and would distribute the primitive words according to certain classes of properties until they were brought to the smallest number of principles, so that this philosophy of words would exactly imitate that of things. But this is an object rather of desire than hope. And I do not wish that the things I said concerning the power of letters and natural signification be accepted as if they can always or for the most part be observed in languages today. For the majority have long since retreated from the original meanings owing to innumerable metaphors, metonymies, and synechdochies. . . . So that the learned man who recently at Paris reviewed my dissertation on knowing the origins of nations on the basis of languages, published in the Miscellanea Berolinensia, said nothing against me when he seemed to raise objections." Clauberg's *Ars Etymologica Teutonum e Philosophiae fontibus derivata* (Duisburgi ad Rhenum, 1663) is reprinted in the *Collectanea Etymologica*, I, 187-252. Leibniz had the highest opinion of this work as well as of Clauberg as a philosopher. See Leibniz, *Otium Hanoveranum*, p. 181: "Descartes would improve some things in physics, but boldness and excessive pride cause displeasure, along with obscurity of style, confusion, and slander. Clauberg, his disciple, has for long been esteemed more highly by me, straightforward, perspicuous, brief, methodical."

33. *Nouveaux essais*, II, ii, 1 (A VI, vi, 283).

34. Davillé, p. 613, with references to letter to Gerhard Meier of 16 Dec., 1692.

35. A I, vii, 629, in letter to Tentzel from Hann., 16/26 March, 1692.

36. *Nouveaux essais*, III, ii, 1 (A VI, vi, 285). This passage concludes: "And in general we should not trust etymologies without an abundance of concurring evidence." Leibniz often states the non-per-saltum principle in linguistic study: "I almost never trust the regularity of etymologies, except when they proceed from language to language following the juxtaposition of location, and not by skipping." (Wieselgren, pp. 31-32, in letter to Sparfvenfelt of 27 Dec., 1698.)

37. A I, v, 31, in letter to Ludolf of 19 (?) Dec., 1687: "There will in time be those who advance the matter further and collect the dialects also of living nations in writing, which will be necessary for completing the harmony of languages."

38. Wieselgren, p. 6, in letter to Sparfvenfelt of 6 Dec., 1695: "In fact, it is a cause of astonishment to me that neighboring nations often have such different languages, as the Germans and the Slavs. Perhaps the ancient nations that were in between, producing a less perceptible transition from one language to the next, have been destroyed."

39. A I, vii, 399, in letter to La Loubère of 5/15 Oct., 1691: "It would be important if we could have quite old and original histories of these countries on the extremity of Asia. As also if we could gain some knowledge of the languages of all the eastern Indies. For it is by this means that we can best make conjectures on the origins of nations. It is sufficiently clear that nearly all the languages of the world known to the ancients are interrelated to a large degree and appear to come from the same source. But when we pass to America and to the extremities and distant places of Asia and Africa, the languages seem to be so different among themselves and from ours that one would say it is another race of animals. But if we proceed from nation to nation in the study of languages, we would draw better conclusions than by this skipping." A month earlier he had made the same point in a letter to Ludolf of 5/15 Sept., 1691 (A I, vii, 366): "No doubt, if the first linguistic change between neighbors produces another dialect, the second and third change would in the end make another language, nor do I strongly oppose those who hold the opinion that most languages in the world known to the ancients have flowed from the same source. But about the Chinese, American, and Africans I have nothing to say in so far as they differ from us by the entire quality of speech not to mention body." It was no doubt with this problem in mind that Leibniz wrote: "I also wish to know what has been or can be discovered on the great question whether America and Asia are joined toward the northeast or whether there is an ocean in between." (Letter of 6 Nov., 1712 in Guerrier, p. 275; this letter asks information about a variety of languages spoken in the Czarist empire and on its far eastern borders.) In the requests Leibniz made to his Russian connections, he stressed the need to have languages marked on maps: "Maps show the borders of states but not those of nations, which the harmony of languages more clearly makes evident." (Letter to Le Fort le Jeune, Hann., 3/13 Aug., 1697, in Guerrier, p. 22-23.) Similarly Guerrier, p. 51, in letter to Huyssen of 7 Oct., 1703: "I find this lack in the description of distant countries, that the languages of the nations are not indicated, which means that we know neither their cognations nor their origins." For a detailed summary of Leibniz' interest in Asian languages and his research program for their study, see "Concept einer Denkschrift Leibniz's über Untersuchung der Sprachen und Beobachtung der Variation des Magnets im Russischen Reiche," in Guerrier, pp. 239-243.

40. Leibniz, *Deutsche Schriften*. Ed. Gottschalk Eduard Guhrauer, II (Berlin, 1840), pp. 478-79. On the use of *pater nosters* in linguistic study, see also A I, vii, 553-54 (letter to La Loubère, 4 Febr., 1692); Michaelis, p. 46 (letter to Ludolf, 17 April, 1692); Kortholt, I, 374 and 416-417 (letters to La Croze of 3 May, 1704, and 28 Dec., 1711).

41. *Discours de métaphysique*. Ed. Georges Le Roy (Paris: Vrin, 1957), p. 41 (in § 6).

42. A I, v, 31: "For nothing is lacking so that learned men, known to you, and in part also youths, can excell within in a short time, when each of them skilled in particular languages is furnished with the Ariadne thread by you."

43. Herder in "Vorrede" to *Des Lord Monboddos Werk von dem Ursprunge und Fortgange der Sprache* (Riga, 1784). In Herder, *Sämmtliche Werke*. Ed. Bernhard Suphan (Berlin, 1877-1913), XV, 179-183.

The History of Linguistics
and Professor Chomsky

In this paper I propose to examine Chomsky's version of the history of linguistics. It is well known that Chomsky turned to this subject after he had published his earlier purely linguistic studies. These studies had already indicated his interest in the history of linguistics, but it was not until the publication of *Aspects* (1965:47-59) that he treated the subject at greater length, in a section on 'Linguistic theory and language learning'. Late in 1966 followed the main work, *Cartesian linguistics*, and two years later *Language and mind,* in which the first chapter and parts of the third were again devoted to the history of linguistics. Transformational generative grammar was linked to antecedents in the 17th and 18th centuries, both as a matter of intellectual interest and to serve the purpose of polemics against its own immediate predecessor in linguistics, the tradition which can be called Bloomfieldian—a tradition which had gone out of its way to show contempt for the work which Chomsky was now raising to a position of respect and admiration. I think it is fair to say that this polemic element is clearly evident in the Chomskyan version of the history of linguistics, for it is the general tendency of this version to elevate 'Cartesian' approaches to the study of language, and to depreciate to

Reprinted from *Language* 46 (1970), 570-585. I have dealt with matters related to the present essay in "'Cartesian Linguistics': History or Fantasy?" *Language Sciences*, No. 17 (October 1971), 1-12. A large literature on the subject has appeared since this essay was written. See esp. André Joly, "La linguistique cartésienne: une erreur mémorable," in *La Grammaire générale: des Modistes aux Idéologues*, ed. by André Joly and Jean Stéfanini (Publications de l'Université de Lille III), pp. 165-199. For a bibliography, see Charles Porset, "*Grammatista philosophans*: Les sciences du langage de Port-Royal aux Idéologues," *ibid.*, pp. 40-43.

an equal or greater degree all empiricist, behaviorist, or associationist procedures in the study of language, whether rightly or wrongly so labeled. One of the first reviews of *Cartesian linguistics* (Kampf 1967) concluded by calling attention to this tendency as Chomsky's special merit. It observed that literary historians had rarely looked at the 17th century conflict between empiricists and rationalists in terms of current learning theory. We are told that, since most of the important figures involved, such as Dryden and Swift, stressed the primacy of experience, 'Locke emerges as the hero, Descartes the villain, from the histories of the conflict. Chomsky forces us, at last, to reconsider the influence of empiricism on the development of science and scholarship.' It should be unnecessary to point out why this statement is absurd, in both fact and interpretation. But it is worth noting that Locke is made out by that reviewer, as by Chomsky, to be a villain, or at least a sort of nincompoop in matters of language and the philosophy of mind. I shall return to that problem, since it has a very direct bearing on my belief that Chomsky's version of the history of linguistics is fundamentally false. I shall make an assumption, which I think will be readily granted: namely, that Chomsky is in fact attempting to give a historical account and is not merely seeking out concepts, statements, and arguments in an unhistorical fashion. Even if this were not the case, there can be no doubt that Chomsky's work has in fact been read and understood as the history of linguistics. It has been assumed that his history gives an adequate account of the main line of development from the middle of the 17th century to the early decades of the 19th century. It may be recalled that the subtitle of *Cartesian linguistics* is 'A chapter in the history of rationalist thought'.

Before proceeding, I shall state what I take to be the criteria of adequacy for such a history, as for any history that falls within the larger territory of the history of ideas.[1] In general there are two: adequate scholarship; and the over-all coherence of the entire history that is presented, without omission or neglect of material that is relevant, either by the writer's own standards or by those of the figures he deals with and cites.

The first criterion, that of scholarship, involves a reasonably comprehensive knowledge of the texts that are used and of the total work of each major figure. What, for instance, will happen to the argument if Du Marsais turns out to have been powerfully anti-Cartesian on the very points that Chomsky takes to be fundamental to Cartesianism? Will not the argument be impaired or perhaps show signs of collapse? Worse yet, what will happen if Du Marsais turns out to have been a professed Lockean? In fact, Du Marsais was both strongly anti-Cartesian and emphatically pro-Lockean. We shall see other examples of this sort of carelessness, omission, and (unfortunately) plain ignorance. These are not examples that have only a peripheral effect on the argument; they affect its very core. There is of course no absolute safeguard against such errors, but in this case the remedy lies within easy reach, since Du Marsais's entire work is compact and easy to survey, thanks also to the very complete index which accompanies the best and presumably complete edition of his works (1797). We may note that, when Chomsky (1966:53-4) does refer to D'Alembert's eulogy of Du Marsais, he uses a passage which is closely preceded by the statement that Du Marsais was anti-Cartesian.[2]

There is also one generally acknowledged avenue to avoidance of the worst errors, namely an adequate acquaintance with the best secondary literature and the best editions. Not only is such acquaintance nearly absent from Chomsky's excursions into history, but he relies on outright inferior sources. For instance, to determine what is commonplace in Locke interpretation, he cites the laughable notes in Fraser's wretched edition of the *Essay* (Chomsky 1968:86). This, incidentally, makes Chomsky the latest—and for a long while the first—denigrator of Locke in the conservative Victorian tradition, in which denigration of Locke was a matter of doctrine. Fraser's edition is the summa of that attitude.

The second basic criterion of historical research is the over-all coherence of the entire presentation, without omission or neglect of relevant material. In this connection, we note that Cartesianism in linguistics is seen by Chomsky to run straight through the German Romantics down to Wilhelm von Humboldt, as illustrated by citations from Herder and both the Schlegels. But these citations occur in works that deal specifically with the origin of language, and in one case even with 'etymology in general'. Neither of these subjects appears, not even according to Chomsky, in Cartesian linguistics or in universal grammar, which in fact by its very presuppositions would seem immune to the time perspective. Would not a little suspicion have been commendable here, suspicion that the history is not quite so simple as we are told? Such suspicion might have directed attention to the problem of the origin of language, as it was viewed in the 18th century. It is true that the secondary literature, which in any event is not cited, would not have shown how strongly Herder was influenced by Condillac; but since the ostensible purpose was to do something new, a relevant opportunity was missed.[3]

Turning now to the history itself, we may ask, first, whether Cartesian linguistics in the shape of the Port-Royal Grammar of 1660 is in fact Cartesian in the sense that is claimed. And, second, we may ask whether Chomsky's version of history is correct, from 1660 through the 18th century into the early nineteenth, if we grant that

there was some sort of linguistic theory embodied in universal grammar, whether we call it Cartesian or not. I shall deal briefly with the
first question and then at greater length with the second, which I
take to be the more substantial part of the entire problem.

All the reviews and discussions I have seen have something important to say about this first question, though none deal with the second
question. There are signs, however, that they take that part of the
history to be generally correct. Both Zimmer 1968 and Salmon 1969
point out that there are significant antecedents of the method and
principles presented by the Port-Royal Grammar. Thus, as Mrs. Salmon
observes, if the postulated Cartesianism is not one of dependence,
but merely one of parallel, then all the Cartesianism vanishes—and,
one might add, the lustrous prestige of the name. Miel 1969 demonstrates the significance of Pascal and of Augustinianism, as indicated
by his title 'Pascal, Port-Royal, and Cartesian Linguistics'. This is
merely another way of saying that the Port-Royal Grammar was indeed a Port-Royal product—that is not without importance, for Locke
was very sympathetic to the Jansenists of Port-Royal; he owned their
words and read them. His political philosophy would seem to have
received significant impulses from Pierre Nicole, who with Arnauld
was responsible for the Port-Royal Logic, which is so closely related
to the Grammar that it must be called its twin. Apart from the last
point about Locke, this could all quite easily have been learned from
the relevant secondary sources, most of it in fact from Sainte-Beuve's
Port-Royal, now one hundred and ten years old, to which Chomsky
makes some convenient references (e.g. 1966:75, 104, 105). It would
also seem potentially dangerous to ignore the fact that the Port-
Royalists had significant disagreements with Descartes—Arnauld, for
instance, over innateness.

But the most substantial discussion is Robin Lakoff's recent review
(1969) of the new edition of the Port-Royal Grammar. She points
out (1) that Lancelot's *Nouvelle méthode pour apprendre facilement
et en peu de temps la langue latine* (1644) offers much more explicit
similarities to Chomskyan linguistics than does the Port-Royal
Grammar; (2) that the third edition of the *Nouvelle méthode* (1654)
is even richer in this respect; (3) that Lancelot credits the improvement of this third edition to his recently gained knowledge of
Sanctius's famous *Minerva, seu de causis linguae latinae* (1587); and (4)
that this work by Sanctius is indeed the historical source of what is
found most admirable in the Port-Royal Grammar. It may be added
that Sanctius appears in turn to be indebted to the speculative grammars of the Middle Ages, a tradition whose relevance was pointed out
as long ago as 1947 by Gilson (1947:7). Chomsky knew Robin Lakoff's

findings before their publication, and he answers her in *Language and mind* (15-6) to the effect that Sanctius merely offered 'a device for the interpretation of texts', but nothing truly like the Cartesianism of the Port-Royal Grammar. The reason for the difference, we are told, is that they were 'in particular, separated by the Cartesian revolution'. Of course, that answer begs the question, since the very point is whether in fact there was a 'Cartesian revolution' in these matters. But there is a more serious side to Chomsky's answer regarding Sanctius and the mere interpretation of literary texts: it entirely disregards the incontestable fact that practically all universal grammarians, including Du Marsais, emphatically and often state their indebtedness to Sanctius, a fact that cannot escape attention even in the most cursory reading.[4] Chomsky cannot avoid censure by referring to the remark early in *Cartesian linguistics* (2-3) that these developments in universal grammar 'have roots in earlier linguistic work'. If that question were to be left open, then the term Cartesian would obviously have to be dropped until its appropriateness could be established. This is only one example of Chomsky's curious procedure in historical research and argument, a procedure in part made possible by his ignorance of the general intellectual history of the entire period under discussion.

I wish to make one more observation about this linguistic work prior to 1660. In her review (170), Mrs. Salmon seeks out earlier uses of the term 'general grammar', and she finds it in J. H. Alsted's *Encyclopaedia* (1630). But, as Jellinek points out (1913:94), Alsted was merely incorporating Christoph Helwig's *Libri didactici grammaticae universalis, Latinae, Graecae, Hebraicae, Chaldaicae*, first published posthumously in 1619.[5] Helwig worked closely with Wolfgang Ratke, who also in 1619 published his *Allgemeine Sprachlehr*. The title page of this work had a rather elaborate device, crowned by the significant words 'Ratio vicit, vetustas cessit'; that is, antiquity and old authority and tradition have lost to the triumph of reason (Ising 1959, end of 'Einleitung'). Bacon, in his *Advancement of learning* (1605:II.xvi.4), a passage that is for some reason generally ignored in this context, says that there are two kinds of grammar, one 'popular'—in the Latin of *De augmentis scientiarum* (1623:VI.i) he says 'literaria'—and the other 'philosophical, examining the power and nature of words, as they are the footsteps and prints of reason'. A few pages later he says: 'Knowledge that is delivered as a thread to be spun on, ought to be delivered and intimated, if it were possible, in the same method wherein it was invented.' This means that the method is a pedagogical problem, a problem in learning theory and practice, designed to shorten the job of learning. All the great general grammars arose in the context of this problem including those of Sanctius, Ratke, Helwig, Comenius, Lancelot, Du Marsais, and Condillac, to mention only a few. And they were often accompanied by what would appear to be greatly exaggerated claims for the efficiency of the method. Sanctius, for instance, claimed that he could teach Latin in eight months, Greek in twenty days, astronomy in eight or ten days, philosophy and music in a month or less (Weiss n.d., 610-11).[6] The method is, of course, that of reason, as the Ratichian motto reminds us, and it is often stated explicitly that reason would relieve the burden of memory, hence the shortening of the time required in learning the material. Du Marsais, for instance, observed that since the rules are nothing but general observations, they ought to be founded on reason alone. Once they have been comprehended, he went on, "We use only the memory of reason, so to speak, and this memory is never the slave of words." (1797:I.38). It is in this light that we must understand the frequent occurrence of the word 'method' in the titles already mentioned, as well as in the *Linguarum methodus novissima* of Comenius, who in his pansophy developed this doctrine in greater detail than any other 17th century figure. Bacon's critique of the idols of man must also be understood as a statement concerning method. But most famous is, of course, Descartes's *Discourse on the method of rightly conducting the reason and seeking truth in the sciences*. Readers who are familiar with Descartes's famous dream on the night of 10 November 1619 will see more clearly how profoundly his preoccupation with method typifies the dominant philosophical and pedagogical concerns of his time.

The art of speaking and the art of thinking, the grammar and the logic, are two faces of the same coin. As Gilson said in 1947, summing up the principles of the masters of grammar in the thirteenth century: the man who knows one grammar does not know all languages, but he knows all grammars, for there is only one, that of the intelligence whose operations are identical in all men, the universal grammar of the human mind (1947:7). Though I am not sure I understand Chomsky on this point (on which he is never very clear), no universal grammar postulates anything other than reason as the underlying framework or abstract apparatus of all grammars. They never postulate a separate linguistic something, though Chomsky talks vaguely about 'the forms of thought' and innate ideas. Du Marsais, for instance, rejected innate ideas out of hand. To be a universal grammarian, it is enough to be a rationalist.

Let me now turn to the second problem, whether Chomsky renders a correct account of the history of linguistics between 1660 and the romantic period around 1800. His account takes for granted that everything of value in 18th century linguistic theory is Cartesian. It follows further from Chomsky's treatment of Locke that nothing derived from him can be either Cartesian or valuable in this context, and thus also that a Lockean linguistics would be incompatible with a Cartesian linguistics, an idea which we may then reasonably assume would also have reached the awareness of those who were practicing either one or the other. The facts, however, are incontestably the very reverse of these conclusions.

Let me begin with the key figure, Condillac, though he is never mentioned by Chomsky. Even a cursory reading in the vast body of literature on language in the eighteenth century will show that Condillac is by all odds the most important figure, both as a theorist and by virtue of his influence. Significantly, Descartes's name is notably absent from all discussions that specifically deal with language, though references to the masters of Port-Royal and to Locke occur frequently. Condillac's first and most influential work was the *Essai sur l'origine des connoissances humaines*, first published in 1746 with the subtitle, 'a work in which all that concerns the human understanding is reduced to a single principle'. The English translation of 1756 had the subtitle 'a supplement to Mr. Locke's Essay on the human understanding'. This description is correct, and no reader can fail to see Condillac's dependence on Locke, a relationship he often and fully acknowledges. Curiously, Condillac's *Essai* and Chomsky's *Language and mind* have this in common, that they are both 'linguistic contributions to the study of mind', which is the subtitle of the latter work.

Locke's *Essay* suggested that reflection goes to work as soon as sensation has given it material to work on. Thereafter the mind may further gain ideas of its own operations—that is, ideas of reflection. Reflection is a power of thinking, but Locke did not explain how that power of thinking gains control over the vast variety of material on which it works. He did, however, suggest that this control steadily grows; there is, so to speak, a progress of the mind both in the individual and in mankind at large. This progress is suggested in a variety of ways, but especially by references to children and to language. In Book II of the *Essay*, for instance, we find a number of suggestive observations. Here Locke says he is apt to think that words may very much direct our thoughts 'towards the originals of men's *ideas*' (II.xv.4). In another passage he says: 'We may observe that mankind have fitted their notions and words to the use of common life and not to the truth and extent of things . . . This, by the way, may give us some light into the different state and growth of languages' (II.xxviii.2). And further: 'When children have, by repeated sensations, got ideas fixed in their memories, they begin by degrees to learn the use of signs.

And when they have got the skill to apply the organs of speech to the framing of articulate sounds, they begin to make *use of words* to signify their *ideas* to others' (II.xi.8). He had also made it plain that words often play an active role in thinking, especially the words for the complex ideas of mixed modes. Words are abbreviations of our manifold experience, and this fact of abbreviation makes it possible for us to handle experience and knowledge in thought. This concept of abbreviation is, of course, also fundamental in universal grammar and Condillac. Neither Locke nor Condillac ever assumed that reason and its manifestation in reflection were not innate; in line with the new science and Newton, they were not interested in the *why* but in the *how*. As Locke said, 'Man is by nature [i.e. innately] rational', and 'God commands what reason does' (cf. Aarsleff 1969a:107-10). To Locke, everything that man could ever know, he owed to the light of nature, by which he meant the two inalienable, powerful, innate, creative faculties of sense-experience and reason. And to Locke, of course, the use of language and words was creative, as any reader of the *Essay* must know. That is also precisely why a doctrine of the creative origin of language could be framed by using materials offered by Locke. A recent book on Condillac (Knight 1968) says that to him reason was 'acquired', which, taken as a statement about what Condillac said and meant, is plain nonsense.

But Locke left Condillac with the job of reducing the workings of the understanding to a single principle. To Condillac this single principle was 'la liaison des idées', that is, the connection of ideas, which is also innate and beyond explanation.[7] It is, so to speak, what gravity is in Newton's physics, which was the model and impulse for this reduction to a single principle. It is the key to the progress of the mind; it makes it possible for reflection to increase and gain increasing control over its materials. This control is gained by the institution of arbitrary, articulated, verbal signs, each connected with a particular idea.

This all-important act of institution would seem inconceivable without the prior occurrence of some natural signs that provide reflection with the suggestion for the making of arbitrary, verbal signs. Condillac himself raises that objection (1746: 22b), saying that he will provide the answer when he gives his account of the origin of language. Thus the key question about the beginnings of the exercise of the understanding has been converted into a question about the origin of language. The problem is solved in this fashion. Man shares with the animals the innate tendency to make certain natural gestures in response to fear, joy, fright, love, etc. Such gestures constitute a rudimentary mode of expression and communication in these simple situations, but for Condillac as well as for Descartes they do not constitute the language that is peculiar to man. Insistence on the non-creative nature of involuntary gestures is by no means specifically Cartesian, though this seems to be widely believed. These gestures include involuntary vocal cries, 'cris de nature', which humans will invariably hear each other make on the occasions that give rise to them. If we imagine two human beings together, both will make the same noise when frightened, for instance, by an approaching lion; but if one of them makes that cry on seeing a lion, the other will react as if he also saw the lion even when in fact he did not. Here the cry has already functioned as a warning against the initially unnoticed danger. Reflection will now be quick to realize that the voluntary and deliberate production of the same sign will have the effect of warning against an approaching lion, even when the man making the warning is not himself endangered and thus not making the cry involuntarily. By such natural and chance events, reflection will be guided to see the possible use of instituted, arbitrary signs—in other words, the origin of language. Thus it is not correct to say, as is in fact almost universally believed, that Condillac explains the origin of language by convention or agreement. He was quite aware of the nugatory quality of that doctrine, and he found ways of overcoming it by first giving the innate power of reflection suggestions from the involuntary 'cris de nature'. Hence Rousseau's familiar passage on the dilemma posed by any attempt to 'explain' the origin of language has no force against Condillac's argument, and was in fact not levelled against it; when Rousseau presents his account of the origin of language some pages later, in the second part of his *Discourse on the origin of inequality among men* (1755), he follows Condillac.

The progress of the mind becomes a question of the progress of language. The history of thought—in the characteristic, 18th century sense—can be pursued in the origin of language. It must be firmly understood that this study is purely conjectural, a fact that was made perfectly clear by Condillac, Rousseau, and Herder. It is fully as conjectural as Locke's state of nature, from which in fact it undoubtedly received strong impulses. In *Inequality* (1755: 190-1), Rousseau says: 'I have here entered upon certain arguments and risked certain conjectures . . . It is by no means a light undertaking to distinguish properly between what is original and what is artificial in the actual nature of man, or to form a true idea of the state which no longer exists, perhaps never did exist, and probably never will exist; and of which it is, nevertheless, necessary to have true ideas, in order to form a proper judgment of our present state.' Discussions of the state of nature and of the origin of language do not pretend to offer historical truths. The enterprise is entirely theoretical and designed to illuminate our concept of the nature of man. The chasm which Chomsky rightly says divides the eighteenth and the nineteenth centuries in the matter of linguistics is chiefly a matter of the latter century's failing to see and fully grasp that theoretical mode. A typical instance of this failure of understanding is offered by a passage in Renan's *De l'origine du langage* (1858:41-2). Referring to Condillac and his contemporaries, he says: "They addressed themselves to theoretical questions before they had dedicated themselves to the patient study of precise details. . . . Eighteenth-century philosophy had a strong penchant for artifical explanations in everything that pertains to the origins of the human mind." The 19th century had lost the 18th century's fundamental conviction, its first theory we might say, that of the uniformity of human nature. It thus also failed to see the fundamental distinction between nature and art, and it did not grasp the theoretical, conjectural quality of the state of nature, which it took to be misdirected quasi-history. To the 18th century, however, this difference existed between the state of nature and the origin of language: that if language was man-made, then man might hope to gain some firm insight into the history of man and thought by a study of the things that pertain to language, e.g. etymology as then understood. Here no doubt lies the ultimate reason why the concept of progress in the social sciences first arises in the context of the study of language, in the latter half of the 18th century.

I have found it necessary to give this brief account of the theoretical question of the origin of language as it was first introduced by Condillac, partly because the matter is almost without exception grossly misrepresented (the only writer who has really grasped it is Franco Venturi in his brilliant book *La Jeunesse de Diderot*, 1939); and partly because it shows Locke's dominant position in linguistic theory in the 18th century. Condillac's *Essai*, and specifically its account of the origin of language as an essential aspect of the philosophy of mind, immediately had a powerful impact. The first work to take up its problems was Maupertuis' *Réflexions philosophiques sur l'origine des langues et la signification des mots* (1748), soon to be followed by Diderot's letters *On the blind* (1749) and *On the Deaf-mutes* (1751), and by at least twenty individual works in German, French, and English before Herder's prize essay of 1770. In addition, Diderot's and D'Alembert's *Encyclopédie* deliberately, on the suggestion of Condillac's *Essai*, gave all matters relating to language a prominent place in that great work.

At this point, according to Chomsky and his sharp rejection of

Locke in favor of Descartes—indeed, by his entire account of the history of linguistics—we should expect an immediate reaction against universal grammar. Nothing of the sort happens. It is a fact that Condillac's *Essai* caused an immediate revival of universal grammar without the slightest sense of conflict, and the topic was at once so completely fused with interest in the origin of language that the term 'grammaire générale' was soon used for both. In his famous article on etymology, first published in the sixth volume (1756) of the *Encyclopédie*, Turgot observed that study of the origin of language is indispensable 'to comprehend at large and from a proper point of view the general theory of speech and the march of the human spirit in the formation and progress of language . . . This theory is the source which gives rise to the rules of that grammaire générale which governs all languages and to which all nations submit though believing to follow only the caprice of usage' (1913:505).[8] This fusion is not surprising. Both modes in the study of language made the same basic assumptions regarding reason and the uniformity of human nature, and both were directed toward the same subject matter and aim; only their methods of approach were different. When Condillac in the 1760s wrote a universal grammar for the young Prince of Parma, he began with two chapters on the origin of language—necessarily, he said, 'since one must have some knowledge of the origin of language before undertaking to decompose [analyse] it' (1775: 435a). Why so? Because 'the history of the human mind has shown me the order I need to follow in the instruction of the Prince', and because 'the art of speaking is none other than the art of thinking and reasoning, which develops as the languages become more perfect' (1775:403a).

This fusion also reached all aspects of the subject matter of universal grammar; what the latter did atemporally, the study of the origin of language did on the scale of time, as a theoretical problem in development. One basic problem in universal grammar is the matter of inversion, which in current terms deals with deep and surface structure. In the *Letter on the deaf-mutes* (1751), Diderot took up the same problem in the light of gestures, opening with the statement that he thought it would be appropriate to begin with a consideration of the origin of language (1751: 349). Similarly, the Port-Royal Grammar had assumed that some word classes, such as nouns and verbs, were primary in relation to others. Pronouns, for instance, were mere handy abbreviations or convenient substitutes for nouns. In the terminology of the Port-Royal Grammar, they had been 'invented' to fulfill that function. Study of the origin of language converted this question into that of which parts of speech came first and how the others were introduced and formed. The same fusion is again evident in the many articles on linguistic matters in the *Encyclopédie*, written largely by Du Marsais and after his death by Beauzée and Douchet. It is an amusing fact that Chomsky, unaware, reminds us of that fusion by citing Herder as an exponent of linguistic Cartesianism. To postulate any influence of universal grammar on Herder is demonstrably false; to detect the overwhelming influence of Condillac is demonstrably true. In fact, what Chomsky sees here is not even a matter of fusion, but simply a reflection of Locke's rationalism through Condillac.[9]

The fusion occurred only because Condillac had revived the theory of language and thus had also given new life to universal grammar. After its initial publication in 1660, the Port-Royal Grammar was republished in 1664, 1676, 1679, and 1709, but then not again till 1754 with the notes of Duclos. At that time the publishers said that it had long been unobtainable, which is what is always said when an old book has recently come into demand. The Port-Royal Grammar did not appear in English until 1753, though there had been translations of Lamy's *Art of speaking* in 1676, 1696, and 1708. In his article on 'Encyclopédie' (1755: 429) in the *Encyclopédie*, Diderot observed that the philosophy of language was so recent that there had not been time to make adequate provision for it when that great work was being planned; it will be recalled that the first volume appeared in 1751. But, he went on (450), they would do the best they could to remedy their serious omission, and had been fortunate to engage Du Marsais to write those articles. At no point is there the slightest suggestion that there was any conflict between universal grammar and the origin of language.

The neglect of universal grammar, its revival after 1746, and its fusion with the origin of language are all summed up in the career of Du Marsais. Near the end of his life, he gained recognition because of his connection with the *Encyclopédie*, but he was then over seventy. He received the highest praise from Condillac, Diderot, and D'Alembert, but he had spent most of his life in near poverty, making a meager living by teaching Latin. His work on universal grammar was ignored; and apart from a few short pieces published during his life, many of his writings were published only after his death, on the strength of the reputation he had gained from the *Encyclopédie*. Of the great seven-volume work on language he had in mind, only the volume *Des tropes* was published during his lifetime; and, as he bitterly remarked, it was so little understood that a wellwisher congratulated him on the publication of his work about the tropics. That was in 1730.

His first work, and an important instance of his linguistic theory, is the *Exposition d'une méthode pour apprendre la langue latine* (1722). His method was this: he arranged the Latin phrases according to the 'ordre naturel', and then placed the corresponding French phrases underneath in interlinear translation. This procedure obviously involves the related problems of inversion and construction or syntax, two subjects on which he gave special proof of his brilliance as a universal grammarian. On his source and authority for this method, he said: 'I could cite a great many authorities, and among others that of Mr. Locke in his *Thoughts concerning education*, in order to justify what I say here, that learning by routine should precede the rules' (1797:I.27). Instruction in formal grammar should be kept to a minimum until the pupil could, as Locke said, 'read himself *Sanctii Minerva* with Scioppius and Perizonius's notes' (1693: 272). Du Marsais's *Exposition* was immediately attacked by the Jesuit *Journal de Trévoux*; and the following year, in 1724, Du Marsais published a defense, which cited Locke at considerable length and included a list of 'a large number of learned men of the first order' who had advocated the same method. The list went like this: 'Scaliger, Sanctius, Vossius, Scioppius, M. le Fèvre de Saumur, le père Lamy, Locke, M. l'abbé de Dangeau, and a large number of others' (1797:I.145). It might be added, incidentally, that Locke's library contained the grammars of all the men mentioned in that list, except one that was published after his death.[10]

It can be shown that Du Marsais belonged to radical, Lockean groups in France, and his philosophy shows it. He held basic views of mind, thought, and the understanding that are entirely incompatible with the version of innateness which Chomsky takes to be essential to the principles of universal grammar. In a short piece on the qualities of the good philosopher, published in 1743, he said: 'The philosopher is a human machine like any other man; but it is a machine which, by its mechanical constitution, reflects on its movements' (1797:VI.25). In the same piece he observed, about the nature of thought, that 'it is in man a sense just like sight and hearing, depending like them on an organic constitution' (VI.28).[11] In another piece, 'De la raison', first published in 1770, he observed: 'The only means of instruction we have as individuals are either our own experience or authority. Experience is either exterior, that is, furnishes us with ideas of sensible objects; or interior, that is, furnishes us with ideas of the operations of the mind [entendement] ; there is the common source of all our knowledge; it is impossible to acquire ideas in any other fashion' (1797:VI.9). Some of the articles Du Marsais wrote for the *Encyclopédie* are clearly Lockean and quite incompatible with Descartes: 'Abstraction' (1797:IV.29-41), 'Adjectif' (IV.85-110), 'Education' (V.183-212), and 'Fini' (V.291-94). Very outspoken is a section 'Remarques sur l'idée' (V.319-22), which occurs in the *Logique*, a work from which Chomsky frequently cites other passages at length. In the early nineteenth century, Degérando observed: "The analogy of the views of Du Marsais with the theories of Locke is still more striking, and it is clear that he had thought deeply on the matter. His excellent article on abstraction is a kind of abridged version of Locke's *Essay*." (quoted from Krauss 1962:519). More recently, Ricken has observed (1964:554): "It seems at first sight a paradox but is a fact that Du Marsais supported the foundation of his rationalist syntax on Locke." No Cartesian could hold the views which Du Marsais in fact did hold— that is, no Cartesian in Chomsky's sense. But apparently, universal grammar of the highest order can be done not only without those Cartesian views, but can be excellently done on a Lockean basis.

This brings me to my final point, which is perhaps also the most crucial: Chomsky's view of Locke. It is hard to discuss, since Chomsky on the one hand has a very strong antipathy to Locke, yet never even gets close to saying anything precise about him; he is never quoted and never reported, though some notes from the Fraser edition are thrown into the argument. Chomsky thinks, one suspects, that Locke postulated thinking to be controlled by association or some sort of behaviorist principle. This of course is an old myth, though the very position of association of ideas in the *Essay* is the strongest and most obvious reminder of Locke's rationalism: he calls the association of ideas a 'sort of madness' precisely because it upsets the normal and natural procedures of rational and ordered thought. Unfortunately, there is in fact good reason to doubt that Chomsky has read Locke's *Essay*, just as we have seen evidence that he has not read any of the many passages that prove Du Marsais' Lockeanism. He observes (1968: 70) that Locke's critique of innateness had 'little relevance to any familiar doctrine of the seventeenth century.'[12] The arguments Locke gave against it had already been met, we are told, by such people as Lord Herbert of Cherbury in his *De veritate* (1625). In *Cartesian linguistics*, Chomsky cites Herbert at length (60-2), but the curious thing is that he cites from the very chapter and the very passages which Locke discusses in Book I of the *Essay* (I.iii.15-20, iv.8-18). This discussion is by far the most extensive of any that Locke offers on any philosopher named in the *Essay*. It would certainly have been relevant to note that fact, and perhaps also, if one disagrees with Locke so strongly, to show why Locke's critique of Herbert is unacceptable, and why Herbert is correct that it is one of our innate ideas that there is a deity and that this deity should be worshipped.

The fact of the matter is that Locke's understanding of innateness is so radical that it does not touch that of Descartes. According to Locke, unless the child knows at birth those pretended innate truths and is ready to speak them at once, they cannot be innate. This would among other things mean that the very words in which they would have to be spoken must also be innate. In *Cartesian linguistics* (1966: 66-7), Chomsky quotes at length from Descartes' *Notes directed against a certain program*. Even the passages cited should have alerted him to the fact that Descartes is not quite saying what Chomsky thinks or wants Descartes to be saying. But the preceding paragraph leaves less doubt. Here Descartes says: 'I never wrote or concluded that the mind required innate ideas which were in some sort different from its faculty of thinking; but when I observed the existence in me of certain thoughts which proceeded, not from extraneous objects nor from the determination of my will, but solely from the faculty of thinking which is within me, then, that I might distinguish the ideas or notions (which are the forms of thought) from other thoughts *adventitious* or *factitious*, I termed them *innate*. In the same sense we say that in some families generosity is innate, in others certain diseases like gout or gravel, not that on this account the babes of these families suffer from these diseases in their mother's womb, but because they are born with a certain disposition or propensity for contracting them' (1647: 442). Chomsky elsewhere would appear to be saying that he will not accept such mere dispositions, propensities, or operations as the sort of innateness he postulates and takes to be fundamental to universal and Cartesian grammar.

Again arguing against Locke, Chomsky observes in *Aspects* (1965: 34): 'In studying the actual character of learning, linguistic or otherwise, it is of course necessary to distinguish carefully between these two functions of external data—the function of initiating or facilitating the operation of innate mechanisms and the function of determining in part the direction that learning will take.' Failure to make this distinction, we are told (203), is what vitiates Locke's critique of innateness. This is curious, for I cannot think of a more beautiful example of the extended application of this distinction than Locke's derivation of the law of nature from the play of the innate faculty of reason on pain and pleasure, uneasiness and happiness, to guide man toward that unalterable law which Locke also calls the 'divine law' and 'the law of reason'. It is worth recalling the profound sense and aim of Locke's argument against innateness, a sense he makes emphatically clear at the end of Book I of the *Essay*. Locke wished to make certain that all claims to truth must argue on public, not on private and esoteric, grounds—with good reason. Locke was painfully aware of the potential tyranny of any doctrine of innateness, a doctrine that would therefore subvert the grand passion that illuminates all Locke's work, his desire for toleration. Regarding some men's claim to know innate principles, Locke observes that 'it put their followers upon a necessity of receiving some doctrines as such . . . in which posture of blind credulity, they might be more easily governed by and made useful to some sort of men, who had the skill and office to principle and guide them. Nor is it a small power it gives one man over another to have the authority to be the dictator of principles and teacher of unquestionable truths, and to make a man swallow that for an innate principle which may serve to his purpose who teacheth them' (I.iv.25).

I must conclude with the firm belief that I do not see that anything at all useful can be salvaged from Chomsky's version of the history of linguistics. That version is fundamentally false from beginning to end—because the scholarship is poor, because the texts have not been read, because the arguments have not been understood, because the secondary literature that might have been helpful has been left aside or unread, even when referred to. The nearly hysterical reception that has greeted *Cartesian linguistics* has already had its consequences. The book catalogs are bursting with announcements of series that will reprint all that pertains to 'Cartesian linguistics', and texts are being read as if they were Cartesian when in fact they are not. Universal grammar is profoundly important in the history of linguistics, but Chomsky's account fails to grasp both the nature and the history of that importance. In the meantime, other equally important aspects of the study of language in history are being ignored. A good example is Leibniz. He took the study of words, of dialects, of etymology and meanings to be worth practically all of the time he spent on the study of language (his 'philosophical language' is not concerned with natural languages and is thus another subject). In the as yet unpublished 'Epistolaris de historia etymologica dissertatio', he cites at least two hundred little-known works from the 16th and 17th centuries (cf. Aarsleff 1969b). These works constitute a very significant body of work pertaining to the history of the study of language. Yet, with a very few exceptions, they are totally forgotten and ignored today; they do not appear in attempts to deal with the history of linguistics, and are not listed in the reprint catalogs. Professor Chomsky has significantly set back the history of linguistics. Unless we reject his account, we will for a long while have no genuine history, but only a succession of enthusiastic variations on false themes.

Notes

1. Elsewhere (Aarsleff 1967:3-11) I have tried to state what I take to be the proper principles in the history of the study of language.

2. The matter cited by Chomsky is in d'Alembert 1757:lxx-lxxii; but he is quoting from Sahlin 1928. D'Alembert's observations on Du Marsais's anti-Cartesianism are on pages lxvii-lxix.

3. Some of the problems dealt with in this essay are treated more fully in Aarsleff 1974.

4. Du Marsais refers to the authority of Sanctius in 1797:I.19, 68, 114, 143-4, 145, 152-3; IV.213; V.33, 36. In some of these contexts he also refers to the masters of Port-Royal; but when he does so specifically, it is never to the grammar of 1660, but to 'leur sçavante Méthode latine' (I.19), to 'la méthode de P. R. de l'hellénisme' (V.33), and to 'la méthode latine de P. R.' (V.36). This is significant, and it clearly supports and strengthens Robin Lakoff's argument.

5. In an unpublished manuscript in the Niedersächsische Landesbibliothek, Hannover, MS IV, 469, fol. 73 v, Leibniz says: "Besides, to certain grammars of particular languages is added a universal grammar, which Christoph Helvic (a professor at Giessen), was perhaps the first to undertake; his universal grammar, referring especially to the Latin, Greek, Hebrew, and Chaldaic languages, appeared at Giessen in 1619 in quarto. In our time a French scholar has undertaken a universal grammar, entitled *Grammaire raisonnée*, which is by no means to be spurned. Here belongs also Caramuelis's *Grammatica audax*." This passage would appear to have been written very late in Leibniz' life, presumably within a few years of his death. In a note to his 1667 work, Leibniz wrote (1930:279) "Moreover the knowledge of languages especially pertains to memory and the learning of signs whence instruction begins; it is either transmitted by usage or by the rules of the art of grammar, which we have aplenty for the usual languages, but Christoph Helvic has produced a general one, and recently a French author *de la Grammaire raisonnée*." These notes could have been written as late as 1709. In all his life of busy writing, Leibniz made very few references to the Port-Royal grammar (probably no more than five), all of them so general that it is doubtful whether he actually knew the work. This is a remarkable fact considering that Leibniz spent the years 1672-76 in Paris, where he frequently saw Antoine Arnauld.

6. For a characteristic example of the great expectations that were placed in the method and its capacity to shorten the process of learning, see Mersenne 1640.

7. Elsewhere (Aarsleff 1967:18) I say that 'Condillac wished to demonstrate that reflection could be derived from sensation.' I am now convinced that that statement is false.

8. In the quoted passage, Turgot speaks of 'the march of the human spirit in the formation of speech and progress of language'. In the 18th century literature on the subject, this phrase becomes standard, almost rhetorical, on that subject. It should be compared with the passage from d'Alembert, p. lxxii (quoted by Chomsky 1966:54), with its significant description of Du Marsais.

9. Elsewhere (Aarsleff 1974) I give additional material on Herder and his dependence on Condillac. A common source of error is the assumption that Herder's *Über den Ursprung der Sprache* gives a correct account of Condillac. That assumption is not justified, and it is no substitute for reading Condillac's *Essai*. This confusion has led to the further assumption that Herder disproved Condillac's account of the origin of language. He did not. Condillac

gave an account of the origin of language as speech, while Herder in the first part of the prize essay asserted that language is the same as 'Besonnenheit' or 'Reflexion' and that it need not be spoken to be language. Herder used the word Sprache for both language and speech.

10. See Harrison & Laslett 1965, nos. 845b, 1114, 1307, 2202, 2543, 2987.

11. There has been some argument over whether Du Marsais was in fact the author of 'Le philosophe' (see Dieckmann 1948, Krauss 1962). There is, however, no doubt that he was felt by many to be the probable author. But it is plentifully evident that Du Marsais's Lockeanism and anti-Cartesianism do not hang on this problem.

12. In Aarsleff 1964:60-63 I argue that Locke's critique of innateness was specifically directed against certain doctrines which were widely publicized in England in the 1650s. They were of a linguistic nature, being derived from Boehme's doctrine of the language of nature. I now have stronger reason to believe my identification is correct. Chomsky (1966: 94) refers to my article.

References

Aarsleff, Hans. 1964. "Leibniz on Locke on language." *American Philosophical Quarterly* 1.165-88. Repr. above pp. 42-83.

———. 1967. *The study of language in England 1780-1860.* Princeton.

———. 1969a. "The state of nature and the nature of man in Locke." *John Locke: problems and perspectives,* ed. by John W. Yolton, 99-136. Cambridge.

———. 1969b. "The study and use of etymology in Leibniz." *Studia Leibnitiana. Supplementa,* 3.173-89. Wiesbaden. Repr. above pp. 84-100.

———. 1974. "The tradition of Condillac: the origin of language in the eighteenth century and the debate in the Berlin Academy before Herder." *Studies in the history of linguistics,* ed. by Dell Hymes. Bloomington: Indiana University Press, pp. 93-156. Repr. below pp. 146-209.

D'Alembert, J. Le Rond. 1757. "Eloge de Du Marsais." In Du Marsais 1797:I.xxxi-xci.

Bacon, Francis. 1605. *Advancement of learning.* In: *The Works of Francis Bacon,* ed. by James Spedding, R. L. Ellis, and D. D. Heath, London, 1857-74 [reprinted, Stuttgart-Bad Cannstatt, 1963], vol. 3, pp. 253-491.

———. 1623. *De augmentis scientiarum.* (*Ibid.,* vol. 1, pp. 413-840.)

Chomsky, Noam. 1965. *Aspects of the theory of syntax.* Cambridge, Mass.

———. 1966. *Cartesian linguistics,* New York.

———. 1968. *Language and mind.* New York.

Condillac, E. de. 1746. *Essai sur l'origine des connoissances humaines.* In: *Oeuvres philosophiques,* ed. by Georges le Roy, I.1-118. Paris, 1947.

———. 1775. *Cours d'études pour l'instruction du Prince de Parme: Introduction au cours d'études & Grammaire.* (*Ibid.,* 395-513.)

Descartes, R. 1647. "Notes directed against a certain program." In: *The philosophical works of Descartes,* tr. by Elizabeth S. Haldane and G. R. T. Ross, 1.429-50. Cambridge, 1967.

Diderot, D. 1749. *Lettre sur les aveugles.* In: *Oeuvres complètes de Diderot,* ed. by J. Assézat, I.275-342. Paris, 1875.

———. 1751. *Lettre sur les sourds et muets.* (*Ibid.,* 343-428.)

———. 1755. "Encyclopédie." (*Ibid.,* XIV.414-503; Paris, 1876.)

Dieckmann, Herbert. 1948. *Le Philosophe: texts and interpretation.* St. Louis.

Du Marsais, César Chesneau 1797. *Oeuvres.* 7 vols. Paris.

Gilson, Étienne. 1947. *Discours prononcés dans la séance publique tenue par l'Académie Française pour la réception de M. Étienne Gilson le jeudi 29 mai 1947.* Paris.

Harrison, John, and Laslett, Peter. 1965. *The library of John Locke*. Oxford.

Herbert, Edward. 1625. *De veritate*, tr. by Meyrich H. Carré. Bristol, 1937.

Herder, J. G. 1770. *Abhandlung über den Ursprung der Sprache*, ed. by Hans Dietrich Irmscher. Stuttgart, 1966.

Ising, Erika. 1959. *Wolfgang Ratkes Schriften zur Deutschen Grammatik (1612-1630)*. Berlin.

Jellinek, M. H. 1913. *Geschichte der neuhochdeutschen Grammatik*, I. Heidelberg.

Kampf, Louis. 1967. Review of *Cartesian linguistics*, by N. Chomsky. *College English* 28.403-8.

Knight, Isabel F. 1968. *The geometric spirit: the Abbé de Condillac and the French Enlightenment*. New Haven.

Krauss, Werner. 1962. "L'énigme de Du Marsais." *Revue d'Histoire Littéraire de la France* 62.514-22.

Lakoff, Robin. 1969. Review of Grammaire générale et raisonnée. *Language* 45.343-64.

Leibniz, G. W. von. 1667. "Nova methodus discendae docendaeque jurisprudentiae." In: *Sämtliche Schriften und Briefe*, sechste Reihe, 1.259-364. Darmstadt, 1930.

Locke, John. 1693. *Some thoughts concerning education*. In: *The educational writings of John Locke*, ed. by James L. Axtell, 109-325. Cambridge, 1968.

———. 1706. *Essay concerning human understanding*, 5th ed., ed. by John W. Yolton. 2 vols. London, 1961.

Maupertuis, Pierre-Louis Moreau de. 1748. "Réflexions philosophiques sur l'origine des langues et la signification des mots," In: *Oeuvres de M. de Maupertuis*, I.259-85. Lyon, 1756.

Mersenne, M. 1640. Lettre de Mersenne à Comenius. In: *Correspondance du P. Marin Mersenne*, ed. by Cornelis de Waard and Bernard Rochot, 10.263-274. Paris, 1967.

Miel, Jan. 1969. "Pascal, Port-Royal, and Cartesian linguistics." *Journal of the History of Ideas* 30.261-71.

Renan, Ernest. 1858. *De l'origine du langage*. In: *Oeuvres complètes*, ed. by Henriette Psichari, 10.9-123. Paris, 1958.

Ricken, Ulrich. 1964. "Condillac's *liaison des idées* und die *clarté* des Französischen." *Die Neueren Sprachen* 1964.552-67.

Rousseau, J. J. 1755. *Discourse on the origin of inequality*. In: *The social contract and Discourses*, tr. by G. D. H. Cole. New York, 1950.

Sahlin, Gunvor. 1928. *César Chesnau du Marsais et son rôle dans l'évolution de la grammaire générale*. Paris: Presses Universitaires de France.

Salmon, Vivian. 1969. Review of *Cartesian linguistics*, by N. Chomsky. *Journal of Linguistics* 5.165-87.

Turgot, A. R. J. 1756. "Etymologie." In: *Oeuvres de Turgot*, ed. by G. Schelle, 1.473-516. Paris, 1913.

Venturi, Franco. 1939. *La jeunesse de Diderot (1713-1753)*. Paris.

Weiss, Charles. n.d. "François Sanchez [Sanctius]." *Biographie Universelle* 37.610-11.

Zimmer, Karl E. 1968. Review of *Cartesian linguistics*, by N. Chomsky. *International Journal of American Linguistics* 34.290-303.

Locke's Reputation
in Nineteenth-Century England

In 1890 C. S. Peirce wrote a review of A. C. Fraser's recent book on Locke, published to coincide with the bicentennial of Locke's *Essay*. Peirce remarked that "Locke's grand work was substantially this: Men must think for themselves, and genuine thought is an act of perception. . . . We cannot fail to acknowledge a superior element of truth in the practicality of Locke's thought, which on the whole should place him nearly upon a level with Descartes." This estimate of Locke was not the common opinion in England during the nineteenth century. This opinion was reflected in Fraser's book which, Peirce remarked, could not "be said to be a sympathetic account of [Locke]. The biographer seems to see no charm in his hero, and is perpetually speaking of his want of imagination; which only means he was not given to unpractical dreaming."[1] Locke had his knowledgeable critics and defenders—for instance Dugald Stewart and John Stuart Mill—but the common opinion ranged from extreme hostility and contempt to condescending criticism of isolated minor points. His style was deplored, his philosophy was called unoriginal and a mere unacknowledged plagiarism of Gassendi and Hobbes; he was said to have so thoroughly misunderstood Descartes that he had merely repeated him with new errors; he was said to owe his philosophical reputation entirely to his advocacy of the popular argument for political freedom or merely to the intellectual circumstances of his time; he was held accountable for Condillac's rejection of reflection and reason; he was knocked down with a few bare sentences loosely drawn from Leibniz; he was said to have made the mind a puny, passive,

Reprinted from *The Monist* 55 (1971), 392-422.

mechanical thing. He was called a sensualist, a materialist, a sceptic, an atheist, and a utilitarian though at the same time—and not without contradiction—he was generally, especially by his critics, styled (in his own words) a "great lover of truth," a plain and simple, well-meaning and religious man. To the nineteenth century Locke meant the *Essay*, and the history of the *Essay* was in large measure the history of modern thought, of the eighteenth century. Precisely for this reason there was something nearly sinister about him, in spite of his good personal character. "Locke, himself a clear, humble-minded, patient, reverent, nay, religious man," said Carlyle, "had paved the way for banishing religion from the world."[2]

It was one of the prominent characteristics of nineteenth-century writing on Locke that it often ran into the sort of patronizing rhetoric that suggests small knowledge of its subject. Many shared Joseph De Maistre's opinion that Locke was the evil genius of the eighteenth century, an opinion expressed in some eighty ranting pages of the *Soirées de Saint-Petersbourg*.[3] But for some reason Locke seemed more difficult to get rid of than his progeny. To his dismay, G. H. Lewes found "the sneers and off-hand charges" against Locke so frequent that "I, who had read him in my youth with delight, began to suspect that my admiration had been rash."[4] Writing a few years later, in 1854, Henry Rogers found Locke in a state of "transient obscuration . . . labouring under some . . . partial eclipse at present."[5] William Whewell was no lover of Locke—and one might add not much of a reader of him either. He did not blame Locke for the rejection of innate ideas, which were "in no way necessary to support of independent moral truth," but for adducing,

> as important and instructive facts, all the wretched and disgusting instances of human degradation and depravity, which tend to show how far man may lose his moral nature. To dwell upon such cases has always been a favourite mode of reasoning of those who hold that moral judgments are merely artificial and conventional.[6]

In the same lectures Whewell had, in argument against Locke, observed that, "we believe that [God] intends us to use our rational and moral faculties in discovering what is right and what is wrong. . . . We do not doubt that the Supreme Rule of human action . . . is identical with the Will of God," which is in fact almost precisely what Locke had argued in the most poorly understood—then as even today—chapters in the *Essay*. Had Whewell forgotten—or did he not know—that Locke had built his morality on the doctrine that God "commands what reason does," and that "we are born to be, if we please, rational creatures"?[7] During the entire nineteenth century, most writing on Locke presents a strange mixture of opinion, ignorance, and hostility. In 1829, Henry Brougham expected that a new opportunity to discuss Locke would "doubtless be presented by some of the controversial tracts that are likely to arise out of the present publication,"[8] that is by Peter King's *Life of Locke*, which appeared in that year, but hardly a work that one would expect to cause controversy. Locke was not a neutral subject.

Thus Locke's reputation in the nineteenth century presents a problem, and it is the aim of this essay to give an account of that reputation. It is not my purpose to examine whether he exercised any direct and genuine influence, though I suspect that the answer must be in the negative, except perhaps for John Stuart Mill. Similarly, I shall not systematically inquire into the validity of the interpretations and opinions that are offered, a task that would carry me far beyond the limits of this essay. On this matter we all face a common difficulty, as acute today as it was in the nineteenth century, namely the absence of an enlightened, reliable, and commonly received interpretation of Locke's philosophy. During the last twenty years, Locke scholarship has been better and livelier than it ever was, but the false and vacuous platitudes that fill the common literature are still much the same. Thus Locke's reputation in the nineteenth century has relevance even today. But the legitimacy of my concern with reputation as distinct from influence rests on the simple fact that what was written and known about Locke was more often a matter of opinion than of study and knowledge. The *Essay* was "one of those books which had been so thoroughly assimilated by that part of the world which cares in the most cursory manner for speculative subjects, that large numbers of people naturally suppose themselves to have read it, when in point of fact they never have."[9] Comments to the effect that the *Essay* in fact had very few readers, even among men who professed to know it, can be cited from the beginning to the end of the century, and they would hardly be less justified today than they were then. Sadly, this was as true of the common writer as of the common reader. The literature time and again reveals the truth of Robert Vaughan's observation in 1847, "that the opinions of men in relation to [Locke] have been formed from the writings of his opponents, or from the writings of men who, while professing to be his disciples, perverted his doctrines, and not from an adequate study of his own works."[10]

The nineteenth century did not lack access to Locke. The tenth edition of the *Works* appeared in 1801, and there were four more in the course of the century, in 1812, 1823, 1826, and 1854.[11] The twenty-first edition of the *Essay* was issued in 1805, the thirty-second in 1860, and there were more before the end of the century, including

Fraser's edition which has long been considered authoritative though its editorship is deplorable and its extensive notes useless as soon as they go beyond mere matter of fact. These notes constitute a warehouse of the unsympathetic nineteenth-century interpretations of Locke, which have thus been passed on to succeeding generations, who, it seems, have generally put trust in them. Some of the other works were also published separately, a few of them several times— thus the *Conduct of the Understanding* no less than ten times. But it was of course especially the *Essay* that was in demand, and to smooth the way it was often read in abridgments, encouraged by Locke's own admission that he would "not deny but possibly it might be reduced to a narrower compass." In addition to the three abridgments which had already appeared before 1800, at least half a dozen new ones came on the market before 1900, in Dublin and Cambridge, where the *Essay* was a set text, and in London.[12]

The fondness for abridgments may perhaps also be seen in relation to Locke's style, on which Sir William Hamilton in 1830 made a classic and often-cited comment: "In his *language*, Locke is, of all philosophers, the most figurative, ambiguous, vacillating, various, and even contradictory, as has been noticed by Reid and Stewart, and Brown himself; indeed we believe by every author, who has had occasion to comment on this philosopher." But he went on to make a wise comment which few have heeded: "The opinions of such a writer are not, therefore, to be assumed from isolated and casual expressions, which themselves require to be interpreted on the general analogy of his system."[13] But on this matter opinion was divided. With some justice, Dugald Stewart found that Locke's style resembled "that of a well-educated and well-informed man of the world, rather than of a recluse student who made an object of the art of composition."[14] But Hazlitt observed that Locke stated

> . . . his arguments with so many limitations and with such a variety of expression to prevent misapprehension, that it is often difficult to guess at his real meaning. There is it must be confessed a sort of heaviness about him, a want of clearness and connexion, which in spite of all his pains, and the real plodding strength of his mind he was never able to overcome.[15]

Finally, before I take up some particular figures and issues, there is a pattern that deserves comment: Locke's standing at Oxford and Cambridge. At Oxford the heads of colleges had decided already in 1704 that tutors should not read the *Essay* with their students, a decision which Locke, writing to Anthony Collins, took "as a recommendation of that book to the world, as you do, and I conclude, when you and I next meet, we shall be merry upon the subject. For this is certain that, because some wink or turn their heads away, and will not see, others will not consent to have their eyes put out."[16] And thus the matter stood at Oxford far into the nineteenth century. In 1847, Henry Hallam remarked that if Oxford presumed to speak of Locke—"her chief boast"—as "'the sophist Locke,' we may console ourselves by recollecting how little influence such a local party is likely to obtain over the literary world."[17]

In this as in other respects, Cambridge was different from Oxford. Here the *Essay* and Paley's *Principles of Moral and Political Philosophy* had "long formed . . . prominent subjects of instruction,"[18] a fact which now that the reaction against Locke and the eighteenth century set in caused much embarrassment and determined efforts to remedy. Some years earlier, in 1821, Dugald Stewart had identified the source of the difficulties that Cambridge was soon to encounter. At Cambridge the *Essay*

> was for many years regarded with a reverence approaching to idolatry; and to the authority of some distinguished persons connected with that learned body may be traced . . . the origin of the greater part of the extravagancies which, towards the close of the last century, were grafted on Locke's errors, by the disciples of Hartley, of [Edmund] Law, of Priestley, of Tooke, and of [Erasmus] Darwin,[19]

all of whom, except for Priestley, were Cambridge men. With this heritage, within a scheme that made moral edification an important aspect of college life, the young must be fortified against alluring and corrupting influences. Thus Cambridge became the center of anti-Lockeanism from the middle 1830s, beginning with Adam Sedgwick's *Discourse on the Studies of the University* and culminating in William Whewell's tenure of the chair of moral philosophy since 1839, exacerbated perhaps by the fact that Mill was beginning to become the dominant influence at Cambridge. Sedgwick and Whewell delivered some of the strongest and most widely read attacks on Locke during the entire century. In 1841, in a letter that dealt chiefly with theological education, Whewell wrote: "I have already used my influence to introduce an Anti-Lockian philosophy, and intend to use it for other good purposes."[20]

The course of Locke's reputation may be divided into three periods. The first extends from the beginning of the century to 1829, the year that saw the publication of Victor Cousin's astoundingly successful *Cours de l'histoire de la philosophie*, which devoted eleven lectures to Locke. The second period is marked by an intensification of the debate, with Sedgwick and Whewell, drawing support from Cousin, on one side, and Mill on the other, both sides having their supporters. This debate had ebbed out by 1860. The last period repeats the arguments on both sides in a lower key without sharp confrontations. Still, in spite of the excellent works of Fox Bourne and Leslie Stephen during this period, many unsympathetic and unfounded interpretations of Locke are passed on to a largely unsuspecting audience by Fraser's edition of the *Essay* in 1894. For each of these three periods, I shall take up a number of representative figures and issues.

Locke's inferiority to German transcendentalism is one of the basic themes of Locke criticism during the nineteenth century. It makes its appearance at the very beginning of the century in Henry Crabb Robinson's account of his life at the German universities. He was "a little touched now and then by [Schelling's] contemptuous treatment of our English writers," especially of Erasmus Darwin and Locke. He was impressed by seeing one hundred and thirty "enthusiastic young men eagerly listening to the exposition of a philosophy which in its pretensions is more aspiring than any publicly maintained since the days of Plato and his commentators—a philosophy equally opposed to the empiricism of Locke, the scepticism of Hume, and the critical school of Kant."[21] He had found that understanding Kant meant

> refutation of Locke's (or rather Aristotle's) famous principle, that there is nothing in the intellect which was not before in sense, or that all our conceptions (ideas) are derived from sensation. According to the empirical system, as stated in its utmost consistency by Horne Tooke, man has but one faculty, that of receiving sensation from external objects.[22]

Here in the last phrase, though obvious nonsense in regard to Locke, we find one of the chief charges against Locke, repeated over and over again throughout the century, thus proving how little capable people were of understanding and reading Locke, in spite of many cogent and well-documented arguments to set the matter straight.[23]

The chief exponent of German transcendentalist dislike and even contempt for Locke is of course Coleridge. On 23 December 1810, Crabb Robinson reported Coleridge's opinion, which contains so many commonplaces that it deserves to be quoted in full:

> As usual he spoke with contempt of *Locke's* Essay. It led to the destruction of Metaphysical Science by encouraging the unlearned to think that with good sense they might dispense with study. The popularity of *Locke's* Essay he ascribed to his political position: he was the advocate of the new dynasty against the old and as a religious writer against the infidel, tho' he was but an Arian! And the *national* vanity was gratified. He and Newton were pitted against Leibniz. It was to lessen Leibniz that Voltaire set up Locke. He assented to my remark that Atheism might be demonstrated out of Locke—he praised Stillingfleet as the opponent of Locke's Essay.[24]

These were themes which Coleridge had already fully developed in a series of long letters to Josiah Wedgwood during the early months of 1801, when Coleridge was contemplating a work "on the originality and merits of Locke, Hobbes, and Hume . . . confident that I can prove that the Reputation of these three men has been wholly un-merited."[25] Clearly, if both Hume and Locke could be reduced to the detestable Hobbes, the battle was won. A few years later, in 1805, a comment in the *Notebooks* raised the spectre of the philosophy of utility, though held by religious men: "Almost all men nowadays act and feel more nobly than they think, yet still the vile cowardly selfish calculating Ethics of Paley, Priestley, Locke and other *Erastians*, do woefully influence and determine our course of action."[26]

Coleridge went to great lengths to deny Locke all originality; even after sincere and careful study, he "could never discover any one thing to account for that prodigious impression that seems to have been made, either in the novelty of the sentiments or in the system of those which are peculiar to it."[27] In 1824 he wrote in a notebook:

> Grant me Gassendi, Hobbes, Des Cartes De Methodo, and Spinoza . . . and I will undertake to produce a duodecimo volume containing in a con-nected form every principle of the Essay . . . the whole sum and detail with exception only of Locke's Admitted Errors—nay, all that has been since added by Locke's Followers, on Association and the application of the same to the principles of Language and of general conceptions.[28]

Both in the letters to Wedgwood and in the later lectures, Coleridge was especially eager to show that Locke's "Innate Ideas were Men of Straw, or scarcely so much as that—and that the whole of Mr. Locke's first Book is a jumble of Truisms, Calumnies, and Misrepresentations." They were men of straw because Locke had made a great pother over nothing by failing to see that he and Descartes "held precisely the same opinions concerning the original Sources of our Ideas," a theme which often recurs during the nineteenth century. Having detailed Locke's intellectual inferiority, Coleridge wished that Newton's name could find a more worthy associate, "we should say Bacon and New-ton, or still better perhaps, Newton and Hartley." To the eighteenth century, following Voltaire, Newton and Locke were the two great philosophical benefactors of mankind, but the nineteenth century, retaining its admiration for Newton, naturally wanted to dissociate him from Locke—it became much like a game of musical chairs to see how the good guys and the bad could be joined and disjoined.[29] Oddly, it was not till late in the century that Bacon was called an empiricist; he was almost universally and uncritically praised, Coleridge going so far as to call him "our English Plato."[30]

In 1809, William Hazlitt issued a "Prospectus of a History of Eng-lish Philosophy"[31] which briefly stated the confused opinions he delivered in his "Lectures on English Philosophy" during the early months of 1812, though not published until 1836 at a time when the attack on Locke was at its height. In the "Prospectus" he stated his basic and often repeated theme that

> Hobbes . . . was indeed the father of modern philosophy. . . . He was by nature a materialist. Locke assisted greatly in giving popularity to the same scheme, as well as by espousing many of Hobbes's metaphysical principles, as by the doubtful resistance which he made to the rest. And it has of late received its last polish and roundness in the hands of some French philosophers, as Condillac and others (116).

Thus Locke is denied originality, later efforts to "supply the deficiencies of the Essay" merely having reduced its philosophy to the purity of the *Leviathan* (128). By comparison with Hobbes, Berkeley, Hume, and Hartley, Locke was "a mere common practical man" (180). Locke's admission of reflection had been "very awkwardly and inartificially made" (149). Hazlitt therefore wished to prove that "ideas are the offspring of the understanding, not of the senses. . . . There is a common principle of thought, a superintending faculty . . . and it is by means of this faculty that man indeed becomes a reaonable soul" (151). Hazlitt's attempt to deal with "Liberty and Necessity" shows how little he, like most of his century, understood the chapter "Of Power" in the *Essay*'s Book Two. That Hazlitt's lectures did not have much success is understandable. They are tedious and confused, being made up chiefly of page-long citations from Hobbes and Locke. But he was the first Englishman of the century who publicly stated a number of persistent commonplaces about Locke.

While Coleridge's opinions filtered out to the public in *The Friend, Table Talk,* and the *Statesman's Manual,* Dugald Stewart was publishing his famous supplement to the *Encyclopaedia Britannica,* the *Dissertation Exhibiting the Progress of Metaphysical, Ethical, and Political Philosophy since the Revival of Letters in Europe.* It was published in two parts in 1815 and 1821; during the rest of the century it was often cited as an authority, deservedly.[32] Solid and well informed, the *Dissertation* argues cogently against the most serious misinterpretations of Locke, though Stewart was by no means an uncritical or even a sympathetic observer of Locke. Convinced that the *Essay* had been "much more generally applauded than read," he was eager to "vindicate the fame of Locke, not only against the censures of his opponents, but against the mistaken comments and eulogies of his admirers, both in England and on the Continent" (205). He insisted first of all, rightly I believe, that Locke was primarily a rationalist; he had prepared the thinking part of his readers, to a degree till then unknown, for the un-shackled use of their own reason. This has always appeared to me the most characteristical feature of Locke's Essay; and *that* to which it is chiefly in-debted for its immense influence on the philosophy of the eighteenth century (223).

As a consequence, Stewart found that Locke had been misrepresented on two issues: on innate ideas and on the power of moral judgment. Supporting, or rather conveying, his argument by very full citations, Stewart shows that Locke's doctrine unjustly "has been confounded with those of Gassendi, of Condillac, of Diderot, and of Horne Tooke." Various detached passages might seem to justify this "superficial view . . . yet of what weight . . . are these passages, when com-pared with the stress laid by the author on *Reflection*, as an original source of our ideas, altogether different from *Sensation*?" Locke could not be held accountable for Condillac's opinion that "our ideas are nothing more than *transformed* sensations" (224-7), a claim which more than any other, the *Essay* notwithstanding, to the nineteenth century constituted the essence of "Locke's system" and clear proof of his sensualism and ultimate materialism. Similarly, Stewart argued that the philosophy of the French *Encyclopédie* was based on a mis-taken view of Locke. He concluded, again rightly, that to Locke an innate idea signified "*something* coeval in its existence with the mind to which it belongs, and illuminating the understanding before the external senses begin to operate."[33]

Stewart also found, again rightly, that an often-cited passage in Leibniz did not bear the interpretation it was often given, both before and after Stewart. With reference to the *Essay*, Leibniz had said, "nihil est in intellectu quod non fuerit in sensu, *nisi ipse intellectus*." These last three words were often cited triumphantly as an unanswerable refutation of Locke. But Stewart did not see now the *nisi ipse intel-lectus* could be urged as an objection against a philosophy which had given reflection such a large role in the making of knowledge. "To myself," Stewart said, "it appears, that the words of Leibniz only convey in a more concise and epigrammatic form, the substance of Locke's doctrine" (233-6). If Stewart had known Leibniz' critique of Locke in the *Nouveaux essais*, he would have found even stronger reason to see no conflict between Locke and Leibniz on this point.[34]

Again, on the power of moral judgment, Stewart insisted that Locke had been misunderstood, citing Locke's words that "there is a law of nature, as intelligible to a rational creature and studier of that law, as the positive laws of commonwealths" (241). As an example to illustrate the common error of making Locke responsible for the doctrines of eighteenth-century "systems," Stewart cited the case of Hartley, who had clearly stated that he differed from Locke on a basic point: "It appears to me," Hartley had said, "that all the most complex ideas arise from sensation, and that *reflection is not a distinct source*, as Mr. Locke makes it" (237). It is doubtful, however, whether Stewart is right in his contention that most of the eighteenth-century philosophers who invoked Locke were in fact directly indebted to Gassendi. Whether owing to genuine misunderstanding or deliberate selection, Locke's doctrines had been misrepresented by his admirers.

But few paid attention to Stewart's refutation of false interpretations; Locke's opponents in the nineteenth century were not ready to relieve the *Essay* of responsibility for Diderot, Helvetius, and the Condillac of the "transformed sensations." Stewart could only conclude with resignation that the misapprehensions about Locke were

> so very general, and at the same time so obviously at variance with the whole spirit of his Essay, as to prove to a demonstration that, in point of numbers, the *intelligent readers* of this celebrated work have hitherto borne but a small proportion to its purchasers and panegyrists (237).

If he had been able to look into the future, Stewart would have learned that the proportion of good readers would remain much the same. The admirers of one century had sufficient authority to have their interpretations accepted without question by the opponents of the next. The great stumbling block was the opening book about "innate notions," rejection of which seemed to conflict with the admission of reflection. Stewart found it

> fortunate for Locke's reputation, that, in other parts of his *Essay*, he has disavowed, in the most unequivocal terms, those dangerous conclusions which, it must be owned, the general strain of his first book has too much the appearance of favouring.[35]

At the end of the 1820s, Carlyle made Locke responsible for all the spiritual disasters of the time, in spite of his admiration for "the estimable character of the man." Locke had caused philosophy "to treat itself popularly," while in Germany it "dwells aloft in the Temple of Science, the divinity of its inmost shrine; her dictates descend among men, but she herself descends not." He traced the disastrous course through Hume to the dictum of Cabanis that "as the stomach secretes Chyle, so does the brain secrete Thought." This was the discovery of the French who followed in Locke's footsteps, "and what then was Religion, what was Poetry, what was all high and heroic feeling? Chiefly a delusion." Metaphysics itself "from Locke's time downwards, has been physical; not a spiritual philosophy, but a material one."[36]

The second stage of Locke's reputation, marked by the deepest contempt for Locke, opened in 1829 with the publication of Cousin's *Cours de l'histoire de la philosophie . . . du XVIIIe siècle*, a course of twenty-five lectures delivered that year, of which the last eleven were devoted to Locke. It immediately gained a reputation that is astounding even among the opponents of Locke, for it is doubtful whether any writer has ever been so completely misrepresented at such length—half the length of the *Essay* which was the only subject of the lectures devoted to Locke. The *Cours* is an unending succession of what truly deserves the name of nonsense. Though Cousin deals only with the *Essay*, he is determined to find in it only what he found in the most heinous doctrines of French sensualism. Only the fact that few read the *Essay* combined with the already well-established dislike of Locke can explain the success of these lectures. Already in 1830, Sir William Hamilton remarked that Cousin's history was "the most important work on Locke since the *Nouveaux essais* of Leibniz."[37] The *Cours* was noted and cited in England long before the publication of the first translation in 1852, and the lectures on Locke were soon separately published, first in English in America in 1834, and later in London in 1851. In the universities where Locke was taught, it became a set text along with the *Essay*.[38] Compared with Cousin's *Cours*, the publication, also in 1829, of Peter King's *Life of Locke* was hardly noticed, though it might have served to correct a number of misapprehensions.[39]

It would be ungracious, even were it possible, to tire the reader with an account of Cousin's nonsense. He is determined to find that the *Essay* "comprehends almost all the sensualistic tradition which concerns the eighteenth century." "The essential character of sensualism is, as we have seen, the negation of all the great truths which escape the senses, and which reason alone discovers"[40] —one thinks of Stewart's wise insistence that the general effect of the *Essay* was to instill respect for reason. Cousin's observations on Locke's conception of enthusiasm may be taken as a typical example of his mode of interpretation. I trust all readers of the *Essay* will recall that Locke's rationalism finds lucid expression in the two related chapters on "The Association of Ideas" and "Enthusiasm." But Cousin blames Locke for making a satire of enthusiasm, for to Cousin, enthusiasm is a "state of reason which listens to itself and takes itself as the echo of God upon earth, with the particular and extraordinary characters which are attached to it." Thus he concludes that "enthusiasm is a rational fact which has its place in the order of natural facts and in the history of the human mind."[41] Perhaps the reader needs to be reminded that Cousin is indeed offering a critique of Locke, not merely making an adventitious personal remark on enthusiasm. To many this was welcome argument, perhaps even wisdom.

Cousin was ably and severely refuted in the *Edinburgh Review* in 1834.[42] Though Locke "distinctly recognises original faculties, and active powers of mind, wholly independent of experience," Cousin is determined "to contract the comprehensive doctrines inculcated by Locke within the narrow limits of his class of Sensation." Thus, the reviewer concludes, it is "obvious that M. Cousin has wholly misapprehended the purport and spirit of the philosophical system which he undertakes to subvert. This error is by no means peculiar to M. Cousin. It is entertained by the majority of continental critics."[43]

A dozen years later, G. H. Lewes in his *History of Philosophy* demonstrated the falsity of Cousin's account of Locke, suggesting that he as well as Whewell could barely have read Locke, yet their criticisms were "samples of the style in which the great master is spoken of by his most modern critics. Let them be sufficient warning to the reader of what he is to expect from the partisans of the reaction against Locke, and his followers; and stimulate him to the careful study" of Locke's works.[44] But Whewell at least did not take Lewes's advice, as we shall soon see. The following year, in 1847, Robert Vaughan observed that it was from such works as Cousin's exposition of Locke "and scarcely at all from the examination of the Essay itself, that the opinions prevalent on the continent with regard to the system of Locke have been derived. Nor must we forbear to add, that this last remark applies to English reading and authorship, hardly less than to those of our neighbours." After a closer examination of Cousin's arguments, Vaughan concluded, with a dig at one of Cousin's great admirers, that "one tenth of Sir William Hamilton's learning and acuteness would suffice to make it abundantly plain, that if viewed simply as an exposition of Locke, the lectures of Cousin are worse than worthless."[45] But they were far from useless to Locke's critics in England.

When Adam Sedgwick's *Discourse on the Studies of the University* was published late in 1833 it made a sensation, running through three more editions within the next two years with new material added in support of its argument. Originally delivered as a sermon at the Commemoration of Benefactors in the Chapel of Trinity College on 17 December 1832, it became within a week the object of an earnest request for publication. Appending a list of names in support of this request, Whewell wrote to Sedgwick that "the rising generation . . . declare that their intellectual culture requires that you should print and publish your sermon."[46] Sedgwick's *Discourse* is a reminder that Cambridge was not merely a place of learning, but also of Christian education, of moral edification. Consequently Locke had much to do with the "intellectual culture" of its young men. The first part of the *Discourse* deals with the study of "the laws of nature," recommending the study of Newtonian philosophy because it "teaches us to see the finger of God in all things animate and inanimate" (14). Unlike many of Locke's critics, Sedgwick is a strong advocate of natural religion, a theme he surprisingly does not at all seem to have detected in Locke. The second part argues for the study of the classics, but it is the final part that is the weightiest and longest. It is devoted to "the study of ourselves as individuals and as social beings," including "ethics and metaphysics, moral and political philosophy, and some other kindred subjects of great complexity, hardly touched on in our academic system, and to be followed out in the more mature labours of after life" (10). The author had explained the real issue in the original Preface. "He has," he said, "attacked the utilitarian theory of morals, not merely because he thinks it founded on false reasoning, but because he also believes that it produces a degrading effect on the temper and conduct of those who adopt it" (vii). It was in this context that he discussed Locke and Paley.

Sedgwick states all the adverse Victorian commonplaces about Locke. Every chapter of the *Essay* bears "marks of deep thought . . . and above all, of a lofty independent spirit, holding allegiance to no authority but that of truth" (47). But in spite of this conventional tribute, Sedgwick finds only fault with the *Essay*. It has "almost overlooked . . . the distinction between innate ideas and innate capacities," and "of the imaginative powers" Locke "hardly says one word, or speaks of them only to condemn them," though "it is by the imagination, more perhaps than by any other faculty of the soul, that man is raised above the condition of a beast" (48-49). But the most calamitous fault of the *Essay* was its omission of "the faculties of moral judgment." It had, for instance, omitted conscience which is a "heaven-born rule of action" that has been "implanted in our bosoms by the hand of our Maker, to preside there and pass judgment on our actions." In a passage of characteristic but quite meaningless rhetoric, Sedgwick observed that if the mind had no "innate knowledge"—those are indeed his words—it must also be without

> innate feelings and capacities—a piece of blank paper, the mere passive recipient of impressions from without. The whole history of man shows this hypothesis to be an outrage on his moral nature. Naked he comes from his mother's womb . . . and as for knowledge, his soul is one unvaried blank;

yet has this blank been already touched by a celestial hand, and when plunged in the colours which surround it, it takes not its tinge from accident but design, and comes forth covered with a glorious pattern (52-54).

It is natural to wonder whether Sedgwick had read the long chapter "Of Power" in Book Two of the *Essay*, the chapter that is by far the most important in relation to Locke's ethics and moral philosophy. Sedgwick had indeed read it, but probably not very closely. It was nineteenth-century doctrine that this chapter was hardly worth reading, or as Sedgwick said, "there is no one who does not regard his dissertation on *power* as crude and obscure" (47). In a later passage that deals more closely with Locke's chapter "Of Power," Sedgwick shows that he had misunderstood its entire argument in a very elementary sense. His conclusion is:

> The determination of the human will has ever been considered a dark and difficult subject of inquiry. One cause of this may be, that it takes place more by passion and affection than by reason; and we should be almost justified in affirming, that the will is never determined by reason only, unless some affection be superadded (68-69).

If Locke's doctrine is true, then man is in a state of "absolute moral necessity," a conclusion also reached by Cousin, who would appear to have been read by Sedgwick though he does not make reference to Cousin. If Sedgwick had made a better effort to understand Locke, he would have found a great deal to admire as being in harmony with his own sentiments; but Locke had been too deeply compromised by his followers to receive a sympathetic reading. In a sense the *Discourse* was successful; the editions followed quickly, and it seems to have been widely read and caused much debate. But its argument did not hold up very well, partly because it argued passionately for the fixity of species in the edition of 1850 that was to be the last. In this edition the 94 pages of the *Discourse* were preceded by a Preface of 442 pages and followed by an appendix of 228. Sedgwick made sure that a copy was sent to Balmoral for the Prince Consort to read.[47]

We have already seen that William Whewell was delighted to be able to use his influence against Lockian philosophy at Cambridge. With sections on Locke in two of his works, he became perhaps the greatest and most influential of the Victorian denigrators of Locke, in his *Philosophy of the Inductive Sciences* (1840) and in the *Lectures on the History of Moral Philosophy in England* (1852).[48] The entire *Philosophy* was in a way directed against Locke. In the letter dedicating the work to Sedgwick, his close friend at Trinity ("our common Nursing Mother," "the College of Bacon and of Newton"), he wrote with reference to the *Discourse*:

The same spirit which dictated your vigorous protest against some of the errors which I also attempt to expose, would have led you, if your thoughts had been more free, to take a leading share in that Reform of Philosophy, which all who are alive to such errors, must see to be now indispensable. To you I may most justly inscribe a work which contains a criticism of the fallacies of the ultra-Lockian school.

In the text, Whewell paid the conventional tribute that Locke himself did not intend to throw doubt "upon the certainty of either human or divine knowledge," but he coupled Locke with Condillac's "transformed sensations," saying that the French writers consistently followed Locke's doctrines in their rejection of reflection, "which formed an anomalous part of his philosophy." He suggested that Locke merely repeated Hobbes, who was too unpopular for his ideas to have much effect. Locke was unoriginal but popular; he owed his authority

mainly to the intellectual circumstances of the time. Although a writer of great merit, he by no means possesses such metaphysical acuteness or such philosophical largeness of view, or such a charm of writing, as to give him the high place he has held in the literature of Europe.

He stated his own intuitionism by insisting, against Locke as he thought, "on the activity of the mind, as the necessary basis of all knowledge."

In the *Lectures on Moral Philosophy*, Whewell restated these opinions with even greater hostility to Locke, clearly revealing his incomprehension or ignorance of the chapter "Of Power," whose main thesis of course is that right conduct is the result of the dictates of reason prevailing over desire. If Whewell had understood Locke on this point, he would, much like Sedgwick, have had reasons for agreeing with him. Still, in the "Introductory Lecture," Whewell identified two opposed kinds of moral philosophy. "Dependent morality" has "asserted Pleasure, or Utility, or the Greatest Happiness of the Greatest Number, to be the true end of human action" while "independent morality" regulates "human action by an internal principle or relation, as Conscience, or a Moral Faculty, or Duty, or Rectitude, or the Superiority of Reason to Desire" (ix). Naturally, Whewell sides with independent morality, which should also have made him side with Locke. Ignoring the argument in which it occurs, he cites Locke's sentence beginning "good or evil are nothing but pleasure and pain," to demonstrate that Locke "belongs to the school of moralists who reject the independence of morality, and reduce moral good to a dependence on something else, namely, the pleasure which it produces." This was a consequence that followed from Locke's rejection of innate ideas which justified his French followers in discarding reflection "as a merely ceremonious expression" and asserting as Locke's great doctrine, that all our ideas are derived from the senses. Now *this* doctrine concerning ideas irresistibly fastens upon us the ethical tenet, that right and wrong are some modifications or other of bodily good and ill, that is, bodily pleasure and pain. And thus Locke's name is made the badge of the Sensualist School of morals (70-72).

Whewell admitted that Locke would have rejected this position, for he "really did cherish many views and speculations which were altogether at variance with the spirit and tendency of the Sensualist system of morals," an admission that typically illustrates the peculiar contradictions which Locke's critics so often faced but did not attempt to resolve. They were at all cost determined to have Locke the way they wanted him. As was also common, Whewell had an explanation which condescendingly deprived Locke of any merit for holding such edifying opinions, for these were "probably the remnants of his education in the philosophical school which preceded him" (70-72). Locke is again made unoriginal, an author with a flair for writing up old doctrines in a popular form and style. He has been considered as

the founder and master of the New Philosophy . . . but I think it will be acknowledged, by any one who carefully looks into the literary history of the subjects on which he wrote, that he originated little or nothing. All the distinctive opinions which he maintained had already been asserted, and very widely entertained (69-70).

But Whewell's evident incomprehension of the passages in the *Essay* that are relevant to his own morality shows that he was in no position to determine Locke's originality. Locke had become a whipping post. What his critics really meant but did not wish to attack too directly was the utilitarian philosophy. Both Sedgwick and Whewell were answered by John Stuart Mill.

Mill answered Sedgwick's *Discourse* in 1835 in a severe, sarcastic, and spirited essay.[49] This essay is also a scathing critique of Paley as a superficial, even simple-minded writer on morality, as well as an attack on Cambridge for producing nothing better than the *Discourse* on the subjects it deals with. On innate ideas, Mill makes the proper but in the nineteenth century nearly futile correction that Sedgwick had failed to see Locke's distinction between innate ideas and innate faculties. Sedgwick "shows no signs of having read any writer on the side of the question which he attacks, except Locke and Paley, whom he insists upon treating as the representatives of all others who adopt any of their conclusions" (47-8), an observation that holds true not only of Sedgwick but of practically all Locke's critics, with the possible exception of Coleridge. Mill makes another criticism which has equally wide application. Sedgwick had called it the greatest fault of the *Essay* that it took a much too limited view of "the capacities of man," "depriving him both of his powers of imagination and of his moral sense." "Are words altogether without meaning to the Professor," Mill asked, "that he can write in [this] manner . . . with the fact looking him in the face from his own pages, that it is entitled *An Essay on the Human Understanding*? Who besides Mr. Sedgwick would look for a treatise on the imagination under such a title?" (48). But though there would have been good reason to do so, Mill does not enter into discussion of Locke's chapter "Of Power" and its argument, thus giving the impression that he perhaps himself tended to see it rather in the eighteenth-century tradition.

Whewell's *Lectures* were answered by Mill in the year of their publication.[50] This fascinating and brilliant essay demonstrates how Mill with his much deeper knowledge of philosophical texts and their arguments can bare the hollowness and over-all inconsistency of the sorts of arguments that were advanced by Sedgwick and Whewell. In the eighteenth century, orthodox religion and ethics were attacked "on the ground of instinctive feelings of virtue, and the theory of moral taste or sense. As a consequence of this, the defenders of established opinions, both lay and clerical, commonly professed utilitarianism." But when Godwin and Bentham founded a moral philosophy on utility, a reversal occurred. "Utility was now abjured as a deadly heresy, and the doctrine of *a priori* or self-evident morality, an end in itself, independent of all consequences, became the orthodox theory" (170). Here Mill clearly identifies what is no doubt the chief source of the confusion about Locke that is so characteristic of the nineteenth century. The remedy had been found in German philosophy: "The tone of religious metaphysics, and of the ethical speculations connected with religion, is now altogether Germanized; and Dr. Whewell, by his writings, has done no little to impress upon the metaphysics of orthodoxy this change of character." Two tendencies had developed, one anti-inductive (Descartes, Spinoza, Leibniz, Kant, Schelling, and Hegel), the other inductive, which thanks to the "speculations of Bacon and Locke, and the progress of the experimental sciences, gave a long period of predominance to the philosophy of experience" (171). This had led to the paradoxical situation that some thought it possible to profess "themselves Baconians in the physical department, remaining Cartesians in the moral." These were themes which Mill had already dealt with in his wonderful essay on "Coleridge" in 1840.[51]

In this essay he had identified Bentham and Coleridge as the typical representatives of the two tendencies, the radical and the conservative, "the one pressing the new doctrines to their utmost consequences; the other reasserting the best meaning and purposes of the old." He believed that "these two sorts of men, who seem to be, and believe themselves to be, enemies, are in reality allies. What was really hateful and contemptible was that which preceded them, and which each, in its way, has been striving now for many years to improve" (146). On the question of the "sources of our knowledge," he found that "the truth . . . lies with the school of Locke and Bentham," but he also admitted that "the doctrines of the schools of Locke stood in need of an entire renovation," for on the Continent this philosophy had taken the form of

> .the shallowest set of doctrines which perhaps were ever passed off upon a cultivated age as a complete psychological system,—the ideology of Condillac and his school; a system which affected to resolve all phenomena of the human mind into sensation, by a process which essentially consisted in merely *calling* all states of mind, however heterogeneous, by that name (128-9).

In England the situation was much the same. Thus Mill occupies an intermediary position, eager to reconcile the two opposites by enlightening each regarding their misinterpretations.[52] The confrontation of Whewell and Mill in 1852 marks the culmination of the great public debate over Locke's merits. During the rest of the century it became less lively and was much softened. It now only remains to take a look at a few representative discussions.

In 1854, when Locke's *Works* were reissued, Henry Rogers wrote a remarkable essay in the *Edinburgh Review*.[53] He did something never before attempted in the nineteenth century and rarely done before or since; he considered Locke's philosophy not only as it was contained in the *Essay* but in all his works. He referred not only to the *Thoughts Concerning Education*, the political philosophy, and the controversy with Stillingfleet (which few had cited), but also to the *Reasonableness of Christianity* and even to the commentary on the Epistles of St. Paul. He argued powerfully against Cousin and countered the common opinion that Locke was "almost ignorant of what his predecessors had written, and such a very Troglodyte in metaphysics that he was not properly acquainted even with such writers as Descartes or Hobbes" (390), an opinion that was bound to arise in a century that was fast becoming so compulsively scholarly and name-parading that the absence of names was taken for lack of learning. He argued against the common interpretation of Book One on "Innate Notions," against holding Locke "responsible . . . for the extravagancies of the Sensational schools, especially of the French," and said that "Locke would have recoiled with abhorrence from all attempts of men of the Condillac and Condorcet stamp to reduce all knowledge to sensation" (404). He quite properly insisted "on the possible degradation of Locke's real meaning occasioned by the adventitious limitation of the term 'experience,' [so as to include only sensation, thus excluding reflection] as we do not recollect that any critic has expressly referred to it" (407). He saw the best proof that Locke rejected sensationalism in his letters to Stillingfleet, "and we wonder that those remarkable productions have not been more frequently cited in the criticism of Locke" (417). He found that "Locke's words [have] been so often quoted, misquoted, perverted, and supplemented, and such a voluminous body of controversy raised about them that . . . it is difficult to recognise Locke's true lineaments" (405). Historically, Locke had never been so well examined since Stewart's *Dissertation*, which Rogers often invoked as authority. He concluded in the hope that his observations would give "our youthful readers a more just conception of the character and value of Locke's philosophy than, we think, is always current in the present day; or stimulate them to make themselves masters of his principal writings" (453).[54]

In 1855, Edward Tagart, a Unitarian divine, published a long, rather dull defense of Locke, entitled *Locke's Writings Historically Considered*. He saw the great tradition in Bacon, Locke, and Hartley with associationism as its greatest product; he naturally had much admiration for Priestley and was therefore critical of all the Scottish philosophers, even of Dugald Stewart. Finding Locke "the most philosophical of Christians, the most Christian of philosophers" (424), he insisted on the Christian nature of what he saw as the great tradition. It is characteristic that Tagart did not face Locke directly, but rather defended him against the opinions of his critics.

This is also the plan of a much better book, indeed a brilliant book, by Thomas E. Webb called *The Intellectualism of Locke*, published at Dublin in 1857. "What if the Empiricism of Locke be one of the *fables convenues* of Philosophy?" he asked. "This is the fact which it is the object of this Essay to establish, and it is on the establishment of this fact that I rest Locke's claims to be regarded as a great thinker" (17). It was Webb's aim to demonstrate that the postulated incompatibility of Locke and Kant did not exist, an attempt that may be somewhat paradoxical, but which still produced what may well be considered the most exciting single book on Locke's philosophy written during the nineteenth century. The book is marked by very close knowledge of the *Essay* and by an uncommon awareness of the precise meanings of words and terms in Locke where they differ from current meanings, a matter that has generally, today as much as then, caused a vast number of misunderstandings. He also very astutely made an observation similar to one we have already seen in Mill. "Warburton remarks," Webb said, "as a characteristic of the controversies of his own times, a strange propensity in the Clergy to mistake their friends for their enemies, and as strange a propensity in the Freethinkers to mistake their enemies for their friends." Locke had been "canonized by the Schools whose principles he devoted his energies to subvert," Webb went on to observe, "he has been anathematized by the Schools whose doctrine it was the great object of his Philosophy to enforce" (160).[55]

Webb also made an observation which deserves serious attention in relation to Locke's own context in the seventeenth century, a matter very rarely considered: "According to Locke, our experimental knowledge was the result of a species of pre-established harmony. . . . Experience, in short, was the result of the correspondence between external reality and thought. But Locke's successors abandoned this position" (172). At Dublin in 1862, Webb was followed by William H. S. Monck with his *Critical Examination of M. Cousin's Lectures on Locke*, which is a very able book and all that anybody needs to know about Cousin on that subject.

The rest of the century saw the publication of a number of conventional pieces, though marked by a somewhat better and freer knowledge of Locke than had previously been the rule. In Masson's *Recent British Philosophy* (1865) we find an exposition that differs little from what is normal even today, one hundred years later. The terms "empirical philosophy" and "empiricism" are for the first time used directly and extensively about Locke. Masson did see Locke as a sensationalist, finding Leibniz' *"nisi intellectus ipse"* a "staggering blow to Lockian philosophy." Locke's empiricism could not stop short of sensationalism (27-30). But the last quarter of the century also saw the publication of Fox Bourne's still unsurpassed *Life of Locke* and of Leslie Stephen's great work on *English Thought in the Eighteenth Century*, which was itself an attempt to straighten out the history of the Lockian tradition.[56]

I began with a citation from C. S. Peirce's review of Fraser's book on Locke. It did not strike the usual note, but there was another review that did.[57] The reviewer, W. L. Courtney, took pride in Locke's Englishness, his typical practical common sense. "It is to Locke above all that we owe that distinguishing mark of English philosophy—its empirical character" (93). Hence he blamed Fraser for "the occasional tendency to rewrite Locke's doctrines in the language of later idealism." But Courtney also maintained that Locke would not even "allow the innateness of capacities or potential faculties of knowing," finding

Locke's *tabula rasa* "an impossible thing; the mind is not passive, but active. . . . We can never do without the *ipse intellectus* in giving an account of the birth and growth of knowledge" (107-8). He concluded that Locke was "in himself . . . a mass of inconsistencies"(122).

Locke's reputation in the nineteenth century is an interesting example of how a philosopher and his philosophy can become so embroiled in controversy that it becomes nearly impossible to get back to the starting point. But it also shows that Locke was still very much alive; otherwise, the nineteenth century would not have fought its own battles by projecting them into the reading of Locke. It was not a very clear view of Locke that came out of these battles. During the next seventy years there has been no comparable controversy over Locke and his philosophy, but we have been left with the confusion that is our heritage from the nineteenth century.

Notes

1. *Nation*, 51 (25 September 1890), 254-55. Peirce observed that Fraser "in a paragraph" had well disposed of "the insufferable sophistry of T. H. Green."

2. "Goethe" in *Critical and Miscellaneous Essays* (5 vols.; New York, 1899), Vol. I, p. 215 [198-257]; the figures in parentheses indicate the page span of the essay.

3. *Oeuvres complètes*, Vol. 4 (Lyon, 1884), pp. 299-381, "Sixième entretien." De Maistre was much admired by William Whewell and his friends; see my *Study of Language in England 1780-1860* (Princeton, 1967), pp. 227-29, 236-37, 241.

4. *History of Philosophy from Thales to Comte* (5th ed., 2 vols.; London, 1880), Vol. 2, p. 246; first published 1845-1846 as a *Biographical History of Philosophy*.

5. *Edinburgh Review*, 99 (April, 1854), 384 [383-454]: "John Locke: His Character and Philosophy," which is also in Rogers, *Essays* (3 vols.; London, 1855), Vol. 2, pp. 1-96.

6. *Lectures on the History of Moral Philosophy in England* (London, 1852), p. 71; Whewell was no doubt especially thinking of the text cited in *Essay* i, iii, 9, which Locke had discretely retained in the Latin original. Locke's use of evidence drawn from travel accounts and from the observation of "idiots, savages, and madmen" was as much deplored in the nineteenth century as it had been admired in the eighteenth. The next quotation is from the same text, p. xxi.

7. For my own interpretation of Locke on this matter, see "The State of Nature and the Nature of Man in Locke" in John W. Yolton (ed.), *John Locke: Problems and Perspectives* (Cambridge, 1969), pp. 99-136, esp. pp. 108ff. The quotations from Locke are in *Works* (9 vols.; London, 1794), Vol. 6, p. 11 (*Reasonableness*); and Vol. 2, p. 337 (*Conduct of the Understanding*, §6).

8. *Edinburgh Review*, 50 (October, 1829), 1 [1-31].

9. James Fitzjames Stephen, *Horae Sabbaticae* (3 vols.; London, 1892), Vol. 2, p. 108. (Hereinafter cited as HS.) On pp. 106-73, this volume contains four essays on Locke first published in the *Saturday Review*: "Locke's Essay," 22 (29 December, 1866), 795-97 [HS, 106-22]; "Locke as a Moralist," 23 (19 January, 1867), 73-5 [HS, 123-39]; "Locke on Government," 23 (16 February, 1867), 206-208 [HS, 140-56]; and "Locke on Toleration," 23 (9 March, 1867), 305-307 [HS, 157-73]. These are good essays, though in "Locke on

Government," Stephen seems to be the first to give currency to the mistaken notion that there is some conflict between the reputed empiricism of the *Essay* and the rationalist doctrines accepted in the *Two Treatises*.

10. "Locke and his Critics" in the *British Quarterly Review*, 5 (May, 1847), 292 [289-337], reprinted in Vaughan's *Essays on History, Philosophy, and Theology* (2 vols.; London, 1849), Vol. 1, pp. 59-120. This essay was a review of ten recent books on philosophy, including V. Cousin's *Cours de l'histoire de la philosophie*, Adam Sedgwick's *Discourse*, and the histories of philosophy by G. H. Lewes and J. D. Morell. In the entire nineteenth-century literature, this is the best, most well informed, and in its interpretation most correct essay on Locke's philosophy; it is well worth reading today. Vaughan was a Congregationalist minister; it is characteristic—and of course not accidental—that some of the most reliable essays on Locke were written by independent divines.

11. H. O. Christophersen, *A Bibliographical Introduction to the Study of John Locke* (Oslo, 1930), p. 89.

12. *Ibid.*, pp. 95-96. To his listings should be added *An Abridgment of Locke's Essay* by Louisa Capper (London, 1811), which frankly admitted that it was "calculated for the superficial reader" (p. viii). Pringle-Pattison's familiar abridgment of 1924 had reached its sixth printing in 1950, and since the Second War two other abridgments have appeared. The effect of thus putting Locke's philosophy into a narrow compass should not be underestimated. On this subject, see C. B. Martin's Introduction to *Locke and Berkeley, a Collection of Critical Essays*, eds. C. B. Martin and D. M. Armstrong (New York: Doubleday Anchor Original, 1968).

13. *Edinburgh Review*, 52 (October, 1830), 189 [158-207], a review of a recent French translation of Reid under the title "Reid and Brown."

14. *Dissertation* (1821) in *Collected Works*, ed. Sir William Hamilton (11 vols.; Edinburgh, 1854-1860), Vol. 1, p. 213.

15. *Complete Works of William Hazlitt*, Centenary Edition, ed. P. P. Howe (21 vols.; London, 1930-1934), Vol. 2, p. 162, in "Lectures on English Philosophy" delivered early in 1812, first published in 1836. Contrary opinions can be found. Johann Gottlieb Buhle found that Locke had an excellent style, "which is a model of its kind, though admittedly its special beauty can be fully grasped only in the original," in *Lehrbuch der Geschichte der Philosophie* (6 vols.; Göttingen, 1800-1804), Vol. 6, Part 2, p. 1001. Buhle's account of Locke is critical but sound. The Germans began to produce large-scale histories of philosophy in the late eighteenth century; they soon went through new and enlarged editions, and a few were translated into English both in England and America. William Enfield did a version of Brucker's *Historia critica philosophiae* (first published at Leipzig in 6 vols. 1742-1767), published in London in 2 vols. 1791, 1819, and 1837; it highly praises Locke. Wilhelm Gottlieb Tennemann's *Grundriss der Geschichte der Philosophie für den akademischen Unterricht* was published at Leipzig in 11 vols., 1798-1819, several volumes in the meantime being reissued, revised and enlarged. He placed Locke among "Anhänger der empirischen Schule." Though both Buhle and Tennemann have a Kantian orientation, they give a much better and more systematic account of Locke than anything that was available in England. They also both had detailed bibliographies. It is clear that they were widely used, even cribbed in England. There is a copy of Tennemann annotated by Coleridge in the British Museum. Sir James Mackintosh remarks on these histories in *Edinburgh Review*, 27 (October, 1816), 190.

16. H. R. Fox Bourne, *The Life of John Locke* (2 vols.; London, 1876), Vol. 2, p. 523 (Locke to Collins, 21 Feb. 1703/4).

17. *Introduction to the Literature of Europe* (3 vols.; Boston, 1854), Vol. 3, p. 387, in a note added in 1847. This work was first issued 1837-1839. On these pages, Hallam speaks of Book III of the *Essay* as the most admirable, an opinion shared by Dugald Stewart, John

Stuart Mill ("that immortal Book"), Macaulay, and James Fitzjames Stephen. Stewart in *Dissertation* spoke, p. 210, of "the third book (by far the most important of the whole), where the nature, the use, and the abuse of language are so clearly and happily illustrated." He referred to it, as was commonly done, as "the logic of Locke" and was surprised at Oxford's "partiality for the logic of Aristotle of which Locke has so fully exposed the futility" (*ibid.*, p. 214).

18. Sedgwick, *Discourse* (London, 1835), p. 46.

19. *Dissertation*, p. 215; Stewart also observes that "it was in the Scottish universities that the philosophy of Locke, as well as that of Newton, was first adopted as a branch of academical education" (p. 551).

20. Mrs. Stair Douglas, *The Life and Selections from the Correspondence of William Whewell*, D. D. (London, 1881), p. 248 (letter to Julius Charles Hare, 8 December, 1841). In *The Study of Language in England*, esp. pp. 211-63, I have dealt with the Trinity circle's role in fighting the Utilitarians by attacking what was seen as their linguistic philosophy and its consequences, derived from Horne Tooke who claimed Locke as his chief intellectual ancestor. The plan for a new English dictionary, the one that became the *Oxford English Dictionary*, was conceived as an anti-Utilitarian and ultimately anti-Lockian move. This matter forms a significant aspect of Locke's reputation in the nineteenth century.

21. Thomas Sadler (ed.), *Diary, Reminiscences, and Correspondence of Henry Crabb Robinson* (3 vols.; London, 1869), Vol. 1, pp. 128-29 (6 June, 1802).

22. *Ibid.*, p. 139 (1802).

23. Crabb Robinson's *Diary*, etc. was not published until 1869, but in these passages we find the use of "empiricism" and "empirical" that has given rise to modern usage, which invariably—though wrongly—contrasts Locke's reputed empiricism to rationalism, a contrast that would not have made sense to Crabb Robinson, Coleridge, and Dugald Stewart who saw correctly that empiricism contrasted with idealism. The term was not nearly so common in the nineteenth century as it has become since. Robinson's use of it at this time demonstrates its German origin in this sense; the term is of course Kantian, and it had been used by Buhle and Tennemann, who as early as 1797 had concluded his translation of Locke's *Essay* into German with an often-cited "Abhandlung über den Empirismus in der Philosophie, vorzüglich den Lockischen." In English its first public appearance was perhaps in David Brewster's *New Edinburgh Encyclopaedia*, 2d American Edition (New York, 1819), Vol. 12 in the article "Locke," who is said to have "been charged with inconsistency in supporting this doctrine of the empirical origin of our ideas by a multitude of unsatisfactory proofs," though even here Crabb Robinson's usage comes closer to our own. The terms—the noun and the adjective— are not used in this sense by Coleridge, Hazlitt, Lewes, Vaughan, and Henry Rogers. In David Masson's *Recent British Philosophy* it is made equivalent to "Lockism," and thus seems to have gained currency in this context only by 1865: "Though it may be against Locke's will, his Empiricism cannot stop short of Sensationalism." Masson, 3d ed. (London, 1877), pp. 27-30 (1st ed. 1865). In the *Edinburgh Review*, 36 (October, 1821), 240, Sir James Mackintosh refers to "the German word 'empirical'" in a discussion of suitable terms.

24. Roberta Florence Brinkley (ed.), *Coleridge on the Seventeenth Century* (Durham: Duke University Press, 1955), p. 97. This is a fuller and presumably more correct text than the one in Crabb Robinson, Vol. 1, p. 313.

25. Earl Leslie Griggs (ed.), *Collected Letters of Samuel Taylor Coleridge*, Vol. 2, 1801-1806 (Oxford, 1956), p. 707 (letter to Thomas Poole, 16 March, 1801).

26. Kathleen Coburn (ed.), *The Notebooks of Samuel Taylor Coleridge*, Vol. 2, 1804-1808 (New York, 1961), entry 2627.

27. Kathleen Coburn (ed.), *The Philosophical Lectures of Samuel Taylor Coleridge*, hitherto unpublished (London, 1949), p. 376. These lectures were given during the winter of 1818-1819; part of Lecture 12 and most of Lecture 13 are devoted to Locke. They reflect

the record of study that is presented in the letters to Wedgwood. As already indicated in some of the quoted passages, Coleridge credited Locke's reputation to accidental historical circumstances; for the details see Griggs, Vol. 2, pp. 701-03.

28. Brinkley, p. 99.

29. See Griggs, Vol. 2, pp. 683-86; Coburn (ed.), *Lectures*, pp. 373-83. In an often-cited passage, Sir William Hamilton had said regarding innate ideas that he had "no doubt that had [Descartes] and Locke expressed themselves with the clearness and precision of Scotus, their opinions on this subject would have been found coincident both with each other with the truth." Thomas Reid, *Philosophical Works*, ed. by Sir William Hamilton (2 vols.; Edinburgh, 1895), Vol. 2, p. 782.

30. Masson, p. 27, as late as 1865 seems hesitant to link Bacon with empiricism: "The general tenor of Bacon's writings leaves an impression as if he had given a splendid impulse to Empiricism." It is worth observing that the term 'empiricism' and its cognates are not used in Macaulay's famous and influential essay on Bacon (1837).

31. Hazlitt, *Complete Works*, Vol. 2, pp. 111-19. Here and in the following, page references will be given in the text when the work cited is obvious.

32. *Collected Works*, Vol. 1, pp. 1-527 with important "Notes and Illustrations" following. We are only concerned with Part II "Progress of Metaphysics during the Eighteenth Century," here occupying pp. 206-484. Sect. I, pp. 206-51, is devoted to Locke; Sect. II, pp. 252-86, to Leibniz conjointly with consideration of Locke. Already in 1810, Stewart had published two essays on Locke in *Philosophical Essays*; these are in *Collected Works*, Vol. 5, pp. 55-86, "On Locke's Account of the Sources of Human Knowledge, and its Influence on the Doctrines of his Successors"; and pp. 120-36, "On the Influence of Locke's Authority upon the Philosophical Systems which prevailed in France during the latter Part of the Eighteenth Century." These essays make much the same points as the *Dissertation*, but are somewhat more critical of Locke; Stewart had gained greater sympathy for Locke between 1810 and 1821. I shall be concerned only with the *Dissertation*.

33. *Ibid.*, pp. 236-39. I do not agree with Stewart's identification, in the same passage, of Locke's innate ideas wth the Cartesian doctrine. I think Locke had something else in mind; see "Leibniz on Locke on Language," above, p. 61. I also believe that the usual view of Condillac's "transformed sensations" is a misinterpretation. "Sensation" here does not mean the same as in Locke, and attention to Condillac's own revisions and later additions to his works shows that he was very eager to retain the full autonomy of reason as the principle behind reflection. See my essay on "The Tradition of Condillac" in *Studies in the History of Linguistics*, ed. Dell Hymes (Bloomington: Indiana University Press, 1974). Repr. below pp. 146-209.

34. Sir James Mackintosh rightly pointed this out in his review of the *Dissertation*, Part II, in the *Edinburgh Review*, 36 (October, 1821), 220-67. On pp. 247-48, he cogently cited the passage of Leibniz' *Nouveaux essais* that begins, "perhaps the opinions of our able author [Locke] are not so far from mine as they appear to be" (from "Préface"), as well as the passage in II, i, § 2, which would especially have pleased Stewart; having cited the famous words that have often been used against Locke, "there is nothing in the intellect that was not before in sense, with this exception: save only the intellect." Leibniz said: "This agrees pretty well with the author of the *Essay*, who ascribes a considerable part of our ideas to the reflection of the mind on its own nature" (in *Akademie Ausgabe*, Series 6, Vol. 6 (1962), pp. 51-52 and 111). The "nisi ipse" passage in Stewart was taken from a letter to Fr.-W. Bierling of 28 October, 1710, in L. Dutens (ed.), *Leibnitii opera omnia* (6 vols.; Geneva, 1768), Vol. 5, pp. 358-59. In Lecture 13 [Coburn (ed.), p. 383], Coleridge had already cited Leibniz in the spirit Stewart rejected. Leibniz's aphorism was tossed back and forth for the rest of the century in arguments or assertions about the meaning of Locke's innate notions.

35. In 1820 appeared the *Lectures on the Philosophy of the Human Mind* by Thomas Brown, Stewart's disciple and his successor in the chair at Edinburgh. These lectures had

been delivered within the previous ten years. He admired Locke for trying to fix the limits of human knowledge in order to escape "perfect scepticism." He rejected, much like Stewart, the common opinion that Condillac and the "French metaphysicians" had rightly understood Locke, thus "conferring on Mr. Locke a praise which they truly meant to do him honour, but praise which the object of it would have hastened to disclaim." In nineteenth-century Britain, Brown was one of the few philosophers who rightly observed that Condillac's *Essai sur l'origine des connoissances humaines* (1746) did not advocate the doctrine commonly attributed to the *Traité des sensations* (1754), and that Condillac was not a materialist. See *Lectures* (19th ed., London, 1851), pp. 12-13, 207-10.

36. *Critical and Miscellaneous Essays*, Vol. 1, pp. 76 and 215, and Vol. 2, p. 64; from "The State of German Literature" originally in *Edinburgh Review*, 46 (October, 1827), 304-51; "Goethe" in *Foreign Review*, 2 (1828), 80-127; and "Signs of the Times" in *Edinburgh Review*, 49 (June, 1829), 439-59.

37. *Edinburgh Review*, 52 (1830), 191. Hamilton also observed that, "the French philosophers are . . . in my opinion, fully justified in their interpretation of Locke's philosophy; and Condillac must, I think, be viewed as having simplified the doctrine of his master, without doing the smallest violence to its spirit," in *Lectures on Metaphysics and Logic* (2 vols.; Edinburgh, 1882), Vol. 2, p. 198. The 11th edition of the *Encyclopaedia Britannica* (1911) contains a very long article on Cousin by John Veitch, who says that Cousin "left several new, just, and true expositions of philosophical systems, especially that of Locke and the philosophers of Scotland."

38. In his excellent *Critical Examination of M. Cousin's Lectures on Locke* (Dublin, 1862), p. 4, Monck remarks on "the general dissatisfaction with which M. Cousin's criticisms have been regarded for some years in this University" (Trinity College, Dublin), where he was read along with the first three books of the *Essay*. The *Cambridge University Calendar for the Year 1868*, p. 31, lists among the "regulations for the moral sciences tripos" under the heading "Mental Philosophy," the required reading of Locke's *Essay* and Cousin's *Philosophie de Locke*.

39. Henry Brougham wrote a review, favorable both to Locke and to King, in the *Edinburgh Review*, 50 (October, 1829), 1-31.

40. *Course of the History of Modern Philosophy*, trans. O. W. Wright (2 vols.; New York, 1852), Vol. 2, p. 429.

41. *Ibid.*, pp. 392-93. Since Cousin elsewhere cites Leibniz's now familiar aphorism against Locke, it is curious that he has not read Leibniz on enthusiasm in the *Nouveaux essais*.

42. Vol. 59 (July 1834), 359-73; the author of this review has not been identified.

43. *Ibid.*, pp. 368-69. The reviewer also observes that regarding space, "the doctrines of Locke and of Kant, though apparently so different, may be easily reconciled with one another, and are both essentially true." This is also the argument of Thomas E. Webb's *The Intellectualism of Locke* (Dublin, 1857). The *Dictionary of National Biography*, First Supplement, rightly calls Webb's book "brilliant though paradoxical."

44. Lewes, *History*, Vol. 2, pp. 266-71. Lewes wrote an article on "Moral Philosophy of France" in the *British and Foreign Review*, 15 (1843), 353-406, in which he called Cousin a charlatan.

45. *British Quarterly Review*, 5 (1847), 293 and 299. On p. 298, Vaughan correctly observed that J. D. Morell in his popular *Historical and Critical View of the Speculative Philosophy of Europe* (1846) adopted all the "French misconceptions of Locke."

46. John Willis Clark, *The Life and Letters of the Reverend Adam Sedgwick* (2 vols.; Cambridge, 1890), Vol. 1, p. 401.

47. *Ibid.*, Vol. 2, p. 186.

48. The *Philosophy of the Inductive Sciences* (2 vols.; London, 1840), devoted two

chapters to Locke, in Vol. 2, pp. 457-81, under the titles "Locke and his French Followers" and "The Reaction against the Sensational School." These chapters (nos. 14 and 15 in Book xii) were both included in *The Philosophy of Discovery* (London, 1860), pp. 201-24. In these chapters the influence of Cousin is evident; he is cited several times, and it is observed that "M. Cousin himself . . . has argued very energetically and successfully against the doctrines of the Sensational School." Whewell also mentions de Maistre's "vigorous critique" of Locke. The *Lectures* were published in 1852, devoting part of the "Introductory Lecture," pp. ix ff., and pp. 69-77 to Locke and Clarke.

49. *London Review*, 1 (April, 1835), 94-135. I am using the text in the *Collected Works of John Stuart Mill*, Vol. 10, pp. 31-74 (Toronto, 1969): *Essays on Ethics, Religion and Society*, eds. J. M. Robson, F. E. L. Priestley, and D. P. Dryer. (Hereinafter cited as *Mill*.)

50. *Westminster Review*, 58 (October, 1852), 349-85; in *Mill*, pp. 165-201.

51. *Mill*, pp. 117-63; it was first published in the *London and Westminster Review*, 33 (March, 1840), 257-302.

52. Mill's determination to retain a balanced view is expressed in his Preface to *Dissertations and Discussions* (1859) in *Mill*, pp. 493-94. His own essay on Sedgwick's *Discourse* might give the impression, Mill said, of "more complete adhesion to the philosophy of Locke, Bentham, and the eighteenth century than is the case," but the subsequent essays on Bentham and Coleridge would rectify that impression; the essay on Whewell's moral philosophy would in turn correct the impression of any too great sympathy for the reaction of the nineteenth century agains the eighteenth.

53. *Edinburgh Review*, 99 (April, 1854), 383-454.

54. Two years later H. L. Mansel delivered a lecture at Magdalen College, in which he showed that Locke was neither the disciple of Hobbes nor the parent of Condillac, and Mansel rejected the usual interpretation of Leibniz's aphorism. See "On the Philosophy of Kant" in *Letters, Lectures and Reviews* (London, 1873), pp. 157-85. In 1864 he again dealt with Locke in an essay on "Freethinking—its History and Tendencies," *ibid.*, pp. 291-336.

55. This observation had also been made in one of Coleridges letters to Josiah Wedgwood; see Griggs, Vol. 2, pp. 701-702.

56. In 1877 the *Westminster Review*, 107 (N.S. 51), 163-95, carried a review of the lives by Fox Bourne and Peter King and of Locke's *Works*; it is sympathetic to Locke.

57. *Edinburgh Review*, 173 (January, 1891), 92-122.

The Tradition of Condillac: The Problem of the Origin of Language in the Eighteenth Century and the Debate in the Berlin Academy before Herder

> Passion, interest, inadvertency, mistake of his meaning, and a thousand odd reasons or capriccios men's minds are acted by (impossible to be discovered) may make one man quote another man's words or meaning wrong. He that has but ever so little examined the citations of writers cannot doubt how little credit the quotations deserve where the originals are wanting, and consequently how much less quotations of quotations can be relied on. This is certain, that what in one age was affirmed upon slight grounds can never after come to be more valid in future ages by being often repeated.
>
> Locke, *Essay* IV, xvi, 11.

> The ordinary words of language and our common use of them would have given us light into the nature of our *ideas*, if they had been but considered with attention.
>
> Locke, *Essay* III, viii, 1.

Introduction

It is the primary aim of this essay to identify and examine the intellectual background of one of the best-known and most influential works in the history of the study of language, Herder's *Über den Ursprung der Sprache*. It was written in response to a prize-essay topic set in 1769 by the Berlin Academy, which at the time had debated the problem of the origin of language for some twenty years. In Berlin as well as in Paris, London, and Edinburgh, the characteristic eighteenth-century formulation of this problem had been introduced by a single immensely influential work, Condillac's *Essai sur l'origine des*

Reprinted from *Studies in the History of Linguistics*, ed. by Dell Hymes (Bloomington: Indiana University Press, 1974), pp. 93-156.

146

connoissances humaines (1746). This work has largely been forgotten; the Berlin Academy debate it caused has been ignored; and Herder's *Ursprung* has been read with very slight knowledge—or none at all— of its historical context. It has been almost universally misinterpreted both in regard to its doctrines and its originality. My essay consists of two parts of roughly equal length. Part I deals, first, with Condillac's *Essai* in history, that is, with the reasons for its being so widely ne- glected or misunderstood; and, second, in order to remedy the effect of these misconceptions, with three basic features of linguistic theory in the mid-eighteenth century. Space does not permit detailed and systematic exposition of the argument of the *Essai*, which I hope the reader will find encouragement to read on his own, in its entirety. Part II deals with the first and most striking effect of the *Essai*, the debate on the origin of language in the Berlin Academy. Beginning in the years around 1750, this debate continues unbroken until the spring of 1771 when Herder's *Ursprung* was awarded the essay prize. I shall close my essay with some observations on the position of Herder's essay within the context I have attempted to identify and explain.

It will be useful to make a brief remark about the term "origin of language." It is cumbersome always to say "the linguistic theory that underlies and finds expression in efforts to deal with the question of the origin of language," but the term must be so understood. Unfor- tunately we lack such neat terms as "universal grammar" and "uni- versal grammarian," which are readily understood to involve linguistic theory. To remedy this need for a term that formally parallels "uni- versal grammar," I have where appropriate used "origin of language" without the definite article. It is characteristic that the late eighteenth century and the early nineteenth understood the terms "universal grammar" and "grammaire générale" to include the problem of ori- gin of language in its Condillacian formulation. The historical legiti- macy of this usage will become clear in the course of my analysis.

I. Origin of Language in the Mid-Eighteenth Century

It is common knowledge that the eighteenth century was vitally interested in the origin of language. It is safe to say that no other century has debated that question with greater zeal, frequency, con- sistency, and depth of insight. The truly creative period was intense and brief. It began in 1746 with the publication of Condillac's *Essai*, and it ended twenty-five years later in the final month of 1770 when Herder, during his sojourn in Strasbourg, hurriedly wrote his prize- essay, which appeared in print in January of 1772. With a singleness of origin that is rare in the history of ideas, the fountainhead of this debate was the *Essai*,[1] which in turn drew its inspiration from Locke's *Essay*. This indebtedness is not my present subject, but it may be briefly indicated by citing the subtitle to the *Essai* in the first edition: "A work in which all that concerns the human understanding is reduced to a single principle." Similarly, the subtitle of Thomas Nugent's English translation (1756) correctly made the same point in slightly different words: "A supplement to Mr. Locke's Essay on the Human Understanding." Within this philosophical context in Locke, Condillac was heavily indebted to one other English work, William Warburton's *Divine Legation of Moses* (1737-1741), where Condillac had found the doctrine of the language of action or gestures which occupies a crucial position in his argument.[2] In a general way, like most of his French contemporaries, Condillac was also under the influence of the current conception of Newtonian philosophy as known chiefly through Voltaire's *Eléments de la philosophie de Newton* (1738).

In France the debate was taken up by Diderot, Rousseau, Turgot, de Brosses, by Condillac himself in subsequent works, by a large number of articles in the *Encyclopédie*, as well as in a variety of pieces by other figures. In Berlin the problem was introduced in 1748 by the expatriate Frenchman Maupertuis in his *Réflexions philosophiques sur l'origine des langues et la signification des mots*. Cross influences soon passed between Berlin and Paris, and the debate also reached Scotland as seen in two distinguished works, which fall outside my present plan. The first was Adam Smith's "Considerations concerning the first Formation of Languages," first published in 1761.[3] The second was the first volume of Lord Monboddo's brilliant *Of the Origin and Progress of Language* (1773).[4] To these two, a third, less substantial work may be added, Joseph Priestley's *Course of Lectures on the Theory of Language, and Universal Grammar* (1762). But apart from the decisive roles of Locke and Warburton, other English writers also exercised a continuing influence both on general and on particular aspects of· the debate, whether in the original or in French and German translations. A few names and titles will immediately call this strain to mind: Shaftesbury, Berkeley, Francis Hutcheson's *Inquiry into our Ideas of Beauty and Virtue* (1725 and often reissued, French translation 1749, into German 1762), Thomas Blackwell's *Inquiry into the Life and Writings of Homer* (1735), James Harris's *Three Treatises* (1744), Robert Lowth's *De sacra poesi Hebraeorum Praelectiones academicae* (1753, reissued in Germany with notes by J. D. Michaëlis 1758-1761), and John Brown's *Dissertation on the Rise, Union, and Power, the Progressions, Separations, of Poetry and Music* (1763).

Condillac's Essai *in History*

THE *ESSAI* NEGLECTED AND MISUNDERSTOOD

The chief piece in the puzzle is Condillac's *Essai*. With that piece lost, forgotten or ignored there is no hope of gaining a clear and coherent understanding of the debate, of its basic issues, and of the historical sequence of events that tie it together. Secondary, tertiary, or irrelevant pieces have been introduced to fill the empty space in an attempt to achieve some semblance of order—Rousseau, Hobbes, and even Plato and Aristotle. Benfey's *Geschichte der Sprachwissenschaft* uses all four, but makes no mention of Condillac.[5] Before coming to Herder, Heymann Steinthal's *Ursprung der Sprache* makes brief mention of Plato and of Dietrich Tiedemann's *Versuch einer Erklärung des Ursprunges der Sprache* (Riga, 1772), which judged on Steinthal's account, is wholly secondary and which in any event had no influence.[6] Cassirer's chapter on "The Problem of Language in the History of Philosophy" in the first volume of *The Philosophy of Symbolic Forms* has been widely regarded as a history of the problem that is our present concern. It should not be considered in that light. Herder again emerges in a manner that is contrary to the facts, but in a footnote to the opening of this chapter Cassirer rightly observes that "a comprehensive work on the history of the philosophy of language is still a desideratum."[7] P. A. Verburg in *Taal en Functionaliteit* (1952) deals with Condillac in scattered fashion, quite failing to grasp the nature of his thought and especially of the *Essai*. Verburg explores the relationships with Hobbes and Leibniz, who have no historical relevance to the *Essai*, but ignores the impact of Locke.[8]

Hans Arens's *Sprachwissenschaft* (1955) sees Condillac as a typical representative of the French "rationalistisch-psychologische Betrachtung," which, we are told, is characterized by "intellectual impatience and intolerance toward life that can only be mastered mathematically when it is conceived as pure mechanism." For the study of language, we are told, the result is that "language is not at all seen as the mode and expression of life, but throughout as a mere logical system of signs for concepts and the statement of propositions."[9] Against this travesty of Condillac, indeed of the dominant strain of mid-eighteenth century French thought, there is no remedy except the obvious one: a reading of the *Essai*. Arens's judgment denies Condillac the very qualities that were central to his conception of the nature of man and of his progress and achievements in all modes of expression from poetry and art to philosophy and mathematics. It totally misconceives the nature of Condillac's doctrine that, "good sense, intellect, reason and their contraries equally result from the same principle, which is the connection of ideas one with the other; rising still higher, we see that this connection is produced by the use of signs; and that, consequently, the progress of the human mind depends entirely on the proficiency we demonstrate in the use of language. This principle is simple, and it casts great light on this matter. So far as I know, I am the first person to have recognized it."[10] One consequence of such neglect of Condillac is that prominent aspects of Herder's *Ursprung* will appear more original and new than they in fact were. Herder was not the first to stress the primacy and legitimacy of poetic expression in comparison with philosophical discourse. Arens illustrates the nature of Condillac's thought by citing one passage from the posthumously published *Langue des calculs* (1798) and another from the *Essai*, both of which quite fail to indicate the nature of Condillac's argument. These citations are so bizarre as to preclude any suspicion of influence in the very quarters where that influence was most powerful.[11]

Of course, it may be argued that some of these works were not really setting out to explore historical relationships, and it is true that some of them are not very clear about their methods and intentions. There can be no doubt, however, that these works have indeed been read as if they were giving quite adequate and reliable historical coverage. They have been considered authoritative, and they are typical of a large number of other works that present either the same story or the same kind of story. All of them appear to be the victims of quite obvious misconceptions about the eighteenth century that were first confidently asserted as truth during the nineteenth century. In the second chapter of his *De l'origine du langage*, Ernest Renan deals briefly with the French *philosophes*, then dismisses their work as irrelevant: "They addressed themselves to theoretical questions before they had dedicated themselves to the patient study of precise details. . . . Eighteenth-century philosophy had a strong penchant for artificial explanations in everything that pertains to the origins of the human mind," words that contrast strangely with the mystical rhapsodies which Renan substitutes for clear statement whenever he approaches the need for explanation or for some sort of conclusion, as for instance in the final pages of *De l'origine*.[12] His manner is characteristic of the nineteenth-century belief that the eighteenth century was trying to "explain" the origin of language when in fact it was trying to explore and perhaps explain the nature of mind and man.

It is reasonable to ask why Condillac's *Essai* has been ignored. In general, I think that the strong international position of historical and comparative philology in German scholarship of the last century and the reflection of this prominence in the historiography of the subject have tended to favor earlier German work pertaining to the study of language. But more specifically I think there are two reasons: The overwhelming attention paid to Herder as the single focus of all attempts to deal with the history of the problem; and, second, the seemingly trivial fact that the title of the *Essai* gives no indication that a theory of language and its origin is the center of the entire argument of the *Essai*. I shall deal with each in turn.

(a) *Herder as focus*. The longest, most detailed attempt to come to grips with the refractory philosophy of Herder's *Ursprung* is a typical example of this failure to see the relevance of Condillac. Hansjörg A. Salmony has devoted nearly the first half of his book on *Die Philosophie des jungen Herder* (1949) to a discussion of the *Ursprung* and its argument, making a determined effort to resolve its seeming—or perhaps real—contradictions and ambiguities in order to explain what Herder really meant. In the process Salmony produces an explication of Herder which in fact closely resembles Condillac's argument. This turn is so extraordinary that it would not seem possible were it not for the fact that Salmony clearly reveals his total ignorance of the *Essai*. He simply has not read it, though he has a great deal to say about what he takes to be its doctrine, depending largely on his faith in the reliability of Herder's own statements concerning it—thus following the curious procedure of taking a primary text, *in casu* the *Ursprung*, to be also a trustworthy secondary text on a work which for the purpose of the examination at hand should itself have been considered a primary text. Salmony regularly makes reference to well-established scholarly works that support his analysis, a fact which clearly shows how widely and authoritatively Condillac has been ignored.

A few typical instances will reveal the absurdities that result. It is the thesis of the *Essai*, we are told, that "language is nothing but the development of 'cries of emotion,' it is in its origin not above man, not divine, but below man, animalistic." Both the *Essai* and Condillac's other works reject this view. This common error is in part made possible by ignoring Condillac's basic distinction between natural gestures and "les cris naturels" on the one hand and on the other the artificial and, in this sense arbitrary, vocal signs of the language and speech that is uniquely human. In the same context, again revealing ignorance of what the *Essai* says, Salmony tells us that, "in the *Langue des calculs* is shown how an articulate language gradually emerges from an original language of gestures (langue d'action), a language, it is expressly said, that does not merely serve the needs of communication and outward understanding, but above all comprehension. . . . Here the talk is no longer about the animalistic origin of language, of the 'noises' and 'cries of emotion.'"[13] In his own book, Salmony says, "the subject is throughout the origin-of-language theory of the *Essai*, never of the far more important one in the *Langue des calculs*."[14] Salmony seems aware that if the argument he recognized in the *Langue des calculs* had been presented in the *Essai* in 1746, as in fact it was at great length, then this fact would have had very considerable consequences for the possibility of a link between Condillac and Herder. But Salmony's ignorance of the *Essai* and hence of the true chronological relationship protected him against that painful possibility. The unfinished *Langue* was written in the last years before Condillac's death in 1780 and first published in the *Oeuvres* of 1798.

Naturally, any evidence that Herder during the 1760s was acquainted with Condillac's *Essai* would have forced Salmony to reconsider his argument, but here again he shares the universal silence of scholars, though the evidence has been in print for nearly one hundred years. In a note to *Fragmente III* (1767), Herder observed: "The German Library [a serial publication] has brought to my attention a book that I now leaf through with delight. The second part of the *Essai sur l'origine des connoissances humaines* has observations that cast light on my fragment 'on the ages of language.'"[15] This acquaintance with Condillac would seem to go back to the years 1763-1764, when Herder wrote a brief piece called "Allgemeine Betrachtung über die Sprachen," which consists of excerpts from the *Essai*.[16] In his perplexity, Salmony uses the common expedient of paying more attention to Rousseau than a strict examination of the historical context will justify. Salmony's one hundred pages on Herder's philosophy of language is not only long and detailed and pursued with great determination in regard to historical correctness; his treatment also offers a compendium of common errors, thus raising neglect of Condillac to the level of confident doctrine.

(b) *The Title*. The second reason for neglect of Condillac is perhaps more obvious than the first and also rather distressing: the title of the *Essai* says nothing about language. It does not reveal that more than a third of it bears the title "De l'origine et des progrès du langage,"[17] nor of course that the origin of language is pivotal in the entire argument concerning "l'origine des connoissances humaines." This lesson could, however, have been learned from Condillac's contemporaries, who were not mistaken. Rousseau's *Discours sur l'origine et les fondemens de l'inégalité parmi les hommes* (1755) has been the most common substitute to fill the gap left open by ignorance of the

Essai. The most famous and often cited passage has this rarely cited beginning: "Permit me for a moment to consider the troubled question of the origin of languages. I could restrict myself to citing or repeating here the researches which Condillac has made on this matter, all of which clearly confirm my opinion and which perhaps gave me the first idea of it."[18] Similarly, Diderot in the opening paragraph of his *Lettre sur les sourds et muets* (1751) observes, "I could have addressed myself to Condillac or to Du Marsais, for they have also treated the matter of inversions."[19]

Other obvious references can easily be cited; but they are hardly needed since all major and minor items in the debate clearly reveal their debt to the *Essai*, to its problems and its issues, including significant passages in Condillac's own *Traité des sensations* (1754), *Traité des animaux* (1755), and his *Cours d'études* (1775). The argument of the *Traité des sensations* has perhaps offered the chief cause for misunderstanding. In the *Lettre sur les aveugles* (1749),[20] Diderot had pointed out that the *Essai* came very near to saying the same thing as Berkeley in the *Three Dialogues between Hylas and Philonous*, though ostensibly Condillac would be opposed to Berkeley's idealism, a point well taken and its occasion already obvious in the opening sentence of the *Essai*: "We never step outside ourselves; and we never perceive anything but our own private thought." In the *Sensations* Condillac had gradually endowed a statue with the senses of smell, taste, hearing, and vision, none of which alone or together give any assurance of the existence of anything outside ourselves. But adding finally touch and motion, it gains—in the words of Georges le Roy—"in an incontrovertible manner the sense of something existing outside." Thus Condillac passes from "l'idéalisme au réalisme," paradoxically borrowing suggestions from Berkeley's *New Theory of Vision*. Still, as le Roy rightly observes, "Condillac's psychology is not materialist, as some have found it possible to believe by making it similar to Diderot's; it implies an undiluted spiritualism."[21]

The statue demands a moment's attention. The *Traité des sensations* is generally reputed to contain the fullest and most characteristic version of Condillac's conception of man. This conception, it is believed, offers a purely mechanistic and materialist account of the nature of man and his knowledge, as if Condillac in that work had offered "enough to account for the richest intellectual and emotional experiences man knows," to use the words of a recent publication on Condillac.[22] In other words, the *Sensations* has been read as if it were a "traité des connaissances humaines," when it is in fact precisely what its title says and no more. It is not, as has been believed, about the whole subject of man and the understanding. The statue is a structural device designed to show that the sensations suffice to produce a habitual and instinctive assurance of the existence of the outside world, which was all Condillac set out to do in order to meet Diderot's charge of Berkelianism. Existing not in society but in total isolation and lacking all but the most rudimentary form of reflection as well as the use of signs and language, the statue is forever debarred from attaining the nature of man. It is quite literally and in a profound sense speechless.

This conception of the statue was already clear in the first, 1754 edition of the *Sensations*, as le Roy clearly demonstrated in 1937 in his book on *La psychologie de Condillac*: "In fact, the *Treatise on the sensations* does not have the exclusive character it has often been given. It does not deny the role of language in the development of the mental faculties, and consequently it does not constitute a refutation of the *Essai*. It deals solely with the operations of mind that precede the acquisition of languages, and it limits itself to the analysis of those operations."[23] In this book, however, le Roy did not consider some very significant additions on this very point to the final version of the *Sensations* which Condillac prepared during the last years of his life. These additions strongly underscore the meaning of the statue's lack of language, as if Condillac was eager to make this point especially clear, thus further reducing any possibility of conflict with the *Essai*. In one of these revisions, the marginal summary reading "conclusion de ce chapitre" has been replaced by these words: "Its knowledge is only practical; and the light that guides it is merely instinct." A new paragraph has then been added, containing these passages: "It analyzes naturally, but it has no language. But an analysis that is made without signs can only give very limited knowledge. . . . Thus when I treat the ideas that the statue acquires, I do not mean to say that it has knowledge of which it can render an exact account to itself: it has only practical knowledge. All the light it has is properly speaking instinctive, that is to say, a habit of conducting itself according to ideas of which it does not know how to render account to itself. . . . To acquire knowledge of theory, it is necessary to have a language: for the ideas must be classified and determined, which presupposes signs employed according to method."[24] In fact, late in life Condillac appears to have been eager to insist on his continuing commitment to the argument of the *Essai*. In his final revisions in *De l'art de penser* he added a note to a chapter entitled "De la nécessité des signes." The note said: "After the printing of my *Essai*, from which the largest part of this work is drawn, I have completed the demonstration of the necessity of signs, in my *Grammar* and in my *Logic*."[25]

In fact, the statue hardly differs from the animals in the *Traité des animaux* (1755), as a few passages from that work will show: "There are somehow two selves in each human being: the self of habit and the self of reflection," and "the self of habit suffices for the needs that are absolutely necessary to the preservation of the animal. But instinct is only this habit deprived of reflection." This is precisely what was also true of the statue. But "the measure of reflection we have beyond our habits is what constitutes our reason." Like the statue, the animals have only "des connoissances practiques," but not of theory, "for theory presupposes a method, that is, convenient signs for the determination of the ideas, for arranging them in order and for gathering the results." Thus "our mind is not of the same nature as that of the beasts," and it is no wonder that man, "who is as superior in regard to organic being as by the nature of the spirit that animates him, alone has the gift of speech."[26]

Thus the decisive difference between man and beast lies between the statue and man, not between the statue and the beast. The *Essai* had already been perfectly clear on this point: "From all the operations we have described results one that, so to speak, crowns the understanding: it is reason. . . . [which] is nothing but the knowledge of the manner in which we are obliged to rule the operations of mind," and "we are capable of more reflection in proportion as we have more reason. Consequently, this last faculty produces reflection."[27] The unique instrument of this reflection is "la liaison des idées," which ensures control over the memory by means of those signs which men in society by mutual aid have instituted for that purpose. And "language is the most palpable example of the connections we form voluntarily," unlike the mere association of ideas which, not being voluntary, also is not subject to our control, a distinction Condillac makes frequently and clearly. This "liaison" itself is, like reason behind it, natural and innate; it is "uniquely in the nature of the mind and the body. That is why I regard this connection as a first and fundamental experience, which should suffice to explain all the others."[28] Thus in Condillac as in Locke, reflection is a powerful, active, creative, innate faculty, Professor Chomsky *non obstante*; and it is precisely for this reason that Condillac, building on Locke, could present a theory of the creation of human language.

ROUSSEAU

If the full title of Condillac's *Essai* made it possible to overlook the relevance of that work in the history of linguistic philosophy, one may ask why the same fate did not befall Rousseau's *Discours sur l'origine et les fondemens de l'inégalité parmi les hommes*. It has not been ignored, no doubt because Rousseau has continued to maintain his place in literature. The *Inégalité* was published in German in 1756, while the *Essai* appeared in German only in 1780. Rousseau and his contemporaries took Condillac for granted, while later generations have tended to remember only Rousseau. The fact that some passages on language in *Inégalité* have been used to fill the gap left open by neglect of Condillac has caused perhaps the most widely held misconception of the question concerning the origin of language. Owing to Rousseau, it has been believed that the entire question had only received shallow treatment, as if all previous accounts had assumed that primitive man must have been a full-fledged philosopher—in the manner of contemporary man—in order to create the first language. Rousseau put the dilemma succinctly: "If men have had need of speech to learn to think, they have had still greater need of knowing how to think in order to invent the art of speaking."[29] This dilemma in turn resolves itself into the question whether language or society came first. Rousseau gives up: "To whoever wishes to undertake it, I leave the discussion of this difficult problem, which has been more necessary: society already formed for the institution of languages, or languages already invented for the creation of society."[30] The dilemma is obvious enough, but it has been forgotten that Rousseau is, at this point, making the prior assumption that the primitive man he is here considering leads an absolutely solitary life, that men, "having neither a fixed abode nor any need one for the other, met perhaps barely twice in their lives, without recognizing each other and without speaking."[31] It is only after he has made this basic assumption that Rousseau lapses into his first and best-known digression on the origin of language.

At the beginning of Part Two of the *Inégalité*, however, Rousseau returns to the question of the origin of language, and this time he can give an account that closely follows that of Condillac since he is now making a different assumption about the stage of development man has achieved: man already has the rudiments of social organization. Need has given him "some crude idea of mutual interactions." He has also, still independently of language and speech, developed "some sort of reflection, or rather a mechanical prudence that indicated the precautions most necessary for his safety."[32] Now the origin of language creates no difficulty: "Inarticulate cries, many gestures, and some imitative noises must have been for a long time the universal language, which, with the addition in each country of some articulate and conventional sounds—of which the institution, as I have already said, is not too easy to explain—produced particular languages, but these were rude and imperfect and nearly such as are to be found today among some savage nations."[33] This agrees well with Condillac, and it is this second conception that is taken up in Rousseau's posthumous *Essai sur l'origine des langues* (1781).[34]

It is obvious that Rousseau's two passages on the origin of language are not contradictory, since they rest on very different assumptions. The former is not a valid critique of Condillac, and the second closely follows him, but it is only the former that has been remembered and cited as if it touched Condillac's argument. It is easy to see the fatal consequences of that error. Condillac later gave a good answer to Rousseau's first passage.[35]

LINEARITY OF SPEECH

Now, if Condillac is misunderstood and ignored, there is a good possibility that Rousseau will also be misunderstood. This has in fact occurred, even where it was perhaps least to be expected. Citing an observation of Rousseau's on what is usually called the linearity of speech, Jean Starobinski has remarked: "He recognized perfectly the specific difference, the temporal order. Thus he anticipates the observations of Ferdinand de Saussure."[36] If the implication is that this idea is original with Rousseau, then the statement is not correct. Rousseau had himself been anticipated by several others. Condillac's *Essai* had already shown how the inescapable linearity of speech had forced man to decompose the initial unitary signs of the language of action into discrete, arbitrary signs of human language, thus making analysis and ordered reflection possible.[37] Later he gave this idea prominence in his theory of language: "If all the ideas that compose a thought are simultaneous in the mind, they are successive in discourse: it is languages that provide us with the means of analyzing our thoughts."[38] An entire thought is instantaneous, like a painting; it has no succession in time. This idea had also been forcefully stated by Maupertuis in his *Réflexions*, as we shall soon see. And in the *Lettre sur les sourds et muets*, Diderot had observed that "our mind is a moving picture from which we paint ceaselessly . . . the mind does not go step by measured step like expression. The brush executes only in the process of time what the painter's eye embraces in a flash. The formation of languages demanded the decomposition."[39] Thus the linearity of speech was, also before Rousseau, a central doctrine in the philosophy of language that found expression in conjectures on the origin of language. This doctrine held a place of equal importance in universal grammar. We shall later see that this common agreement was one of the reasons why origin of language and universal grammar were completely fused soon after the publication of the *Essai* in 1746, a fusion that would seem highly unlikely, indeed impossible, if certain current dogmas about the history of linguistics, about the so-called "Cartesian" linguistics and Lockian thought, had any validity.

I have tried to correct some basic misconceptions which for the most part have their origin in factual errors and inadequate knowledge about the heroic age—a name it deserves—of linguistic theory in the eighteenth century. I shall now take up three misconceptions of a more general nature. They concern: the true import of analysis and understanding in terms of origins; the meaning, more specifically, of asking questions about the origin of language; and, thirdly, the reputed conflict between universal grammar and Lockian philosophy.

Three Basic Features of Linguistic Theory in the Eighteenth Century

ORIGINS

The eighteenth century explored the origins of all aspects of man's institutions and works: Society and the state with their laws and rules of obligation, the arts (whether poetry, music, painting, sculpture, or architecture), the crafts, the mind, thought, and language. It was the best mode of explanation and analysis they knew, just as understanding in terms of structure is perhaps the dominant and most natural mode in our time. This approach in terms of origins was man-centered, and its chief object was to get down to principles, to what was basic and natural or innate in man's being as he came from the Creator's hand, as distinct from what man had created by means of his "active faculties" as Locke called them, from what in the terminology of the eighteenth century was called artificial. What man had by nature, in addition to his body, was the light of nature, which to Locke, Du Marsais, and Condillac meant the two innate, active creative powers of reason and sense experience.[40] "Principle," said Condillac, "is the synonym of beginning, and it is in this meaning that it has first been used."[41] A large number of specific statements to this effect can be found, but we may take one from an early piece by Herder, his "Versuch einer Geschichte der lyrischen Dichtkunst," which he wrote in 1764 at a time when he had been reading Condillac's *Essai*. This passage will also show how the metaphor of organic growth is used to enforce this conception: "But it is not merely amusing but also

necessary to investigate the origin of the things that we wish to understand rather fully. Here a part of history obviously escapes us, and
how much does not history serve to explain the whole? And what is
more, the most important part of history from which everything else
is subsequently derived. For like the tree from the root, so the progress and flowering of an art must be derived from its origin. It contains the entire being of its product, as the entire plant with all its
parts lies enveloped in the seed; and I could not possibly from the
later state gain elucidation to the same degree that my explanation
achieves in genetic terms."[42] During the years he spent in Königsberg,
1762-1764, Herder took notes from Kant's lectures, including a passage that clearly shows how the question of origin was designed to
separate the natural from the artificial. In a section on "Quellen der
Sittlichkeit," at this point in relation to Hutcheson's *Inquiry*, Herder
took this note: "In order to distinguish what is art from nature, we
must push toward the origin, just as we are accustomed to distinguish
traditional beliefs (proverbial sayings) from certainty. We would need
to study the consciousness of primitive tribes, and this is far better
than ours which is the product of art. Rousseau has examined it."[43]

The search for origins is thus an attempt to get down to basic principles, to what is by nature as opposed to what is by art. But this
method would make no sense without the unquestioning acceptance
of a particular doctrine that is one of the great commonplaces of the
eighteenth century: the doctrine of the uniformity of human nature
in all ages and climes. Again, there is hardly a major figure of that
century who has not given it direct statement, for instance David
Hume in his familiar statement that "mankind is so much the same,
in all times and places, that history informs us of nothing new and
particular." Similarly Du Marsais observed: "The different avenues
that different peoples have taken to express themselves are subject to
the two sovereign rules of uniformity and variety; there is uniformity
in the essential nature of thought, and variety in the avenue followed
and in the expression."[44] In Locke's words, "Men, I think, have been
much the same for natural endowments, in all times."[45] This doctrine
of uniformity had an important consequence, again shared by all the
men we are concerned with. Referring to his *Essay*, Locke wrote:
"All therefore that I can say of my book is, that it is a copy of my
own mind, in its several ways of operation. And all that I can say for
the publishing of it, is that I think the intellectual faculties are made,
and operate alike in most men."[46]

The doctrine of uniformity and its corollary in the universal relevance of self-examination are equally fundamental in Descartes and

Locke, but the use of the genetic method in philosophical inquiry was an example set by Locke and eagerly pursued in the eighteenth century with the full weight of his authority. This procedure was applied in the philosophy of mind and the understanding as well as in pedagogy and political philosophy. It should be recalled that knowledge of Locke had a much wider base in the eighteenth century than it has had since. In fact, today the most that can generally be assumed is a skimpy acquaintance with the *Essay*, even for people who pretend to know what it says. Many are still the victims of nineteenth-century conservative thought, to which denigration of Locke was a matter of doctrine. Many still use A. C. Fraser's edition of the *Essay*, now over seventy years old. Toward that edition there can only be one intelligent attitude: to consider it a curious piece of Victoriana. Both the text and the information about it are very unreliable, and the notes are outright laughable.[47] Being spared that monster, readers in the eighteenth century were much better off than many readers and scholars are today, whether they read the *Essay* in the original or in translation. But the eighteenth century also read the *Thoughts concerning Education* (12 printings in French and at least one German by 1747), which as we shall see had a significant influence on Du Marsais; and the *Two Treatises of Government* (five printings in French by 1755, one German in 1718). Locke was much more than the *Essay*, and something quite different from the sort of empiricist he has later—much later—been made out to have been. In our terms Locke was, like Descartes, a rationalist, a matter to which I shall return.

It is too obvious to require demonstration that the *Essay* exhibited the genetic approach and that Locke is chiefly responsible for its popularity during the eighteenth century. There is so to speak, in Locke's own words, "a progress of the mind" both in the individual and in mankind at large. This progress is suggested in a variety of ways, but especially by the consideration of children and languages. In Book II of the *Essay*, for instance, we find a number of suggestive observations. Locke says he "is apt to think [words] may very much" direct "our thoughts towards the originals of men's *ideas*," while in another passage he remarks, "that mankind have fitted their notions and words to the use of common life and not to the truth and extent of things. . . . This, by the way, may give us some light into the different state and growth of languages."[48]

But Locke himself had not pursued the origin of language. In the *Second Treatise of Government*, however, he had used the postulate of a hypothetical or conjectural state of nature for the purpose of identifying the basic rules of moral and political obligation. This procedure aimed at reaching back beyond the artificial accretions—the customs, laws and rules of government—of particular societies as they had been known in history. The conception of this conjectural state was of course supported by much relevant knowledge, drawn from all periods and places in history, but especially from travel accounts of distant and presumably more primitive and certainly different societies. This sort of information corresponded, so to speak, to the experimental knowledge which the scientists could produce in the laboratory, where nature could easily be separated from art to reveal its uniform natural laws.[49] Similarly, the philosophical question of the origin of language as first formulated by Condillac sought to establish man's linguistic state of nature in order to gain insight into the nature of man, indeed into the unique nature of man. Consequently, in addition to the method, the political philosophy of Locke and Condillac's origin of language have much in common, most strikingly perhaps a common interest in what has rightly been called comparative anthropology, nourished by travel literature. Owing to this similarity between the uses of the state of nature in political and in linguistic philosophy, they have also frequently been misunderstood in similar ways.

The state of nature itself was hypothetical construct, a model it might perhaps be called today, and the charge often brought later that Locke fooled himself about history is entirely beside the point. Neither Locke nor the eighteenth century made any such mistake. In *Inégalité*, for instance, speaking of the state of nature, Rousseau said: "The researches we may enter into on this subject must not be taken as historical truths, but merely as hypothetical and conditional reasonings, designed more properly to throw light on the nature of things rather than showing their actual origin, like the reasonings our physicists engage in all the time on the formation of the world." He wanted to be sure this point was not misunderstood. A few pages earlier, in the Preface, he had observed: "I have hazarded some conjectures, not so much in the hope of solving the problem as with the intention of elucidating it and reducing it to its proper form. . . . For it is not a light undertaking to separate what is original from what is artificial in the actual nature of man, and to gain a good understanding of a state that no longer exists, perhaps never existed, probably never will exist, and concerning which it is all the same necessary to have well-founded ideas in order to form a proper judgment about our present state."[50] This is the capital point: the search for origins concerned the present state of man, not the establishment of some "historical" fact or "explanation" of how things actually were at some point in the past.

The nineteenth century was so saturated with a factual historical view that it could not see the attempt to deal with origins in any other light, thus failing utterly to comprehend what the previous century had been up to. Renan's critique is typical, clearly demonstrating this failure of understanding. Referring to Condillac, Maupertuis, and Rousseau on the origin of language, Renan observed: "They considered man with the present mechanism of his faculties, surreptitiously displacing this mechanism into the past, ignoring the profound differences that must exist between the first ages of mankind and the present state of his consciousness."[51] It was in fact precisely this difference between early man and modern man that the eighteenth-century philosophers were interested in, and they took it to be the result of a process of development or progress that had occurred owing to man's artificial accomplishments, which in turn had their source in man's nature, in his innate mental make-up. By rejecting the uniformity of human nature, Renan lost the distinction between natural and artificial man; consequently the eighteenth century could no longer be understood. More than that, it became, in so far as this view was involved, an object of contempt.

Locke's political philosophy and Condillac's origin of language share another significant agreement. In both cases the method rules out that divine origin can be admitted, even though one may on other grounds accept it. In the *First Treatise of Government* Locke had rejected the argument that the grounds of political authority could be derived from the lordship of Adam and his descendants; he had also insisted on Adam's ordinary humanity, as it has been called. Condillac, at the very beginning of his section on the origin and progress of language in the *Essai*, had rejected the relevance of the story of Adam and Eve, for when they came from the hand of God, they were, "by extraordinary assistance placed in the state of reflecting and communicating their thoughts." It was not, he said, sufficient for "a philosopher to say that something has been accomplished by extraordinary means." It was his duty to explain "how it could have been accomplished by natural means."[52] Similarly, Rousseau observes with regard to his hypothetical state of nature that religion tells another story, but religion "does not forbid us to form conjectures based solely on the nature of man and the beings around him, on what mankind could have become if it had been left to itself."[53] Herder was of the same opinion. In the early "Versuch einer Geschichte der lyrischen Dichtkunst" already cited, he devoted several pages to the task of showing the uselessness of referring to divine origin, for it fails to explain anything: "And what is the use of this hypothesis: poetry has a divine origin; it still demands its own explanation. It explains nothing, for all it says is: I see effects that I cannot derive from natural causes: so they come from God—a charitable conclusion that suspends all further investigation. . . . Ignorance, fear, superstition, three sisters that rule so many ages and nations, have as we know more than once drawn a cloud over many things in nature whose causes we can now explain without wonder or magic. In these matters a philosopher must be as impatient as Shandy was with his brother Tobias when the former would make trial and the latter with raised hands and enraptured eyes cried to him, 'Brother, it comes from God.' 'Brother Tobias,' he exclaimed, 'you are cutting the knot without philosophy.'"[54] The method is conjectural, the postulate of divine origin can have no relevance. Its acceptance would of course also have meant that man's career would not be a record of progress, but a sorry story of decay and corruption, a doctrine which early in the next century was in fact advocated by the two conservative and anti-Lockian writers Joseph de Maistre and Louis de Bonald, who both had a considerable influence on anti-Lockian English thought in the nineteenth century.[55]

ORIGIN OF LANGUAGE

With these considerations in mind, it will, I hope, be obvious that the question of the origin of language did not aim at historical and factual explanation of states of language in the past. It was as hypothetical as the state of nature in political philosophy, and like the latter, its aim was to understand man in the present. But among all the accomplishments of man that might be inquired into, language was the most important because it was admitted that man could have achieved very little without signs and language. In Condillac's words: "The progress of the human mind depends entirely on the proficiency we demonstrate in the use of language."[56] To inquire into the origin of language is therefore the same as inquiring into man's understanding and knowledge. It may be a bit crude, but still have truth and brevity, to say that Condillac transformed Locke's theory of knowledge, his inquiry into "the original, certainty, and extent of human knowledge" as Locke called it at the beginning of Book I of the *Essay*, into a theory of the origin of language just as Locke had turned political philosophy into a question about the state of nature. Condillac's gestures and "les cris naturels" form the only "language" that is natural to man; it is the immediate expression of the passions. This "language," therefore, is not the specifically human language and speech that form the aim of Condillac's inquiry, but thanks to man's unique possession of reason this gestural language suggests the utility of signs and the possibility of developing artificial, voluntary signs. Of these natural signs, Condillac said: "Little by little the use of signs extends the operations of mind, and these in turn, being exercised more, perfect the signs and make their use more familiar. Experience proves that these two factors lend mutual aid to each other."[57] This passage indicates why the origin of language has a crucial function in Condillac's account of the origins of the human understanding. Without language and signs, man's innate capacity for reflection, his reason, could not have shown itself and developed. The connection between the first part of the *Essai* ("Des matériaux de nos connoissances et particulièrement des opérations de l'âme") and the second ("Du language et de la méthode") is indicated by this sentence: "It seems that we would not know how to use signs of institution if we were not already capable of sufficient reflection to choose them and to attach ideas to them. How then, someone will perhaps object, can the exercise of reflection be acquired only by the use of signs? I answer that I shall meet that difficulty when I give the history of language."[58]

Thus the question of the origin of language is a question about the nature of language and the nature of thought, a means therefore of gaining knowledge of the progress of mind and the history of thought. Without the linearity of speech, no progress could have occurred. In Condillac's words: "If a thought has no succession in the mind, it does have succession in discourse, where it is decomposed into as many parts as the ideas it contains. As this happens we can observe what we do in thinking, we can render account of it to ourselves; we can consequently learn to conduct our reflection. Thinking becomes an art, and it is the art of speaking," a view in which Condillac entirely agrees with the Port-Royal Grammar, whose subtitle was "l'art de parler," just as its companion piece, the Port-Royal Logic, had the subtitle "l'art de penser."[59] All participants in the debate accepted the principles expressed in Monboddo's two statements that "it appears, that, from the study of language, if it be properly conducted, the history of the human mind is best learned," and that he "could not give the philosophical account I proposed, of the origin of language, without inquiring into the origin of ideas."[60] The origin of language and universal grammar agreed that language cannot be seriously studied without reference to mind.

The function of Condillac's treatment of the origin of language in his argument about the human understanding clearly shows that the question of the origin of language had serious epistemological implications. Maupertuis's *Réflexions* opened with this statement: "The signs by which men have designated their first ideas have so much

influence on all our knowledge that I believe that researches into the
origin of languages and on the manner in which they have been
formed, deserve as much attention and can be as useful in the study
of philosophy as other methods that build systems on words with
meanings that have not been thoroughly examined."[61] When pressed
by a critic that he had in fact not said much about the origin of language, Maupertuis answered: "The composition and decomposition
of the signs of our perceptions and their relations to the perceptions
themselves constitute nearly all our knowledge and make it function
at their pleasure. It is with the aim of estimating the value of this
knowledge that I am treating this problem in mechanics and not at
all, as Mr. Boindin thinks, in order to explain the mechanics of the
languages themselves."[62] Another good example of this epistemological concern is Diderot's *Lettre sur les sourds et muets*, which takes
up the origin of language in connection with the problem of inversion. Franco Venturi has rightly stressed this aspect of the origin-of-
language problem. The subject of that *Lettre* is, in Venturi's words,
"problems that are in a particular sense esthetic and epistemological."[63]

UNIVERSAL GRAMMAR AND ORIGIN OF LANGUAGE

Though historically related to different philosophical doctrines—
one Lockian and the other now popularly supposed to be Cartes-
ian- both origin of language and universal grammar saw language as
the distinguishing feature that set man apart from the animals and
both assumed that the study of language could give insight into mind
and the nature of man. Both saw language as the most striking proof
of man's creativity; the use of language was itself creative and in turn
the condition for all further creativity. Accepting the axiom of the
uniformity of human nature, both aimed first at understanding the
universal properties of language. They were, as Maupertuis warned
his readers, not interested in knowing why Londoners said "bread"
but Parisians "pain."[64] Today no one will deny that these are prominent qualities of universal grammar. We are all indebted to Chomsky
for restoring universal grammar to its rightful place of importance in
linguistic theory and history, for dismissing the ignorant, hostile, un-
comprehending, and incompetent accounts which were the run of
the mill not so long ago. Partisan history is no history.

But it would seem that these rationalist qualities are not granted
to the mid-eighteenth century concern with the origin and progress
of language. Yet, there cannot be any doubt that this concern exhib-
its those qualities as clearly as does universal grammar. Both modes
in the study of language were directed to the same subject matter

and aim; only their methods of approach were different. When Condillac during the 1760s prepared a grammar for the young Prince of Parma, he began with two chapters on the origin of language; necessarily so, he said, "for before undertaking the decomposition of a language, we must have some knowledge of the manner in which it has been formed."[65] Why so? Because "the history of the human mind showed me . . . the order I should myself follow in the instruction of the Prince," and because "the art of speaking is the art of thinking and the art of reasoning, which develop in the same measure as languages approach perfection."[66] These passages, incidentally, remind us of the very important—and I take it obvious—fact that both universal grammar and origin of language are closely allied to the theory of learning and the problem of the acquisition of language. Universal grammar and the origin of language became fused. What one did atemporally in terms of structure alone, the other did on the scale of time. It is no accident that the first great collected editions of Du Marsais and of Condillac appeared within one year of each other—in 1797 and 1798—during the Directory, and it was natural that Destutt de Tracy should remark a few years later on the greatness of the Port-Royal Grammar, but regret, "that they did not either in their grammar or in their logic enter into greater detail on the formation of our ideas."[67]

This view of the basic utility of forming conjectures on the origin and progress of language is already evident in Condillac's *Essai*, though he was later to become more explicit in this regard. It comes out in such statements as, "should not words stand in the same relation to ideas in all the sciences as do Arabic numerals to ideas in arithmetic?"[68] and "why is it that arithmeticians have such precise ideas? The reason is that, knowing how they are produced, the arithmeticians are always prepared to compose and decompose them so as to compare them in terms of their relations."[69] This conception did not mean that Condillac took the first speaking men to have been full-blown philosophers, for the first language was still intermixed with gestures and owed its origin to the passions: "It is to the poets that we owe the first and perhaps also the greatest obligations,"[70] a view that has often been denied to Condillac in favor of Herder.

One of the central concerns of universal grammar was the problem of inversion, which in current terms involves the matter of deep and surface structure, like the problem of ellipsis. This problem was equally important in origin of language. In the *Lettre sur les sourds et muets*, Diderot dealt with that question by considering it in the light of gestures. To discuss the matter of inversion, he said, "I believe that it is

relevant to investigate how languages were formed."[71] Similarly, the
Port-Royal Grammar had assumed that some word classes—such as
those of the noun and the verb—were primary in relation to other
classes, which were only abbreviations or convenient substitutes for
the former, as most of the pronouns were for nouns. These latter
classes had therefore been "invented" to fulfill those functions. The
origin of language converted this problem into the problem of which
came first and how the others were formed and introduced. This
intimate and happy alliance of universal grammar and origin of language is clearly stated in Turgot's article "Étymologie," first published
in volume six of the *Encyclopédie* in 1756. Referring to origin of language, he wrote: "It is easy to see how indispensable these prelimin-
aries are to comprehend at large and from the proper point of view
the general theory of speech and of the march of the human mind in
the formation and progress of language. . . . This theory is the
source that generates the rules of the universal grammar that governs
all languages, to which all nations submit in the belief of following
merely the whims of usage."[72]

In this fusion of universal grammar and the origin of language, Du
Marsais is a special and very instructive case. As a universal grammarian he has no rival except Claude Lancelot and Antoine Arnauld,
and Chomsky leaves no doubt about his importance. But Du Marsais
gained recognition only late in life when he was engaged to write articles on language and related philosophical subjects for the *Encyclopédie*. At the time of his death at eighty in 1756, he had completed a
large number of articles—both short and long—covering the beginning
of the alphabet through the entry "Grammairien." As early as 1749,
Condillac praised his *Des Tropes* (1730), regretting that Du Marsais
had not yet given the public a complete grammar.[73] Diderot also
often referred to Du Marsais with great respect.[74] But until the concluding years of his life, Du Marsais's work on universal grammar was
ignored, and he himself lived in poverty, moving from one insignificant post to another. His short "Exposition d'une méthode raisonnée
pour apprendre la langue latine," appeared in 1722; a brief Preface to
a larger work on "Les véritables principes de la grammaire, ou nouvelle grammaire raisonnée pour apprendre la langue latine" was published in 1729, but of the great work he had in mind only *Des Tropes*
appeared during his lifetime—and on that work he was complimented
by a well-wisher who thought it was a history of the tropical regions.[75]
The *Logique*, the essay on "Inversion," and the "Fragment sur les
causes de la parole" were not published until 1769, and still other
writings only in the *Oeuvres* of 1797.

In philosophy Du Marsais was strongly anti-Cartesian—he maintained, for instance, that animals are not automatons.[76] His work on universal grammar was closely tied to the practical job of teaching Latin by which he tried to make a living for the better part of his life. His method was this: He arranged the Latin phrases according to the "ordre naturel" and placed the corresponding French words underneath in interlinear translation. This method obviously involves the related problems of inversion and construction or syntax, two subjects on which Du Marsais gave special proof of his brilliance as a universal grammarian. On his authority for this method, he said: "I could cite many authorities, including that of Mr. Locke in his Treatise on the Education of children, in order to justify what I am saying here, that routine ought to precede rules; but in a manner that pertains to good sense and can be supported by experience, authorities are pointless."[77] Actually Locke had not advocated changing the Latin word order to make it more nearly follow the "ordre naturel," but he had implied the same principle by suggesting that the child should begin with "some easy and pleasant book" and that the English interlinear translation should be "made as literal as it can be." Instruction in formal grammar should be kept to a minimum until the pupil could, as Locke said, "read himself 'Sanctii Minerva,' with Scioppius and Perizonius's notes."[78] By using this method, Du Marsais similarly argued that the child would first gain a sufficient command of the new language by "routine"; only after instruction and learning by routine should the pupil turn to grammar. His mode of teaching was attacked by the Jesuit *Journal de Trévoux* in May of 1723 in a review of Du Marsais's "Exposition." The following year Du Marsais published an answer, defending his method and citing Locke at greater length. This defense included a list of "a large number of learned men of the first order," who had advocated the same method: "Scaliger, Sanctius, Vossius, Scioppius, M. le Fèvre de Saumur, le P. Lamy, Locke, M. l'abbé de Dangeau, and a large number of others."[79] Du Marsais enrolled Locke among the universal grammarians.

This is not the place to demonstrate in detail that Du Marsais followed Locke not only on this particular point, but in philosophy in general. But a few quotations will show that Du Marsais held basic views of mind, thought, and the understanding that are incompatible with the version of innateness which Professor Chomsky takes to be essential to the fundamental principles of universal grammar. In 1743 Du Marsais published a short piece on the chief virtues of the good philosopher. In this piece, "Le philosophe," he said among other things: "The philosopher is a machine like any other man; but it is a machine that, owing to its mechanical constitution, reflects on its motion." In the same piece he had this to say about the nature of thought: "Thought is one of man's senses, like seeing and hearing, like them dependent on an organic constitution."[80] In another short piece, "De la raison," first published in 1770, he said: "The only means of instruction we have are either our own experience or authority. Experience . . . is either exterior, which means that it provides us with ideas of sensible objects; or interior, which means that it provides us with ideas of the operations of the understanding; there is the common source of all knowledge; we cannot acquire ideas by any other means."[81] No Cartesian, in Chomsky's sense, could hold those views. In sum, Du Marsais was heavily indebted both to the Port-Royal Grammar and to Locke, and he was decidedly anti-Cartesian in philosophy on the very points that have in recent years been held most essential to the strength of universal grammar as a linguistic theory.

Far from being averse to each other, universal grammar and origin of language interpenetrated each other. This union apparently did not spoil universal grammar, for we are told by Chomsky that "the tradition of philosophical grammar . . . flourished from the seventeenth century through romanticism."[82] There is in fact strong evidence in favor of the argument that universal grammar as a philosophical and theoretical discipline, on the level of a Du Marsais, had fallen into desuetude during the first half of the eighteenth century, gaining fresh importance only after origin of language, thanks to Condillac, had created renewed interest in linguistic theory. After its initial publication in 1660, the Port-Royal Grammar was published in 1664, 1676, 1679, and 1709, but then not again till 1754 with the notes of Duclos. At that time the publishers said that it had long been unobtainable, which is what they always say when an old text has recently come into demand. In England, the Port-Royal Grammar did not appear in English until 1753, though there had been translations of Lamy's *Art of Speaking* in 1676, 1696, and 1708. Universal grammar was revived only after Condillac's *Essai*, precisely because the *Essai* had successfully raised important problems in the theory of language.

Of course, Du Marsais's own lack of success is the best demonstration that universal grammar had declined into merely practical and specific applications. It might perhaps be argued that the revival of universal grammar in 1754 was designed to counter origin of language as a linguistic theory, but the historical facts do not offer the slightest foundation for such an interpretation. Equally groundless would be the argument that what remained of value was exclusively the contribution of universal grammar. Chomsky admires Herder, F. Schlegel, A. W. Schlegel, Coleridge, and Wilhelm von Humboldt as exponents of certain doctrines and views which Chomsky derives from "Cartesian" linguistics, but which in fact derive from the tradition of linguistic theory that took shape around the origin of language problem. Indeed the references to Herder and to both the Schlegels occur in works that deal specifically with origin of language, in one case even with "etymology in general." Both of these are subjects which nowhere appear in "Cartesian" linguistics or universal grammar, which would in fact seem immune to time perspective.

LOCKE, CONDILLAC, AND PROFESSOR CHOMSKY

There is especially one basic confusion which has followed in the wake of Chomsky's pronouncements on the history of linguistics. It has come to be believed that it is a uniquely "Cartesian" doctrine that human language consists of arbitrary, voluntary signs and not of vocal gestures that are the mere expression of the passions. This doctrine is not only much older than Descartes, but fundamental in Locke and Condillac. Locke insists over and over again that the "signification of sounds is not natural, but only imposed and arbitrary," brought about by "a voluntary imposition whereby such a word is made arbitrarily the mark of such an idea."[83] In Condillac, the voluntary and arbitrary nature of the vocal sign in human language is even more prominent than in Locke, who had not systematically discussed origin of language. In the *Essai*, Condillac says that there are three kinds of signs, accidental, natural, and "les signes d'institution." Neither of the first two is "species-specific" to man since he shares them with the animals. Thus instituted signs alone effect the uniqueness of human language and speech. "But as soon as a human being begins to attach ideas to the signs he has himself chosen, we find his memory formed. . . . Here we begin to perceive the superiority of the human soul over that of animals. For, on the one hand, it is certain that it is not within their reach to attach their ideas to arbitrary signs; and on the other, it seems certain that this inability does not proceed entirely from the organisation. Is not their body as proper for the language of action as ours?"[84] Thus in Locke as well as in Condillac, "the force that generates language is indistinguishable from that which generates thought," to use Chomsky's own words, though he would presumably deny this view to Locke and does not find it in Condillac for the painful reason that Condillac is not once mentioned in any piece of writing by Chomsky that I have ever seen. The insistence on the creative aspect of language and speech among the Romantics—chiefly of course in Germany—derives from Condillac's *Essai*. Recalling Condillac's discussion of artistic creativity in the long section on the origin and progress of language, one wonders how it has been possible to miss this point—except of course owing to what in fact happened, both in the past and today: neglect of Condillac's *Essai*.[85]

As an expression of his own interpretation, Chomsky cites a passage from d'Alembert's "Éloge de Du Marsais," to the effect that his object of study was "the march of the human mind in the generation of its ideas."[86] In the literature of the time, this phrase is used over and over again to refer to origin of language, but never to universal grammar alone. In *Language and Mind*, Chomsky says that he has "been describing the problem of the acquisition of knowledge of language in terms that are more familiar in an epistemological than a psychological context, but I think that this is quite appropriate."[87] This statement also perfectly describes the enterprise of Condillac and his followers in their concern with origin of language.

It is true that Chomsky in *Cartesian Linguistics*[88] states that his chief concern is with the content and present-day significance of Cartesian doctrines, not with their transmission and the historical situation. But unfortunately, if one sets out to do part of the history, one does not escape the consequences of making a selection that ignores other contemporary work. These consequences mean not only historical distortion and error—which might be considered by some an academic matter of little relevance—but also the loss and neglect of other work which would seem to be relevant and deserve attention by the same criteria that are applied to universal grammar. Condillac and others are ignored, while features of later linguistic theory are assigned exclusively to the "Cartesian" tradition, when in fact, as we have seen, they have a different source.

I think it will be granted that all the writers in question—including the ones who figure in Chomsky's work—were neither unintelligent nor befuddled. Consequently we have no reason to assume that they carelessly or stupidly overlooked the sort of incompatibility between "Cartesian" and Lockian linguistics which Chomsky's argument certainly entails. I therefore see only one possibility, that there is something seriously wrong with Chomsky's facts and argument. We have before us a private myth which is already well on its way to becoming a public one. This distortion of the history of the study of language need not surprise us. That "history" has always, with few exceptions, been a succession of partisan stances, as in the standard nineteenth-century works on the subject as well as in the later denigration of universal grammar that was fashionable until recently. By Chomsky's own frequent admission, this situation is unfortunate, for he often deplores the virtual absense of reliable, precise, in-depth work on the history of the study of language. In these misunderstandings, the crucial figure is Locke, who receives very strange treatment from Chomsky, so strange in fact that it is hard to see what the point about him is, except that he is assigned the role of villain, or at best is made out to have been a fool or nincompoop in matters of linguistic theory. This matter deserves closer attention.

Both *Cartesian Linguistics* and *Language and Mind* make a number of statements about Locke's conception of innateness, but the reader will look in vain for as much as a single precise reference to Locke's text, or even for a correct report of what he says. *Language and Mind*, however, makes a reference to two notes by Fraser in his edition of the *Essay*, the edition I have mentioned above. In the text to which Chomsky appends this note, he says: "Locke's critique had little relevance to any familiar doctrine of the seventeenth century. The arguments that Locke gave were considered and dealt with in quite a satisfactory way in the earliest seventeenth-century discussions of innate ideas, for example those of Lord Herbert and Descartes, both of whom took for granted that the system of innate ideas and principles would not function unless appropriate stimulation took place. For this reason, Locke's arguments, none of which took cognizance of this condition, are without force [note 14]; for some reason, he avoided the issues that had been discussed in the preceding half-century."[89] In note 14, Chomsky says that "this observation is commonplace," and then proceeds to cite two notes in the Fraser edition as authority.[90] The observation may be commmplace because Fraser's edition, with its silly notes, has been so widely used. But this observation will not be found in informed works—including eighteenth-century works—that deal seriously with Locke and with what he said and meant. The remark that Locke on this point took no account of what had been said during the rest of the seventeenth century is astounding, so astounding that one must wonder how—and whether—it can be made by anyone who has read the *Essay* (even in Fraser's edition), and who has made an effort to acquaint himself with the best secondary literature, which though not necessary could have offered welcome aid.

A reading of the *Essay* itself is enough to show that Locke was not the sort of empiricist we have generally been told that he is, for instance in the "commonplace" observations of Fraser's notes. If there is a typical empiricist version of the philosophy of mind, it is surely that of Hume, who took the mind to be nothing but a train of ideas held together by association. This is a view that is totally foreign to Locke, and the very position of the association of ideas in the *Essay* is the best reminder of it. To Locke the association of ideas is a disturbing, non-constructive, uncontrollable feature of thought precisely because such association interferes with the normal exercise of reason, even to the point where it may subvert reason. Locke calls it "madness": "I shall be pardoned for calling it by so harsh a name as *madness*, when it is considered that opposition to reason deserves that name and is really madness."[91] If by rationalism is meant the doctrine that reason is the principal source of certain knowledge as well as of all ordered knowledge even when not certain in that sense, then Locke was surely a rationalist, in spite of all that we have been told to the contrary—chiefly by Victorian conservatives.

It might have seemed more germane to the entire question to have talked about rationalism but Chomsky for some reason generally prefers to talk instead about innateness, even about the "Cartesian postulation of a substance whose essence was thought."[92] On the matter of innateness the confusion is complete and so basic that it may not be worth further consideration until Chomsky abandons dependence on Fraser's notes as authority for what are commonplace views of Locke's philosophy. The confusion is complete because the doctrines of innateness which Chomsky attributes to both Descartes and to Locke are doctrines which neither of them held. *Cartesian Linguistics* quotes a long passage from Descartes' "Notes directed against a certain Programme" in support of the interpretation of Descartes' conception of innateness which that book presents. But Chomsky does not cite the passage which immediately precedes it. This is a long passage, but it will be necessary to quote it in its entirety: "*In article twelve* he [Regius who had criticized Descartes on innateness] appears to dissent from me only in words, for when he says that *the mind has no need of innate ideas, or notions, or axioms,* and at the same time allows it the faculty of thinking (to be considered natural or innate), he makes an affirmation in effect identical with mine, but denies it in words. For I never wrote nor concluded that the mind required innate ideas which were in some sort different from its faculty of thinking; but when I observed the existence in me of certain thoughts which proceeded, not from extraneous objects nor from the determination of my will, but solely from the faculty of thinking which is within me, then, that I might distinguish the ideas or notions (which are the forms of these thoughts) from other thoughts *adventitious* or *factitious,* I termed the former '*innate*.' In the same sense we say that in some families generosity is innate, in others certain diseases like gout or gravel, not that on this account the babes of these families suffer from these diseases in their mother's womb, but because they are born with a certain disposition or propensity for contracting them."[93] In other words, what is produced by the "faculty of thinking" (*facultas cogitandi*) is what Descartes calls innate. This agrees with Locke, who uses the terms reason, reflection, that powerful faculty, and similar terms, and who derives all knowledge from the light of nature, from the "faculties [man] is endowed with by nature." To Locke these innate faculties were reason and the capacity for sense experience—sensation or sense-perception to Locke being much more than a picture in the back of the eye or something automatic for which a passive mind would suffice.[94]

Locke's agreement with Descartes on this point will be clear to anyone who has read the *Essay*, but it also emerges from certain notes, which Locke wrote in response to a critique of his conception of innateness: "Of those who say there are innate laws or rules of right and wrong, 'tis reasonable to demand a list of them, & he that cannot produce what he soe tells of 'tis plain folly." And: "If moral Ideas or moral rules (which are the moral principles I deny to be innate) are innate, I say children must know them as well as men. If by moral principles you mean a faculty to finde out in time the moral difference of actions . . . this is an improper way of speaking to cal a power principles; I never deny'd a power to be innate, but that which I deny'd was that any Ideas or connection of Ideas was innate."[95] It is surprising that it could have been missed that Locke and Descartes do not use the term innate in the same manner, and that owing to this difference, it is possible for them to have the same conception of what is in fact natural and innate to the mind. Locke will not allow the term to be used of any idea or notion or principle unless it is already full-blown, actual, and known to the child from the mother's womb. In the long passage I have cited, Descartes made the same point, though having stated that qualification, he did allow himself the use of the term innate.

Writing to Locke in 1704, his intelligent friend Anthony Collins observed: "There can be nothing advanced contradictory to the design of the *Essay of Human Und.* but on the Principle of Innate Ideas, in that sense they are refuted by the Author in the *1st* book."[96] In the *Essay* Locke took up Lord Herbert of Cherbury's *De Veritate* on innateness. Lord Herbert had listed five innate principles "imprinted on the minds of men by the hand of God." Locke lists them and then observes: "Though I allow these to be clear truths and such as if rightly explained, a rational creature can hardly avoid giving his assent to, yet I think he is far from proving them innate impressions *in foro interiori descriptae*."[97] To Locke self-evident propositions, for instance, are innate in Descartes' sense. To Locke all men are by nature rational and God "commands what reason does." When the *Essay* first came out, some quite intelligent men took it to be a metaphysical treatise in the Cartesian manner. It may also, owing to many misrepresentations on this point, be recalled that Leibniz did not say that the *Essay* offered the philosophy expressed in the familiar words "nihil est in intellectu quod non fuerit in sensu." Leibniz cited the whole statement, concluding "excipe: nisi ipse intellectus." This, Leibniz said, "agrees well enough with the author of the Essay, who seeks the source of a good part of our ideas in the reflection of the mind on its own nature."[98] It may also be recalled that Locke had great sympathy for the Jansenists and their philosophy, which of course is the philosophy characteristic of the Port-Royal and preeminently of Antoine Arnauld. During his years in France, Locke translated some of the essays in Pierre Nicole's *Essais de morale*, which would appear to have had a decisive influence on his political philosophy. Nicole was, except for the last years, a close associate of Arnauld, with whom he collaborated on the *Logique ou l'art de penser*.

If Locke had a single passionate thought that informed his entire life and work, it was toleration and the belief that men could live in Peace. Innateness as commonly used was inimical to this belief, and Locke's philosophy was immediately in conservative, orthodox, and bigoted circles taken to be dangerous heresy. If the inhabitants of South America, for instance, did not share the moral rules and religious beliefs which their Spanish conquerors took to be a necessary and innate part of the make-up of decent men, then they were treated accordingly, as animals rather than as men. In the eighteenth century Professor Chomsky's innateness did not have a single philosophically respectable defender. To Locke it was in the interest of toleration and peace to postulate that all men could learn or come to assent to what had been revealed by the light of nature. But it was intolerable and had violent and inhuman consequences to claim that there are certain rules they must know. At the end of Book I, "Of Innate Notions," Locke said: "Nor is it a small power it gives one man over another to have the authority to be the dictator of principles and teacher of unquestionable truths, and to make a man swallow that for an innate principle which may serve to his purpose who teacheth them." These principles or "universal truths" were "discovered by the application of those faculties that were fitted by nature to receive and judge them, when duly employed about them."[99] Claims to truth must be argued on public, not on private and esoteric, grounds.

Chomsky's version of Locke's philosophy—in so far as it is possible (and fair) to judge on the slender evidence we are offered—is plainly false. The consequence of that error is historical chaos.[100]

II. The Debate in the Berlin Academy

Arens has observed that universal grammar was the dominant French concern in the mid-eighteenth century, while origin of language received only slight attention. But in Germany, he says, the emphasis lay on origin of language since universal grammar made a late appearance in Germany. We are further told that German work on the study of language in this period was, by contrast to French work, informed by a strong anthropological view.[101] I hope I have shown that the historical facts do not offer the slightest support to Arens's thesis; it is a conventional myth. The problem of the origin of language is brought to Germany from France only a few years after the publication of Condillac's *Essai* in 1746, by the president of the newly reconstituted Berlin Academy, Pierre-Louis Moreau de Maupertuis (1698-1759).

On his arrival in Berlin, Maupertuis had found German metaphysics "une étrange science," which he took to be the fault of the Germans rather than of metaphysics. With a true sense of the moment, he introduced his new audience to the question of the origin of language and its attendant philosophical problems. Outside the Academy the climate was very favorable indeed. Within it, Maupertuis raised a debate that was to lead directly to the prize topic which Herder answered in his *Ursprung*.

The Debaters and Their Writings

I shall now, in chronological order, take up the communications on the philosophy, nature, and origin of language which belong to the Academy debate before Herder. For each item, I shall provide an exposition of its main argument and a brief discussion, but space does not permit detailed observations. On the whole, I shall assume that the reader will draw his own conclusions on the basis of the material I have presented in the first part of this paper.

MAUPERTUIS AND THE REVIVAL OF THE ACADEMY

When Frederick the Great became King of Prussia in 1740, he soon made plans to put new life into the Berlin Academy. Though founded by Leibniz in 1700 with great expectations and ambitious plans, it had declined into narrow provincialism, and it had quite failed to gain any stature among the learned societies of Europe. The King reorganized the Academy, himself wrote its new statutes, and invited Maupertuis—then a French scientist of acknowledged international standing and a member of both the Académie des Sciences in Paris and of the Royal Society in London—to become its first president. Maupertuis assumed the presidency in May of 1746, and he officially remained in that post until his death in the house of Johann Bernoulli at Basel on 27 July 1759. During most of his years in Berlin, he was plagued by the disease from which he died, consumption, as well as by the unpleasant and bitter controversy with Voltaire, who by his greater prestige and by merely being read, has put Maupertuis's reputation under a cloud ever since. Still, in terms of work and influence, these were fruitful years for Maupertuis and for the Academy, which prospered under his guidance and under the benevolent patronage of the King.

The statutes of the Académie Royale des Sciences et Belles-Lettres, to use its official name, were unique in one respect; they made provision for all branches of knowledge, for the sciences as well as for the humanities. In addition to the two classes of natural science and mathematics (which in London and Paris were the subjects of the Royal Society and of the Académie des Sciences), the Berlin Academy had a third class for "philosophie spéculative" and a fourth for "belles-lettres." It was expressly stated that the new society should include the subjects which in London and Paris were covered by the scientific societies as well as the subjects which in Paris were the province of the Académie des Inscriptions et Belles-Lettres. This organization did not come about without controversy and discussion, but the solution brought the Academy into line with Leibniz's organization of the first Berlin Academy. It was determined that the third class, "the class of speculative philosophy shall treat logic, metaphysics and ethics," while the fourth, "the class of belles-lettres shall comprise antiquities, history and languages."[102] It is significant that both prize-topics and all the communications on language dealt with here, except two, belong to the third class, that is, to philosophy rather than to what we would call literature and philology. It was further stipulated that any member could make communications outside his own class and that the weekly Thursday-night meetings should be plenary sessions, that is, not be divided according to class, and that each should in turn be devoted to one of the four subject classes. The importance and uniqueness of this arrangement are obvious. Without it Maupertuis, for instance, would have had no opportunity to speak to his fellow members on the philosophy of language. Writing late in 1747, Maupertuis expressed reservations about the inclusion of metaphysics, but at the same time affirmed his determination to make the best of it, "if I had laid down the organisation of the Academy, perhaps I would not have had the courage to introduce such a class; but since I found it there, I am happy that it is there, and I can only hope that it will make a good figure in the world." The remaining years of his life were chiefly devoted to "philosophie spéculative," which he wished to raise to a higher and international level, above the German provincialism he had found on his arrival.[103]

For obvious reasons, the official language was French, but papers in German and Latin were permitted, and regular provision was made for their translation into French. It should be emphasized that Maupertuis's contemporaries in Berlin considered him to have a deeply religious and spiritual outlook. "M. de Maupertuis," said Formey, "was a very religious man." Formey also believed that Maupertuis's two papers on the origin of language were not only the best of their kind but also the best of all his writings.[104] Maupertuis was inordinately fond of animals (birds, dogs, deer, and monkeys), kept a whole menagerie around him in his living quarters, and made great efforts to interbreed them in the most unlikely combinations. Maupertuis made extended visits to France and Paris during the summer of 1746, and from the spring of 1753 until the summer of 1754. He again left for France in June of 1756 and never returned to Berlin. It is significant information that Maupertuis, during his second visit to Paris, "took great pleasure in the conversation of Condillac and took great interest in the undertaking of the Encyclopédie, of which the first volumes had then recently appeared."[105]

MAUPERTUIS, *REFLEXIONS* (1748)

In the late 1740s Maupertuis wrote his *Réflexions sur l'origine des langues et la signification des mots*,[106] which was first published at Paris in 1748 in a dozen copies in order to see what reception it would get. Since the problems it takes up are so clearly linked to those of Condillac's *Essai* of 1746, there would seem to be little doubt that the *Réflexions* was suggested by the *Essai*. In fact, they offer a critique and conclusions very similar to the Berkeleian consequences which Diderot had also found in the *Essai*. Maupertuis had been in Paris during the summer of 1746, and we are told that he meditated on the interrelations of material existence and thought during the winter of 1746-1747.[107]

Maupertuis's essay illustrates how conjectures on the origin of language are put in the service of epistemology. His problem is this: Accepting the uniformity of human nature and the identical workings in all of perception and reason, that is the light of nature, all men will also have the same experience of nature (vii); their perceptions will be the same and thus also their knowledge of the structure of reality. But men's knowledge is in fact not based directly on these common perceptions; men have of necessity become creatures of language, and their knowledge is about signs which owe their origin "to simple and rude human beings who at first formed only the few signs they needed to express their ideas" (iv). Men have fixed their attention on and given signs to widely differing parts of the original perceptions. Hence translation among distant languages is virtually impossible, and signs have no strict philosophical validity in regard to reality—an idea also found in Bacon, Robert Boyle, and clearly in Locke. We are barely born before we hear an infinity of words which express rather the prejudices of our speech community than the first ideas of our minds: "We retain these words, we attach confused ideas to them; and voilà, we soon have provision for the rest of our lives, most often without being advised to probe into the true value of these words and the certainty of knowledge they can give us, or make us believe that they possess" (iii).

These considerations underlie the opening statement (already cited above) of the *Réflexions*: "The signs by which men have designated their first ideas have so much influence on all our knowledge that I believe that researches into the origin of languages and on the manner in which they have been formed, deserve as much attention and can be as useful in the study of philosophy as other methods that build systems on words with meanings that have not been thoroughly examined." We may therefore expect to learn a great deal from the comparison of distant languages, "because in the construction of languages we can discover the vestiges of the first steps taken by the human mind." Comparison of contiguous and related languages—such as English and French—will not offer insight, for "the expressions of ideas are there segmented in the same manner, and consequently the comparison of these languages with one another cannot teach us anything" (ii). Consequently, speakers of such languages "have followed pretty much the same path, and the branches of knowledge have taken nearly the same turn" (v). In these observations Maupertuis reveals the characteristic eighteenth-century interest in comparative anthropology and in the relativity of men's achievements, a theme also prominent in Locke. Maupertuis's concern was not entirely theoretical, however, for during his scientific expedition to Lapland in 1736 to measure the flatness of the earth toward the pole, which had been predicted by Newton, he had not failed to pay attention to the Lapp language.

But in his approach to the problem, Maupertuis actually takes another course, for two reasons. No language is really primitive enough to give us the information we need, and, second, the only substitute Maupertuis can think of also has nothing to offer. He admits that he has no memory whatsoever of his own first ideas, of what happened when he first opened his eyes and formed his first conclusions "at the age when my mind, with fewer ideas, would have been easier for me to recognize than it is today because it was, so to speak, more itself" (vi). He finds only one remedy, to imagine that, having totally lost all memory of all his previous perceptions and of all the judgments of reason he has made, he suddenly again confronts the world with the light of nature alone at his disposal. He will then, as also postulated by Condillac, have the sort of single, unanalyzed, simultaneous perception or thought which we can only express by a collection of words such as "I see a tree" (vii). He would have other perceptions and ideas, for instance "I see a horse." These would all have single expressions—A, B, etc.—so long as they had the form "I see" plus object. But the large number of single perceptions and their signs would soon become unmanageable, forcing man to have recourse "to another language" (viii). The two examples above would become CD and CE, and similarly "I see two lions" and "I see two ravens" would become decomposed into CGH and CIK. Again, H for "lions" and K for "corbeaux" will no longer do if we want to describe those animals, "for to analyze these aspects of perceptions, another subdivision of signs would be necessary" (x). Further , new signs will be needed for the use of other senses, as in "I hear sounds, I sense flowers." Thus our knowledge soon ceases to be about our immediate perceptions. Language and words take over, and hence also the possibility of error. The very nature of our knowledge becomes determined by language, which it alone makes possible. What we call our sciences depend so intimately on the manner in which we have designated our perceptions, "that it seems to me that the questions and propositions would have been altogether different if other expressions had been created for the first perceptions" (xii).

Man has now, for better or worse, become a creature of language, and he finds himself in a dilemma. If human memory had been sufficient to the task of remembering all its single perceptions, we would never have fallen into the perplexities which are caused by language.

As a remedy for our shortness of memory, we achieve economy by means of decomposition. The consequences have been momentous, "it seems to me that none of the questions that perplex us so much today would ever have entered our minds" (xiii). As soon as we began to analyze and give signs to different parts of our perceptions, "we have misconceived our task: we have taken each of the parts of the expressions for things; we have combined the things among themselves, in order to discover in them the relations of agreement and opposition, and in this fashion was born what we call our sciences" (xiii). Thus the result: "One can say that memory is opposed to judgment," or as he expressed it more carefully in the answer to Boindin, "This construction of languages is the cause of our errors and the origin of so many difficulties that we find insoluble. . . . What we have done to relieve memory has thrown the judgment into error."[108] It would appear that the alternative to error is piecemeal, scattered, unmanageable knowledge and the impossibility of science. The danger becomes evident when we consider the traditional concepts of substance and mode.

The substance of a tree is said to inhere in its extension, not in its greenness, but "that derives from the fact that in the established language we have agreed to call *tree* whatever has a certain figure independently of its greenness" (xvi). It is not obvious that we—or the first speaker—might not have fixed on the greenness and made it as inseparable from the concept of tree as we now consider its extension to be. If men of the same country who have long reasoned together have difficulty agreeing on their ideas, what can we imagine if we gained contact with a distant and to us entirely unfamiliar nation whose first ancestors had built their language on different principles? We could not possibly understand each other. The different quality of their philosophy and knowledge would not, however, derive from a difference in their first perceptions, "but I believe that it would derive from the language to which each nation is accustomed, from this fixing of signs on different parts of perceptions: a fixing that includes much that is arbitrary and which the first human beings have been able to do in several different ways; but which once done in this or that manner, invariably causes this or that propostion and has a lasting influence on all our knowledge" (xix).

So far, it is clear that Maupertuis has offered a critique of the argument of Condillac's *Essai*, which had not explored the errors that are consequent upon words. We have seen that Diderot's remark on the Berkeleian consequences of the *Essai* had made Condillac somewhat advance the fund of knowledge which man could gain in his prelinguistic state. This revision occurred in the *Traité des sensations* with the device of the statue; but it is tempting to assume that Maupertuis's observations may have given additional force to Diderot's remarks.[109]

In the concluding pages of the *Réflexions*, Maupertuis explores the problem in a somewhat different manner which clearly shows the influence of Berkeley. A man may not only have the perception that is expressed in the words "I see a tree," but also "I think of a tree" . . . "I dream of a tree," "I have dreamt of a tree," which together strengthen the conviction of the reality of the tree's independent existence, thus producing the perception "I have seen a tree," joined with the circumstances of place, having seen the same tree before, having returned and seen it again, etc. He will arrive at "I have seen a tree," in other words he will gain conviction that the tree does in fact have existence apart from perception, or as Maupertuis says: "This last perception transmits its reality onto the object, so to speak, and forms a proposition on the existence of the tree as being independent of the self" (xxi-xxv). But we may also say "there are sounds," though we know very well that what is 'out there' are only vibrations not at all like what we hear and call sounds. Our tree may be in the same situation, "neither this image nor the tree resembles my perception" (xxvi), and even the sense of touch will not convince him otherwise. He concludes with the admission, "there is a cause on which all our perceptions depend, *for nothing is what it is without reason*. But what is this cause? I cannot penetrate to it, for nothing in me resembles it. Let us stay within the bounds that have been prescribed for our intelligence" (xxviii).[110]

The *Réflexions* was not published for a wider public until 1752, when it was included in the first volume of Maupertuis's *Oeuvres*, published at Dresden. In the meantime it had been seen by the Parisian man of letters Nicolas Boindin, who wrote some brief critical remarks on it, suggesting that its entire thesis might have dangerous consequences to religious belief. The final words of his critique were: "Thus, though this work would not at first sight seem to invite criticism, it is nonetheless certain that one could draw very dangerous conclusions." These remarks were first published in Boindin's *Oeuvres* in 1753, two years after his death, and Maupertuis found them so important that he in turn wrote an answer, first printed in 1756.[111] Boindin was the most notorious and unregenerate atheist of his day, and the only member of the Académie des Inscriptions et Belles-Lettres never to have been the subject of an official eulogy, facts which suggest that Boindin's real intent was to embarrass Maupertuis—or whomever he took to be the anonymous writer—in order to promote his own atheism.[112] In any event, in his answer Maupertuis reiterated his position that his analysis of the origin of language not only explained "the existence of material being, but that it annihilates any distinction that one would make of the two modes of existence, one in the mind, and the other outside." Maupertuis compared himself to Berkeley, who had attacked the system of our errors only by toppling its pinnacles, while Maupertuis, as he says of himself, "we undermine it at the foundations: an edifice very different from the famous tower of which the confusion of languages prevented the building in the plains of Senar, this one having been built exclusively by the abuse or forgetting of the signification of words."[113]

The *Réflexions* was not read in the Academy, but it could have been known there after the Dresden edition of 1752. In addition, Maupertuis's interest in language also found expression in other ways. In a very well-attended public assembly on 18 June 1750, he spoke on "Les Devoirs de l'académicien," concluding with remarks on the desirability of exploring the possibility of framing a universal language of learning, "a language more regular than all our languages, which have only been formed little by little; easier and that can be understood by all," a subject which had occupied Leibniz and which, as we shall see, continued to occupy the Berlin Academy, in fact as late as the first decades of the nineteenth century.[114] A few years later, in the *Lettre sur le progrès des sciences* (1752), he reported that travelers to the Pacific Islands had there seen "savages, hairy and with tails, a species midway between monkeys and us. I would rather have an hour's conversation with them than with the most refined mind of Europe."[115] He also observed that the Patagonians ought to be better known, not so much for their large stature but rather because "their ideas, their knowledge, their history would be still another matter of interest."[116] In the same work in a section entitled "Expériences métaphysiques," Maupertuis remarked on language and the original knowledge of men and on their interdependence. He then suggests that one could raise several groups of children in isolation to find out whether, for instance, the differences among languages that are now so obvious, were introduced by the fathers of separate families on a common original language, or whether the different modes of expression were different from the very beginning. "This experiment would not merely instruct us on the origin of languages; it could tell us many other things on the origin of ideas themselves and on the fundamental notions of the human mind." The philosophers have talked long enough on this subject without giving an answer; perhaps the natural philosophers will provide the answer, "they would at least give us their knowledge without distortion."[117] This sort of experiment was again, as we shall see, to be mentioned in the Berlin Academy.

BEAUSOBRE (1755)

On 18 September 1755, Louis Isaac de Beausobre read a paper called "Reflections on the changes of living languages with reference to orthography and pronunciation," a subject he pursued in three additional papers delivered over the next three years.[118] This is a rather conventional and unexciting piece. The most perfect language can be found only among the dead languages, and Beausobre prefers Latin. We should aim to prevent those changes which it is within our power to control and find suitable restraining remedies for the rest. Orthography is obviously a great stabilizer, and we ought rather to let pronunciation follow spelling than change spelling to conform to our speech, as had been advocated by Duclos in the notes to his edition of the Port-Royal Grammar (1754). Our alphabet does not in any event have enough letters to record the number of distinct spoken sounds—a point Herder was later, in the *Ursprung*, to bring against Süssmilch. Etymology is a great aid to memory and should not lightly be allowed to disappear from view—"it is a torch that lights a dark path for us, thus sparing us the pains of remembering the turns and windings," an old argument about the mnemonic utility of etymology. It also has another familiar importance: "Everything is precious that can help us to understand the progress of the human mind."

Beausobre's essay contains no interesting philosophical observations, no profound critical insights, but it compares well with many other similar pieces written during these years, whether in Germany, in France, or in England. It also offered a certain amount of information that could be useful and suggestive to others. This essay would appear to be indebted to Diderot's famous article "Encyclopédie," which had appeared in volume five (1755) of the *Encyclopédie*. Oddly, it also shows some affinity with Turgot's article on "Etymologie," which was published in volume six the following year. As a remedy against the changes that occur in living languages, Diderot had advocated referring the roots of a modern changing language to those of a dead one—either Latin or Greek—which is fixed and does not change. He also was much concerned about the growing difference between spelling and pronunciation, advocating the creation of a phonetic alphabet, "a systematic alphabet in which the same sign does not represent different sounds or different signs." Diderot considered it essential to transmit our present pronunciation to posterity. It was his concern to ensure that the *Encyclopédie* would not be rendered obsolete by becoming linguistically inaccessible to later generations.[119]

MAUPERTUIS, "DISSERTATION" (1756)

On 13 May 1756, Maupertuis read a paper with the title, "Dissertation on the different means employed by men to express their ideas."[120]

This piece lacks the philosophical depth of the earlier *Réflexions*. It is rather a collection of astute observations on several subjects. Its opening is reminiscent of Condillac, which is perhaps no accident when we recall that Maupertuis a few years earlier had met Condillac in Paris. We can, Maupertuis says, imagine a variety of means of communication—"des cris naturels," gestures, musical notation, etc.—but no such language has been known both to arise and to be maintained naturally. The choice has for a number of reasons fallen on speech. The number of words in a given language is proportioned to the number of ideas, hence among "the most spiritual nations," we find more words and finer distinctions than among "the most rude," who would have only just enough to get along, and in some cases perhaps not even that. In the course of time it was observed that a large number of ideas referred to objects that could be conceived independently of others, and for these were formed the words we call substantives. Adjectives were originally modifications of these words. Verbs were formed separately to refer to actions, and so forth, but Maupertuis does not intend to go into detail about the parts of speech, which differ from language to language. They are the grammarian's business. Maupertuis will rather deal with the general principles which have guided all peoples in the formation of languages.

He then briefly reverts to the argument of the *Réflexions*. Actually men did not at first make all these distinctions, but expressed everything in a single "word," for example "I have killed a great bear" would not have been divided up into so many words but would have been a single expression (xiii). Soon shortness of memory caused decomposition, just as the reverse may occur in a language that is already well developed. "It is for this reason that we have introduced technical words into the most perfect languages as well as many abbreviated expressions that contain entire phrases."

After a digression on systems of writing (xiv-xxix), Maupertuis raises the difficult question of the causes of the diversity of languages if we are to assume that all mankind has its ultimate origin in a single family. Even if a million changes should have occurred, would we not expect to find a large number of words that are still the same? Of course we would, but we find that it is in fact not so. A certain number of "authors who are scholars rather than philosophers" (xxxi) have claimed to find words in modern languages that have the same signification as in the languages that are said to be old and original. But this, says Maupertuis, proves nothing; it is purely a matter of statistical chance among such a vast number of words, so that all the etymologists prove is that they themselves know a very large number of words in many different languages. To understand the diversity of languages, we must then either believe in the miracle that is told of the Tower of Babel, or we must assume that when the dispersal took place men had not yet begun to speak. Though he does not say so outright, he clearly believes that the latter is the case. The independent origin of many languages is an unstated assumption of the earlier *Réflexions*, whose problem would disappear if they could all be known to have had a single origin. Maupertuis concludes that each language has had its beginning in the family: "As each isolated family becomes a people and its needs and ideas multiply, it forms a language and writing, in the manner we have explained; and today there is no nation however small that does not have its own" (xxxiii).

This diversity is obviously inconvenient, and learned men have tried to find a remedy. Maupertuis will not imitate them, but merely make some general observations. To hope that one could ever gain adoption of a spoken universal language is utterly foolish. It is, however, possible to consider a written one, though it would have to be more than a mere device for easy translation. If the nature of ideas could be fixed and ordered according to their priority, their generality, etc., it would be possible to create a corresponding set of characters. But how is it possible to hope that men could ever come to agree on the same ideas, when they cannot even agree on such ideas as space and the vacuum, which some say are the first and most fundamental of ideas, while others maintain that they do not even exist. If Descartes and Malebranche had made a written philosophical language, Locke and Newton would never have understood it (xl). This sort of thing is possible only where a few, very simple ideas are involved, as in arithmetic, algebra, and music. Maupertuis is convinced that each nation will keep the language it has, though many of the factors that cause difficulty are not essential to languages and could perhaps be removed or simplified—inflections and conjugations, for instance, could be made uniformly similar and regular. Here the essay ends, seemingly unfinished. It became the immediate occasion for the next event in the debate.

SÜSSMILCH (1756)

In the autumn of the same year, on 7 and 14 October 1756, Johann Peter Süssmilch—best known for his highly original demographic studies—read two papers on the divine origin of language. These papers were not published until 1766, with the title *Versuch eines Beweises, dass die erste Sprache ihren Ursprung nicht vom Menschen, sondern allein vom Schöpfer erhalten habe*. In the Preface, signed 13 May 1766, Süssmilch explained that the first draft went back some ten years when his interest in the subject had first been roused by a paper read by Maupertuis—it later becomes clear that Süssmilch is referring to the "Dissertation." Desiring to re-examine his own argument, Süssmilch had held up publication, but a stroke three years ago had now made him decide to publish his papers without further revision. The mere act of publication as well as the dedication of the essay to the members of the Academy would seem to suggest that Süssmilch was eager to reintroduce his argument into the debate at this time. He was right that publication was timely, for both Herder's prize-topic and the answer are closely related to the *Versuch*, which is an excellent piece—cogently argued, lucid, and tightly organized.[121] Its author died less than a year after publication in March of 1767.

Süssmilch's thesis is simple: "Language is the means to the use of reason, but without language the use of reason is not possible, without it we cannot attain abstract and general concepts and their ready use; consequently we cannot link conclusions and cannot reason, thus also not perform other things that without exception depend on the use of reason."[122] Briefly, the argument takes this form. Language is either divine or human. If human it must be either natural or artificial. But since we say that the sounds made by animals are natural and also observe that they are the same for the same species all over the world, human language cannot be natural in that sense. Only arbitrary audible forms will do. Language must then be artificial, and if so it must have come about either by complete accident or by design, that is by free choice and the exercise of reason. Accident can be ruled out since it would entail complete disorder and irregularity, which apart from the uselessness of such a language is disproved by our observation that all languages, also primitive ones, have "Regeln der Vollkommenheit und Ordnung," that is design. Consequently any human language must be the work of reason and wise choice. But the prerequisite for such design is the perfect use of reason, which involves abstraction, reflection, and ratiocination. These, however, cannot occur without the prior possession of the use of signs. Thus man cannot have invented language, either instantly or gradually. Its origin must then lie outside man in a higher and more intelligent being. God was the creator and the first teacher of language, which by a miracle was communicated to man in the beginning.[123] How this may have happened Süssmilch does not propose to examine since his proof is entirely philosophical, though he hopes it will offer a convincing refutation of all enemies of revelation.

A few points in this cogent argument deserve attention. Condillac had argued that an adequate capacity for silent reflection precedes the first invention of arbitrary vocal signs, which in turn is followed by a steady extension of the effect of reflection. The process is gradual and has its origin in a latent capacity for the use of reason. Süssmilch will allow nothing of the sort. His argument rejects that possibility; the conclusion of his argument is in accord with Revelation—but not derived from it. The *Versuch* presents a philosophical argument, not a string of scriptural citations.[124] To Süssmilch, language as a human accomplishment has nothing in common with the arts, which, he admits, indeed do seem to have had simple beginnings and to have undergone gradual growth toward greater perfection.[125] Second, the very uniformity of grammar—i.e., universal grammar—and the arbitrariness of the signs become sources of proof: "This formal agreement forces us to go back to the one and only teacher and creator of language. Free arbitrariness in the choice of signs and their accidental nature puts an end to all sophistry. The form of language is not like the form of a bird's nest or a beehive, which owing to innate instincts must always be formed in the same fashion."[126]

An Appendix citing *Inégalité* has Condillac's name, but Süssmilch notes that he has not seen the work in question, the *Essai*; it might have been useful, he admits, but he has decided to make do with Rousseau. Having been the occasion for the *Versuch* in the first place, Maupertuis's analysis is rejected, while the dilemma of the first passage on language in Rousseau's *Inégalité* is accepted, though Süssmilch ignores the pre-social state of man in that passage as well as the Condillacian argument offered later in the passage on post-social man. The *Inégalité* had come to Süssmilch's attention—in Moses Mendelssohn's German translation of 1756—only after he had finished the first complete draft. He had then decided not to take account of it in his *Versuch*, except to mention in an appendix at the end that he found himself in basic agreement with it. For the first time since Condillac's *Essai*, genuinely new views had been introduced into the debate by Süssmilch's brilliant *Versuch*. The power and influence of his argument are clearly revealed also before their publication in 1766.

MICHAËLIS'S PRIZE-TOPIC (1757-1759)

In the public assembly of 9 June 1757, a significant event occurred: the Academy announced its first prize-topic on language. The problem was set for "la classe de philosophie spéculative" and had the following form: "What is the reciprocal influence of the opinions of a people on the language and of the language on opinions?" It was further specified that the answer should first, by means of suitable examples, show "how many forms and irregular expressions there are in languages, obviously created by the particular opinions held by the peoples, among which these languages have been formed." This, it was felt, would be the easier part and merely preliminary to the more essential task "of showing in certain turns of phrase proper to each language, in certain expressions, including the roots of certain words, the sources of particular errors or the obstacles to the acceptance of particular truths." Finally, these two parts would, it was hoped, lead to "very important observations. Having shown how a particular quality of mind produces a language, and how this language in turn gives to the mind a more or less favorable inclination toward true ideas, one could explore the most practicable means to remedy the shortcomings of languages."[127]

It will hardly require demonstration for the reader to see that both the topic and the directions have their source in issues raised by Maupertuis—in fact the opening sentence of the *Réflexions* had formulated the problem. But we have even more precise evidence. In his *Cours d'études pour l'instruction du Prince de Parme*, Condillac devoted the last chapter of Book III of the *Cours d'histoire* to "L'influence des langues sur les opinions et des opinions sur les langues." It opens with this statement: "It is Maupertuis who, in the name of the Academy at Berlin, formulated the problem I am about to discuss." There would seem to be no room for doubt that these words refer to our present concern, the prize-topic for 1759.[128]

In the public assembly of 31 May 1759, the secretary, Samuel Formey, announced that the prize had been awarded to an essay submitted by the distinguished Göttingen professor of Semitic languages, Johann David Michaëlis.[129] On the same day a rather fantastic and otherwise unimportant member of the Academy, André-Pierre le Guay de Prémontval, wrote his congratulations to Michaëlis: "I am happy that I have doubly contributed to the outcome, both as the author of the proposed question and as one of those who voted for you."[130] Given Prémontval's understandable eagerness to attract what little importance he could to himself, I see no reason to accept this claim, which in any event would not change the fact that the problem

had been introduced by Maupertuis. A footnote to the English translation of Michaëlis's essay, taken over from the French translation by
J. B. Merian (1762),[131] explains that the problem had arisen in connection with a point in the philosophy of Wolff, on which Prémontval
had read two confused papers on 16 May 1754, one on the principle
of sufficient reason and the other on the law of continuity.[132] This
note also gives an interesting insight into partisanship in the Academy
and shows how observations on language were expected to provide
solutions to philosophical problems: "It is proper even to take notice
that M. de Prémontval having shewn that the falsity of the demonstration becomes manifest, on thinking, or on translating into French,
whereas in the Latin and German expression, it remains strangely enveloped and intricate; and this it was which gave rise to the important
question, on the influence of language on opinions, and of opinions
on language. Never had the bulk of the German nation been misled
by the Wolffian philosophy, had not the two languages, which are
most familiar to them, the German and Latin, been more accommodated than the French, to the sophism, on which the whole is founded.
This, perhaps, is one of the most remarkable passages in the history
of the human mind."

Michaëlis's answer was greatly admired and was soon published in
German (1760), in French (1762), in English (1769 and 1771), and
in Dutch (1771). The French translation, from which the English was
made, contained some important supplements, of which the chief
dealt with the possibility of framing a successful universal language
of learning—the answer is no, and Michaëlis's discussion still stands as
one of the best on that subject.[133]

Michaëlis's answer is spirited, well informed on the general nature
of the debate, and clearly reveals the hand of an accomplished philologist. It has been almost wholly forgotten, and even in contexts, such
as Herder, where it is highly relevant, it figures not at all, wrongly, or
only briefly—often with misinformation. Space does not permit analysis and discussion here. One point, however, demands attention.
Michaëlis had not dealt with the origin of language, but near the end
of his essay he had emphasized the close connection between that
problem and his own. He suggested that the Academy might some
day direct its attention to this topic: "How would a language arise at
first among men who formerly had no language, and little by little
attain its present perfection and elaboration?"[134] It is obvious that
this question is an invitation to reconsider the entire problem of the
origin of language since Condillac's *Essai*. It is also obvious that the
formulation of the question makes an assumption which had been

rejected by Süssmilch's *Versuch*. The Academy took the suggestion, and some readers may already have recognized the topic for which Herder's *Ursprung* gained the prize in 1771. The next item in the debate repeated Michaëlis's question and again invited the Academy to make it the topic of a prize-essay.

FORMEY (1762)

On 15 July 1762, the Academy's perpetual secretary, Samuel Formey, read a very lively paper which presented a summary of the present state of the question accompanied by an outline of a practical experiment designed to give a factual and irrefutable answer. The title of Formey's paper is: "Survey of the principal means that have been employed to discover the origin of human language, ideas, and knowledge."[135] Its aim was to offer proof of the Süssmilch thesis, and its occasion was a passage Formey had found in Michaëlis's supplement on the universal language, added to the French translation. "The tendency to link ideas with sounds is natural to man," Michaëlis had said, "and if we had not when born found a ready-made language, we would not have hesitated to invent one." Having confidently offered this assertion as if it were incapable of contradiction, Michaëlis had proceeded to suggest the essay topic which has been cited above. "I deny equally both the principle and the consequence," Formey commented. If men had been abandoned on the surface of the earth without language, without a certain fund of knowledge, and without reason to handle that knowledge in order to satisfy their most basic needs, they would have remained the most imperfect of animals, indeed they would rather have failed to survive beyond the first generation. To Formey the state of nature is a phantasm, it has no explanatory value since it will always begin with conjectures that man started out with something, with certain abilities. Consequently Formey concludes, "there is no other primitive language than the one the first man spoke because God had taught it to him." Plain reasoning has brought Formey to this conclusion, but for the sake of gaining more universal grounds of conviction he would rather have facts. He would therefore suggest an experiment which, though Formey does not mention it, by a clever argumentative turn harks back to a proposal already made by Maupertuis in 1752 under the title "Expériences métaphysiques."

The experiment must last at least two generations, says Formey. Take a dozen children of the same age, bring them up with everything they need—food, clothing, and every other care but do not ever allow anyone to say a word in their presence, and when they grow up, do not show them any product of art and science; do not even allow them to see how their food is prepared. What will happen when they reach adolescence and youth? They will no doubt follow the only passion we can attribute to them, and soon they will have children—if we can imagine that they will know how to go about satisfying their desires. But how will the mother know how to take care of the child, never having had occasion to learn it by observation? How will the child find the mother's milk when even the mother probably will not know enough to give it to the child? And if the natural families cannot find subsistence, do we need to ask questions about the invention of language and the satisfaction of man's most basic needs? Add further that in actuality the first generation of men, unlike the one in the experiment, would not have enjoyed the benefit of having been taken care of in infancy and childhood. If at any point the merest vestige of language should occur, Formey would willingly admit defeat. As for himself, "the more I think of it, the more I believe that the pure state of nature is an illusion, a plain absurdity, a manifest contradiction; the more I am strengthened in the thought that the Supreme Being, the author of our existence, is also the author of our first ideas and even of the habitual ability we have for their expression." He is also convinced that he has found the answer to Rousseau's remarks on the state of nature in the Preface to Inégalité, especially to Rousseau's question: "What experiments would be necessary to gain knowledge of natural man? And by what means can these experiments be made in the midst of society?"[136] Formey's essay and Süssmilch's Versuch supported the same thesis, and they were published in the same year. The debate was rapidly reaching the impasse which found its issue in Herder's Ursprung.

TOUSSAINT (1765)

On 13 June 1765, François-Vincent Toussaint read a paper called, "Of the conclusions that can be drawn from the language of a nation in regard to its culture and customs."[137] In spite of the promising title, this essay is a very conventional performance, almost as if Toussaint— who had recently become a member—knew that papers on language were popular, but did not quite know how the problems were discussed. We are told, for instance, that German is the most methodical of all languages, the least mixed in with exotic terms, the best preserved, and that it has undergone the fewest changes: "It proclaims solid human beings full of good sense of whom the inconstancy of fashions and the influence of foreign intercourse have not gained control." These are familiar themes, but they appear out of place in the debate on the nature of language.

SULZER (1767)

The last paper to concern us was read in 1767 or possibly in 1768, by Johann Georg Sulzer, "Observations on the reciprocal influence of reason on language and of language on reason."[138] The title is enough to show that Sulzer opposed Süssmilch and Formey, but beyond that his argument is not very clear. On the whole Sulzer presents a weak version of Condillac, seeming rather to follow some of the more doctrinaire articles in the *Encyclopédie*. The origin of language is a difficult problem, Sulzer observes, for without reason how could language develop and how reason without language? Finding themselves in this dilemma, even great philosophers have found no other explanation than miraculous origin, but Sulzer believes that supernatural causes cannot be admitted till natural causes have been proved to fail. The purpose of his essay, however, is not to examine the entire question, but merely to make some thoughtful observations on the interdependence of language and reason. Sulzer seems not entirely aware how many problems he is raising, but a cry of despair in the middle of the essay shows that he did feel the consequences: "It is infinitely easier to sense how these things have come about than to describe clearly the conduct of the mind in its operations."

His problem is this: "What would the conduct of mind have been like for a man who set out to seek signs suitable for the presentation of ideas, and by what means has he found these signs?" He finds the method rather easy. We cannot follow history back to the twilight of reason, but fortunately we have another source of information. What instructed man does today can tell us what "l'homme brute" did before he had language. Experience must begin by analysis of perception before words can be made. This is the first step toward language, and the next is equally simple. To find words for objects, all he needed to do was to imitate "the very sounds by which these objects proclaim themselves." It is no surprise to the reader that Sulzer believes the first invention of language was not at all difficult and did not surpass the capacities of "un homme brute." His assurance, is, of course, incompatible with the arguments of Condillac, Maupertuis, Süssmilch, and Formey; one wonders how it was possible to ignore them in a paper on this subject at that time unless even a poor argument against Süssmilch's thesis was considered better than none at all.

How then, asks Sulzer, did man first find words for things which are not associated with sound in any way? Quite easily, we are told. He changed an "old" word a bit and gave it a new meaning, or he used metaphor, the association of ideas being common to all men: "This talent is innate in man, the most rude nations have it as well as those closest to the state of the brute, even those human beings that are born deaf and mute. Attention combined with a little reflection is enough to put it to use. Thus it belonged to man before his language was formed." If we could recover these first radical words, Sulzer believes it would be possible "to show exactly the path the mind has followed in arriving at the significations most removed from the first sense." Etymology then receives its conventional tribute: "Let us note here that the etymological history of languages would be the best history of the progress of the human mind." It is especially by virtue of this optimism, this characteristic rhetoric about "la marche de l'esprit humain"—a phrase we have met before—that Sulzer has much in common with contemporary French discussions and very little with the Berlin debate which had preceded his own contribution.

So far Sulzer has shown how man could find or make the elements of language. He will now consider their role in man's progress toward cultivated reason. The question of the relationship between language or words and reason is quite lost sight of, in any serious sense. Words are an aid to memory, abridge the operations of the mind, and promote invention and discovery, as exemplified in the work of Linnaeus. These points are all very conventional. Though Sulzer does not himself say so, the words he has so far considered are all nouns; he has followed the simplest form of the argument that finds the origin of language in invention with reference to first sensations of objects. Verbs, he says, are formed by modification of already existing forms; exactly how we are not told, though Sulzer believes that these modifications are for the most part the result of chance. He concludes that the grammatical perfection of a language is the outcome of reason and genius. Language and reason interact to improve each other. The degree of sophistication of a language is measured by its capacity for compact expression. Hence to learn such a language is to learn to think and improve one's taste. The perfection of language and eloquence is as important as the discovery of new truths. The progress of reason depends both on the scientists and on "les beaux-esprits." Sulzer's paper quite lacks the force of argument that would be required to decide the issue in favor of the human invention of language, against Süssmilch and Formey. The question remained open. One or two years later, in the late spring of 1769, the Academy set the topic for 1771, Herder's topic. With this topic the debate also closed. Condillac's *Essai*, the fountainhead of the debate, was nearly twenty-five years old.

HERDER (1769-1771)

Following Michaëlis's suggestion, the topic for 1771 was given in this form: "Supposing that human beings were left to their natural faculties, are they in a position to invent language? And by which means will they achieve this invention on their own?" It was further specified that "a hypothesis is expected that explains the matter clearly and meets all the difficulties."[139] Corresponding to these two divisions, Herder divided his answer in two parts with these super-scriptions: "Has mankind left to its natural faculties been able to invent language on its own?" and "The manner in which man most suitably could and must have invented languages." The answer to the first question is yes, as summarized in these assertions: "Endowed with the capacity for thought that is peculiar to him and this capacity for thought (reflexion) for the first time being given free exercise, man has invented language. . . . This capacity for thought is his unique quality and essential to his species: so also language and his own invention of language. The invention of language is as natural to him as his being human."[140] At least since the nineteenth century it has become an unquestioned dogma that this doctrine is Herder's entirely new and original contribution to the problem of the origin of language, indeed that "the age of the philosophy of language opens with Herder's prize essay."[141] Belief in this dogma has been coupled with the equally unfounded dogma that all previous natural (as dis-tinct from divine) explanations had given language a purely animalistic origin, most often with specific reference to the example of Condillac. It will now, I hope, be clear to my readers that all participants in the debate (perhaps with the exception of Sulzer) had emphatically as-serted that man's possession of reason and reflection is the foundation of human language and that animals, not having reason and reflec-tion, also are without such a language. Herder had arrived at a doc-trine which had been fully argued in Condillac's *Essai* in so far as it involves reflection and language.

It would be easy to draw up a catalog of close similarities between Herder and Condillac, in spite of the fact that the existence of such similarities has been ignored or denied, though always (as in the case of Salmony) with little or no knowledge of the *Essai*. The doctrine of the intimate connection between "Volksgeist" and language has gen-erally been held one of Herder's most important contributions to the thought of his age. But the second part of the *Essai*, the part Herder had read by the middle 1760s, contains such statements as these: "Everything confirms that each language expresses the character of the people who speak it." "Of all the writers, it is with the poets that the genius of languages gains the most lively expression." And "For anyone who understands them well, languages would be a painting of the character and genius of each people. He would see how the imag-ination has combined ideas according to the given outlook and the passions."[142] It is true that at the time these ideas were, so to speak, in the air, but Condillac was the first to give them a firm place in the theory of language and its origin.

There is, however, one very significant difference between the Condillacian argument and the argument Herder presents in the first part of the *Ursprung*. Though this difference has very considerable consequences, it has not to my knowledge been noted in the secondary literature. To Condillac and his followers language meant language *and* speech. Without including articulated, arbitrary, vocal signs language could have meant nothing in their argument. But in the first part of the *Ursprung*, the part that has generally been considered a deliberate and successful refutation of Condillac's doctrine, Herder deals exclusively with "die innere Entstehung der Sprache."[143] Only in the second part does "Sprache" also mean speech, though Herder throughout the *Ursprung* uses the term "Sprache" without remarking on the distinction, except when he later adds "äussere" and "innere." The reader is alerted to this use of "Sprache" in such passages as these: "The first sign distinguished in consciousness was a word of the soul. It is the invention of human language." "The savage, man alone in the forest would have had to invent language for himself, even if he had never spoken it. . . . It is incomprehensible to me how a human soul could be what it is except by the fact that it would have to invent language for itself, already without mouth and society." And "More than one language have one name for 'word' and 'reason,' 'concept' and 'word,' 'language' and 'cause,' and this synonymy contains its entire genetic origin."[144] This "innere Sprache" is in other words a complete language of concepts, a doctrine that is entirely foreign to the argument of Condillac's *Essai*, which therefore is not touched by Herder's assertions. Herder's doctrine would also seem to conflict with his own argument about the creation of speech in the second part of the *Ursprung*, for here Herder holds a doctrine of the mutual development or progress of reason and speech. It would further seem to conflict with Herder's belief that language in the beginning has no grammar, that is, language considered as speech.[145] It is this sort of disagreement and inconsistency between the parts of the *Ursprung*—and it has long been admitted (though almost as if it were a special virtue) that the essay contains many such inconsistencies—that has necessitated a number of not very successful attempts at interpretation which fill up the literature. Curiously, more than one interpreter has, like Salmony, unknowingly offered a reading that comes close to presenting Condillac's argument.

The Academy's official report on the *Ursprung* reveals the distance that separates well-informed, contemporary judgment from later opinion. According to this report, Herder had argued that the origin of language was not divine, but "purely animalistic, that is to say it proceeds from the combination of the organic structure of man with the mental faculties located in a body that is so organized and from the circumstances in which the animal that has this organization and these faculties finds itself placed." Herder's name deserved to be mentioned with those of Diderot, Rousseau, and Condillac, "as much owing to the power of reasoning with which he, like them, sounds the depths of metaphysics as owing to the respect he shows toward them as he departs more or less from their views."[146] A dozen years after the award of the prize, the Academy published the report, which Johann Bernhard Merian had read on the day of the award, 6 June 1771. What Merian saw in the *Ursprung* were, for instance, such Condillacian principles as these: "Human language depends so immediately on reflection, that only one step remains to lead man to this important discovery," and that man has "a nature essentially different from animal nature. And this difference is produced solely by the power of reflection, of recording these thoughts and linking them by means of language."[147] I find Merian's report correct and neutral, but modern readers conditioned by the conventional views would hardly recognize it as an analysis of the *Ursprung*, let alone as an exposition of Herder's linguistic philosophy.

A detailed examination of Herder's essay falls outside the limits of this paper. Such an examination will demand consideration of his reading, of his writings both before and after 1770, of his position vis-à-vis Kant, Hamann, Mendelssohn, Abbt, and others. Thanks to the important work of Professor Irmscher we may hope to see the publication of much relevant, hitherto unpublished material. But in the present context it will seem reasonable to try to give a few preliminary answers to the problems we are facing: Why has the *Ursprung* received such curious and on the whole (it must be said) ignorant treatment? And why did Herder give very inadequate, indeed on significant points, false accounts of contemporary work on the origin of language? These two questions are interrelated, but I shall begin with the second.

There are first of all the known facts about the conditions under which Herder wrote the essay, hastily in Strasbourg during the last months or even weeks of 1770. Many of the texts he did not have at hand, and physically he was troubled by a recent eye operation; and there may have been other personal factors. Condillac is the text. We have seen that Herder some five years earlier had come upon the

Essai, been excited by it, and taken notes from it. But in all the references he makes to the *Essai*—whether earlier or in the *Ursprung*—he talks only of volume two, that is the volume of the original edition which contained the second part of the *Essai*, the part with the long section on the origin and progress of language. If it can be assumed that Herder had never read the first part, he would have had no way of understanding the important role of reflection in Condillac's argument. Herder would also have been ignorant that the origin of language in the *Essai* merely forms part of a larger argument about the origin of human knowledge and understanding. Further, the later writings on the origin of language, including those I have dealt with in this paper, had addressed themselves directly to the problem of the origin of language without systematically placing it in Condillac's full context. Thus, if Herder had not read Part One of the *Essai*, it becomes understandable that he could criticize the adequacy of the argument he found in Part Two at the very same time as he unwittingly reconstructed the missing part in Condillac's manner. Herder's surprising misrepresentation of the argument of the *Essai* could in fact have come about without his knowledge. It might be argued that even Part Two would have given Herder a better understanding of Condillac than he shows. This objection carries little weight, however, for in the *Ursprung* Herder is never very precise even about the arguments of texts he did have at hand. We know, for instance, that he did have a copy of Süssmilch's *Versuch*, though he still misrepresents its argument.[148] My suggestion that Herder had not read the first part of Condillac's *Essai* will solve the most perplexing problem about the *Ursprung*.

But why has the context of the prize-essay been studied so carelessly, if at all? First of all, I think, because the *Ursprung* by its very style carries the reader along; it is forceful, direct, irreverent, and clever. More important, no doubt, is its central position in the national tradition of German literature. After the *Ursprung*, Herder's reputation steadily increased until he became the authority, the seeming originator of the ideas he had laid down in his youthful essay. Herder was believed, even on Condillac. But this neglect of the context could hardly have persisted right down to the present day if the nineteenth century had not corrupted our understanding of the eighteenth. For complex reasons I shall not go into, post-romantic scholarship has lent its enormous prestige to the truly silly belief that Condillac, among many others, was a mechanistic, materialist philosopher. Herder became one of the intellectual heroes of romanticism because it was believed that he had rescued the origin of language from "the

Enlightenment conception of language as a still-to-be-added faculty, so to speak, to fully developed man," from "intellectual impatience and intolerance toward life that can only be mastered mathematically when it is conceived as pure mechanism"—statements that speak nonsense about the material we have examined though they purport to say something true about that very material.

One thinks with gratitude of Franco Venturi's brilliant insight concerning the significance of studying the discussions of the origin of language among the *philosophes*: "Detailed attention to this discussion ought to be one of the best means to gain true understanding of the Enlightenment, to discover the force and intellectual vigor that to this day constitute its greatness; and I believe we can hereby come to grasp the extremely complex but very interesting moment when the claims that have been made on the subject of the creative power of the human mind coincide with the first esthetic discoveries that open the way to romantic and modern theories."[149]

Thus I end where I began, with Condillac. His influence is decisive, the issues he raised in the *Essai* first created the problem of the origin of language in its most powerful and philosophical form. Rarely in intellectual history has a single work raised a European-wide debate so quickly yet continued to dominate the debate for so long, whether in Germany, France, or England. And that debate has much greater unity and quite a different meaning, wider implications, and greater relevance than has generally been admitted and understood.[150]

Notes

1. The best edition of Condillac is *Oeuvres philosophiques de Condillac*, ed. Georges le Roy, 3 vols. (Paris: Presses Universitaires de France, 1947-1951). Hereafter referred to as Condillac, followed by volume and page number (with a and b for each column); to facilitate cross reference to other editions of Condillac, I shall also give the section, chapter, and paragraph numbers necessary for identification. Of the relevant secondary literature, the following may be mentioned: Georges le Roy's *La Psychologie de Condillac* (Paris, 1937) and his Introduction to the *Oeuvres* I, vii-xxxv. Franco Venturi's excellent chapter entitled "La lettre sur les sourds et les muets" in his *Jeunesse de Diderot (1713-1753)*, tr. Juliette Bertrand (Paris, 1939), pp. 237-282; this chapter, which also deals with Condillac and Rousseau, offers one of the best discussions of the problem of language and its origin in the mid-eighteenth century. Ulrich Ricken, "Condillac's *liaison des idées* und die *clarté* des Französischen" in *Die Neueren Sprachen 1964*, pp. 552-567. Hans Aarsleff, *The Study of Language in England 1780-1860* (Princeton, 1967), pp. 18-34; on p. 18 I say that Condillac wished to reduce reflection to sensation, but now consider that false. The single principle by which he wished to explain the mind was "la liaison des idées" ("the connection of ideas"), a principle that was designed to imitate the power of the concept of gravity in Newtonian philosophy. Condillac makes it clear that "la liaison des idées" is not the same as association of ideas.

2. On Wharburton, see Aarsleff, pp. 21-22.

3. Adam Smith's essay was first published in *Philological Miscellany* (London, 1761), pp. 440-479. Since the third edition of *Theory of Moral Sentiments* (1767), it has generally been part of that volume. In the years immediately preceding, Smith had written a review of the early volumes of the *Encyclopédie*. See Aarsleff, pp. 103-104, and "Wilhelm von Humboldt and the linguistic thought of the French idéologues," below p. 353, note 29.

4. This work was suggested by Monboddo's reading of a review of Nugent's English translation. See Aarsleff, pp. 36-42.

5. (München, 1869), pp. 283 ff.

6. 2nd ed. (Berlin, 1858), pp. 1-10.

7. Ernst Cassirer, *The Philosophy of Symbolic Forms*, tr. Ralph Manheim, vol. I *Language* (New Haven, 1953), 117-176. First German edition 1923.

8. (Wageningen, 1952), pp. 357-367. Verburg deals with Condillac after Monboddo.

9. (Freiburg/München, 1955), p. 89. Arens's section on the "Französische Richtung: rationalistisch-psychologische Betrachtung," including the selections from Condillac, is repeated unchanged in the second "durchgesehene und stark erweiterte Auflage" (Freiburg/München, 1969), pp. 106-119, (1st ed., pp. 88-102).

10. Condillac I, 36b (*Essai* I, ii, § 107).

11. See also Guy Harnois, *Les Théories du langage en France de 1660 à 1821* (Paris, 1928), pp. 43-50. Harnois admits the importance of the *Essai* in a few sentences, but then goes on to the *Grammaire*, first published in 1775.

12. Renan, *De l'origine du langage* in *Oeuvres complètes*, ed. Henriette Psichari, vol. VIII (Paris, 1958), 9-123; the quoted matter is on pp. 41-42. This is the expanded version of 1858 (first version 1848).

13. Salmony, *Die Philosophie des jungen Herder* (Zürich, 1949), p. 42.

14. *Ibid.*, p. 67. This is one of the many passages that show Salmony's ignorance of the *Essai*.

15. *Herders Sämmtliche Werke*, ed. B. Suphan, vol. I (Berlin, 1877), 529. The part to which Herder refers is Condillac's long section on the origin of language. This edition will hereafter be referred to as Suphan.

16. Suphan II (Berlin, 1877), 370. Cf. A. Warda, "Ein Aufsatz J. G. Herders aus dem Jahre 1764," in *Euphorion*, Ergänzungsheft No. 8 (1909), pp. 75-82, where Condillac's *Essai* is also mentioned.

17. Condillac I, 60-104. The entire *Essai* covers pp. 3-118.

18. *Inégalité*, ed. Jean Starobinski in Rousseau, *Oeuvres complètes*, vol. III (Paris: Pléiade, 1964), 146; *Inégalité* covers pp. 109-223, hereafter referred to as *Inégalité*. It should be recalled that Rousseau spent a year as tutor to Condillac's nephews, made his acquaintance, and later met him again in Paris: "I am perhaps the first who has seen his significance and understood his importance. . . . He was then working on the *Essai*, which is his first work." Condillac had difficulty finding a publisher, but Rousseau put him in touch with Diderot, who then arranged for publication. At the time the three philosophers met regularly for a weekly dinner and conversation. See *Confessions*, end of Book VII.

19. Denis Diderot, *Oeuvres complètes*, vol. I (Paris, 1875), ed. J. Assézat, p. 349. This edition will hereafter be referred to as AT.

20. AT I, 275-342, see esp. 304-305. On 21 August 1749, Condillac wrote to Gabriel Cramer: "Are you familiar with the work by Diderot entitled *Letter on the blind for the benefit of those who have sight*? I shall tell you no more about it, for it praises me too much." See Condillac, *Lettres inédites à Gabriel Cramer*, ed. Georges le Roy (Paris, 1953), p. 54.

21. Le Roy, "Introduction" in Condillac I, xix-xx and xxiii. For the interesting relationship between the *Essai* and *Sensations*, see *ibid.*, pp. xvii-xxi. On the non-materialist and religiously devout tendency of Condillac's teaching, see also Henri Bédarida, *Parme et la France de 1748 à 1789* (Paris, 1928), pp. 412-416.

22. Isabel F. Knight, *The Geometric Spirit, the Abbé de Condillac and the French Enlightenment* (New Haven, 1968), p. 106. This work can only tend to perpetuate conventional errors about Condillac. The title is curious; in the *Essai* II, ii, §52, Condillac says: "We have four famous metaphysicians, Descartes, Malebranche, Leibniz, and Locke. The last is the only one who was not a geometrician, and how much superior he is to the other three!" Condillac I, 117b.

23. P. 175. See pp. 166-176, with citations given p. 166, to which other citations could be added.

24. Condillac I, 267b-268a (*Sensations* II, viii, §35). The other additions reinforce this point: an entirely new introduction to Part IV on p. 298, and a new paragraph on p. 307a in IV, v, §4. In this second version of the *Sensations*, Condillac made even more extensive revisions and additions on the matter of touch and motion; these are duly noted in le Roy's book from 1937. I have not had access to the 1754 edition of the *Sensations*, but am following the indications given in le Roy's own excellent edition of the *Oeuvres philosophiques*. It is hard to understand why le Roy himself both in the Introduction to the *Oeuvres* as well as in some footnotes to Condillac's text should have forgotten the good insight of 1937. It would seem to be mere inadvertence since he offers no argument one way or the other. Also, though le Roy has noted the additions I have just listed, he does not take account of them although they greatly strengthen his argument of 1937. I therefore find his note in Condillac II, 536 inexplicable.

25. Condillac I, 731, in note to *L'Art de penser* I, vi.

26. The first three passages are in Condillac I, 363-364 (in *Animaux* II, v); the last two on p. 371b (end of II, vii) and p. 361b (II, iv).

27. Condillac I, 33a and 36b (in *Essai* I, ii, §92 and §107).

28. Condillac I, 29a and 14a-b (in *Essai* I, ii, §77 and §15). On Condillac's distinction between the voluntary and the involuntary connection of ideas, of which only the latter corresponds to Locke's "association of ideas," see also Condillac I, 29-30 (*Essai* I, ii, §§79-84); I, 400 (in "Discours préliminaire" to *Cours d'études*); I, 727-729 (*L'Art de penser* I, v); and II, 221 (in *Histoire moderne* XX, beg. of ch. x).

29. *Inégalité*, p. 147.

30. *Ibid.*, p. 151.

31. *Ibid.*, p. 146.

32. *Ibid.*, pp. 165-166.

33. *Ibid.*, p. 167. The different layers, so to speak, of natural man in Rousseau have been pointed out by A. O. Lovejoy in "The supposed Primitivism of Rousseau's *Discourse of Inequality*," in *Essays in the History of Ideas* (New York: Capricorn Books, 1960), pp. 14-37. It would have illuminated Lovejoy's argument if he had considered the place of language in this context.

34. *Oeuvres complètes* (Paris: Hachette, 1905), I, 370-408. The parts of this essay that concern language were almost certainly written in 1754 to form one of the long notes to *Inégalité*. See P. M. Masson, "Questions de chronologie rousseauiste" in *Annales de la Société Jean-Jacques Rousseau* IX (1913), 45-49. There is a recent edition of Rousseau, *Essai sur l'origine des langues*, ed. Charles Porset (Bordeaux: Ducros, 1970).

35. Condillac I, 433a-b (in *Grammaire* I, ii). Jean Morel in "Recherches sur les sources du Discours de l'inégalité," in *Annales de la Société Jean-Jacques Rousseau* V (1909), 119-198, deals with both passages in the section "Condillac et Rousseau," but does not discriminate between them (pp. 143-160).

36. "Rousseau et l'origine des langues" in *Europäische Aufklärung. Herbert Dieckmann zum 60. Geburtstag*, eds. Hugo Friedrich and Fritz Schalk (München-Allach, 1967), p. 294.

37. See Venturi, pp. 247-249, and Ricken, pp. 559-561.

38. Condillac I, 436b (*Grammaire* I, iii). See also I, 430a (*Grammaire* I, i). This idea is also fully developed in *Logique* (1780) I, chs. ii-iii in Condillac II, 374-378, and earlier in a somewhat different manner in the original ch. xvii "De l'usage des systêmes dans les arts," in *Traité des systêmes* (1749) in Condillac I, 212-214.

39. AT I, 369. A few years later, Diderot stated the same principle in much greater detail in the article "Encyclopédie" in the *Encyclopédie* vol. V (1755); see AT XIV (Paris, 1876), 433-435. With a somewhat different conception, the idea is developed in Bernard Lamy, *L'Art de parler* (Paris, 1676) pp. 4-9. It is also in Du Marsais, *Oeuvres* (Paris, 1797), III, 381, 385 (in "Fragment sur les causes de la parole"). Further references in Aarsleff, p. 15n.

40. Cf. Du Marsais: "When we say *the light of the mind*, this word light is taken metaphorically: for as light, in its proper sense, makes us see corporal objects, so the faculty of knowing and perceiving enlightens the mind and puts it in a position to draw sound conclusions." *Oeuvres* II, 120, in *Des Tropes* (1730).

41. Condillac II, 403b (*Logique* II, vi).

42. Suphan XXXII (Berlin, 1899), 86-87; "Versuch" covers pp. 85-140.

43. Hans Dietrich Irmscher, ed., *Immanuel Kant. Aus den Vorlesungen der Jahre 1762 bis 1764. Auf Grund der Nachschriften Johann Gottfried Herders* (Köln, 1964), p. 92 (= *Kantstudien. Ergänzungsheft* No. 88).

44. *Oeuvres* I, 23, in "Exposition d'une méthode raisonnée pour apprendre la langue latine" (1722), which covers pp. 1-41.

45. *Works* (London, 1794) II, 361, in *Conduct of the Understanding*, written 1697, first published 1706, in French 1710, 1732; in German 1755.

46. *Works* II, 139, in "Mr. Locke's Reply to the Bishop of Worcester's Answer to his Letter" (1697). The qualifications "much the same" and "most men" are designed to take account of men whose minds are for some reason or other deficient. Locke took for granted that man is wholly different from the animals in his capacities.

47. The best edition of Locke's *Essay* is the 5th (1706), the last to receive Locke's own revisions. This text is available in John Locke, *An Essay concerning human Understanding*, 2 vols., ed. John W. Yolton (London & New York: Everyman's Library Nos. 332 & 984, 1961). The claim made by Fraser for his edition and prominently repeated on the cover of the Dover reprint, no doubt in good faith, that it is "collated" is simply not true in any meaningful sense of that word. In French the *Essay* was read in Pierre Coste's translation of 1700, which had Locke's approval and which included a number of revisions which were first published in English in the 5th edition. German translation 1755 and 1757; Latin at London 1701, Leipzig 1709 and 1731, Amsterdam 1729. There were ten printings in French by 1787, all but two before 1759.

48. *Essay* II, xv, 4, and II, xxviii, 2. The key passage is III, i, 5, which is perhaps the most frequently quoted passage of the *Essay*. It is cited in Condillac I, 87a (*Essai* II, i, § 103). Of course, these passages became suggestive because they were imbedded in a work which invested them with profound meaning and rich implications.

49. It is well known that books on voyages and travels constituted a very large part of Locke's own library and that he took special care to acquire everything of this sort that was published. See John Harrison and Peter Laslett, *The Library of John Locke* (Oxford, 1965), pp. 18, 27-29 (= *Oxford Bibliographical Society Publications*, New Series, XIII). Richard Ashcraft, "John Locke's Library: Portrait of an Intellectual," *Transactions of the Cambridge Bibliographical Society* V (1969), 47-60.

50. *Inégalité*, pp. 133 and 123.

51. Renan, *De l'origine*, p. 42 (ch. ii).

52. Condillac I, 60a (*Essai* II, i, §0). It is worth noting that Locke in the *Essay* III, vi, 44-51, argues strongly for Adam's ordinary humanity also in regard to language, concluding:

"The same liberty also that Adam had of affixing any new name to any ideas, the same has anyone still especially the beginners of languages, if we can imagine any such."

53. *Inégalité*, p. 133.

54. Suphan XXXII, 99, but see the entire passage pp. 92-101. It should be noted that this was written before the publication of Süssmilch's *Versuch* in 1766. Cf. *Über den Ursprung der Sprache* in Suphan V (Berlin, 1891), 52: "The divine origin explains nothing and nothing can be explained from it." The anecdote of Shandy and Tobias would seem to come from Kant; see Herder's letter to Hamann (17 April 1768), which deals with the subject of divine origin, in Johan Georg Hamann, *Briefwechsel*, eds. Walther Ziesemer and Arthur Henkel, II (Wiesbaden, 1956), 408-409. In a lecture on the origin of language, Joseph Priestley observed: "Notwithstanding the powers of speech might have been communicated, in a considerable degree, to the first parents of the human race; yet, since it is natural to suppose it would be only sufficient for the purpose of their own condition, we may perhaps conceive more justly of the manner in which language was improved from so small a beginning as is represented in the lecture." *A Course of Lectures on the Theory of Language, and Universal Grammar* (Warrington, 1762), pp. 237-238.

55. On de Maistre's and Bonald's influence in England, see Aarsleff, pp. 227-229.

56. Condillac I, 36b (*Essai*, I, ii, § 107).

57. *Ibid.*, I, 61b (*Essai* II, i, § 4).

58. *Ibid.*, I, 22b (*Essai* I, ii, § 49).

59. *Ibid.*, I, 403b ("Discours préliminaire").

60. See Aarsleff, p. 38n. On the principle that language cannot be studied without reference to mind, see a firm statement in Du Marsais, *Oeuvres* V, 95-96 (at the end of his article on "Construction" (1754)). It may be useful to recall Du Marsias' definition of "Esprit": "By this word *mind*, we here understand the faculty we have of conceiving and imagining. It is also called *understanding.*" *Oeuvres* V, 316.

61. *Oeuvres de Mr de Maupertuis* I (Lyon, 1756), 259-260.

62. *Ibid.*, p. 294.

63. Venturi, p. 238.

64. *Oeuvres de Mr de Maupertuis* I (Lyon, 1756), 260.

65. Condillac I, 435a (*Grammaire* I, ii). The *Grammaire* as well as the *l'Art d'écrire, l'Art de raisonner, l'Art de penser,* and the *Histoire ancienne* and the *Histoire moderne* all formed part of the *Cours d'études pour l'instruction du Prince de Parme.* The *Cours* was written between 1758 and the end of 1766, but not published until 1775. *L'Art de penser* is largely made up of passages from the *Essai.*

66. Condillac I, 403a ("Disc. prélim.").

67. Harnois, p. 33.

68. Condillac I, 42a (*Essai* I, iv, § 5).

69. *Ibid.*, p. 105b (*Essai* II, ii, § 9).

70. *Ibid.*, p. 101b (*Essai* II, i, § 153).

71. AT I, 349.

72. *Oeuvres de Turgot*, ed. Gustave Schelle, 5 vols. (Paris, 1913-1923), I, 505. ("Étymologie" covers pp. 473-516.) Of all the work on language produced in France in the eighteenth century, Turgot's "Étymologie" proved most congenial to the nineteenth-century philologists; to Renan, "Only Turgot is an exception; he seems to have had the most advanced views on language." *De l'origine*, p. 42. I agree with Venturi, p. 394, that Turgot is not typical; he made no original contribution to origin of language, and even his article on etymology was based on work by de Brosses. See Aarsleff, p. 36n.

73. Condillac, I, 214 (in a note to the original ch. xvii of the *Traité des systèmes*). Condillac and Du Marsais knew each other personally; see Condillac I, 735b (in note to the end

of *l'Art de penser* I, vi, a note that is interesting also for other reasons).

74. AT I, 349, 414 and XIV, 429.

75. The "Exposition" is in Du Marsais' *Oeuvres* I, 1-41; the "Véritables principes," *ibid.* I, 265-279.

76. D'Alembert, "Éloge de du Marsais" in Du Marsais, *Oeuvres* I, lxvii.

77. *Oeuvres* I, 27.

78. *Works* (1794), VIII, 152-164, in § § 163-169 of *Thoughts concerning Education.* This edition of Sanctii *Minerva* is from 1687 and was in Locke's library; he also had another edition from 1664 before Perizonii notes were added. He owned Lancelot's grammars of Italian and Spanish, Lamy's *l'Art de parler*, and Cordemoy's *Discours physique de la parole*. See Harrison and Laslett, *Library of John Locke*, Nos. 845b, 1114, 1307, 2202, 2543, 2544, 2987.

79. *Oeuvres* I, 145; cf. pp. 102-104. Du Marsais' "Remarques sur les articles LII et LIII des Mémoires de Trévoux du mois de May 1723" are in that volume pp. 83-146. M. le Fèvre de Saumur presumably refers to Tannegui le Fèvre, *Méthode courte et facile pour apprendre les humanités grecques et latines* (Saumur, 1672), published in English in 1721, 1723, and 1750. It was in Locke's library, No. 1114.

80. *Oeuvres* VI, 25 and 28. There has been some doubt whether Du Marsais wrote "Le philosophe"; see Herbert Dieckmann, ed., *Le Philosophe*, Texts and Interpretation (St. Louis, 1948) and Werner Krauss, "L'énigme de Du Marsais" in *Revue d'histoire littéraire de la France* LXII (1962), 514-522. There is no doubt whatever about his Lockianism and his strong anti-Cartesianism; see for example these articles written for the *Encyclopédie*: "Abstraction" and "Adjectif" in *Oeuvres* IV, 29-41 and 85-110; and "Education" and "Fini" in *Oeuvres* V, 183-212 and 291-294. Very outspoken is a section "Remarques sur l'idée" (in V, 319-322), which occurs in the *Logique*, a work from which Professor Chomsky often cites other passages at length.

81. *Oeuvres* VI, 9; cf. also pp. 16-21 on reason and faith, closely following Locke. Cf. Ricken, p. 554: "It seems at first sight a paradox, but is a fact that Du Marsais based his rationalist theory of syntax on Locke." See also quotation from Degérando in Krauss, p. 519. Our knowledge of the intellectual milieu in which Du Marsais moved just prior to his first publication in 1722, also indicates closeness to Lockian thought; see Ira O. Wade, *The Clandestine Organization and Diffusion of philosophic Ideas in France from 1700 to 1750* (Princeton, 1938), pp. 98-101.

82. *Language and Mind* (New York, 1968), p. 19.

83. *Essay* III, iv, 11 and ii, 1.

84. Condillac I, 21b (*Essai* I, ii, § 46). In the correspondence with Gabriel Cramer, having been asked to explain the prerogative of arbitrary signs over natural ones, Condillac observes that this problem is the key to his insistence on "la nécessité absolue des signes" (by which he means arbitrary signs). So long as man has only natural cries, he is bound to nature and thus not free; the arbitrary signs over which he has control and which alone constitute human language, free him from that dependence, but in turn make him culture bound; granted that man has reason and reflection, language and knowledge are products of man's social being and of social intercourse. See Condillac, *Lettres*, pp. 83-86 (in letter written between September 1750 and January 1752) and again pp. 101-105 (which was also written during those years).

85. *Cartesian Linguistics* (New York, 1966), pp. 13 ff.

86. *Ibid.*, pp. 53-54.

87. *Language and Mind*, p. 77.

88. *Cartesian Linguistics*, pp. 1-2, 75-76.

89. *Language and Mind*, p. 70.

90. *Ibid.*, p. 86.

91. *Essay* II, xxxiii, 4. It must be recalled that Condillac's "liaison des idées" is not the same as Locke's association of ideas. In the standard French translation of the *Essay* Locke's term was rendered "association des idées." See also note 28 above.

92. *Language and Mind*, p. 6. Professor Chomsky sometimes says "innate" and "innateness," and "innate ideas," at other times "rationalist" and "rationalism," though in all cases he seems to intend his words to carry the same meaning. That usage is curious, and it disregards necessary and time-honored distinctions. There would in fact seem to lie some deeper and more serious confusion behind this terminological mistiness.

93. *The Philosophical Works of Descartes*, trs. Elizabeth S. Haldane and G. R. T. Ross, 2 vols. (Cambridge, 1967), I, 442. Since I cited the long passage from "Notes directed against a certain Programme" in January of 1969 in order to show that this text cannot be used to set Descartes and Locke apart on this important matter, it has come to my attention that the very same passage has been cited at least twice for the same purpose. It was used in 1801 by Coleridge to show that Locke's "Innate Ideas were Men of Straw," because Locke and Descartes "held precisely the same opinions concerning the original Sources of our Ideas." See Earl Leslie Griggs, ed., *Collected Letters of Samuel Taylor Coleridge*, vol. II (1801-1806) (Oxford, 1956), pp. 681-686 (in letters to Josiah Wedgwood of 18 and 24 February 1801). The same passage was cited again in 1821 by Sir James Mackintosh, who found that "it may well be doubted, whether [Locke's ideas of reflection] much differed from the innate ideas of Descartes." See *Edinburgh Review* XXXVI (October 1821), 235-236. Dugald Stewart also believed that Locke had been misrepresented on innate ideas and that he was essentially a rationalist. See Stewart's *Dissertation*, Part II (1821) in *Collected Works*, ed. Sir William Hamilton, 11 vols. (Edinburgh, 1854-1860), I, 206-251 and 553-556, esp. pp. 223 ff. Mackintosh's discussion occurs in a review of the *Dissertation*, Part II. See above, "John Locke's Reputation in Nineteenth-Century England." It is evident that present-day assumptions—or more often dogmas—about the opposition between rationalism and empiricism form a characteristic late-Victorian heritage of largely conservative inspiration.

94. In this respect Locke agreed with, for instance, Antoine Arnauld. See Arnauld's argument against Malebranche in *Des vraies et des fausses idées*, especially ch. v in Arnauld, *Oeuvres* XXXVIII (Paris, 1780), 198.

95. John W. Yolton, *John Locke and the Way of Ideas* (Oxford, 1956), p. 56.

96. *Ibid.*, p. 57.

97. *Essay* I, iii, 15. In this chapter, sections 15-20, Locke cites and discusses Lord Herbert on innateness, using the very chapter and passages in Herbert which Professor Chomsky cites with approval in *Cartesian Linguistics*, pp. 60-62. Thus Professor Chomsky takes Herbert to be relevant and familiar, yet says that "Locke's critique [of innate ideas] had little relevance to any familiar doctrine in the seventeenth century" (*Language and Mind*, p. 70). Since the *Essay* also discusses Herbert on innateness in I, iv, 8-18, these sections offer by far the most extensive discussion of any named philosopher anywhere in the *Essay*. Of course, even if the *Essay* had not said a word about Lord Herbert, it is a matter of plain knowledge that its discussion of innateness was indeed relevant to doctrines held in the seventeenth century.

98. *Nouveaux essais* II, i, 2 (in the Akademie Ausgabe of Leibniz, series 6, vol. VI (1962), 111; cf. also *ibid.*, p. 55). In 1821 Stewart cited the entire "nihil est . . . nisi ipse intellectus" passage from a Leibniz letter of 1710, observing that Leibniz' words "only convey in a more precise and epigrammatic form, the substance of Locke's doctrine" (*Dissertation*, Part II, pp. 233-236). In his review of the *Dissertation*, Mackintosh for the first time in England cited the similar passages from the *Nouveaux essais* to the same effect (*Edinburgh Review* XXXVI, 247-248). Again in 1854, Henry Rogers made the same point with similar citations (*Edinburgh Review* XCIX (April 1854), 421-422). In 1819, Coleridge had drawn the opposite lesson; see *The Philosophical Lectures of Samuel Taylor Coleridge*, ed. Kathleen Coburn (London, 1949), p. 383. Coleridge several times repeated that interpretation elsewhere.

99. *Essay* I, iv, 25; cf. I, iii, 20.

100. For matter relevant to the argument I have presented here, see my essay "The State of Nature and the Nature of Man in Locke" in John W. Yolton, ed., *John Locke: Problems and Perspectives* (Cambridge, 1969), pp. 99-136. In the essay on "Leibniz on Locke on Language," above pp. 60-61, I have tried to identify the doctrine of innateness—a linguistic one—against which Locke was arguing. I believe the identification is correct.

101. *Sprachwissenschaft*, pp. 102-103. So also in the 2nd ed. (1969), pp. 119-120.

102. Adolf Harnack, *Geschichte der Königlich Preussischen Akademie der Wissenschaften zu Berlin*, 3 vols. (Berlin, 1900), I, 300.

103. Harcourt Brown, "Maupertuis *philosophe*: Enlightenment and the Berlin Academy," in *Studies on Voltaire and the Eighteenth Century* XXIV (1963), 258-259. The history of the Berlin Academy is set forth in Harnack's magnificent *Geschichte*, which is of the first importance for all studies in the thought of the eighteenth century; for the present subject see especially I, 247-394, where the statutes will be found pp. 299-302. Convenient biographies of most of the members mentioned below will be found in Christian Bartholmèss, *Histoire de l'Académie Prusse depuis Leibniz jusqu'à Schelling, particulièrement sous Frédéric-le-Grand,* 2 vols. (Paris, 1850-1851). See also Samuel Formey, "Éloge de Monsieur de Maupertuis" in *Histoire de l'Académie Royale des Sciences et Belles-Lettres* 1759 (imprint 1/66), pp. 464-512. I have given the official title of the Academy's proceedings normally referred to as the *Mémoires*, hereafter abbreviated *Mém.*, followed by year and in parenthesis the year of publication. Emil du Bois-Reymond has a good biography of Maupertuis in *Sitzungsberichte der Königlich Preussischen Akademie der Wissenschaften zu Berlin 1892* (Januar bis Mai), pp. 393-442. This item is also in *Reden von Emil du Bois-Reymond*, 2 vols. (Leipzig, 1912), II, 426-491. An indispensable guide and source of information concerning the early years is Eduard Winter, *Die Registres der Berliner Akademie der Wissenschaften 1746-1766* (Berlin: Akademie-Verlag, 1957). For each of the 855 meetings (until 17 July 1766), it gives a list of the members present and the business of the meeting. I shall refer to it as Winter, followed by number and date. It should be remembered that somewhat less than half of the communications read in the weekly sessions were actually printed in the *Mém.*, though some papers were later published separately.

104. Formey, "Éloge," pp. 505 and 495-496.

105. Pierre Brunet, *Maupertuis*, 2 vols. (Paris, 1929), I, 161. Condillac was unanimously elected member on 4 December 1749 (Winter No. 153). During the time when he had sought refuge in Berlin, de la Mettrie was proposed for membership on 27 June 1748 and elected regular member on 4 July 1748 (Winter, Nos. 92 and 94).

106. The relevant items are in vol. I of *Oeuvres de Mr de Maupertuis*, nouv. éd. corrigée et augmentée (Lyon, 1756). This volume contains: "Avertissement" by Maupertuis, with some useful information, pp. 255-257; *Réflexions*, pp. 259-285; Boindin's "Remarques," pp. 287-291; Maupertuis's "Réponse," pp. 293-309. Both the *Réflexions* and the later "Dissertation" are divided in short paragraphs, to which I shall make reference in the text with the appropriate Roman numeral.

107. M. L. Dufrenoy, "Maupertuis et le progrès scientifique," in *Studies on Voltaire and the Eighteenth Century* XXV (1963), 572.

108. *Oeuvres* (Lyon, 1756) I, 299-300.

109. See letter of Condillac to Maupertuis (à Segrez 12 August 1750) in which he thanks him for the gift of "l'Origine des Langues," which he knew by reputation but had not yet seen, copies being scarce. Condillac adds that he is now himself working on "la génération du sentiment" (Condillac II, 535). Owing to his poor eyesight, Condillac did not write a long answer until 25 June 1752 (*ibid.*, 535-538). He finds the *Réflexions* very philosophical, precise and fruitful, but regrets that Maupertuis has not dealt with the question, "how the

progress of the mind depends on language. I have attempted it in my *Essai* . . . but I have been mistaken and given too much to signs." We have already seen that Condillac later in life was eager to reassert the doctrine of the *Essai*.

110. The words underlined by Maupertuis remind us of his well-known familiarity with Leibniz. The concluding four paragraphs of the *Réflexions* deal with the problem of duration and have been seen to relate to Kant.

111. In the *Oeuvres* (Lyon, 1756) in vol. I, as Maupertuis explains in the "Avertissement."

112. L. Gossman, "Berkeley, Hume and Maupertuis," in *French Studies* XIV (1960), 322, suggests that Boindin's remarks were actually written by Turgot, but the only reason given is reference to Turgot's "Remarques critiques sur les Réflexions philosophiques de Maupertuis" (1750). I see no force in that suggestion. Boindin's "Remarques" were published in his *Oeuvres*, and Maupertuis in his answer clearly assumes that the writer was the famous atheist. Turgot's critique was not published until du Pont de Nemours' edition of the *Oeuvres* (Paris, 1807-1811). Turgot's critique offers a strange instance of incomprehension or perhaps of stubborn unwillingness to argue on Maupertuis's grounds. According to Turgot, words are tied directly to things, things are directly experienced as they are; since all men have the same sense experience, their ideas are correspondingly identical.

113. *Oeuvres* (Lyon, 1756), I, 298-299. For a typical nineteenth-century opinion of eighteenth-century discussions of language, see Benfey's remarks on the *Réflexions* in his *Geschichte der Sprachwissenschaft*, pp. 283-285. The quality of his remarks is suggested by this passage: "If we did not know that human wisdom and folly always go hand in hand, it would be incomprehensible how such an exceptionally intelligent man could arrive at such truly ill-considered nonsense."

114. Winter No. 176. Printed *Mém.* 1753 (1755), pp. 511-521; also in Maupertuis, *Oeuvres* (Lyon, 1768. Olms Reprint, 1965) III, 283-302 (this matter p. 297).

115. *Oeuvres* (Lyon, 1768) II, 383.

116. *Ibid.*, II, 388.

117. *Ibid.* II, 429-430.

118. Winter No. 399. Printed *Mém.* 1755 (1757), pp. 514-529. The other three papers were not printed in the *Mém.* See Winter Nos. 424 (25 March 1756), 476 (7 July 1757), and 501 (16 February 1758).

119. AT XIV, 435-441.

120. Winter No. 430; printed in *Mém.* 1754 (1756), pp. 349-364. It is worth noting that, though given in 1756, this essay was printed in the volume for 1754, which was published in 1756. It is also in *Oeuvres* (Lyon, 1768) III, 435-468.

121. Winter Nos. 444 and 445: "Mr. Süssmilch read a paper in German in which it is proved that languages could not have a human origin but that they come directly from God." In 1745, Süssmilch had read a paper (published in *Mém.* for that year, pp. 188-203) under the title, "Réflexions sur la convenance de la Langue Celtique, et en particulier de la Teutonique avec celles de l'Orient, par lesquelles on démontre que la langue Teutonique est matériellement contenue dans les Langues Orientales, et qu'elle en descend" (Harnack, *Geschichte* III, 554). Between 1746 and his death, Süssmilch read no less than 32 papers, most of them on demography, but seven of them on linguistic matters. These were not printed in the *Mém.* In addition to Nos. 444 and 445, see Winter Nos. 143, 255, 469, 696, and 709.

122. *Versuch*, pp. 33-34.

123. *Ibid.*, pp. 14-17.

124. Thus in the study of language Süssmilch's *Versuch* would seem to be one of the first works to stress the conflict between faith and natural explanation, between the divine act and gradual development. This conflict has since taken many forms, but when, during the 1830s and 1840s in England, it involved the opposition of Genesis and geology, language

was invoked on the side of Genesis. See Aarsleff, pp. 207-209, 223-225. See also C. C. Gillispie's excellent *Genesis and Geology* (Cambridge, Mass., 1951).

125. *Versuch*, p. 54.

126. *Ibid.*, p. 83. The excellence of Süssmilch's argument needs to be stressed; one fears that scholars who make disparaging remarks about him are ignorant of his outstanding contributions to demography and have not read the *Versuch*. His work on demography easily makes him the most important and creative member of the Academy during the years we are here concerned with, possibly with the exception of Euler. Robert T. Clark, Jr., in his *Herder, his Life and Thought* (Berkeley, 1955), p. 131, observes: ". . . Süssmilch, a member of the Academy, although one wonders how he got in." Clark has the *Versuch* in mind! More recently, it has been remarked: " . . . those who ascribed the origin of language to God —in the last analysis owing to mental ineptitude and laziness (Süssmilch)." One must hope that people who associate the *Versuch* with "Ratlosigkeit und Bequemlichkeit" have not read it. See Manfred Krüger, "Der menschlich-göttliche Ursprung der Sprache, Bemerkungen zu Herders Sprachtheorie," in *Wirkendes Wort* XVII (1967), 8. For an informed discussion, see Bruce Kieffer, "Herder's treatment of Süssmilch's theory of the origin of language in the *Abhandlung über den Ursprung der Sprache*: A re-evaluation." *The Germanic Review* 53 (1978), 96-105.

127. Winter No. 472. The formulation of the question and the directions will be found in the first part of *Mém.* 1770 (1772), "Histoire de l'Académie," with separate pagination, p. 25. Also briefly in Harnack, *Geschichte*, II, 306.

128. Condillac II, 90-94. In a footnote the editor refers to Maupertuis's two papers. These are of course highly relevant, but Condillac's words—"a proposé"—are so specific that they can well bear my reading.

129. Winter No. 554.

130. J. G. Buhle, ed., *Literarischer Briefwechsel von Johann David Michaëlis* I (Leipzig, 1794), 152.

131. (London, 1769), p. 46.

132. Winter No. 344. Printed *Mém.* 1754 (1756), pp. 418-442.

133. It was read to the Academy on 13 March 1760 and was, like the original essay, in German. Winter No. 587.

134. *Beantwortung der Frage von dem Einfluss der Meinungen in die Sprache und der Sprache in die Meinungen* (Berlin, 1760), p. 78. It may be recalled that Johann Georg Hamann in *Kreuzzüge des Philologen* (Riga, 1762), included an unfavorable discussion of Michaëlis's essay under the title "Versuch über eine akademische Frage." See Hamann, *Sämtliche Werke*, ed. Josef Nadler, II (Wien, 1950), 119-126. For a brief account of Michaëlis's essay, see Aarsleff, pp. 143-147.

135. Winter No. 682. Printed in *Mém.* 1759 (1766), pp. 367-377. Since this and the remaining pieces are brief, I shall not give further page references. In 1757, Formey had brought out an edition of Du Marsais's *Des Tropes*; he had been shocked by French indifference to it and found it difficult to obtain a copy (see "Avis des éditeurs" in Du Marsais, *Oeuvres* I, xiii). Formey had some correspondence with Condillac; see the interesting letter from Condillac to Formey (Paris, 25 February 1756) in Condillac II, 538-541.

136. *Inégalité*, pp. 123-124. See also the informative notes on pp. 1295-1296.

137. Winter No. 808. Printed in *Mém.* 1765 (1767), pp. 495-505. This paper and Beausobre's were printed in the "Classe de Belles-Lettres." All the other papers as well as the two prize topics, Michaëlis's and Herder's, belonged to the "Classe de Philosophie Spéculative."

138. *Mém.* 1767 (1769), pp. 413-438. Winter's *Registres* end with 18 July 1766.

139. *Mém.* 1770 (1772), "Histoire" p. 28. It is striking proof of the popularity of the question that the Academy received no less than thirty-one answers.

140. *Ursprung* in Suphan, V, 34.

141. Bruno Liebrucks, *Sprache und Bewusstsein*, vol. I *Einleitung. Spannweite des Problems* (Frankfurt am Main, 1964), p. 48.

142. Condillac I, 98b, 103b (*Essai* II, i, § §143, 161, 162).

143. Suphan V, 64, 194.

144. *Ibid.*, V, 35, 38, 47.

145. *Ibid.*, V, 82-83: "Since every grammar is only a philosophy of the language and a method for its use, it follows that the more original the language, the less grammar is there in it," a view which I should think will rule out that Herder can be cited as an example of "Cartesian" linguistics. Cf. Condillac I, 442-443 (*Grammaire* I, vi): "Slowness of progress does not prove that they [languages] have been formed without method; it only proves that the method has been perfected slowly," and "the system governing languages must be fundamentally the same throughout; consequently all languages have common rules." (in Condillac I, 435a; *Grammaire* I, ii). Though not published until 1775, the *Grammaire* was finished no later than 1766.

146. *Mém.* 1771 (1773), pp. 17-20, in "Histoire."

147. *Mém.* 1781 (1783), pp. 388 and 404 in "Analyse de la Dissertation sur l'Origine du Language, qui a remporté le prix en 1771."

148. Suphan V, 20-21, 40-41.

149. Venturi, pp. 238-240. Among the Herder interpretations I have seen, I know only one exception to the conventional view; it is Hans Dietrich Irmscher writing in the "Nachwort" to his recent edition of the *Ursprung* (Stuttgart: Reclam, 1966), p. 140: "Condillac affirms the animalistic origin of language in his *Essai*. What we use as a highly differentiated means of understanding is nothing other than a continuous development of what man among other things also shares with the animals. Herder has completely made this thesis his own." Though I cannot agree with this interpretation of Condillac, the second statement is correct, and to my knowledge unique. Irmscher's text in the Reclam edition follows that of the Suphan edition.

150. I am happy to note that the arguments of this essay have raised discussion that takes issue with some of the interpretations offered here. Two fruitful studies are : Herder, *Traité sur l'Origine de la langue, suivi de l'analyse de Mérian et des textes critiques de Hamann*. Introduction, traduction et notes de Pierre Pénisson (Paris: Aubier-Flammarion Collection Palimpseste, 1977). Wolfgang Pross, *Johann Gottfried Herder: Abhandlung über den Ursprung der Sprache*. Text, Materialien, Kommentar (München: Carl Hanser Verlag [1980], in: Reihe Hanser Literatur-Kommentare, vol. 12).

Condillac's Speechless Statue

It is widely recognized that Condillac occupies a commanding position in the intellectual life of Europe during the latter half of the eighteenth century. Between 1746 and the year of his death in 1780, at the age of sixty-five, he published a number of works that caused excitement and influence not only in France, but also in Germany, England, and Italy. In France his importance and influence is acknowledged by Diderot, d'Alembert, Rousseau, Turgot, and de Brosses (to mention only the best-known names among his French contemporaries), and the French *Encyclopédie* is heavily indebted to him. As early as 1748, his philosophy was introduced in Germany by Maupertuis, who had recently become president of the Berlin Academy; he raised a Condillacian discussion of language, man, and knowledge that lasted over the next twenty-five years, culminating in Herder's *Abhandlung über den Ursprung der Sprache*.[1] In England Condillac gave the impulse to several works, of which Lord Monboddo's great work *Of the Origin and Progress of Language* is the best known. Given this wide influence on figures who were themselves significant and influential, it is clearly a matter of importance to know and understand Condillac well. Since the nineteenth century, his place in intellectual history has in fact not been well understood, and it is for this reason that I wish to examine the crucial question in Condillac's philosophy: the role that language plays in his understanding of the nature of man. This problem can be approached in several ways, but

Reprinted from *Studia Leibnitiana. Supplementa* XV (1975), 287-302. (Akten des II. internationalen Leibniz-Kongresses, Hannover 17.-22. Juli 1972.)

210

perhaps the most revealing avenue is to ask why Condillac's statue doesn't speak. The first part of my essay will deal with this problem. In the second part I shall try to indicate the kinds of misunderstanding Condillac has suffered and explore some of the reasons for it.

I

That the statue neither speaks nor is in a position to learn to speak is evident enough, but why is that so? Since the nineteenth century, commentators and historians have either not seen the problem or have offered interpretations that carry the implication that the statue speaks or is so placed that it could if it should choose to do so, in other words that the full gift of language is within its reach, thus being able to rise to "the richest intellectual and emotional experiences of man," to cite a recent statement that is representative of the conventional understanding of Condillac.[2] You may recall that the statue occurs in the *Traité des sensations*, first published in 1754, but written during the years immediately following 1749. This work is commonly seen as the most important expression of Condillac's philosophy, even as a thoroughgoing revision or rejection of the arguments and principles presented in the *Essai sur l'origine des connoissances humaines* (1746).[3] You may recall that the statue is gradually brought to life as Condillac endows it with the five senses one by one, first smell, then taste, hearing, and vision in that order, none of which alone or together give the statue any assurance of the existence of anything outside itself. But being finally endowed with the sense of touch and with motion, it gains enduring awareness and conviction that there is indeed a world outside itself. This conclusion was the aim of Condillac's entire argument, for it was his answer to Diderot who in his *Lettre sur les aveugles* (1749)[4] had suggested that Condillac was a Berkeleian idealist on the basis of the emphatic opening of Part One of the *Essai*: "Whether we raise ourselves, to speak metaphorically, to the heavens or descend into the abyss, we never step outside ourselves and we never perceive anything but our own private thoughts."[5]

Bound within its sparse mode of being, the statue develops a certain measure of mental life and even a certain crucial success, in spite of the fact that the statue throughout remains "un homme isolé," a point repeatedly stressed by Condillac. It is successful because it learns enough to ensure its own preservation. This accomplishment it shares with man, or with human beings, for when the ideas we owe to the five senses are joined together, "they give us all the knowledge that is necessary for our preservation."[6] This capacity for preservation is acquired by experience, that is by interaction with nature, because the statue naturally seeks the attainment of pleasure and the avoidance of pain. It learns to recognize its basic needs, "ses besoins," which Condillac calls "the knowledge of a good that it finds it is necessary for itself to have . . . it is in this fashion that pleasure and pain will always determine the exercise of its faculties."[7] Thus, "the order of its studies is determined by its needs."[8] The statue's needs are limited to those natural ones that relate to its preservation: "To eat, to protect itself against any adversity or to defend itself against it, and to satisfy its curiosity: those are all the natural needs of the statue."[9]

In order to meet the needs that secure its preservation, the statue is capable of learning from experience. It develops certain rudimentary mental capacities, guided by its innate, natural tendency to avoid pain and gain its opposite, pleasure: it can remember sensations it has had in the past; these sensations, Condillac calls "idées intellectuelles" which are distinguished from the mere "sensations actuelles" it happens to have at any particular moment in the present. Memory makes it possible for the statue to compare past sensations with actual and present sensations.[10] By this means it can, for instance, compare and judge regarding differences in size. It learns from nature and it learns naturally owing to those faculties that are part of its nature. It also has the power of imagination which is a heightened form of memory: "Imagination is memory itself, brought to the full vivacity of which it is capable."[11]

When we note that the statue cannot merely have sensations, but also remember, imagine, and judge, we may feel that Condillac has already moved a good distance away from the mechanical sensualism, let alone materialism, that is generally attributed to him.[12] For whereas actual sensation is passive, the other powers are active, and this activity is in the "mind" of the statue—Condillac never tires of insisting on the activity of the mind. In all his works this activity is crucial to his argument: yet practically all interpretations make it their chief point to assert that man and his mind are entirely passive according to Condillac, a fact that shows how profoundly he has been misunderstood since the nineteenth century. Thus though his argument is certainly directed against innate ideas as commonly understood, it still retains mentalism—it may be recalled that Du Marsais, with whom Condillac was personally acquainted, also forcefully rejected innate ideas. To say, therefore, as has often been said (indeed along with passivity it is one of the commonplaces of the interpretation of Condillac), that he reduced Locke's reflection to mere sensation, thus allowing only a single source of ideas and knowledge, is a mere play on words that quite fails to produce any conviction. It is true that a few phrases may seem to support that interpretation, but only if—and that is a very great if—they are read out of context without regard for his argument.[13] Condillac often insists that his entire method is guided by observation of the operations that are open to our inspection. He maintains the temporal priority of sensation, just as Locke had also argued that reflection cannot go into action and reveal itself until sensation has furnished the mind with materials to work on.

So far I have dealt with the statue's abilities, and it is evident that they do not at all suffice to make it a human being. I shall now deal with the limitations. But before proceeding it must be mentioned that there are two versions of the *Traité des sensations*, the original 1754 version, which I have used so far, and the later version that was presented in the *Oeuvres complètes* published in 1798. The second version contains the entire text of the 1754 version, but adds a number of new passages.[14] Thus the second version does not present a new argument, but strengthens and clarifies the original argument. The new passages underscore Condillac's commitment to the argument of the *Essai* in 1746, a commitment that is also indicated by some of his later works.[15] This fidelity to his first work is important since it has most often been either ignored or denied with serious consequences for the understanding of Condillac's position and influence in the intellectual history of the latter half of the eighteenth century.

Let me now turn to two passages that are new in the second version. The first occurs in Section II at the end of the long Chapter viii entitled "Of the ideas that a human being can acquire when limited to the sense of touch." Here the description of the final paragraph has been changed from "Conclusion de ce chapitre" to "Its knowledge is only practical; and the light that guides it is merely instinct." He has then added a passage on the severe limitations imposed on the statue owing to its lack of language: "Its method in the acquisition of ideas is to observe in succession, one after the other, the qualities it attributes to objects: It analyzes naturally, but it has no language. But an analysis that is made without signs can only give very limited knowledge . . . and since it has not been possible to put them in order, the collection must be very confused. Thus when I treat the ideas that the statue acquires, I do not mean to say that it has knowledge of which it can render an exact account to itself: It has only practical knowledge. All the light it has is properly speaking instinctive, that is to say, a habit of conducting itself according to ideas of which it does not know how to render account to itself, a habit which when acquired guides it safely, without any need for it to recall the judgments that made it assume that habit. But as soon as its ideas have taught it how to conduct itself, it no longer thinks of it and it acts by habit. To acquire knowledge, it is necessary to have a language: for the ideas must be classified and determined, which presupposes signs employed according to method. See the first part of my grammar or my logic."[16] The second passage enforces the same point: "If you recall that I have demonstrated how much signs are necessary in order to produce distinct ideas of any kind, you will tend to believe that I attribute more knowledge to the statue than it can acquire. But we must make a distinction . . . between knowledge of theory and practical knowledge. To have those of the first kind we need a language."[17]

Thus the answer to the question why the statue does not speak is simple: because it cannot. It is in a profound sense speechless. And it is speechless because it exists all by itself, in total isolation. The progress of knowledge, which must include "les connoissances de théorie," depends on the development of man's innate capacity for reflection, and this development can occur only with the aid of man's greatest artificial accomplishment, speech and language, that is by means of voluntarily created arbitrary signs which record experience, give structure to reality, make communication and thus also tradition possible, make past knowledge retrievable, and allow the combination of ideas according to any deliberate plan.[18] Thus language, knowledge beyond what is needed for mere preservation (in the form of unreflective habit turned into instinct), and the progress of mind are all functions of society. This was also the argument of the *Essai*, which is not superseded or subverted by the *Traité des sensations*. Though the statue served to answer Diderot's observation about Condillac's seeming commitment to Berkleian idealism, the statue remains on the mental level of the animals.

A brief consideration of Condillac's next work will show what I mean. The aim of the *Traité des animaux* (1755) is well known; it was to show that the animals are not, as the Cartesians held, mere automatons. They think in certain rudimentary ways exactly like the statue: they acquire ideas, learn from experience, judge, compare and discover, meet the needs of preservation, develop habits, act by instinct, and have no language. Again like the statue, they gain some practical but no theoretical knowledge. But the *Traité des animaux* is not merely about animals, it is also about man. In a chapter "De l'instinct et de la raison," we encounter these passages: "There are somehow two selves in each human being: the self of habit and the self of reflection. . . . The measure of reflection we have beyond our habits is what constitutes our reason. . . . The instinct of animals has only practical knowledge for its object: it does not lead to theory; for theory presupposes a method, that is, convenient signs for the determination of ideas, for arranging them in order and for gathering the results. Ours embraces both theory and practice: it is the effect of a method that has become second nature. But every human being endowed with language has a means of determining its ideas, to arrange them and to appropriate the results: it has a method more or less perfect."[19] Thus we can make this chart:

Statue, animals	Man
moi d'habitude	moi de réflexion
instinct	raison, réflexion
connoissances pratiques	connoissances de théorie
animals: cris naturels but no language	voluntary, arbitrary signs, language
satisfaction only of needs of preservation	satisfaction of needs beyond preservation

The contrast between the statue and the animals on the one hand and man on the other is a contrast between Nature and Art.

If some animals are known to live in groups or societies, we may ask why they do not have language. Condillac's answer is: "It is not surprising that only man, who is as superior in regard to organic being as by the nature of the spirit that animates him, has the gift of speech."[20] Here again Condillac is repeating doctrine that he had already advanced in the *Essai* in 1746. Here he said: "From all the operations we have described results one that, so to speak, crowns the understanding: it is reason . . . [which] is nothing but the knowledge of the manner in which we are obliged to rule the operations of mind." Later in the same chapter, he says in summing up: "We are capable of more reflection in proportion as we have more reason. Consequently, this last faculty produces reflection."[21] Thus Condillac emphatically says that reason is fundamental in the nature of man. It places him in a realm of being and potentiality that is altogether different from that of the animals. Reason is the sine qua non of language.

In this light the common belief that Condillac is a sensualist or a materialist appears very odd indeed. In 1937 Georges le Roy said: "In fact, the *Treatise on the sensations* does not have the exclusive character it has often been given. It does not deny the role of language in the development of the mental faculties, and consequently it does not constitute a refutation of the *Essai*. It deals solely with the operations of mind that precede the acquisition of languages, and it limits itself to the analysis of those operations."[22] Condillac's statue does not have the means of rising "to the richest intellectual and emotional experiences of man." The statue and the argument in which it moves underscore the central and crucial importance Condillac assigned to speech and language in his philosophy of the nature of man. Almost blinded by an altogether different mode of looking at language, the nineteenth century missed Condillac's point and turned him into their own image of the superficial philosopher, sensualist, materialist, or whatever he was called. For the nineteenth century that may be understandable, but it is distressing to find these views repeated today in books that lay claims to understanding, and scholarship. And if, as may well be argued, Condillac is the most important and influential philosopher of the French enlightenment, not least as seen in the *Encyclopédie*, then this error is more than odd; it gets in the way of intellectual history.

II

Let me now indicate briefly some of the ways in which this stubborn misunderstanding and ignorance of Condillac have arisen. I think there are four main factors, and I shall consider each in turn.

The first is this: in the tradition of intellectual history dating from the early decades of the nineteenth century, Condillac's philosophy of language has been found most fully and typically represented by his last, unfinished, and posthumous work *La langue des calculs*, which was first published in the *Oeuvres complètes* (1798). This view makes two serious errors. Condillac's *Langue des calculs* presents only a particular aspect of his philosophy of language, and it is not, for obvious reasons, the work by which he gained such enormous influence during the latter half of the eighteenth century. Inspired by Garat and occurring during the years of the Directoire, the publication of the *Oeuvres* in 1798 was designed to serve the purposes of a new philosophy of signs, man, and the progress of knowledge; this philosophy was made the foundation of the radical educational program promoted by the Directoire. (The same intention had guided the first publication of the *Oeuvres* of Du Marsais in 1797.) The best known exponent of these views is Destutt de Tracy; during 1796 and February of 1798, he read five papers to the Institut national which in August of 1798 (a few months after the appearance of Condillac's *Oeuvres*) were published in the *Mémoires* under the title "Mémoire sur la faculté de penser." A few years later began the publication of

Destutt de Tracy's *Élémens d'idéologie*. His main text was the *Traité des sensations*, and the *Langue des calculs* came to be seen as a "Programmschrift" for a radical doctrine of man and education. The *Essai sur l'origine des connoissances humaines* received attention only in so far as it satisfied these needs.

The consequences have been overwhelming, for as soon as the reaction set in, Condillac became chiefly known and understood in the version of his thought that had been presented by Destutt de Tracy and the *idéologues*. Condillac and the *idéologues* became the victims of the violent reaction that from the early decades of the nineteenth century was directed against eighteenth-century thought and the Revolution. This distorted, even contemptuous view of Condillac was presented to vast audiences in the lectures and writings of Victor Cousin who gained astonishing influence both in France and England. For similar reasons, Cousin also gave a very peculiar account of Locke which had a powerful effect in England—it is the sort of version of Locke's philosophy Professor Chomsky has recently taken to be a "commonplace," something that is true and obvious. In the history of the study of language, one example will serve to show the effect. Both in the first and second edition (1955 and 1969) of his great commentated anthology *Sprachwissenschaft*, Hans Arens bases his account of Condillac on the *Langue des calculs*. Summing up, he says about Condillac's philosophy that it is characterized by "intellectual impatience and intolerance toward life that can only be mastered mathematically when it is conceived as pure mechanism." For the philosophy of language we are told that the consequence is the following: "Language is not at all seen as the mode and expression of life, but throughout as a mere logical system of signs for concepts and the statement of propositions."[23] Clearly, such ignorance precludes historical understanding. It also removes the possibility that German interest in the problem of the origin of language, as in Herder for instance, might be heavily indebted to Condillac.

The second source of confusion about Condillac springs from the simple matter of chronology. After the publication of the *Essai* in 1746, writings on the philosophy and especially the origin of language followed in close succession so that it is important to follow the sequence of publication before deciding on questions of priority and influence. In fact, most major figures, not merely in France, explicitly state their indebtedness to Condillac, but even these statements have often been ignored. The most serious, indeed fateful error is the tacit assumption that Condillac said nothing about language until the publication of his *Cours d'études* in 1775, the work that includes his

Grammaire, L'art d'écrire, L'art de raisonner, and *L'art de penser,* or the publication of his *Logique* in 1780. The *Cours d'études* was written between 1758 and the end of 1766, and its basic linguistic doctrines are already in the *Essai;* thus Condillac expressly says that the greater part of the *L'art de penser* is drawn from the *Essai,* a fact that must be obvious to any reader even without such assurance. A few examples drawn from the recent secondary literature will show the consequences of failing to pay attention to the chronology. An article from 1938, says that Diderot in 1751 in the *Lettre sur les sourds et muets* found the origin of language in gestures and inarticulate cries and then goes on to observe, with reference to the *Cours d'études,* that this doctrine was later taken up, as the article says, by "Condillac himself."[24] Now, this doctrine forms a fundamental part of the argument of Condillac's *Essai,* from which Diderot took it with explicit acknowledgement to Condillac. Many other similar examples could be cited. Jean Starobinski, for instance, finds that the principle of the linearity of speech is first found in Rousseau, though it also is crucial in the philosophy of the *Essai.*[25] Both Diderot and Rousseau have often been credited with doctrines which they themselves credited to Condillac—which shows that even Diderot and Rousseau are not always being read with much care.

A third cause of confusion lies in the nineteenth century's immersion in a strict historical view, combined with positivism, that altogether blocked understanding of the conjectural and theoretical mode of eighteenth-century thought. This mode did not aim at establishing historical fact and did not claim to have done so. A typical instance of this failure of understanding is found in Renan's *De l'origine du langage.* Renan says of Condillac and his contemporaries, with disapproval of course: "They addressed themselves to theoretical questions before they had dedicated themselves to the patient study of precise details. . . . Eighteenth-century philosophy had a strong penchant for artificial explanations in everything that pertains to the origins of the human mind."[26] The nineteenth century failed to see the import of the eighteenth century's distinction between nature and art, and without that distinction Condillac becomes incomprehensible.

Finally, there is a fourth factor that has caused endless confusion: the tendency, prompted one suspects by desire, to see a sharp division between the philosophies of language in France and Germany, as if they fall in altogether separate compartments. There is even a word for it: Herder is said to belong to the "Deutsche Bewegung." In his *Sprachwissenschaft* Arens makes it a principle that whereas the French busied themselves with universal grammar, the special linguistic province of the Germans was the question of the origin of language: "Related to the orientation of the time toward general problems about mankind and especially to 'universal grammar,' is also the problem of its origin, in France treated more peripherally, in Germany, where philosophical grammar only appears much later, for a long time a current topic."[27] As already mentioned, it can easily be demonstrated that the philosophy of Condillac's *Essai* and especially its long section on the origin of language were debated in the Berlin Academy, deliberately chosen and introduced by Maupertuis. It was this debate that caused the formulation of the two prize-topics that were answered by Johann David Michaëlis and Herder. It was not a problem which in that form had a German origin. A book that offers perhaps the most detailed discussion we have of Herder's *Abhandlung* and its philosophy of language shows the confidence with which Condillac's *Essai* is ignored. The author of this book shows no knowledge of the *Essai*, but—and that is fantastic—takes the *Abhandlung* as a reliable secondary source. Ignorant of the *Essai*, he then assures the reader that in his book, "the subject is throughout the origin-of-language theory of the *Essai*, and . . . never of the far more important one in the *Langue des calculs*." In this work, the author says, "is shown how an articulate language gradually emerges from an original language of gestures (langue d'action), a language, it is expressly said, that does not merely serve the needs of communication and outward understanding, but above all comprehension. . . . Here the talk is no longer about the animalistic origin of language, of the 'noises' and 'cries of emotion.'"[28] The implication is clearly that if Herder had known the doctrine of the *Langue des calculs*, then the story would have been altogether different. The problem is indeed bothersome, for the brief passage on the origin of language and the language of action in the latter work merely recapitulates what Condillac had presented and argued at much greater length in the *Essai*. This total misunderstanding becomes especially curious when we consider that there has for at least seventy years been published proof that Herder as early as 1764 had read Part Two of Condillac's *Essai*, that is the very part which, under the title "Du langage et de la méthode," contains the long section entitled "De l'origine et des progrès du langage," which takes up a full third of the entire *Essai*. One feels tempted to see a conspiracy of silence to keep the "Deutsche Bewegung" free of French influence.

I am of course suggesting that Herder, along with the other participants in the debate in the Berlin Academy, was directly and profoundly influenced by Condillac's *Essai*. Remembering that human speech and language (with its voluntary, arbitrary signs) is exclusively a product of 'réflexion,' is it possible to read this often-quoted statement from Herder's *Abhandlung*, always cited as his basic and original doctrine, without immediately thinking of the *Essai*: "Endowed with the capacity for thought that is peculiar to him and this capacity for thought (reflexion) for the first time being given free exercise, man has invented language." Or we may consider the following doctrines that are taken to be so typical of Herder: "Everything confirms that each language expresses the character of the people who speak it." Or the doctrine that, "Of all the writers, it is with the poets that the genius of language gains the most lively expression." Or this: "For anyone who understands them well, languages would be a painting of the character and genius of each people. He would see how the imagination has combined ideas according to the given outlook and the passions."[29] Or the related and equally celebrated doctrine that the first speech occurred in stituations of strong emotion and reactions to nature. These doctrines are all fully stated and argued in the *Essai*, from which the quotations are taken. I may add this: It is often dogmatically asserted that Wilhelm von Humboldt continued the study of language in the tradition of Herder and Hamann; this claim is taken to be so safe that no one seems to have bothered to substantiate it. Though I think I have an extensive knowledge of Wilhelm von Humboldt's writings and of his often very revealing correspondence, I have never found any evidence that this claim can be substantiated and much that casts it seriously into doubt. It is, however, evident and universally admitted that Humboldt's interest in anthropology, already strong during the 1790s, did not find its locus in the study of language until the years in Paris and immediately following, during the journeys to the Basque Provinces and Spain. His orientation may be Kantian, though there is much uncertainty about precisely how, but his early linguistic writings clearly show the influence of the philosophy he encountered in Paris, where he moved much in the circles of the idéologues and where he read all of Condillac's major works as soon as they came out in the late spring of 1798. He may have said that he didn't agree with them, have contrasted their philosophy with Kant's, and much else. But it remains significant that his orientation towards language occurs precisely at this time and within the spirit of the thought of Condillac and the idéologues. The reputed similarity of the linguistic thought of Herder and von Humboldt (and of course others) may be a common but separate indebtedness to similar sources rather than a tradition that links Herder and Humboldt sequentially. But this, so far as I know, is a possibility that has never been considered, yet it is in large measure demonstrable and much more plausible than the unsubstantiated (sometimes even fabricated) claims that are assumed to take care of the matter.[30]

Without trying to summarize, let me briefly conclude in this fashion. The speechless statue of the *Traité des sensations* shows the supreme role that Condillac assigned to language in the nature of man, mind, and knowledge; in this respect the *Traité* merely follows the argument of the *Essai*, which separately considered would have served equally well for our purposes. Wide ignorance of the *Essai*, misunderstanding of the *Traité*, and unquestioning faith in a number of curious historical errors have obscured the intellectual history of the latter half of the eighteenth century. If we pay attention to the texts and to the context of intellectual cross-influence of that period, we may be able to see things in a better and more interesting light.

Notes

1. For some of the matters treated in the present essay, for instance on the role of Maupertuis, see "The Tradition of Condillac," above; it will be referred to as Aarsleff 1974. There is striking proof of Condillac's popularity and of the exposure given to his thought in the four volumes of Panckoucke's *Encyclopédie méthodique* that are devoted to "Logique et Métaphysique" (Paris, 1786-1791). Looking only at vol. 1, the "Discours préliminaire" (pp. xv-xvi) explains that, "this Dictionary is therefore a compilation of the best treatises, dissertations and articles on metaphysics and logic. . . . In the light of this plan, the reader will understand that it is chiefly Locke and Condillac who have provided most of the articles." Thus the article "Ame" (pp. 27-71) reprints on pp. 49-71 all of Condillac's *Essai* Part I, section ii "L'Analyse et la génération des opérations de l'âme." This article refers to the entry "Langage," pp. 597-621a, which reprints all of the 14 chapters in Part I of Condillac's "Grammaire." "Association des idées," pp. 158a-161a, simply reprints the famous chapter from Locke's *Essay* Book II, ch. xxxiii. The article "Idée," pp. 497a-554a, reprints on pp. 505-535b Locke's *Essay* Book II, chs. 1-xii, and on pp. 535b-545a, *Essay* Book II, chs. xxix-xxxi. These are merely random examples, but enough to show that Locke and Condillac were not likely to be forgotten.

2. Isabel F. Knight, *The Geometric Spirit, the Abbé de Condillac and the French Enlightenment* (New Haven: Yale University Press, 1968), p. 106. This book perpetuates conventional errors about Condillac, but the very fact of publication shows how firmly established they are. The fundamental error is the opinion that it was Condillac's chief aim to make the mind altogether passive and to reduce Locke's reflection to mere sensation. This error has found support in the subtitle of the *Essai* (found only in the 1746 edition), which said, "a work in which all that concerns the understanding is reduced to a single principle." This has been interpreted to mean sensation. But the argument makes it clear that Condillac means "la liaison des idées," and in the *Essai* (Part II, sect. II, ch. iii, §43) he expressly says so: "Philosophers have often asked whether there is a first principle of our understanding. . . . It seems to me that everyone can consult his own experience to be assured of the truth of the foundation of this work. Perhaps we shall even be convinced that the connection of ideas is without comparison the simplest, the clearest and the most fruitful principle. At the

very time when its influence was not noted, we were indebted to it for every improvement made by the human understanding." Both in the *Essai* and other writings, Condillac stresses that "la liaison des idées" is voluntary, the expression of reason and reflection, and thus different from the involuntary association of ideas. In the *Essai* this distinction was not always made evident in the terminology, though on occasion it was; but when Condillac in his later writings cited his own *Essai*, for instance very extensively in *l'Art de penser* (which forms part of the *Cours d'études*), he took care to clear up the terminology. Where the *Essai*, for instance, had said "Locke has revealed the greatest danger in the connection of ideas," the same sentence in the latter work reads "association of ideas." In the English translation of the *Essai*—as *An Essay on the origin of Human knowledge* (London, 1756)—the translator Thomas Nugent carefully distinguished between the "connexion of ideas" and the "association of ideas." Coste's widely read French translation of Locke's *Essay* of course rendered "association of ideas" as "association des idées." It is astonishing that Isabel F. Knight in the *Geometric Spirit* without question or even discussion assumes that the "liaison des idées" is the same as Locke's "association of ideas."

3. For the text of Condillac I am using the edition of Georges le Roy, *Oeuvres philosophiques de Condillac*, 3 vols. (Paris, 1947-1951); to make cross-reference to other texts possible, I shall give not only page references to the le Roy edition, but also the appropriate place by part, section, chapter, and paragraph. Since all the texts that concern us here are in vol. I, I shall merely give the page reference. The misunderstanding of Condillac and the eighteenth century I am dealing with, we owe especially to Victor Cousin; for Cousin's influence in this regard, see "Locke's Reputation in nineteenth-century England."

4. *Oeuvres complètes*, I (Paris, 1875), ed. by J. Assézat, pp. 304-305.

5. *Essai*, p. 43a (I, I, i, § 1).

6. "Extrait raisonné du Traité des sensations," p. 325a.

7. *Traité des sensations* (hereafter TS), p. 228a (I, ii, § 25). It is well known that the statue was widely used in the philosophical literature of the time; for a listing see le Roy's note TS, p. 222. Cf. Condillac's "Réponse à un reproche qui m'a été fait sur le projet exécuté dans le Traité des sensations," pp. 318-319.

8. TS, p. 300b (IV, i, § 7). On pleasure, pain, uneasiness (inquiétude), etc., Condillac was drawing on Locke's *Essay* Book II, with special attention to the great ch. xxi "Of Power." This is plain not merely in the nature of Condillac's argument, but also in his terminology. This was a prominent aspect of Locke's philosophy which the nineteenth century either ignored or misunderstood; Locke was better understood by the eighteenth century than by the nineteenth. See Aarsleff, "The State of Nature and the Nature of Man in Locke," in: *John Locke: Problems and Perspectives*, ed. by John W. Yolton (Cambridge University Press, 1969), pp. 99-136.

9. TS, p. 303b (IV, ii, § 7).

10. TS, pp. 266b-267a (II, viii, § § 29-31).

11. TS, p. 229b (I, ii, § 29).

12. These charges later became commonplace. A review of TS in the Jesuit-dominated *Journal de Trévoux* (March 1755, pp. 641-669) wrote: "Some critics hold that this system of the sensations breathes an odor of materialism, a hateful suspicion that should not be advanced without the most telling proof. As for ourselves, we believe that the spirituality of the soul forms an essential part of this treatise and that without this doctrine the entire system would lack all consistency."

13. I have commented on this in note 2 above.

14. The revisions are indicated in the le Roy edition which I follow.

15. This is especially evident in *De l'art de penser*, which is for the most part made up of passages from the *Essai*; Condillac even added a footnote to this effect, p. 731a (I, vi):

" . . . my *Essai* . . . from which the greater part of this work is drawn." Condillac makes the same point p. 735b (in footnote near the end of I, vii): "Experience has confirmed me in these reflections, which I would not have added here if I had not already stated them in my *Essai*. . . . which I copy here as in many other places. I must also proclaim that many writers have copied this *Essai*, for one might think that I am copying them in what I write on the art of thinking. Plagiarist metaphysicians are I don't know how common."

16. TS, pp. 267b-268a (II, viii, §35). The cited passage relies on an argument that is fully presented in *Essai*, pp. 19-23 (I, II, chs. iv-v).

17. TS, p. 298, in the introduction to Part IV that was not in the 1754 version. *Essai*, p. 43b (I, IV, i, §11) contains a passage that very nearly describes the state of the statue: "Deprive a superior being's mind of the use of written signs. . . . Deny it the use of speech. . . . And finally, take away the use of every kind of signs . . . [and] you will have an imbecile."

18. Condillac often, right from the *Essai* on, stresses the mutual interaction of reflection on the one hand and signs and language on the other, e.g., *l'Art de penser*, p. 733a (I, vi): "Thus signs and reflection are causes that lend each other mutual aid, reciprocally contributing to their progress. . . . In fact, how much reflection has it not required to form the languages, and how great is not the aid that languages lend to reflection?" This does not subvert Condillac's basic axiom that reason and reflection are primary, given in the nature of man, prior to language; language is man's chief artificial creation. Since the notion that the mind "generates" something (as in "generative grammar") has recently become familiar in particular contexts, it is worth noting that the same principle is frequently invoked by Condillac, as indicated by his use of the words "engendre" and "génération." It is an astonishing though conventional error to say that according to Condillac man "has acquired reason," that he wished to "eliminate all autonomous activity from the mind," that he "had deprived reflection of its autonomy by making it depend upon the mechanical association of ideas" (Knight, *The Geometric Spirit*, pp. 147, 29, 37).

19. *Traité des animaux*, pp. 362a-365b (II, v). Hereafter TA.

20. TA, p. 361b (II, iv).

21. *Essai*, pp. 33a (I, II, xi, §92) and 36b (I, II, xi, §107).

22. *La psychologie de Condillac* (Paris, 1937), p. 175.

23. Destutt de Tracy's five papers were published as "Mémoire sur la faculté de penser" in *Mémoires de l'Institut national des sciences et arts. Sciences morales et politiques*, I (Thermidor an VI [1798], 283-450). Arens *Sprachwissenschaft*. (1st ed. (1955), p. 89; 2nd ed. (1969), pp. 106-107.

24. H. J. Hunt, "Logic and Linguistics: Diderot as 'grammairien philosophe," in: *Modern Language Review* 33 (1938), 218; cf. Jacques Proust, "Diderot et les problèmes du langage," in: *Romanische Forschungen* 79 (1967), 1-27. On the *Cours d'études*, see Luciano Guerci, "La composizione e le vicende editoriali des Cours d'études di Condillac," in: *Miscellanea Walter Maturi* (Torino: G. Giappichelli, 1966), pp. 185-220. (= Università di Torino, Facoltà di Lettere e Filosofia; Storia. vol. 1.)

25. On the linearity of speech, see Aarsleff 1974, above, pp. 157-158.

26. Renan, *Oeuvres complètes*, ed. Henrietta Psichari, 8 (Paris, 1958), pp. 41-42. On conjectural or theoretical history, see Aarsleff, *The Study of Language*, pp. 110-111. On its later career, see J. W. Burrow's excellent *Evolution and Society: A Study in Victorian social Theory* (Cambridge University Press, 1966).

27. *Sprachwissenschaft*, 1st ed., pp. 102-103; 2nd ed., p. 120.

28. Hansjörg A. Salmony, *Die Philosophie des jungen Herder* (Zürich, 1949), p. 42.

29. *Essai*, pp. 98b (II, I, xv, §143) and 103b (II, I, xv, §§161-162).

30. In one of his earliest pieces on language, written 1801 or 1802, Humboldt wrote this

statement (which is incompatible with a passage in Herder's *Abhandlung* that is often cited to show the core of his doctrine): "Each spoken word was an attempt to make oneself understood by someone else. Isolated man would never have hit upon the idea of speaking. For the aptitude for language is inseparably linked with the aptitude for sociability. A speechless human community is absolutely a contradictory concept. Either man lives in isolation bent toward the earth like animals in the forest, or he walks upright with the same being as his peers." "Fragmente der Monographie über die Basken" in *Gesammelte Schriften*, ed. Albert Leitzmann, vol. VII, part 2 (Berlin, 1907), pp. 596-597. The dating is Leitzmann's *ibid.* p. 604. This view is retained in Humboldt's later and best known works, e.g. vol. VI, 155, 159 and VII, part I, 36. H. B. Acton gives an excellent account of "The Philosophy of Language in Revolutionary France," in: *Proceedings of the British Academy* 45 (1959), 199-219. To François Picavet's classic, *Les idéologues* (Paris, 1891), can now be added the studies by Sergio Moravia, *Il tramonto dell' illuminismo. Filosofia e politica nella società francese (1770-1810)* (Bari: Laterza, 1968), and *Il pensiero degli idéologues. Scienza e filosofia in Francia (1780-1815)* (Firenze: "La Nuova Italia," 1974). For a discussion of the secondary literature (chiefly within the last generation) and bibliography on the study of language in the eighteenth century see Aarsleff, "The eighteenth century, including Leibniz" in *Current Trends in Linguistics*, vol. 13, *The Historiography of Linguistics*, ed. Thomas A. Sebeok et al. (The Hague: Mouton, 1975), pp. 383-479. On Humboldt, see the essay below on "Wilhelm von Humboldt and the linguistic thought of the French idéologues."

Thomas Sprat

Thomas Sprat was born in 1635 at Beaminster in Dorset and died at Bromley in Kent on 20 May 1713. His famous *History of the Royal Society* has occupied an important place in the history of science.

Sprat was one of several children born to Thomas Sprat, a poor parish curate who held B.A. and M.A. degrees from Oxford, and his wife, who was the daughter of a Mr. Strode of Parnham, Dorset. From this "obscure birth and education in a far distant country," as he later described it, he entered Wadham College, Oxford, in November 1651, receiving the B.A. in June 1654 and an M.A. three years later. At Wadham, Sprat became a member of the active and soon influential circle that launched him on his surprising and varied career as the historian and defender of the Royal Society and as a man of the church. He became the favorite and protégé of John Wilkins and formed close associations with other members of the scientific group that gathered around Wilkins during those years, especially with Christopher Wren, Seth Ward, and Ralph Bathurst. Although Sprat may possibly have attended their meetings, there is no record of his having done so and no indication that he ever engaged in the sort of scientific work that was their interest.

In 1659 Sprat's first publications appeared. One was a poem, "To the Happy Memory of the Late Lord Protector," dedicated to Wilkins for "having been as it were moulded by your own hands, and formed under your government," and charged with devoted admiration for

Reprinted from *Dictionary of Scientific Biography*, C. C. Gillispie, editor-in-chief (New York: Scribner's), XII (1975), pp. 580-587.

Cromwell as the great savior who had led his people into the promised land. Sprat's loyalties were always pliable, a fact often noted by his contemporaries, for he later served Charles II, James II, and William and Mary with the same devotion he had expressed for Cromwell. In politics he became a staunch Tory, a defender of the divine rights of kings, and a strong exponent of high church doctrines. He has, not without reason, been called a time-server. In 1659 Sprat also published a poem in praise of the poet Abraham Cowley, written "in imitation of his own Pindaric odes," thus gaining the nickname "Pindaric Sprat." Cowley, who was also known as a promoter of natural philosophy, returned the favor in his "Ode to the Royal Society," prefixed to Sprat's *History of the Royal Society*, when he said that "ne'er did Fortune better yet / Th' Historian to the Story fit."

Sprat's close association with Cowley had important consequences. In accordance with the poet's will, Sprat was charged with the publication of his *English Works*, published in 1668 and often reprinted, for which he wrote "Account of the Life and Writings of Abraham Cowley." Cowley may also have brought Sprat to the attention of George Villiers, second duke of Buckingham, who by the late 1660s was Wilkins's patron. Having been ordained early in 1660, Sprat later that year gained his first ecclesiastical office through the influence of Cowley and the duke, who also helped him to some of his later preferments. During most of the 1660s and perhaps longer, Sprat was the duke's chaplain, and in 1675 he was appointed one of the three trustees for part of Buckingham's estate, a position that may have helped to pay for his well-known love of good living. In August 1676 he became one of the king's chaplains, soon rising steadily to canon of the Chapel Royal, Windsor, near the end of 1680; dean of Westminster in September 1683; and bishop of Rochester in November 1684, holding the last two offices until his death. In 1676 Sprat married Helen, Lady Wolseley, of Ravenstone, Staffordshire, an event that later in that year led Robert Hooke to note in his diary that he "saw fat Tom Sprat joyd him of marriage." Sprat was survived by his wife, who died in February 1726, and by a son, Thomas, archdeacon of Rochester. They were all buried in Westminster Abbey.

Although he was a prominent figure in his time, Sprat's fame today rests entirely on his *History of the Royal Society*, first published in 1667. Its 438 pages constitute a large and puzzling work on an institution barely seven years old when the book appeared. Since its concerns and their implications touched all major aspects of contemporary affairs, not least religion, the infant Royal Society quickly became involved in controversy and detraction, against which even the good fortune of royal patronage proved insufficient. Neither its present position nor its controversial origins during the past twenty years, open to many unwelcome interpretations, was strong enough to allow it to ignore this opposition without risking serious damage to its reputation and success, which depended on wide cooperation and not least on considerable financial support.

It was the first design of the *History* to explain the nature, organization, work, and aims of the Royal Society to the public, thus showing that the promotion of its affairs was a national, even a patriotic, enterprise that promised both a healing of the wounds left by the recent turbulent events and great material benefits. The *History* was a piece of public relations, even of propaganda. The material that went into it was carefully supervised and selected, and its omissions and suppressions are as significant as its contents. It is not an impartial document; and it gave such strong impetus to renewed controversy that it may be doubted whether the Royal Society would not, at least in England, have been better off without this premature piece of justification. The formidable Henry Stubbe said a few years later that Sprat's work was "a nonsensical and illiterate history." It is a curious irony that the early Royal Society has been the center of similar debate in the extensive recent literature on its history.

The *History* is divided into three parts without separate titles. Part one (pp. 1-51) presents a survey of ancient, medieval, and Renaissance philosophy that is meant to show "what is to be expected from these new undertakers, and what moved them to enter upon a way of inquiry different from that on which the former have proceeded." With exaggeration that mars the conciliatory tone, the Royal Society "most unanimously" follows in the footsteps of antiquity except in "matters of fact: for in them we follow the most ancient author of all others, even Nature itself." It proposes to honor the ancients by being their children rather than their pictures. Here, and often in the rest of the work, Sprat's strong words are reserved for "downright enthusiasts" and the "modern dogmatists," whom he compares to the recent "pretenders to public liberty," who became the greatest tyrants themselves. This political theme recurs forcefully throughout the work—for instance, in a later passage eulogizing Charles I as the royal martyr who followed the "divine example of our Saviour." Sprat finds agreement between the growth of learning and of civil government. Already in this first part Bacon is, as it were, the Royal Society's patron saint, "who had the true imagination of the whole extent of this enterprise, as it is now set on foot." Even members and friends of the Society must have known that this respect for Bacon as the sole intellectual ancestor was exaggerated; but it was necessary in order to rule out the thought of any foreign influence or indebtedness, which an impartial judge would readily have admitted. Both Gassendi and Descartes had been read and admired in England.

Part two (pp. 52-319) contains the history proper and is chronologically divided into three sections. The first (pp. 52-60) relates the prehistory of the Royal Society up to the first regular meeting on 28 November 1660, tracing its origin exclusively to the meetings that were held "some space after the end of the Civil Wars at Oxford, in Dr. Wilkins his lodgings, in Wadham College." Contradicted repeatedly in the seventeenth century, this brief account has dominated most discussions of Sprat's work and has recently formed the center of much fruitless argument. It will be considered more closely below.

The second section (pp. 60-122) covers the period between the first meeting and the granting of the second royal charter in the spring of 1663. At this time Sprat was proposed for membership by Wilkins and was duly elected. When ninety-four original fellows were elected on 20 May, in accordance with the provisions of the new charter, the Royal Society was firmly established with a large and varied membership. This section is not historical. It explains the nature and aspirations of the Society; its organization, membership, meetings, subject matter, and method of inquiry; its careful interpretation of evidence; and "their manner of discourse," a subject that has received more than its fair share of comment in the secondary literature. These pages contain a panegyric on "the general constitution of the minds of the English" and the special prerogative of England, "whereby it may justly lay claim to be the head of a philosophical league above all other nations in Europe," owing to the "unaffected sincerity," "sound simplicity" of speech, and "universal modesty" that characterize the English as a nation.

This section contrasts the need for cooperative labors and shared verification with Descartes's contemplative method, explains that a division between teachers and scholars is not "consistent with a free philosophical consultation," and suggests that the Royal Society seeks to satisfy the same ambition as the one which at Babel was punished by a "universal confusion" because it "was managed with impiety and insolence." But true knowledge cannot be separated from "humility and innocence": since the Society's amibtion "is not to brave the Creator of all things, but to admire him the more, it must needs be the utmost perfection of humane nature."

At this point Sprat observed that the preparation of the *History* had been interrupted for more than a year by the plague (which caused the Royal Society to discontinue its meetings from June 1665 to February 1666) and the great fire of London during the first week of September 1666. Thus, although parts of the rest of the work may have been written before, it was not printed until after this date.

The third section (pp. 122-319) of part two tells the story of the Royal Society's work since the spring of 1663. Its first division (pp. 122-157) deals with its reputation and correspondence abroad, and with the encouragement it has received at home from professional and social groups and from the royal family. It concludes with epitomes of the charter of 1663 and of the statutes that had been prepared between June and the end of that year. As late as April 1667 Wilkins was, by order of the Council, directed to prepare these epitomes for the *History*.

The second division (pp. 158-319) of the third section of part two presents fourteen instances "of this their way of inquiring and giving rules for direction . . . from whose exactness it may be guessed, how all the rest are performed," interspersed with Sprat's comments. These papers, not in chronological order, were read before the Royal Society between February 1661 and November 1664. Most of them were also printed in other contemporary publications; and they were drawn from the Society's records under the careful supervision chiefly of Wilkins, who received orders regarding their selection between the end of 1664 and April 1667. The choice was clearly designed to be representative and to have wide appeal both to scientific and, not least, to practical and even lucrative interests. At the end of this part, Sprat confidently observed, "If any shall yet think [the Society] have not usefully employed their time, I shall be apt to suspect, that they understand not what is meant by a diligent and profitable laboring about Nature."

Finally, part three (pp. 321-438) is an apology for the Royal Society that tries to meet all conceivable objections to its enterprise, thus giving a telling picture of the Society's conception of itself in relation to contemporary society, thought, and opinion. Among the many young men against "the enchantments of enthusiasm" but had also helped to save the university itself from ruin. The Society is also This matter obviously caused some concern, for in the brief account of the Wadham meetings Sprat claimed that they had not only armed many young men against "the enchantments of enthusiasm" but also had helped to save the university itself from ruin. The Society is also a great ally of religion, leading man "to admire the wonderful contrivance of the Creation" so that his praises "will be more suitable to the Divine Nature than the blind applauses of the ignorant," unlike the "enthusiast that pollutes his religion with his own passions." Indeed, experiments are necessary to separate true miracles from falsehoods, and they especially support the Church of England by the agreement that exists "between the present design of the Royal Society and that of our Church in its beginning: They both may lay equal claim to the word reformation." It is Sprat's conviction that "the universal disposition of this age is bent upon a rational religion." Finally, the Society offers great benefits to all manual arts, to trade, to "wits and writers," and to "the interests of our nation." The *History* concludes with a list of all present fellows of the Society up to June 1667.

By early summer the *History* was in the press; in mid-August Pepys saw a copy at the booksellers; at the end of September several persons had read it; and on 10 October 1667 it was presented to the Society by Wilkins, hearty thanks being "ordered to the author for his singular respect to the Society shewed in that book." That it did not, although issued by its printers, bear the Royal Society's imprimatur may indicate some hesitancy to grant it, since this procedure was normal for books encouraged by the Society or written by its fellows, in accordance with the provisions of the royal charter. The *History* sold well, for some six months later Oldenburg reported that the first printing—presumably 1,000 copies—was nearly gone. The work was greatly praised in England and immediately gained the somewhat exaggerated reputation for eloquence and style that has been conventional ever since.

For nearly three years Oldenburg had been announcing the work's imminent publication to his correspondents on the Continent, and at last he could satisfy the inquiries that had kept streaming in. He sent out copies with elaborate covering letters inviting cooperation, an effort that soon proved successful in the form of further inquiries about details of experiments and other matters described in the *History*, although several correspondents complained that their poor English would deny full benefit until they had Latin or French translations. The Royal Society immediately tried to supply them, but only an unsanctioned French translation was published, in identical versions, at Geneva and Paris in 1669 and 1670. Thus, as a careful exercise in public relations, Sprat's work confirmed his hope that "this learned and inquisitive age will . . . think [the Society's] endeavors worthy of its assistance."

From the seventeenth century to the present day, the main problem raised by Sprat's work has always been its historical reliability. As early as 1756, Thomas Birch explained in the preface to his own

History of the Royal Society that part two of Sprat's account was less admired than the others; and he could cite well-informed contemporary opinion for his wish that the history of the Royal Society's "institution and progress" had omitted less and given more facts, and that "the order of time in which they occurred had been more exactly marked." At the very least, Birch was certainly thinking of Sprat's silence on the London meetings in 1645 attended by John Wallis, who in the meantime had given two detailed accounts of them. Their relevance to the prehistory of the Society has been denied—at the cost of creating an unconvincing, ad hoc image of the early post-1660 Society, built on interpretations and arguments so bizarre and ill-informed that they disprove themselves. In addition to Wallis's two accounts, both of which include Wilkins, it is well-known that since the early 1640s Wilkins had taken a strong interest in natural philosophy, was present in London in the mid-1640s, and in other ways was associated with the people he met at those early gatherings.

Clearly, the *History* is not reliable on matters of fact; it cannot, as has been claimed, be considered an impartial account written under the supervision of those who had all the information. They may have had it but not wished to use it all. And if less than dependable on this point, the *History* may be so on others, where similar interests were at stake. Well aware of French competition that might challenge its priority, and understandably concerned about some prominent members' actions and allegiances during the 1640s, the Society's interests demanded that its official history omit information that cast doubt on its pure Englishness, on its agreement with the Church of England, and on its loyalty to the restored monarchy. The early London meetings were embarrassing on all counts. There is good reason to accept Wallis's statement that they were suggested by Theodore Haak, a foreigner who had received the suggestion from his French connections, especially from Marin Mersenne, with whom he had then for some years been in correspondence on matters of this sort. At the time both Haak and Wallis were active in the Westminster Assembly; and Haak was associated not only with Comenian circles but also with Comenius, who by 1660, if not earlier, had become anathema owing to his strong millenarianism and defense of the apocalyptic prophets—no doubt Sprat's strong words against enthusiasm are also aimed at Comenius. Tracing the Royal Society's origins only to Wilkins's Wadham group and Oxford ensured respectability. But there would seem to have been more involved than this.

Fortunately we have a great deal of information about the composition, supervision, and uncertain progress of Sprat's work. Referring to the two secretaries, Oldenburg and Wilkins, and their authority "to publish whatever shall be agreed upon by the Society," Sprat said that he was not usurping their prerogative, "for it is only my hand that goes, the substance and direction came from one of them." That man undoubtedly was Wilkins, and Oldenburg seems to have had little to do with the project. The records abundantly demonstrate that the historical part was closely supervised, not only by Wilkins but also by several small groups of fellows, from 21 December 1664 until it went to press. That the choice fell on Sprat is perhaps not surprising: young, energetic (although, before it was finished, Oldenburg complained that the *History* was in "lazy hands"), available, an intimate of Wilkins and perhaps also recommended by Cowley, he had the time that others, especially Wilkins, could hardly have spared. But it might also—for the sake of distance—have been thought useful that the writer not have lived through the entire history of the last decades. Given the sort of image the Royal Society needed, Wilkins was safer in the background, unknown to the public, than as the official historian. Capable but busy, Oldenburg was no doubt ruled out by his German origin and perhaps by other considerations as well. Sprat was a useful and willing tool.

The first mention of a history dates from May 1663, immediately after the second charter and the election of the ninety-four additional original fellows, when Robert Moray wrote to Huygens that the Royal Society would soon publish a small treatise about itself. At the end of the year, again in a letter to Huygens, this work was for the first time called the "history of the Society," intended to accompany the statutes when they were printed, which was believed to be soon. Nothing was heard of the project until November 1664, when Oldenburg wrote to two correspondents that the history was nearly finished and would "we hope, be published soon," and informed Boyle that Sprat intended to give it to the printer in early December. Brouncker, Moray, Wilkins, Evelyn, and others had read it; "but we are troubled," Oldenburg added, "that you cannot have a sight of it, before the publication," for he was worried "whether there be enough said of particulars, or . . . whether there are performances enough for a Royal Society, that has been at work so considerable a time." So far there was no indication that the Society had supervised the work; but within a month, and then repeatedly, well before the plague caused the meetings to be discontinued, it began active supervision and selection of suitable materials for Sprat. There is no doubt that this change was caused by the publication, in May 1664, of Samuel Sorbière's *Relation d'un voyage en Angleterre*, addressed to the

French king in the form of a letter dated 25 October 1663 (with a dedication dated 12 December). Sorbière had spent three months in England, beginning in early June 1663, seeing several prominent members of the Society, attending a number of its meetings, and becoming a member on the same day as Christiaan Huygens.

The *Relation* was soon answered by Sprat in the form of a long letter addressed to Christopher Wren, dated 1 August 1664 and published in 1665 under the title *Observations on Monsieur de Sorbière's Voyage Into England*. It was an unfair and defamatory pamphlet, in which Evelyn may have had a share, commensurate with the provocation Sprat felt, "for having now under my hands the History of the Royal Society, it will be in vain for me to try to represent its design to be advantageous to the glory of England, if my countrymen shall know that one who calls himself a member of that assembly has escaped unanswered in the public disgraces, which he has cast on our whole nation." A brief view of the reasons for this violent reaction will explain the aim and reliability of Sprat's *History*.

Sorbière was a somewhat unsteady and superficial character with considerable talent and flair. Some unwise political implications of the *Relation* had caused such strong displeasure in both England and Denmark that Louis XIV banished Sorbière to Nantes; but before the end of the year he had been pardoned, partly owing to the intercession of Charles II through diplomatic channels. Having also heard that some members of the Royal Society were preparing an answer, the king ordered them to desist. Thus the issue in fact concerned the Royal Society alone. As was usual in contemporary travel accounts, Sorbière had made some critical observations on individuals and on English history and institutions, but in general the *Relation* gave a very favorable picture of England and especially of the Royal Society. Sprat, however, dealt only with the criticism, often with obvious misrepresentation of his source. He chided Sorbière for reducing the Society to triviality in his account of its meetings, although clearly no such effect was either intended or expressed. He rejected Sorbière's statement that Hobbes was Bacon's follower in natural philosophy, "between whom there is no more likeness than there is between St. Gregory and the Waggoner." Sorbière's intimacy with Hobbes was a strong irritant: they met several times during Sorbière's English visit—in fact, one of his reasons for going to England was to see Hobbes, whose early work he had translated into French in the 1640s. Worst of all, Sprat claimed—again incorrectly—Sorbière had said that the Royal Society relied upon books for its knowledge of nature and that it divided into sects and parties, the mathematicians holding to

Descartes and the men of general learning to Gassendi, "whereas neither of these two men bear any sway amongst them." With the exception of Hobbes, wisely not mentioned in that work, these matters were all made prominent in the *History*, which also shared with the *Observations* Sprat's patriotic defense of English politics and religion, about which Sorbière had said much that was now better forgotten.

Sprat's suppressions are equally telling. He does not refer to Sorbière's statements that he went to England to see his friends and to inform himself about the state of science in England; that the Royal Society's history was being prepared (the first public mention); that as secretary of the Montmor Academy in Paris he knew Oldenburg, who while in Paris as tutor to Boyle's nephew Richard Jones had "constantly" attended its meetings from the spring of 1659 to the spring of 1660, a matter easily attested by other sources and well known to the Society, which in fact had very cordial relations with that Academy during the early 1660s; and that the establishment of the Royal Society had been preceded by the establishment of the Montmor Academy. The official beginning of the latter is placed in 1657, but it was known to have its ancestry in Mersenne's meetings during the 1640s, which through Haak connect with the early London meetings in 1645. Sprat's silence on the Montmor Academy is notable also in the *History*, which cites only a single institution akin to the Royal Society, although only as a "modern academy for language"—the French Academy, well-known for its hostility to natural philosophy in those very years. This undoubtedly was the crux of the matter: only by suppressing all mention of the London meetings and of the Montmor Academy in favor of Wilkins's Wadham circle was it possible to preserve priority and originality for the Royal Society, for Bacon, and for England.

There is finally one aspect of Sorbière's *Relation* that could not escape any informed reader. Addressed to Louis XIV, the work clearly had as its primary aim, very cleverly pursued by a judicious balance between praise and criticism, to goad the king into official support and patronage for a French academy of science, an effort Sorbière is known to have begun before he went to England, just as the French king is also known to have sought secret intelligence of the state of learning in England at the same time, the eventful spring of 1663. The publication of Sorbière's *Relation* had created a crisis. Sprat put aside his *History* to write his *Observations*, and the Royal Society intervened with its supervision late in 1664 because it felt that it was now openly in a race with Paris and shared Oldenburg's fears that the *History*, in its late 1664 version, did not say enough about details and accomplishments for a society that had "been at work so considerable a time." Thus Sprat's *History* is thoroughly unreliable as history in our sense of the word. Far from ensuring impartiality and truth, the supervision was designed to suppress known but discomfiting facts. That the work also, in this respect, was transformed into a piece of propaganda shows the Society's sense of its vulnerability.

For these reasons, whatever the truth (which may not now be ascertainable) Sprat's *History* cannot be used to refute such accounts as Gian Domenico Cassini's, in *Recueil d'observations faites en plusieurs voyages* (1693), to the effect that on his return to England in 1660, Oldenburg "gave the occasion for the formation of the Royal Society." The general attitude of the Society to the whole matter may be reflected in its reaction to the suggestion that Sorbière be omitted from the lists of the Society, made and favored on 13 November 1666 in a meeting of the Council—which, however, did not have power of final decision. The following day, a vote taken at a meeting of the Society showed fourteen in favor of continuance, eight against.

Sprat was only thirty-two when the *History* was published but never again took any part in the Society's affairs, although he remained a member until his death. Owing to his increasingly conservative politics and his services to changing monarchs, he soon assumed many high offices in the church, although not so high as he had hoped and others expected; he did not become archbishop of York when that see fell vacant in 1686. During the reign of James II, he was an active member of the "infamous" ecclesiastical commission but ultimately terminated its effectiveness when he resigned in August 1688, refusing to prosecute the clergy who had not read the king's Declaration for Liberty of Conscience, although three months earlier he had himself caused much displeasure in London by insisting that it be read in Westminster Abbey. In May 1685 Sprat brought out a tendentious account of the Rye House Plot, written at the request of the king; but he later evaded James's command to write an account of the Monmouth Rebellion. Only a few years later he assisted at the coronation of William and Mary.

Sprat often preached in London, where Evelyn heard him no fewer than seventeen times between 1676 and 1694, always with the greatest praise for "that great wit Dr. Sprat." The sermons extol the monarchy and reason with as much spirit as they denounce "the Romish tyranny" and "the Anabaptistical Madness and Enthusiastical Phrensies of these last ages."

In May 1692, Sprat was the victim of a fantastic blackmail attempt, complete with a forged incriminating document secretly placed in a vase in his palace, purporting to show that he was involved in a conspiracy to restore James II. It caused him great embarrassment, with house arrest and close examination by his peers, before the forgery was found out. For the rest of his life Sprat celebrated the day of his deliverance. He wrote a vastly entertaining account of the plot and the intriguing characters who perpetrated it. It may be argued that this is his best piece of writing.

Estimates of Sprat's character have not been unanimous, either by his contemporaries or by posterity. Gilbert Burnet was not one of his friends, but on Sprat's death he wrote a sketch for which there is support in other contemporary sources: "His parts were bright in his youth, and gave great hopes: but these were blasted by a lazy, libertine course of life, to which his temper and good nature carried him without considering the duties, or even the decencies of his profession. He was justly esteemed a great master of our language, and one of our correctest writers." Swift said that Burnet's estimate was false. Still, both the *Observations on Sorbière's Voyage* and the *History of the Royal Society* show qualities that would seem to have belonged also to the man.

Bibliography

1. Original Works. There is a mimeographed bibliography by Harold Whitmore Jones and Adrian Whitworth, "Thomas Sprat 1635-1713. Check List of His Works and Those of Allied Writers" (Queen Mary College. Univ. of London. 1952). The *Observations on Monsieur de Sorbière's Voyage* was reissued in 1668, and again in 1709 in a volume that also contained the first English translation of Sorbière's *Relation* and of François Graverol's "Memoirs for the Life of M. Samuel Sorbière." The *Relation* was published in German and Italian in 1667 and 1670. Sprat's *History* was reissued at London in 1702, 1722, and 1734. It has recently been made available in a facsimile reprint "edited with critical apparatus by Jackson I. Cope and Harold Whitmore Jones" in the series Washington University Studies (St. Louis, Mo., 1958). The introduction and notes are useful also for bibliography, but are weak on the actual *History* itself, paying more attention to contemporary controversy, especially to Joseph Glanvill and Henry Stubbe. Unfortunately, this edition does not supply an adequate table of contents and, astonishingly, has no index. Some of Sprat's sermons were printed during his lifetime, but these are all among the ten printed in *Sermons Preached on Several Occasions* (London, 1722). None of the sermons heard by Evelyn is among them. *A True Account and Declaration of the Horrid Conspiracy to Assassinate the Late King Charles II at the Rye-House* was reissued in 3 vols., Edmund Goldsmid, ed., as Collectanea Adamantaea, XIV (Edinburgh, 1886). *A Relation of the Late Wicked Contrivance of Stephen Blackhead and Robert Young, Against the Lives of Several Persons, by Forging an Association Under Their Hands*, 2 pts. (London, 1692), is in *Harleian Miscellany*, VI (London, 1745), 178-254. Sprat's few poems were often reprinted in various collections during the eighteenth century.

II. Secondary Literature. There is no full life of Sprat, and the materials for one hardly exist. There is a very brief life in E. Curll, *Some Account of the Life and Writings of the Right Reverend Father in God, Thomas Sprat, D.D.* (London, 1715); it also contains Sprat's will. Much detail is in H. W. Jones, "Thomas Sprat (1635-1713)," in *Notes and Queries*, 197 (5 Jan. 1952), 10-14 and (15 Mar. 1952), 118-123; these form a supplement to the entry in the *Dictionary of National Biography*. There is much information about Sprat and his *History* in most of the well-known seventeenth-century sources. The most important are the following. Thomas Birch, *The History of the Royal Society*, 4 vols. (London, 1756-1757), has been reissued in facsimile reprint by A. Rupert and Marie Boas Hall as Sources of Science, no. 44 (New York-London, 1968): it has a very incomplete index of names and subjects at the beginning of vol. 1. Since Birch's order is strictly chronological, the information drawn from that work can be readily identified. *The Correspondence of Henry Oldenburg*, A. R. and M. B. Hall, eds., II-VII, covers 1663-1672 (Madison, Wis., 1966-1970). Of comparable importance is the correspondence of Christiaan Huygens, in *Oeuvres complètes de Christiaan Huygens*, 22 vols. (The Hague, 1888-1950), with relevant material in II-VII. Sprat's name occurs often in the *The Diary of John Evelyn*, 6 vols. (Oxford, 1955), with much information in the excellent notes by the editor, E. S. de Beer.

Balthasar de Monconys, *Journal des voyages de Monsieur de Monconys*, 3rd ed., 3 vols. in 4 pts. (Paris, 1695 [1st ed. Lyon 1665-1666, in 3 vols.]), III, 1-170, deals with the six weeks the author spent in England, where he often saw Sorbière and attended meetings of the Royal Society; where the two accounts cover the same matters, Monconys agrees with Sorbière. *Parentalia, or Memoirs of the Family of the Wrens*, Christopher and Stephen Wren, eds. (London, 1750), has some information about Sprat. Sprat has an entry in Anthony à Wood, *Athenae Oxonienses*, Philip Bliss, ed., IV (London, 1820), cols. 727-730.

Indispensable for reference is *The Record of the Royal Society*, 4th ed. (London, 1940), which prints the charters and the statutes. General bibliography for the Royal Society can be found in *Isis Cumulative Bibliography 1913-1965*, Magda Whitrow, ed., 2 vols. (London, 1971), II, 749-751; and in Marie Boas Hall, "Sources for the History of the Royal Society," in *History of Science*, 5 (1966), 62-76. Two relevant studies that have appeared since the Hall work are Charles Webster, "The Origins of the Royal Society," *ibid.*, 6 (1967), 106-128 (a review and critique of Margery Purver, *The Royal Society: Concept and Creation* [London, 1967], which is informed by a doctrinal faith in the historical integrity of Sprat's *History*, but the arguments that support this faith are unbelievable); and Quentin Skinner, "Thomas Hobbes and the Nature of the Early Royal Society," in *Historical Journal*, 12 (1969), 217-239.

Valuable for information and bibliography about French academies is Harcourt Brown, *Scientific Organizations in Seventeenth-Century France (1620-1680)* (Baltimore, 1934), to be supplemented by Albert J. George, "The Genesis of the Académie des Sciences," in *Annals of Science*, 3 (1938), 372-401. To Vincent Guilloton goes the credit for first showing that the cause of the Sorbière-Sprat controversy lay in the Royal Society, although he uses only a few of the available sources: "Autour de la *Relation du voyage de Samuel Sorbière en Angleterre*," in *Smith College Studies in Modern Languages*, 11, no. 4 (July 1930), 1-29. Important further information is in three studies by André Morize: "Samuel Sorbière et son *Voyage en Angleterre*," in *Revue d'histoire littéraire de la France*, 14 (1907), 231-275; "Samuel Sorbière," in *Zeitschrift für französische Sprache und Literatur*, 33 (1908), 214-265, with bibliography of Sorbière's MSS and printed works on 257-265; and "Thomas Hobbes et Samuel Sorbière. Notes sur l'introduction de Hobbes en France," in *Revue germanique* (Paris), 4 (1908), 193-204. There is a useful essay on Sorbière's philosophical orientation in A. G. A. Balz, *Cartesian Studies* (New York, 1951), 64-79.

Sprat's *History* and the problem of English prose style have been treated in a number of not very fruitful literary studies. The most significant is Francis Christensen, "John Wilkins and the Royal Society Reform of Prose Style," in *Modern Language Quarterly*, 7 (June 1946), 179-187 and (Sept. 1946) 279-290. For general background there are the relevant chapters in R. F. Jones, *Ancients and Moderns*, 2nd ed. (Berkeley-Los Angeles, 1961; paperback, 1965).

John Wilkins

John Wilkins was born in Northamptonshire in 1614 and died in London in 1672. Active and influential throughout his life, he left an enduring mark on English life and thought as man of the church, theologian, popular writer on science, and academic and scientific administrator.

Wilkins's career coincides with the most eventful period in modern English history—the years just before the Long Parliament to the decade after the Restoration and the formation of the Royal Society. It was not an easy time for an active man to retain influence and office, but Wilkins managed owing to his habit of prudence and a spirit of moderation and tolerance. In 1643 he subscribed to the Solemn League and Covenant and in 1649 he took the engagement of loyalty to the English Commonwealth. He was trusted by Cromwell, whom he advised on the need for a national church and episcopacy against presbytery. After the return of Charles II in 1660, he submitted to the Act of Uniformity and soon enjoyed the favor of the restored monarchy. Still, only the most unforgiving royalists ever questioned his integrity. Throughout his life, he gained and retained the friendship and respect of men of the most diverse political and religious persuasions. No doubt such personal qualities as charm, ready conversation, and energy played their part in his success, but the deeper reason would seem to lie in his commitment to beliefs that transcended the exclusive interests of any particular faction. From the first to the

Reprinted from *Dictionary of Scientific Biography*, C. C. Gillispie, editor-in-chief (New York: Scribner's), XV (1976), pp. 361-381.

last, all his writings advocate scientific and religious views that by the time of his death had proved that they represented the temper of the times. The new science had triumphed, and the liberal Anglican theology known as latitudinarianism was, thanks to him, on the rise under such men as John Tillotson, Edward Stillingfleet, and Simon Patrick.

Both in print and action, Wilkins was committed to a set of principles and beliefs—generally known as natural theology—which he was the first fully to formulate and advocate in England. He never questioned the importance of the Bible and revelation as sources of faith, and in this respect his thought differs from what later became known as deism. But his writings are devoted to the argument that moral and religious philosophy can be grounded on natural religion, by which he understood what "men might know, and should be obliged unto, by the mere principles of reason, improved by consideration and experience, without the help of revelation."[1]

Owing to the omnipotence, benevolence, and wisdom of God, both the universe and man are so admirably contrived that man can ensure the welfare of his soul by the mature exercise of the faculty of reason, which is the defining quality of his nature. This faculty reveals to man the natural principles that govern creation, thus providing him with knowledge that "may conduce to the proving of a God, and making men religious," by making him understand that "such a great order and constancy amongst" the heavenly bodies "could not at first be made but by a wise providence, nor since preserved without a powerful inhabitant, nor so perpetually governed without a skillful guide."[2]

Similarly, man is endowed with a natural principle that makes him seek moral good "as a rational voluntary free agent,"[3] owing to his steady inclination "to seek his own well-being and happiness," so that "nothing properly is his duty, but what is really his interest," which is another argument "that the author of his being must be infinitely wise and powerful."[4] Man's natural desire for happiness is as certain as the descent of heavy bodies,[5] an example that Wilkins also used to illustrate the fixed laws that rule nature. Both man and nature are governed by laws that ensure the harmony of religion and science.

Consistent with these arguments, Wilkins stated the deistic principle that the salvation of the heathen is not a problem for man to decide; since "God has not thought fit to tell *us* how he will be pleased to deal with such persons, it is not fit for us to tell *Him* how he ought to deal with them."[6] In his writings, Wilkins often used the wise testimony of the ancients to support the knowledge and arguments advanced by the new science. Whether we call some of his writings scientific and others religious is a matter of emphasis; they all have the same aim: to guide man's conduct toward moral virtue, religious devotion, and ultimately the hope of salvation. The pursuit of happiness, even comfort, in this world is man's legitimate interest.

But reason alone is not sufficient. Man is also naturally "a sociable creature . . . having only these two advantages to his protection, Society and Reason . . . Adam in the state of innocence could not be happy, though in Paradise, without a companion."[7] This is a theme Wilkins stresses again and again; it is the foundation of his constant advocacy of conciliation, moderation, and tolerance, often in contexts that refer to "all that confusion and disorder, which seem to be in the affairs of these times."[8] The instrument that ensures the benefits of social intercourse is language: "Every rational creature, being of an imperfect and dependent happiness, is therefore naturally endowed with an ability to communicate his own thoughts and intentions; that so by mutual services, it might the better promote itself in the prosecution of its own well-being."[9] As useful knowledge, both natural and moral, is a function of cooperation, so successful cooperation is a function of communication; the improvement of natural knowledge and language is the response to the "two general curses inflicted on mankind," after the fall of Adam, "the one upon their labors, the other upon their language."[10] After the anniversary meeting of the Royal Society on 30 November 1667 (in which the annual election of officers also took place), Pepys recorded that some members went out for dinner, he himself choosing to sit next to Wilkins "and others whom I value." With his last work, *An Essay Towards a Real Character and a Philosophical Language*, then in the press, Wilkins stated that "man was certainly made for society, he being of all creatures the least armed for defence, and of all creatures in the world the young ones are not able to do anything to help themselves . . . and were it not for speech man would be a very mean creature." Wilkins is the chief source of the Royal Society doctrines about language and style; knowledge based on mere words and phrases has "in it this intrinsical imperfection, that 'tis only so far to be esteemed, as it conduces to the knowledge of things," words themselves being merely "the images of matter." To treat them otherwise is to fall into "Pygmalion's phrenzy."[11]

Wilkins's view of useful knowledge determined his attitude toward the three chief sources of authority: the Bible, antiquity, and books. Using arguments that today are perhaps best known from Galileo's *Letter to the Grand Duchess Christina*, Wilkins repeatedly rejected scriptural authority in natural philosophy, a principle to which all the new scientists were committed; if theology is allowed interference with philosophy, then the status of the latter is endangered as an independent source of the wisdom of the creator. In his first publication, Wilkins stated the principle in these terms: "It is not the endeavor of Moses or the prophets to discover any mathematical or philosophical subtleties; but rather to accommodate themselves to vulgar capacities, and ordinary speech, as nurses are wont to use their infants."[12] On scientific matters, he was also fond of citing contradictory scriptural passages, just as he criticized those among his contemporaries "who upon the invention of any new secret, will presently find out some obscure text or other to father it upon, as if the Holy Ghost must needs take notice of every particular which their partial fancies did over-value."[13]

He treated classical authors in much the same way as the Bible, using citations to suit his purposes both for and against his own principles, those in the latter category being dismissed as contrary to reason and experience. But he rejected outright the superior authority of antiquity: "In such learning as may be increased by fresh experiments and new discoveries, it is we are the fathers, and of more authority than former ages, because we have the advantage of more time than they had."[14] He was aware that the vast public structures of the Egyptians, Hebrews, Greeks, and Romans might be used to argue against the inferiority of their mechanical knowledge; he answered that if we have nothing of the sort nowadays, the reason does not lie in our knowledge, for "mechanical discoveries are much more exact now," but rather in the fact that "we have not either the same motives to attempt such works, or the same means to effect them as the ancients had." By this he meant that great wealth and power, then concentrated in the hands of a few, were now more widely diffused. "There is now a greater equality amongst mankind and the flourishing of arts and sciences has so stirred up the sparks of men's natural nobility, and made them of such active and industrious spirits, as to free themselves in a great measure from that slavery, which those former and wilder nations were subjected unto."[15]

The belief in the leveling and ennobling effect of the new knowledge found expression in Wilkins's attitude toward "bookish" men and mere bookish learning. Antiquity having slighted the mere manual and practical arts as "base and common," such studies had come to be neglected for hundreds of years, with grave consequences for the well-being of man. But the mechanical arts are just as worthy as the old and honored liberal arts such as logic and rhetoric, indeed "that discipline which discovers the general causes, effects, and proprieties of things, may truly be esteemed as a species of philosophy." Since all studies ought "to conduce to practice as their proper end," book learning is often rightly considered mere "pedantry." Wilkins was eager to overcome the prejudice that studies pertaining to the mind deserve greater respect than those that deal with material things. It was in this spirit that he devoted his *Mathematical Magick* to practical mechanical devices and labor-saving inventions "whereby nature is in any way quickened or advanced in her defects," for these are in fact "so many essays, whereby men do naturally attempt to restore themselves from the first general curse inflicted upon their labors." Wilkins's scientific writings are all of a popular nature, written not for the learned, but for "such common artificers, as are well skilled in the practice of these arts, who may be much advantaged by the right understanding of their grounds and theory." For this reason he wrote in English, referring on the authority of Ramus to the German practice of public lectures given in the vernacular, "for the capacity of every unlettered ingenious artificer."[16] Though he defended the universities on several occasions, Wilkins was aware that they must justify their teaching in terms of real use and benefit to mankind, a view that made him one of the principal advocates of university reform at Oxford and Cambridge.[17]

Wilkins's scientific writings constitute a single, well-conceived educational program to reach a larger audience outside the confines of traditional learning, both to promote natural philosophy and to lend dignity to the practical arts. He announced this program in the opening of his first publication, saying that it was his desire to "raise up some more active spirit to a search after other hidden and unknown truths; since it must needs be a great impediment unto the growth of sciences, for men still to plod on upon beaten principles, as to be afraid of entertaining anything that may seem to contradict them."[18] In this task of popular education, Wilkins's importance can hardly be overestimated. He laid the foundation for the wide participation and interest that the Royal Society enjoyed during its formative years.

The means of this success was pedagogical flair, shown both in his capacity for clear and interesting exposition, always without any suggestion of condescension, and in the choice of subjects, which in the context of the times were sensational. Was the moon inhabited? Could man find a means of flying to it? Was it much like the earth with mountains and oceans? Was the earth a planet? Could man navigate under water, lift heavy weights with little effort, or communicate effectively by other means than ordinary speech? The very titles were catchy—he did not shun the title *Mathematical Magick*, although it was certainly against his principles to suggest that there was any magic in the study of natural philosophy.[19] His more serious purpose was to gain acceptance for the new science, to bring the work of Copernicus, Kepler, Galileo, Gilbert, Mersenne, and others to the attention of his countrymen. Against the authority of the Bible, antiquity, and book learning, he answered that "we must labor to find out what things are in themselves, by our own experience, and a thorough examination of their natures, not what another says of them." Natural religion will prevail; disorder, strife, and sectarianism will vanish when disputes are resolved by giving "soft words but hard arguments."[20] There is no important principle in Thomas Sprat's *History of the Royal Society* that had not earlier been argued by Wilkins. "The universal disposition of this age," wrote Sprat, "is bent upon a rational religion." In his first work Wilkins said that the opponents of new views too often submitted to authority, a point he enforced by saying that "our opposites . . . too often do *jurare in verba magistri*," thus citing the well-known line in Horace from which the Royal Society drew its motto *Nullius in verba*.[21]

There is, finally, another aspect of Wilkins's character that bears some relation to his career and influence: unlike most of his scientific and ecclesiastical associates, he was a man of the world. After their first meeting, Robert Boyle remarked that Wilkins's "entertainment did as well speak him a courtier as his discourse." Anthony à Wood observed that Wilkins was "bred in the court, and was a piece of a traveller, having twice seen the prince of Orange's court at the Hague, in his journey to, and return from, Heydelburg, whither he went to wait upon the price elector palatine, whose chaplain he was in England."[22] Without such social attainments, Wilkins's sphere of activity would hardly have reached so far beyond his humble origins.

Early Career. Wilkins was born at the Northamptonshire house of his maternal grandfather, the puritan divine John Dod, who was known for an exposition of the Ten Commandments. His mother, Jane Dod, had four children in her marriage to Walter Wilkins, an Oxford goldsmith who died in 1625. John Aubrey reports that the father was "a very ingenious man with a very mechanical head. He was much for trying experiments, and his head ran much upon the perpetual motion." In a second marriage, to Francis Pope, Jane Dod had a son, Walter, who remained close to Wilkins.[23]

After schooling at home, Wilkins began grammar school at the age of nine under the noted Greek and Latin scholar Edward Sylvester, and in May 1627 he matriculated at New Inn Hall, Oxford (later united with Balliol College). He soon transferred to Magdalen Hall, where his tutor was the Baptist divine John Tombes. He graduated B.A. 20 October 1631, and gained the M.A. degree on 11 June 1634; at this time Wilkins was tutor in his college, one of his students being Walter Charleton, who thereby "profited much beyond his years in logic and philosophy."[24] A few years later he was ordained and became vicar of Fawsley. At this time he is reported to have become chaplain to William Fiennes, first viscount Saye and Seale, who was then a supporter of the Puritans and later sat in the Westminster Assembly. But in 1641 Wilkins dedicated his *Mercury* to George Lord Berkeley (1601-1658), signing himself "your lordship's servant and chaplain." His desire to move in high places was further gratified when he became chaplain to Charles Louis, the prince elector Palatine, the king's nephew. The elector lived in England during a good part of the 1640s, befriending the parliamentary party in the hope of securing the restitution of his lost possessions. During the early months of 1646, Wilkins was officially engaged as preacher at Gray's Inn; during these years he also preached at the Savoy.[25]

On 13 April 1648, the Parliamentary Visitors made Wilkins warden of Wadham College. The holder of this office was required to take the degree of doctor of divinity, but on 5 March 1649, the Visitors gave him a year's dispensation, since Wilkins was "at this time in attendance on the prince elector, and cannot in regard of that service have time to do his exercise, and all other things necessary unto that degree."[26] He took the degree on 19 December the same year. Since this occurred at the time when Charles Louis was returning to Heidelberg to take possession of the lands that had been restored to him as a consequence of the Peace of Westphalia, we may surmise that it was at this time that Wilkins made his visits to the Continent and to The Hague.[27]

Beyond these sparse facts, we have little information about Wilkins's life during his formative years. No doubt he spent most of them in Oxford and London. It was in London that he participated in the meetings that were devoted, as John Wallis recorded, to "what has been called the New Philosophy or Experimental Philosophy," these meetings having been convened at the suggestion of Theodore Haak. It is an interesting conjunction that they began during the Westminster Assembly, of which Wallis was then secretary. For a better view of Wilkins's early career, we have his writings and some reasonable conjectures about his associations.

Although published two years apart, the *Discovery* (1638) and the *Discourse* (1640) can be considered a single work. Addressed to the common reader, the primary aim was to make known and to defend the new world picture of Copernicus, Kepler, and Galileo by showing its agreement with reason and experience against subservience to Aristotelian doctrines and literal biblical interpretation. Kepler and especially Galileo's *Siderius nuncius* (1610) and Matthias Bernegger's Latin translation (1635) of the *Dialogue Concerning the Two Chief World Systems* are frequently cited, along with a wealth of other references from the literature that had appeared within the last generation. The work is polemical, but unlike Campanella's *Apologia pro Galileo* (1622), which is cited with approval, it constantly turns the reader's attention to the positive arguments that may be drawn from rational interpretation of observable phenomena. The central argument was borrowed from Galileo: the moon is not a shining disk or whatever else men have imagined, but a world with natural features much like the earth. And if so, then the moon might also be inhabited, although Wilkins does not find sufficient grounds to say what sort of beings the inhabitants are, thus neatly avoiding the touchy question of whether they are descendants of Adam. Further, if the moon shares natural features with the earth, then the argument could be extended to form a uniformitarian view of the constitution of the entire universe, thus breaking down the Aristotelian doctrine of fixed, hierarchical spheres that obey laws other than those of the sublunar world. In both the first and the second work, Wilkins is careful to warn the reader at the outset that he is not pretending to write a precise treatise expounding unquestionable truths; but though much might still be doubtful, he is confident that the hypotheses he defends will, against all prejudice, be granted conformity with observable phenomena and with simplicity of explanation. In the 1640 edition of the *Discovery*, Wilkins added the sensational idea that it might be possible to contrive a way of flying to the moon, thus taking up a suggestion already known in England from Francis Godwin's *Man in the Moone* (1638). In the latter part of the second work, Wilkins supports his argument for the movement of the earth by reference to William Gilbert's suggestion that the earth is a lodestone. Bacon had argued against Gilbert on that point. Both works make few and only general references to Bacon, quite insufficient to attribute any important inspiration to him.

The *Discovery* and the *Discourse* have a wealth of references to recent literature—at least some thirty in each, of which nearly a dozen are new in the second work. They suggest that Wilkins found his occasion in the controversy that grew up in the wake of Philip van Lansberge's *Commentationes in motum terrae, diurnum et annuum*

(1630). This work was opposed by Libertus Fromondus both in *Anti-Aristarchus, sive orbis-terrae immobilis* (1631) and in *Vesta, sive Ant-Aristarchi vindex adversus Jac. Lansbergium* (1634), in which he defended the proscription of Copernican doctrine first issued by the congregation of cardinals in 1616 and reiterated in 1633. Fromondus was Wilkins's chief anti-Copernican opponent in both works; only the second work contains Alexander Ross's *Commentum de terrae motu circulari* (1634), which opposes both Lansberge and Nathaniel Carpenter. With a wide and mature command of the literature, Wilkins was engaged in international controversy. There can be no doubt that he succeeded in his aim of gaining acceptance for Copernicus, Kepler, and Galileo in England.[28]

We may wonder why Wilkins, still only in his middle twenties, took up the controversy with so much energy and conviction. In the *Discovery*, the "Epistle to the Reader" states that the work is "but the fruit of some lighter studies," finished in a few weeks; but the extensive reading adduced in both works could hardly have been so quickly mastered. The subject must have required longer preparation, perhaps during his student days and while he was tutor in his college. Henry Briggs, who died in 1630, was the first Savilian professor of geometry; in London he had been close to William Gilbert and Edward Wright, and in Oxford he became acquainted with John Pell and Theodore Haak, who was in Oxford during the later 1620s. Briggs was a strong Copernican and scorned astrology as "a system of groundless conceits," a view that was shared by his Savilian colleague in the astronomy chair, 1621-1643, John Bainbridge, who in London had belonged to the circle of Briggs and Nathaniel Carpenter. Both had been professors at Gresham College before coming to Oxford. It seems reasonable to assume that Wilkins had learned something from either or both of these men, who most closely illustrate the interest and orientation that characterized his career from the beginning.

Only a year later, in 1641, Wilkins published another book on a a popular subject, entitled *Mercury, or the Secret and Swift Messenger, Showing How a Man May With Privacy and Speed Communicate His Thoughts to a Friend at Any Distance*. It mentions such old tricks as baking secret messages into loaves of bread, but Wilkins's chief interest was cryptography, of which he gives a wealth of examples, all ready for use. But he also deals with cryptology or secret communication by speaking, either by involving the sense in metaphors and allegories or by changing old words or inventing new ones as is done by thieves, gypsies, and lovers; and with "semeology," that is communication by signs and gestures, as used for instance by deaf mutes.

Thus *Mercury* is not merely a practical guide in the use and decoding of ciphers, but a broadly based discussion of the means of communication, or what today would be called semiotics. The opening chapter states the basic principle that men are born with a natural ability to communicate, capable of learning any language in the same manner as they can master "other arts and sciences"; but men are not born with a single language that is natural to all mankind, for if this were so men would retain it so that all men would have a "double language, which is evidently false." In other words, like Mersenne, Wilkins rejected the natural-language doctrine then advocated by Robert Fludd. Wilkins ridiculed cabalistic interpretations of the sort that was again to occupy him in controversy with John Webster, who attacked the universities for neglecting Jacob Boehme's mystical linguistic doctrines. At the same time, Wilkins saw that the Babelistic multiplicity of languages was a great hindrance to the promotion of arts and sciences, men now wasting much time merely learning words instead of addressing themselves directly to the study of things. Citing such well-known instances as Arabic numerals, astronomical and chemical signs, and musical notes, he devoted a chapter to the possibility of creating a universal character as a remedy for the Babylonian confusion. It outlines the principles he was later to follow in his final work. At the end of *Mercury*, Wilkins notes that though his work can be used to serve unlawful purposes, it can also be used to uncover them. If the abuse of useful inventions is a reason for suppressing them, he observes, "there is not any art or science which might be lawfully professed."[29]

After dealing with communication and the second curse on mankind in *Mercury*, Wilkins next turned to the remedies for the first curse, inflicted upon man's labors. This pattern shows how closely Wilkins, with most of his contemporaries, related his concerns to the biblical story of man's terrestrial life. His *Mathematical Magick* (1648) is divided in two parts: "Archimedes or Mechanical Powers" and "Daedalus or Mechanical Motions." These titles might suggest an emphasis on the theoretical problems that had occupied much of the literature on mechanics during the previous generation, but the work is almost wholly devoted to the practical uses of mechanical devices with only enough theory to give the reader a sense of scientific initiation and understanding. The address "To the Reader" explains that the present work forms part of the same educational efforts as Wilkins's previous publications by showing how "a divine power and wisdom might be discerned, even in those common arts which are so much despised." The book's aim was "real benefit," both for gentlemen in the improvement of their estates, as in the draining of mines and coalpits, and for "common artificers" in gaining a "right understanding of the grounds and theory" of the arts they practice. It is therefore a short book, a compendium of knowledge otherwise only available in large, expensive volumes in Latin rather than the vernacular, "for which these mechanical arts of all other are most proper."

The first part deals with the balance, lever, wheel, pulley, wedge, and screw in that order, all illustrated with line drawings and pictures. Then follow chapters that show how the combination of these devices may produce "infinite strength" so as to "pull up any oak by the roots with a hair, lift it up with a straw, or blow it up with one's breath," all illustrated with rather sensational pictures. The second part treats a miscellaneous collection of strange devices and possibilities, such as flying machines, moving and speaking statues, artificial spiders, the imitation of sounds made by birds and man, a land vehicle driven by sails, a submarine, Archimedes's screw, and perpetual motion. This is a strange, almost baroque assembly, but all of these subjects had already been discussed in the extensive literature on which Wilkins drew, and a few years later a speaking statue was among the wonders shown to visitors at Wadham College. Automata were a legitimate scientific interest. There is little theory here, even scant hope of practical success, but much excitement. Learned fancies were being shared with a lay audience. It would be a mistake, however, to think that Wilkins was being frivolous. Even in the 1660s the Royal Society was not averse to the pursuit of such projects. There was as yet no clear distinction between what we consider good science and technology as opposed to fruitless speculation. The same scientific success that brought about the disenchantment of the universe also raised technological hopes that entered the realm of magic. Wilkins knew that wonder is the chief impulse to serious study and experiment.

A closer look at the sources of *Mathematical Magick* yields interesting information both about Wilkins's orientation and about the dating. It can easily be seen that many of the line drawings and illustrations are taken from other works along with the principles and devices they illustrate. The most recent work cited is John Greaves's description of the Egyptian pyramids, *Pyradomographia* (1646). But the works on which he chiefly relied were Guidobaldo del Monte's *Liber mechanicorum* (1577) and Marin Mersenne's *Cogitata physico-mathematica* (1644).[30] The use of Mersenne is much too extensive to have been introduced in a late revision; if therefore we take seriously Wilkins's statement in the dedication to Charles Louis that "this discourse was composed some years since, at my spare hours in the university," we must conclude that he devoted a good part of his time to university affairs during the mid- and late 1640s, a fact that may explain his sudden appointment to the wardenship of Wadham in 1648. Yet those affairs left him time to write the book, perform his official preaching duties in London, attend the early scientific meetings there, and serve as chaplain to the elector. Wilkins clearly managed his diverse functions with considerable energy.

Wilkins's explanation and illustration of the six traditional mechanical devices relied chiefly on Guidobaldo; a mere visual comparison of the handsome pages of the *Liber mechanicorum* with Wilkins's modest book makes this dependence obvious. Following Pappus, Guidobaldo had reduced all these devices to the same working principle as the lever—with the exception of the wedge, which he also discussed in terms of the inclined plane without making a clear choice between the two. Wilkins altogether omitted the inclined plane, but did not reduce the wedge to the lever principle as he did for the balance, wheel, pulley, and screw, presumably because he did not wish to burden his lay readers with the finer points of theory in a work which in any event limited to the barest minimum the mathematical principles offered by his sources.[31] In the order of the six devices, however, Wilkins followed Mersenne by treating the wheel before the pulley, but he did not use Mersenne's somewhat more complicated analyses. Thus the reader of *Mathematical Magick* would not have gained a sense of the long controversy over the proper understanding of these devices, revived in 1634 by Mersenne's *Les méchaniques de Galilée*.[32] From Mersenne, Wilkins also borrowed his account of the "glossocomus" or "engine of many wheels," with the analysis and illustration that shows how it works like a series of interlocking levers.[33] In addition he cited works other than the *Tractatus mechanicus* from the *Cogitata*: on the bending and power of bows,[34] on the flattening of a bullet fired against a wall,[35] and on the submarine.[36] Wilkins's debt to Mersenne is so heavy that it deserves closer attention. Mersenne is cited in the *Discovery*, the *Discourse*, and in *Mathematical Magick*. He is not mentioned in *Mercury*, but the general subject of this work forms the very core of Mersenne's own enquiries: the phenomena of communication, language, and the possibility of creating a philosophical language. It would be correct to say that Wilkins's scientific writings together present a popular version of Mersenne. The affinity of interests and orientation was too close to stem from common reliance on the same literature. The plurality of worlds was the only subject that separated them, but for Wilkins this was only a tentative suggestion of no systematic importance, confined to the

Discovery and not repeated. Mersenne's position on the Copernican doctrine was sufficiently ambiguous not to create any problem.[37]

Mersenne and Wilkins shared the conviction that religion and morality have a rational basis, that the grounds of religious belief are not tied to the retention and defense of Aristotelian doctrines, that a rational explanation of nature is possible when firmly based on sense experience and experiment, that this explanation would be mechanical and quantitative, that man is essentially different from the animals by virtue of possessing reason, that man alone is capable of language and communication, and that the growth of knowledge is a function of communication. Both were opposed to magic and the irrational, and for this reason they opposed the belief in the magical and occult powers of words, a doctrine then chiefly associated with Jacob Boehme and Robert Fludd. Language is not part of nature, it can tell us nothing about the essences of things, and thus cannot give "real knowledge" about the things of creation. It is conventional and man-made— "a man is born without any of them, but yet capable of all," Wilkins said. If this were not so, then it would not be possible to maintain that reason and experience together form the exclusive source of scientific knowledge. Thus the nature of language is the crucial problem in the epistemology of the new science. This fact explains some evident similarities between Mersenne, Wilkins, and Locke; as Mersenne felt bound to engage in a sustained critique of Fludd, so Locke argued against Boehme and his English disciple John Webster with his doctrine of "innate notions."[38] On these grounds Mersenne repeatedly argued that only God can know the essences of things and their true causes. Like Locke, he was convinced that certainty cannot be achieved in physics, "for we do not know the true reason of the effects we clearly see, and which we submit to our uses."[39]

Wilkins stated the same principle in 1649: "In our natural enquiries after the *efficient* causes of things, when our reason is at a stand, we are fain sometimes to sit down and satisfy ourselves in the notion of occult *qualities*; and therefore much more should be content to be ignorant of the *final* cause of things, which lie more deep and obscure than the other."[40] On this central doctrine, Mersenne and Wilkins disagreed with Bacon's goal of penetrating into "the nature of things." This principle severely limits the extent to which Bacon can be said to have guided and informed the new science in England. Bacon in fact played a small role in Wilkins's thought, in no way comparable to Mersenne's role. Mersenne and Wilkins also admired Gilbert on points that Bacon did not accept. As *Mathematical Magick* shows, Wilkins also followed Mersenne in taking an interest in automata;

they focused attention on interesting problems. In all their conduct and affairs, both Mersenne and Wilkins showed admirable openness and tolerance, of men as well as of opinions. In spite of the dramatic outward differences of their lives, they offer a beautiful example of the unifying, even irenic effect of the new science, in accordance with their mutual aim.[41]

If with Wilkins's contemporaries we grant that he was the chief promoter of the new science in England—not only by virtue of his writings, but also owing to his personal encouragement of individuals and his success in the shaping of scientific organization before and after the official formation of the Royal Society—then his alliance with Mersenne has far-reaching consequences for the belief that the Rosicrucian enlightenment was the seed-bed of the sort of natural philosophy that it was the aim of the Royal Society to promote. No attempt to assess Wilkins's importance can ignore these problems. Fludd and Mersenne do not go together. The groups they represent are not separated by their interest in a philosophy of nature, but they are set apart by their basic methods and principles, and it is this latter criterion that is crucial. Neither does one owe anything to the other regarding the need for formal cooperation and exchange of knowledge in a college (whether invisible or not) or an academy, for this need had been advocated by Mersenne as early as 1623; it was met by Théophraste Renaudot's conferences as early as 1629 and by Mersenne's own Academia Parisiensis at least by 1635. The ubiquitous presence of Hartlib and others shows nothing except a shared interest in natural philosophy and its results, although this presence has been the chief prop of the Rosicrucian argument. The wide tolerance of men like Mersenne and Wilkins should not be construed to mean positive approval. It has been argued that Continental influences reached England through The Hague, owing to the presence there of the exiled Queen Elizabeth of Bohemia, who for well-known reasons made some political use of such men as Hartlib and John Dury (Durie) as well as their contacts with circles that may, at least in part, be called Rosicrucian. In these matters the queen relied heavily on the services of the roving ambassador Sir Thomas Roe. On these grounds it has been argued that John Wallis's account of the first London scientific meetings in 1645 "seems to give a curiously 'Palatinate' coloring to the origins of the Royal Society."[42]

The weakness of this argument is obvious: it ignores the fact that The Hague was the home of a very different intellectual group that had lively contacts with London. It was through these contacts that Mersenne became more widely known in England. During these years, from 1633 until his death in 1649, the English ambassador at The Hague was Sir William Boswell, whose chief business of course was not with the exiled Palatinate queen, but with the court of the House of Orange. A strong royalist and a Laudian, he was successful in preventing Dutch intervention in the Civil War during the 1640s. At the center of this group in The Hague was Constantijn Huygens, whose political, cultural, and intellectual importance is well known. Huygens's correspondence shows that he was on intimate terms with Boswell,[43] and they shared many scholarly interests, including musicology. As secretary to Prince Frederic Henry of Orange, Huygens was Boswell's main contact with the court. He corresponded with both Descartes and Mersenne, as did Boswell although those letters are lost. Huygens regularly transmitted mail from Mersenne in Paris to recipients in Holland, including Descartes; Boswell occasionally did likewise. Between mid-summer of 1639 and August 1640, Boswell lived in London, and it was during this period that Haak initiated his lively correspondence with Mersenne at the encouragement of Boswell, "with whom Haak seems to have enjoyed a long-lasting and close acquaintance," beginning in 1638.[44] As was to be expected, it is evident that the contents of Mersenne's letters became widely known in London, just as these contacts were in part responsible for Mersenne's close English ties during the early 1640s.[45]

Having already cited Mersenne in his first two publications, Wilkins may have written *Mercury* on a hint from Mersenne transmitted through Haak. At the beginning of this book, Wilkins tells the reader that it was occasioned by a reading of Francis Godwin's *Nuncius inanimatus, or The Mysterious Messenger* (1629), which he had mentioned in the *Discovery*. It is tempting to think that his renewed interest in speedy and secret communication was related to the fact that Haak had sent Mersenne a copy of Godwin's little book, soon receiving the well-founded judgment that it "was indeed very animated because it teaches us nothing, saying not a word about its secret of communication. What is the use of writing, 'I know such and such things,' but not tell; that is to make fun of the readers."[46] In line with this critique, Wilkins's purpose in *Mercury* was precisely to remove linguistic mystification and the secrecy of ciphers by bringing the technique out in the open. It is no wonder that Wilkins kept informed about Mersenne, so that soon after its publication in 1644 he made the *Cogitata physico-mathematica* the main source of his *Mathematical Magick*. It was at this time, in 1645, that Haak called the first London meetings, which not only discussed scientific subjects but also performed experiments. Wallis's list of the topics shows no

Rosicrucian inclination, and the meetings themselves were most likely suggested by the success of Mersenne's Academia Parisiensis.[47] It was the group around Huygens and Boswell at The Hague that exerted a decisive influence in England. The chief foreign vehicle of this influence was Mersenne, its chief beneficiary was Wilkins. The Royal Society is in large measure the record of the nature and success of this influence.[48]

The Oxford Years. In 1648 Wilkins entered upon the second stage of his career. Oxford had come under increasingly severe strains during the 1640s. College finances were in disarray, new admissions dropped precipitously, teaching duties were only fitfully performed, and the academic community was torn into factions aligning royalists and men of the old stamp against Parliamentarians, feuding over religious observances, the inviolability of college statutes, the curriculum, the proper conduct and morals of students and teachers, and even proper modes of personal appearance and attire. This situation was intensified by the frothy presence of extreme Anabaptist agitators who acknowledged no authority but their own private revelations. The crisis came to a head after the victorious Parliamentary forces under Fairfax entered the town. On 1 May 1647, Parliament passed an ordinance which empowered a committee to look after "the better regulating and reformation of the University of Oxford, and the several colleges and halls in the same, and for the due correction of offences, abuses, and disorders, especially of late times committed there."

Within the next year the Parliamentary Visitors came to Oxford, ejected the old warden of Wadham College, and appointed Wilkins, who took charge on 13 April 1648. It proved a wise choice. At the age of thirty-four, he must have impressed the authorities by his accomplishments in the university and in his varied public offices as well as by his forceful advocacy of new learning, his moderation in religious affairs, his energy, and his extensive connections. Under the guidance of a man who was not considered a bigot, the college admissions soon rose steeply, including a large number of country gentlemen and "cavaliers," a fact that may also have helped improve the finances. It is universally acknowledged that Wadham was a distinguished college during Wilkins's wardenship. Among the new fellows of Wadham who came to Oxford from Cambridge were Seth Ward and Lawrence Rooke, "who was much addicted to experimental philosophy." They were joined by other men migrating from London and the scientific meetings there to continue their work in Oxford. They met at various places, including Wadham, where Wilkins created a laboratory. They included the nucleus of the future Royal Society: John Wallis, Jonathan Goddard, William Petty, Ralph Bathurst, Thomas Willis, and Robert Boyle, to whom Wilkins wrote on 6 September 1653: "I should exceedingly rejoice in your being stayed in England this winter, and the advantage of your conversation at Oxford, where you will be a means to quicken and direct our enquiries." Not long after, Boyle took up residence in Oxford.[49] The meetings were also attended by some of the able students who came to Wadham. The most brilliant was Christopher Wren, Wilkins's special protégé in his early career. Among the others were Wilkins's half-brother Walter Pope, Thomas Sprat, William Lloyd, William Neile, and Samuel Parker.

These men and their activities created an air of modernity and intellectual excitement in the university which suited Wilkins's desire to introduce the new philosophy in a manner that at the same time demanded discipline and significant achievement. He would hardly have been disturbed that his circle was in low repute among the Aristotelians, Galenists, and "those of the old stamp, that had been eminent for school and polemical divinity, and disputations and other polite parts of learning, [who] look upon them very inconsiderably, and their experiments as much below their profound learning and the professors of them."[50] This was precisely what reform was about and why so many sought Wilkins's advice and encouragement. When Oldenburg in the spring of 1656 settled in Oxford for a while, he was glad to find lodgings near Wilkins and Wadham, waxing poetic in his description of the new garden's "design and cultivation, where pleasure rivals utility and ingenuity industry."[51] Created at no small expense, the expansion and layout of this formal garden was one of Wilkins's first innovations. It was exquisitely executed with various mechanical wonders, a Doric temple, and on a mound, a statue of Atlas carrying the world on his shoulders. The garden shows a characteristic aspect of Wilkins's knowledge and orientation, as does his fondness for music.[52] When the warden's friend, the royalist John Evelyn, visited Wadham in July 1654, he was fascinated by the curiosities he was shown. There were not only scientific instruments, but also a "hollow statue which gave a voice and uttered words" and transparent, elaborately adorned apiaries built in the shape of castles and palaces, but constructed so as to make it possible to take out the honey without destroying the bees.[53] In those days science and ingenuity were visual.

While still at the Westminster School, Robert Hooke received a copy of *Mathematical Magick* as a gift from the author; and when a few years later he became a student at Oxford, he attended the scientific meetings and sought Wilkins's advice on his experiments on the art of flying and the making of artificial muscles.[54] Ten years later Hooke concluded the preface to *Micrographia* with an eloquent tribute to Wilkins, describing him as many must have seen him during those years:

> There is scarce any one invention, which this nation has produced in our age, but it has some way or other been set forward by his assistance. . . . He is indeed a man born for the good of mankind, and for the honor of his country. In the sweetness of whose behavior, in the calmness of his mind, in the unbounded goodness of his heart, we have an evident instance, what the true and the primitive unpassionate religion was, before it was soured by particular factions. . . . So I may thank God, that Dr. Wilkins was an Englishman, for wherever he had lived, there had been the chief seat of generous knowledge and true philosophy.

In the midst of this busy life, Wilkins was also a member of several influential university committees, including the delegacy to which the governance of the university was entrusted by its chancellor, Oliver Cromwell, on 16 October 1652. In this work, Wilkins successfully sought to regain for the university and the colleges their lost autonomy, to mediate between contending factions, and to maintain order and discipline. He especially defended the university against the attacks of radical religious factions, both on the governance of the university and its curriculum. One such attack was Webster's *Academiarum examen* (1654), which Wilkins and Ward answered the same year in *Vindiciae academiarum*. It opened with a letter by Wilkins, outlining and rejecting the three main charges. Contrary to Webster's accusations, the university was not a slavish follower of Aristotle but freely opposed him "as any contrary evidence does engage them, being ready to follow the banner of truth by whomsoever it shall be lifted up." Further, the university did not presume to teach what can proceed only from the spirit of God as Webster had charged. And it did not intend to direct its teachings according to the mystical linguistic doctrines of Boehme and "the highly illuminated fraternity of the Rosicrucians." Webster's trust in these authorities, said Wilkins, "may sufficiently convince what a kind of credulous fanatick reformer he is like to prove." Wilkins remained committed to the principles he shared with Mersenne.[55]

There appears to be good reason to accept Tillotson's assessment of Wilkins's achievement in the life of the university: "It is so well known to many worthy persons yet living, and has been so often acknowledged even by his enemies, that in the late times of confusion, almost all that was preserved and kept up of ingenuity and learning, of good order and government in the University of Oxford, was chiefly owing to his prudent conduct and encouragement."[56]

In the spring of 1656, Wilkins married Cromwell's sister, Robina French, which is said to have strengthened his hand with the Lord Protector in the interests of the university.[57]

Cambridge. In 1659 Wilkins made a sudden change of the sort that energetic men, confident of their powers, are prone to make when they, after success in one place, see an opportunity to apply their talents in new territory. After Cromwell's death, Wilkins had become a close adviser to Richard Cromwell, who appointed him master of Trinity College, Cambridge, "thinking he would be as serviceable in that, as he had been in the other university."[58] He took possession in late summer, resigning from the wardenship of Wadham on 3 September 1659. His tenure lasted barely a year. After the king's return to England in May 1660, Henry Ferne was made master, having successfully pressed a claim on the basis of a promise made by Charles I. The reason given was that the statutes did not allow a married master, but without Ferne's intervention this circumstance would hardly have prevented continuation. In a letter of July 1660, "numerously signed," the fellows of Trinity both offered their congratulations on the restoration and requested the reconfirmation of Wilkins, "appointed at their earnest petition, on the death of Dr. Arrowsmith, in 1658."[59]

During his brief association with Cambridge, Wilkins entered the circle of a group of men with whom he, in spite of some differences, had so much in common that he came to be considered one of them. With the Cambridge Platonists, he shared the outlook that was just then coming to be known as latitudinarianism: a commitment to tolerance and comprehension in church affairs, respect for learning, and the principle that the right understanding of religion, both revealed and natural, is essentially governed by reason. At the time of the Act of Uniformity a few years later, Richard Baxter wrote a succinct description of these men. He divided the conformists into three groups: the zealots, those who submitted for a variety of personal and other reasons, and

> those called latitudinarians, who were mostly Cambridge men, Platonists or Cartesians, and many of them Arminians with some additions, having more charitable thoughts than others of the salvation of the heathens and infidels. . . . These were ingenious men and scholars, and of universal principles, and free; abhorring at first the imposition of these little things, but thinking them not great enough to stick at when imposed.[60]

Wilkins's departure from Cambridge was felt as a loss by many, one of them being Isaac Barrow, whom Wilkins helped to the geometry professorship at Gresham College in 1662, the year before Barrow assumed the Lucasian chair at Cambridge. With an uncertain future behind him, Wilkins now gravitated to London and the culmination of his career as the energetic center of the Royal Society.

The Royal Society and the Last Years. In 1660 began the third and last stage of Wilkins's career. He did not have to wait long for ecclesiastical preferment. On 28 January 1661, he was again elected preacher at Gray's Inn,[61] and at the end of the year George Lord Berkeley (1628-1698) presented him with the living of Cranford, Middlesex.[62] On 11 April 1662 he became vicar of St. Lawrence Jewry in London, a living that was in the king's gift; thus he soon gained royal favor.[63] During the 1660s, he held a plurality of other ecclesiastical offices until in 1668 he became bishop of Chester.[64] Wilkins preached regularly at St. Lawrence Jewry, but his main sphere of activity was elsewhere.

During the late 1650s scientific meetings were held at Gresham College. After attending a lecture by Wren on 28 November 1660, the group gathered to discuss a plan for the founding of "a college for the promoting of physico-mathematical experimental learning." It is an unmistakable sign of Wilkins's importance that he was on this occasion appointed to the chair; within the next two weeks, Oldenburg wrote that Wilkins had been elected "president of the new English Academy very recently founded here under the patronage of the king for the advancement of the sciences."[65] Wilkins was still styled president in the first months of the new year, but on 6 March 1661 Sir Robert Moray was chosen president, no doubt owing to his close associations with the king, whose favor was eagerly and successfully sought during the first years. The rest is a familiar story. The society gained its first official charter under royal patronage a few years later, many new members joined, and an astonishing and ceaseless round of activities got under way, lasting with undiminished energy until about the time of Wilkins's death in November 1672, when attendance at meetings began to drop off and a state of seeming exhaustion set in, no doubt in part owing to a financial crisis. It is hard to say whether this decline was related to the loss of Wilkins, but the coincidence is striking.[66]

The records of these years show that Wilkins was busier than any other member in the affairs of the society. From the beginning until his death, he was each year reelected to the council, being also one of the two secretaries, another elective office, until he became bishop of Chester. He was occasionally called vice-president, although the statutes made no provision for such an office. While secretary, he attended practically every meeting and at most of them he was busy doing something: providing recent information, proposing experiments, being put in charge of this and that, appointed to special committees, asked for advice, engaged in fund-raising, and preparing suitably interesting doings for the king's visits. He proposed a very large number of candidates for membership, suggested that Robert Hooke be made curator of the collections, and proposed Nehemiah Grew as curator for the anatomy of plants.[67] At the same time he also supervised the writing of Sprat's *History of the Royal Society* (1667).[68] During the plague in the summer of 1665, Wilkins, Hooke, and William Petty removed to Durdans near Epsom in Surrey to carry out experiments on "improved chariots" and other mechanical devices; their results were reported to the society the following year. This was one of the several subjects of *Mathematical Magick* that occupied the society during the 1660s.[69]

At the beginning of 1668, Wilkins once more became involved in church affairs. After the fall of Clarendon, during the closing months of the previous year, the way was open for an attempt to bring at least some groups of nonconformists into communion with the church, a policy Wilkins had long supported in accordance with the promise made by the king in the Declaration of Breda shortly before his return to England. It was also advocated by the duke of Buckingham, now the king's first minister. Richard Baxter was approached, but he found himself unable to accept the initial terms of negotiation and requested instead that "two learned peaceable divines" be nominated "to treat with us, till we agreed on the fittest terms." One of them was Wilkins, who drew up a proposal that was revised during further deliberations. Baxter's detailed account shows that Wilkins was a skillful negotiator who tried his best to find a compromise that would satisfy all parties. This proved impossible, and when it became known that a bill for comprehension was ready, Parliament refused to accept it.[70] But Wilkins had Buckingham's patronage, and when the see of Chester fell vacant in August, he was soon appointed and duly consecrated on 14 November 1668.[71] In a diocese known for its large number of Dissenters, he was as lenient to nonconformists as his predecessor had been severe, many being brought into communion with the church owing to his "soft interpretation of the terms of conformity," while others who did not conform were still allowed to preach.[72] Early in 1669, Pepys heard that Wilkins, "my friend . . . shall be removed to Winchester and be Lord Treasurer." Although he discounted this rumor, he added that Wilkins was "a mighty rising man, as being a Latitudinarian, and the Duke of Buckingham's great friend."[73] In the midst of all his activites during the 1660s, Wilkins had also found time to prepare his greatest work, *An Essay Towards a Real Character and a Philosophical Language*, which with the official imprimatur of the Royal Society was presented to it on 7 May 1668.[74]

The *Essay* is the largest and most complete work in a long tradition of speculation and effort to create an artifical language that would, in a contemporary phrase, "repair the ruins of Babel." On one level a mere universal language would accomplish this aim by removing the obstacle that ordinary languages place in the way of common communication, whether in religion, commerce, or science. The universal use of a single language, for example, Latin, would meet this problem, but as Latin lost ground during the early half of the seventeenth century, especially in scientific writings, the need for other solutions was felt with greater urgency. As knowledge grew, in large measure aided by the introduction of common, conceptual, nonverbal symbols (much like Arabic numerals), there seemed to be new hope for the idea of a different sort of language, generally traced back to Ramón Lull, which would refer directly to what knowledge and thought are about, rather than using the imperfect medium of ordinary languages. There was wide agreement with Bacon that in these languages words were a perpetual source of philosophical error, being "framed and applied according to the conceit and capacities of the vulgar sort."[75]

The traditional model for such a language, often cited in the seventeenth century, was the language Adam spoke when he named the animals in his perfect state of knowledge before the fall. In the cabalist tradition, in Boehme and Fludd, it was believed that this language could somehow be recaptured. It was, for instance, seriously believed by some that it could be found by a sort of etymological distillation from all existing languages of the hitherto hidden but original elements of the Adamic language, on the assumption that this language was Hebrew, that Hebrew was the source of all other languages, and that these elements expressed the natures or essences of things. This was the mystical way, repeatedly rejected by Mersenne as nonsense; only God can know the essences of things.

But granting that man can grasp the order of creation by sense experience and reason, it would seem possible for man to comprehend and codify this knowledge in an artificial language based on the study of things. Within the more limited range of fallen man, this language would be a substitute for the lost Adamic language; if complete, it would express all man's knowledge in a methodical, rationally ordered fashion that mirrored the fabric of nature. It would be philosophical and scientific without error. On the practical level, it could be expressed in written or spoken symbols or both. Unlike a universal language, in which knowledge was still tied to the "cheat of words," to use another contemporary phrase, it would deal directly with things. This, it was hoped, would not only make knowledge easier and quicker to attain; it would cause a vast increase in knowledge.

These hopes were sustained by an optimism for which nothing seemed unattainable, similar to other expectations that strike us as equally chimerical, for instance the perpetuum mobile and the squaring of the circle. During the first half of the seventeenth century, a wealth of texts toyed with the possibility of a philosophical language, most of them on the level of groping speculation which never reached articulate statement of basic principles. In addition to these texts, there were many rumors about men who were working on such projects. They were typically surrounded by great secrecy, and there were several instances of offers to reveal the secret for great sums of money. The philosophical language was the exact equivalent of the philosopher's stone. Leibniz brought more conviction, energy, and intelligence to this problem; yet even he never spelled out its full meaning.[76]

Wilkins based his plan on a few basic principles. He assumed that "as men do generally agree in the same principle of reason, so do they likewise agree in the same internal notion or apprehension of things." Now, if the common notions of men could be tied to common marks, written or spoken, then mankind would be "freed from that curse in the confusion of tongues, with all the unhappy consequences of it." These marks would "signify things and not words," conjoined "with certain invariable rules for all such grammatical derivations and inflexions, and such only, as are natural and necessary," all contrived so "as to have such a dependence upon, and relation to, one another, as might be suitable to the nature of the things and notions which they represented." Thus the various marks, with their modifications, would follow an ordered and rational analysis of knowledge. The advantage would be immense, for "besides [being] the best way to helping the memory by a natural method, the understanding likewise would be highly improved; and we should, by learning the character and the names of things, be instructed likewise in their natures."[77]

Wilkins decided, somewhat arbitrarily he admitted, on forty basic genera, which with "diffcrences" and "species" would produce the marks that would give an inventory of the world, so to speak. Thus "world" is a genus (in the "effable" language represented by *da*), which by addition of the second difference, denoting "celestial" (with the effable sign *d*) produces the notion "heaven" (*dad*). "Earth" has the same elements, but to it must be added the mark for the seventh species, denoting this "globe of sea and land." This mark is *y*, so that the effable sign for earth is *dady*. As was soon observed by several critics, this entire system was after all closely tied to English words. Yet, postulating that it followed a natural method, Wilkins believed that it could be mastered in one month.[78] This belief reveals something about the *Essay*'s ancestry, for this was precisely the claim being made by mystical projectors, who, however, had the good reason for their claim that they assumed a strict interpretation of the macrocosm-microcosm harmony. For them, once the Babelistic confusion of ordinary words and false concepts was stripped away, man would regain the Adamic nakedness of pure and complete knowledge. With pure intellect thus restored, the need for memory would vanish; the small traces of it still required would be caused by the last imperfections in the system, much as friction cannot be entirely overcome.

The *Essay* was tainted by its ancestry. In *Mercury*, Wilkins had outlined some of its principles, although only for the creation of a universal language. In the *Vindiciae academiarum*, having ridiculed Webster's mystical advocacy of a genuinely natural, Adamic language, Seth Ward suddenly, as if unrelated to the subject, had said: "It did presently occur to me, that by the help of logic and mathematics this might soon receive a mighty advantage." He then briefly outlined the plan Wilkins executed. "Such a language as this," Ward said, "where every word were a definition and contained the nature of the thing, might not unjustly be termed a natural language, and would afford that which the cabalists and Rosicrucians have vainly sought for in the Hebrew, and in the names assigned by Adam."[79] The evidence shows that it was soon after and with the help of Ward that Wilkins began work on his philosophical language, as he openly admits in the "Epistle to the Reader" in the *Essay*. In rather awkward fashion Wilkins straddled two traditions that to the minds of most observers could not be brought together. Mersenne had clearly outlined the plan of such a language, but stayed clear of the mystical implications; and, in the event, he seems not to have had faith in its practicality, although he took an interest in its theoretical aspects, much as he did in automata.[80] In the *Essay* Wilkins also modified his optimistic statements with great diffidence about the entire plan and avowals of its tentative, incomplete execution, inviting the Royal Society to appoint a committee to examine it and make suggestions for its improvement. It was fortunate for his reputation that the *Essay* came at the end of Wilkins's career.[81]

The publication of the *Essay* put the Royal Society in a difficult situation. Written by one of its best-known members, encouraged and published under its auspices, it caused a crisis of prestige. It had been much talked about before publication, and it was soon distributed both in England and on the Continent. Yet none of the scientific members of the society had much, if any, faith in it, with the exception of Hooke, who mastered it and continued to take great interest in it.[82] Following Wilkins's wishes, the society immediately set up a committee to report on the *Essay*, but within the society this committee was never heard from again.[83] It was, however, decided that the society's "repository" under Hooke would be organized according to the *Essay*.[84] In its outward relations, the society talked up the *Essay* with much exaggeration. Thus after Christiaan Huygens had voiced his doubts to Moray, the latter quickly wrote back that the character was easy to master; the king had already done so and everyone was now following his example.[85]

Outside the Royal Society, a group of men (some of whom were fellows) continued to seek to improve and perfect the philosophical language, but with the exception of Hooke, these were men without scientific prestige in the society.[86] Having himself already written on similar plans, Leibniz soon learned about the *Essay*; he admired it greatly, although he still found it short of his own requirements. In 1680 he wrote of this admiration to Haak, but added that something "much greater and more useful could be made of it, insofar as algebraic characters are superior to chemical signs."[87] But so far as the Royal Society was concerned, the *Essay* was quietly forgotten.

The *Essay* did have one important effect; it set John Ray to work on botanical classification. Wilkins had lost all his belongings in the Great Fire of London, including part of the as yet unpublished manuscript of the *Essay*.[88] But eager to finish it, he enlisted the help of Francis Willoughby and John Ray in October 1666. They prepared the zoological and botanical tables. Ray was at the time perhaps Wilkins's most intimate and devoted friend; he immediately went to work, spending much of the next year helping Wilkins, on several occasions staying for extended periods with him at Chester. But he admitted at the same time that the project did not suit him.

> I was constrained in arranging the tables not to follow the lead of nature, but to accommodate the plants to the author's prescribed system. . . . What possible hope was there that a method of that sort would be

satisfactory, and not manifestly imperfect and ridiculous? I frankly and openly admit that it was, for I care for truth more than for my own reputation.[89]

It is a good question whether Wilkins knew of this criticism, which went to the heart of the matter; the *Essay* did not, as he had intended, follow the "method of nature." After publication, Ray helped Wilkins in amending the tables of natural history, just as he also at Wilkins's request made a Latin translation.[90] Later Ray brought his classifications to a perfection that he had not found it possible to achieve within the system of the *Essay*.[91]

Wilkins was now spending most of his time at Chester, with frequent journeys to London. Suffering from "fits of the stone," he unsuccessfully sought a cure at Scarborough Spa during the summer of 1672. On 10 August 1672, Lord Berkeley, recently arrived from Dublin, was nobly entertained by Wilkins at dinner in the bishop's palace at Chester.[92] On 30 October Wilkins was in London, where he attended, for the last time, a meeting of the Royal Society.[93] But the attacks persisted. Hooke and others administered medication, but to no avail. On 19 November 1672, Wilkins died at the house of John Tillotson, who had married his stepdaughter. At his death he is reported to have said that he was "prepared for the great experiment." The funeral sermon was preached by William Lloyd at the Guildhall Chapel on 12 December; the funeral was attended by a very large crowd, "though it proved a wet day, yet his corpse was very honorably attended . . . there were above forty coaches with six horses, besides a great number of others." He was buried in the church of St. Lawrence Jewry.[94]

In his own time Wilkins's stature and influence were very considerable. He was committed to a policy of tolerance that allowed compromise both in political and ecclesiastical affairs, based on the conviction that natural and revealed religion together with the new science proved a benevolent, providential order which, if rightly understood, ensured that mankind could live happily and peacefully, even prosperously, in this world. For this reason, his influence was divided between such men as Hooke, Boyle, and Ray on the one hand, Tillotson, Stillingfleet, and Patrick on the other. In this sense he shaped the temper of England in the latter half of the seventeenth century and left a significant impression on the eighteenth. His influence was acknowledged by John Ray both in the *Wisdom of God Manifested in the Works of the Creation* (1691) and *A Persuasive to a Holy Life* (1700), with the telling subtitle, "From the Happiness Which Attends It Both in This World and in the World to Come." In science, Hooke's tribute in the *Micrographia* leaves no doubt of Wilkins's importance, although he did not make any direct contribution to science. Even those, like Anthony à Wood, whose party loyalties made them caustic critics of men with similar careers, were sparing in their criticism of Wilkins. The age is full of testimonies that are echoed in Gilbert Burnet's summary of Wilkins's character: "He was naturally ambitious, but was the wisest clergyman I ever knew. He was a lover of mankind, and had a delight in doing good."

Notes

1. *Of the Principles and Duties of Natural Religion*, 8th ed. (London, 1722), p. 34; 1st ed. (London 1675). It was published from Wilkins's papers by his literary executor, John Tillotson, who in the preface explains that the first 12 chapters (pp. 1-165) were left ready for the press by Wilkins. They constitute the greater part of bk. 1, entitled "Of the Reasonableness of the Principles and Duties of Natural Religion." The rest was put together by Tillotson from "the materials left for that purpose," including all of bk. II, "Of the Wisdom of Practicing the Duties of Natural Religion." There are two references (pp. 48, 55) to Tillotson's sermon *Of the Wisdom of Being Religious* (1664), but these may be insertions and thus do not necessarily determine the time of composition. William Lloyd's *Sermon Preach'd at the Funeral of the Right Reverend Father in God, John Wilkins, D.D., Late Bishop of Chester* is included.

2. *A Discourse Concerning a New Planet, Tending to Prove, That 'Tis Probable Our Earth Is One of the Planets* (London, 1640), in *The Mathematical and Philosophical Works*, 2 vols. (London, 1802), I, 257. The *Discourse* comprises I, 131-261; it was published anonymously.

3. *Principles and Duties*, p. 17.

4. *Ibid.*, p. 73.

5. *Ibid.*, p. 17. Marin Mersenne had used the same metaphor: "Mechanics can teach how to live well, namely by imitating heavy bodies that always seek their center in that of the earth as the spirit of man must seek his in the divine essence, which is the source of all spirits." Dedication in *Les méchaniques de Galilée*, Bernard Rochot, ed. (Paris, 1966), p. 14.

6. *Ibid.*, p. 346.

7. *Sermons Preach'd Upon Several Occasions*, 2nd ed. (London, 1701), p. 236, 1st ed. (London, 1677, repr. 1680, 1682). There is a preface by the editor, John Tillotson. The axiom that man is a sociable creature is credited to Aristotle and, as often in Wilkins, supported by reference to the Stoics, especially Seneca.

8. *A Discourse Concerning the Beauty of Providence in all the Rugged Passages of It* (London, 1649), p. 65. Similar references occur in *Sermons*. The text of the 9th sermon (pp. 263-287) is Ecclesiastes 4:9—"Two are better than one." Its opening words call Ecclesiastes "a discourse from the most profound principles of reason and philosophy." Like Isaac Barrow, Wilkins had a marked preference for the Wisdom Books (see H. R. McAdoo, *The Spirit of Anglicanism* [London, 1965], p. 239). The 11th sermon (pp. 327-357) and 12th sermon (pp. 359-390) inculcate public spiritedness and cooperation; the theme of the 13th sermon (pp. 391-427) is moderation, followed by a sermon on the evils of vengeance and wrath.

9. *Mercury, or the Secret and Swift Messenger* (London, 1641; 2nd ed., 1694), in *Mathematical and Philosophical Works*, II, 1. *Mercury* comprises II, 1-87; it was published anonymously.

10. *Mercury*, II, 53; these are the opening words of ch. 13, "Concerning an Universal Character, That May Be Legible to All Nations and Languages."

11. *Sermons*, p. 184. The nature of language and the sociability of man were discussed in one of Théophraste Renaudot's conferences, 21 May 1635, with views that agree with Mersenne and Wilkins. *Recueil général des questions traictées ès Conférences du Bureau d'Adresse*, II (Paris, 1660), 458-463; 1st ed. (Paris, 1636). Wilkins had great influence on prose style, both in scientific discourse and in sermons. This is succinctly pointed out by Gilbert Burnet, *History of his Own Time*, 6 vols., 2nd ed. enlarged (Oxford, 1833), I, 347-348. See also Francis Christensen, "John Wilkins and the Royal Society Reform of Prose Style," in *Modern Language Quarterly*, 7 (1946), 179-187, 279-290, and esp. W. S. Howell, *Eighteenth-Century British Logic and Rhetoric* (Princeton, 1971), pp. 448-502. Wilkins's basic stylistic doctrine is already stated in the last section of *Ecclesiastes, or a Discourse Concerning the Gift of Preaching as It Falls Under the Rules of Art*. This section, "Concerning Expression," says that "obscurities in the discourse is an argument of ignorance in the mind. The greatest learning is to be seen in the greatest plainness. The more clearly we understand anything ourselves, the more easily we can expound it to others. When the notion itself is good, the best way to set if off, is in the most obvious plain expression," 3rd ed. (1651), p. 128; 1st ed. (1646). This was Wilkins's most popular work, often reprinted and steadily expanded, also after his death, having reached at least ten printings and its 7th ed. by 1693.

12. *The Discovery of a World in the Moon, Or, a Discourse Tending to Prove, That 'tis Probable There May Be Another Habitable World in That Planet* (London, 1638), in *Mathematical and Philosophical Works*, I, 19. The *Discovery* comprises I, 1-130; it was published anonymously. The 1640 printing contains chapter 14 on the possibility of flying to the moon. Since 1640, the *Discovery* and the *Discourse* have been published together; there was a 5th ed. in 1684. As Wilkins indicates, the words quoted here are taken from Edward Wright's preface to William Gilbert's *De Magnete* (1600). On the same point, Wilkins also refers to John Calvin's *Commentaries on the First Book of Moses, Called Genesis* (see the translation by John King [Edinburgh, 1847], pp. 84-87, 141, 177, 256). I see no evidence that Wilkins knew Galileo's *Letter* with its closely similar arguments, first published in Italian with Latin translation in 1636. In 1640 Wilkins devoted chs. 3-6 of the *Discourse* (I, 149-203) to the same issue, again citing Calvin (now including the *Commentary on the Psalms*), many passages from the Bible and the Church Fathers, and also such modern writers as Girolamo Zanchi, Franciscus Valesius, Christoph Clavius, Gaspar Sanctius, and Mersenne. Their religious and scientific allegiances were diverse: Sanctius and Clavius were Jesuits, the latter a friend of Galileo but opponent of Copernican astronomy; Zanchi studied at Padua and died at Heidelberg where he served the Palatine rulers; Valesius was a Spanish physician; Mersenne, often cited by Wilkins, took an ambiguous attitude toward Copernicus, but found no scriptural evidence for a charge of heresy, as Wilkins pointed out in the *Discourse* (I, 160). Cf. William S. Hine, "Mersenne and Copernicanism," *Isis*, 64 (1973), 18-32. Zanchi (1516-1590) was a Reformed theologian of pronounced irenic tendencies. His use by Wilkins at this time is noteworthy because he was also, along with especially Hugo Grotius, an authority with William Chillingworth in the *Religion of Protestants* (1638). See the excellent study by Robert R. Orr, *Reason and Authority, the Thought of William Chillingworth* (Oxford, 1967). There are other suggestive similarities between Chillingworth and Wilkins. Thus *Principles and Duties*, p. 27, cites the last section in bk. II of Grotius's *De veritate religionis Christianae* for the very same purpose as Chillingworth in *Religion*, ch. 6, sect. 51.

13. *Discourse*, I, 172.

14. *Ibid.*, I, 138. Cf. *Discovery*, "To the Reader": "It is a false conceit for us to think that amongst the ancient variety and search of opinions, the best has still prevailed." (In the *Mathematical and Philosophical Works* [1802] this "To the Reader" is placed at the front

of vol. I, before "The Life of the Author.") Mersenne makes the same point in *Questions inouyes* (Paris, 1634), pp. 144-148.

15. *Mathematical Magick, or the Wonders That May Be Performed by Mechanical Geometry* (London, 1648), in *Mathematical and Philosophical Works*, II, 127, 131. *Mathematical Magick* comprises II, 89-260, but the dedication to the prince elector Palatine and "To the Reader" are placed at the very front of vol. I. There was a 4th ed. in 1691.

16. *Mathematical Magick*, "To the Reader." For the other points, often repeated in his writings, see the opening chapters, *ibid.* (II, 91-97); cf. *Sermons*, p. 254.

17. *Sermons*, p. 254.

18. *Discovery*, "To the Reader."

19. *Mathematical Magick*, "To the Reader," points out that the title was suggested by Cornelius Agrippa, *De vanitate scientiarum*, ch. 42.

20. *Discourse*, I, 136-137, 134.

21. *Discovery*, I, 14. The full line in Epistle I, 14, reads *Nullius addictus jurare in verba magistri* ("Not pledged to echo the opinions of any master") but the entire context of lines 10-18 is relevant. It was John Evelyn who suggested the motto. In "Praefatio ad lectorem" of the *Quaestiones in Genesim*, Mersenne had recalled the same Horatian passage for precisely the same purpose, against Aristotelian authority and in favor of our own experience of phenomena; Wilkins cited this work in the *Discovery* and in the *Discourse*. See Robert Lenoble, *Mersenne ou la naissance du mécanisme* (Paris, 1943), p. 224; cf. p. 222.

22. R. E. W. Maddison, *The Life of the Honourable Robert Boyle* (London, 1969), p. 85 (Boyle to Hartlib, 14 September 1655); Anthony à Wood, *Athenae Oxonienses*, Philip Bliss, ed., III (London, 1817), col. 971. Wood's information is also in Walter Pope, *Life of Seth Ward* (London, 1697), p. 29.

23. The information often given that Wilkins was born at Fawsley, Northamptonshire, is not certain; see Barbara J. Shapiro, *John Wilkins 1614-1672. An Intellectual Biography* (Berkeley, 1969), pp. 12-13, 254-255.

24. Wood, *op. cit.*, IV (1820), col. 752. Edward Sylvester also taught Chillingworth.

25. Reginald J. Fletcher, *The Pension Book of Gray's Inn, 1569-1669* (London, 1901), pp. 355-357. There is good reason to accept the explanation that it was Wilkins's "skill in the mathematics that chiefly recommended him" to Charles Louis, "his Electoral highness being a great lover and favourer of those sciences, in which he must needs have been very agreeable to his Chaplain, who was entirely of the same turn and temper." See vol. VI (1756), 4266, in *Biographia Britannica*, 7 vols. (London, 1747-1766); this very full and well-informed article is the best biographical account of Wilkins (it covers pp. 4266-4275 and was most likely the work of Thomas Birch).

26. Montague Burrows, ed., *The Register of the Visitors of the University of Oxford from AD 1647 to AD 1658* (London, 1881), p. 22, Camden Society, n.s. 29.

27. It is not clear whether Wilkins made two journeys during 1648-1649, or whether one of them occurred earlier or, less likely, later. Charles Louis spent most of the years between 1644 and his return (May 1649) in England. In 1644 he was invited to attend the sessions of the Westminster Assembly (Bulstrode Whitelocke, *Memorials* [London, 1732], p. 108). Wilkins was formally accepted by the Assembly on 25 September 1643.

28. It is hard to accept Grant McColley's argument that Campanella's *Apologia* is the main source of both the *Discovery* and the *Discourse*. The reason is not merely that the two writers had little in common except their defense of Galileo, but especially that Wilkins used the important literature published since the *Apologia* (1622), including Galileo's own *Dialogue* in the Latin translation (1635). See "The Debt of Bishop Wilkins to the *Apologia pro Galileo* of Tomaso Campanella," in *Annals of Science*, 4 (1939), 150-168; Campanella, *The Defence of Galileo*, tr. by Grant McColley, in *Smith College Studies in History*, 22, nos. 3-4

(April-July 1937), intro.; "The Ross-Wilkins Controversy," in *Annals of Science*, 3 (1938), 153-189. All these items have much useful information, although they are committed to a view of conflict between science and religion that is now outmoded. Ross answered Wilkins in *The New Planet no Planet* (London, 1646). The entry on Wilkins in *Biographia Britannica* plausibly suggests that the *Discourse* was not merely a treatise on the new astronomy but written as a defense of Galileo: "It was the first just treatise of its kind, and more effectually exposed the folly and absurdity as well as cruelty of the proceedings in the Inquisition by taking no direct notice of them" (*op. cit.*, p. 4268). It is remarkable that Wilkins's defense on the question of biblical authority uses the same arguments as Galileo in the *Letter to the Grand Duchess*, which was presumably not known to Wilkins.

29. Like his two previous books, *Mercury* cites a wealth of sources, both ancient and modern, with some fifty in the latter category. Among the most important are Johannes Trithemius, *De polygraphia* and *De stenographia*; Hermannus Hugo, *De origine scribendi* (1617); and Gustaphus Selenus, *De cryptographia* (1624)—the author's name is a pseudonym for the learned Duke August of Braunschweig-Lüneburg. In 1630 John Pell had written "'A Key to Unlock the Meaning of Johannes Trithemius' in His Steganography; Which Key Mr. Pell the Same Year Imparted to Mr. Samuel Hartlib." (See Wood, *Fasti Oxonienses*, Philip Bliss, ed. [London, 1815], I, 463.) Like the *Discovery* and the *Discourse, Mercury* was published anonymously, but the dedication is signed "J. W." It has five commendatory poems at the front, two of them addressing the author as their friend: Richard Hatton, who entered Magdalen Hall, Oxford, on 7 July 1637; and Richard West, who matriculated at Christ Church, Oxford, on 15 February 1633; both presumably knew Wilkins at Oxford, which adds a little to the sparse information we have of Wilkins's life during those years. Another poem is by Sir Francis Kynaston, the center of a literary coterie at court, who in 1635 founded Musaeum Minerva, an academy for young noblemen. Wilkins was clearly getting known in wider circles.

30. Among other recent works are Pierre Gassendi, *Vita Peireskii* (1641); A. Kircher, *De Magnete* (1643); and Mario Bettini, *Apiaria universae philosophiae mathematicae in quibus paradoxa et nova pleraque machinumenta ad usus eximios traducta et facillimis demonstrationibus confirmata exhibentur*, 2 vols. (Bologna, 1641-1642).

31. Wilkins mentions Guidobaldo among his chief sources. An abbreviated version of the *Mechanicorum Liber* is in *Mechanics in Sixteenth-Century Italy*, tr. and annotated by Stillman Drake and I. E. Drabkin (University of Wisconsin Press, 1960), pp. 239-328. It includes, on a reduced scale, the line drawings and illustrations of the original. In the final pages of *Mathematical Magick*, Wilkins discussed Archimedes's screw with reference to Guidobaldo's *De cochlea* (1615). This device also interested Mersenne.

32. The only point on which Wilkins may be indebted to Galileo is the subject "concerning the proportion of slowness and swiftness in mechanical motions" (*Mathematical Magick*, II, 146-148), which shows similarity with chapters 1 and 5 of *Les méchaniques* (see Rochot, ed., pp. 23-25, 32-34), but it is possible that Wilkins could also have found this in some other source. In that work Galileo did not deal with the wedge, but explained the rest on the principle of the lever. The Mersenne work in question is *Tractatus mechanicus theoricus et practicus* (96 pp.) contained in the *Cogitata physico-mathematica*, which was ready from the press on 1 April 1644. This collective volume also contains other pieces to which Wilkins refers. Mersenne explained the screw in terms of the inclined plane, the balance and the wheel in terms of the lever, and the pulley and the wedge in terms that combined the lever and the inclined plane. During the 1630s, Descartes also treated these devices in a number of letters to Mersenne (about August-October 1630 and again at greater length on 13 July 1638) (see C. de Waard *et al.*, eds., Mersenne, *Correspondance*, II [1937], 602-620, and VII [1962], 347-375); and in the letter to Constantijn Huygens 5 October 1637 (Descartes, *Correspondance*, Ch. Adam and G. Milhaud, eds. II [Paris, 1939], 31-41). These letters do

not all offer the same explanations, but Descartes had a low opinion of Guidobaldo's reduction of the pulley to the lever principle, while Galileo found Guidobaldo the best of all writers on these subjects (see Rochot, ed., p. 77).

33. *Mathematical Magick*, II, 137, 135, 138, 148; cf. *Tractatus*, pp. 39-43. Mersenne's term is *glossocomus*. With the same name, this device was also discussed and explained on the principle of interlocking levers, with illustration, in Bettini, *Apiaria*, I, pt. 4, 31-34, with reference to the source in bk. VIII of Pappus, *Mathematicae collectiones* (1588). This book gave an account of the mechanics of Hero of Alexandria, of which the full text was not known until the late nineteenth century. Pappus attributed the term *glossocomus* to Hero, who is also the source of other terms in the technical vocabulary of mechanics. First published in the late sixteenth century, both his *Automata* and *Pneumatics* were very influential, clearly seen, for instance, in Salomon de Caus, *Les raisons des forces mouvantes avec diverses machines tant utilles que plaisantes. Aus quelles sont adjoints plusieurs desseings de grottes et fontaines* (Frankfurt, 1615). Book 1, theorem XVI, on the lifting of heavy burdens by the multiplication of forces, has an illustration that bears a striking resemblance to Wilkins's illustration in *Mathematical Magick*, II, 143. De Caus's garden designs found expression in the garden at Wadham College, for instance the mound with a statue (cf. de Caus, bk. II, problem X; bk. I, problem XII, deals with perpetual motion). In John Bate, *The Mysteries of Nature and Art* (London, 1634), bk. 1, "Of Water Works," is a popular exposition of Hero's *Pneumatics*, with illustrations from the Italian edition, showing how to make mechanical chirping birds and the like, all subjects that also fascinated Mersenne and Wilkins, who was clearly much indebted to this tradition stemming from Hero. De Caus was active in England and Heidelberg in the early seventeenth century. On de Caus, see C. S. Maks, *Salomon de Caus 1576-1626* (Paris, 1935).

34. *Ibid.*, II, 162; cf. Mersenne, *Ballistica et acontismologia* in *Cogitata*.

35. *Ibid.*, II, 174; cf. *De hydraulicus et pneumaticus phaenomenis*, pp. 149-153.

36. *Ibid.*, II, 188-194, "Concerning the Possibility of Framing an Ark for Submarine Navigations"; cf. *De hydraulicus*, pp. 207-208, and *Tractatus de magnetis proprietatibus*, pp. 251-259. In the former, Mersenne, like Wilkins, referred to the submarine constructed by Cornelis Drebbel, who was also known for his work on other devices, including the perpetuum mobile; the name recurs elsewhere in Mersenne. Already in 1634, Mersenne had asked in question 21 of the *Questions inouyes*, pp. 84-89, "Peut-on faire des navires, et des bateaux qui nagent entre deux eaux." The same work opened with one of Wilkins's favorite topics, "A sçavoir si l'art de voller est possible," a problem that recurs in the *Cogitata* (e.g., *Tractatus mechanicus*, p. 41). It is curious that Wilkins already in the *Discovery* (I, 118) had discussed why a man under water does not feel the weight of the water above him, a subject Mersenne treated in the *De hydraulicus*, pp. 204-206. *Mathematical Magick* (II, 192) credits information about an especially accomplished French diver to a note to *Tractatus de magnetis*, placed in the pagination of *Harmoniae liber*, p. 368 (also part of the *Cogitata*). For the greater part of his career, Drebbel was active in England, where he died in 1633. During his stay in London in the early 1620s, Constantijn Huygens was intimately acquainted with Drebbel's projects and inventions, which were also widely discussed later in the century by Boyle, Wren, and Hooke, in addition to Wilkins. See Gerrit Tierie, *Cornelis Drebbel (1572-1633)* (Paris-Amsterdam, 1932); and L. E. Harris, *The Two Netherlanders Humphrey Bradley and Cornelis Drebbel* (Cambridge, 1961), pp. 119-227.

37. See Hine, cited at end of note 12. Some time around 1660, Isaac Newton took extensive notes from the *Mathematical Magick*; see Frank E. Manuel, *A Portrait of Isaac Newton* (Cambridge, Mass., 1968), pp. 11, 49. The same notebook also has long excerpts from Bate, *Mysteries*, bk. III, "Of Drawing, Washing, Limming, Painting, and Engraving." See E. N. da C. Andrade, "Newton's Early Notebook," in *Nature*, 135 (1935), 360.

38. The term is in Webster's *Academiarum examen* (1654); see "Leibniz on Locke on Language," above, p. 61.

39. *Questions inouyes*, pp. 69-74, where Mersenne also argues that certainty is possible in mathematics since it deals with quantities, it is "a science of the imagination or of pure intellect, like metaphysics, which is not concerned with any other object than what is possible in the absolute."

40. *Discourse Concerning the Beauty of Providence*, p. 71. Belonging to the year of the king's execution, this sermon argued that, "we may infer, how all that confusion and disorder, which seems to be in the affairs of these times, is not so much in the things themselves, as in our mistake of them" (p. 65). It is characteristic of Mersenne and Wilkins that moral and religious arguments jostle statements of scientific principle. In this text Wilkins often cites the Stoics, especially Seneca.

41. For an excellent introduction to Mersenne, see A. C. Crombie's article in *Dictionary of Scientific Biography*, IX (1974), 316-322. Wilkins's programmatic advocacy of the Copernican system, contrasted with Bacon's equally strong rejection of it, obviously limits the role that can be assigned to Bacon in the creation of English science in the seventeenth century—"It is the absurdity of these opinions that has driven men to the diurnal motion of the earth; which I am convinced is most false," wrote Bacon. See Lisa Jardine, *Francis Bacon: Discovery and the Art of Discourse* (Cambridge University Press, 1974), p. 77.

42. Frances Yates, *The Rosicrucian Enlightenment* (London, 1972), p. 182; cf. p. 183: "We have thus here a chain of tradition leading from the Rosicrucian movement to the antecedents of the Royal Society." See also p. 175 and the reference to H. R. Trevor-Roper there.

43. Boswell has a brief entry in the *Dictionary of National Biography*; there is a much fuller life in *Autobiography of Thomas Raymond and Memoirs of the Family of Guise of Elmore* (London, 1917), G. Davis, ed., pp. 69-80 (Camden Society, third series, vol. 18). Boswell was one of the literary executors of Bacon's estate, possessing among other things the important writings edited by Isaac Gruter, *Francisci Baconi de Verulamio scripta in naturali et universali philosophiā* (Amsterdam, 1653). In 1651, Gruter published another manuscript in Boswell's possession, William Gilbert, *Du mundo nostro sublunari philosophia nova*, often known as "Physiologia nova." Bacon used this work in some of his writings, though without citation. Mersenne knew of this work, writing to John Pell, on 20 January 1640, that Gilbert had written on "Selenography or the geography of the moon, which however has not been published" (*Correspondance*, IX [1965], 52). The most likely source of this information is surely Boswell. Boswell also had a collection of John Dee's papers, some of which he intended to publish himself (C. H. Josten, ed., *Elias Ashmole 1617-1692*, 5 vols. [Oxford, 1966], II, 1242; IV, 1372). This was known to Hartlib, who recorded it in the "Ephemerides" in 1639; he said there and later repeated (see Davis, p. 77) that Boswell attributed "all his proficiency in learning whatever it be, to the goodness" of Dee's Preface to Euclid. There is no compelling reason to believe that respect for that Preface means commitment to cabalistic doctrines; it is perhaps wiser to accept Leibniz's opinion that Edward Kelley was an impostor who abused Dee. Boswell was secretary to Lord Herbert of Cherbury in 1620 while the latter was ambassador at Paris. There are references to Boswell in *De Briefwisseling van Constantijn Huygens* (1608-1687), J. A. Worp, ed., 6 vols. (The Hague, 1911-1917). (These are vols. XV, XIX, XXI, XXIV, XXVIII, XXXII in the series *Rijks geschiedkundige Publicatiën*.) The Mersenne *Correspondance* is of primary importance.

44. Pamela Barnett, *Theodore Haak* (The Hague, 1962), p. 32. Wood, *Athenae Oxonienses*, IV, 280, has an instructive list of Haak's "many great and learned acquaintance," including John Williams, John Selden, Henry Briggs, John Pell, Wilkins, and Boswell, "who encouraged him to keep and continue his correspondence with the learned Mersennus, and others of later time." Wood says of Boswell: "He was a learned man, a great encourager of learning,

zealous for the Church of England, faithful in the execution of his embassy, and highly valued by eminent persons" (*Fasti*, I, 332). In the 1640s, Haak and Boswell helped Pell to academic appointments in Holland.

45. In 1639 and 1640, Hartlib's "Ephemerides" show knowledge of the Mersenne-Haak correspondence; during Boswell's stay in London at this time, there is also information about him. For information about Haak, see the entry in *Dictionary of Scientific Biography*, IV (1972), 606-608.

46. *Correspondance*, XI (1970), 412 (to Haak, 4 September 1640). Mersenne also wrote to Haak on other subjects that occur in Wilkins, e.g., universal language, underwater navigation, and flying (XI, 417, 408, 435). On 16 November 1640, he wrote to Haak: "You are right when you say that neither God nor the sciences are bound by languages, and in fact, any one language is fit for the expression of everything." This statement expresses both his own and Wilkins's rejection of mystical linguistic doctrines (XI, 420).

47. Christoph J. Scriba, "The Autobiography of John Wallis," in *Notes and Records of the Royal Society*, 25 (1970), 40.

48. During the mid-1640s both Wilkins and Haak, himself a native Palatine, were associated with Charles Louis. Both his mother's and his own letters have been extensively published; the letters give no indication that Rosicrucian influence could have come from that source, or even that the writers had any interest in it. An informative recent article is G. A. Benrath, "Die konfessionellen Unionsbestrebungen des Kurfürsten Karld Ludwigs von der Pfalz (*d.* 1680)," in *Zeitschrift für die Geschichte des Oberrheins*, 116 (1968), 187-252.

49. Boyle, *Works*, Thomas Birch, ed., 6 vols. (London, 1772), VI, 633; this is one of the few Wilkins letters on record. At this time, Wilkins found a place at Wadham for the instrument maker Christopher Brooke (or Brookes), "purposely to encourage his ingenuity" (see Wood, *Fasti*, I, 403; also E. G. R. Taylor, *The Mathematical Practitioners of Tudor and Stuart England* [Cambridge, 1954], p. 234; this book has a valuable alphabetical collection of brief biographies [pp. 165-307], followed by a list of works in chronological order [pp. 311-441]).

50. Anthony à Wood, *The History of the Antiquities of the Colleges and Halls in the University of Oxford*, John Gutch, ed., 2 vols. (Oxford, 1792-1796), II, pt. 1, 633-634. Though seen with a somewhat prejudiced eye, this is one of the chief sources for the history of Oxford in this period, with the relevant material on pp. 501-708. Another important source is Montague Burrows, *Register of the Visitors*. The handiest narrative source is Charles Edward Mallet, *A History of the University of Oxford*, 3 vols. (London, 1924-1926). See esp. vol. II, *The Sixteenth and Seventeenth Centuries* (1924).

51. *Correspondence*, A. R. and M. B. Hall, eds., I, 94 (letter to Edward Lawrence, April 1656).

52. See T. G. Jackson, *Wadham College* (Oxford, 1843), on the gardens (with illustration), pp. 211-212, on music, p. 117; there is an account of a famous musical evening at Wadham in "The Life of Anthony à Wood," in *Athenae Oxonienses*, I (1813), xxxii.

53. *Diary*, E. S. de Beer, ed., III, 105-110 (1-13 July 1654).

54. R. T. Gunther, *Early Science at Oxford*, VI (Oxford, 1930), *The Life and Work of Robert Hooke*, pp. 5-9.

55. The two pieces have been reprinted in Allen G. Debus, *Science and Education in the Seventeenth Century: the Webster-Ward Debate* (London, 1970). In his letter to Ward, Wilkins nearly verbatim repeats some passages from the opening chapter of his *Discourse Concerning the Gift of Prayer* (1651; 9th ed., 1718) on the three gifts requisite in a minister.

56. "To the Reader," in *Sermons*. Tillotson was specifically rejecting some critical remarks in Wood's *Historia et Antiquitates Universitatis Oxoniensis* (1674), which was a Latin version done by John Fell from Wood's English manuscript. Wood was much displeased with

this version, both because of its bad Latin and because Fell had taken the liberty of inserting his own comments, of which the depreciation of Wilkins was one. In the late summer of 1654, some of the Wadham fellows made official complaint about Wilkins's conduct of college affairs, but after due consideration the charges were rejected by the Visitors; it is not clear what the issue was. See Burrows, *Register*, pp. 394-397.

57. She had previously been married to Peter French of Christ Church, also a man of some importance in the university. Tillotson married a daughter of that marriage. It is an often repeated error that Wilkins on this occasion gained permission to marry from Cromwell, then chancellor of the university; the Wadham statutes had already been altered in 1651 so as to permit the warden to marry—one wonders whether Wilkins contemplated marriage at that time or whether he was acting on principle. See Jackson, *Wadham College*, p. 116. In June 1670, Wilkins was the only bishop to favor a divorce act, then pending (see Edmund Ludlow, *Memoirs*, C. H. Firth, ed., 2 vols. [Oxford, 1894], II, 503). Robina Wilkins died in 1689; she and Wilkins had no children.

58. Mark Noble, *Memoirs of the Protectoral-House of Cromwell*, 2 vols. (London, 1787), I, 314.

59. *Calendar of State Papers, Domestic*, 1660. In preparation for the appointment, Wilkins had been incorporated doctor of divinity at Cambridge on 18 March 1659.

60. *Reliquiae Baxterianae* (London, 1696), pt. I, p. 386. Baxter especially sought the churches where he "heard a learned minister that had not obtruded himself upon the people, was chosen by them, and preached well (as Dr. Wilkins, Dr. Tillotson . . .)" (*ibid.*, p. 537). Gilbert Burnet made the same point, counting Benjamin Whichcote, Ralph Cudworth, Henry More, and John Worthington along with Wilkins among "the divines called Latitudinarians." "At Cambridge," he wrote, Wilkins "joined with those who studied to propagate better thoughts, to take men off from being in parties, or from narrow notions, from superstitious conceits, and a fierceness about opinions" (*History of His Own Time*, I, 340). I see no reason at all for the opinion, heard in the eighteenth century and repeated by John Tulloch, that Wilkins "was a Calvinist . . . of a somewhat strict type" (*Rational Theology and Christian Philosophy in England in the Seventeenth Century*, 2 vols. [Edinburgh, 1872], II, 442). The terms "latitude-men," "latitudinarian," and "latitudinarianism" first occurred in the 1660s in a pejorative sense, but were soon adopted as the common term. In 1662, the term was used to refer to the men we call the Cambridge Platonists with stress on the connection between them and the mechanical philosophy. (The generic term Cambridge Platonists did not occur until after the middle of the nineteenth century.) See the pamphlet by S. P., *A Brief Account of the New Sect of Latitude-Men Together With Some Reflections on the New Philosophy*. (S. P. is traditionally identified as Simon Patrick, who was also the first English translator (1680) of Grotius's *De veritate*.) There is an illuminating contemporary account in Edward Fowler, *The Principles and Practices of Certain Moderate Divines of the Church of England (Greatly Misunderstood) Truly Represented and Defended* (London, 1670). Thus this book was published soon after the failure of the bill for comprehension. Fowler calls the latitudinarians "persons of great moderation" and says they are also called "rational preachers" and "moral preachers." He names More, Cudworth, John Worthington, Joseph Mede, and Chillingworth. John Beardmore said that Wilkins "was looked upon as the head of the *Latitudinarians*, as they were then stiled." See "Some Memorials of the Most Reverend Dr. John Tillotson . . . Written Upon the News of His Death [1694] by J. B.," in Thomas Birch, *The Life of the Most Reverend Dr. John Tillotson*, 2nd ed. (London, 1753), p. 390. The term "latitude" is given prominence by Chillingworth: "This Deifying of our own Interpretations, and tyrannous inforcing them upon others; this Restraining of the World of God from that latitude and generality, and the Understandings of Men from that liberty, wherein Christ and the Apostles left them, is, and hath been the only Fountain of all the Schisms of

the Church . . . the common Incendiary of Christendom" (*Religion of Protestants*, ch. 4, sect. 16; in this passage Chillingworth cites the agreement of Zanchi). The two chief influences on Tillotson were Chillingworth and Wilkins. Ernst Cassirer's *Die Platonische Renaissance in England und die Schule von Cambridge* (Leipzig-Berlin, 1932), opens with the surprising opinion that the Cambridge Platonists were hostile to the new mechanical philosophy and had little understanding of it. With characteristic misjudgment, R. F. Jones believed that Samuel Parker's *A Free and Impartial Censure of the Platonick Philosophy* (Oxford, 1666) was "a vigorous attack" on the Cambridge Platonists; in agreement with the common use of the term "Platonic" at that time, it was a critique of the chief opponents of the new philosophy, *i.e..*, enthusiasts and Rosicrucians of the sort illustrated by John Webster, whose *Academiarum Examen* Jones, astonishingly, calls "the most important expression of the new scientific outlook between Bacon and the Restoration" (*Ancients and Moderns* [paperback ed., 1965], pp. 188, 108). For reliable information and interpretation, see Marjorie Nicolson, "Christ's College and the Latitude-Men," in *Modern Philology*, 27 (1929), 35-53, and McAdoo, *The Spirit of Anglicanism*.

61. Fletcher, *Pension Book*, 435-436.

62. White Kennett, *Historical Register* (London, 1706), p. 576. Wilkins succeeded Thomas Fuller on 10 December 1661. The appointment shows Wilkins's life-long association with the Berkeley family, this George Berkeley being the son of the man to whom *Mercury* was dedicated.

63. Kennett, p. 658; Wilkins succeeded Seth Ward, who became bishop of Exeter.

64. Some of these offices are listed in R. B. Gardiner, *The Registers of Wadham College*, pt. I, 1613-1719 (London, 1889), p. 171.

65. *Correspondence*, I, 406 (Oldenburg to Boreel, 13 December 1660). The term "physico-mathematical" may have been heard before, but it brings to mind the title of Mersenne's *Cogitata physico-mathematica*; was it perhaps Wilkins who had brought in the proposal?

66. Wilkins willed £400 to the Society.

67. Among the candidates Wilkins proposed were Haak, John Hoskins, Francis Willoughby, Edward Bysshe, George Smyth, Thomas Sprat, Henry Power, Henry More, John Ray, Anthony Lowther, and Ralph Cudworth. *The Record of the Royal Society of London*, 4th ed. (London, 1940), does not list Cudworth among the members, contrary to statements in the recent literature, e.g., J. A. Passmore, *Ralph Cudworth* (Cambridge, 1951), p. 2; and McAdoo, p. 121. These statements would seem to be correct.

68. I have dealt with that important function in the entry on Thomas Sprat, reprinted above.

69. Thomas Birch, *History of the Royal Society*, 4 vols. (London, 1756-1757), II, 30, 41, 60, 63, 66, 74, 89. Durdans was the property of Lord Berkeley. On his return from Oxford on 7 September 1665, Evelyn stopped at "Durdans by the way, where I found Dr. Wilkins, Sir William Petty and Mr. Hooke contriving chariots, new rigs for ships, a wheel for one to run races in, and other mechanical inventions, and perhaps three such persons together were not to be found elsewhere in Europe, for parts and ingenuity." Samuel Pepys was interested in the same matter; see entries in his *Diary* under 11 and 22 January 1666. See also letter from Hooke to Boyle, 8 July 1665, in Gunther, *Early Science*, VI, 248.

70. Baxter, *Reliquiae*, pt. III, pp. 23 ff.; Burnet, *History*, I, 477. On the Comprehension scheme, see Norman Sykes, *From Sheldon to Secker, Aspects of English Church History 1660-1678* (Cambridge, 1959), pp. 71-75. At this time Sir Matthew Hale and Wilkins "came to contract a firm and familiar friendship," so close that "there was an intimacy and freedom in [Hale's] converse with Bishop Wilkins that was singular to him alone." See Gilbert Burnet, *The Life and Death of Sir Matthew Hale, Kt. Sometime Lord Chief Justice of His Majesty's Court of King's Bench* (London, 1700). Hale was also close to James Ussher and Baxter.

71. Burnet, *History*, I, 464; Evelyn's description in *Diary* under that date. Benjamin Whichcote succeeded Wilkins as vicar of St. Lawrence Jewry.

72. Kennett, *Register*, pp. 815, 817, 921.

73. Pepys, *Diary*, 16 March 1669.

74. In a meeting of the Royal Society on 29 October 1662, "Dr. Wilkins was put in mind to prosecute his design of an *universal language*" (Birch, *History*, I, 119).

75. See "Leibniz on Locke on Language," pp. 57 and 78 (note 43).

76. Albert Heinekamp, "Ars characteristica und natürliche Sprache bei Leibniz," in *Tijdschrift voor Filosofie*, 34 (1972), 452; this article is an excellent treatment of the subject. The classic treatment is Louis Couturat, *La logique de Leibniz* (Paris, 1901), esp. chs. 2-5. A briefer discussion is found in L. Couturat and L. Leau. *Histoire de la langue universelle* (Paris, 1907), with a section on Wilkins, pp. 19-22. Paolo Rossi, *Clavis universalis, arti mnemoniche e logica combinatoria da Lullo a Leibniz* (Milan, 1960), is the best history of the subject. In the literature, both primary and secondary, the *locus classicus* for the philosophical language is Descartes's letter to Mersenne, 20 November 1629 (Mersenne, *Correspondance*, II, 323-339), written in response to a project of which Mersenne had sent him a copy. The subject is often mentioned in the Mersenne correspondence, but unfortunately the notes, usually so informative, attached both to the Descartes letter and others on the same subject are very confused; this confusion has gradually been cleared up in recent volumes. It is an index of the low conceptual level of much recent secondary writing on this popular topic that it fails to make the distinction between a merely universal and a philosophical language; this has made it possible for some to argue that the philosophical language came about by a sort of evolutionary growth of stenography.

77. Wilkins, *Essay*, pp. 20-21.

78. *Ibid.*, pp. 51-52, 398, 454.

79. Debus, pp. 214-216 (original pagination, also given there, pp. 20-22). Ward's basic outline does not state anything that had not been said earlier.

80. For the relevant passages in Mersenne, see references given in notes 50-51 to the entry on Mersenne in *Dictionary of Scientific Biography*, IX, 322. Cf. Lenoble, *Mersenne*, pp. 514-518; Eberhard Knobloch, "Marin Mersenne's Beitrag zur Kombinatorik," in *Südhoffs Archiv*, 58 (1974), 356-379.

81. There are useful illustrations in E. N. da C. Andrade, "The Real Character of Bishop Wilkins," in *Annals of Science*, I (1936), 1-12. An informative account is Jonathan Cohen, "On the Project of a Universal Character," in *Mind*, 63 (1954), 49-63. Although weak on the intellectual and philosophical context there is much useful detail on contemporary projects in Vivian Salmon, *The Works of Francis Lodwick. A Study of his Writings in the intellectual Context of the Seventeenth Century* (London, 1972). In a monograph entitled *Zum Weltsprachenproblem in England im 17. Jahrhundert. G. Dalgarno's 'Ars signorum' und J. Wilkins' 'Essay' (1668)* (Heidelberg, 1929; *Anglistische Forschungen*, Heft 69), Otto Funke argued that Bacon was the inspiration for such projects and that Wilkins was in large measure indebted to Dalgarno. Funke does not consider Mersenne. In a useful article on "The Evolution of Dalgarno's *Ars Signorum*," in *Studies in Language and Literature in Honour of Margaret Schlauch* (Warsaw, 1966), pp. 353-371, Vivian Salmon, along somewhat similar lines, argued that "without Dalgarno, Wilkins would never have begun the task which led to the *Essay*" (p. 370); the evidence, including troublesome questions of dating and personal relationships, does not warrant that conclusion. Neither Funke nor Salmon considered the cogent contemporary discussion in Robert Plot's *Natural History of Oxfordshire* (London, 1677), pp. 282-285, which concludes that the question must be left open. Anthony à Wood is the source of the persistent belief that Wilkins cribbed from Dalgarno's *Ars signorum*, saying that the author showed it, before it went to press, to Wilkins, "who from thence taking a

hint of a greater matter, carried it on, and brought it up to that which you see extant" (*Athenae Oxonienses*, III, 970; this opinion is repeated in the entry on Wilkins in the *Dictionary of National Biography*). Benjamin DeMott has unconvincingly argued for strong Comenian influence on Wilkins ("Comenius and the Real Character in England," in *Publications of the Modern Language Association*, 70 [1955], 1068-1081; "The Sources and Development of John Wilkins' Philosophical Language," in *Journal of English and Germanic Philology*, 57 [1958], 1-13). He rests his argument chiefly on the claim for the irenic religious effect of the philosophical language, but this is a common claim that cannot be used for such identification, but the fundamental difficulty is that what Comenius had to say on this subject was not original. DeMott ignores Mersenne. Salmon argues against DeMott in "Language-Planning in Seventeenth-century England," *In Memory of J. R. Firth* (London, 1966), pp. 370-397. R. F. Jones, "Science and Language in England of the Mid-Seventeenth Century," in Jones, *The Seventeenth Century* (Stanford, 1951; original publ. 1932), was always a poor guide and is now thoroughly outmoded. Jorge Luis Borges's quaint essay "The Analytical Language of John Wilkins" has brought Wilkins and the *Essay* to the attention of the literati (in *Other Inquisitions 1937-1952*, Ruth L. C. Sims, trans. [New York, 1966], pp. 106-110). See also the entries on Bochme, in *Dictionary of Scientific Biography*, II (1970), 222-224; and on Comenius, *ibid.*, III (1971), 359-363.

82. R. T. Gunther, *Early Science in Oxford*, vol. VIII, *The Cutler Lectures of Robert Hooke* (Oxford, 1931), pp. 150-152, with illustration (reproduced in Andrade). Hooke found it "so truly philosophical, and so perfectly and thoroughly methodical, that there seems to be nothing wanting to make it have the utmost perfection." Hooke's faith in the philosophical language is closely related to his belief in demonstrability in natural science, a belief not shared by his scientific colleagues in the Royal Society.

83. Since this is true also of other committees appointed by the Society during these years, the failure to report cannot be taken as evidence one way or the other.

84. This had been suggested by Wilkins in the "Epistle dedicatory" of the *Essay*. See also Sprat, *History of the Royal Society*, p. 251. Hooke called memory a "repository." His conception intimates a link with the mnemonic tradition; in John Willis's *The Art of Memory* (London, 1621; later reissued), *repository* is the word for the memory device of "an imaginary house or building."

85. Huygens, *Oeuvres*, VI, 397 (Huygens to Moray, 30 March 1669); *ibid.*, p. 425 (Moray to Huygens, 16 April 1669).

86. This correspondence is in the Aubrey MSS in the Bodleian Library, Oxford. They have recently been examined by Vivian Salmon in "John Wilkins' *Essay* (1668): Critics and Continuators," in *Historiographia Linguistica*, 1 (1974), 147-163. Great efforts were made to elicit a plan from Seth Ward, but when it finally came it was found disappointing, inclining "too much to Lullius" (MS Aubrey 13, fol. 113v, Thomas Pigott to Aubrey at Hooke's, Oxford, 14 April 1678).

87. Leibniz, *Philosophische Schriften*, C. I. Gerhardt, ed., 7 vols. (Berlin, 1875-1890). VII, 16.

88. On this occasion Seth Ward helped Wilkins to a precentorship at Exeter; see Pope, *Life of Seth Ward*, p. 56.

89. Ray to Martin Lister (7 May 1669), quoted in Charles E. Raven, *John Ray* (London, 1950), p. 182. Ray repeats this judgment in several other letters of the same years.

90. Several Continental scholars, including Leibniz, had called for a translation. Ray's translation is known to have been in the archives of the Royal Society for more than a century, but has since been lost. As late as May 1678, Aubrey wrote to Ray: "I have at length gotten my desire, viz. an able Frenchman to translate the real Character into French. It is Dr. Lewis du Moulin." W. Derham, *Philosophical Letters of Ray* (London, 1718), p. 144.

91. There is an illuminating discussion of these problems in Philip R. Sloan, "John Locke, John Ray, and the Problem of Natural System," in *Journal of the History of Biology*, 5 (1972), 1-53. Locke said in the *Essay*: "I am not so vain to think that anyone can pretend to attempt the perfect reforming the languages of the world, no, not so much as of his own country, without making himself ridiculous" (Book III, ch. II, paragraph 2). This represents the general view of the Royal Society. There is cogent criticism of Wilkins's *Essay* in *Reflections Upon Learning* (1699) by the antiquary and critic of the new science, Thomas Baker; see *Reflections*, 4th ed. (1708), pp. 21-22.

92. *Calendar of State Papers, Domestic*, 1672.

93. *Diary of Robert Hooke*, 1672-1680, Henry W. Robinson and Walter Adams, eds. (London, 1935), p. 11.

94. The death is reported in Hooke's *Diary* under 19 November: "Lord Bishop of Chester died about 9 in the morning of a suppression of the urine." On the next day, he had more details: "Dr. Needham brought in account of Lord Chester's having no stoppage in his uriters nor defect in the kidneys. There was only found 2 small stones in one kidney and some little gravel in one uriter but neither big enough to stop the water. 'Twas believed his opiates and some other medicines killed him, there being no visible cause of his death, he died very quickly and with little pain, lament of all." The cause of Wilkins's death continued to be a matter of debate. In 1695, the physician Edward Baynard published "An Account of the Probably Causes of the Pain in Rheumatisms; as also of the Cure of a Total Suppression of Urine, not caused by a Stone, by the Use of Acids," in *Philosophical Transactions of the Royal Society*, 19 (Jan.-Feb. 1695), 19-20. Baynard suggests that Wilkins's case was falsely diagnosed.

Bibliography

I. Original Works. In addition to the works in the notes, see the following: *A Sermon Preached Before the King on March 7, 1669* (London, 1669). *A Sermon Preached Before the King on March 19, 1671* (London, 1671). These two sermons are not reprinted in Tillotson's collection of fifteen sermons.

When the *Discovery* and the *Discourse* were first published together, in 1640, they appeared under the title *A Discourse Concerning a New World and Another Planet in Two Books*. Several of Wilkins's works have been issued in reprints in recent years. *The Mathematical and Philosophical Works* (London, 1708) is the first collection of the works covered by that title. They are here placed in chronological order of publication with separate paginations and title pages. This edition opens with a "Life of the Author and an Account of His Writings," and closes with "An Abstract of Dr. Wilkins's *Essay Towards a Real Character and a Philosophical Language*." The contents are the same as in the 1802 edition.

II. Secondary Literature. This literature is given in the notes. Our knowledge of Wilkins's life derives chiefly from the early biographical writings: William Lloyd's funeral sermon; Walter Pope, *The Life of Seth Ward . . . With a Brief Account of Bishop Wilkins, Mr. Lawrence Rooke, Dr. Isaac Barrow, Dr. Turberville, and Others* (London, 1697); John Aubrey, "John Wilkins," in *Aubrey's Brief Lives*, Oliver Lawson Dick, ed., (Ann Arbor, 1957), pp. 319-320; A. à Wood, *Athenae Oxonienses*, Bliss, ed., III (1817), cols. 967-971, but this rich source has much relevant information scattered throughout the four volumes. This is also true of Wood, *Fasti Oxonienses*, and *History of the Antiquities of the Colleges and Halls in the University of Oxford*, John Gutch, ed. See also Pierre Bayle, *A General Dictionary, Historical and Critical. . . .* John Peter Bernard, Thomas Birch, John Lockman, eds., 10 vols. (London, 1734-1741), X, 160-164. The best biographical entry on Wilkins is the one in *Biographia Britannica*; see n. 25. It is much better than the entry in the *Dictionary of National Biography*. These sources have formed the bases of entries in biographical reference works since the eighteenth century, with the accretion of more or less reliable anecdotal matter from other sources.

Since Wilkins was so widely known in his own time, he is mentioned in most contemporary records, some published long ago and some only recently, such as the diaries of John Evelyn and Samuel Pepys, Birch's *History of the Royal Society*, the correspondence of Henry Oldenburg, and *The Diary and Correspondence of Dr. John Worthington*, James Crossley, ed., 2 vols. in three parts (Manchester, 1847, 1855, 1886, with vol. II, part II edited by R. C. Christie). (These are vols. 13, 36, and 114 in the publications of the Chetham Society.)

On Wilkins and Wadham College, the most important treatment is Jackson's *Wadham College*, but see also J. Wells, *Wadham College* (London, 1898), pp. 69-87. Patrick A. W. Henderson, *The Life and Times of John Wilkins* (London, 1910), is chiefly about Wadham College. The best modern biography is Dorothy Stimson, "Dr. Wilkins and the Royal Society," in *Journal of Modern History*, 3 (1931), 539-563. Neither J. G. Crowther, *Founders of British Science* (London, 1960), nor E. J. Bowen and Sir Harold Hartley, "John Wilkins," in *The Royal Society, Its Origins and Founders*, Sir Harold Hartley, ed. (London, 1960), pp. 47-56, offer anything new, and they are not reliable. For some reason, the subject of Wilkins at large has proved an open field for guesswork and partisan interpretation. The intellectual history of England in the mid-seventeenth century has been treated in a number of recent books that show great diversity of interpretation, e.g., Christopher Hill, *Intellectual Origins of the English Revolution* (Oxford, 1965), and Frances A. Yates, *The Rosicrucian Enlightenment* (London, 1972); this literature tends to be occupied with polemics rather than substance. Barbara J. Shapiro, *John Wilkins 1614-1672. An Intellectual Biography* (Berkeley, 1969), has some new biographical information, but does not meet its claim to being an intellectual biography. Based on a small part of the relevant literature, Henry G. van Leeuwen presents an illuminating discussion of his subject in *The Problem of Certainty in English Thought 1630-1690* (The Hague, 1963). He argues that Chillingworth's discussion was followed by Tillotson, which is correct, but then postualtes that Wilkins and Glanvill, learning from Tillotson, "secularized" the argument for the benefit of science and the Royal Society. Simple chronology is enough to refute that interpretation. The deeper problem, however, is that van Leeuwen ignores Wilkins's early writings except *Mercury*, and that he makes a distinction between religion and science (as is also clearly shown in the notion of secularization) that is not warranted by the texts and the intellectual framework of the time; the term "natural religion" should be a sufficient reminder of that fact. (Van Leeuwen also states that *Mathematical Magick* was composed, "like most of [Wilkins's] earlier works, during his school days" [p. 56].) Shapiro rightly argues against van Leeuwen (pp. 232-316); see also Shapiro, "Latitudinarianism and Science in Seventeenth-Century England," in *Past and Present*, no. 40 (July 1968), 16-41. Marjorie Hope Nicolson's *Voyages to the Moon* (New York, 1948) is the classic treatment of a subject that has come to be associated with Wilkins. There is an excellent account of Wilkins in H. R. McAdoo, *The Spirit of Anglicanism. A Survey of Anglican Theological Method in the Seventeenth Century* (London, 1965), esp. pp. 203-231; it is the most important recent treatment of Wilkins. See also the bibliographies under the entries for Theodore Haak and Thomas Sprat in the *Dictionary of Scientific Biography*.

I have also used material contained in five lectures I gave under the auspices of the Program in the History and Philosophy of Science at Princeton University in the spring of 1964, entitled "Language, Man, and Knowledge in the 16th and 17th Centuries."

An Outline of Language-Origins Theory since the Renaissance

Why a "Conference on Origins and Evolution of Language and Speech" would wish to hear about the history of the subject is a good question. Is this history at all relevant to current study and research? It would be presumptuous for me to say, since I cannot claim to have any close knowledge of the interesting work that has been done in recent decades. This, at least, is certain: since the possession of language and speech has always been considered the chief characteristic of the human species, the question of origin has also been considered fundamental in any attempt to understand the nature of man and what distinguishes him from other animals. Most major philosophers and most philosophical systems have dealt with the problem in one way or another; in fact, so universal has this interest been that its absence, as in Kant, has been cause for wonder. Plato, Aristotle, the Stoics, the Epicureans, the Church Fathers, Thomas Aquinas, Luther, the German mystics, Jacob Boehme and Robert Fludd, Marin Mersenne, John Locke, and, following him, most eighteenth-century philosophers would readily have understood the question in its present formulation, although they would have given quite different answers. A meeting of physicists would hardly schedule a paper on past doctrines concerning the constitution of the solar system; it would simply not appear sufficiently instructive to be worth the time and effort in that context. Is our situation different? It would again be presumptuous for me to say, but given the difficulty of the problem, it is at least

Reprinted from *Origins and Evolution of Language and Speech*, ed. by Stevan R. Harnad, Horst D. Steklis, and Jane Lancaster. *Annals of the New York Academy of Sciences* 280 (1976), 4-17.

possible that we may learn something, both positively and negatively, from a knowledge of past discussion of the question.

The problem is difficult, because it has traditionally been seen as the central question about the nature of man. It has been bound up with other fundamental questions such as intelligence, reason, thought, man's social nature, political philosophy, and the progress of knowledge. In its classic eighteenth-century formulation, the origin of language and speech was the key to the question of the history of thought, of mankind. This complex mixture of speculation and some empirical information that was often cogent is illustrated in Lord Monboddo's great work from the 1770s, *Of the Origin and Progress of Language*. This work shows a feature that is common to all such treatments: it is intimately involved with contemporary assumptions and philosophical doctrines. Arguing against Humean scepticism, Monboddo did not arrive at his discussion of the origin of language until he had devoted two long sections to epistemology and to the social and political nature of man. Yet, he was convinced that the origin of language occupied a central place in what he, according to a typical eighteenth-century formulation, called "the natural history of man," for, as he said, "it is by language that we trace, with the greatest certainty, the progress of the human mind," a view that would have gained the emphatic agreement of Locke, Leibniz, and Condillac.

The eighteenth century did not share the attitude of Dr. Johnson, who found little merit in "Lord Monboddo's strange speculation on the primitive state of human nature"; it was, Johnson said, "all conjecture on a thing useless, even were it known to be true. Knowledge of all kinds is good; conjecture, as to things useful, is good; but conjecture as to what it would be useless to know, such as whether men went upon all fours, is very idle." Unlike Dr. Johnson, we do share the eighteenth century's curiosity about these matters; if at all possible, we do want to know whether men ever went upon all fours, and especially whether the higher primates could learn to speak and why they do not. But seen in the context of his time, Johnson was right to stress that this was all a matter of speculation and conjecture. Some twenty years later, the Scottish philosopher Dugald Stewart called Adam Smith's essay "Considerations Concerning the first Formation of Languages" (1761) an example of "conjectural or theoretical history." The eighteenth century did not fool itself that it was establishing facts about the primitive state of mankind; it sought reasoned plausibilities with the chief intent of separating man's natural endowments from his artificial accomplishments; the chief product of man's art was language, which, in turn, was the foundation of the progress of thought and knowledge. It is one of the curious quirks of history that the nineteenth century became so compulsively historical in the factual sense that it misinterpreted the eighteenth century on this important point, with the significant consequence that linguistic philosophy came to be ridiculed as useless and jejune, "unempirical" speculation quite unworthy of serious attention by right-minded scholars; that is, by university professors who, from the limited but dominant perspective of their chairs in comparative-historical philology, collectively saw themselves as the sole legitimate authority on all matters relating to the study of language.

My own business, so to speak, is intellectual history, and it is in this manner that I propose to deal with the subject. This means that I am more interested in what has been said than in the question whether past discussions fit current conceptions; it is often forgotten or ignored that adequate attention to the former problem is the indispensable prerequisite to an informed handling of the latter. Needless to say, in the short time we have, I can only deal with a small part of the wealth of material that is available. After a single example from antiquity, I shall jump to the seventeenth and later centuries.

Nearly 2,500 years ago, Herodotus told the story of an Egyptian king who wished to know which nation was the oldest on earth. He therefore contrived to have two children brought up in isolation from all speech in order to find out what language they would speak if left to their own devices. He was disappointed to learn that the first word they spoke was not Egyptian but Phrygian, thus proving that the Phrygians were the oldest nation. I mention this anecdote because it shows the consistency with which the problem and the experiment designed to solve it have recurred. As late as the eighteenth century, the same experiment was proposed, though it was at the same time admitted that it could not be performed, for obvious reasons. History records several similar experiments, usually with the answer that the language the children spoke was Hebrew. But even if the experiment could not be performed, the same problem drew attention to so-called wolf-children; that is, children who for some reason had lived isolated from other humans, growing up among animals. The most familiar example is perhaps the "Wild Boy of Aveyron," who a few years ago was the subject of a beautiful movie, based on the account of the French doctor, Jean Itard, written in 1801. It is a sign of the philosophical interest in such children that reports began to occur with increasing frequency from the latter half of the seventeenth century; cases were discussed by Leibniz, Condillac, Monboddo, and many others. I am sure it is well known that these children did not speak and never learned to speak if they had lived in isolation beyond the early, speech-learning years of childhood. The communication of deaf-mutes was also a lively subject in the seventeenth century and especially in the latter half of the eighteenth, chiefly owing to Condillac's philosophy of communication and language.

If we jump some two thousand years to the Renaissance, we find a different conception of the problem, which now began to receive much serious attention. Argument and counterargument developed views that led directly to the eighteenth century. The formulation that remained dominant far into the seventeenth century was based on the Old Testament, with a strong admixture of Jewish mysticism as found in the cabalistic doctrines that became known in the west after the expulsion of the Jews from Spain in 1492, a year which for that reason marks a watershed in linguistic philosophy and speculation. It is well known that Genesis contains two profoundly influential linguistic statements: Adam's name-giving in Chapter 2 and the story of the Babylonian Confusion in Chapter 11. The first is the source of the powerful conception of Adam as archetypal man, in every respect, of course, but chiefly in the matter of language. The dominant interpretation of the act of name-giving was turned into a doctrine of the origin of language in this fashion. This act occurred before the Fall when Adam was in a state of perfect, nearly divine knowledge. Thus his "names" bore a natural relation to the animals they named, simply because there must, so it was postulated, have been perfect harmony between word and thing; words could not be merely accidental or based on some sort of agreement that arbitrarily assigned a sound to the animal named. This idea led to the doctrine, heard even late in the seventeenth century, that Adam, also after the Fall, was both the greatest philosopher and the greatest etymologist who ever lived. Since all mankind descended from Adam and Eve, all languages had a single origin and exhibited certain common features. We may find this conception useless or fanciful, but it had great value in stimulating linguistic study, for instance in the search for what we call linguistic universals. It was generally postulated that this first language was Hebrew, a belief which in turn led to a great deal of comparative study that was much more fruitful and competent than the nineteenth century's inordinate pride in its own comparative, historical philology, has allowed us to know. Leibniz, for instance, had great respect for this work, which he knew intimately.

Now, we might think that the Babylonian Confusion put an end to these doctrines. But with some exceptions, that was not the case. The Confusion was open to several interpretations; one of them was that though the single language of mankind had been scattered into mutually unintelligible forms of speech, it was still possible that the original elements of the pre-Babylonian natural language had been preserved in the new languages. Thus, though the present languages could not be seen to be natural in the Adamic sense, they were still not the product of conventional agreement which arbitrarily assigned certain sounds to stand for certain things. This belief raised the hope that determined etymological study might reveal the forms of the original natural language. There were, in fact, people who made vast collections of words in the largest possible number of different languages on the assumption that it would be possible to arrive at the original elements of the Adamic language by some sort of etymological distillation, so to speak. This may seem nearly idiotic, and few seventeenth-century figures put any trust in it, but the need to argue against this doctrine was fruitful.

The conception I have described is properly called mystical, although it pretended to offer something like empirical means to recapture the Adamic protolanguage. But there was another, much more influential and genuinely mystical, linguistic mode, best illustrated by Jacob Boehme. In his moments of God-given inspiration, Boehme claimed that he was given direct insight into the natures of things and that he understood the Adamic language; thus words became, in these moments, direct revelations of the essences of things; that is, language became again genuinely natural, as it was to Adam. Each word revealed the nature of the thing, almost as a chemical formula does to us. In this conception there is a strong admixture of cabalistic lore and Renaissance neoplatonism.

Such claims did not remain confined to the province of religion. On the contrary, if Boehme and such cabalistic figures as Robert Fludd were right, then it would, by this means, be possible to gain real, scientific knowledge of the constitution of things in nature by the proper study of words and language. This seems so utterly fantastic to us that we may hesitate to believe that these views could pose a threat to science, but this is in fact precisely what happened, and for this reason the advocates and practitioners of the new science felt compelled to argue against them. Thus it was seriously maintained by some, also in England, that science must not neglect this potential source of knowledge. If, for instance, the word "gold" could be understood in proper cabalistic fashion, it would give us information about the essence of gold itself. The chief thrust of Locke's *Essay* is an argument against this view, and it was for this reason he argued that we can never know more than what he, defiantly, called the "nominal essence" of gold. This term was defiant because it implied a rejection of the mystical understanding of essence. In this sense it can be said that Locke's *Essay* was a handbook in the epistemology of the new mechanical philosophy, or what we call science, practiced and advocated by the "Royal Society of London for the Promotion of Natural Knowledge."

It is in this light that Locke's argument against "innate notions," as he called them, must be understood, an argument in which the Royal Society found itself involved owing to attacks upon it conducted in these terms, most characteristically by a man named John Webster, whose text used the very terms that occur in Locke's counterargument. It has rightly been said that "Locke certainly considered the doctrine of innateness as having its foundation in the abuse of words." On these points, arguments closely similar to Locke's had previously been advanced both by his close and admired friend Robert Boyle and by Descartes's correspondent Marin Mersenne. Time does not permit closer consideration of Marin Mersenne, who in the first half of the seventeenth century was the influential advocate of mechanical philosophy. A large part of his extensive writings are therefore devoted to argument against the cabalistic doctrines of Robert Fludd, in the same manner that Locke later argued against other statements of the same doctrines. For this reason, Mersenne is the most innovative and influential writer of the first half of the seventeenth century on the nature of language, although there would seem to be no evidence that he directly influenced Locke; the close similarity of their arguments is explained by their common opposition to the same doctrines and their common commitment to the same mechanical philosophy.

Like Locke, Mersenne argued forcefully that we can never know the internal constitutions of things, that language is purely conventional (as opposed to natural in the Adamic sense), and that all the knowledge that is open to us in these matters must rely on the external manifestations of things. Like Locke, he took reason to be the fundamental, defining characteristic of man, the source of his uniqueness and all his artificial accomplishments, and the basis of all knowledge that truly deserves the name. Locke was a great admirer of the Port-Royal logic and grammar, a fact that is also evident in the *Essay*. The contrast and conflict between so-called empiricism and rationalism is a nineteenth-century invention, advanced in the context of a conservative reaction against contemporary philosophical doctrines, in the interest of a characteristic Victorian ideology. Further, this view did not remain unopposed during the nineteenth century; Coleridge, who was no mean judge, said that Locke and Descartes held "precisely the same opinions about the original sources of our ideas." Locke's argument against innateness is one among several that were aimed at doctrines well known in the seventeenth century. Locke did not present what has been called a "caricature" of seventeenth-century rationalist philosophy. His discussion of the association of ideas is incontrovertible evidence of his rationalism; to Locke the association of ideas is what he called "a sort of madness," because it interferes with the rational procedures of genuine knowledge. This distinction was observed during the eighteenth century, very clearly, for instance, by Condillac, who made the same distinction between the involuntary association of ideas on the one hand and the voluntary "connection of ideas" which is governed by reason.

In the *Essay*, Locke did not address himself directly to the problem of the origin of language, but by devoting a separate book, Book III, to what he called "language and words in general," he placed the problem of language at the center of his epistemology; it is a mistake, however, to assume that all Locke had to say about that problem is contained in Book III. The whole tenor of his genetic psychology was an invitation to further exploration. He made some suggestive remarks that bore directly on the subject; for instance, when he observed that he was "apt to think that the names of things may very much direct our thoughts to the originals of men's ideas." He repeatedly dismissed the doctrine of natural language, just like Mersenne, for example, when he said that "words . . . came to be made use of by men as the signs of their ideas, not by any natural connexion that there is between particular articulate sounds and certain ideas, for then there would be but one language amongst all men [a point, incidentally, also made by Mersenne and others]; but by a voluntary imposition, whereby such a word is made arbitrarily the mark of such an idea. . . . Words in their primary or immediate signification, stand for nothing but the ideas in the mind of him that uses them, how imperfectly soever or carelessly those ideas are collected from the things which they are supposed to represent" (*Essay* III, ii). In the philosophy and study of language, Locke's influence was immense during the eighteenth century, credited by all who wrote on the subject, including the universal grammarian Du Marsais, who rejected outright the Cartesian doctrine of innateness.

It has already been pointed out that wolf children began to gain increasing attention from the latter half of the seventeenth century. The same is true of the higher primates, though the arguments and speculations derived from this source long remained uncertain, since the information was based not on observation of living specimens but on the anatomy of dead bodies. The most influential text was a book published in 1699, Edward Tyson's learned and much-admired *Orang-Outang, sive homo sylvestris, or the Anatomy of a Pygmie compared with that of a Monky, Ape, and a Man.* For our purposes, the crucial point was Tyson's finding that the ape had organs of speech as perfect as those of man. This led him to the observation, embarrassing to a number of assumptions, that "there is no reason to think that agents do perform such and such actions because they are found with organs proper thereunto; for . . . apes should speak, seeing that they have the instruments necessary for speech" (pp. 51-52). This claim tended to support the uniqueness of man, in line with the Cartesian doctrine that animals are mere machines, a doctrine that proved fruitful by eliciting arguments against its plausibility based on closer observation of the behavior of animals. Tyson's account was given wider currency when it was repeated in Buffon's influential *Natural History*. Strange as it may seem at first, Monboddo enrolled the orang-outang in the species man in order to elevate the special stature of man. Monboddo found support for his argument in the fact that the orang-outang used tools much like man, in this case a sort of walking-stick, which from the late fifteenth century right through Tyson and Buffon remained a conventional detail of the iconography of this primate, pictured in half-upright position supporting himself with this stick. If it is true that orang-outangs use tools, then Monboddo was so far right; but the situation is curious. Since apes had not been reliably observed in their natural habitats, the stick really offered no authoritative evidence at all. In fact, one rather suspects that the stick was introduced, first in 1486, because it would have offended religious doctrine to show a monkey that walked erect on his own two feet alone, for this posture was traditionally taken to be the exclusive privilege of man as a sign of the divine favor which no other creature than man enjoyed.

Let me now turn to the work of Condillac. In 1746 he published, in French, a work called *An Essay on the Origin of Human Knowledge*; he readily admitted his debt to Locke—in fact, the English translation (1756) bore the subtitle, "A Supplement to Mr. Locke's *Essay*." The importance of Condillac can hardly be overestimated. His influence is pervasive on the French *Encyclopédie*, as well as on European thought in general during the latter half of the eighteenth century. In France his influence soon became apparent in the work of Diderot, Rousseau, Turgot, and many others, who acknowledged their indebtedness; in Germany the thought of his *Essay* was debated in the Berlin

Academy, leading directly to Herder's prize essay on the origin of language (1772); in Edinburgh it became, indirectly, it seems, the chief impulse for Monboddo's great work. In his later works, Condillac continued to expound and extend the philosophy of the *Essay*.

The core of Condillac's doctrine is this. He posits axiomatically that man is a social creature, thus agreeing with Locke and, for that matter, the Bible; that man has the capacity for sense experience; and that he is rational. These features we cannot explain, but experience shows that we have them. Animals do not have reason, though they are capable of certain rudimentary forms of thought. With these natural endowments, how has man gained the knowledge he has? The answer is that the deliberate use of arbitrary signs, in the form of language and speech, is the indispensable instrument without which man would have remained in the condition of the animals. The crucial element in the origin of human knowledge is the origin of language, a problem that involves the question of the nature of language. His procedure is a search for basic principles, for as Condillac said, "principle is synonymous with beginning." In typical eighteenth-century fashion, he is using the search for origins to separate nature from art. Language is man's greatest and most decisive artifical creation, and it is in turn the foundation of human knowledge.

Condillac's *Essay* is divided into two parts, the first on the operations of the mind, the second on "language and method." The basic argument of the first part is this: Condillac says that he is examining the present state of man; that is, after the Fall, and not before, when it was possible to have ideas prior to the use of the senses. All knowledge must therefore begin with simple perception. If an act of perception is accompanied by consciousness of having a perception, it is attended by attention; this capacity for attention makes it possible for the mind to note changes in its perceptions, in their disappearance and recurrence. When the latter occurs, the result is reminiscence, which is the beginning of experience, for without it every moment would appear to be the first in our existence. It cannot be explained, but is assumed to have its foundation in the nature of the union of body and mind. Attention has the further effect of linking certain perceptions together in such a manner that they become inseparable; one will recall the other. This connection is the source of imagination, memory, and contemplation. Imagination occurs when the attention is so full as to recall the perception of an object as if it were present. Memory occurs when the reproduction is less complete, making present in the mind not all the connected perceptions but only some of them, such as the circumstance in which the object was first perceived.

The mind may, for instance, be able to recall the name of a flower or the place where it was first seen, but fail to recall its odor and other details. Both imagination and memory, and by extension contemplation, depend on the connection of ideas which is the product of attention, whose force and selection are governed by the needs that accompany particular situations. Thus situations of strong emotion—such as fear, delight, love—are especially fruitful, a principle also familiar in eighteenth-century aesthetics, in large measure owing to Condillac. As yet, however, both imagination and memory are beyond the active control of the mind, for neither will occur except by the chance encounter of a perception that elicits a particular imagination or memory. It is this circumstance that raises the possibility of an active and deliberate use of signs; if the mind could somehow have a sufficient stock of signs at its disposal, it would also be able to control and master its past experience; it would, so to speak, have a reliable retrieval system.

There are three kinds of signs to consider. First, accidental signs, which are obviously beyond our deliberate control. Secondly, natural signs, "or the cries which nature has established to express the passions of joy, of fear, or of grief, etc." They are uttered involuntarily in the situations that give rise to them; they are, in fact, vocal gestures, of the same order as other natural expressions of the face, arms, hands, or the whole body. If a particular passion and the accompanying vocal gesture have occurred often, they will become linked so that one will elicit the other. "Then it is," says Condillac, "that this cry becomes a sign, but this imagination will not acquire any habit till it has been heard by chance; consequently this habit will be no more in man's power than" is the case with accidental signs. Finally, there is a third kind of sign, "instituted signs, or those which we have chosen ourselves, and bear only an arbitrary relation to our ideas." It is on the use of this internalized stock of signs that all knowledge and its progress depend, for they open the way for the exercise of reflection, which means deliberate and productive control over thought and the materials of past experience. Reflection is given in the nature of man; it is the expression of reason, which, Condillac says, "crowns the understanding." We are capable of higher degrees of reflection in proportion to our reason. From these admittedly small beginnings, the progress of language and knowledge is made possible, the use of arbitrary signs and the capacity for reflection mutually helping each other to higher and higher degrees of intellectual control.

It is at this point that the crucial question of the origin of language enters the argument. Condillac says: "It seems that we would not know how to make use of instituted signs, if we were not already capable of sufficient reflection to choose them and attach ideas to them; how then, it may be asked, can it be that the exercise of reflection is only acquired by the use of signs?" He answers: "I shall meet that difficulty when I give the history of language."

The origin of language is the subject of the second part of the *Essay*. It begins with the second kind of signs, natural cries, which form part of the gestural "language of action" that is natural to man. It is not part of the instituted language and speech, whose origin Condillac seeks to explain; without reason and the innate capacity for reflection, nothing would happen. Since the language of action is natural, it is the same in all, and when heard or observed it elicits the same passion that first occasioned it. Similar situations would occur along with the vocal gestures appropriate to them, so far, involuntarily. By such repetition, the early human creatures would in time gain the power to recall a certain range of such gestures at will and thus also to reproduce them as signs for the information of others; that is, communication. For instance, the sign or gesture indicating fright at the approach of a lion could, by one person who was not directly threatened, be deliberately produced to alert another who was in danger; this act would involve the exercise of reflection, a procedure tantamount to using the original, involuntary sign with the function of a deliberate arbitrary sign. Thus man would gradually, by slow degrees and in the long process of time, as Condillac often emphasizes, come to do by reflection at will what he had previously done by instinct alone. The deliberate use of a few simple signs would extend the operations of the mind and facility of reflection; the signs would in turn be improved, increase in number, and grow more firmly familiar. The mind and the use of signs would interact to the mutual advantage and progress of both. At this stage it became possible to create the language whose origin Condillac is seeking, the use of deliberately created arbitrary signs. This is the importance of instituted signs, which alone will serve this purpose. Condillac said: "The natural cries served early man as a model for a new language. They articulated new sounds, and by repeating them several times with an accompanying gesture indicating the objects they wished to note, they accustomed themselves to give names to things." He stresses that for a very long time, the language of action would coexist with the new language, both of them simultaneously serving together in the process of communication. This also came to form an important element in Romantic esthetics, for example, regarding poetic meter.

There are several other aspects of Condillac's thought that are interesting, but they do not concern us here; the outline I have given does not exhaust his philosophy of language. In the closing years of the eighteenth century, his philosophy was taken up with special eagerness by the French *idéologues*, who, for a while, until they were suppressed by Napoleon as politically dangerous, exercised considerable influence. When Wilhelm von Humboldt lived in Paris in the late 1790s, he was especially close to the *idéologues*, and it is clear that it is to them that he owes both the beginning of his linguistic philosophy as we know it and a number of its fundamental features. This indebtedness has been obscured, ignored, or denied by a scholarly tradition that has found his intellectual background exclusively in German sources. The mention of Wilhelm von Humboldt calls to mind a prominent feature of Condillac's philosophy of language; this feature is that the use of language is creative, in its beginning and continuing in every act of speech. If we were to enroll Condillac in the tradition of so-called empiricism, this feature of creativity would not belong here, according to some recent views. The importance of creativity is even textually evident in Condillac's frequent use of such terms as "generate," "generating," "generation," and similar terms (in their French equivalents, of course). This, you may recall, is a view that has often been associated chiefly or exclusively with Humboldt.

Condillac belongs in the tradition of linguistic philosophy that began in the seventeenth century with such innovative figures as Mersenne and Locke. Although this tradition incorporated some views already familiar in antiquity, it began as a reaction against the mystical linguistic doctrines that were seen to pose epistemological difficulties for the new science. The views represented by Descartes were not new, and they did not conflict with the Locke tradition, as shown by the case of Du Marsais, among others. There is thus an intimate connection between this tradition and the philosophy of the new science. This important aspect of intellectual history has received little attention; indeed, it has generally been ignored or denied, owing to subservience to the nineteenth century.

We can speculate on the reasons why this tradition fell into neglect and even disrepute, a situation that has rightly been seen as an impoverishment of the study and philosophy of language. Briefly said, the nineteenth century became so overpoweringly successful in creating its own mode of philological, historical language study that all linguistic problems that did not fit this mode came to be considered trivial, irrelevant, or worse yet, unscholarly and unscientific. In that century, therefore, professional students of language had little to offer that is relevant to our present concern, the origin of langue. In fact, one could say that there was a regression. In Condillac's century, there was little fear that the study of language posed a threat to religious belief, but during the next century it did enter into this set of problems. When other sciences, especially geology, with such works as Sir Charles Lyell's *Principles of Geology*, were felt to cast doubt on fundamental points of Victorian orthodoxy, language and especially its origin were invoked as proof of the evident and necessary intervention of divine power. This situation gave rise to a number of arguments about the origin of languge, best known perhaps from the writings of Max Müller, who argued that the origin relied on a special act of divine favor, operative only on that occasion and for that purpose. This argument denied the principle of uniformitarianism, which had become established in geology (and in other moments in history in the other sciences), an especially dangerous principle, it was felt, because it raised doubts about the biblical account of the flood. These controversies are now forgotten, but they were prominent in England during the midnineteenth century, indicated, for instance, by the fact that the British Association for the Advancement of Science, meeting in Oxford in 1847, considered this problem at great length in the attempt to support orthodoxy on arguments derived from the philosophy of language. It is significant that the men who were active on the side of orthodoxy were the same who denigrated Lockean philosophy on conservative grounds. Thus, questions which in the eighteenth century had commanded wide interest and assent among students of language were in the nineteenth century taken over by ethnologists, anthropologists, and by Charles Darwin, who took an active part in this controversy, seen for instance in *The Descent of Man*. William Dwight Whitney wrote extensively on the origin of language, chiefly in often virulent controversy against Max Müller. The effect of this religious controversy and of the new comparative philology was to put the great linguistic tradition of the previous centuries out of court among professional students of language. And so, on the whole, it has remained until recent years; both the school of Bloomfield and later, dominant schools of linguistic study have given little encouragement to serious work on the question of the origin of language.

Still, it would not be correct to say that the eighteenth century was altogether forgotten. It has often been noted that the Linguistic Society of Paris, in the second clause of its bylaws, in 1866 expressly prohibited the discussion of the origin of language. But this prohibition had little effect, and it was deplored by prominent French linguists, notably Michel Bréal, who said he could not imagine that the study of language would retain much relevance and vitality if this question was removed from its domain. Although himself the French translator of Bopp's *Comparative Grammar*, Bréal was also the first and most severe critic of the German school of comparative philology, which he referred to in terms that show he took the period of its dominance to mark a course of increasing narrowness and triviality, even silliness, in the study of language. For Bréal this period covered the fifty years from 1816 to 1866; that is, from Bopp to Schleicher. Bréal spoke with great admiration of the *idéologues* and the eighteenth century. In this revival of respect for the Condillac tradition, he was not alone; among several other well-known exponents of the same admiration was Hippolyte Taine. This is of some importance, for Saussure knew Bréal well, and Saussure seems also, from other sources, to have been under positive influence of the eighteenth century, a fact that must immediately appear evident to anyone familiar with the literature. Both the doctrine of the linearity of speech and of the arbitrariness of the linguistic sign are fundamental in Condillac and his followers.

To conclude, I have tried to outline the major stages in the history of the philosophy of language since the Renaissance as it bears more narrowly on the problem of the origin of language. The doctrine of natural language typically illustrated by speculation on Adam's name-giving was dominant during the sixteenth and much of the seventeenth centuries. It would be both ungracious and false to think that this tradition of study was useless; on the contrary, within its clear definition of basic views and assumptions, much useful work was done. I have further tried to show how this linguistic philosophy elicited counterarguments and new modes of study, prominently in Mersenne and Locke, and that this new orientation formed the foundation of linguistic philosophy during the eighteenth century. I have paid some attention to Condillac, not merely because he seems to me to hold considerable inherent interest, but also because his importance is now increasingly coming to be realized. I cannot conceive that any history of linguistics, or indeed any intellectual history, will be worth much unless Condillac is granted the prominent place he demands. Finally, I have tried to sketch why the nineteenth century has tended to obscure our view of the accomplishments of the previous centuries, when the subject of this conference was also a vital issue. Behind the course I have followed lies the belief that a good understanding of the history of the study of language will result in some significant revisions of the generally accepted structure of intellectual history. The history of the study of language, like the history of science, is not a small parochial affair that should aim merely to fit the pieces into the sort of history we already have. Among the benefits of this enterprise may be that it will lend respect and perhaps some useful impulses to speculation and study that will enlighten our understanding of the nature of language and the origins and evolution of language and speech.

References

Gordon W. Hewes's *Language Origins: A Bibliography*, second revised and enlarged edition (The Hague: Mouton, 1975), in two parts, is a magnificent guide to the extensive literature. Tyson's book has been issued in facsimile (1966, Dawson's, London), with an introduction by Ashley Montagu. There is a relevant essay by the Dutch anatomist Peter Camper, "Account of the Organs of Speech of the Orang Outang," with proof of "the true organical reason . . . the absolute impossibility there is for the Orang and other monkies to speak," in *Philosophical Transactions of the Royal Society*, 1779, 69: 139-159. The English translation of Condillac's *Essay* has been reissued in the series Scholars' Facsimiles and Reprints (1971 Gainesville, Fla.) but the French text is preferable. On wolf children, see Lucien Malson, *Wolf Children and the Problem of Human Nature* (1972, Monthly Review Press), with a list of recorded cases from 1344 to 1961 on pp. 80-82; this volume contains Jean Itard's *The Wild Boy of Aveyron*. (This book was first published in French under the title *Les Enfants Sauvages*, Paris, 1964.) See also Frank Tinland, *L'homme sauvage* (1968, Payot, Bibliothèque Scientifique, Paris). On Mersenne, see A. C. Crombie's excellent article, with full references, in *Dictionary of Scientific Biography* 9, 1974, 316-322. On Jacob Boehme, see *ibid.* 2 (1970), 222-224, with bibliography. There is an interesting essay by Robert Wokler on "Tyson and Buffon on the Orang-utan," in *Studies on Voltaire and the Eighteenth Century* 155 (1976) 2301-2319. On John Webster, Locke, and related questions see "Leibniz on Locke on Language." On Condillac and on the nineteenth century, see *The Study of Language in England 1780-1860* (Princeton 1967), especially Chapters 1 and 6. "Locke's Reputation in Nineteenth-Century England," "Condillac's Speechless Statue," "Thoughts on Scaglione's *Classical Theory of Composition:* The Survival of 18th-century French Philosophy before Saussure," in *Romance Philology* 29 (1976), 522-538. On "Cartesian linguistics," see "The History of Linguistics and Professor Chomsky," "Cartesian Linguistics: History or Fantasy?" *Language Sciences* No. 17: 1-12, October 1971 and the "Epilogue" to "The eighteenth Century, including Leibniz," in *Current Trends in Linguistics*, Vol. 13, the *Historiography of Linguistics* (The Hague: Mouton, 1975), pp. 383-479. On Condillac, see also "The Tradition of Condillac."

Bréal vs. Schleicher: Reorientation in Linguistics during the Latter Half of the Nineteenth Century

William Dwight Whitney often observed that Germany was the home of language study. Owing to its great prestige, comparative Indo-European philology gained a prominent place in the universities, until about 1840 at the expense of natural science, which had to make its way against the prestige of *Naturphilosophie*. This philosophy was the close relative of philology, both being expressions of Romantic thought and aspirations. Thanks largely to Wilhelm von Humboldt's educational philosophy and the reforms he instituted both in secondary and higher education, philology gained recognition and regular academic chairs in at least a dozen German Universities. This institutionalization ensured advances, but ultimately also caused rigidity, insensitivity, and even hostility to innovation. Pointing forward to Ferdinand de Saussure's linguistic thought, the radical innovation that occurred during the later decades of the nineteenth century did not take place in Germany, where the new developments, though important, stayed closer to accepted institutional forms. It occurred in France, and Michel Bréal was its first and chief spokesman.

It is this innovative reaction that I wish to examine. Where and when did it first appear? Who spoke for it? What were the issues? Who were the targets of the critique? What were its sources? What

First published under the title "Bréal vs. Schleicher: Linguistics and Philology during the latter half of the nineteenth Century," in *The European Background of American Linguistics*. Papers of the third Golden Anniversary Symposium of the Linguistics Society of America, ed. by Henry M. Hoenigswald (Dordrecht: Foris Publications, 1979), pp. 63-106. Written later, the essays on "l'âme and Saussure" and on "Michel Bréal, 'la sémantique,' and Saussure" deal with other aspects of the developments that are the subject of the present essay.

293

principles did it adopt? Needless to say, given the limitations of space and time, this can only be a sketch, but it seems worth doing in order to question what would appear to be the widely held though unexamined assumption that all later study of language has been spun out of the Bopp tradition.

The Problem

The problem is obvious. If it is argued that with Bopp the study of language was somehow transformed and codified, then we are left with the consequence that the domain of language study has been severely diminished. But if we take history seriously, this is not a satisfactory solution. Both before and after the dominance of the Bopp tradition, the study of language has covered a much wider territory, a fact that cannot be ignored except by making a number of ad-hoc decisions, e.g., that only with Bopp did the study of language become 'scientific,' a claim that has been repeated in the 1930s with exclusive reference to Bloomfield's *Language*; or that Bopp was the first to study language for its own sake, as if motivation (whether imputed or real, if determinable at all) were sufficient to establish legitimacy—on that principle many figures have no place in the history of science, e.g., Copernicus, Brahe, Kepler, Mersenne, Boyle, Newton, and Linnaeus.[1] Among the sources of this distortion, the most prominent is respect for a historiographical tradition that was ideologically designed to celebrate the Bopp tradition and its institutional status; this respect is sustained by a positivist view of natural science that was cogently criticized even in the nineteenth century. The matter reached absurdity in the 1860s when it was dogmatically claimed that language was a natural organism with its own life and laws independent of speakers, and that as a consequence the study of language was—or ought to be—a natural science.

It was at this point that the reaction set in. In 'Schleicher and the physical theory of language' (1871), Whitney wrote that Schleicher's 'deserved reputation as a philologist . . . gives à dangerous importance to his opinions as a . . . student of the theory and philosophy of language. There is, unfortunately, no necessary connection between eminence in one of these characters and in the other' (299). Whitney was making the now familiar distinction between philology and linguistics.[2] The occasion for the reaction was chiefly Schleicher's two pieces (1863, 1865) on what he took to be the implications of Darwin's recently published *Origin of species* for the study of language. It is surely to put our own intelligence and judgment on a very low level not to recognize the embarrassing, inconsistent, and even offensive nonsense stated in these pieces. Take, for instance, this passage, with its obvious racist implications: "We can now see that certain nations, for instance the Indian tribes of North America, already owing to their infinitely complicated languages truly luxuriating in forms, are not suited for a role in history and have therefore now decayed into regression and even extinction. It follows with high probability that not all organisms advancing on the way toward becoming human would have developed themselves upward to the point of forming a language." This is on the level of the most vulgar journalistic readings of Darwin. The previous page has this remarkable statement: "Like all languages of historically important nations, the languages which we now speak are senile linguistic specimens" (1865:27).[3]

The 1890s

By the 1890s the reaction was evident; it will therefore be useful to look at a few examples that point both forward and backward. They show that the reaction and the innovation were designed to overcome Schleicher and the tradition he stood for. During this decade, Saussure wrote some well-known notes that spoke critically of the German tradition and its final embodiment in "Schleicher's laughable attempt that collapses under its own ridiculousness"; Schleicher was a "complete mediocrity, which does not exclude pretensions." By contrast Saussure wrote, citing Whitney, "'language is a human institution.' That changed the axis of linguistics." The linguistic sign is arbitrary: *cow, vacca,* and *vache* can all mean the same thing.[4] The credit and the criticism are clearly assigned to Whitney and Schleicher, neither of them French and both then dead. It is useful to bear in mind that credit and blame that is fixed on distant and dead figures, may have their aim closer to home. Thus in the 1890s the *Revue de linguistique* held closely to the Schleicher line, consistently criticizing the men who, like Bréal and Meillet, were associated with the Société de linguistique de Paris and its publications. A good example of such strategic displacement, as it may perhaps be called, is the nineteenth-century critique of Locke and the eighteenth century which was in fact aimed at the contemporary utilitarian philosophy.[5]

During the same decade Bréal published his *Essai de sémantique* (1897), which, as he and others made clear, dealt with a subject that had occupied him for thirty years, e.g., his early essays (1866b, 1868b).[6] Bréal studied, he said, "the intellectual causes that have presided over the transformation of our languages" (5); he wished his study to say something about the language now spoken and to have general utility. Like Jespersen, Bréal was deeply involved in problems of language teaching and educational reform. Bréal argued against Schleicher's doctrines of organicism and the decay of language, against these habits of thought, "that one would rather have expected in some disciple of the mystical school," by which he meant Herder and German romanticism. He rejected anthropomorphism and the abuse of metaphor that gave literal sense to such locutions as the birth, struggle, propagation, and death of words and languages (4). He studied language in its social dimension, as a means of communication that was constantly being shaped by its speakers. Near the end of the *Essai* he revealed where his own sympathies lay; speaking against organicism and the philologists who declared that man counts for nothing in the development of language, he wished to be done with this phantasmagoria: "Our forefathers of the school of Condillac, those idéologues who for two generations were the target of a certain school of criticism, were closer to the truth when they said, in their simple and honest fashion, that words are signs. . . . they have no other existence than the signals of the wireless telegraph" (255). In a favorable review, Meillet observed that Bréal's book was "one of the rare books on linguistics that have immediate interest for sociology" (Meillet 1903-04:640; cf. Meillet 1898). In his obituary of Bréal, Meillet said that everything in the *Essai* "is reasonable and intelligible; the kind of latent mysticism that survives owing to the fact that historical linguistics arose in the midst of the romantic period is entirely banished from Bréal's book" (1916a:17). Meillet also said on at least two occasions that "Bréal and Ferdinand de Saussure were the two masters who gave the French school of comparative grammar its particular quality" (1915:120). Referring to the *Essai* and Bréal's semantic studies, Meillet also stressed Bréal's rationalism (1930:227).[7]

Among the representative works of the 1890s is also Jespersen's *Progress in language* (1894) which by its very title announced its opposition to Schleicher's doctrine of linguistic decay.[8] Jespersen concluded: "On every point our investigation has led us to scepticism with regard to the system of the old school of philology" (126). Exposing the comic inconsistencies of Schleicher's discourse, Jespersen rejected the dogma that linguistics is a natural science, by contrast taking for his guide "an idea expressed long ago and with considerable emphasis by Wilhelm von Humboldt, that language means speaking, and that speaking means action on the part of a human being to make himself understood by somebody else." The virtue of a language is measured by its efficiency, that is, its ability to accomplish "much with little means, or, in other words . . . to express the greatest amount of meaning with the simplest mechanism" (12-13). Schleicher had contrasted the Gothic *habaidêdeima* with English *had* to show how "our words, as contrasted with Gothic words, are like a statue that has been rolling for a long time in the bed of a river till its beautiful limbs have been worn off, so that now scarcely anyting remains but a polished stone cylinder with faint indications of what once it was" (11).[9] Jespersen drew the opposite conclusion, citing all fifteen forms of the Gothic for "had" against the single English form—and in so doing he not only opposed Schleicher but repeated both example and argument from Bréal's "De la forme et de la fonction des mots" (1866b).

Bréal's early essay reads like a blueprint for Jespersen's *Progress*. Reading Bopp and Schleicher, said Bréal, "one could believe one was in fact reading a treatise on the geology of the world or witnessing a series of crystallizations of speech." He respected "this purely empirical method which has produced the results that modern linguistics is proud of." But he immediately proceeded to state the qualification that reveals his own orientation: "But must we believe that the science we study consists exclusively in this observation of the exterior forms of language? . . . We do not think so. We must make sure that the description of human language does not make us forget man, who is both the beginning and the end, for in language everything proceeds from him and addresses itself to him" (1866b:249). The science of language must study both the forms and functions of words. It must include what he later called 'sémantique,' i.e., "la signification des mots" (243). The mere empirical observation of forms is insufficient, for "it makes us ignore the first cause of the transformation of languages, which is not furnished by the analysis of words, but which must be sought in ourselves" (257). The principle that the history of languages follows is not its own: "It always keeps in step, if not with political history, at least with the intellectual and social history of the people" (264).

Bréal's concentration on the social and communicative dimension of language is already prominent in his earliest writings before he could have read Whitney. Citing Humboldt, he agreed with Jespersen that, "there is no language apart from us; even when engraved on stone or brass, said Wilhelm von Humboldt, languages have only an ideal existence. Words exist only the moment when we think and understand them" (265). Consequently he did not admit any necessary connection between the decadence of words and that of thought;

words may retain their function in spite of 'mutilations,' as illustrated by the forms *habere* and *avoir*. They can also cut themselves loose from their etymological meanings, which thus are not the final criteria if we wish to understand the language we speak now—and that was Bréal's chief interest. He was therefore also committed to the uniformitarian doctrine that the creation of idioms, i.e. languages, did not occur merely at the point of origin (as, e.g., Max Müller felt compelled to argue by his postulate of an initial, never-repeated linguistic miracle): "We create them at every moment, for all the changes they undergo are our work" (265). Bréal shared Whitney's and Jespersen's interest in the problem of the origin of language as a legitimate question for linguistic scholars; he was committed to the characteristic eighteenth-century doctrine of the continuing creation of language. It is not surprising that Bréal and Jespersen cited each other, and that both Bréal and Victor Henry in reviews gave high praise to Jespersen's book.[10] Bréal referred to Jespersen on the unnecessary luxury of a redundant multiplicity of endings. Jespersen credited this observation to J. N. Madvig who as early as 1836, in one of his first critiques of German philology, had written: "The entire development of forms in predicate and attribute (I hardly dare speak this heretical truth) is a mode of decorative luxury that has its source in the helplessness of the young language, in its striving for clarity with norms not yet fixed and clear, or in its childishly repetitive fussiness" (1971:66 [28]).[11] Jespersen's book is one long illustration of Madvig's admiration for the "praise-worthy simplicity of English," a point Madvig first made in the context of rejecting F. Schlegel's and K. F. Becker's organicism. Caught in this prejudice, said Madvig, these linguists "become inconsistent when they confront the English language with its extreme simplicity of forms. It can be denied neither that the people who speak it have rich and lively notions, nor that the language was capable of power and terse fullness and could express the most profound thought" (1971:50, 65-66 [6, 26-28]; 1836; Jespersen 1894: 32-35). It is striking evidence of the tradition linking Schlegel and Schleicher that Madvig so early fixed the same critique on the former that a generation later was aimed at the latter. Madvig, Bréal, and Jespersen all saw this link. It is brought out by the example of Chinese; to Schlegel it was a language governed by purely exterior and mechanical rules as opposed to the mysterious organic perfection of early Indo-European; Jespersen reversed these relations.[12]

Citing a few prominent examples, I have tried to show that during the 1890s it became evident on all sides that the study of language was being transformed. Saussure, Jespersen, and Meillet stated the principles which they continued to argue and develop; Saussure in the *Cours*, Jespersen in subsequent writings (for instance in *Language* (1922) which verbatim includes large parts of *Progress*), and Meillet by his well-known commitment to the sociological aspects of language and its study. Bréal's *Essai de sémantique* was often re-issued. The reaction against the German tradition was triggered by Schleicher and continued to be aimed at his French devotees. The central principle of this innovation held that language does not have independent existence as a product of nature, but is the expression of human activity. It is an institution, its function is communication, its being is social, and the linguistic sign is arbitrary. Since historical study alone cannot take account of these factors, it provides an insufficient basis for the understanding of the system or structure of language at any given moment. Disengagement from history means interest in the present state of language. Owing to Saussure's teaching during the Paris years, the distinction between diachronic and synchronic study was taking shape. "It is well known," said Meillet, "that linguists study language from two points of view. Sometimes they observe and describe the state of a language at a given moment, and at other times they follow the transformations of a language in distinct successive periods of its history" (1900-01:597).[13] Bréal, Whitney, and Jespersen took a genuine interest in the problem of the origin of language. Here as in other respects, the reaction against the romantic tradition meant a revival of the classical eighteenth-century philosophy of language.

Madvig

The reaction and the new orientation that showed so clearly in the 1890s were not new. The first articulate and consistent critic was J. N. Madvig, who between 1832 and 1881 published a number of essays in Danish devoted to general linguistics or to what Charles Thurot in a review called 'grammaire générale' (Thurot 1875:16).[14] In 1842 Madvig gave this summary of his linguistic theory: language is "in its origin a product of the activity created by the drive toward statement and communication among individuals who live together. It is a system of signs for notions and their combinatory relations expressed by articulate sound, interconnected and mutually determined in regard to its parts. The signs have value by the acknowledgement and sanction of those who participate in the language and owe their meaning only to this acknowledgement and by virtue of it." To this he joined the uniformitarian principle "that the act of language formation was none other than the one by which the actual language that exists today was created as an understandable and ready means of communication; the origin of language cannot be at variance with its being and life, its form of existence" (1971:86 [55-56]).[15] Madvig therefore ridiculed the notion of the decadence and decline of language (e.g., 1971:240 [267-68]; 1856-57). The linguistic sign is arbitrary, "consequently the sound of words bears no natural and necessary relation to conception and its object" (1971:89 [59]; 1842). Language is the work of man, created to serve the social needs of communication. As early as 1841, he had blamed "Bopp and his school for ignoring that language fully formed is the real thing, and that the true value of a word is not in its origin but in what it has become for those who were speaking and writing the language," a point Madvig often stressed, thus coming close to making the distinction between diachronic and synchronic study (Thurot 1870:381).[16]

Madvig saw comparative philology as an auxiliary discipline to history. He rejected the notion of organicism as mere metaphor, both generally and with references to F. Schlegel: "The error of the other school shows in the obscure and foggy conception and talk of language as an independent organism (how it was created I cannot imagine) that grows of its own accord; because it is forgotten that even the smallest modification, initiated by a human individual, in the use of a single word of a particular language, came to be continued and established by others" (1971:88 [58-59]; 1842).[17] Consistent with the doctrine of institution and the arbitrariness of the sign, he sarcastically rejected the notion of sound symbolism as a piece of mysticism (1971:89-92 [59-63]). He maintained that words take their origin in concrete, sensible things: "That all language formation begins with the naming of conceptions of sense is a proposition that follows simply from the nature of language and the necessary manner of its growth and formation" (1971:98 [72]; 1842; cf. 51 [6]).[18] Madvig often criticized "an erroneous estimation, often prominent in the more recent empirical study of language, of the importance of what is physical and phonetic in language in relation to the true intellectual content. Scholars speak as if they hope to seize the life and nature of language in the soundlaws, but true scholarship in the study of individual languages lies altogether elsewhere, in the full comprehension of the actually present (or past) vocabulary and system, in the firm recognition and further examination of meanings and usages in all directions, in the clear grasp of syntactical rules in all their flexibility and of the cooperation of all constituent parts in the construction of clear and exact speech" (1971:192 [200]; 1856-57).[19] Thus like

Bréal, Madvig found the omission of syntax and semantics a serious error, citing Jacob Grimm's statement that syntax lies half outside grammar (1971:203 [215]; 1856-57).

Since languages are the work of man, Madvig places much emphasis on the principle that the grammatical categories are universal and thus do not reveal intellectual or cultural aspects of particular languages and their speakers; the presence or absence of gender, for instance, does not indicate spiritual superiority or inferiority.[20] By contrast he found, like the eighteenth century, that the linguistic relativity principle operates in the lexicon, in "what is often called the more material aspect of language, largely independent of what pertains to intellect, that is in the vocabulary and, inseparable from it, in the stock of meanings. It is here that we find the national richness of conceptions that has become manifested in expression" (1971: 338; 1842).[21]

This survey shows that Madvig's philosophy of language was, as Jespersen said, "on the whole rationalistic" (1894:59); it was anti-romantic.[22] There is no major and hardly any minor aspect of the critique of the German tradition that set in after Schleicher that had not in the previous generation been advanced by Madvig.[23] As some of the cited passages show, Madvig knew that his views were unorthodox. Though a classicist, he did not find antiquity superior to modern times, not even classical literature; and he wondered how Goethe and Schiller could reconcile their admiration for Greece and Rome with the practice of slavery and the position of women in those societies. He supported educational reforms that reduced the classical curriculum to make room for modern languages and natural science.

In the preceding pages I have deliberately avoided citation of statements that Madvig made after 1866. The reason is this: By 1871 it had come to his attention that Whitney's *Language* (1867, based on lectures given during 1864 and January 1865) came uncomfortably close to presenting principles and ideas already argued in Madvig's Danish publications. Ten years later, Madvig was more explicit in a lecture "Was ist Sprachwissenschaft?" given at Oslo and the same year (1881) published in Sweden (where a translation of Whitney 1875a had just appeared in 1880). Referring to Whitney 1867 and 1875a, Madvig, in 1881, found "a remarkable similarity between the observations on the nature and life of language developed there and those that I have briefly sketched in the first part of this lecture." He concluded: "I must say with great emphasis that the ruling and basic ideas in Whitney's writings on the relation of sound and meaning, on the origin of language, on its source in the naming of sensible things, on the creation of inflexional forms and the full right of modern languages for equal standing with the older languages with their greater richness of inflexions, etc., etc.—were stated by me in part 25 years before the appearance of Whitney's first publication, in part more than ten years ago, and what is more, often with greater succinctness and precision." Madvig still rejected the suggestion of any dependence on Whitney's part, though not without adding, "but the agreement in thought and expression still seems remarkable and striking to me" (1971:356-57).[24]

Whatever the truth—and it would be well worth knowing, though that is hardly possible today—the similarities are indeed striking, even in minor details that emerge from a consecutive reading of Madvig and Whitney. In any event, the near unanimity of Madvig, Whitney, and Bréal on so many principles can be read as an example of what in the history and sociology of science is called 'multiples' (the term is Robert K. Merton's (1973)), that is, the simultaneous but independent appearance of the same discoveries, a phenomenon that has lately received a good deal of attention as an especially fruitful means of historical insight, though it has not penetrated the history of linguistics. We see, for instance, that the social nature of language that later emerged as the linkage between linguistics and sociology was neither new nor forgotten; stressed by Locke, it was central in the classical eighteenth-century tradition and was throughout the nineteenth century recognized in England, e.g., by the Utilitarians and John Stuart Mill. It is only when the German tradition is considered the norm that the social dimension appears to require special explanation. This fact, along with many others, suggests that it is rather German philology, no matter how prominent it was for some fifty years, that must be seen as a special phase and not as the norm, if we are to gain both coherence and order, that is to say understanding in the history of linguistics. As Madvig, Whitney, Bréal, and others insisted, comparative historical grammar and philology do not encompass all of the study of language.

Whitney

Since the principles that are often credited to Whitney are already in Madvig, there is no need to detail them. A couple of points deserve mention, however. In *Language* (1867), Whitney did not make any critical comment on Schleicher, quite the contrary, perhaps because Schleicher was then still living. But Whitney does remark that to speak of language "as having independent and objective existence, as being

an organism or possessing organic structure, as having laws of growth
. . . all these are figurative expressions, the language of trope and
metaphor" (35). Still, Whitney never quite abandoned this conception,
as the title of his second book (1875a) shows.[25] This aspect of Whitney would seem to be related to another that is more important: the
pervasive historical positivism that marks all his work, as, for instance,
in the opening pages of *Language*. For Whitney no study and explanation of linguistic phenomena was valid unless it was historical. In this
respect he differed greatly from Madvig and Bréal, who was well aware
of this trait in Whitney. Bréal called Whitney a "positiviste convaincu"
by contrast to Max Müller's orientation as a follower of Herder
(Bréal 1900).

Bréal

The reaction against Schleicher began in France during the 1860s.
The first unmistakable sign was Bréal's decision to translate not
Schleicher's *Compendium* (1861-62) but Bopp's *Vergleichende Grammatik*.[26] The first volume of this translation (1866) opened with a
long Introduction (dated 1 November 1865) which clearly staked out
the views that Bréal was soon to develop. The comparative method
could best be learned, Bréal observed, from Bopp's work, the source
and example of German linguistic scholarship, which, Bréal said, was
characterized by the accumulation of detailed observations while
general questions were put aside or only lightly touched as being the
last rather than the first a science should solve (iv). Thus Bréal very
early introduced the theme that was to play such a prominent role in
the reaction, the German indifference to theory. Bréal admired Bopp
precisely because his sober scholarship had overcome the linguistic
mysticism which Bopp's teacher Windischmann, drawing on Herder,
shared with the Schlegels, with Creuzer and Görres. "Bopp did more
than anyone," said Bréal, "to dispel the mystery in which these
lofty minds—lofty but friends of the twilight—were pleased to envelop the first productions of human thought" (viii-x).[27] Throughout
the Introduction, Bréal was sharply critical of F. Schlegel on the
same points that were soon brought against Schleicher: the organicist
doctrine, the abuse of metaphor, the belief in the original mysterious
perfection of language and its later decadence, the romantic notion
of "a mysterious education which the genius of mankind or at least a
privileged portion of the human family might have received in its infancy" (xxiv). He knew that Schlegel's book *Über die Sprache und
Weisheit der Indier* (1808) after the initial chapters (which as I have

shown elsewhere depend heavily on Sir William Jones's *Anniversary Discourses* (Aarsleff 1967:115-161)) got lost in "a thick fog of hypotheses," which Wilhelm von Humboldt and Bopp also found troublesome (see, e.g., Bopp, 1866:225-230 (§108). Bréal also knew that Schlegel, "like others, took his knowledge from the *Asiatic Researches*," whose facts he adapted "to a chronology of his own invention and to a preconceived philosophy of history" (x-xiii).[28] After citing Jones's famous passage on the affinity of Sanskrit and other Indo-European languages, Bréal underscored that at the beginning of Sanskrit studies, "Sanskrit is presented as the sister language and not as the mother language of the European languages" (xviii-xix), a significant fact that seems to have been widely forgotten in the later historiographical tradition, which is marked by ignorance of Jones's *Discourses* except for isolated quotation of the statement of affinity repeated by Schlegel, like so much else he read in Jones. In the concluding pages of the Introduction (xxxviii ff), Bréal pointed out, as had Madvig, that Bopp had concentrated on "la phonétique et la théorie des formes" at the expense of syntax. Bréal's Introduction states virtually all the criticisms that he and others were to bring against the German tradition.

A few years later, in December 1867, Bréal delivered an opening lecture at the Collège de France on "Les progrès de la grammaire comparée" (printed 1868) in which he set forth his critique of comparative grammar in more detail. In the same year he also appeared as editor of a French translation of Schleicher's two pieces (1863, 1865) on linguistic Darwinism. Bréal's lecture was published in the first volume of the *Mémoires de la Société de Linguistique de Paris*, which Whitney reviewed the same year. Here Whitney observed that one of the most interesting pieces in the volume was "by Bréal, one of the soundest and most esteemed of the younger philologists of France," treating, Whitney said, "of the 'Progress of Comparative Grammar,' and it is a careful and suggestive exposition of the errors into which students in this branch are liable to fall" (Whitney 1868).[29] Reviewing the same publication, Gaston Paris also called attention to Bréal's essay, a piece that was replete, as one would expect, he said, "with sharp and penetrating observations that gain special interest because they involve a subject very much alive today: the present state and disagreements (one could almost say schisms) in German scholarship" (Paris 1868a:248).

The same year Paris also reviewed the French translation of Schleicher. He commented critically on Schleicher's statement that languages are natural organisms: "All these words can only be applied to the individual life of an animal and if such metaphors are used rightly in linguistics, we must take care not to be fooled. The development of language does not have its cause in itself, but in man, in the physiological and psychological laws of human nature; for that reason it differs fundamentally from the development of species, which is the exclusive result of the conjunction of the essential conditions of the species with the exterior conditions of the milieu. If we fail to keep in mind this all-important distinction, we fall into evident confusion." In conclusion he cited Bréal's very brief preface to the effect that even those who did not share Schleicher's ideas would find them stimulating (Paris 1868b).[30]

It is abundantly clear that Bréal initiated the reaction against Schleicher and the German school. In 1866, in "De la forme et de la fonction des mots," he argued that comparative grammar offered a purely exterior study of words which needs to be illuminated and checked by the study of meaning (1866b:243), that there is no necessary link between the decay of words and that of thought, that language study must not forget that man is both its ruling principle and its end, and that the history of language goes hand in hand with the intellectual and social history of its speakers. His social orientation and semantic aim were already firmly stated by 1868.[31]

Without questioning Bréal's originality, we may ask: What sources did he draw on, what mode of language study did he admire as an answer to the shortcomings of comparative philology? Owing to his frequent historical references, the answer is simple: the classical eighteenth-century tradition. I have already cited the well-known passage in the *Essai de sémantique* expressing admiration for Condillac and *les idéologues*, but similar statements occur throughout Bréal's writings. Among his most forceful early statements is another opening lecture, "Les idées latentes du langage" (1868b), which is a companion to "De la forme et de la fonction des mots." It is the thesis of this essay that the mere exterior mode of comparative grammar must be supplemented by "this collection of principles and observations of which Port-Royal gave the first model and which is known as general or philosophical grammar." Since it is the aim of universal grammar to show the interrelations of the operations of mind and linguistic expression, it is not opposed to the analysis of forms. On the contrary, "it is much more correct to say that universal grammar will find an abundance of relevant and well-founded materials in the observations of [present-day] linguistics" (299). The essay is devoted to the well-known concept of sub-audition or ellipsis, so central in universal grammar; Bréal proposes to examine what one could call "interior ellipsis, if it was not more appropriate to call this order of phenomena by the more general name *the latent ideas of language*" (301).

Bréal argues that there is no exact correspondence between meaning and form; the outward forms of language only incompletely express thought and would not be able to express even the simplest and most elementary thought unless the mind did not constantly come "to the aid of speech and supplied the remedy for the insufficiency of its interpreter by the insights it draws from its own resources. Our habit of filling in what is missing and clarifying the uncertainties of language is so familiar that we are barely aware of it" (300). This is not a deficiency; on the contrary, a language that at any given moment represented what is in the understanding and which gave expression to what went on in the mind, would become a nuisance, "for it would be necessary for language to change itself with each new notion, or that the operations of mind always remained the same, in order not to shatter the mechanism of language" (301). In other words, "our understanding completes what is only indicated" (303). The source of these currently familiar ideas is well known, as we are reminded by this statement: "The entire syntax has its pattern in the mind and if formal differences have later more or less separated the parts of discourse, it is because language has assumed the imprint of the intellectual activity it represents. It is our mind that animates the word with a transitive force, connects and subordinates propositions, and deprive certain words of their proper signification in order to make them serve as the articulations and as the joints of discourse. The unity of the proposition and of the phrase, no less than that of the word, is the work of the mind" (320).

As in Madvig, the consequence is the rejection of the doctrine that expressed forms—such as genders, cases, etc.—measure the cultural or spiritual quality of languages and their speakers. Languages use different means to achieve similar ends, thus all are qually good: "We must not in human beings of another race than ours deny *a priori* the existence of any notion that is not marked by a special sign in their language. The mind penetrates the fabric of languages and covers even its empty spaces and interstices. By not admitting a nation to have ideas other than those that are formally represented, we run the risk of neglecting perhaps what is most vital and original in its intellectual make-up"(322). To illustrate what he had in mind, Bréal used an image already well-known in the seventeenth century: that of a painting which the mind observes differently at a distance and close-up. Standing back, it is easy to tell the background from the foreground and note light and shadow though the canvass is bathed in the same light. Close-up it all becomes unconnected details, but again standing back "our sight, yielding to

long habit, blends the color nuances, distributes the light, puts the features together again and recomposes the work of the artist" (321).[32]
It is the mind that interprets and creates what is there on the canvas.

Bréal's two essays "De la forme et de la fonction des mots" and
"Les idées latentes du langage" present a reaffirmation of the principles of universal grammar, which must, he argues, complement
comparative philology if we are to achieve a fuller understanding of
language; this understanding must include syntax and what he then
called the significations of words. Historical knowledge of forms may
contribute to, but does not by itself create or constitute this understanding. Universal grammar relates the phenomena of language to
mind, and it is in these terms that syntax must be studied. In this
reaction against the insufficiency of historical study, he is advocating
synchronic study. When Saussure in the *Cours* wished to explain the
terms diachronic and synchronic, he referred the former to the Bopp
tradition and the latter to "the grammarians inspired by traditional
methods," of which Saussure gave the Port-Royal grammar as an
example: "It is interesting to note that their point of view on the
question that is occupying us is absolutely irreproachable. Their program is strictly synchronic" (118).[33] Further, for Bréal universal
grammar does away with the romantic doctrine, also combatted by
Madvig, that the richness or poverty of existing forms can be used to
assess the spiritual or cultural 'merit' of languages and their speakers;
it does away with the very real racist elements that are inherent in
much nineteenth-century philological doctrine. Finally, Bréal is,
again with Madvig and the classical eighteenth-century philosophy of
language, committed to uniformitarianism: "Thus we must not place
the origin of languages only at the beginning of races: we create them
every moment, for the changes they undergo are our work" (1866b:
265).[34]

Bréal's knowledge of eighteenth-century doctrine also shows in
several of his other essays, e.g., in 1879 when he discussed a theme
that is central in Condillac, "le génie de la langue." Recalling Quintilian's metaphor of words as counters or coins with conventionally accepted values (used by Bacon, Hobbes, Locke, Leibniz and many
others, with the implication that words are arbitrary signs), Bréal repeated Locke's observation that our thinking and speaking routinely
run on words rather than on concepts and things: "We think only
by means of words, or rather we think the words, for this linguistic
instrument is even more indispensable than we think . . . we imitate
the bankers who when they handle values treat them as if they were
the coin itself, because they know that at a given moment they could

change them for the coin." This is a way of saying that what matters to the speakers is the current value system; its history or origin is at that point irrelevant, though the study of it may yield another kind of knowledge.[35] The subject of the influence of language on mind, said Bréal, had often been treated to excess by the German school, which, however, had failed to notice that it is stated in Rousseau's *Émile*: "Reason alone is universal, the mind has its own particular form in each language, a difference that may well in part be the cause or the effect of national qualities." In his theoretical writings, Rousseau credited the points of linguistic philosophy to Condillac, as did Diderot, de Brosses, and many other contemporaries. Bréal concluded this essay with mention of the problem of the origin of language, "to which modern linguistics pays little attention," but which was so important during the previous century. Comparative philology had made the error of believing that early Indo-European roots were close to the primitive form of language, but "there are centuries of speech behind them," an assertion also made by Madvig against the German school (1879:1009-1010).[36] In this context Bréal again rejected the organic metaphor and the doctrine that linguistics is a natural science.

In the 1890s Bréal again mentioned the problem of the origin of language in a discussion of Renan's early opinions on this subject. As a disciple of German thought, Renan had set himself against the slow and gradual creation of language: "He recoils at the image of mankind gradually developing its intellect, winning its titles to honor one by one. In this, he stands in direct opposition to the eighteenth century, to the philosophy of Condillac, Maupertuis, Condorcet, Volney. He is the disciple of German philosophy of the beginning of this century, which expressly dedicated itself to the task of contradicting and refuting the school of Condillac. He found his nourishment in the writings of Friedrich Schlegel, of Wilhelm von Humboldt, who themselves were the inheritors of Herder and were under the impact of his thought" (1893:11).[37] There is no doubt where Bréal stands. His reaction against Schleicher and the German school drew on the classical eighteenth century tradition.

The Revival of Eighteenth-Century Thought

In his respect for the previous century Bréal was not alone. A few years before Bréal in the *Essai* (1897) praised Condillac and the *idéologues*, Durkheim had traced the origins of sociology not to contemporary English and German thought but to Montesquieu: "All the force that today carries us in the direction of social problems has its source in our own eighteenth-century philosophers. In this brilliant group of writers, Montesquieu stands out among the rest" (Durkheim 1892:25). The revival of the eighteenth century formed part of the turn against the philosophy of Victor Cousin and his school, which for nearly a generation ruled as nothing less than the official philosophy. The hallmark of this school was denigration of eighteenth-century philosophy and especially of Condillac and the *idéologues* (Aarsleff 1976b:532-533; Fox 1973:452-58). There were all along writers who did not accept this version of Condillac, but by the 1850s the turn in favor of the eighteenth century was evident.

Cournot is credited with the creation of mathematical economics, but he was also a philosopher of science and an intellectual historian of distinction (Granger 1971). He defended Condillac against the neglect and disdain he had suffered. In his two great philosophical works, Cournot devoted several chapters to language (1851:II, 1-89; 1861:II, 53-118). In the first of these chapters, opening "a language is a system of signs," Cournot stressed the necessity of instituted signs; he also devoted a long section to the subject of "the linear order of discourse" (1851:II, 58ff), in which he said: "One of the radical imperfections of spoken or written discourse is that it constitutes an essentially linear series; that its mode of construction obliges us to express successively, in a linear series of signs, relations which the mind perceives or ought to perceive simultaneously and in another order and to dislocate in the expression what belongs together in thought or in the object of thought" (1851:II, 68).[38]

A few years later, Cournot was joined by Taine (1868 [1857]) in his severe critique of the school of Cousin. Here Taine also criticized the rule of metaphor: "This can be called the metaphysics of metaphors; here failures of style become the errors of science; false language produces false thinking; qualities and powers being compared to beings, they become beings; perverse expression perverts truth" (1868:245). Taine's major philosophical work *De l'intelligence* (1870), opened with 60 pages under the title "Les Signes." In the Preface Taine stated that he had carefully noted his three principal debts: "The first, very fruitful, sketched and affirmed by Condillac . . . the second belongs to Stuart Mill; the third . . . to Bain." In 1869, Henri Weil's long-neglected book (1844) was re-issued on Bréal's suggestion.[39] By the 1880s Renan remarked that Cousin's philosophy had now been forgotten for twenty years. During these decades there was also a strong reaction against Comtian positivism, forcefully stated by the greatest French scientists of the time, Claude Bernard (1865, see, e.g., 306) and Louis Pasteur (1882). The innovation begun by Bréal during the 1860s formed part of a broad movement in French intellectual life during the latter half of the nineteenth century. It is well known in art and literature. It also found expression in educational reform (in which Bréal was an important figure), in the creation of new chairs and disciplines, and in the publication of a large number of new journals which give the best understanding of the intellectual vitality of the period.

If we now recall the views of the 1890s sketched earlier in this paper, it will I think be evident that these views were not new then. They date back to the 1860s; their first exponent was Bréal, who in his reaction against Schleicher and the German tradition deliberately reintroduced the philosophy of the eighteenth century. Language serves the needs of communication; it is instituted by man and constantly controlled and modified by the mind's activity; it is social, and, being instituted, words are arbitrary signs. The origin of language is a legitimate linguistic problem. Language is not an organism that has independent existence, the study of language is not a natural science, but must be pursued with reference to mind, man, and social life. Universal grammar contains principles that are crucial to the success of this study. The mere historical study of language is not enough. The distinction between diachronic and synchronic study emerges naturally in the reorientation that assigns a new role to historical study. This critique of the German tradition was stated by Madvig during a span of thirty years prior to Bréal and Whitney. The interrelations, if any, between the two latter and Madvig are not clear, but it is evident that Bréal precedes Whitney on the points that have been credited to the latter. Both chronology and the interpretation to which some details are open, raise the question whether Whitney was drawing on Bréal. It seems to me evident that Madvig's and Bréal's work is superior to Whitney's, though Whitney may have stated the same views with more quotable force, so to speak (although not always consistently). In several respects, Whitney is also old-fashioned and doctrinaire compared to Madvig and Bréal, e.g., in his positivism. It seems to me that Madvig gave a good assessment of Whitney when he wrote: "Whitney treats his subject with great learning, sober clarity and openness to the facts; he is less good at dialectically disentangling and demolishing the fabric of false theories; he does not take up the *metaphysics* and does not always penetrate deeply enough" (1971: 395 [v]; 1875).

I do not see that one can accept as historically correct the statement made in the opening chapter of Saussure's *Cours*: "The first impulse was given by the American Whitney, the author of *The Life and Growth of Language* (1875)." This is not surprising, on the contrary; scholars and scientists have often proved mistaken about the history of their discipline and even about the sequence of their own work (e.g., Newton). In the same chapter, Saussure remarked correctly (though somewhat inconsistently with the words about Whitney): "It was not till around 1870 that scholars began to explore the conditions of the life of languages. They saw that the correspondences that unite them are only one aspect of the phenomenon of language, that comparison is only a means, a method of reconstructing the facts." But Saussure was inconsistent once more when he said with reference to the neogrammarians that, "thanks to them, language was no longer looked upon as an organism that develops of its own accord, but as a product of the collective mind of linguistic groups. It was at the same time understood that the notions of philology and comparative grammar were erroneous and insufficient." Madvig, Bréal, and Gaston Paris had said that before 1870. Saussure concluded that one could not say that the neogrammarians, in spite of their great services, had covered the entire field of linguistics. In a footnote to this passage, at the end of the chapter, Saussure restated Bréal's objection to taking metaphors for reality.

Meillet said that Saussure taught the principles of the *Cours* in Paris during the 1880s. In that case, we have an illustration of a principle that was well stated by Claude Bernard in 1865: "Though I recognize the superiority of great figures, I nevertheless think that in the particular or general influence they have on the sciences, they are always necessarily more or less a *function of their time*" (310). Today this is a view that is widely accepted in the history of science and intellectual history; the innovative ideas of individuals play an important role, but they occur in particular contexts. In that sense it seems to me that Bréal deserves credit—I don't say greater credit, for he has hardly received any. It seems obvious to me that there can be no doubt of his importance; in the linguistic reorientation that occurs in the late decades of the nineteenth century, he is the first innovator (though the problem remains of Madvig's share in these events). Bernard's axiom (also stated in the seventeenth century) undercuts what has been called the 'heroic' theory of science, the notion that great geniuses make discoveries, that ideas pure and simple change the world, and that progress is a linear, cumulative succession of such discoveries quite independently of their context. The 'heroic' theory has little use for the intellectual context, except perhaps to set off genius by contrast, and hardly any for such other historical features as social life and conditions.[40] The pure objectivity of science lives in the upper spheres of the life of the mind.

For such a view, there cannot be a history of science or of any discipline; there can only be heroes and saints set off against numskulls and perhaps even villains. This is a positivist doctrine; truth was in the nature of things from the beginning, but has lain hidden owing to prejudice, superstition, and the rule of religion; the past has been a conspiracy against the enlightened present. This is a simple-minded view of things, but it is the typical nineteenth-century version of science and its history; it is the view that makes it possible to accept the absurd belief, doctrinal in the history of linguistics, that with Bopp and a few Germans the study of language, at a stroke, became 'scientific,' or if you wish with Bloomfield in the 1930s (though having more than one contender seriously weakens the doctrine). The decisive innovation that occurred in the study of language during the latter half of the nineteenth century, chiefly in France, shows how false that version of history is. What happened cannot be spun out of the German tradition, whether by positive development or reaction. The postulate that the study of language became 'scientific' with Bopp is equivalent to saying that there is no history of science before Newton or whomever one may choose as god. This is so absurd that one must ask why it should be necessary even to talk about the matter, silly things usually going away by themselves.

The History of Linguistics

Why haven't they gone away in the history of linguistics as they have in the history of science? It cannot merely be because the history of science is older than that of linguistics. The latter had the benefit of the example of the former, yet has not taken the lesson. With some simplification, it is true to say that the history of science was created by Paul Tannery and George Sarton (Taton 1976; Merton 1975). Both were committed to the positivist progress doctrine of pure science, but they were also admirable scholars who set standards that have never been known in the history of linguistics. Alexandre Koyré (Gillispie 1973) placed the history of science firmly in the context of intellectual history on the principle that insight and understanding are subverted if the work of the past is judged by current doctrines. His ground rule was that, "the mania of searching for 'precursors' has very often falsified the history of philosophy beyond remedy." The progress doctrine is methodologically useless. As method it cannot even reveal what progress has in fact occurred.[41] The notion that the 'scientific' study of language began only with Bopp turns all previous work into what is at best unscientific anticipations. The chief reason for the failure of the history of linguistics lies elsewhere.

The history of science has shown something that is also open to observation around us: as soon as a discipline has become institutionally successful, usually in the universities as was the case of philology in nineteenth-century Germany, it tends to create a history that meets the ideological needs of its practitioners. A good example occurred in the seventeenth century; the Royal Society was barely half a dozen years old when it created such a story in Sprat's *History of the Royal Society* (1667). Quite contrary to facts that were well known to contemporaries, it established the myth that the new science was almost wholly an English creation, that Bacon was its father, and that Mersenne, Gassendi, and Descartes had nothing to do with it; it also failed to mention that the early English scientific meetings followed French example (Aarsleff 1975b, 1976a). Sprat's work satisfied the need for a sense of institutional identity that demanded ceremonial affirmation of the exclusive Englishness of the new science. Benfey's and von Raumer's great histories (1869, 1870) celebrated the scientificness and Germanness of comparative philology; they are still the best general histories we have and nearest to what Tannery and Sarton did for the history of science. It is this self-serving institutional folk-history that has been believed, as we see, for instance, in the notion that all later study of language must be spun out of the Bopp tradition. One of the consequences is that we have the claim that there is a powerful "Schleicherian paradigm,' something that is rather like saying that the final codification of the phlogiston theory was the great, forward-looking principle in chemistry. The phlogiston theory played a fruitful role in the history of chemistry, but the future of chemistry depended on its rejection. In this sense, Bréal was the Lavoisier of linguistics.

But if the history is false, what made and still makes it possible? There are, in fact, several competing histories of linguistics; the Bloomfieldians had their comforting version, and the later orthodoxy waited barely ten years for its retrospective historical construction. Linguistics seems to have a special need for such comforts, which may suggest a certain insecurity about its own status. This variety of incompatible histories is good evidence that something is wrong. It might be argued that the problem is lack of knowledge and scholarship; this is true, just as it is true that good work is enough even in the absence of grandiloquent talk about methodology, which remains empty without good examples of its practice. Many works in history, intellectual history, the history of art, and the history of science have had deep methodological significance without saying a word about method but merely illustrating it. If matters are not so simple in linguistics, the chief reason is that its history is still wedded to the typical nineteenth-century positivist faith in progress, in Baconian induction, in the 'heroic' theory of science as the work of geniuses who make discoveries of long-hidden truths. This is an unsophisticated view by any standard.

The matter of Boppian philology and linguistics after Schleicher has much in common with problems posed by science in the nineteenth century. According to the Baconian orthodoxy, theory was not respectable; the collection of facts was the heart of the matter, followed by description and classification. Claude Bernard's teacher and predecessor, the physiologist François Magendie met disappointment in theoretical work, so he said to Bernard that he compared himself 'to a ragpicker: with my spiked stick in my hand and my basket on my back, I traverse the field of science and I gather what I find' (Grmek, 1974). Darwin made frequent public avowals of respect for plain induction, but in their work both Magendie and Darwin fortunately ignored it. The history of linguistics is dominated by very simple views of the nature both of history and of science. For general orientation in intellectual history, the choice will typically fall on such guides as Loren Eisely.[42] So long as the search for knowledge is guided by such method, the result will fit the conventional expectation. Arens's useful anthology (1969) is heavily biased toward German work, as is indicated, for instance, by the astonishing omission of Turgot's influential essay on etymology, by the misrepresentation of Condillac and the French tradition, and by the omission of Madvig.[43] Borst's great *Turmbau* undertakes to fit linguistic events into broad conventional categories, without the least indication that those events may be not merely derivative of their intellectual contexts, but themselves have contributed toward the making of those contexts (Aarsleff 1975c:418-420). The work that is done in the history of linguistics is almost without exception the product of linguists working on the side. The history of science did not become what it is until it was no longer the work of scientists. The difference is not a question of finding enough time; it is primarily a question of orientation.

Let me give a few examples. The 'heroic' theory of science reveres discovery and invention, and by the same token plays down or ignores the context. Thus Sir William Jones gets credit for the discovery of Sanskrit and its affinity with certain other languages; an easily detachable and quotable passage from the second "Anniversary Discourse" is one of the fixtures of histories of linguistics. The story then goes that this passage presents all that he did for the study of language, that it really contains no proof, that it was merely a lucky, impressionistic insight, and that in any event others before him had said much the same thing. Indeed they had. Jones's achievement is not the 'discovery,' but the lucid presentation of the method of comparative language study within the full sequence of his "Anniversary Discourses," all carefully structured to form a single argument. Concentration on his 'discovery' not only simplifies the story, but it also has made it possible to give F. Schlegel credit for what Jones did. This is the version of history that has become gospel, so successful that the "Discourses" are evidently not read even by those who write as if they know them. Comparative philology becomes "eine deutsche Wissenschaft." A quotation from Bréal given above said bluntly and correctly that Schlegel drew on the *Asiatic Researches*, in which, of course, the "Discourses" were first published.

The problem raised by the case of Jones is this: if he was not the first to make some such discovery, why is he almost universally associated with it? Why was he successful at least to that degree? The chief reasons would seem to be these: Firstly, he was already before he went to India and took up Sanskrit a man of recognized intellectual stature in several subjects, including linguistics; thus much was expected of him. Secondly, he presented his 'discovery' in a systematic context that gave it abundant meaning and implications; he created a method. And thirdly, he had the means and foresight to see that without a learned society to promote the study of India and without a publication to make this new knowledge available, the world would not be any the wiser. None of the previous proponents of the discovery came anywhere near meeting these conditions. It may be argued that the impact also came at the right time; that certainly counts for something, but it is not a sufficient explanation. If Leibniz, for instance, had made a similar statement in an equally rich methodological context and published it in, say, the *Journal des Sçavans*, would it have been ignored? This example reveals not only the consequences of the discovery fixation, but also how historical facts that can be quite readily known are ignored in order to make possible, create, and then maintain the ad-hoc mythical history that satisfies the ideology: Schlegel gets credit for what he learned from others. The history of English science in the seventeenth century performed a similar vanishing trick on its debt to France. Like patriotic and even chauvinist history, such distortions and vanishing tricks are not uncommon. But it is unusual and rather distressing that the history of linguistics remains so attached to its old folk-history, often stated with great solemnity as befits ceremony.[44]

Just as the 'heroic' theory causes the failures that result from the discovery fixation, so it cannot take account of recurrences and repetitions, that is, the statement of closely similar or even identical arguments and principles at widely separated periods. Since the theory demands that achievement is not forgotten if publicly known, counterexamples must be explained away by some ad-hoc story. Recurrences are embarrassing; if unrelated, they question the progress doctrine; if related, they cast doubt on the originality of all but the first known proponent. Seeming instances of the former sort will often on closer inspection prove to belong with the latter. It is the unrelated recurrences that are the most interesting, for they raise illuminating questions about the intellectual contexts and the reasons for the repetition. Were the contexts similar, and if so how similar? And if not seemingly similar, why the repetition? The history and sociology of science have called attention to this problem, to what Robert K. Merton with reference to multiple discoveries calls a "strategic research site."[45]

Uniformitarianism would seem to be a case in point. It is characteristic of the history of ideas, of its weakness, that it does not find this principle until the word had been created, that is around 1840. But there is an analogue in the early seventeenth century in the discussion and controversy that followed Galileo's writings on Jupiter's moons, on the surface of the moon, etc. Indeed, the rejection of the hierarchical Aristotelian universe (with its fixed spheres, etc.) marks the assertion of a uniformitarian view of nature. Marin Mersenne was involved in these events, and he also asserted uniformitarian principles with regard to language. The new science demanded the rejection of the Adamic language doctrine in favor of the view that language is man-made, its aim communication, its being social, and that words are arbitrary signs (Crombie 1974; Aarsleff 1976a). The epistemology of the new science could not get along with the essentialism of the Adamic language doctrine—this is what Locke's argument against innate ideas is about. Owing to Mersenne, one of the conferences of Théophraste Renaudot, held during the late 1630s, debated precisely the same problem that was the topic of Herder's prize-essay some 140 years later. Since there is, it seems, no demonstrable connection between the two events, the implications are suggestive and should prove instructive.

During the nineteenth century uniformitarianism again became an issue both in linguistics and in science; two hundred years apart the controversy took much the same form. The issue joined linguistics and science because the doctrine that words somehow have natural meaning cropped up again in romantic linguistic philology, reflected in renewed interest in Boehme. Darwinian theory faced opponents committed to essentialism. Both in science and linguistics as well as in their interrelations the nineteenth century is in large measure a replay of the seventeenth; there are a good many more examples than I can mention here. Thus the reassertion of the arbitrariness of the linguistic sign and all that goes with it (that languages are institutions, social, etc.) is perhaps the central theme of the linguistic innovation that took place in the later decades of the nineteenth century. This is also true of the seventeenth century; Mersenne and Locke both (without any direct connection) made the arbitrariness of the linguistic sign a cardinal principle, a principle that is best known from Locke's *Essay*, which was the chief source of eighteenth century linguistic philosophy. It is therefore not surprising that there are evident similarities between Locke and the eighteenth century on the one hand and what we read in Saussure on the other.

To return to the intellectual history of the nineteenth century, let me examine two principles that occupy Claude Bernard in the *Introduction* (1865); both are related to the matter discussed in the previous pages. We have seen that both Magendie and Darwin ignored the rules of classical Baconian induction just as it was at the peak of its reputation. There is a rich literature on this subject; an understanding of this problem and how it was debated and worked out during the middle stretch of the century is fundamental to achieving a grasp of the intellectual history of that century, including the study of language.[46] Bernard addressed himself to his problem with great boldness. He argued that no worthwhile observation occurs without imagination and prior hypothesis, that method alone is barren, "and it is an error made by certain philosophers to have attributed too much power to the method in this respect" (a reference to the positivists), that excessive commitment to preconceived theories and ideas blocks discovery and causes poor observation, that induction and deduction cannot be separated, and finally that (as was to be expected) "Baconian induction has become famous and been made the foundation of all of the philosophy of science. Bacon, however, did not understand the procedure of the experimental method" (54, 67, 71, 79, 86). The reaction against Schleicher and the German school was similar to this critique of mere method, of simple induction. Bernard and Bréal stand in similar relations to the traditions that reigned in their disciplines.

The second principle in Bernard parallels the argument that comparative philology is not all of linguistics. Writing of the interrelations of anatomy and physiology, Bernard said that the anatomical perspective had hitherto dominated; he granted that anatomical study would naturally appear first, "but I believe that this principle is false in so far as it lays claim to being exclusive and that it has now become harmful to physiology, after having rendered very great services, which I would be the last person to contest. In fact, anatomy as a science is simpler than physiology and consequently it should be subordinated to it instead of ruling it. In a word, I believe that physiology, the most complex of all the sciences, cannot be fully elucidated by anatomy" (157-58). What especially marked physiology was the study of living things, "in a word, to know anything about the functions of life, they must be studied in the living state" (160). It is obvious that Bernard's defense of physiology and the study of living specimens against the anatomical tradition and its advocates closely resembles the case of language study around 1870, also in so far as there is a well-known historical link between the early history of comparative philology and anatomy—Sir William Jones had attended John Hunter's famous Croonian lectures and makes reference to them several times in the "Anniversary Discourses," and Friedrich Schlegel's debt to Cuvier is well known. Both physiology and Bréal's linguistics are linked to the philosophy of science which Bernard stated more openly than Darwin ever did, though both gained eminence by following it. There are perhaps few legacies of the nineteenth century that have had a greater impact on the twentieth than Darwinism and the ideas that found expression in Saussure's *Cours*. There are affinities between their historical situations. It is perhaps not entirely idle, therefore, to note that both have had their greatest impact concurrently during the last generation.

No purely internal history of a science or a discipline can achieve coherence and lead to the sort of understanding that yields a sense of explanation. It is only by inclusion of external factors that genuine intellectual history becomes possible. The prerequisite is disengagement from the conventional patterns and from subservience to the institutional bias of folk-history. This argument is presented with great cogency in Ravetz's excellent book on *Scientific Knowledge and its Social Problems* (1970). Let me quote a suggestive passage from that book: "Until the nineteenth century, no field of natural science had such internal and social strength that its leaders could, or even wished to, reject all external components of value from its work. The 'purity' of science seems to have been developed first in the university environment of nineteenth-century Germany, where the natural sciences struggled to win a place alongside the established humanistic and philological disciplines. With the eventual establishment of university science on a large scale in all advanced countries in the earlier part of this century, the ideology of purity also became a convenient means of preserving the autonomy of an increasingly expensive social activity. By the entirely natural processes of the formation of folk-history, the tradition of the purity of science was extended back in time to the origins of modern science, and across to all fields of scientific inquiry" (164-65).[47]

In the first part of this paper I have tried to illustrate, and in the latter part I have argued that the history of linguistics is rather out of it if we set its conceptual framework, its understanding of history and science, against the method, practice, and achievement of intellectual history and of the history of science. This problem was also the subject of my Introduction to *The study of language in England 1780-1860* (1967). It was clear to me then that the available histories were of little use as to substance and that they followed a method which had all the deficiencies I have described above. I argued, consequently, that if the history of the study of language was to be more than a largely unconnected record of events, it would need to expand its territory, that the study of language in any period is so closely bound up with the intellectual context—such as science, philosophy, theology, and ruling ideology—that this context must be known and related to language study, and that the history of linguistics must both relate to the results of the history of science and learn from its example. The terms internal and external history were not then around, but that was what my argument was about. I also pointed to the chief obstacle to a viable history by referring to the consequences of "a positivist conception of the forward march of history, of progress, a conception that will invariably give less than the history that is my concern. With this sort of outlook, no history of learning or scholarship can ever achieve more than a deceptive coherence." I illustrated by giving examples from the seventeenth to the nineteenth centuries, including an example to which I have also referred in this paper: "Even natural science did not have its origin in unalloyed, disinterested, nearly angelic objectivity about the phenomena of nature, though it is still widely believed, indeed often dogmatically asserted against the testimony of the evidence, that the early Royal Society had only the purest of scientific motives." My book was, I said, "an essay in the application of that method." The method for which I argued has general import, and I presented it in those terms. In the body of the book I showed how intimately language study was bound up with events in physics, chemistry, geology, religious thought, church politics, and the philosophical controversies of the time. I also cited Alexandre Koyré's words quoted earlier in this paper. I am eager to call these facts to the readers' attention; they are easy to check. The reason is this: In recent years my argument about the method—clearly noted in several reviews—has made repeated appearances in the writings of E. F. K. Koerner in contexts that not only leave my Introduction unmentioned but also misrepresent what the book does and is about; this can only tend to prevent his readers from knowing what my Introduction says and what my book is about. The most recent version of his misrepresentation says this: "It seems . . . that the author hoped the reader would, through some kind of osmosis, absorb the 'method' from the thicket of positivistically gleaned historical facts . . . nowhere in the book are guidelines of procedure mapped out which could, *mutatis mutandis*, apply to any other period in the history of the linguistic debate."[48] Let me repeat. I did not leave the method to osmosis, and I did not confine my examples to a narrow time-span. That this sort of misrepresentation can get into print not once but several times has been a serious liability for the history of the study of language.

Notes

1. Koerner 1972a:216 says: "Bopp's work is surely the first important step towards the positivistic attitude which attempts to study language for language's sake (and not in order to gain insight into the culture, philosophy and literature of earlier periods of mankind), a trend which became very powerful during the last decades of the nineteenth century." This statement is typical of the sort of ad-hoc myth by which the conventional history is maintained.

2. In Whitney 1867, this distinction was intimated but not made explicit, e.g., p. 241, and in the subtitle "Twelve lectures on the principles of linguistic science," though the substance of the book went beyond mere philology. Whitney 1875a:315 stated the distinction: the comparative method "is insufficient as applied to the whole study—the science of language." On the distinction, cp. Hjelmslev 1937:10.

3. Maher 1966 argues that the 'tale' of Schleicher's Darwinism is "wholly apocryphal," but this goes against the plain dictionary meaning of Darwinism and Darwinian, the latter meaning a follower of Darwin as the term was used soon after 1859 of dozens of figures by themselves or others, even though what they claimed had little or no basis in an understanding of the *Origin of Species*. Schleicher's two pieces protest emphatic adherence to what he took to be Darwinism, though he had of course earlier, like others, treated language study as a natural science. Even on the criteria for Darwinism that Maher accepts (p. 2 in quotation from Wellek), Schleicher fits, e.g., by his commitment (1863:4-5) to "Kampf ums Dasein," that is "the struggle for existence," which is the title of the chapter in which Darwin, with mention of Malthus, introduces the concept of natural selection. As will be seen below, the reaction against the F. Schlegel-Schleicher doctrines was also a reaction against their racism. There is relevant material in Poliakov 1971.

4. Some of Saussure's notes will be found in Jakobson 1971. For the original, see Godel 1954, esp. pp. 59-60.

5. See, e.g., the opening words of Hovelacque 1877: what marks modern linguistics is that it has recognized and proclaimed "that there was a *life of language*, that each language inevitably passed through certain biological periods; in other words, that it shared the common lot of all organisms, of all natural functions. The truth of this fact strikes the eyes of all observers." Cf. Whitney's review of Hovelacque 1876: "It has far too much of fact and too little of inference and reasoning for a manual of science . . . His main authority is Schleicher, than whom a more untrustworthy guide in these matters could not well be found; and he adopts and puts nakedly forward, without any attempt to establish or to refute the reasoning by which they have been repeatedly overthrown, such dogmas as that the study of language is a natural and not a historical science; that languages are born, grow, decay, and die, like all living creatures" (Whitney, 1876). On a widely held view of Locke during the nineteenth century, see Aarsleff 1971, which also has information about Victor Cousin and his critique of the eighteenth century.

6. See Bréal's own remarks 1897:6-7. The word 'sémantique' was introduced by Bréal in 1883: "As this study deserves to have a name, we shall call it 'sémantique,' that is to say the science of significations" (1883:133). The term was already in common use, that is without explication, in the late 1880s, e.g., by Gaston Paris and Victor Henry. The *Revue de linguistique et de philologie comparée* carried a very unfavorable review by Paul Renaud, saying that Bréal's *Essai* "makes one think of *La Pluralité des mondes* explicated, in regard to form, by a rival of Renan, and that is to say everything." The same review also argued against Bréal's critique of organicism and "the life of language" (Renaud 1898). Renan referred to Bréal as "my friend and colleague," but Bréal criticized Renan's linguistic philosophy, as will be seen below. So far as I know, the first time Bréal used the term 'sémantique' was in a letter of 14 April 1879 to Angelo de Gubernatis: "I am also preparing a book on the intellectual laws of language on which I have been working for some years: that's what one could call 'la sémantique.' You heard a sample of it when you came to my lecture." See Ciureanu 1955:460.

7. The first two editions of the *Essai* (1897, 1899) contained two supplementary essays, to which two more were added in the 3rd ed. (1904), one of which is entitled "La linguistique est-elle une science naturelle?" Here (pp. 312-314) Bréal again criticized "la théorie mystique," which he had already identified in 1866a:viii, xxiiif. In this context he made one of his not infrequent remarks about the racist implications: "They imagined a distant past which they decorated with all sorts of qualities that recent eras have lost. At the bottom of all these speculations lay disdain and contempt for reason. A certain arrogance of caste was also part of it; the idea of privileged races, among whom they didn't forget to place themselves, could not fail to please. This personal aspect shows in the expression *indo-germanic*, created to designate one of the great families of languages." Bréal was born in 1832 of French-Jewish parents at Landau in what was then the Bavarian Rhineland: during the reaction following the coup d'état in 1852, he was one of several Jewish students excluded from the École normale. See Gerbod 1965:333.

8. Jespersen 1894 is, as the author says (*ibid.*, p. v), "to a certain extent an English translation of" Jespersen 1891, which also makes reference to Bréal.

9. This passage is cited from the beginning of the second chapter in Schleicher 1869:34. Jespersen also cited "Schleicher's opinion that English shows 'how rapidly the language of a nation important both in history and literature can sink.'" (15).

10. Bréal 1896; Henry 1894, 1896:15. Jespersen referred to Bréal 1876 as a "sober critical article" (1894:114).

11. The figure in square brackets is the page reference to Madvig 1875. The date is that

of the year of the Danish text. I have not had access to the Danish text of Madvig's essays. Bréal 1897:25 refers to Jespersen 1894:33-36. It is curious that Bréal echoes Madvig on a point that I don't see in Jespersen: "Language is deprived of this somewhat childish luxury."

12. See esp. Jespersen 1894:80-111. In various ways, Chinese has been a sort of linguistic test case since at least the seventeenth century, e.g., in Leibniz.

13. In the same review, Meillet stated his sociological view, "language is a social institution of which the conditions of existence and development could be understood only from a sociological point of view" (598), already advanced in one of his earlier publications: "Of all social facts, language is without doubt the first that has been studied scientifically" (opening words of Meillet 1893). Meillet took credit for this view: Bréal, he said, "saw clearly that language is an organ of society. But he would not have been happy to say that language is a social fact, as I did the day I succeeded him and as Ferdinand de Saussure did at Geneva in his course in general linguistics" (1930:226). Meillet credited the synchronic, diachronic distinction to Saussure, who "was especially eager to mark the contrast between two ways of looking at linguistic facts: the study of language at a given moment and the study of linguistic development in time" (1913-14:183). Meillet saw the *Cours* as representing Saussure's teaching in Paris: "I never attended Saussure's course in general linguistics. But it is well known that Saussure's thought was formed very early. The doctrines he explicitly taught in his course in general linguistics were those that already distinguished his teaching of comparative grammar twenty years ago at the École des Hautes Études when I was a student. I recognize them such as it was often possible to imagine them then" (1916b:33). Cf. Mauss 1900: "The language of a society is nothing but a social phenomenon" (141). The interest in the social aspect of language had political implications; see, e.g., this passage in Worms 1894 about James Darmesteter: "He was among those who encouraged the students to 'go to the people,' to make friends with the workers, to dedicate themselves to working for popular education and judicious social improvement." Cf. Mauss 1937.

14. Before Madvig 1875, only Madvig 1843 (from a Danish text 1841) had appeared in German.

15. It is generally believed that the uniformitarian principle, when it makes its appearance in the study of language, had been suggested by Lyell's writings on geology. But Madvig's use of this principle in 1842 was almost certainly independent of Lyell. I say more about uniformitarianism below.

16. Thurot is quoting from Madvig 1843:17; Madvig 1971:327-36 has only excerpts from this essay. Cf. Madvig, "No historical-etymological study can replace the systematic, mind-oriented description of the use of forms, which, if it is to have genuine substance, requires a competent capacity for abstraction and logical clarity" (1971:203 [216]; 1856-57). Cf. also this passage from M. Cl. Gertz's detailed lecture notes (1866): "Thus the importance of comparative language study is fundamental; but we should not forget that the proper linguistic study of an individual language aims at the understanding of what has value and use in this individual and fully finished, actually existing language, at insight into the phenomena of the language. For only this, what has value and is used, is the truth of the matter; whatever else comparative language study can accomplish is only secondary matter which has nothing to do with the phenomena of the individual language and does not promote its completeness" (1971:391).

17. Cf. "But no one will, on sober reflection, build anything on usage that is so metaphorical as that of organism when it is used of language" (1971:332, 1832). On F. Schlegel see 1971:50, 169 [5, 169]; 1836, 1856-57. Madvig ridiculed the talk of "das Tiefe und Geheimnisvolle," e.g.: "If it should now seem to somebody that I have effaced all that is deep and mysterious in the structure of language, I can only answer that I have endeavored myself and encouraged others to do their best to look with penetration and without illusion

into the deep in order to discover actual forms and to gain a true conception of what goes on there. Perhaps some will also be of the opinion that my approach lowers the importance of linguistic science. Comparative language study shall show us what it can, the affinity of languages and the coherence of their development, but it is not its aim to promise explanations of aspects of intellectual life that lie outside its province" (1971:252 [283-284]; 1856-57). Cf. 1971:173 [175]; 1856-57.

18. The doctrine of the 'sensible' origin of all words is important in the seventeenth century, best known perhaps from Locke's famous statement that became one of the most frequently cited texts in the linguistic philosophy of the eighteenth century (See, e.g., Aarsleff 1967:31). It is also in Bréal, e.g., 1866b: 251.

19. In this passage Madvig uses the word 'phonetic' in a sense that is strange to us, but common before the word late in the century took the meaning we now are accustomed to. See, e.g., this passage in Renan, referring to Bopp and his followers: "What especially gives this method its soundness is phonetics. The theory of sound change is the true base of comparative grammar" (1878:1215). It was in opposition to this sense of the term that Bréal created his term 'sémantique', "the science which I have proposed to call 'sémantique' by contrast to phonetics, the science of sounds" (1897:9; it was during the 1890s that Rousselot became director of the first phonetic laboratory thanks to Bréal's support and influence). Cf. Madvig: "I will first of all strongly emphasize the intellectual and inner aspect of language (but as it is actually grasped and known, not as an incomprehensible mystery) as that which poses the fundamental and most important task of language study, in opposition to the exaggerated prominence that is given to what is outward and pertains to sound" (1971: 276 [315]; 1871).

20. See, e.g.: "Thus speaking at large, the grammatical categories have in all nations a common content, given in the nature of its outlook and limited to it" (1971:122 [105]; 1856-57). Cf. "We must emphasize that reality does not give any cause to begin our language study with the presupposition of a certain normal grammatical structure or a direct relationship between the particular constitution of the language and language families on the one hand and the intellectual disposition of nations on the other" (1971:126 [111]). Much of Madvig's argument is directed against Wilhelm von Humboldt whom he found the most interesting exponent of the views he opposed. Madvig especially criticized Humboldt's efforts to identify Kantian categories in grammar; these categories were designed to refer to real relations, while Madvig held that grammar and language express only the work of the mind, its 'Vorstellungsart.' His critique therefore is not aimed at the classical eighteenth-century doctrine.

21. The entire essay (1842) on "Verhältnis und Stellung der Sprachen in der Kulturentwicklung" (1971:337-344) is devoted to this subject.

22. On Madvig's philosophy of language, see also Friis Johansen 1971. Siesbye 1887-88: 124-38. Jensen 1963:44-87. DeMauro 1969 (esp. 76-77, 173) has pointed to the importance of Madvig and his similarity with Bréal. I have earlier indicated my general agreement with DeMauro, suggested by the fact that we have both independently cited the same passage in Thomsen 1902:38, for the same purpose (DeMauro 58-59; Aarsleff 1967:8).

23. Madvig also briefly stated some of the same views in his writings on Latin and Greek grammar and syntax; in their German and French translations, these works were widely reviewed in the *Revue critique*, chiefly by Charles Thurot (who called Madvig "le premier latiniste de l'Europe" (1870:380)), during the years when Bréal was one of its editors. Thurot began teaching at the École normale in 1861; in 1868 he published his well-known *Notices et extraits de divers manuscrits latins pour servir à l'histoire des doctrines grammaticales au Moyen Age.*

24. Madvig first mentioned the Whitney matter in a footnote to the Danish text of his

essay of 1871 (1971:468). This note was omitted in the German text in Madvig 1875, where he instead made the same point more prominently in the "Vorrede" (1971:394-395 [iv-v]). He returned to it in 1881, as we have just seen, and again in his memoirs, where he wrote (in Danish): "Whitney, who is a man of extensive and independent studies, has raised objection to this supposition, and I am willing to let it fall, but still wish to maintain and stress that the truth of what I have said in the works in question is confirmed by the unrelated appearance and development of the basic arguments in two so widely separated places" (1887:256). A German version is 1971:401. The matter is discussed in the editor's Introduction and notes (1971:37, 468-469). It would seem clear that Madvig's decision to bring out the German version of some of his essays in 1875 was caused by these events. Madvig's memoirs were dictated in 1884 and early 1885.

25. See also 1867:46 which takes back part of what he said on p. 35. Henry 1887 opened with the observation that "before and especially after the great work of Whitney [1875a] , much has been said about the life of language; but I am not sure there is always perfect agreement on the value and implication of this term." The publication of A. Darmesteter 1887 caused much discussion of this issue. Inconsistencies on fundamental principle are not uncommon in Whitney; thus 1867:373-74 argues that "language is no infallible sign of race," though "it still remains true that, upon the whole, language is a tolerably sure indication of race." Whitney doesn't hesitate to speak of a "superior race," of "barbarism," and the like. Later in the same book, he contradicts himself: "The extent to which the different races of men have availed themselves of language, to secure the advantages placed within their reach by it, is, naturally and necessarily, as various as are the endowments of the races . . . Language makes each community, each race, a unit" (446-47). Such thinking was rejected both by Madvig and by Bréal.

26. The significance of this decision was noticed, e.g., by Egger 1873; it was also pointed out by Meillet 1916a:12. It was Egger who advised Bréal to undertake the translation (Bréal 1866a:lvii). Bréal 1866a has only few mentions of Schleicher, none of them critical; Schleicher was then still living, and Bréal may not yet have known Schleicher 1863, 1865. Bréal 1866a is dated 1 November 1865. On p. liv, Bréal gives mildly qualified praise to the *Compendium*. Bréal was never so outspokenly and impatiently critical as Whitney. For an interesting discussion of events and figures (including Bréal and Gaston Paris) in the 1870s, see Dionisotti 1972.

27. One of the notable facts about Bréal is his close knowledge of German life, intellectual history and literature; he published extensively on the history and organization of German education (see, e.g., 1884) and he also wrote on German literature. In France he was throughout his career, though chiefly during the early years, deeply involved in the reform and administration of education (see, e.g., 1886). He was one of the chief organizers of the École pratique des Hautes Études (established in 1868 largely on the German model), a close adviser to Victor Duruy and Jules Simon, and for a period of ten years inspector general of public instruction for higher education (from 1879 to 1888 when the post was discontinued for budgetary reasons). His writings on these subjects show that his interest in the social dimension of language was not merely scholarly; it was also a practical concern. He was opposed to the ruling elitist education which divided the people in two nations that linguistically did not understand each other: "We have two nations in France: one thinks, reads, writes, debates and contributes to the European cultural movement, the other is unfamiliar with this exchange of ideas going on around it, or if it tries to enter this exchange, it resembles a man suddenly thrown into a conversation that has been going on for a long time before he came in which he hears names being pronounced and issues debated that are all equally beyond his knowledge" (1886:76). In the same book (1886:398-99), Bréal also made one of his critical remarks about assigning national differences to inherent racial

features. He constantly tried to join public and academic interest; he regularly contributed to at least half a dozen journals of general circulation. He was an early member of the Société de linguistique de Paris, its secretary from 1868 until his death in 1915 (during the Paris years choosing Saussure as joint secretary, whom Bréal had also proposed for membership), and its most active member. There is a close link between Bréal's linguistic and public stature during the last four decades of the century; no attempt to understand his importance can ignore this link, well known in the history of education on all levels. In this respect, he resembles Madvig who played a prominent role in similar reforms, for a while as minister of education.

28. Madvig made the same point 1971:50, 169 [5, 169]; 1836, 1856-57. Whitney (1871: 311) talked of F. Schlegel as representing the "antediluvian period of linguistic science."

29. The next year Whitney voiced his critique of Schleicher in the obituary devoted to him (a practice, incidentally, quite foreign to Bréal's urbane temper): Schleicher was "a vehement champion of the paradox that a language is a 'natural organism,' growing and developing by internal forces and necessary laws; and his statement and defence of his doctrine are so bald and extreme as to be self-refuting; he was not unskilled as a naturalist, and his studies in natural history, by some defect in his logical constitution, seems to have harmed his linguistics" (1869:70).

30. In this review, Gaston Paris referred to his own opening lecture at the Sorbonne in 1867, in which he had also opposed the abuse of metaphor, and to Bréal 1866b on the same question. Paris repeated the passage on metaphor in his review of A. Darmesteter 1887 (Paris 1887:66). For a cogent critique of organicism and the organic metaphor, see Tarde 1896. The occasion for Whitney 1871 would also seem to be the same French translation of Schleicher, cited near the end of that essay with the remark that "even so sound and careful a philologist as M. Bréal has been misled into giving the inauspicious beginning [of the series] an implied sanction by letting his name appear alone upon the title-page, as author of the Introduction . . . and in it he indicates—though, in my opinion, in a manner much less distinct and decided than the case demanded—his at least partial non-acceptance of Schleicher's views." As Paris's review shows, there were no grounds for this petulant observation; Bréal never used Whitney's sledgehammer methods, and his views on Schleicher were already clear enough. In 1869, Bréal published a review of Benfey 1869, remarking that Benfey was too indulgent on F. Schlegel's theory of flexions and that the history was distorted by rather strong patriotic sentiments, "one could be led to believe that there has not been room for any advanced intellectual culture between the civilization of antiquity and the scholarly activity that today has its chief home in Germany and that these two periods are separated by an intellectual desert. We cite these passages merely to show that German patriotism is not always exempt from these outbursts of boastfulness with which it rightly takes issue when found in other nations." This critique was well founded, raised often both then and later, by men of different nationalities. It is worth noting that this, like other statements to the same effect, was written before the Franco-Prussian war.

31. E. F. K. Koerner writes: "Bréal's sociologism can, as we believe, be traced to Whitney's *Vie du langage* (Paris 1875), and thus it is conceivable that the sociological tradition in linguistics was initiated by the American linguist who was the first to incorporate sociological notions (probably under the influence of Spencerian ideas) into the study of language" (1973:227). As already shown, Bréal's view of linguistic 'sociologism' was independent of Whitney, argued by Bréal prior to any possibility of dependence on Whitney. The indebtedness, if any, is rather the other way round. I have also pointed out the quite obvious fact that the social nature of language is the common view, from Mersenne and Locke to Madvig, Mill, and the Utilitarians; it is its absence in the German school that is remarkable, not its presence elsewhere. Whitney is not "the first to incorporate sociological notions . . . into

the study of language," a contention that is typical of the sort of historical distortion that is the consequence of fixation on the German tradition as the norm. Further, if Bréal were to have found this view in Whitney, there is no reason to think it would be from Whitney 1875a. In his Introduction (dated 27 August 1872) to vol. IV of the translation of Bopp, Bréal referred to Whitney 1867 (in the 2nd ed., London 1868) as "a work too little known in France." He repeated this reference in Bréal 1873. Collin 1914:28 intimates that Whitney 1875a was translated into French by Bréal; that of course is possible, but Collin gives no reason for the attribution, his work is so sloppy as not to inspire confidence, and the carefully catalogued Whitney Papers in the Yale Library do not indicate any communication between Bréal and Whitney such as one might expect if Bréal were the translator.

32. In a note to 1868b:322, Bréal wrote: "While writing these lines, I thought of Schleicher's book, *Die Untersuchung von Nomen und Verbum in der lautlichen Form*." Since Schleicher had recently died, Bréal added: "I had no idea that scholarship had just lost this eminent scholar." In 1871, Whitney conducted a somewhat similar argument, which he illustrated with an image so similar to Bréal's that one is tempted to see a connection. Whitney said: "Now it is easy to throw a group of objects, by distance and perspective, into such apparent shape as shall obscure or conceal their true character and mutual relations. Look at a village only a little way off . . . so in language: if you insist on standing aloof from the items of linguistic change and massing them together, if you will not estimate the remoter facts by the nearer, you will never attain a true comprehension of them" (1871:313-14). Whitney 1875 (48-49), in discussion of form and meaning, also resembles Bréal's discussion of form and function. There are striking similarities between Bréal 1866b, 1868b and Madvig. Thus in 1836, Madvig wrote: "It is a great error to assume that the general sense of the relation that lies in the outlook is not just as much there for the speaker when it has no particular sign, because there was no need for it and it had no occasion to be formed or has disappeared, as when the sign exists" (1971:52 [8]). In a note to the German text 1875, Madvig said that the entire passage had been shortened in the German version, because he had since, in 1856-57, dealt with the subject at greater length. The longer passage in the Danish text of 1836 is given in German translation pp. 410-12. It seems to me clear that Bréal's argument is very similar to Madvig's, except that Madvig does not refer to the Port-Royal and universal grammar. I find this puzzling and see no easy way to account for it. Is it a 'multiple'?

33. Cf. *ibid*.: "Classical grammar has been blamed for not being scientific; still, its basis is less open to criticism and its object better defined than is the case with the linguistics begun by Bopp." Cf. also: "To synchrony belongs entirely what is called 'universal grammar'" (141).

34. Wells 1973 credits linguistic uniformitarianism to Max Müller, without mention of Madvig and Bréal. That the classical eighteenth-century doctrine was uniformitarian must be evident to any reader of its chief exponent, Condillac; as in Bréal, it is a consequence of the mind's constant activity in the use of language, manifest also textually in Condillac's frequent use of the word 'generate' and its derivatives to describe this linguistic activity. Müller's critics would not have granted that he was uniformitarian, precisely because he did not apply this principle at what was for them the crucial point: the origin of language. See quotations on uniformitarianism above, esp. from Madvig.

35. On this metaphor and a characteristic nineteenth-century version of it, see Aarsleff 1967:233-34. Koerner 1974 says that my book is about "the historical background which led to the formation of the Philological Society of London in 1842, rather than a history of linguistics." The book is no more about the Philological Society than *Bleak House* is about Yorkshire because part of the action is set there. Koerner also says that the "detailed index . . . unfortunately does not seem to include the often very informative footnotes." The index in fact has very close to 200 references to the footnotes, each one clearly indicated by

the letter n after the page number, and thus readily observable even at a hasty glance. This is typical of Koerner's unreliability, whether it is a question of misrepresentation or plain ignorance of the items he reports on.

36. Here Bréal again states the uniformitarian principle: "If we could have witnessed this evolution, we would no doubt have discovered the action of the same laws that we recognize in the transformation of the modern languages" (1879:1010).

37. Bréal knew that Renan had later substantially changed his position; see, e.g., Renan 1878. Bréal is referring to Renan's *L'avenir de la science*, written in 1848, but not published until 1890 with a fascinating introduction that shows how profoundly the intellectual context had changed over the intervening forty years. First in 1871, Madvig made a similar critique of Renan (1971:288 [331-32]). In 1875, he added footnotes on the same matter to his earlier writings (1971:88, 124 [58, 109]).

38. At this point, Cournot continues with this image: "The matter would be evident to everyone if it were a question of describing in words a system composed of discontinuous parts, such as a clockwork—not to say a painting or a landscape." On p. 73, Cournot wrote of "the linear order which is imposed by the essential nature of language." The linearity of discourse is central in Condillac's philosophy of language, see Aarsleff 1974, above pp. 157-158. Cournot's distinction and importance became increasingly known toward the end of the nineteenth century. The *Revue de métaphysique et de morale* devoted a special issue to him in May 1905 (vol. 13, 291-543); a brief headnote says that the late Gabriel Tarde had planned a new edition of Cournot's works, "almost unattainable today." Nothing came of it then, but an edition of Cournot's complete works is now being published in response to the same need that Tarde identified seventy years ago. The nature of Cournot's work and the knowledge of him at that time obviously have significant implications for the history of the study of language and its intellectual locale during the nineteenth century.

39. There were eleven editions of Taine's *Philosophes* by 1912. The re-issue of Weil 1844 in 1869 appeared in the *Collection philologique*, edited by Bréal, in which the two Schleicher pieces had been published the previous year. Weil's book was re-issued again in 1879. Weil's reference in the title to *grammaire générale* is not casual; the Introduction refers to the discussion between Beauzée and Batteux, "ces savants estimables." Weil began teaching in Paris at the École normale and the École pratique in 1861 and taught there until his retirement in 1892. The Taine passage is in the Preface to the 4th edition (1883).

40. To serve the ends of folk-history, a figure is often placed in a benighted context that makes him shine the more in the dark, though this flattering ad-hoc context is pure myth. Thus it is often said that in Herder's time it was dangerously unorthodox to believe that the original language was not Hebrew and that the short Mosaic chronology was not authoritative; the result is to make Herder shine. It is possible that such beliefs were held by some Lutheran country pastors, but that is not the claim which is made about the intellectual context. It is nonsense. Mersenne, for instance like the majority in the seventeenth century, rejected both. Another strategy is to claim that a particular figure is so unique that he suffered no influence at all; this attempt to safeguard claims for originality is of course self-defeating, for such claims are empty unless the possibilities of influence have been examined. It is not the aim of intellectual history to reduce individual originality, but to make it possible to identify it. It is no slur on Newton to know what he owed to Kepler.

41. Another sort of ad-hoc strategy is the claim, ridiculed by Madvig and many others, about "das Tiefe und Geheimnisvolle." Thus when it is suggested that Herder owes much to Condillac, it is claimed that Herder's theory "is surely thought through more deeply and consistently," without any attempt whatever to demonstrate what this means. The words are merely hortatory.

42. In 1972b:274, Koerner referred to a passage in Wilhelm Scherer (1875) that related Darwin to Malthus. Koerner, however, doubted "very much that this is correct, since Malthus was mainly concerned with the economic considerations influencing the growth or decline of the population, not with ideas of selection, survival of the fittest, and the like." Thus Koerner at one stroke showed elementary ignorance of both Darwin and Malthus. He also demonstrated that he had not read the Scherer passage with much care, for it says that Darwin has "by his own admission borrowed from Malthus' demographic laws." As any reader of the *Origin of species* and other writings by Darwin (e.g., the *Autobiography*) knows, Darwin's reading of Malthus played a crucial role in the inception of evolutionary theory. When Koerner published a revised version of his 1972b essay, he tried to correct his error, now saying that Scherer's suggestion "has been confirmed in recent years" (1976:694). For this confirmation, Koerner refers to Young 1969:110, n. 3. But that footnote is not on that subject at all, and Young naturally does not give confirmation of a fact that has been known not only by scholars but by ordinary readers for more than 100 years. Later in the same essay (125-28), Young does in fact give some of the relevant passages for the sake of analysis. Koerner is also of the opinion that Darwin was "in the final analysis really nothing more than a synthesizer and popularizer of ideas prevailing in the natural sciences of his time" (1973:4).

43. It is notable, however, that Arens says: "The Swiss de Saussure was undeniably the leader of French linguistics, even if we recognize as its founder Bréal, who with innumerable writings since 1862 had made himself known as mythologist, philologist, and linguist" (1969:443).

44. Since I wrote that chapter, Paul Diderichsen informed me that Louis Hjelmslev "on many occasions in lectures and discussion with great emphasis maintained that it is Jones (and not the Germans) who deserves the honor of being the founder of comparative philology" (see Aarsleff 1976b, 1530). For advancing that argument with documentation that I should think would have gone some way toward making the argument at least plausible, a German reviewer, writing in a reputable German journal, accused me of 'prejudice' pure and simple, without the slightest effort to examine what I offered in support. This is understandable; the purpose of the accredited story is not to be history, but to ensure that the faith is kept, that the mythical folk-history is respected. See Nickel 1969; cf. Lämmert 1967. It has also been argued that Jones was not followed up with the immediate excitement that is by some taken to be proof of major accomplishment. Even if this doubtful criterion is accepted, the conclusion does not follow in this case. The nine discourses were delivered during the years 1784-92, and published in the annual volumes of the *Asiatic Researches* beginning in 1788 at Calcutta, which was some six months away from Europe. Given the well-known events of European history during those years, it is not difficult to imagine how slowly these volumes got around. Contemporary correspondence testifies to eager but most often frustrated anticipation. A German translation of some pieces came out during the late 1790s, a pirated English edition began to appear in 1798 (followed by at least two more), and finally a French translation of the first seven volumes appeared at Paris in 1805, with notes and commentary by such famous men as Cuvier. Obviously, the argument about failure to elicit reaction does not stand up. The reason might readily have been suspected, but the history of linguistics is not given to such circumspection; besides, it might lose the day for F. Schlegel and the conventional folk-history. Schlegel was lucky to get into print when he did, with Jones's matter at the beginning of the volume and his own "thick fog," as Bréal said, at the back. On the 'heroic' theory and the discovery fixation, see Merton 1973:343-412. I am referring to the chapter on "Sir William Jones and the New Philology" in Aarsleff 1967: 115-61.

45. There is a rich and recent literature on the sociology of science; Merton 1973 is among the most important, a collection of essays published over the last decades. Among others may be mentioned Ben-David 1960, 1964, 1970, and 1971, as well as Ben-David and Zloczower 1962; the early chapters of Ben-David 1971 should be ignored. The two items by Clark (1968a and 1968b) suggest that a similar investigation of the competing publications of the Société de linguistique de Paris and the *Revue de linguistique* could prove fruitful. See also Clark 1973, esp. ch. 6.

46. Darwin has for a number of reasons attracted great attention during the last ten years; this distinguished literature is important both as intellectual history and for its methodological example and insight. Ghiselin 1969 is excellent and basic. Hull 1973 has an introduction that is especially illuminating on Darwin's scientific method in the context of the time, e.g., on essentialism. It also reprints fifteen contemporary reviews by well-known figures. Robert M. Young has written a large number of fascinating essays that are also methodologically significant; among these may be mentioned his essays 1969, 1971, 1973. The *Dictionary of Scientific Biography* is the indispensable and authoritative reference work. For a cogent critique of the history of ideas, both method and results, see Skinner 1969.

47. The great importance of Ravetz 1970, just quoted, needs to be emphasized. Both for knowledge and method, see also Ravetz 1972, 1973. The items listed in notes 45, 46, and 47 lead on to additional literature.

48. Koerner 1976:387. Thus this revised version substitutes equally patent misrepresentation for what appeared in the first version, 1972b. In November of 1972, I spoke to Koerner about the misrepresentation of my book in his essay; I received no answer. Thinking that I might hear by letter, I waited till the end of January 1973, then wrote up the facts in a letter; I quickly received the reply that Koerner hoped I would forgive him that he did not have the time to answer. I then wrote Aarsleff 1973, which was immediately published in the same journal that had published Koerner 1972. (Aarsleff 1973 contains essentially what I had said in my letter.) The editor of the volume in which Koerner 1976 has recently appeared was told of Aarsleff 1973 and the misrepresentations of Koerner 1972b. One of the important aspects of Ravetz 1970 is that it discusses honesty and integrity in writing, citation, and editing, not merely as a matter of personal obligation, but as a duty to the subject and the discipline. See esp. pp. 176-83 and 245-59.

References

Abbreviations: *BSL   Bulletin de la Société de Linguistique de Paris,* Paris.
      DSB   Dictionary of Scientific Biography
      RC   Revue critique d'histoire et de littérature

Aarsleff, Hans 1967. *The study of language in England 1780-1860.* Princeton University Press.
———1971. "Locke's reputation in nineteenth-century England." *The Monist* 55:392-422. Repr. above.
———1973. "A word on Koerner's historiography of linguistics." *Anthropological Linguistics* 15 (March). 148-50.
———1974. "The tradition of Condillac: The problem of the origin of language in the eighteenth century and the debate in the Berlin Academy before Herder." *Studies in the History of Linguistics,* ed. by Dell Hymes (Bloomington, Indiana) pp. 93-156. Repr. above.
———1975a. "Condillac's speechless statue." *Studia Leibnitiana. Supplementa XV—Akten des II. Internationalen Leibniz-Kongresses Hannover,* 17-22. Juli 1972. Vol. 4:287-302. Repr. above.

———1975b. "Thomas Sprat." *DSB* 12:580-87. Repr. above.

———1975c. "The eighteenth century, including Leibniz." In: *Current Trends in Linguistics*, vol. 13, *Historiography of Linguistics*, ed. by Thomas A. Sebeok, assoc. eds. Hans Aarsleff, Robert Austerlitz, Dell Hymes, Edward Stankiewicz (The Hague/Paris: Mouton), part I, 383-479.

———1976a. "John Wilkins." *DSB* 14:361-81. Repr. above.

———1976b. "Thoughts on Scaglione's *Classical theory of composition*: The survival of 18th century French linguistic philosophy before Saussure." *Romance Philology* 29:522-38.

Arens, Hans 1969. *Sprachwissenschaft*. 2nd ed. Freiburg/München, Alber.

Ben-David, Joseph 1960. "Scientific productivity and academic organisation in nineteenth-century medicine." *American Sociological Review* 25:828-43.

———and A. Zloczower 1962. "Universities and academic systems in modern societies." *European Journal of Sociology* 3:45-84.

———1964. "Scientific growth: A sociological view." *Minerva* 2:455-76.

———1970. "The rise and decline of France as a scientific centre." *Minerva* 8:160-79.

———1971. *The scientist's role in society. A comparative study*. Englewood Cliffs, Prentice-Hall.

Benfey, Theodor 1869. *Geschichte der Sprachwissenschaft und orientalischen Philologie in Deutschland seit dem Anfänge des 19. Jahrhunderts, mit einem Rückblick auf die früheren Zeiten*. München, Cotta.

Bernard, Claude 1865. *Introduction à l'étude de la médecine expérimentale*. Collection Garnier-Flammarion 1966.

Bopp, Franz 1866-1874. *Grammaire comparée des langues indo-européennes*, tr. by Michel Bréal. Paris. 5 vols. I 1866; II 1868; III 1869; IV 1872; V 1874.

Borst, Arno 1957-63. *Der Turmbau von Babel*. Stuttgart, Hiersemann.

Bréal, Michel 1866a. "Introduction" to Bopp 1866:I i-lvii.

———1866b. "De la forme et de la fonction des mots." Bréal 1877:243-66. First publ. in *Revue des cours littéraires de la France et de l'étranger*, 4th year, No. 5 (29 Dec. 1866), 65-71.

———1868a. "Les progrès de la grammaire comparée." Bréal 1877:267-94. First publ. in *Mémoires de la Société de Linguistique de Paris* I (1868), 72-89. Given at Collège de France 9 Dec. 1867.

———1868b. "Les idées latentes du langage." Bréal 1877:295-322. Separately published 1868.

———1869. Review of Benfey 1869. *RC* 8 (18 Dec.), 385-89.

———1873. Review of Whitney 1873. *RC* 13 (22 Feb.), 113.

———1876. "Les racines indo-européennes." Bréal 1877:375-411. First publ. *Journal des savants* 1876:632-52, as a review with subtitle "Examen critique de quelques théories relatives à la langue mère indo-européenne."

———1877. *Mélanges de mythologie et de linguistique*. Paris, Hachette.

———1879. "La science du langage." *Revue scientifique*, 2nd ser., vol. 8 (26 April 1879), 1005-11.

———1883. "Les lois intellectuelles du langage: Fragment de sémantique." *Annuaire de l'Association des études grecques en France*, 17:132-42.

———1884. *Excursions pédagogiques*. Paris, Hachette. First ed. 1882.

———1886. *Quelques mots sur l'instruction publique en France*. Paris, Hachette. 5th ed. (410 pp.), First ed. 1872 (151 pp.).

———1893. Review of Renan 1890. *Journal des savants*, January 1893, 5-17. Republished in *BSL* 8 (1894), lviii-lxviii, as Obituary with title "M. Ernest Renan et la philologie indo-européenne."

———1896. Review of Jespersen 1894. *Journal des savants* 1896, 381-89, 459-70.

———1897. *Essai de sémantique (Science des significations)*. Paris, Hachette.

———1900. Obituary of Max Müller. *Académie des inscriptions et belles-lettres. Comptes rendus*. 2 Nov. 1900, 558-64.

Ciureanu, Petre, ed. 1955. "Lettere inedite di Michel Bréal, Gaston Paris e Emile Littré." *Convivium* July-Aug.:1955:452-466.

Clark, Terry N. 1968a. "Émile Durkheim and the institutionalization of sociology in the French university system." *European Journal of Sociology* 9:37-71.

———1968b. "The structure and functions of a research institute: the *Année sociologique*." *European Journal of Sociology* 9:72-91.

———1973. *Prophets and Patrons: The French University System and the Emergence of the Social Sciences*. Cambridge, Mass.: Harvard.

Collin, Carl S. R. 1914. *A bibliographical guide to sematology*. Lund, Blom.

Cournot, Antoine-Augustin 1851. *Essai sur les fondements de nos connaissances et sur les caractères de la critique philosophique*. 2 vols. Paris.

———1861. *Traité de l'enchaînement des idées fondamentales dans les sciences et dans l'histoire*. 2 vols. Paris.

Crombie, A. C. 1974. "Marin Mersenne" *DSB* 9:316-22.

Darmesteter, Arsène 1887. *La vie des mots étudiée dans leurs significations*. Paris, Delagrave.

De Mauro, Tullio 1969. *Une introduction à la sémantique*. Paris, Payot. Original Italian 1966.

———1973. See Saussure 1916.

Dionisotti, Carlo 1972. "A year's work in the seventies." *Modern Language Review* 67:xix-xxviii.

Durkheim, Émile 1892. *Montesquieu et Rousseau, précurseurs de la sociologie*. Note introductive de Georges Davy. Paris: Les Classiques de la Sociologie, 1953. Original Latin thesis, Bordeaux 1892.

Egger, E. 1873. Review of Bopp 1866-74. vols. 1-4. *Journal des savants* 1873. 473-88.

Fox, Robert 1973. "Scientific enterprise and the patronage of research in France 1800-70." *Minerva* 11:442-72.

Friis Johansen, Karsten 1971. "Einleitung," in Madvig 1971. 1-46.

Gerbod, Paul 1965. *La condition universitaire en France au XIXe siècle*. Paris.

Ghiselin, Michael T. 1969. *The triumph of the Darwinian method*. Berkeley, California.

Gillispie, Charles C. 1973. "Alexandre Koyré." *DSB* 7:482-90.

Godel, R. 1954. See Saussure 1954.

Granger, G. 1971. "Antoine-Augustin Cournot." *DSB* 3:450-54.

Grmek, M. D. 1974. "François Magendie." *DSB* 9:6-11.

Henry, Victor 1887. Review of A. Darmesteter 1887. *RC*, n.s. 23:282-85.

———1894. Review of Jespersen 1894. *RC* n.s. 38:501-04.

———1896. *Antinomies linguistiques*. Paris, Alcan.

Hjelmslev, Louis L. 1937. "An introduction to linguistics. Inaugural lecture on appointment to the Chair of Comparative Linguistics at the University of Copenhagen." *Essais linguistiques. Travaux du Cercle Linguistique de Copenhague* 12 (1959), 9-20.

Hovelacque, A. 1876. *La linguistique*. Paris.

———1877. "La vie du langage." *Études de linguistique et d'ethnographie*. Paris. Pp. 1-13.

Hull, David L. 1973. *Darwin and his critics: The reception of Darwin's theory of evolution by the scientific community*. Cambridge, Mass., Harvard.

Jakobson, Roman 1971. "The world response to Whitney's principles of linguistic science." Silverstein 1971:xxv-xlv.

Jensen, Povl Johs. 1963. "Madvig som Filolog." *Johann Nicolai Madvig. Et Mindeskrift.* 2 vols. Copenhagen 1955-1963. II.1-209.

Jespersen, Otto 1891. *Studier over Engelske Kasus. Med en Indledning: Fremskridt i Sproget.* Copenhagen, Klein.

———1894. *Progress in language with special reference to English.* London, Swan Sonnenschein.

Koerner, E. F. K. 1972a. *Bibliographia Saussureana 1870-1970.* Metuchen, N. J., Scarecrow Press.

———1972b. "Towards a historiography of linguistics. 19th and 20th century paradigms." *Anthropological Linguistics* 14, no. 7:255-80.

———1973. *Ferdinand de Saussure. Origin and development of his linguistic thought in western studies of language. A contribution to the history and theory of linguistics.* Braunschweig, Vieweg.

———1974. "Annotated chronological bibliography III, 1962-1972." *Historiographia linguistica* 1:351-84.

———1976. Revised version of Koerner 1972b. Herman Parret, ed. *History of linguistic thought and contemporary linguistics.* Berlin, De Gruyter. Pp. 685-718.

Lämmert, Eberhard 1967. "Germanistik eine Deutsche Wissenschaft." In book under that title. Edition Suhrkamp no. 204, pp. 7-41.

Madvig, J. N. 1843. *Bemerkungen über verschiedene Puncte des Systems der lateinischen Sprachlehre und einige Einzelheiten derselben.*

———1875. *Kleine philologische Schriften.* Vom Verfasser deutsch bearbeitet. Leipzig, Teubner.

——— 1887. *Livserindringer.* Copenhagen: Gyldendal.

———1971. *Sprachtheoretische Abhandlungen.* Im Auftrage der Gesellschaft für Dänische Sprache und Literatur, hrsg. von Karsten Friis Johansen. Copenhagen, Munksgaard.

Maher, John P. 1966. "More on the history of the comparative method: The tradition of Darwinism in August Schleicher's work." *Anthropological Linguistics* 8, no. 3, part II. 1-12.

Mauss, M. 1900. Review of J. Deniker. *Les races et les peuples de la terre* (Paris 1900). *Année sociologique* 4:139-43.

———1937. "In memoriam Antoine Meillet (1866-1936)." *Oeuvres* III (1969) 548-53. First publ. in *Annales sociologiques* ser. E, fasc. 2 (1937) 1-7.

Meillet. A. 1893. "Les lois du langage." *Revue internationale de sociologie* 1:311-21, 860-70.

———1898. Review of Bréal 1897. *RC* n.s. 45:141-43.

———1900-1901. Review of Wilhelm Wundt, *Völkerpsychologie*, I *Die Sprache* (Leipzig 1900). *Année sociologique* 5:595-601.

———1903-1904. Review of Bréal 1897, 3rd ed. (1904). *Année sociologique* 8:640-41.

———1913-1914. "Ferdinand de Saussure." Meillet 1951:174-83.

———1915. "La linguistique." *La science française.* 2 vols. *Exposition universelle et internationale de San Francisco.* 2:117-24.

———1916a. Obituary of Michel Bréal. *BSL* 20:10-19.

———1916b. Review of Saussure 1916. *BSL* 20:32-36.

———1930. "Michel Bréal et la grammaire comparée au Collège de France." Meillet 1951: 212-27.

———1951. *Linguistique historique et linguistique générale.* vol. II. Nouveau tirage. Paris, Champion.

Merton, Robert K. 1973. *The sociology of science. Theoretical and empirical investigations*, ed. by Norman W. Storer. University of Chicago Press.

———1975. "George Sarton." *DSB* 12:107-14 (with Arnold Thackray).

Nickel, Gerhard 1969. Review of Aarsleff 1967. *Anglia* 86:163-66.

Paris, Gaston 1868a. Review of *Mémoires de la Société de Linguistique de Paris*, 1 (1868). *RC* 5:248.

——1868b. Review of Schleicher 1868. *RC* 6:241-44.

——1887. Review of A. Darmesteter 1887. *Journal des savants* 1887:65-77, 149-58, 241-49.

Pasteur, Louis 1882. *Discours de réception à l'Académie française.* 27 April 1882.

Poliakov, Léon 1971. *Le mythe aryen. Essai sur les sources du racisme et des nationalismes.* Paris, Calman-Lévy.

Raumer, Rudolf von 1870. *Geschichte der germanischen Philologie, vorzugweise in Deutschland.* München, Oldenburg.

Ravetz, Jerome R. 1970. *Scientific knowledge and its social problems.* Oxford University Press.

——1972. "Francis Bacon and the reform of philosophy." *Science, medicine and society in the renaissance. Essays to honor Walter Pagel,* ed. by Allen G. Debus. 2 vols. New York, Watson, 2:97-119.

——1973. "Tragedy in the history of science." *Changing perspectives in the history of science. Essays in honour of Joseph Needham.* London. Ed. by Mikuláš Teich and Robert Young. Pp. 204-22.

Renan, Ernest 1878. "Des services rendus aux sciences historiques par la philologie." *Oeuvres complètes,* ed. by Henriette Psichari, 8 (1958), 1213-32. First publ. in *Revue bleue* 1878.

——1890. *L'avenir de la science.* Paris, Calman-Lévy.

Renaud, Paul 1898. Review of Bréal 1897. *Revue de linguistique* 31:60-67.

Saussure, Ferdinand de 1916. *Cours de linguistique générale,* ed. by Tullio de Mauro. Paris 1973. Payot.

——1954. "Notes inédites de F. de Saussure," ed. by R. Godel. *Cahiers Ferdinand de Saussure* 12:49-71.

Scherer, Wilhelm 1875. Review of German version of Whitney 1867 (München 1874). *Preussische Jahrbücher* 35:106-11.

Schleicher, August 1863. *Die Darwinsche Theorie und die Sprachwissenschaft.* Weimar. Böhlau.

——1865. *Über die Bedeutung der Sprache für die Naturgeschichte des Menschen.* Weimar. Böhlau.

——1868. *La théorie de Darwin et la science du langage. De l'importance du langage pour l'histoire naturelle de l'homme,* traduit par M. de Pommard. Paris: Franck. (*Collection philologique,* fasc. 1, avec un avant-propos par M. Michel Bréal.) Translation of Schleicher 1863, 1865.

——1869. *Die deutsche Sprache.* 2nd ed. Stuttgart, Cotta. First ed. 1860.

Siesbye, O. 1887. "Nogle ord til minde om Johan Nicolai Madvig." *Nordisk Tidsskrift for Filologi,* n.s. 8:81-150.

Silverstein, Michael, ed. 1971. *Selected writings of William Dwight Whitney.* Cambridge, Mass. and London, MIT Press.

Skinner, Quentin 1969. "Meaning and understanding in the history of ideas." *History and Theory* 8:3-53.

Stankiewicz, Edward 1974. Review of Koerner 1972a. *Semiotica* 12:171-79.

Taine, Hippolyte 1868. *Les philosophes classiques du XIX siècle en France.* Paris. First ed. 1857 entitled *Les philosophes français du XIXe siècle.* 12 editions by 1912.

——1870. *De l'intelligence.* 2 vols. Paris, Hachette.

Tarde, Gabriel 1896. "L'idée de 'l'organisme social'" *Revue philosophique* 41:637-46.

Taton, René 1976. "Paul Tannery." *DSB* 13:251-56.

Thackray, A. See Merton 1975.

Thomsen, Vilhelm 1902. *Sprogvidenskabens Historie. En kortfattet Fremstilling*. University, Copenhagen.

Thurot, Charles 1870. Review of Madvig, *Grammaire latine. RC* 9:380-87.

———1875. Review of Madvig 1875. *RC* 18:241-45.

Weil, Henri 1844. *De l'ordre des mots dans les langues anciennes comparées aux langues modernes: Question de grammaire générale*. Re-issued 1869 and 1879.

Wells, Rulon 1973. "Uniformitarianism in linguistics." *Dictionary of the History of Ideas. Studies of Selected Pivotal Ideas*. 4:423-31.

Whitney, W. D. 1867. *Language and the study of language*. New York, Scribner.

———1868. Review of *Mémoires de la Société de Linguistique de Paris*. vol. 1. *Nation* 6:331.

———1869. Obituary of August Schleicher. *Nation* 8:70.

———1871. "Schleicher and the physical theory of language." Whitney 1873:298-331. First publ. in *Transactions of the American Philological Association for 1871* (35-64) under the title "Strictures on the views of August Schleicher respecting the nature of language and kindred subjects."

———1873. *Oriental and linguistic studies*. New York, Scribner Armstrong.

———1875a. *The life and growth of language: An outline of linguistic science*. New York, Appleton.

———1875b. "Are languages institutions?" *The Contemporary Review* 25:713-32. Also publ. under the title "Streitfragen der heutigen Sprachphilosophie." *Deutsche Rundschau* 4 (1875) 259-79.

———1876. Review of Hovelacque 1876. *Nation* 22:98.

Worms, René 1894. Obituary of James Darmesteter. *Revue internationale de sociologie* 2: 745-47.

Young, Robert M. 1969. "Malthus and the evolutionists: The common context of biological and social theory." *Past and Present* No. 43:109-45.

———1971. "Darwin's metaphor: Does nature select?" *The Monist* 55:442-503.

———1973. "The historiographic and ideological contexts of the nineteenth-century debate on man's place in nature." *Changing perspectives in the history of science. Essays in honour of Joseph Needham*, ed. by Mikuláš Teich and Robert Young. London. Pp. 344-438. London, Heinemann.

Zloczower. See Ben-David 1962.

Wilhelm von Humboldt and the Linguistic Thought of the French *Idéologues*

In this essay I propose to examine the relationship between the philosophy of the *idéologues* and Wilhelm von Humboldt. Based on the thought of Condillac, this philosophy unfolded with great vigor during the late 1790s, especially in the work of Destutt de Tracy, precisely during the years when Humboldt resided in Paris where he is known, as I shall show, to have had close contacts with the *idéologues* and their work. The central doctrine both in their philosophy and in Humboldt's is the so-called principle of linguistic relativity with its associate doctrines of the ultimate subjectivity of speech and its social nature. These doctrines have generally been credited to Humboldt alone with some dependence on Herder, and they have been seen as especially characteristic of a romantic view of language. In an earlier essay on "The Tradition of Condillac" I have argued that Herder himself was in fact indebted to eighteenth-century French linguistic thought and especially to Condillac.[1] In this essay I argue both that there are no grounds for the claim that Humboldt drew on Herder, and, secondly, that Humboldt himself built on the similar though later version developed by the *idéologues*. The admitted similarity of the thought of Herder and Humboldt on some, though as we shall see not all points derives from common indebtedness to the same tradition and cannot be explained by sequential influence that

This is a revised version of an essay first published in French: "Guillaume de Humboldt et la pensée linguistique des Idéologues." In: *La Grammaire générale: des Modistes aux Idéologues*, ed. by André Joly and Jean Stéfanini (Publications de l'Université de Lille III, 1977), pp. 217-241.

links Humboldt to Herder. Thus, if I am right, both Herder and Humboldt drew on eighteenth-century sources that have generally been considered incompatible with romantic thought. But this creates a dilemma, for both of them are among the foremost exponents of the philosophical doctrines that shaped the literature and criticism of romanticism. Obviously, then, my argument raises doubts about the conventional understanding of the nature and background of these doctrines. In this sense the present essay is a contribution to comparative criticism.

On 15 November 1798, Humboldt wrote to Christian Gottfried Koerner about his life in Paris, where he had arrived almost a year earlier. In spite of reservations, so typical of his changing moods, he stated emphatically, "dass mein Aufenhalt hier in meinem Denken Epoche macht" (1940. 62). ("That my residence here opens a new period in my thinking.") Humboldt's letters have often been cited to show that it was around 1800 that his chief interest became centered on language and its philosophy as the best means of studying man, the individual, and society. On 20 December 1799, he wrote to F. A. Wolf: "In the future I feel that I shall devote myself more exclusively to language study, and that a thorough and philosophically oriented comparison of several languages is a task that I can shoulder after some years of serious study" (GW V. 214). Two years earlier he had written to Koerner: "For the culture of a nation, there is simply nothing that's more important than its language" (1940. 54; 2 Dec. 1797). On 16 June 1804 he again wrote to Wolf, this time from Rome: "Basically everything I work at, also my Pindar, is language study. I believe I have discovered the art of using language as a vehicle to range over the highest and the lowest levels of the world and its multiplicity, and I am steadily becoming more engrossed in this view" (GW V. 266).

At the end of the year he spent in Germany between his return from France in the late summer of 1801 and his departure for Rome in the autumn of 1802, Humboldt felt restless and depressed, again eager to travel, as he admitted in a letter to Schiller (1962. II, 264; 22 Oct. 1803). He had already on 6 February 1802 written to Mme de Staël that he was planning to return to Paris, though there were little problems about "this favored plan, but which I hope to overcome" (1916. 436). But instead of returning to Paris, he went to Rome as Prussian resident accredited to the Vatican. During these years, until his return to Germany in 1808, he was immersed in language studies, based both on the materials his brother Alexander had brought from America and on the rich holdings of the Vatican library. But these studies were guided by the stimulation he had received in Paris. It was in Paris that he first found his philosophical and intellectual vocation in the study of language as well as the orientation and basic principles that guided that study. His exposure to French thought was crucial.

It is this relationship between Humboldt and the *idéologues* in the busy late 1790s that is the subject of this essay. Two sorts of problems present themselves. The first concerns the simple question why this relationship has been ignored in the extensive literature, both old and recent and almost entirely German, that has been devoted to the history and nature of Humboldt's thought. The second concerns some of the basic doctrines. I shall deal with each in turn.

The State of Humboldt Studies

Though it is admitted that Humboldt's decisive turn to language occurred around 1800, this turn has usually been explained by such general observations as that it was a natural consequence of his exposure to another language and culture in France or that in 1799, "during his first Spanish travels, his interest shifted almost imperceptibly from the national character to the national language and thus to language in general" (Ruprecht 1963. 218). Accounts that attempt to be somewhat more precise postulate that Humboldt was indebted to Herder and Hamann, to "die deutsche Bewegung"—the German movement—and to Kant. Or to gain continuity they seek the beginning in his classical studies under F. A. Wolf. Regarding Kant, it may be observed that since Humboldt had gone through several periods of intense study of Kant already by 1793, the inspiration and decisive impulse can hardly be found there. Chronologically the same is true of Wolf, who, however, in so far as he had a philosophy of language, held views of the sort that Humboldt encountered in Paris. With regard to Herder and "die deutsche Bewegung," the matter is somewhat more tangled though no less clear; it will be taken up later.

Humboldt study is in a state of self-imposed retardation, stubbornly ignoring the rich materials that have come into print during the last hundred years, chiefly in the Akademie-Ausgabe (Humboldt 1903-1937) that began publication in 1903. Especially important are the detailed Paris diaries (AA XIV-XV). This attitude is illustrated in a recent essay: "From Rudolf Haym (1856) we have the thorough, still unsurpassed biography that also treats the linguistic work in detail. It is now again available in reprint (1965) and may be cited here above and in place of all other studies" (CT 535).[2] Haym's work enjoys deserved stature as an expression of its time, but as plain biography its value today is severely limited by the simple fact that, given its date, Haym lacked access to the very large body of documentation that has become available only in this century. Including the hitherto unpublished and revealing early writings as well as the Paris diaries and much of the correspondence, this material makes Haym's biography woefully inadequate in regard to both facts and interpretation. Since Haym there have been many shorter biographies and treatments of special aspects of Humboldt's life and thought, but they have all, with a single exception, failed to undertake any significant revision. Though limited by the sources, Haym's chapter on the years 1797-1802 made no effort to explore what was going on in Paris during those years or even to name the men Humboldt was already then known to have associated with. The long section on "Sprachwissenschaft" (pp. 429-560) is the source of the opinion that Humboldt worked from Kant, was indebted to Herder, and owed nothing to French thought.

For whatever reason, Haym's limitations were not entirely those of his sources. This fact emerges clearly from a comparison with Gustav Schlesier's earlier and longer biography (1843-1845), published when the available materials were still more limited—Schlesier had only the first four volumes of the edition of *Gesammelte Werke*. For the years 1798-1808 (II, 1-133), Schlesier's treatment is much more complete than Haym's, and many of his insights have been confirmed by later publication. He made a serious and successful effort to understand the Paris scene. He knew that "among the scientific researches of the French, it was especially studies devoted to nature and to language that stood out brilliantly. Such names as Lalande, Geoffroy Saint-Hilaire, Cuvier, Delambre and others illuminated the study of nature; in language study it was partly classicists, partly linguists that distinguished themselves" (II, 18). Schlesier knew that the French were then busy with general and comparative language study, cited Silvestre de Sacy as an example, and remarked that "Humboldt began at this time more and more to direct his interest toward general language studies." Schlesier understood the role of signs in contemporary linguistic thought, knew that Basque was already then a subject of linguistic interest in Paris, and concluded his section on Humboldt's linguistic studies (II, 484-539) with an observation whose importance has been forgotten since Haym: "Paris had already at the beginning of the century become the center of modern language study; here the researches of the English were first continued, who along with their Asiatic realm had also won the core language of the indo-germanic group of languages." Unlike Schlesier, Haym did not even suggest that French thought played a role in Humboldt's development. Perhaps Haym has been valued because he kept Humboldt safely within the German tradition, but for those who expect a biography to offer reliable information and interpretation, Schlesier has stood the test of time much better than Haym. It is this unfounded yet enthusiastic faith in Haym that has been responsible for the unscholarly retardation of Humboldt studies.

The only exception is a brilliant book that has been ignored by most and maligned by many because it demythologizes the idealized nineteenth-century image of Humboldt presented by Haym. This is Kaehler's *Wilhelm von Humboldt und der Staat. Ein Beitrag zur Geschichte deutscher Lebensgestaltung um 1800*, first published in 1927 and re-issued in 1963, the year of Kaehler's death. Fully using the new material on the Paris years, Kaehler shows that this period was decisive for Humboldt's intellectual development in general and for his political philosophy in particular (see esp. pp. 153-176).[3] Kaehler points out, for instance, that the new materials disprove Haym's claim that Humboldt in Paris took little interest in what was going on around him, being chiefly preoccupied with the past (Kaehler 490). The hostile reception of Kaehler's brilliant book reveals the retardation of Humboldt studies that has been caused by subservience to Haym.

Herder and Humboldt

The belief that Humboldt was deeply indebted to Herder's *Abhandlung über den Ursprung der Sprache* (1772) is generally credited to Haym's Humboldt biography and to the fuller statement of this opinion in his biography of Herder (1880-1885. II, 408-409). This opinion has recently been reaffirmed by Gipper-Schmitter and other interpreters, e.g., in such statements as this: "With Herder's prize essay begins the era of linguistic philosophy" (Aarsleff 1974, above p. 195).[4] Neither in 1856 nor in 1885 did Haym substantiate this claim, nor did he consider the possibility that there might be other sources. The repetition in 1885 is puzzling, for in the meantime Steinthal (1858) had argued against any such dependence in a book that is still the most substantial treatment of the problem. Pott (1876) accepted Steinthal's argument on this point. Since Haym ignores both Steinthal and Pott, the reassertion of his claim in 1885 cannot be cited against their findings. Gipper-Schmitter, however, put trust in Haym as an answer to Steinthal and Pott (CT 520).[5]

Feeling hard pressed on this sensitive point, Gipper-Schmitter argue that Herder is "repeatedly mentioned" in Humboldt's letters and diaries, that he knew Herder personally, corresponded with him, and even gave the title—but no more—of Herder's prize essay in the notes he took on his teacher Engel's tutorials in philosophy. All this is true, but it surely does not help the argument. Herder's name occurs in the diaries and notes, but without any indication that the subjects help support the claims that are being made. It is known that Humboldt corresponded with Herder, but the authoritative bibliographical source (Goedeke) does not indicate that the letters have been printed. If Gipper-Schmitter know of any such correspondence and its contents, which of course is crucial, it would be important to know the particulars. The mention of the title in the notes proves nothing; first, because we all have old notes taken in school with titles of books with contents we never knew or have long since forgotten; second, because if this argument is used, it must also be noted that Condillac is cited on the very next page along with other potentially relevant names. In other words, Herder does not at all occupy a privileged position in Humboldt's tutorial notes.

In the printed letters Herder's name occurs rarely, except in those to Schiller and *An eine Freundin* (Humboldt 1962 and 1909). In spite of the frequent mention of Herder in the Schiller letters, the subjects of those passages have no relevance whatever to our problem.[6] In the letters *An eine Freundin* we find the longest passage on Herder that I know of in Humboldt's letters. It concludes: "He was philosopher, poet, and savant, but he was not truly great in any of these disciplines" (II, 313-316; 6 Oct. 1833). The implications of this passage are similar to what we find in a curious entry in the Paris diary that records Humboldt's unfavorable impression of Bernardin de St.-Pierre; it ends: "For the most part he is surely missing his vocation and makes the mistake of entering a field in which he is bound to lose—how far can it be said that he has a head much like Herder's?" (AA XIV, 383-385; 27 Dec. 1797). Is it likely that Humboldt would have written about Herder in such terms if he had felt deeply indebted to him, or that he would have failed to single out Herder's contribution to the philosophy of language? Still, begging the question, Gipper-Schmitter conclude: "It is thus entirely beyond question that Humboldt knew Herder's writings" (CT 520). These efforts do not dispel doubts about Humboldt's debt to Herder. On the contrary, they tend rather to strengthen them. And the question still remains, if Humboldt really knew Herder's essay in 1785-1786 when he took notes on Engel's tutorials and if, as claimed, it meant anything to him, why did it not have any effect until much later when he was in Paris?

The insistence on Humboldt's debt to Herder's essay also raises other problems. Herder wrote on language throughout his career, and the views presented in his early writings differed much from those of the later writings. It is generally agreed, for instance, that Herder's preface (1784) to the German translation (done at his suggestion) of Monboddo's *Of the Origin and Progress of Language* is an admission that he no longer stood by the doctrines of his earlier essay (1772). But those who link Herder and Humboldt make no distinctions; they read Herder's prize essay as an expression of what is said to be the foundation of the romantic philosophy of language, as distinct from the rationalist-materialist doctrines they reserve for the French, thus setting Herder and Condillac apart. Neither Herder himself nor his contemporaries saw things that way. The Berlin Academy's initial report on the prize-essay said that for Herder the origin of language, "is purely animalistic, that is to say, it is a result of the combination of the organic structure of man with the mental faculties that reside in a body so organized, and of the circumstances in which the animal is placed." The longer report from the same time but published later, said that according to Herder, "human language depends so closely on reflection that only one step more will guide man to this important discovery," and that man has "a nature that is essentially different from that of the animals. And this difference is entirely produced by the ability to reflect, to record our thoughts, and to link them by means of language." These reports give Herder an unmistakable Condillacian cast on these basic principles, strikingly evident in the role he assigned to reflection.[7]

Ernst Cassirer and others who ignore Condillac single out "this emphasis on reflection, which Herder, in his essay on the origin of language, considers the crucial intellectual factor of all verbal creation" (1933. 52). Without any mention of Condillac or French philosophy, Lammers says: "Humboldt has clearly recognized the excellence of Herder's point of view. He has made the concept of reflection his own . . . Herder's concept of reflection is for Humboldt the foundation of the nature of thinking" (1936. 50-51). Gipper-Schmitter cryptically observe that "Herder's 'Besonnenheit' and 'Réflexion' are more profoundly and consistently thought through than the 'réflexion' of his predecessors" (CT 575).[8] Such passages make the failure of the conventional history apparent.

In the 1790s Humboldt wrote a brief set of notes "Ueber Denken und Sprechen" (AA VII, 581-583)—"On Thinking and Speaking"—that may well be his earliest specific statement on this subject that was to become so central for him. These notes contain these three basic principles: that thinking relies on reflection; that reflection is advanced by artificial manmade signs that segment the spatially un-differentiated 'painting' seen by the eye; and that these signs, being vocal, necessarily follow in temporal sequence, in other words the principle of the linearity of speech that plays a fundamental role in Condillac's argument. This combination of interrelated principles bears close resemblance to what we find in Condillac (also born out by other details in the notes), perhaps especially as set forth in the *Grammaire* of the *Cours d'études*. This combination is not in Herder. I am not saying that Humboldt drew directly on Condillac. He may have for in the late 1790s while in Paris he took very extensive notes on Condillac; but whatever the source, Condillac is in it.[9]

It might be argued that the Berlin Academy reports were biased in favor of doctrines foreign to Herder's thought, but this solution is not possible. Herder was deeply troubled by the reaction of Hamann, whose reading of the *Abhandlung* agreed with the Academy's. In February 1772, Herder wrote to his future wife about his fears concerning the consequences of the publication of his prize-essay: "It is a disaster, I wish it didn't exist. Today I wouldn't write it for anything, and never again write anything like it" (Düntzer and Herder 1856-1857. III, 178). In May the situation was still more serious: "I have not deserved Hamann's review; it is obviously nothing but a spiteful lampoon" (Düntzer and Herder 1861-1862. II, 27).[10]

Herder was in fact very familiar with French thought, a fact that is rarely mentioned in the secondary literature—perhaps for fear that doing so would open a Pandora's box of embarrassment? There is clear documentary evidence that Herder read at least Part II of Condillac's *Essai sur l'origine des connoissances humaines* (1746)—the part that deals with the origin of language—during the years prior to the writing of the prize-essay. Though this evidence has long been in print and is of obvious importance, it is never mentioned.[11] It is also known that Herder during these years took notes on articles in the French *Encyclopédie*, chiefly on matters "qui concernent la grammaire" (Dobbeck 1961. 146). We also know that Herder's library was rich in French literature. These holdings stand out not merely numerically, but also by the fact that they contain "the writings of literally all the better-known representatives of the French Enlightenment, including those that are both philosophically and politically the most radical" (Stolpe 1966).[12]

I see no way around the conclusion that there are no grounds for accepting the conventional claim, based on Haym, that Humboldt in

Herder's prize-essay found a new romantic linguistic philosophy that satisfied his reputed distaste for the reputed materialism and sensationalism of Condillac and his followers. In fact, this claim seems to be a mid-nineteenth-century myth that has never been supported by evidence; owing to its ideological appeal, the myth has been taken for history. At the time its plausibility relied on the belief, still widely credited, that French and German thought were separated by a gulf that precluded mutual interrelations and continuity, indebtedness, and influence. Both in France and Germany this view formed part of the reaction against the French Revolution and eighteenth-century thought. But some of those who were involved in events around 1800 did not see it that way, e.g., Humboldt and Friedrich Schlegel.[13]

The Basic Doctrine

There are two interlocked principles that form the foundation of Humboldt's linguistic thought; they occur together thoughout his work. The first is the ultimate subjectivity of language; the second is what he called "un désir irrésistable de sociabilité" (AA III, 323), that drives men to speak in order to communicate and be understood. By its social nature and function, language mediates between the individual and society, thus largely overcoming the subjectivity by expressing—indeed by cooperatively creating—the shared universe of thought that is determined by common needs and mutual interests. Since the diversity of mankind finds expression in individual languages, linguistic study becomes the chief instrument of the study of man, of anthropology.

Humboldt first laid down these principles in one of his earliest writings on these questions, written during the years 1801-1802 when he was immediately under the impact of his recent exposure to French philosophy. In "Fragmente der Monographie über die Basken" (first published in 1907) he wrote: "It would never have occurred to an isolated human being to hit upon the notion of speaking. For the predisposition for language is inseparable from the predisposition for sociability." Still, the subjective element cannot be removed entirely: "Not even in the most advanced culture and when it concerns the simplest things does one person fully and thoroughly understand another" (AA VII, 596-597). The principles of the "Fragmente" are repeated in Humboldt's great work on the Kawi language, first published just after his death and generally considered the most mature expression of his thought. The repetition occurs in a section on

"Natur und Beschaffenheit der Sprache überhaupt" (AA VII, 52-65) —on "the Nature and Constitution of Language in general"—which is often cited as an especially concise statement of Humboldt's basic ideas.[14] Here he wrote about language, the individual and society: "The reciprocal effect of the individual on language becomes more evident when we consider that the individuality of a language exists only in a metaphorical sense, while the true individuality lies only in the speaker at any moment. At a given word, no man thinks directly and precisely the same as another" (AA VII, 64). Let us take a closer look at these principles and their background.

Among the ideas that have been used to link Herder and Humboldt is Herder's principle that "each human being 'in the true metaphysical sense' speaks his own language, a thought that also recurs in Humboldt" (CT 527).[15] Condillac stated this principle twice in the *Essai*: "It is enough to study a human being for a while to learn *his language*; I say his language, for everyone has his own according to his passions," and "the same words spoken by the same mouth have quite different significations" (*Oeuvres* I, 98b and 107b).[16] In the fundamental article on etymology in the *Encyclopédie*, Turgot likewise observed that "neither two human beings, nor perhaps the same human being at different times, attach precisely the same idea to the same word" (1756. 108).[17] Many other examples can be cited to show that Herder's principle is not original with him. The most representative linguistic statement of the *idéologues* was the "Mémoire sur la faculté de penser" by Destutt de Tracy, who was an avowed follower of Condillac. He was very explicit on the subjectivity of language and developed this principle and its implications in great detail. He wrote:

> We hardly ever have perfect assurance that the particular idea we have formed owing to a particular sign, by these means, is exactly in every respect the same as the idea attached to it by the person we got it from and by other persons who use that sign. . . . And there is more: we have agreed that every sign is perfect for its inventor. So far so good; but strictly speaking that holds true only in the moment of invention: for when he uses the same sign at another moment in life or in another disposition of mind, it is not at all certain that he himself brings together exactly the same collection of ideas under that sign as the first time. (1798. 412).[18]

As soon as we turn to the question how this subjectivity is overcome, we again see that Humboldt is within the Condillac tradition along with Destutt de Tracy.

Destutt de Tracy's "Mémoire" is rich in arguments and principles that appear again in Humboldt. Thus with reference to the principle of subjectivity, de Tracy says that it must be admitted that "these imperfections of signs, being inherent to their nature or rather to our nature, are irremovable," for "if we note that these signs have no meaning until we have formed our own idea of what they represent, we see that it follows that a fully formed idea is something absolutely intransmissible" (1798. 414, 419).[19] Like Humboldt later, de Tracy argues that this imperfection is in large measure corrected both by experience and by the steady intersubjective testing and adjustment of private conceptions that occur in the social exchange of speech, a process he calls "la rectification successive des premières idées" (1798. 447).[20] In the "Fragmente" Humboldt restated the same principle: "Each spoken word was an attempt to make oneself understood by another person. It would never have occurred to an isolated human being to hit upon the notion of speaking" (AA VII, 596).[21] As was to be expected, Humboldt repeated the same point in the passage of his last work to which I have already referred: "In other words, the conception is translated into actual objectivity without at the same time being deprived of its subjectivity. This can only be accomplished by language. As an outward phenomenon, however, language develops only socially, and a human being understands himself merely in so far as he has tentatively tested the understandability of his words on others" (AA VII, 55).[22]

For de Tracy, the *idéologues*, and Humboldt these two interlocked principles of subjectivity and sociability gave language its central role both in the study of man—in anthropology—and in the education of man, i.e., in the process Humboldt called "Bildung." They all believed in the educability of man toward perfection. Following F. A. Wolf, Humboldt made Greek the chief instrument of this education in the schools. It is interesting, therefore, that Wolf rested his rationale on Condillacian principles.[23]

Surely the reader has already noticed that our subject in the preceding pages has been the principle of linguistic relativity, or rather its foundation. It has been called a "genuine discovery" of Humboldt's (Gipper 1965. 10), a view that is conventional and ubiquitous. Far from being his discovery, it is commonplace eighteenth-century doctrine, stated, discussed, and argued frequently right into the early nineteenth century, chiefly in French writings and never so busily as by the *idéologues* during the 1790s, amply illustrated in de Tracy's writings. It is the foundation of their anthropology. It is abundantly illustrated in Degérando's "Considérations sur les diverses méthodes à suivre dans l'observation des peuples sauvages."[24] This doctrine had been stated and developed in Condillac's *Essai*, most obviously in the long chapter "Du génie des langues" (*Oeuvres* I, 98a-104a), summarized in the sentence: "Everything confirms that each language expresses the character of the people who speak it." It is the subject of the "Réflexions" of Maupertuis, who framed the topic for which J. D. Michaëlis gained the prize of the Berlin Academy in 1759, with the telltale title *Von dem Einfluss der Meinungen in die Sprache und der Sprache in die Meinungen (On the Influence of Opinions on Language and of Language on Opinions)*. And Michaëlis's essay in turn formulated the topic to which Herder addressed himself in his *Abhandlung* (Aarsleff 1976. 535-536; 1975b. 397-398 and 431-433; for further details see Aarsleff 1974, repr. above).

The relativity principle and its subjective basis are a consequence of the epistemology that Condillac took over from Locke. This epistemology and its revolutionary linguistic effect were first developed in the seventeenth century when the new science rejected the Adamic language doctrine — the doctrine of divine origin — with its postulate that words somehow refer directly to things, like a nomenclature that constitutes an inventory, in favor of the view that we can know only the external manifestations of phenomena. Thus, language being manmade, even words for physical objects are not certain. Words refer not to objects but to ideas we have in our minds. Here is the cause of linguistic subjectivity. Ideas may be "bundled" differently among individual speakers of the same language and among different languages. Words, said Locke, are like knots that tie bundles of ideas together. Mistaken trust in words has caused the assumption that they refer directly to things, as if there were a reliable "double conformity" between thing-idea and idea-word. Therefore Locke made it a principle that it is often impossible to do a faithful translation from one language into another.[25]

This principle is so basic that it is discussed in a host of writings, often under the rubric "génie des langues." There would be no need to learn it directly from Locke or Condillac. The double-conformity principle recurs in Humboldt's work on the Kawi language in the section already cited that contains a summary of basic eighteenth-century linguistic philosophy: "The entire manner of the subjective perception of objects is necessarily carried over into the formation and use of language. For the word originates precisely in the perception, it is not a copy of the object itself, but of the image the object creates in the mind." The consequence is this familiar doctrine, already noted in the seventeenth century: "Since all objective perception is unavoidably mixed with subjectivity, it follows that we, even independently of language, can consider every human individuality as having its own view of the world. But it becomes still more so by language.

With objects man lives chiefly according to the manner in which language brings them to him, indeed since his feelings and actions depend on his conceptions, exclusively so" (AA VII, 59-60).[26] The linguistic relativity principle is not Humboldt's discovery.

The relativity principle is the foundation of interest in national languages and dialects, of Herder's "Volksgeist." Also in this respect Herder and "die deutsche Bewegung" are merely the beneficiaries of contemporary French philosophy. This has had a profound effect on the poetic practice of romanticism and on the criticism that supported it, evident in Wordsworth, for example. The wide acceptance of this principle also shows in the fascinating answers the Abbé Grégoire received to the questionnaire he sent out to all parts of France in the early 1790s in connection with the plan to impose a single "langue de la liberté" on all of France in order to strengthen the central political and educational power of the government. One of the questions said: "What is the respective influence of the local dialect on customs and of these on your dialect?" One typical answer was: "The influence of local idiom on customs is, I believe, absolutely nil: it is customs that influence language: Du Tremblay, in his treatise on languages, says: 'It is with entire nations as with an individual person. Their language is the living expression of their customs, of their genius, of their inclinations, and a study of the language suffices to penetrate the entire thinking of their soul and all the passions of their heart. Thus each language is necessarily tied to the perfections and shortcomings of its speakers'" (Certeau 1975. 223).[27] This is, if you wish, pure Herder, pure Condillac, pure romantic doctrine—which suggests that the concept and history of romanticism may stand in need of revision.[28]

The respondent concluded his answer with a citation from the *Encyclopédie* and Voltaire on "le génie des langues." Other answers to Grégoire's questionnaire tell the same story—and the respondents had not read Herder or the *idéologues* or Humboldt. Most insisted that their local dialects were cherished by their speakers and indestructible. The unification plan was adopted but was not put into effect, though barely half the population of France had a command of Parisian French.

Conclusion

The conclusion is not in doubt. A few years before he came to Paris, Humboldt had written a sketch for a comparative anthropology, "Plan einer vergleichende Anthropologie" (first published in 1903, but written in 1795), in which he counted language among the mere outward manifestations of man: "All the external aspects can be summed up in physical build and demeanor, stature, color of the face and hair, physiognomy, language, gait, and gestures in general," while he identified "the internal differences" with feelings, inclinations, and passions (AA I, 399). His "anthropologische Wende"—"anthropological turn"—that placed language in a very different relationship had not yet occurred.

The Paris diaries show that Humboldt spent much time in the company of the men and women who represented the intellectual and philosophical life of the day. He formed a close friendship with Mme de Staël (continued in an extensive correspondence), often visited Diderot's daughter Marie Vandeul, had lively and frequent discussion with Condorcet's widow, and was regularly a guest at the house of the aging Mme Helvétius at Auteuil, where since long before the Revolution she had kept the salon that is known as the Society of Auteuil, aptly called the Port-Royal of the *idéologues*, just as Mme Helvétius has been styled "notre-dame d'Auteuil." In its early years, from 1771 on, her salon had been frequented by the *philosophes*, including Condillac and Franklin, and it was now the gathering place of their philosophical descendants. It was the chief visible and continuous link between the years before and after 1789. On one of these occasions Humboldt noted in his diary "the usual people there." They were the *idéologues* whose names occur most frequently of all in the diary: Cabanis, Volney, de Tracy, Sieyès, Degérando, Roederer, Jacquemont, Joseph Dominique Garat, Ginguené, St.- Pierre, and Laromiguière. Most of them were members of the second class of the Institut National, devoted to "les sciences morales et politiques," and especially of the first section whose subject was "analyse des sensations et des idées," that is, the philosophy that stemmed from Condillac. Cabanis identified the subject of this section: "Physiology, the analysis of ideas, and ethics are merely three branches of one and the same science which can rightly call itself *the science of man*." To the passage was added this note: "That's what the Germans call *anthropology*; and under this title they in fact comprise the three principal subjects we are talking about" (I, 126).

Humboldt's sudden turn to linguistic anthropology occurred in this milieu. He took over not merely an orientation but also basic principles that form the core of his linguistic philosophy. All that he later wrote on this subject shows how heavy his debt was. In this sense Humboldt was one of the *idéologues*. What he said in the letter to Koerner—"that my residence here opens a new period in my thinking"—became truer than he could have realized when he wrote those words barely a year after his arrival in Paris.

I am aware that many will find this conclusion surprising, even absurd, but I see no way around it. And since it has never been seriously considered—or considered at all—I know of no argument against it. There are examples, however, of similar surprises. Recently Eugenio Coseriu has shown that the typological distinction between analytic and synthetic languages generally attributed to A. W. Schlegel, in all its essentials owes its formulation to Adam Smith in his "Considerations concerning the first Formation of Languages" (1761), a work that was widely popular in France in the late eighteenth century. Yet, as Coseriu points out, the historiography of the subject has never taken note of this fact.[29]

Similarly, in a large, critical, well-informed, and excellent book on Alexander von Humboldt, Charles Minguet has severely criticized the conventional biographies, chiefly German: "The biographical studies devoted to him chiefly by German specialists leave great gaps, the consequences of a remarkable methodological deficiency. . . . Humboldt we are told is the product of the 'Goethe-Zeit,' his philosophy we are again told is that of 'Goethe-Herder.' . . . Hanno Beck, for example, mentions neither Diderot nor the *Encyclopédie* in his Humboldt biography!" (64-65). Minguet also points out that these simplicities are the work of "les classificateurs impénitent"—of impenitent classifiers—who put trust in conventional but unfounded categories such as empiricism and rationalism. Thus Minguet undertakes an exciting revaluation of Alexander von Humboldt that takes full account of his debt to French thought at the same time as he advances a severe critique of German historiography. It is evident that our understanding of Wilhelm von Humboldt demands similar revision for the same reasons.

Finally, it is widely believed that the philosophy of the *idéologues* was forgotten and never again played a role in linguistic thought. This is not true. When in the 1860s, led by Michel Bréal, the reaction set in against the fifty-year dominance of German philology, the *idéologues* were again taken seriously. Bréal wrote: "Our forefathers of the school of Condillac, those *idéologues* who for two generations have been the target of a certain school of criticism, were closer to the truth when they said, in their simple and honest fashion, that words are signs." In the context of this renewed respect for the thought of the eighteenth century, which was not confined to linguistics, both Bréal and Otto Jespersen cited Humboldt with approval. Following Bréal, Jespersen took as his guide, "an idea expressed long ago and with considerable emphasis by Wilhelm von Humboldt, that language means speaking, and that speaking means action on the part of a human being to make himself understood by somebody else." The *idéologues* and Humboldt were revived together because they stressed that the study of language must be man centered. It was after all Destutt de Tracy who, perhaps following Rousseau, was the first to call language "une institution sociale."

Notes

1. On Condillac, see Aarsleff 1974 and 1975a, both repr. above. The argument of this paper was given earlier formulation in lectures at Princeton in May 1971 and at the universities of Gothenburg, Trondheim, Oslo, and Edinburgh in the spring of 1972.

2. Cf. Gipper 1965. 3:"This account is unsurpassed and can be most highly recommended." I often refer to the essay by Gipper and Schmitter because their treatment is a compendium of conventional writing and opinion on the subject, full of further references.

3. Kaehler does not treat Humboldt's linguistic studies. For a distressing but typical example of the virulence and feeble argument with which Kaehler is attacked and dismissed, see Menze 1965, esp. pp. 18ff.

4. Haym 1856. 472, also cited Humboldt's admitted respect for A. F. Bernhardi's *Anfangsgründe der Sprachwissenschaft* (1805), but its date precludes that this work can have played a role in Humboldt's turn to language; the same is true of Bernhardi's *Sprachlehre* (1801-1803).

5. Gipper-Schmitter also cite other sources for the occurrence of "nearly verbal agreements" between Herder and Humboldt. But the given similarities are in fact not verbal but conceptual and could just as well derive from other sources; no alternatives are considered.

6. On 6 November 1795 Schiller asked for advice on books for the study of Greek. In his answer (20 November 1795) Humboldt mentioned C. G. Ewerbeck's translation of James Harris's *Hermes, oder eine philosophische Untersuchung über die Sprache und die allgemeine Grammatik* (1788), "of which a good German translation is among my books" (Humboldt 1962. I, 228). The recommendation of *Hermes* is interesting also for the reason that it had great stature in Paris, where François Thurot in 1796 brought out a translation at the encouragement of the linguistic philosophers, especially of Garat, to whom the translation is dedicated.

7. Hamann's critique and the Academy report have recently been made available in French translation in Pénisson 1977. For Condillac the origin of language is not animalistic, but the product of 'réflexion,' which is exclusively human. For details, see Aarsleff 1975a on "Condillac's speechless statue," repr. above. In CT 528, Gipper-Schmitter put trust in an incomprehensible argument that tries to attach different meanings to Herder's 'Besonnenheit' and 'Reflexion.' It is curious that Herder himself and his readers today have not considered that his critique of Condillac (1772. 17-18) seems unfounded, and that Herder some ten pages later advances the argument he seemed to reject in Condillac. Similarly Herder's argument (*ibid.*, 20 ff) about the narrow sphere of animal activity coupled with reliable instinct as opposed to man's wider sphere, less reliable instinct, and the means and need to find compensation for that weakness are closely parallelled by Condillac's argument in *Traité des animaux* in the chapter "De l'instinct et de la raison" (*Oeuvres* I, 362-365), a work to which Herder has just referred. This chapter also drew Humboldt's attention.

8. At this point they suggest that regarding Degérando, "we must here take influence from Herder into account," on the grounds that Degérando in 1804 published an obituary of Herder. Apart from the inherent weakness of that argument, even small knowledge of the relevant literature makes the suggestion implausible.

9. On the linearity of speech see Aarsleff 1974, above p. 157, and 1976, 533, n. 21. Lammers (pp. 31-33) prints two hitherto unpublished pieces on syntax ("Wortstellung") and grammar. If we accept his suggestion that they go with "Ueber Denken und Sprechen," my argument about the relation of Condillac is strengthened. Lammers suggests that the watermark dating, 1795-1796, for "Ueber Denken und Sprechen" may need to be revised forward a few years toward 1801, which means that it may be a fruit of the Paris years. There would on other grounds seem to be good reason for this revision, which also strengthens my argument.

10. Several interpreters (e.g., CT 523-524) have tried to resolve the conflict between Hamann and Herder by arguing that Herder also accepted the divine origin of language, contained in the view that man was created with the capacity for language. Since that view is also Condillac's, however, it obviously cannot be used to set Herder and Condillac apart. Herder anticipated this argument in regard to the controversy with Hamann: "You see that he [Hamann] actually wishes to postulate divine origin, but in fact only postulates it in human terms" (Düntzer and Herder 1861-1862. I, 334; to Nicolai 2 July 1772).

11. See Aarsleff 1974, above p. 152. These passages are omitted from Erich Heintel's widely used anthology, *Herders Sprachphilosophie* (Hamburg: Felix Meiner, 1960).

12. Of the total of 7747 items, by far the largest is the category of belles-lettres with 2302 items, no fewer than 934 of them in French followed by 679 in German. Library lists must be used with caution, but along with other evidence the numbers are telling.

13. In 1802-1803, Friedrich Schlegel wrote some critical "observations sur l'ouvrage de Charles de Villers, *La Philosophie de Kant*," in which Villers had argued for the superiority of Kantian philosophy over French *idéologie*. Schlegel did not share that view: "This opposition does not exist, it is not even possible. . . . It is clear that in all of French *idéologie* there is hardly anything that idealism cannot accept, especially when it is treated with the precision and in the truly scientific spirit that one observes in Destutt de Tracy's *Projet d'éléments d'idéologie* . . . *Idéologie* would be an excellent introduction to the principles of transcendental philosophy, too much neglected by German writers" (Schlegel 1802-1803. 544-545). In August 1804 Humboldt wrote a letter that would seem to show that he shared that view. He wrote of the richness that is found "in the field of empirical philosophy that is now being so culpably neglected" (1939. 170). He was writing against the tendency of a recent review of French philosophy in the *Intelligenzblatt der Jenaischen Allgemeinen Literaturzeitung*, which had said: "They seemed barely to suspect that philosophy needs a foundation, and in their examination of the real nature of knowledge they did not go beyond Locke and Condillac, whose sensualism was touched up with the physical-metaphysical ideas of Bonnet and others." Eduard Spranger has argued that Humboldt's "more strictly Kantian period" is limited to the years 1789-1798, and has pointed to the fact, often ignored, that Humboldt "repeatedly declares that the spiritual is merely the finest bloom of the material" (1908. 63, 87). Spranger considered this thesis incompatible with Kantianism. The Paris diary, which does not cover the last year in Paris, shows that Humboldt fought bravely on Kantian grounds against French philosophy, but it is evident that he found ways of accommodation. The materialist-sensualist interpretation of Condillac has often been dismissed, rightly, both at the time by, e.g., La Harpe, Laromiguière, François Thurot, and Degérando, and by later and recent interpreters. This interpretation belongs to the political reaction that began when Napoleon in January 1803 reorganized the Institut National to do away with its Class II, the arena of the *idéologues*, calling it "this nest of pestilential ideology." For related matters, see Aarsleff 1976. 527-529, and Aarsleff 1971.

14. Cf. Lammers: "For these preliminary statements actually contain all the basic principles that became the norm for Humboldt's later linguistic studies" (p. 61).

15. This is a point that has often been made with the same intent. Cf., e.g., "A number of Humboldt's general problems are laid down as seeds in Herder; but we also encounter specific observations, such as the individual differences of the conceptions we attach to words" (Scheinert 1908. 184).

16. The former passage is repeated in *L'Art de parler* in this form: "It happens that the same words in different mouths, and often in the same, have very different meanings" (*Oeuvres* I, 762). This principle is an inescapable consequence of Locke's epistemology. Cf. Locke, *Essay*, Book III, ch. ii, par. 8: "But that they *signify* only men's peculiar *ideas* . . . is evident in that they often fail to excite in others (even that use the same language) the same *ideas* we take them to be signs of . . . [so] that no one hath the power to make others have the same *ideas* in their minds that he has, when they use the same words that he does." Cf. also *ibid.*, par. 1.

17. On the opening page of the same article, Turgot said: "The circumstances that by their recurrence determine the meaning of a word in the mind of each individual are never exactly the same for two individuals."

18. De Tracy's "Mémoire" consists of five papers read to the Institut in 1796 and in February 1798. The quoted passages are repeated *verbatim* in de Tracy 1801. 315. Humboldt mentioned de Tracy's "Mémoire" in the Paris diary already on 27 February 1798 (AA XIV, 426), though it did not appear in print until August of that year. On 20 May (AA XIV, 470) Humboldt was visited by de Tracy, who gave full particulars of the contents and of his argument; this shows how closely and deliberately Humboldt kept informed about these matters. There are many other close similarities between de Tracy and Humboldt. About the difference between man and animals, Condillac repeatedly stated that "it is not surprising that man, who is superior both by virtue of his organic being and by the nature of the spirit that animates him, alone has the gift of speech" (*Oeuvres* I, 361b). This is an eighteenth-century commonplace often asserted, e.g., by de Tracy who says that for language to be possible, "thus prior to language, we must have the means of reciprocally understanding each other . . . and this means can only be the consequence of our being, a necessary effect of our organic being" (1801. 267). Humboldt makes the same point. Secondly, in the "Mémoire" (402f, repeated in 1801, 245f) de Tracy, like Condillac, cited the observation of children who had grown up in isolation from human society (the "enfants abandonnés" or "enfants sylvestres"), pointing out that they can live a long while without language. In the "Fragmente" Humboldt wrote: "Human beings could for a long while lead an animal existence, and it is proved in recent time by children who have been found in the wild" (AA VII, 595). It was during Humboldt's Paris years that the Aveyron boy was found and brought to Paris for study.

19. In de Tracy 1801 the former passage has this form: "These imperfections of signs are inherent to their nature or rather to that of our intellectual faculties. . . . Thus it is impossible to do away with them entirely" (p. 317). This passage also recurs in 1801. 311 in slightly different form.

20. Cf. de Tracy 1801. 352: "We can never be entirely certain that our interlocutors comprise precisely the same combinations as we do under the same signs; so that in using them we often deceive ourselves and do not understand others. There in large measure is the source of the gradual rectification that we observe in our ideas during early life as well as the change in our mode of conceiving the same objects in different periods of our lives and the difference of opinions among speakers on the ideas expressed by certain words."

21. Cf. de Tracy 1801. 322: "An isolated human being would never have conceived the idea of making a language for himself."

22. For a French translation, see Humboldt 1974.

23. See the passage in Wolf 1807. II, 863-870, which develops the argument at length, concluding: "For exercises in the ability to think carried out on languages . . . spur us on to reflect on the world of the intellect as we treat the signs of our ideas themselves as objects."

24. This essay, dated September 1800, is available in the two items given under Degérando 1800. For discussion and references, see Stocking 1964. Degérando's essay has a wealth of later Humboldtian ideas which for reasons of space cannot be discussed here. It is, of course, possible that Humboldt knew Degérando's essay.

25. See Aarsleff 1964, above pp. 54, 76n37. The chief passages in Locke's *Essay* are in Book III, ch. v, and in Book II, ch. xxii, par. 2-6. This doctrine was stated by Marin Mersenne in the 1620s and 1630s; see Crombie 1974 for excellent discussion and references and also the article on John Wilkins repr. above. It was in this context that the Conferences of Théophraste Renaudot, on 4 January 1638, discussed the same topic that Herder answered 132 years later: "Whether men would form a language not having learned any other."

26. See also AA III, 314, and the Introduction to "Agamemnon" (AA VIII, 129-133) on which Humboldt was at work during the Paris years. Depending heavily on Cassirer, Hansen-Løve finds the source of the subjectivity principle in Kant, then attributes its linguistic consequences to Humboldt's "Copernican Revolution," as he calls it. Since Hansen-Løve in conventional fashion pays no attention whatever to French philosophy, he misses the fact that the revolution had already occurred. In a useful article Weimann (1965) has shown anticipations of linguistic relativity in Bacon and Locke, but argues that they were forgotten; thus the day is saved for the traditional historiography — and for Humboldt — although the fact is precisely that the historiography of which we are the victims has failed to see the continued importance of the principle through the seventeenth and eighteenth centuries.

27. The cited text is Jean Frain du Tremblay, *Traité des langues* (1703). Here the quoted words are preceded by this passage: "Speech is the mirror of the soul . . . man paints for himself in his language. In fact, what can man talk about except the abundance of his heart, of what he thinks, knows, and loves?"

28. I have briefly discussed the grounds and implications in 1976. Some of the consequences are treated in "Wordsworth, Language, and Romanticism," repr. below pp. 372-381.

29. Adam Smith's essay was first published in the bibliographically elusive *Philological Miscellany* (London, 1761), pp. 440-479. Since the third edition of the *Theory of Moral Sentiments* (1767) it has generally formed part of that volume. In the years immediately preceding, Smith had written a review of the early volumes of the *Encyclopédie*. It may be noted that the same typological distinction was already made by the Abbé Gabriel Girard in the opening chapter of *Les vrais principes de la langue française* (1747), where the two types are called "langues analogues" and "langues transpositives." Girard's work was in fact Smith's source. In French Adam Smith's essay was first published as part of the article "Langue" in the *Encyclopédie méthodique. Grammaire et Littérature*, 3 vols. (Paris 1782-1786). The essay was published separately at Paris in the year IV of the Revolutionary calendar (1795-1796), and it was included in Mme de Condorcet's translation of *Théorie des sentiments moraux*, 2 vols. (Paris, 1798), where the translation is not the same as in the *Encyclopédie méthodique*. These volumes also contained her own "Lettres sur la sympathie" addressed to Cabanis, her friend at Auteuil. On 16 July 1798, Humboldt took extensive notes on her "Lettres" (AA XIV, 541-543), which he also discussed both with her and with others (*ibid*. 552, 561).

Bibliography

Abbreviations: AA, see Humboldt 1903-1937
CT, see Gipper 1975
GW, see Humboldt 1841-1852
Oeuvres, see Condillac 1947-1951

Aarsleff, Hans. 1964. "Leibniz on Locke on Language." Repr. above.

———1967. *The Study of Language in England 1780-1860*. Princeton University Press.

———1971. "Locke's Reputation in nineteenth-century England." Repr. above.

———1974. "The Tradition of Condillac." Repr. above.

———1975a. "Condillac's speechless Statue." Repr. above.

———1975b. "The Eighteenth Century, including Leibniz." *Current Trends in Linguistics*, vol. 13, *Historiography of Linguistics*, ed. by Thomas A. Sebeok with associate editors Hans Aarsleff, Robert Austerlitz, Dell Hymes, Edward Stankiewicz. The Hague and Paris: Mouton. Part I. 383-479.

———1976. "Thoughts on Scaglione's *Classical Theory of Composition*: The Survival of 18th-century French Philosophy before Saussure." *Romance Philology* 29. 522-538.

Cabanis, Georges. 1956. *Oeuvres philosophiques*. ed. by Claude Lehec and Jean Cazeneuve. 2 vols. Paris: PUF.

Certeau, Michel de, Dominique Julia and Jacques Revel. 1975. *Une Politique de la langue. La Révolution française et les patois: L'enquête de Grégoire*. Paris: Gallimard.

Condillac. 1947-1951. *Oeuvres philosophiques de Condillac*, ed. by Georges le Roy. 3 vols. Paris: PUF.

Coseriu, Eugenio. 1970. "Adam Smith und die Anfänge der Sprachtypologie." *Tübinger Beiträge zur Linguistik*, ed. by Gunter Narr. 3. 15-25.

Crombie, A. C. 1974. "Marin Mersenne." *Dictionary of Scientific Biography*. IX. 316-322.

Degérando. 1800. "Considérations sur les diverses méthodes à suivre dans l'observation des peuples sauvages." *Revue d'anthropologie*, 2nd ser., 5 (1883), 133-182.

———1800. *The Observation of Savage Peoples*, tr. by F. C. T. Moore, with a preface by E. E. Evans-Prichard. Berkeley: University of California Press. 1969.

Destutt de Tracy. 1798. "Mémoire sur la faculté de penser." *Mémoires de l'Institut National. Sciences morales et Politiques*. I. 283-450.

———1801. *Projet d'éléments d'idéologie à l'usage des écoles centrales de la République française*. Paris.

Dobbeck, Wilhelm. 1961. *Johann Gottfried Herders Jugendzeit in Mohrungen und Königsberg 1744-1764*. Würzburg.

Düntzer, H. and F. G. Herder. 1856-1857. *Aus Herders Nachlass*. 3 vols. Frankfurt a. M.

———1861-1862. *Von und an Herder. Ungedruckte Briefe aus Herders Nachlass*. 3 vols. Leipzig.

Encyclopédie méthodique. Grammaire et Littérature. 3 vols. Paris. 1782-1786.

Gipper, Helmut. 1965. "Wilhelm von Humboldt als Begründer moderner Sprachforschung." *Wirkendes Wort* 15. 1-19.

———and Peter Schmitter. 1975. "Sprachwissenschaft und Sprachphilosophie im Zeitalter der Romantik." In same vol. as Aarsleff 1975b above. Part I. 481-606.

Goedeke. Karl. 1959. *Grundriss zur Geschichte der deutschen Dichtung aus den Quellen*. Zweite neu bearbeitete Auflage. vol. 14, ed. by Herbert Jacob. Berlin: Akademie-Verlag. On Humboldt pp. 502-578.

Hansen-Løve, Ole. 1972. *La Révolution copernicienne du langage dans l'oeuvre de Wilhelm von Humboldt*. Paris: Vrin.

Haym, Rudolf. 1856. *Wilhelm von Humboldt. Lebensbild und Charakteristik*. Berlin.

————1880-1885. *Herder nach seinem Leben und seinen Werken dargestellt.* 2 vols. Berlin.

Herder, J. G. 1772. *Abhandlung über den Ursprung der Sprache,* ed. by Hans Dietrich Irmscher. Stuttgart: Reclam. 1966.

Humboldt. Wilhelm von. 1841-1852. *Gesammelte Werke,* ed. by Carl Brandes. 7 vols. Berlin.

————1903-1937. *Gesammelte Schriften,* ed. by the Königlich Presussischen Akademie der Wissenschaften. 17 vols. Berlin.

————1909. *Briefe an eine Freundin,* ed. by Albert Leitzmann. 2 vols. Leipzig.

————1916. "Wilhelm von Humboldt und Frau von Staël," ed. by Albert Leitzmann. *Deutsche Rundschau* 169. 431-442. See also vols. 170 and 171.

————1939. *Briefe an Karl Gustav von Brinkmann,* ed. by Albert Leitzmann. Leipzig.

————1940. *Briefe an Christian Gottfried Köerner,* ed. by Albert Leitzmann. *Historische Studien,* No. 367.

————1962. *Der Briefwechsel zwischen Friedrich Schiller und Wilhelm von Humboldt.* 2 vols. Berlin: Aufbau Verlag.

————1974. *Introduction à l'oeuvre de kavi et autres essais,* tr. by Pierre Caussat. Paris: Seuil.

Kaehler, Siegfried. 1927. *Wilhelm von Humboldt und der Staat.* Göttingen.

Lammers, Wilhelm. 1936. *Wilhelm von Humboldts Weg zur Sprachforschung.* Berlin.

Menze, Clemens. 1965. *Wilhelm von Humboldts Lehre und Bild vom Menschen.* Rattingen bei Düsseldorf.

Minguet, Charles. 1969. *Alexandre de Humboldt.* Paris: Maspéro.

Penisson, Pierre. ed. 1977. *Herder: Traité sur l'origine de la langue,* suivi de l'analyse de Mérian et des textes critiques de Hamann. Paris: Aubier. Flammarion.

Pott, A. F. 1876. *Wilhelm von Humboldt und die Sprachwissenschaft.* Berlin.

Ruprecht, Erich. 1963. "Die Sprache im Denken Wilhelm von Humboldts." *Die Wissenschaft von deutscher Sprache und Dichtung.* Festschrift für F. Maurer. Stuttgart. Pp. 217-236.

Scheinert, Mortiz. 1908. "Wilhelm von Humboldts Sprachphilosophie." *Archiv für die gesamte Psychologie.* 13. 141-195.

Schlegel, Friedrich. 1802-1803. "Observations sur l'ouvrage de Charles de Villers, *La Philosophie de Kant.*" *Kritische Friedrich Schlegel Ausgabe,* vol. 18 (1963), 538-547. The title of this volume is *Philosophische Lehrjahre 1796-1806, nebst philosophischen Manuskripten aus den Jahren 1796-1828,* ed. by Ernst Behler.

Schlesier, Gustav. 1843-1845. *Erinnerungen an Wilhelm von Humboldt.* 2 vols. Stuttgart.

Spranger, Eduard. 1908. "Wilhelm von Humboldt und Kant." *Kant-Studien* 13. 37-129.

Steinthal, Heymann. 1858. *Der Ursprung der Sprache im Zusammenhang mit den letzten Fragen des Wissens: Eine Darstellung der Ansicht Wilhelm von Humboldts, verglichen mit denen Herders und Hamanns.* Berlin.

Stocking, George. 1964. "French Anthropology in 1800." *Isis* 55. 134-150.

Stolpe, Heinz. 1966. "Johann Gottfried Herders Handbibliothek und ihr weiteres Schicksal." *Goethe.* Neue Folge des Jahrbuchs der Goethe-Gesellschaft. 28. 206-235.

Turgot. 1756. "Etymologie." *Encyclopédie.* VI. 98-111.

Weimann, Karl-Heinz. 1965. "Vorstufen der Sprachphilosophie Humboldts bei Bacon und Locke." *Zeitschrift für deutsche Philologie.* 84. 498-508.

Wolf, F. A. 1807. "Darstellung der Alterthums-Wissenschaft." *Kleine Schriften.* ed. by G. Bernhardy. 2 vols. (1869). II. 808-895.

Taine and Saussure

Today Taine is so little known that it may be useful to say at the outset that he was a French critic, philosopher, and historian who by his contemporaries was considered the dominant intellectual figure during the last forty years of the nineteenth century. I shall give more information on that point later.[1]

In a review of a book on modern German thought, Taine observed in 1869 that the author saw a difference between the German and French ideas of God. "He is right," said Taine, "all conceptions, among them that one, differ from one race to another. . . . unable to translate it, we have made it French; but becoming French, it has lost its true sense. By the same token, *God, Gott,* do not find their equivalent in our *Dieu.* With ideas that are so important, the nuance is everything; and to understand the full value of such a word in the speech of our neighbors, we must brave the risks of psychology."[2] The following year saw the publication of Taine's major philosophical work, which is also the key to his entire oeuvre, *De l'Intelligence.* Here he made the same observation with new pairs of examples, arguing that their significations are not the same except in a limited way, owing to the dissimilarity of the objects and emotions in the speakers' minds.[3] The full meaning of a word, including its value, is a function of the cultural system in which it occurs. In *De l'Idéal dans l'art* (1867), Taine had already introduced and developed the concept of

This is an expanded version of an essay first published in *The Yale Review* 68 (1978), 71-81. A French version appeared in *Romantisme,* nos. 25-26 (1979), 35-48.

valeur as a feature that is characteristic of an epoch in the history of art; the historian must note the changes of value between epochs, for such changes create new systems.[4] In Ferdinand de Saussure's *Cours de linguistique générale* (1916) *valeur* also plays an important role. English *sheep* and French *mouton* can have the same significations, but not the same *valeur*. Each word has its place in the system that determines its value.[5]

In the chapter on "La valeur linguistique," Saussure also made a statement that has now been cited so often that it has become a commonplace, like a key to his linguistic thought: "Language can also be compared to a sheet of paper: thought is the recto and sound the verso; we cannot cut one side without also cutting the other. So also in language, sound cannot be isolated from thought, or thought from sound."[6] The linguistic sign is a psychic entity with two surfaces, intimately related and recalling one another. Everyone knows that he called them the *signifiant* and the *signifié*. This principle and the striking metaphor that illustrates it are also in Taine's great work.

In the opening book on "Les signes" in *De l'Intelligence*, Taine argued that we think by means of signs, which for him are not only words but anything mental that goes into thinking; they are rarely full sensations, but usually faded or vague images of sensations. But we cannot think effectively unless these various kinds of images are linked to the signs we call words, which are themselves a special and privileged kind of images. This process Taine calls substitution. Thus "a general and abstract idea is a name, nothing but a name, the name that signifies and comprises a series of similar facts."[7] Like Locke, Taine held that sensation does not reveal substances, but only the signs we take for facts. For Taine "the physical world is reduced to a system of signs," or in Saussure's words, "every material thing is already a sign for us."[8] Taine, Saussure, and Wilhelm von Humboldt all dismissed the belief that language is a nomenclature. They agreed with Locke that words stand for ideas we form of things, not for things themselves as people generally believe by erroneously postulating a reliable "double conformity," as Locke called it, between thing-idea and idea-word.[9]

Near the end of the first volume of *De l'Intelligence* Taine came to the crucial point in his argument: how do physical and mental events connect? Many philosophers, he said, have argued that these two kinds of events are heterogeneous; they say that the image is internal while the sensation comes from the outside. Since they perpetually diverge, no common point can be found. Taine answers that they are not different events, but a single event known under two different aspects. This explanation satisfies Taine because it does not rely on any imaginary or unknown third element. He concludes that the two kinds of separate events previously postulated are always of necessity bound together, "for as soon as they are reduced to a single event with two aspects, it is clear that they are like the verso and recto of a surface, and that the presence or absence of one incontrovertibly entails that of the other. We have a single event with two faces, one mental, the other physical, one accessible to the understanding, the other to the senses."[10] The sheet is his metaphor for the "central event" that "communicates its character to the rest."

But what, he asks, "is the value of each of the two points of view?" That of the understanding (*conscience*) is always direct, the image of the sensation within us, for Taine materially located in the constitution of the brain. But the other aspect, that of external perception, is indirect, for it never gives knowledge of the physical object itself: "In itself this physical and sensible object remains altogether unknown; we know nothing about it except the group of sensations it provokes in us . . . that is to say their constant effects on us, their fixed accompaniments, their signs, nothing but signs, *signs* and *tokens* of things *unknown*." Taine continued: "Thus there is a great difference between the two points of view. By the understanding I attain the fact in itself; by sense I attain only a sign. A sign of what? What is it that is always accompanied, denoted, *signified* by the internal motion of the nervous centers? . . . it is the sensation, the image, the internal mental event." Sharing Saussure's well-known fondness for dichotomies, Taine has analyzed the sign into the purely mental *signifié* and the invariably linked *signifiant* (a term Taine does not use), which, coming from the outside, to us appears physical. We now understand, "why the mental event, being single, must appear double to us; the sign and the event signified are two things that can neither become one nor be separated, and their distinction is as necessary as their connection. But in regard to this distinction and this connection, the advantage is entirely on the side of the mental event; it alone exists. The physical event is merely the manner in which it affects or could affect our senses."[11]

It is evident that Taine's analysis contains all the elements of Saussure's doctrine of signs. For both Taine and Saussure the full range of signs included more than words, but both concentrated on words as the chief kind of mental images. As for Taine, Saussure's "images acoustiques" are only instruments of thought, but in themselves they are nothing until they become "des entités linguistiques" by being joined to concepts. At one point Saussure says that this "unité à deux faces" has been compared to "the unity of the human person, composed of body and soul,"—though he prefers to think of it as the union of hydrogen and oxygen in the chemical constitution of water.[12] We may find this analogy unhappy, but it still shows that Saussure understood what Taine was talking about and that he sought a scientific image that falls into line with Taine's orientation. This preference for scientific illustrations—for crystallization, glaciers, moraines, geological layers, mineralogy, anatomy, spiral shapes, physiology, and "les formules de la science"—is a constant reminder that Saussure was working within the conceptual milieu of Taine's thought. When Saussure said that "without the aid of signs, we would be unable to distinguish two ideas in a clear and certain manner," that "there are no pre-established ideas, and nothing is distinct before the appearance of language," he was following Taine's argument—and as Taine acknowledged, Condillac's. For Taine, the joining of sound and concept formed what Saussure called "a complex unity, physiological and mental."[13]

The two features I have dealt with bring Taine and Saussure so closely together that it would be implausible to argue that the young French-speaking Genevan did not know Taine's work. I shall show below that the similarities extend beyond the two I have discussed. On the question whether Saussure read Taine we have only circumstantial evidence, unless new material turns up. Saussure cites few names, and the records are sparse and cover only limited periods of his life. Records from the early 1890s show that he was then devoting much thought to problems of general linguistics in a manner that later emerged in the *Cours*, but since we have no records from the 1880s, we lack textual evidence for the inception, impulses, and growth of his thought.[14] When he arrived in Paris in the fall of 1880 at the age of twenty-three he had spent three years at the universities of Leipzig and Berlin. He had already published brilliant work, but it gained only slow and grudging acceptance in German scholarship, of which Saussure later wrote privately in severely critical, even contemptuous, terms, especially in regard to its lack of method.

In Paris his work had already been accepted by prominent linguists. Only a year after his arrival he was, thanks to Michel Bréal, entrusted with courses in traditional philology at the École des hautes études, where his teaching, extending to 1891, soon became legendary, not least for its close attention to method. When the *Cours* appeared, his student, colleague, and friend Antoine Meillet observed that he saw in it doctrines Saussure had already taught in Paris twenty years earlier (counting from 1907 when Saussure first gave the course at

Geneva), such as the distinction between diachrony and synchrony.[15] Among his closest friends was the linguist Louis Havet,[16] whose father, also a linguist, had been Taine's teacher and later became his admirer and correspondent. There is good reason to think that the Parisian milieu strongly affected the young Saussure.

In this milieu Taine was the reigning intellectual influence. For this we have the clear testimony of at least two dozen contemporaries, speaking for sociology (Durkheim, Tarde), history and philosophy (Gabriel Monod, Émile Boutroux, François Picavet, Pierre Janet), experimental psychology (Thédodule Ribot), criticism, art, and literary history (Brunetière, Paul Bourget, Maurice Barrès, Gustave Lanson, and Anatole France), all of them areas in which Taine had applied his method.[17] Taine was one of the founders of the École libre des sciences politiques. He reshaped the study of history and extended its range, created experimental psychology, and gave primary impulses to naturalism in literature and to impressionism in painting. He was the first to call public attention to the work of Antoine-Augustin Cournot, who contrasted his admiration for the eighteenth century and for Condillac to the philosophy of Victor Cousin. In the 1880s Nietzsche called Taine the greatest living historian, and it has been suggested that he found the concept of value in Taine.[18] When Ribot started the successful *Revue philosophique* in 1876, it opened with an article by Taine, soon to be followed by other articles by him as well as by detailed discussion of his philosophy. Among Taine's articles was one, based on personal observation, on language acquisition in the child, a subject that also plays a very large role in *De l'Intelligence*. This article so greatly excited Charles Darwin that he dug out and published his own notes taken some thirty years earlier. Taine inspired a large literature on this subject, both in France and in other countries.[19]

For the generation that gained maturity after 1865, Taine's achievement was this. He was the first popular and successful critic of the eclectic, spiritualist, and introspective philosophy which for a generation had ruled France, at times repressively, under the direction of Cousin. Taine proposed instead to apply the method of the natural sciences to the moral sciences. He found this method chiefly in the principles that Cuvier and Étienne Geoffroy Saint-Hilaire had developed in natural history. This method he expounded again and again, most prominently in the Introduction (1863) to *Histoire de la littérature anglaise* and in the prefaces (1858 and 1866) to *Essais de critique et d'histoire*. The Introduction to the *Histoire* outlines a program for what has later been called *histoire totale* or *histoire des mentalités* —a fact widely ignored by later historians, whose estimation of Taine has been determined largely by their rejection, itself ideological, of his *Origines de la France contemporaine*. Already in the 1858-preface to *Essais*, Taine had dismissed the sort of history that is a mass of details and anecdote, "man is not an assemblage of contiguous pieces, but a machine with ordered wheels; he is a system and not a heap." Or in other words, "history is a problem of psychological mechanics."[20] A civilization observes Cuvier's anatomical *loi des dependences mutuelles*, "its parts interrelate like the parts of an organic body." Just as the comparative anatomist can reconstruct an animal if he has a tooth or bone, "similarly in any civilization we find that religion, philosophy, family life, literature and the arts form a system in which any isolated change entails a general change, so that an experienced historian who studies some limited portion of it discerns in advance and almost predicts the qualities of the rest."[21] The concepts of system and structure are fundamental, and the terms occur constantly in Taine's writings. For Taine history embraces all aspects of human life seen as social and collective manifestations. It was a naturalist rather than strictly positivist program — Taine never paid as much attention as is often believed to Auguste Comte, who had considered the study of mind entirely irrational except "through the medium of the brain — we might even say the skull," in Mill's felicitous phrase.[22]

It was this program, this method, and the illustrations he gave that so greatly excited and inspired Taine's contemporaries. On his death in 1893, Anatole France wrote that Taine had inspired his generation around 1870 with "the dynamic cult of life. What he brought us was method and observation, it was a question of fact and idea, of philosophy and history, in short it was science. He set us free from the odious academic spiritualism, from the abominable Victor Cousin and his abominable school . . . he delivered us from hypocritical philosophism." For Durkheim, in a piece of high admiration, Taine had created "l'empirisme rationaliste."[23]

Some of the quotations above show that the concept of system or structure which a later age has found in Saussure was fully developed by Taine with the same broad implications and application that have since been redeveloped from Saussure's linguistic thought. In this sense Taine is a true structuralist. Saussure is also known for his distinction between the social, collective *langue* that forms a structure "où tout se tient," and the individual manifestation that occurs in the *parole*. This parallels a methodological distinction that is also made by Taine and for which he, like Saussure, was criticized. In the second preface to *Essais* Taine noted that his critics had blamed him for neglecting the individual's role by dealing only with "national characteristics and general situations as the only great forces in history." He answered that they forgot that "the great forces are only the sum of inclinations and dispositions of individuals, that our general terms are collective expressions by means of which we, under one of our points of view, bring together twenty or thirty million souls inclined to act in the same way."[24] For Saussure any change in the system of the *langue* is initiated in the *parole*, a contention that many have found paradoxical. But it agrees with Taine's view of culture and history that any change in the system comes from the outside, hence the mandatory attention to "les petits faits" that alert us to such changes. Only in this manner does it become possible to identify causes in history and to understand it.

The distinction between *langue* and *parole* follows from the insistence on structure and system. The same is true of Saussure's distinction between synchrony and diachrony, that is between the study of the material in a given state, "à un moment donné," and the study of features in time and change. Taine made the distinction in the Introduction to his *Histoire de la littérature anglaise* when he identified the three basic cultural forces as race, milieu, and moment. Race embraces the given "interior" force, the milieu the "exterior," and these two suffice for the description of a culture "à un moment donné." But to these two must be added a third, "le moment," "for in addition to the interior and exterior forces, there is the work those forces have already done together, and this work itself plays a role in the making of the one that follows; along with the permanent thrust and the given milieu there is the acquired speed."[25] A few years later, in the 1866-preface to *Essais*, Taine became more explicit. Here he distinguished between the study of "la liaison des choses *simultanées*" and of "la liaison des choses *successives*."[26] Being a system, the former are governed by mutual dependencies (following Cuvier), while the latter is affected by the conditions supplied by the previous system (following Geoffroy Saint-Hilaire). It was Saussure who introduced the terms "synchronique" and "diachronique," of which only the latter is strictly speaking new; the former is old and refers to the study of chronology and the simultaneity of events in history. But he introduced them only after he had observed that the sciences would be wise to pay attention to the axes on which the things they study are situated, "l'axe des *simultaneités*" and "l'axe des *successivités*."[27] The terminological agreements between Taine and Saussure (in this case as in several others also embracing Durkheim) can be extended, though they fall short of the more important conceptual similarities.

Taine was forced to make the distinction between simultaneity and successivity for this reason, often made clear in his writings. Cuvier's principles of comparative anatomy had supplied the method for the study of structural systems. Since Cuvier was totally committed to the fixity of species, his anatomy was entirely synchronic in regard to its objects of study. Though species can be annihilated by geological catastrophes, they are never transformed, and new ones never arise. To take account of change Taine turned to Geoffroy Saint-Hilaire's principles of anatomical connections and balance, developed within comparative embryology. Cuvier strongly opposed Geoffroy's diachrony (as he did Lamarck's), but Taine often expounded both in detail, contrasting Cuvier's "a-historical" method to Geoffroy's "historical" method. Taine explained and illustrated these principles most fully perhaps in De l'Idéal dans l'art; there are clear traces of his exposition in Saussure's discussion of synchrony and diachrony. This work also shows that for Taine the synchronic description of particular epochs must precede diachronic analysis, and that he, like Saussure, took language to be a fundamental cultural fact.[28]

Among today's Saussurian commonplaces are also the linearity of speech and the arbitrariness of the linguistic sign. Taine never expressly discussed either one, but he obviously took both principles for granted—thus without the arbitrariness the principle of valeur would not arise, as Saussure pointed out. Both are, however, basic doctrines in the linguistic philosophy of the eighteenth century, prominent in Condillac and in his disciples late in the century, the idéologues with Destutt de Tracy as the most important figure. Since this work was soon, already by 1800, called the materialist and sensualist foundation of the French Revolution, it became the deliberate aim of the reaction to wash it off the record, as if there had been no respectable French philosophy since the seventeenth century and Descartes, who could so easily be—and was—made to serve the needs of the reaction.

Taine had opened his crusade for the eighteenth century long before the first pages of De l'Intelligence credited the philosophy of signs to Condillac. Often calling him a follower of Condillac, contemporaries counted it one of Taine's greatest services to modern thought that he had restored respect for the philosophy that had been ridiculed, misrepresented, and repressed by the ruling and official academic philosophers. The result was a resurgence of interest in the eighteenth century, and especially in Condillac; it is amply illustrated in French publication during the later decades of the century. In this context the linguistic philosophy gained special prominence. Saussure's two principles of linearity and arbitrariness did not need to be discovered; they were old and could be found in available texts. It is also well known that Taine was the first important admirer of Stendhal, who revered Destutt de Tracy above all other philosophers.

I do not think that my analysis leaves room for doubt that Saussure, like many of his contemporaries, was deeply indebted to Taine—and much more evidence can be adduced than I have space for here. No other source contains all of Saussure's basic linguistic conceptions and methodological principles so tightly locked into a single, fully articulated system; and no set of separate sources presents these elements individually in a manner that so closely resembles Saussure's. What Ribot did for psychology and Durkheim for sociology, Saussure did for linguistics. My argument helps explain certain agreements between the linguistic thought of Saussure and Wilhelm von Humboldt, who was indebted to the linguistic philosophy of the *idéologues* and especially of Destutt de Tracy.[29] My conclusion allows that the thought that found expression in the *Cours* took shape during the Paris years, when Saussure was still a very young man. Taine's writings were often re-issued; when *De l'Intelligence* in 1900 reached its ninth edition, 12,000 copies were in print, an astonishing number for a large and difficult two-volume work. This conclusion overrides many implausible, often ill-informed and conceptually weak arguments that have been presented in the extensive recent literature on Saussure's background. This background has been located almost exclusively in German philological work, often with disregard of obvious chronological problems and silence about Saussure's severe censure of German scholarship.

Among the arguments that have been seriously advanced are the opinions that Saussure owed a wholesale debt to a German book published as late as 1891, that this work in turn may have drawn its "Systembegriff" from eighteenth-century German pietistic theology and philosophy; that the concept of value comes from a German work published as late as 1902, and that the distinction between synchrony and diachrony is merely a restatement of the difference between descriptive and historical-genetic linguistics that had been noted by German philologists.[30] This last opinion is conceptually inadmissible; it simply misses the point, as Hjelmslev forcefully pointed out in 1928.[31]

The concept of system and structure was latent in comparative philology from the beginning, introduced around 1800 by Silvestre de Sacy on Cuvier's model. But it is implausible that Saussure would have recreated it from that source when Taine so fully and often expounded it with great clarity as the core of his method. Comparative philology had not taken account of Geoffroy Saint-Hilaire's diachronic principles. The often debated similarities between Durkheim and Saussure assume a new aspect, for they take their place within mutual indebtedness to Taine. At the same time the chronological problems vanish that are raised by the Durkheim relation. This is also true of Saussure's reputed debt to the Russian linguist Kruszewski and to the Austrian philosopher Heinrich Gomperz, who both cite Taine's *De l'Intelligence* with approval, as well as John Stuart Mill and Alexander Bain to whom Taine also often acknowledged his debt. It was Destutt de Tracy, perhaps following Rousseau, who first gave a name to a prominent principle in Locke and Condillac when he said that language is "une institution sociale," a principle that is crucial in Saussure.[32]

Today Taine is virtually forgotten, and the literature on Saussure has never sought to relate the two figures. But in Saussure's own time Taine was the ruling intellectual influence. It is not surprising that the innovative turn in linguistics should have an extra-linguistic impulse. Established systems are not likely to renew themselves by their own devices, especially not when those systems, then as today, are the jealously guarded pride and property of institutionalized academic hierarchies. The history of Taine's legacy to Saussure illustrates what both maintained: that only external factors change established systems.

Notes

1. For a writer of Taine's importance and influence in his own time, there has been remarkably little interest in him during the last two generations. Few of his writings, and at times none, have been kept in print, and he has also received little attention in the secondary literature. There are several obvious reasons for this eclipse, but I am not concerned with them here. There are now signs that he is gaining increasing attention; see, for instance Jean-Thomas Nordmann, "Taine et le positivisme," *Romantisme* Nos. 21-22 (1978), 21-33. One of the last important writers to pay serious though critical attention to Taine was Jean-Paul Sartre in *L'Imagination* (1936). See *L'Imagination* (Paris: PUF, 1948), pp. 23-28. My own interest in Taine began with Georg Brandes and the desire to gain a better understanding of the intellectual history of the late nineteenth century, including the study of language, than I found in the secondary literature. See: "Thoughts on Scaglione's *Classical Theory of Composition*: The survival of 18th-century French philosophy before Saussure," *Romance Philology* 29 (May 1976), 522-538 (written June 1975); "Wilhelm von Humboldt and the linguistic thought of the French *idéologues*" (written August 1976); "Bréal versus Schleicher." The last two items will be referred to as Aarsleff 1977 and Aarsleff 1979.

2. See Taine's review of Camille Selden, *L'Esprit moderne en Allemagne* (Paris: Didier, 1869) in *Journal de Débats*, 7 February 1869. Substantial parts of this review are reprinted

in Victor Giraud, *Essai sur Taine*, 2nd ed. (Paris: Hachette, 1901), pp. 244-247. Taine's liaison with Camille Selden (whose real name was Elise Krinitz) during the 1860s is well known. See J. Wright, *Un intermédiaire entre l'esprit germanique et l'esprit français sous le Second Empire: Camille Selden, sa vie, son oeuvre* (Paris: Champion, 1931).

3. *De l'Intelligence*, 12th ed. in two vols. (Paris: Hachette, 1911), I, 48; this is the edition to which I shall refer. *De l'Intelligence* was issued twice in 1870, then in 1878 with substantial revisions and additions, again in 1883 with some revisions, thereafter reprinted 1888, 1892, 1897, 1900, 1903, 1906, 1911, 1914, and 1948.

4. *Philosophie de l'art*, 13th ed. in two vols. (Paris: Hachette, 1909) was after 1882 the general title of the work that comprised the five series of lectures, previously published separately, that Taine gave at the *École des Beaux-Arts*, beginning in 1865. *De l'Idéal dans l'art* is here in vol. II, 221-346. See *passim*, but, e.g., p. 234: "In the world of imagination as well as in the world of reality there are different levels because there are different values," and p. 268: "I am speaking of historical epochs. The system of ideas and sentiments that filled a human head in the time of Louis XIV was altogether different from what it is today."

5. Saussure, *Cours de linguistique générale*, ed. Tullio de Mauro (Paris: Payot, 1973), pp. 154-169 "La valeur linguistique." 160: "Forming part of a system, it is endowed not only with a signification but also with a value, and that is something quite different." P. 157: "Values actually remain entirely relative . . . the arbitrariness of the sign makes us understand better why the social fact alone can create a linguistic system. The collectivity is necessary for the creation of values." Since this is the text that has made Saussure's thought known and influential, the "vulgate" text so to speak (hereafter referred to as *Cours*), this is the text I have used unless otherwise noted. In spite of de Mauro's useful and extensive exploration of Saussure's intellectual background, he never mentions Taine; the same is true for the rest of the literature, now very large, on Saussure. I have also used Rudolf Engler's variorum, "édition critique" of the *Cours* (Vol. I, fasc. 1-3, Wiesbaden: Harrassowitz, 1967-1968; vol. II, fasc. 4, 1974). This immense and byzantine edition (hereafter referred to as Engler, ed., *Cours*) offers a wealth of evidence that supports my argument, but too extensive and detailed to present here.

6. *Cours*, p. 157. Cf. p. 99: "Thus the linguistic sign is a psychic entity with two sides."

7. *De l'Intelligence*, II, 259.

8. *De l'Intelligence*, I, 331. Engler, ed., *Cours*, II, 40a [3320.4].

9. The basic text is in Locke's *Essay*, Book II, ch. xxxii, par. 8: "And hence it is that men are so forward to suppose that the abstract *ideas* they have in their minds are such as agree to the things existing without them to which they are referred, and are the same also to which the names they give them do by the use and propriety of that language belong. For without this *double conformity of* their *ideas*, they find they should both think amiss of things themselves, and talk of them unintelligibly to others." Cf. also *Essai*, Book III, ch. v and Book II, ch. xxii, par. 2-6. Thus Locke rejected the idea that language is a nomenclature, and with it the doctrine of the Adamic language and the related postulate of innate ideas as commonly understood. On Humboldt, see Aarsleff 1977, above, p. 346. Cf. *Cours*, p. 97: "Some people regard language, when reduced to its elements, as a nomenclature, that is to say a list of terms corresponding to as many things. . . . The linguistic sign unites not a thing and a name, but a concept and an acoustic image." Cf. Taine, *Histoire de la littérature anglaise*, vol. V, *Les contemporains* (12th ed., Paris: Hachette, 1911), p. 357: "We believe that substances do not exist, but only systems of facts. We consider the idea of substance a psychological illusion. . . . We believe there is nothing in the world except facts and laws, that is to say events and their relations." (In chapter on "John Stuart Mill" first published 1864.) In his book *The Prison-House of Language* (Princeton University Press, 1972), p. 23, Fredric Jameson touches on this matter with the remark: "The vice of Anglo-American

empiricism lies indeed in its stubborn will to isolate the object in question from everything else, whether it be a material thing, and 'event' in Wittgenstein's sense, a word, a sentence, or 'a meaning,'" and he characterizes "this mode of thought" as going back to Locke. I find this incomprehensible. The isolation of object and word is, on the contrary, fundamental in rationalism and the doctrine of innate ideas; it goes with the notion that language is a nomenclature in the manner of the Adamic language. As brought out in his rejection of the "double conformity," Locke's analysis defines the philosophy of signs as it can be traced in Condillac, *les idéologues*, Humboldt, Taine, and Saussure. It is Cartesian rationalism that is "fixiste" and conservative. See André Joly, "La linguistique cartésienne: une erreur mémorable" in *La Grammaire générale: des Modistes aux Idéologues*, ed. by André Joly and Jean Stéfanini (Université de Lille III, 1977), pp. 165-199.

10. *De l'Intelligence*, I, 329. This passage was first published in "Les vibrations cérébrales et la pensée" in *Revue philosophique* 3 (Jan. 1877), p. 7 (where the entire article covers pp. 1-9); it was then included in *De l'Intelligence* in the 3rd (1878) and following editions.

11. *De l'Intelligence*, I, 329-331.

12. *Cours*, p. 145.

13. *Cours*, p. 155, 24. Cf. Engler, ed., *Cours*, I, 16 (in G 3.44a, 89): "It would have been better if linguists had found their ideas elsewhere, perhaps in the natural sciences. Perhaps the scientific tendency would have dawned sooner."

14. See Engler, ed., *Cours*, II, esp. pp. 3-14, Saussure's three inaugural lectures at l'Université de Genève in November 1891.

15. For Saussure's judgment of German linguistics, see, e.g., "Notes inédites de F. de Saussure," *Cahiers Ferdinand de Saussure* 12 (1954), 59: "It will be a subject of philosophical reflection for the future that linguistic science . . . born in Germany, cherished in Germany . . . has never made even a small stir to raise itself to the degree of abstraction that is necessary to govern on the one hand *what one does* and on the other in what sense what one does has legitimacy and justification within the sciences at large. But a second matter for astonishment will be to observe that when this science finally seemed to overcome its torpor, the result is Schleicher's laughable effort that collapses under its own ridiculousness. . . . On the basis of the evidence we have it is obvious that it was a question of utter mediocrity, which does not preclude pretensions." On Saussure's courses, teaching and students in Paris, see Michel Fleury, "Notes et documents sur Ferdinand de Saussure (1880-1891)," *Annuaire 1964-1965*. (École pratique des Hautes Études, IVe section: Sciences historiques et philologiques), pp. 35-67. Meillet followed Saussure's courses 1887-1888, 1888-1889 and substituted for him during his absence 1889-1890. In his review of the *Cours* Meillet wrote: "I never attended Saussure's course in general linguistics. But it is well known that Saussure's thought was formed very early. The doctrines he explicitly taught in his course in general linguistics were those that already distinguished his teaching of comparative grammar twenty years ago at the École des Hautes Études when I was a student. I recognize them such as it was often possible to imagine them then" (*Bulletin de la Société de Linguistique de Paris* 20 (1916), 33). At the time of Saussure's death in 1913, before the publication of the *Cours*, Meillet already credited the synchronic-diachronic distinction to him: "He was especially eager to mark the contrast between two ways of looking at linguistic facts: the study of language at a given moment and the study of linguistic development in time" (*Linguistique historique et linguistique générale*, vol. II nouveau tirage (Paris: Champion, 1951), p. 183). See also Aarsleff 1979, above pp. 299, 295.

16. It is well known that Saussure deeply appreciated Louis Havet's favorable review of his *Mémoire sur le système primitif des voyelles dans les langues Indo-Européennes* (1879) in *Journal de Genève* de mardi 25. Février 1879. Supplément. See also G. Redard, "Ferdinand de Saussure et Louis Havet" in *Bulletin de la Société de Linguistique de Paris* 71 (1976), 313-349.

17. Many of these estimates will be found in "Quelques opinions sur l'oeuvre de H. Taine," *La Revue Blanche* 13 (July-Sept. 1897), 263-295. Others are found in essays on Taine, which by their number and variety also testify to Taine's importance. Cf. André Chevrillon, *Taine. Formation de sa pensée* (Paris: Plon, 1932), p. i: "Taine was the intellectual master of two generations of Frenchmen."

18. See the correspondence between Taine and Nietzsche in *Gesammelte Briefe*, eds. Elisabeth Förster-Nietzsche, Curt Wachsmuth, Peter Gast, III (Berlin, 1905), 198-206. During 1886-1887, Nietzsche sent *Jenseits von Gut und Böse, Morgenröte*, and *Fröhliche Wissenschaft* to Taine. On 11 November 1887, he wrote to Erwin Rohde: "Taine is today the educator of all the more serious scholarly minds in France" (*ibid.*, II (1902), 584). On 4 August 1877 Nietzsche wrote to Malwida von Meysenburg that he was in touch with G. Croom Robertson, "Editor of *the best* philosophical journal [*Mind*] (not only in England, but anywhere); at most Th. Ribot's *Revue philosophique* is its equal" (*ibid.* III, 564). In 1902 J. Segond wrote that Nietzsche had much influenced the concept of value, "and I am not so sure that Nietzsche himself was not in this respect under the influence of Taine, whom he held in high esteem. . . . In fact, in his lectures on *l'Idéal dans l'art* Taine makes the concept of value the center of his studies. . . . And this *creation of values*, does it not proceed from the very spirit of Taine's esthetics?" (in "Quelques publications récentes sur la morale," *Revue Philosophique* 54 (July-September 1902), 263.)

19. Taine, "Note sur l'acquisition du langage chez les enfants et dans l'espèce humaine," *Revue philosophique* 1 (January-July 1876), 5-23, with the 3rd ed. (1878) of *De l'Intelligence* reprinted as a note (I, 357-395). The part on language acquisition in the child was printed in translation in *Mind* 2 (April 1877), 252-259, where Darwin saw it, causing him to publish "A biographical sketch of an infant," *Mind* 2 (July 1877), 285-294, after he had read "M. Taine's very interesting account of the mental development of an infant translated in the last number of *Mind*." *Revue philosophique* 4 (July-December 1877), 17-46, carried an excellent article by Théodule Ribot on "Taine et sa psychologie," which is chiefly a review of *De l'Intelligence*; here (p. 24), Ribot mentioned Taine's observation that *God* and *Dieu* "do not mean the same thing." In *Mind* 2 (July 1877), 366-386, appeared Ribot's fine and informative article on "Philosophy in France." Here he said (p. 377), that Taine's *De l'Intelligence* "and the works of contemporary English psychologists are the only ones to which physiologists and medical men at present have recourse. Till the last few years they used to go to the school of Condillac in search of any psychological explanations of which they had need. This apparently unimportant fact has its significance, for it shows how utterly without influence and authority over men of science the Spiritualist School has been."

20. *Essais de critique et d'histoire*, 12th ed. (Paris: Hachette, 1913), p. iii. *Histoire de la littérature anglaise*, 13th ed., I (Paris: Hachette, 1911), Introduction, p. xxix, "history is a problem in psychological mechanics." Cf. *ibid.*, p. xl: "Just as astronomy is basically a problem in mechanics and physiology a problem in chemistry, so history is basically a *problem in psychology*. There is a particular system of impressions and operations that makes the artist, the believer, the musician, the painter, the nomad, and man in society."

21. *Histoire*, Introduction, p. xxxvi. Here Taine notes that he had already several times explained "the law of mutual dependencies" "especially in the Preface to *Essais* . . . (Seconde Préface de l'édition définitive)." He had in fact already stated it, in slightly different words, in the opening page of the 1858-preface to *Essais*. The Introduction to *Histoire* was first published, in slightly different form, in *Revue germanique* (1 December 1863) under the title "L'Histoire, son présent et son avenir." Practically everything Taine published in book form until 1870 had previously been published in current journals and newspapers, and this remained in large measure true also after 1870; thus the dissemination of his writings was much wider than even his books and their many printings show.

22. John Stuart Mill, review of *De l'Intelligence* in *Fortnightly Review* 14 (July 1870), 121-124. On Taine and Comte see Nordmann, *op. cit.* (note 1 above). When Georg Brandes visited Taine in April of 1870 he was surprised to find that Taine "admits openly that he has only read very little by Comte" (*Georg Brandes's Breve til Forældrene 1859-1871*, ed. Morten Borup (3 vols., København: Reitzel, 1978), I, 215; letter of 25 April 1870). The Brandes correspondence has much useful information about Taine and Renan. Both Claude Bernard in 1865, in *Introduction à l'étude de la médecine expérimentale*, and Pasteur in 1882, in *Discours de réception à l'Académie française*, had rejected Comte's positivism as harmful to science; both were among Taine's admired scientific masters.

23. France, "M. Taine" in *Le Temps* 12 mars 1893, on the occasion of Taine's death. Durkheim in *Revue Blanche* 13 (1897), 287-291: Taine had replaced mere rationalism or empiricism with, "what one could call rationalist empiricism. . . . Accepting for my part the basic principles of this philosophy, as in the account I have given, I am naturally induced to judge Taine's work favorably. . . . Moral science is a living and active reality; it is a system of given facts."

24. *Essais*, p. xxii.

25. *Histoire*, Introduction, p. xxvii.

26. *Essais*, p. xviii.

27. *Cours*, pp. 115-117. The notes on which the *Cours* was based do not use "axe des simultaneités," but have "axe des contemporaneités." For the other term, the notes have both "axe des successivités" and "axe des successibilités." See Engler, ed., *Cours*, p. 177.

28. In *De l'Intelligence* II, 427ff, Taine explained his use of the principles of Cuvier and Geoffroy Saint-Hilaire, concluding: "Similarly, in these human societies whose permanent or changing qualities are the object of history, we are led to understand the totality by means of the elements, which are easy to grasp," and here he again observed that "I have tried to explain this method" in the preface to *Essais* and in the Introduction to *Histoire*. *Ibid.*, p. 441, he concluded, "the whole difference between the two products consists in this, that the first being historical and the second not being historical, the first contains one factor more than the second." In *De l'Idéal*, Taine wrote: "The qualities of the primitive age are the most meaningful of all; in the structure of the language and the species of myths, we discern the future form of religion, philosophy, society and art" (In *Philosophie de l'art*, II, 256).

29. On Humboldt and the *idéologues*, see Aarsleff 1977, above pp. 335-355. In *Projet d'élémens d'idéologie* (1801, p. 261), Destutt de Tracy wrote "Every system of signs is a language." (In the reprint of the 1817-edition, ed. Henri Gouhier (Paris: Vrin, 1970), this is on p. 309). This statement was followed by six pages of examples that constitute the materials for a semiology. In the *Élémens d'idéologie* II, *Grammaire*, Destutt de Tracy used the term valeur in a sense that comes close to Taine's and Saussure's, "we have seen that the uncertainty of the value of the signs of our ideas is inherent, not in the nature of the signs, but in that of our intellectual faculties, and that it is not possible for the same sign to have exactly the same value for all those who use it" (in 1970 reprint of 1817-edition, pp. 378-379; it is also in the first edition, 1804, to which I have not had access). It is this circumstance that necessitates Destutt de Tracy's concept of "the successive rectification of the first ideas," which was taken over by Humboldt; see Aarsleff 1977, above p. 345. In *De l'Intelligence* (II, 34-65), Taine devoted an entire chapter to the psychological aspect of this process under the title "La rectification," where he also analyzed language acquisition in the child in this manner (*ibid.*, II, 48-51 and elsewhere, e.g., II, 267). In a letter of 15 June 1867 to Sainte-Beuve, Taine wrote, "I am writing my treatise *De l'Intelligence*; Condillac and de Tracy knew more about that than Jouffroy. Everything has been vitiated by the antiscientific school of Royer-Collard and Cousin" (*H. Taine, sa vie et sa correspondance* II (Paris: Hachette,

1904), p. 341). It is curious that the recent literature on the term valeur in linguistics finds it in Adam Smith and Turgot, who of course both wrote on language, but not in the more relevant source where it is fully developed, Condillac's *Le commerce et gouvernement considérés relativement l'un à l'autre*, published in the same year, 1776, as Adam Smith's *Wealth of Nations* and before Turgot's *Mémoire sur la valeur et les monnais*, first published 1808-1811, though written 1768. See Georges le Roy, ed., *Oeuvres philosophiques de Condillac*, vol. II (1948), 245: "We must stress the importance that Condillac placed on his theory of value . . . it makes Condillac's work deeply original. . . . it is Condillac's merit, more perhaps than that of anyone else, to have shown that the notion of value is the principle of all economic activity . . . it is equally his merit to have founded the notion of value on that of utility and thus also on need, that is to say on what exists subjectively in the understanding." On the use of the concept of valeur by Michel Bréal, see Aarsleff 1979, above pp. 307-308.

30. The 1891 work in question is Georg von der Gabelentz's *Sprachwissenschaft*. See Eugenio Coseriu, "Georg von der Gabelentz et la linguistique synchronique," *Word* 23 (1967), 74-100. (*Linguistic Studies presented to André Martinet*, Part I. *General Linguistics*.) Here, Coseriu says that it is not a question of coincidence, "but of a true influence of Gabelentz on Saussure" (p. 76); and he concludes: "Thus the influence of Gabelentz on Saussure seems to us beyond doubt. . . . Furthermore, we know today that in 1891 Saussure was still a faithful and respectful disciple of historical linguistics and that it was only by 1894 that he began to reflect methodically on problems of general linguistics" (p. 99). Coseriu's claim is untenable for the good reason that we do not have an unbroken and continuous record of Saussure's development; for the 1880s we have no public autograph documentation at all and for later years only scattered evidence. But Coseriu's claim is also invalidated by the publication in 1974 of Saussure's inaugural lectures in Geneva in 1891. And Meillet told us long ago that Saussure's teaching at Paris in the 1880s contained anticipations of the linguistic thought that found expression in the *Cours*. Since Gabelentz was an admirer of Humboldt, the argument has then been extended to show Saussure's debt to Humboldt. See H. H. Christmann, "Saussure und die Tradition der Sprachwissenschaft," *Archiv für das Studium der neueren Sprachen* 208 (April 1972), 241-255. Christmann says: "On the basis of Coseriu's demonstration we are justified in considering Gabelentz's book the chief source of Saussure's *Cours*" (p. 245). Christmann then identifies six features of structural linguistics in Saussure that are also in Gabelentz, then asks: "Do we now also find them earlier? The answer is yes; we find them together in a linguist who is so well known that it is a wonder how little these relations have so far been known—in Wilhelm von Humboldt. Thus there is a filiation Humboldt-Gabelentz-Saussure, and it embraces not merely isolated thoughts, but decisive features" (pp. 245-246). Quite apart from the new evidence, the Geneva inaugural lectures, published since Coseriu and Christmann wrote, I find the argument unconvincing. The similarities find a much better explanation in Humboldt's—and thus also Gabelentz's—place in the linguistic tradition that Humboldt met in Destutt de Tracy and the *idéologues* and which as we have seen also was central in the thought of Taine. It may further be observed that Gabelentz was primarily a student of Chinese and thus not part of the German philological establishment, and the prior work on Chinese was almost wholly French in the eighteenth-century tradition. H. Rensch, "Organismus-System-Struktur in der Sprachwissenschaft." *Phonetika* 16 (1967), 71-84, suggests that, "the concept of structure which Gabelentz introduced into linguistics" (p. 80), may have its source in eighteenth-century German pietistic theology and philosophy—surely one of the most fantastic suggestions in the literature.

31. Louis Hjelmslev, *Principes de grammaire génerale* (København 1928), p. 57: "The terminology generally adopted that contrasts the 'descriptive' point of view with the 'historical' seems to us altogether false. . . . This terminology is unfortunate, for it reflects a

profound misunderstanding, as if synchronic linguistics did nothing but amass materials while diachronic linguistics alone would be the one that explains."

32. The claims for Kruszevski have been made with reference to his "Prinzipien der Sprachentwickelung" (published in installments in *Zeitschrift für allgemeine Sprachwissenschaft* ["Techmers Zeitschrift"] in vols. 1-5 (1884-1890), going back to an earlier version in Russian of 1883), but the German version at least offers no basis for these claims against Taine, on the contrary since Kruszevski cites Taine as well as sources used by Taine. For Heinrich Gomperz the claims have been made with reference to his *Weltanschauungslehre* vol. 2, part I, *Noologie* (Jena/Leipzig: Diderichs, 1908), which uses the Stoic terms *signans* and *signatum* that are said to correspond to *signifiant* and *signifié*. Again, this suggestion is not plausible, even if we overlook the late date. There would in any event be more reason to cite Gomperz's *Zur Psychologie der logischen Grundtatsachen* (Leipzig/Wien: Deuticke, 1897), which cites both Taine's *De l'Intelligence* as well as sources also used by Taine, especially in the chapter on "Wort und Begriff" (pp. 20-41), but Saussure's debt to Taine is already amply evident before 1897.

Wordsworth, Language,
and Romanticism

In this essay I wish to take a fresh look at the question of romanticism and language in Wordsworth. Other aspects of Wordsworth have in recent years gained new interpretations, but the answers to this fundamental problem have remained much the same for more than a generation, typically represented by M. H. Abrams in *The Mirror and the Lamp* (1953). This old consensus is marked by a few basic features that set the limits of understanding.

It is admitted that Locke is in the background, that language and the ways of knowing, or epistemology, are intimately related, and that these problems were among the first concerns of eighteenth-century thought. With reliance on an old tradition created in the nineteenth century for its own ends, it is believed that this philosophy made the mind entirely passive, whereas the essence of mind and knowing for the romantics was activity. Or, in different terms, it is argued that eighteenth-century philosophy sustained the doctrine of imitation that in turn governed both poetic theory and practice; while romanticism made expression its central concern, with a corresponding philosophy to legitimate its poetry and criticism. The mirror was replaced by the lamp, or rather when the mirror was shattered the lamp suddenly began to cast light. It is further typical of the old consensus that it hardly treats French thought except, if at all, as a hostile element, but for illustrative parallels goes to Germany because, as Professor Abrams says, "in the late eighteenth century, it was the German, more than the English formulations of the new poetics, which

Reprinted from *Essays in Criticism* 30 (July 1980), pp. 215-26.

achieved currency throughout western Europe" (p. 88). This is an en-
trenched opinion of questionable chronological relevance that has
more recently made it possible to rely on a posthumous work by
Wilhelm von Humboldt published in 1835 as the best text—or even
source—for the German romantic philosophy we need to understand
what the problem of language was all about in Wordsworth.[1]

Professor Abrams finds it "remarkable that Wordsworth was more
thoroughly immersed in certain currents of eighteenth-century thinking than any of his important contemporaries," yet insists that "only in
his poetry, not in his criticism, does Wordsworth make the transition
from the eighteenth-century view of man and nature to the concept
that the mind is creative in perception" (p. 103). Though this could
be true, it is the sort of paradox that invites a look for better answers.
After all, Wordsworth admitted in the opening pages of the first Preface (1800), "that there would be some impropriety in abruptly ob-
truding upon the Public, without a few words of introduction, Poems
so materially different from those, upon which general approbation
is at present bestowed," even though he declined for reasons of space
to write "a systematic defence of the theory, upon which the poems
were written."[2] It would surely be odd to imply that he was insensi-
tive to paradox in the heart of the matter he was eager to explain and
to which he repeatedly returned without significant revision or inconsistency. In this brief essay I can merely stake out the general nature
of my argument, which draws on my previous work on the history of
the study and philosophy of language, especially in regard to Condillac
as the central figure who brought about the change that lies behind
the romantic aesthetic and the role it assigned to language.[3]

The basic structure of my argument is this. Wordsworth rejected
the poetic practice and the dominant poetic theory of the last century, but he built his own critical theory on the philosophy of the
same century that had given language a central role in our understanding of the ways of knowing, communication, and the potentialities of
expression. This was the philosophy that had bared "the sad incompetence of human speech" (*Prelude* 6.593) at the same time as it had
shown the impossibility of getting around this imperfection, itself as
fixed and unalterable as gravitation. The task of "separating truth
and sincerity from falsehood and affectation" (II, 82) is a problem of
language, as he had argued in his strictures on Pope's epitaphs which,
he said, "cannot well be too severely condemned" (II, 80). In the
same context he argued that without "minute criticism"—though
"irksome"—the mind "cannot learn the art of bringing words rigor-
ously to the test of thoughts; and these again to a comparison with

things, their archetypes; contemplated first in themselves, and secondly in relation to each other; in all which processes the mind must be skilful, otherwise it will perpetually be imposed upon" (II, 77). It is the active mind—and preeminently the poetic mind—that brings expression close to nature and man's moral being.

The philosophy Wordsworth used had raised fundamental questions about the relations between man and nature, between man and society in the shared linguistic universe, and soon also between literature and society. By whatever lines of transmission, which are not here my first concern (though I think quite as good ones can be found as those generally accepted), Wordsworth based his rejection of the old imitation doctrine and poetic practice on the language-oriented philosophy that was formulated by Condillac, chiefly in his *Essai sur l'origine des connaissances humaines* (1746) and for literary aesthetics also in *De l'art d'écrire* (1775). His thought soon ruled in France, amply illustrated in the *Encyclopédie* as well as in Diderot and others. It found influential followers in Scotland, and in Germany it was taken up by Lessing and Herder, who when cited on these matters is drawing on Condillac. It was popular in France when Wordsworth was there and reached its peak of attention, exposition and influence in Paris during the Directory (1795-1799).

Let me suggest what is involved by beginning with a quotation that will stand for many others that could have been cited. It is a familiar passage on a general principle from a letter of 18 January 1816 to Francis Wrangham, who had asked some questions about the reading of "The White Doe of Rylstone." Wordsworth wrote:

> Throughout, objects (the Banner, for instance) derive their influence not from what they are actually in themselves, but from such as are bestowed upon them by the minds of those who are conversant with or affected by those objects. Thus the Poetry, if there be any in the work, proceeds whence it ought to do from the soul of Man, communicating its creative energies to the images of the external world.

In other words, we know objects only as they are grasped by the mind in a creative though private act, and the nature of this act can be communicated only in the socially shared words of language. Professor Abrams has used this passage to illustrate the expressive theory of romantic aesthetics, "a work of art is essentially the internal made external" (p. 22). But why, we may ask, is this mode the poet's only alternative? For surely it was not mere caprice that made him choose a theory that surrounds both language and the poet's task with so many difficulties.

The answer is indicated by a passage in Locke's *Essay* that sums up his philosophy in terms of its bearing upon language. It occurs in the chapter 'Of true and false ideas' in Book Two.

> It is in our *ideas* that both the rightness of our knowledge and the propriety or intelligibleness of our speaking consists. And hence it is that men are so forward to suppose that the abstract *ideas* they have in their minds are such as agree to the things existing without them to which they are referred, and are the same also to which the names they give them do by the use and propriety of that language belong. For without this *double conformity of* their *ideas*, they find they should both think amiss of things in themselves, and talk of them unintelligibly to others.

It was Locke's aim to reject this delusion of the "double conformity," for as he repeated often, "words . . . stand for nothing but the ideas in the mind of him that uses them." Our perceptions and ideas are private, words are about ideas and not directly about things. This is the source of that "extreme subjectivism" of romantic aesthetics that Professor Abrams illustrates with a passage from Tieck's *William Lovell*: "Indeed, everything that I believe I perceive outside myself can only exist within myself" (p. 347). From Locke's principle—amply argued in the *Essay*—follows a host of consequences that have persisted to the present time. Today we find them in Saussure's *Cours*, but they have played a prominent role ever since Condillac, e.g., in the French *idéologue* and follower of Condillac, Destutt de Tracy, who would seem to be the source of their much better known occurrence in Wilhelm von Humboldt. Among the consequences are the following.

First, since words are abitrary signs for our private ideas, they do not constitute an inventory of the world, a nomenclature, as they did in the Adamic language doctrine against which Locke was arguing. Since it follows that imitation is strictly impossible, the doctrine that prevailed before Wordsworth has lost its foundation. (I shall later mention that this point was not lost on a contemporary who on this matter has been related to Wordsworth.) Second, ideas and notions being private, they are by the same token absolutely incommunicable except through the radically imperfect medium of language—"the sad incompetence of human speech." Each individual has his own language, a principle expressly stated by Locke, Condillac, Turgot, Herder, Destutt de Tracy, and Wilhelm von Humboldt. Third, owing to the privacy of the ideas to which words are tied, this problem is overcome only by the fact that language is a "social institution" (as de Tracy said, perhaps borrowing the term from Rousseau) which embodies the communally shared universe of knowledge and feeling. In so far as words communicate adequately, they do so only because they are submitted to a constant process of "rectification" in the social intercourse of speech within the communal context of shared experience that supplies the means of this rectification. The term is Destutt de Tracy's, who discussed and illustrated his principle in fascinating detail; from this source it was taken up by Wilhelm von Humboldt. De Tracy's writings on the subject date from the late 1790s, a few years before the first Preface of 1800, and de Tracy again published on it just after 1800. There is a sense in which one can see Wordsworth's entire problem as centering on rectification.

The three points just listed involve what is generally called the principle of linguistic relativity, already noted by Locke in his frequent observations on the virtual intranslatability among languages— a consequence of his philosophy of course. Condillac discussed it most fully under the title "the genius of languages." This principle is not, as is widely believed, Humboldt's invention. The language of each society and community reflects experience, both physical and moral, since language is man-made and converses about its speakers' needs and concerns. The consequences of the principle are prominent in Wordsworth. It accounts, for instance, for what may perhaps be called the testing quality of epitaphs. They are the social and local expression of sincere emotion and reverence. We understand why he believes, "that the faults predominant in the literature of every age will be as strongly reflected in the sepulchral inscriptions as any where" (II, 84). And also why he remarks with sadness on the burial of the dead away from their home communities; the survivors' loss is both a linguistic and a moral loss. It is also in this spirit he observes that tombstones in churchyards by the sea "are crowded with metaphors taken from the Sea and a Sea-faring life. These are uniformly in the same strain; but surely we ought not thence to infer that the words are used of course without any heart-felt sense of their propriety" (II, 65).

In fact the principle of linguistic relativity appears in the opening pages of the first Preface as the reason why Wordsworth declined to enter into a detailed systematic defence; it would have taken him too far, "for it would be necessary to give a full account of the present state of the public taste in this country, and to determine how far this taste is healthy or depraved: which again could not be determined, without pointing out, in what manner language and the human mind act and react on each other, and without retracing the revolutions not of literature alone but likewise of society itself." Though the subject cannot be exhausted here, our problem is to gain a sense of what Wordsworth would have said in the longer defence he could envision but did not give.

There was for Wordsworth no alternative to the philosophy he relied on. The medium of poetry is language, it alone can mediate between the subjective and private world of the individual and the public world. Nature and the simple tasks of rural living afford the best referents for the rectification that ensures a primal language best suited to make the internal external without the loss that ends in "falseness and affectation." The mind is not passive either in perception or in speech. For Condillac this creativity lay in reflection and reason which made language possible. Hence Condillac presented the core of his philosophy in terms of a conjectural account of the origin of language, creative in its beginning as in its continuation. Condillac's conception is nowhere more evident than in his well-known but misinterpreted statue (in the *Traité des sensations*), which precisely because it is speechless never rises above the level of the animals. The statue cannot rise beyond the attainment of a "moi d'habitude," or instinct, of "des connaissances pratiques," and thus cannot satisfy any needs above mere preservation; whereas man, thanks to reason and language, has a "moi de réflexion," is capable of theoretical knowledge, and can both conceive and meet needs beyond preservation, that is, all the arts from the simplest to the most exalted. The mind's activity is the fundamental postulate of the philosophy on which Wordsworth based his critical theory. This is true also, of course, of romantic aesthetics at large. The source lies in the philosophy that is usually dismissed as antithetical to romanticism.

Let me turn to another aspect. In the first Preface, Wordsworth had a question and answer: "Is there then . . . no essential difference between the language of prose and metrical composition? I answer that there neither is nor can be any essential difference" (I, 134). Poetry is opposed to "matter of fact, or science," i.e., to rational discourse. Poetry relies on images and on "the manner in which we associate ideas in a state of excitement." The refusal to distinguish poetry from prose on stylistic or linguistic grounds alone rests on the overriding consideration that the medium of both is language. We find the same in Condillac.

De l'Art d'écrire offered an influential treatment of literary aesthetics, especially in the long final chapter called, "Observations on poetic style and incidentally on what determines the quality that belongs to each genre of style." Condillac opened with the question: "How does poetry differ from prose?" He answered that since poetry and prose can deal with the same subject matter, the difference does not lie there. Nor does the intended effect offer means of distinction, for prose often pleases as much as poetry instructs. In both there are as many styles as there are subjects; the difference lies in the style of expression, though never in any absolute sense, only by degrees. But poetry requires more art while at the same time appearing no less natural. At its most pointed, the distinction is that prose presents analysis but poetry images. The essential differences cannot be fixed in terms of prose and poetry, which intermingle across the spectrum, but between the style of the philosopher and the style of the lyric poet; the antithesis of poetry is philosophy. Between these extremities lie all the styles of the genres, which again means that the nuances are so fine that no rule can distinguish them safely in each and every case. I shall pass over a passage that discusses elegance, which Condillac finds troublesome because it differs from one language to another, changes with generations, yet must never fail to appear natural if used at all, a discussion that recalls a similar passage in Wordsworth's Third Essay upon Epitaphs. At the end of the chapter, Condillac argues, like Wordsworth, that poetry must be written in meter.

In the same chapter Condillac also argued that poetry is chiefly characterized by the association of ideas that governs the expression of passion and emotion, while prose, the style of the philosopher, relies on "the connection of ideas," which for Condillac meant reflection and reason. Rules can therefore be given for prose, but not for poetry, and Condillac like Wordsworth steadfastly refused to give any. David Hartley has often been invoked to support interpretations of Wordsworth's understanding of association, but he is a very poor choice over Condillac. The effective and natural use of association depends on too many variable factors; it must take the habits and expectations of the audience into account, and this can only be left to the genius of the poet. Here Condillac respects the consistent relativism that is the consequence of his linguistic philosophy. Hence also the romantic use of local color, which is first of all a linguistic problem, paradigmatically illustrated in Wordsworth's reading of epitaphs. It also follows that rules can never be transferred either from one language to another, or from one age to another. Condillac expressly rejected the notion that anyone becomes a poet by imitating the Greeks. Language is the chief repository of the associations open to the poet; the only general rule Condillac gave is that poets must consult the language men speak. In the same long chapter, he also argued that classical mythology is irrelevant because it has nothing to do with our manners and modes of thinking. For both Condillac and Wordsworth language is the central problem of literary theory and poetic art.

Scholars have pointed out that Wordsworth's discussion of meter and poetry resembles a well-known contribution to the *Monthly Magazine* for July 1796 under the title, "Is verse essential to poetry?" The author was William Enfield, who had earlier been associated with Joseph Priestley's academy at Warrington; the present contribution was one of ten published by him in that magazine during 1796, all on topics that were at the time also being eagerly debated among the *idéologues* in Paris—the first of the contributions discussed the question, "Ought the freedom of enquiry to be restricted?" and was directed against the Bishop of Llandaff whom Wordsworth had addressed in similar terms a few years earlier. Enfield's article on verse and poetry shows close affinity with both Condillac and Wordsworth also on other points than meter. The most interesting point, however, is that Enfield gave clear statement to an obvious argument that I have never seen so bluntly expressed. To a definition that said poetry "is the art of imitating or illustrating . . . every being in nature," he answered: "The obvious objection to this definition [is] that the term *imitation* is improperly used to express the description of objects by arbitrary signs, which exhibit no copy of nature." Condillac's philosophy—and Locke's—had removed the foundations of the imitation doctrine. Since Hugh Blair's *Lectures on Rhetoric and Belles-Lettres* have also been related to Wordsworth, it is relevant to know that they were brought out in French in 1797 during the Directory when the *idéologues* encouraged a number of translations and publications in support of their philosophy, including the first complete edition of Condillac in 1798.

Finally, let me turn to a principle that is universally recognized as being typically romantic, and as such often accompanied with quotation from Herder. It is the one Wordsworth stated at the beginning of the Appendix (1802) to the first Preface: "The earliest poets of all nations generally wrote from passion excited by real events; they wrote naturally, and as men: feeling powerfully as they did, their language was daring, and figurative." Oddly, Wordsworth does not seem to have had an ear for music, and I am not aware that he treated it in the prose writings. But Herder did write on this subject in a passage cited by Professor Abrams (p. 93) from a work published in 1769 shortly before Herder wrote the treatise on the origin of language, at a time when he is known recently to have read Condillac's *Essai*, where music is treated in the manner that later became a romantic commonplace. It was a fundamental point in Condillac's account of the origin of language that language in the beginning was a total union of poetry and music. "Music and poetry are thus naturally born together," he concluded. But he also argued that music and poetry gradually diverged as arbitrary instituted signs were introduced to serve the needs of practical experience and rational thought in response to the needs of the world. Thus the articulateness and utility of language were gained at the expense of the original expressiveness of the first poetic language, while music moved into its own autonomous domain. The poet's dilemma is that he is bound in the medium of a language that was made chiefly to serve the ends of analysis, of philosophy and prose. Since in the beginning all language was naturally poetry, prose is a secondary and more artificial product.

I have argued that Wordsworth's critical defence is deeply indebted to the dominant eighteenth-century philosophy that has generally been dismissed as irrelevant or opposed to his thought. If the argument is well founded, it calls for a radical revision of earlier accounts of the intellectual and philosophical foundations of romanticism. I agree with Professor Abrams that, "what is distinctive in the poetry of Wordsworth and Coleridge is . . . the repeated formulations of [the] outer life as a contribution of, or else as in constant reciprocation with, the life of man the observer"; this is not at variance with the philosophy to which I have appealed. But I cannot agree that their quest, "was an essential part of the attempt to revitalize the material and mechanical universe which had emerged from the philosophy of Descartes and Hobbes, and which had been recently dramatized by the theories of Hartley and the French mechanists of the latter eighteenth century. It was an attempt at the same time to overcome the sense of man's alienation from the world by healing the cleavage between subject and object." It would be more relevant to mention the French organicists (again a vital French contribution to romantic thought). The cleavage of subject and object was irreparable, but the remedy, though imperfect, lay in the very philosophy that had created the cleavage.

I have also argued that the background and understanding we need are found in French thought. This is contrary, I know, to the common practice, but its exclusion should have raised doubts about the old consensus. It is no point against my argument to cite Wordsworth's phrases in "The Convention of Cintra" (1809) about the "pestilential philosophism of France" and "the pellets of logic which Condillac has cast in the foundry of national vanity" (I, 332). Condillac was much more than the logic, but the political and ideological reaction fixed on this work as representative of the philosophy that was being made responsible for the Revolution. After 1800, there were many who like Wordsworth revised their admiration for that tradition, or even concealed their debts. So did Sir James Mackintosh in England

and his friend Mme. de Staël, though her changes of mind were more nuanced. The almost automatic citation of her *De l'Allemagne* (1813) in these contexts is chronologically weak and a poor choice over her genuinely original book *De la littérature considérée dans ses rapports avec les institutions sociales* (1800), which reveals striking similarities with Wordsworth's thought. They were both the disciples of the same tradition, and her book was written several years before she met and travelled with A. W. Schlegel, from whom it is said she learned the "cloudy and sentimentalized version" of romantic thought that is found in her later book (Abrams, p. 91). A. W. Schlegel was also much in debt to French thought. It may well be true that, "the new critical viewpoints were collateral, although at this time still largely independent, in Germany and England" (*ibid.*), but this situation would surely be a puzzle unless some common factor was in the background. The old consensus has never faced this problem.

Our trouble with Wordsworth, language, and romanticism is a nineteenth-century problem. The reaction against the eighteenth century had set in by 1800. Introduced by Napoleon, advocated during the Bourbon Restoration, and celebrated by Victor Cousin, it ruled until the 1850s when Hippolyte Taine successfully revived respect for Condillac and the *idéologues*.[4] But in spite of Taine, who was not an academic, we have been the victims of a scholarly tradition that was created in that spirit by the nineteenth century. Our odd periodization stems from it; the eighteenth-century expert goes home at midnight at the end of the century before another expert takes over the next morning with a new mindset stocked with scholarly constructions about German romanticism and the fantasies of nineteenth-century academia. Our chief problem with the eighteenth century is still the nineteenth century.

Notes

1. See Frances Ferguson, *Wordsworth: Language as Counter-Spirit* (New Haven: Yale University Press, 1977), p. 4 and *passim.*; Gerald L. Bruns, *Modern Poetry and the Idea of Language* (New Haven: Yale University Press, 1974), p. 64 and *passim*. Both use Humboldt's late work on the Kawi language, posthumously published in 1835.

2. All citations are from *The Prose Works of William Wordsworth*, ed. by W. J. B. Owen and Jane Worthington Smyser. 3 vols. (Oxford, 1974). References are given in the text with volume and page numbers.

3. I have in mind my essays on "The Tradition of Condillac," "Condillac's speechless Statue," and "Wilhelm von Humboldt and the linguistic thought of the French *idéologues*."

4. See "Thoughts on Scaglione's *Classical Theory of Composition*: The survival of 18th-century French philosophy before Saussure," in *Romance Philology* 29 (1976), 522-538; and "Taine and Saussure."

Bréal, "la sémantique," and Saussure

In 1891 Bréal answered no to the question whether linguistics is a natural science: "To meet that claim it lacks a crucial qualification, which is that the object it treats does not exist in nature. Language is a human activity: it has no reality apart from the human mind." Vocal signs are the means of communication, but they "have no value except by the ideas we have agreed to attach to them. Everything in language comes from man and addresses itself to him."[1] He was opposing the doctrine which he illustrated by citing Schleicher's words: "'Languages are natural organisms which, independently of the human will and following fixed laws, are born, grow, develop, age and die; thus they also manifest the series of phenomena that we are used to comprehend under the name life. Consequently the science of language is a natural science'" (Bréal 1891. 616; *Sém.* 309).[2] Enveloped in this error, Bréal argued, linguistics had become mere description of outward forms without hope of gaining insight into the nature of language. Several factors had given plausibility to this view: (1) Literal acceptance of the mystical romantic organic metaphor which merged with Schleicher's naturalism—"the mystical theory and the naturalist theory have little by little become one—there are such confluences in the history of ideas" (1891. 619). (2) False scientism combined with fear of seeking principles that are not open to direct investigation.[3] (3) The puzzling duration and identity of language much like but vastly longer than the life of man, though the

A French version of this essay appears in *Histoire, Épistémologie, Langage*, vol. 3, fasc. 1, early in 1892.

very difficulty of setting limits to the beginning and end of languages discredits this view—Latin had continued to exist long after the fall of the Roman Empire, "and in a way one can say that it still exists today, thanks to the Romance languages which are its transformations" (1891. 617; Sém. 311).[4] (4) And the seeming similarity of language change to natural growth. Even in 1891 Bréal found that most linguists were still attached to this naturalism, some on grounds of philosophical conviction, others, he thought, simply for the convenience of exposition, as if they were treating a fourth realm of nature, in addition to the mineral, vegetable, and animal kingdoms that figure in Linnæus, Buffon, and Cuvier.

Schleicher's naturalism had banished mind and will from language and linguistics. Bréal not merely asserted their importance, but shifted the entire orientation of linguistics on to the mind-bound nature of language.[5] He did not wish to dismiss or depreciate the outward and observable phenomena of language, but he did argue that it is the central problem of linguistics to understand how they serve the needs of speakers. He repeatedly stressed this principle, even long before he gave it this formulation in 1891, in a passage which also shows that he was making the distinctions between "langue" and "parole," diachrony and synchrony:

> If the language is simultaneously modified in the mouth of an entire group of persons, that is not because the organs of speech in the same moment, in the entire population, undergo an identical change. In this simultaneous occurrence, there is a more humble and common reason, which is on the one hand the instinct of imitation and on the other the need to understand and to be understood. Speech is first of all a means of communication: it would lose the most essential of its functions if it ceased to serve for the exchange of ideas. (1891. 625; Sém., 323)

It is this dual need to understand and to be understood, and for speech to serve certain intentions, that relates language to mind. Change is not blind, "it is obvious that it is not a question of laws that are inherent in language: they are laws of the mind that manifest themselves in the transformations of speech, in the same way as we observe such changes in the slow evolution of law, of customs, of beliefs" (1891. 618; Sém. 311). A few pages later Bréal enforced this argument in a suggestive passage:

> Language has its residence and its seat in the mind; it would not make sense to think of it in any other way. If it has preceded us, if it survives us, it is because it exists in the mind of our fellow citizens as in ours, because it has existed before us in our parents, and we in our turn transmit it to our children. It is made by the agreement of many minds, by the harmony of many acts of will, some present and acting, the others long since dead

and vanished. It does not diminish the importance of language to grant it only this ideal existence; on the contrary, it means placing it with the things that occupy the first rank and exert the greatest influence in the world, for these ideal existences—religions, laws, customs—are what gives a form to human life. (1891. 619; Sém. 314).[6]

The Saussurean implications are obvious. Treated in the naturalist manner, language is either not open to historical but merely to comparative study or its results can at best be ranged in chronological sequence. In both cases we have what for Bréal was the mode of nineteenth-century linguistics as in Bopp, Schleicher, and neogrammarian doctrine of the 1870s, that is, "la phonétique" or what soon appeared under the name "morphologie."

But like other human institutions that are man's creations, language must be understood in terms of man's liberty and choice in response to need—"for a nation never has any other language than the one it needs" (1866b. 263).[7] Even phonological change cannot be adequately understood except in these terms: "The causes of phonetic changes must be sought in the still little-explored region of consciousness where the actions of daily life are initiated" (1891. 622). It is the dependence of language on man, mind, and social life for the sake of communication by means of conventional signs, that opens the way for linguistics to become a historical science and thus to move from observation and description to theory and understanding because human will is involved: "The entire history of language is a series of efforts more or less deliberate, but stemming from the same source and tending toward the same single end. . . . Here there is no place for any force other than the human will. Thus semantics belongs essentially to history" (1887b. 210). Bréal had expressly introduced the term "sémantique" as the complement to "phonétique" when he first put the new term into print in 1883.[8]

Bréal's two remarkable essays on "L'histoire des mots" (1887) and "Le langage et les nationalités" (1891) offer the most pointed and succinct statement of his sémantique. Both were substantially included in his best-known—though it seems only cited, but seldom read—work, Essai de sémantique (science des significations), first published in 1897 and often reissued.[9] In the programmatic introduction, "Idée de ce travail," he said that the subject had occupied him for the last thirty years. He had in fact argued its basic principles in publications that appeared in the late 1860s, before the formulation of neogrammarian doctrine. His innovation dates from those early years when he had recently assumed the chair in "grammaire comparée" at the Collège de France. His influence is evident already in the 1880s during Saussure's Parisian years. Bréal's sémantique was not, as has long been and is still mistakenly believed, a "semasiologie" that added another item to the inventory of linguistic study. It was a program for a "linguistique générale," and it owed much to Hippolyte Taine. In the Introduction (signed 1 November 1865) to his translation of Bopp's *Vergleichende Grammatik*, Bréal advanced his critique of the tradition, soon followed by two essays in which he argued his own principles: "De la forme et de la fonction de mots" and "Les idées latentes du langage." Both were opening lectures to his well-attended course at the Collège de France, delivered in early December of 1866 and 1868.[10]

Before 1865 Bréal had made a name for himself with writings on mythology in the manner of Adalbert Kuhn and Max Müller, but he now abandoned that interest and later did not wish to recall it. In the Introduction of 1865 he contrasted Bopp's patient study of detail and open-minded spirit of observation to the romantic mysticism of Windischmann, the Schlegels, Creuzer, and Goerres: Bopp "did more than anyone to dispell the mystery in which these lofty minds—lofty but friends of the twilight—were pleased to envelop the first productions of human thought" (1866a. x). For Bréal the typical exposition of this uninhibited speculation was F. Schlegel's *Ueber die Sprache und Weisheit der Indier* (1808), which after its opening chapters got lost "in a thick fog of hypotheses" (p. x).[11] He especially aimed his criticism at two points. First, Schlegel had postulated that the first speakers of Indo-European, owing to special divine favor, had grasped the precise relation between sound and concept with an intuition—"une faculté créatrice"—denied both to less favored languages (such as the Chinese, the Semitic, and the American-Indian languages) and to man today, who, "having lost these faculties, would not know how to explain this relation between the sign and the thing signified which an infallible intuition revealed to our ancestors" (p. xxii). Bréal saw especially three fateful consequences. Schlegel had opened the way for linguistic racism and chauvinism; he had made history, also of language, a story of decay from a state of perfection; and he had violated the uniformitarian principle that for Bréal was the fundamental axiom of all the human or historical sciences. Second, Bréal located the source of these delusions in Schlegel's literal trust in the organic metaphor, which even late in the century still supported the emphasis on "la phonétique" and the doctrine of autonomous sound-change.[12] Bréal did, however, aim his critique also against Bopp, who had treated only "phonetics and the theory of forms" (p. xlii) but paid no attention to syntax.[13] This concentration on the exterior aspects of language tended to sanction the continued rule of Schlegel's mysticism and of Schleicher's naturalism. Bréal later noted that the neogrammarians had not broken that pattern, in spite of their rejection of the old organicism. Bréal had cleared the ground for his own radical innovation.

The two opening lectures in 1866 and 1868 presented a single argument. In both it was Bréal's intent to show that "the history of the forms of language is only half of comparative grammar and that this entirely exterior study of words must always be illuminated and guided by the study of signification" (1866b. 243; cf. 1868. 296). Language study must recognize the two aspects that had generally been separated, form and function. In 1866 he contrasted the Greek study of words in terms of their role in thought or function, to the Indian grammatical study of words in terms of their elements or form, which was much like doing "a sort of chemistry of language" (1866b. 245-246). For the past fifty years, linguists had treated languages in the Indian manner, as naturalists without regard for history, "as the physiologist studies the structure of different organisms." To underscore his point, he added a phrase that was used several times in the same argument by Gaston Paris (on each occasion with reference to Bréal), by Bréal himself (1891. 617; *Sém*. 310), until it found its way into Saussure's *Cours*: reading the great works of Bopp and Schleicher it is, said Bréal, "as if we were being confronted with a description of a fourth realm of nature" (1866b. 248). He concluded that it must be the aim of linguistics to join the two methods: "It is the joining of these two methods that defines historical grammar. The object of this study is to seek in the mind of man the cause of linguistic change" (1866b. 247).

In 1868 Bréal contrasted comparative grammar directly with *grammaire générale*, obviously preferring the latter's effort to relate language and mind, though he noted it had tended to impose mental categories on language without paying sufficient attention to the facts of language. This is the core of Bréal's method and *sémantique*: a revision and extension of *grammaire générale* in the light of empirical study; his preference for *grammaire générale* was shared by Saussure.[14] In 1868 Bréal again argued that language study must be historical; by going beyond Grimm, "we discover the successive formations where the famous student of Germanic thought he witnessed simultaneous variations of the same type. It is in this fashion that our science steadily develops, tending more and more to change its name 'comparative grammar,' which opens the way to ambiguity, for its true name: historical grammar" (1868. 297).

The reason for insisting on history is obvious: what man shapes is, like all his institutions, constantly subject to will and intelligence; understanding is possible only in those terms. Theory and method must take account of the two inseparable aspects that Bréal variously called *forme/fonction, forme/sens, signe/la chose signifiée, corps/ esprit, son/concept, extérieur/intérieur, physiologique/psychologique* that all prefigure the contrast *phonétique/sémantique.* Near the end of the 1866 lecture Bréal said: "The history of language does not follow a principle exclusively its own; it always keeps in step, if not with political history, at least with the intellectual and social history of the people" (1866b. 264). There can be no doubt that Bréal was following Taine's program for the study of the human sciences. This is evident both in the terminology (such as simultaneity and successivity, will and intelligence) and in the overall conceptual framework, soon to be filled out by the role that Taine gave to signs in his fundamental work *De l'Intelligence* (1870). I have argued elsewhere that Saussure was indebted to Taine. It now becomes clear that this debt was intertwined with that of Bréal, for example on the necessarily historical nature of language and its study. "There is only one more step to take," wrote Taine in March of 1866, "so far it has always been a question of the interrelation of things that exist simultaneously; the question now is the interrelation of things in succession" (Taine 1866. xviii). Saussure agreed with Bréal; nineteenth-century language study, as in Bopp and Schleicher, had failed to understand the nature of language and lacked method. This study had been "exclusively comparative instead of being historical. . . . Language was looked upon as having a sphere all its own, a fourth realm of nature" (*Cours,* 16-17).[15] In the context of the same argument, Saussure also agreed with Bréal's statement that "though unpremeditated, the facts of language are nonetheless inspired and guided by an intelligent will" (1887b. 210; *Sém.* 307).[16] Saussure's acceptance of these principles is evident already in his first inaugural lecture at Geneva in 1891, where his debt to Bréal seems beyond doubt.[17]

In 1866 Bréal argued against Schleicher that phonetic change does not cause words to become less adequate for the expression of thought; on the contrary, it often promotes precision and richness of expression. It means progress rather than decay and decadence; fullness of grammatical forms is not an index of racial superiority. In "Les idées latentes du langage" he went further. He argued that the distinct units we call words form only a small part of the means that language puts to use. In addition to the manifest signs we call words, there are others that are just as important, though being "invisible" they have been ignored by linguists in recent generations. Bréal was of course reintroducing one of the basic concepts of *grammaire générale*, subaudition or ellipsis, which he chose to call "latent ideas." What he had in mind was that it is in the nature of language to express ideas only incompletely, that it cannot communicate even the simplest thought, "if the mind did not constantly come to the aid of speech, and unless it supplied the remedy for the shortcomings of its interpreter owing to the capacity for enlightenment that is inherent in it" (1868. 300). A language that at every moment precisely expressed what was in the mind is an impossibility, "for that would demand that language underwent modification with every new notion, or that the operations of mind should forever remain identical not to shatter the mechanism of language" (301), an argument he later repeatedly, like Saussure, brought against the possibility of a philosophical language—or in other words, no viable language can ever be a mere nomenclature. Bréal was postulating what has more recently been called "deep structure." The mind intuits or knows by tradition what is not expressed formally; the understanding completes what language merely indicates (302).[18] For Bréal this aspect of language, latent ideas, had several consequences, of which I can treat only a few.

One of these had a practical aim though a theoretical foundation. The richness and potential of language are not measured by the small number of signs it uses, but by the number of formations this inventory makes possible. Schleicher was wrong, therefore, to deny "*a priori* in men of another race than ours the existence of any notion that is not marked by a special sign in their language. The mind penetrates the fabric of language and covers even the empty spaces and the interstices. . . . Since different languages do not always agree on what they express, they can also differ in regard to what they leave unsaid." This was for Bréal a question of structure, which is the theoretical underpinning: "To explain the structure of a language, it is not enough to analyze its grammar and refer the words to their etymological value. We must enter into the people's way of thinking and feeling" (322). Schlegel's and Schleicher's incipient linguistic racism lacks foundation.

Other consequences, this time of a theoretical nature, stem from Bréal's more than casual statement on structure, just quoted, and from another statement that raised a related issue, that of linguistic units: "The entire syntax has its pattern in the mind. . . . The unity of proposition and phrase just like that of the word is of the mind's making" (320). The example of compounds that do not formally indicate different semantic relations that must still be grasped by the mind, shows that "the two terms of the compound would not make any sense to the mind if the mind did not put together the relation that language leaves without a mark. . . . 'Interior syntax' is what Adlophe Regnier has called this mental work of subordination and association that we are forced to make" (308-309).[19] Different languages use distinct structures to the same ends, as shown by the French phrase "Compagnie d'assurance contre les accidents sur les chemins de fer" and the English phrase "rail road accidents insurance company"—it is one of the puzzling details of Bréal's writings that he often uses fine English examples. He returned to these ideas later when he talked of "formules," "locutions," or "groupes articulés"— the latter a chapter-title in *Essai de sémantique*.[20] He was pointing to what in Saussure's terms are known as syntagmatic relations.

In 1887 Bréal devoted several pages of "L'histoire des mots" to this subject, opening with the statement: "A language does not consist exclusively of words: it consists of groups of words and of phrases" (1887b. 198; *Sém.* 293). Once a word has entered into a phrase, we are no longer concerned with the individual words in it: "It is not the word that forms a distinct unity for our mind: it is the idea. If the idea is simple, it doesn't matter that the expression is complex; the mind perceives only the totality." Like Saussure, Bréal observed that only our habitual attention to writing has obscured this fact; most speakers have no clear and distinct conception of word division, but all the same manage very well "their thought correctly and their speech without making mistakes." The hearer collaborates with the speaker: "The listener concentrates on the idea and unites as a single whole everything that belongs together" (1887. 199).[21] Once made part of a locution, "the word loses its individuality and becomes disengaged from any outside influence" (200; *Sém.* 295).[22] It is clear that syntagms for Bréal belonged to *la langue*, as they did for Saussure.[23]

In the next section, opening "language does not consist merely of words and locutions," Bréal developed another aspect of latent ideas, remarking that he had touched on this matter in his 1868 lecture. Using the four-digit number 2738 as an example, he pointed out that each digit is understood by its place in the sequence, so that "there is thus an element which, though not expressed, contributes to the value of the whole: this element is the order of the digits." Though he does not use the term linearity, he is identifying that principle; the lesson is obvious, "this value of position exists more or less in all languages, and especially in our modern languages," though the linguistic process is not quite so simple and formalized, for here the mind must respect habits already acquired "under the dominance of another state of language." But it is still true that "this appropriation of syntax to a new state of things is, just as much as variation of meaning, a part of semantics"—a passage that also, incidentally, makes it clear that Bréal's sémantique is a "linguistique générale" and not confined to the subject of change of meaning in words (1887b. 205-206).[25] Ten years later Bréal concluded a chapter on compounds with a statement of the principle of binarism: "Whatever the length of a compound phrase, it never comprises more than two terms. This rule is not arbitrary: it pertains to the nature of the mind, which associates ideas in units of two." This is true even when each part of a whole is itself composite (*Sém.* 171).

Bréal's theory of language also contains other basic concepts that reappear in Saussure. His theory clearly employed the distinction between *langue* and *parole*; it is amply illustrated in citations above.[26] *La parole* is at every moment the individual speech manifestation, subject to the speaker's use of the collective *langue* that is given by tradition. On the condition that he is understood, the speaker is free to manage *la langue* by his own will, intelligence, memory, and intention. It is this creative intervention that is responsible for change. The role of will and intelligence creates history, so to speak, so that the study of language must on the one hand be essentially historical and on the other respect the distinctions between simultaneity and successivity that rule in the human sciences. Bréal rarely used these terms, but it is clear (as some of my citations show) that he was working with these principles, and the same holds true for structure. As has already been pointed out, it seems clear that he owed this apparatus to Taine.

Bréal also placed emphasis on the concept of "valeur," which has appeared often in my citations. He had introduced it in 1879: "We imitate bankers who, when they handle values, treat them as if they were the coin itself, because they know that at a given moment they could change them for the coin" (1879. 1010). Thus valeur is intimately related to the distinction between synchrony and diachrony. For a word the only value that counts is the one it has at the moment of speaking, "the people pay no attention to the past: they know only the current meaning" (1887b. 198; *Sém.* 293). The etymology is irrelevant, "the actual and current value of the word exerts such power over the mind that it takes away any awareness of the etymological meaning" (*Sém.* 182)—hence the error of studying language terms of etymology and the past. It is the context that "like the key in music, determines the value of signs" (1887b. 193; *Sém.* 287). This was for Bréal the central principle: "There is a rule that transcends all other rules: Once a sign has been found and adopted for an object, it becomes adequate for the object. We can reduce it materially, but it will always retain its value" (1887b. 204; *Sém*. 301).[27] Values are sustained by structure, by "the action which words in a language exercise on one another at a distance," so that "each new word that is introduced in the language causes a perturbation analogous to the introduction of a new element in the physical or social world" (1887b. 190-191; *Sém*. 284). There is a kind of equilibrium, or as Bréal wrote in 1878, "language, like the world, consists of forces that maintain a state of equilibrium" (1878b. 114).[28]

I have argued that Bréal, beginning in the late 1860s, developed a linguistic theory based on the principles that later emerged in Saussure's *Cours*. Some of these appear in his terminology (such as *langue, parole,* and *valeur*), while other principles are given equally distinct roles in his conceptual framework though they rarely figure in the terminology (such as structure, linearity, binary opposition, syntagmatics, and the distinction between diachrony and synchrony). It is also obvious that for Bréal language is an institution and the linguistic sign is arbitrary. Bréal often said that he was not fond of fancy terminology or of the "esprit de système" it suggested; he was unacademic also in this, that he believed it was possible to write about these matters for a larger public without loss of clarity. His professional contemporaries agreed that he succeeded. In his many reviews Bréal criticized the standard linguistic literature for its obscurity, lack of method, and academic pretention. He had fully argued his theory at least by 1891, several years before the *Essai de sémantique* appeared in 1897 with the subtitle "science des significations," which could just as well have been "science des signes linguistiques." His sémantique was not primarily about change of meaning in words; it was a "linguistique générale." In his perspicacious review Paul Valéry pointed to a reading that shows correct understanding of Bréal: "The researches of M. Bréal support the generalization they suggest. They invite study of all symbolic systems, en masse. Algebra, musical notation, certain kinds of ornamentation, cryptography, etc., are open to semantic analysis. Seen from the point of view of meanings, all these systems and language should, I think, lead to important distinctions among the ways in which mental events are joined together" (Valéry 1898. 259).[29] Bréal's "science des significations" was an example of Saussure's "sémiologie"—"a science that studies the life of signs within society" (*Cours*, 33). In this enterprise Bréal was, like Saussure, indebted to Taine, who had based his account of the understanding—

"l'intelligence"—on a doctrine of signs, also nonlinguistic signs, drawing his chief inspiration from Condillac and his followers.

It is well known that Gaston Paris is among the few scholars to whom Saussure gave prominent mention, for instance for the view that Latin still exists in the Romance languages. But on this point as on other matters of a similar nature, Paris was following Bréal, to whom he regularly acknowledged his debt. In linguistics he called himself Bréal's first disciple, and this is especially true of the rejection of the organicist view of language. Several obituaries observed that Paris was not an original mind, that he borrowed his methods from elsewhere, and that his great role was to teach, organize, and inspire. In the 1880s it was in fact said in Paris that Gaston Paris's scholarly orientation was too German. His acceptance of Bréal's linguistics is contrasted by his continued adherence to romantic doctrines in literary studies. Both with regard to the origin of the Old-French *fabliaux* and to the origin and historicity of the *chansons de geste*, Paris remained the disciple of German and French romantic scholarship, unlike Bréal who in his late work on Homer and the epic argued against doctrines that had the same source as those he throughout his career dismissed in linguistics. It was Joseph Bédier who cut the foundations of Paris's popular literary romanticism in his two astonishing works on *Les Fabliaux* (1893) and on *Les Légendes épiques* (1908-1913). In the latter work Bédier cited Bréal's work on Homer as a model, and he expressly called himself "un esprit réaliste."

Here lies the key to Bréal's entire orientation. It was said at the time that the characteristic cast of French scholarship that emerged in the 1870s was its "réalisme." This meant renewed respect for eighteenth-century philosophy, the rejection of romanticism, independence of German scholarship, and acceptance of uniformitarianism as the fundamental axiom in the human sciences. This axiom entails that past processes do not differ from those that are open to empirical study in the present.[30] For contemporaries it was Taine who had begun and articulated this turn against spiritualism, in favor of what Durkheim with assent and admiration called Taine's "rationalist empiricism." This term also fits Bréal. He was called "un esprit cartésien," and he constantly drew on eighteenth-century philosophy. Near the end of the *Essai de sémantique* he contrasted this philosophy to that of linguistic organicism: "Words are signs, they have no more existence than the signals of the wireless telegraph or than the dots and dashes of the Morse alphabet.

To say that language is an organism is to obscure things and to throw a seed of error into minds. One could just as well also say that writing is an organism. . . . It follows of necessity that linguistics belongs with the historical sciences" (*Sém.* 255-256).[31] Like Taine in philosophy and Durkheim in sociology, Bréal was in linguistics the chief advocate of the eighteenth century, of Condillac and the *idéologues*.

Bréal's role in the history of linguistics has been virtually ignored except for quite frequent disparagement owing to the ignorant error that his sémantique is a semasiology. This attitude was not shared by his contemporaries and students, who did not speak from the narrow perspective of recent reconstructions. Even before Bréal's death in 1915 Meillet said (and later repeated): "Bréal and Saussure were the two masters who gave the French school of comparative grammar its own distinct character" (Meillet 1915. 120). Vendryes wrote as late as 1955 that Saussure's legendary seminars at the École des hautes études (where he owed his position to Bréal) during the 1880s had had "a decisive effect on French linguistics, strengthening the influence of Bréal and especially anticipating that of Meillet" (Saussure 1964. 97; letter of 8 February 1900). Even judging them independently on their own merits, I see no reason to accept the arguments of the extensive literature that says that Saussure's sources are found in the writings of German linguists, either before he came to Paris or after he had left. His linguistic thought was, like Bréal's, a severe critique of the German tradition. Saussure did not arrive in Paris from Leipzig and Berlin with the ideas that generated the *Cours de linguistique générale*, and he did not leave Paris without them. Even Whitney counts for little compared with Taine and Bréal, though it remains a puzzle why Saussure made so much of him, especially of points that few contested such as the social and conventional nature of language. Was the reason perhaps that Whitney was dead and distant, not still living in the Parisian milieu that had inspired the young Saussure? Or simply that he was given the opportunity to write on Whitney for a ceremonial occasion? Bréal was the great innovator who gave French linguistics the distinct and powerful form that by a sort of delayed reaction struck the world in its summa, Saussure's *Cours*. Whether this makes Saussure less original than we have been made accustomed to think depends on one's criteria. His terminology gave it a catching systematic quality, but it was Bréal who supplied the conceptualization that gave the new linguistics its fresh French cast and principles.[32]

Notes

1. Cf. Bréal 1866b. 249: "We must make sure that the description of human language does not make us forget man, who is both the beginning and the end, for in language everything proceeds from him and addresses itself to him." I have treated Bréal in "Bréal vs. Schleicher," but there is little overlap between the two essays. "Taine and Saussure" is also relevant. Readers are invited to pay attention to the terms and concepts "langue," "parole," and "valeur" in the citations from Bréal, on which I shall comment later in this essay. I use the abbreviations *Sém*. for Bréal 1911 and *Cours* for Saussure 1916. All references that are given by year only are to Bréal's writings.

2. 1891 is, with some omissions, included in *Sém*. 309-331, under the title, "La linguistique est-elle une science naturelle?" The topic of 1891 is linguistic chauvinism and racism, which Bréal treated often. Bréal had a sharp eye for the ideological, political, and institutional dimensions of scholarship, but space does not allow their treatment here. He was also an excellent historian of ideas and of linguistics, which is another subject that must be left aside except as it forms part of my subject.

3. Cf. 1887a. 233: "If linguistics has applied itself to the observation of the modifications that occur in the grammatical mechanism, it has not with the same care sought the intellectual causes owing to which this mechanism modifies and renews itself. Linguistics has no doubt been afraid of getting lost in the pursuit of the discovery of principles that are not open to direct investigation."

4. Saussure credits this observation to Gaston Paris, *Cours*. 296, and 1974. 6b-7a, in the first inaugural Geneva lecture, November 1891. On the next point (4), cf. 1887b. 187 (*Sém*. 280): "For to say that words are born, live together and die, isn't it true that that is pure metaphor? To talk of the life of language, to call languages living organisms, is to use figures that will carry us into the midst of dreaming."

5. The study of language seems periodically in need of being reclaimed for man, mind, and social life. It occurred in the seventeenth century in the reaction against the Adamic language doctrine; and it has occurred recently in the reaction against linguistic behaviorism.

6. Cf. 1866b. 265: "Languages have only an ideal existence." 1900. 67: "It is always easy to argue over the moment when a language has been transformed or has ceased to exist: there is a good reason for that. It is that language only has a metaphorical existence."

7. Cf. *Sém*. 204: "Each epoch makes the language it needs."

8. 1883. 133: "In fact, it is on the body and form of words that most linguists have spent all their cleverness: the laws that rule the transformation of meanings have been left in the dark or have been noted only in passing. Since this study deserves to have its name as well as phonetics and morphology, we shall call it 'semantics,' that is to say the science of meanings." Cf. above p. 32/n6.

9. There were new editions in 1899, 1904, 1908, 1911, 1913, and later. The first two editions contained two supplementary essays, of which one was 1887 in somewhat abbreviated form (*Sém*. 279-308). 1891 was included in the edition of 1904 and subsequent editions.

10. These two essays were included in 1878a, to which I make references.

11. Bréal pointed out that these early chapters drew on Sir William Jones; see 1866a. xiii: "Like others, F. Schlegel borrowed his knowledge from the *Asiatic Researches*: he adapted the facts he found there to a chronology of his own invention and to a preconceived philosophy of history."

12. Cf. 1866a. xxiv: only the Indo-European languages truly deserve "the name of languages with flexions; the author continues in the figurative language which he sometimes seems to take literally, that they are the only ones in which the root is a living seed that grows, unfolds and branches out like the organic products of nature." Bréal noted Bopp's

critique of Schlegel's "flexions," "a strange theory which Bopp has expressly contested on several occasions, and contradicted by his life's work" (p. xxii), with reference to *Grammaire comparée*, § 108 (pp. 225-230). Cf. also p. xxvi: "The theory of Schlegel opened the door to mysticism; it contained consequences that involved history as much as grammar, for it tended to prove that man at the beginning had faculties different from those he has today, and that he created something that escapes scientific analysis." Bréal pointed out that Schleicher and Max Müller shared this doctrine.

13. Bréal's usage of "phonétique" for what later, after his time, became known as phonology was common in the nineteenth century. See Aarsleff 1979, above pp. 300 and 323n19. By the time Saussure insisted on retaining this meaning, it was old-fashioned. Cf. *Cours*, 55-56.

14. 1868. 300: "Such study cannot fail to be fruitful, and any disparity between philosophical grammar and empirical grammar should lead to new findings regarding the nature of language and the development of the human mind." Cf. *Cours*, 118: "Classical grammar has been reproached for not being scientific; but its foundations are less open to criticism and its object better defined than is the case with the linguistics inaugurated by Bopp."

15. Saussure's introduction to the *Cours*, on the history of linguistics, relies heavily on Bréal, both 1866a and 1866b; see Saussure 1967-1968. 3-4, where Gautier's notes refer to "Bréal, *Préface* à la *Grammaire comparée* de Bopp." Cf. *Cours*, 411-412, where De Mauro, cites Riedlinger's notes (Saussure 1967-1968. 2-4). It is odd that De Mauro, who elsewhere shows great respect for Bréal, makes no effort whatever to relate Bréal's sémantique to Saussure's *Cours*. Near the end of his introduction Saussure attributes exclusively to the neogrammarians what Bréal had argued earlier; thanks to them, wrote Saussure, "we no longer see language as an organism that develops by itself, but as a product of the collective mind of linguistic groups" (19). Saussure's understanding of the history of linguistics is often not well informed.

16. Cf. *Cours*, 30-31: "Speech on the contrary is an individual act of will and intelligence."

17. Saussure 1974. 3b-8a. The same holds for the other two Geneva lectures. Cf., e.g., 5a: "As we have come to understand better the true nature of the facts of language . . . it has become more evident that the science of language is a historical science and nothing but a historical science." 5b-6a: "What, then, is the second condition implied by the term historical science? It is that the object that is the subject of history . . . represents, in any sense whatever, human actions governed by human will and intelligence." Cf. also Saussure's critique of *grammaire comparée*, *ibid.*, 5a, 14b-15a. Owing to excitement about synchrony, recent Saussure interpretation has lost sight of the fact that his orientation remained firmly historical. Against this misunderstanding, Jonathan Culler correctly insists that "on the contrary, it was precisely because he recognized, more profoundly than his critics, the radical historicity of language that he asserted the importance of distinguishing between facts about linguistic system and facts about linguistic evolution" (Culler 1976. 29).

18. Bréal often stressed this, e.g. here, 312: "Thought is a spontaneous act of mind which no effort coming from outside can set in motion in a direct and immediate manner. All you can do is to provoke my thought."

19. Cf. "syntaxe intérieure" in Saussure 1967-1968. 380, in I R 2.92.

20. Pp. 172-176; the preceding chapter on "Les noms composés" (160-171) is also relevant.

21. Cf. *ibid.*: "But in reality, as soon as the word has become part of an idiomatic formula, we pay attention only to the formula." Cf. *Sém.*, 173: "Everyone knows that the word, in its isolated state, has no very clear existence in the awareness of common speakers and that it is apt to join with what precedes or follows. Our telegraph offices, where words are counted one by one, should have an ample harvest of observations on this subject."

22. Cf. *Sém.*, 174: "These articulated groups do not merely retain entire the signification

of the elements of which they are composed, but they further gain a value that does not belong to them in themselves, but which results from the position they habitually occupy in the phrase."

23. See the first citations in this and the next paragraphs. Cf. 1887b. 201: "Many facts that surprise at first view become clear if we consider this role of locutions in the history of the language."

24. Cf. *Cours*, 172: "These idiomatic turns of phrase cannot be improvised; they are furnished by tradition."

25. These pages of 1887b are omitted in *Sém.* The meaning of *sémantique* is also brought out when Bréal (1887b. 188; *Sém.*, 280) calls Paul's "*Principes de linguistique*" a book devoted to "sémantique." Bréal's translation of the title is also suggestive; he was of course referring to *Prinzipien der Sprachgeschichte* (1880, 2nd ed. 1886), which was never translated into French. On the point he made, Bréal remarked that Paul had often made allusion to this approach, "without, however, having shown the importance of this laborious march of language toward a goal more or less clearly discerned" (1887b. 206).

26. More citations can easily be added, e.g., 1876. 10 (1878a. 373): "It is not surprising that the teaching of language, in its full extent and taken in its true meaning, becomes indistinguishable from general education, because language is the chief instrument of communication among men, and because it is by means of speech that the generations enter into partnership." 1891. 628: It has been said that we are constrained by analogy; on the contrary, said Bréal, "it would be more true to say that we are all, at every moment of the day, creators of language. To limit the part that each of us plays in the production of speech to new expressions, is far too narrow. . . . Analogy is constantly at work, or in other words we are all the time active in the production of speech." (With somewhat altered wording in *Sém.*, 328.)

27. Cf. *Sém.* 152: "The only rule that matters is this: the part that survives takes the place of the whole; the sign, though mutilated, remains adequate to the object."

28. Cf. 1884. 554: "Except in the moments when our attention is directed to the matter of language, this matter is invisible to our eyes. Words have no value for us except as signs of the idea." *Sém.*, 167: "The different parts of a language are mutually dependant." Cf. *Cours*, 116: "For language is a system of pure values exclusively determined by the state of its terms at the moment . . . at each moment [the value] depends on a system of contemporaneous values." *Cours*, 169: " . . . everywhere and at all times this same complex equilibrium of terms that are reciprocally conditioned. Said differently, language is a form and not a substance," a principle that Bréal obviously shared. Cf. also 1891. 629 (*Sém.*, 329): language is not "a mirror that reflects reality: it is a transposition of reality by means of particular signs which for the most part do not correspond to anything that is real." 1886. 238. "Language, this world of convention which reflects the real world."

29. Cf. Thomas 1897. 178: "As practiced by Bréal, semantics is not so much a distinct discipline as a certain manner of understanding and extending linguistics. It is a sort of super-linguistics, an extract, a quintessence of linguistics." Hey 1898. 551: "Bréal's 'sémantique,' however, does not at all coincide with the discipline we have named [semasiology]; 'sémantique' has a much wider territory: it embraces together with phonetics all of the science of language. . . . Semantics is the science of all linguistic phenomena, formal as well as mental, that can be traced back to human intelligence or human will; here belongs, in addition to the doctrine of meaning, the entire mental aspect of etymology, morphology, and syntax."

30. Cf. Saussure on uniformitarianism in *Cours*, 252: "The old school split words into roots, themes, suffixes, etc., and assigned absolute value to these distinctions. . . . There had to be a reaction against these aberrations and the word of command of this reaction was, quite rightly, this: observe what happens in the every-day speech of present-day languages

and do not attribute to earlier periods of the language any process, any phenomenon that cannot be ascertained today." On uniformitarianism, see Christy 1980.

31. Bréal added: "I have avoided comparisons with botany, physiology, geology, with the same care that others have shown in seeking them out. As a consequence, my exposition is more abstract, but I think I can say it is truer." For his own ends Bréal consistently used comparison with architecture to illustrate structure, form, and interrelationships; this is usually also Saussure's practice.

32. Louis Havet was among the first to take up Bréal's sémantique; in 1884 (p. 449) he wrote with reference to the concept Bréal had given a name in print in 1883: "We are too inclined to imagine that all of etymology and linguistics consists exclusively in knowing how to split up a word into prefixes, affixes, suffixes, indixes, roots, endings, differences and other tiny pieces. Is physiology then merely the art of cutting up a chicken or dissecting a man? If we wish our science to make progress, it must, in order to remain precise, continue to pay attention to phonetics, and absorb semantics in order to grow in intelligence." This is spoken in Bréal's spirit.

References

Aarsleff, Hans. 1978. "Taine and Saussure." Repr. above.

——1979. "Bréal vs. Schleicher." Repr. above.

Bopp, Franz. 1866-1874. *Grammaire comparée des langues indo-européennes.* tr. by Michel Bréal. 5 vols. Paris: Imprimerie impériale.

Bréal, Michel. 1866a. Introduction. In Bopp 1866-1874. I, i-lvii.

——1866b. "De la forme et de la fonction des mots." *Revue des cours littéraires de la France et de l'étranger,* 4th year, no. 5 (29 December 1866), 65-71. In: Bréal 1878a. 243-266.

——1868. *Les idées latentes du langage.* Leçon faite au Collège de France pour la réouverture du cours de grammaire comparée, le 7 décembre 1868. Paris: Hachette. In: Bréal 1878a. 295-322.

——1876. "L'enseignement de la langue française." *Revue politique et littéraire* [later *Revue bleue*], July-Dec. 1876, pp. 4-10. Also in: Bréal 1878a. 347-373.

——1878a. *Mélanges de mythologie et de linguistique.* Paris: Hachette.

——1878b. "De l'analogie." In: *Mélanges d'histoire et de philologie.* Bibliothèque de l'École des Hautes Études. Sciences philologiques et historiques, fasc. 35. Paris: Imprimerie nationale. Pp. 101-114.

——1879. "La science du langage." *Revue scientifique de la France et de l'étranger,* 16 (January-July), 1005-1011.

——1883. "Les lois intellectuelles du langage. Fragment de sémantique." *Annuaire de l'association des études grecques en France,* 17. 132-142.

——1884. "Comment les mots sont classés dans notre esprit." *Revue politique et littéraire. Revue Bleue.* 1884, no. 18 (1 November) 552-555.

——1886. "Comment on apprend les langues étrangères." *Revue internationale de l'enseignement,* 11 (January-June), 235-255.

——1887a. "Comment les langues réparent les points faibles de leur grammaire." In: *Mélanges Renier.* Bibliothèque de l'École des Hautes Études. Sciences philologiques et historiques, fasc. 73. Paris: F. Vieweg, Pp. 233-239.

——1887b. "L'histoire des mots." *Revue des deux mondes* 82 (1 July), 187-212.

——1891. "Le langage et les nationalités." *Revue des deux mondes* 108 (1 December), 615-639.

398 Bréal, "la sémantique," and Saussure

——1900. "Introduction à la chronologie du latin vulgaire." *Journal des savants* 1900. 65-77 (February), 137-147 (March).

——1906. *Pour mieux connaître Homère*. Paris: Hachette. (2nd ed. 1911.)

——1911. *Essai de sémantique*. 5th ed. Paris: Hachette. See note 9.

Christy, Craig. 1980. "Uniformitarianism in nineteenth-century linguistics." *Amsterdam Studies in the Theory and History of Linguistic Science* III: *Studies in the History of Linguistics* 20 (1980), 249-256.

Culler, Jonathan. 1976. *Ferdinand de Saussure*. New York: Penguin.

Delesalle, Simone. 1977. "Michel Bréal: Philologie, instruction et pouvoir." *Langages* No. 45 (March 1977), 67-83.

Havet, Louis, 1884. Variétés. *Mémoires de la Société de linguistique de Paris*, 5.442-449.

Hey, O. 1898. Rev. of Bréal, *Sém. Archiv für lateinische Lexicographie und Grammatik* 10. 551-555.

Meillet, Antoine. 1915. "La linguistique." In: *La science française*. Exposition universelle et internationale de San Francisco, 2 vols. 2. 117-124.

Saussure, Ferdinand de. 1916. *Cours de linguistique générale*, ed. by Tullio de Mauro. Paris: Payot, 1972.

——1964. "Lettres de Ferdinand de Saussure à Antoine Meillet, publiées par Émile Benveniste." *Cahiers Ferdinand de Saussure* 21. 91-125.

——1967-1968. *Cours de linguistique générale*. Édition critique par Rudolf Engler. Fasc. 1-3. Wiesbaden: Harrassowitz.

——1974. *Cours de linguistique générale*. Édition critique par Rudolf Engler. fasc. 4. Wiesbaden: Harrassowitz.

Taine, Hippolyte. 1866. Préface de la deuxième édition. In: *Essais de critique et d'histoire*. 12th ed. Paris: Hachette, 1913.

Thomas, Antoine. 1897. "La sémantique et les lois intellectuelles du langage." In: *Essais de philologie française*. Paris: Bouillon. Pp. 166-193.

Valéry, Paul. 1898. Rev. of Bréal, *Sém. Mercure de France* 25 (January-March), 254-260.

Vendryes, J. 1955. "Première société linguistique. La Société de linguistique de Paris (1865-1955)." *Orbis. Bulletin international de documentation linguistique*, 4. 7-21.

Index

Index

Abbreviation, in words and universal grammar, 108
Abbt, Thomas, 197
Abrams, M. H.: on Wordsworth and 18c thought, 372-73, 380; on expressive theory, 374-75
Academia Parisiensis, 252, 254
Academic institutionalization, 5, 18, 32
Act of Uniformity, 239, 257
Adam: as philosopher and etymologist, 25, 59; and words, 47; his name-giving, 59, 281; Besnier on, 59; South on, 59; Boehme on, 60; Leibniz on, 91; Locke on ordinary humanity of, 162; Wilkins on 241; and mankind, 246
Adamic language: and innateness, 9; critique of, 25-26; and linguistic sign, 25-26; and epistemology, 25-26, 282-83, 316-17, 346; and essentialism, 25-27; identity of signifier and signified in, 27; South on, 59; and mysticism, 60; and John Webster, 61, 262; rejected by Boyle and Locke, 61-62; and Boehme, 65, 87, 89, 97n13, 282-83; and German language, 65; Leibniz on, 65-66; and Socinian doctrine, 80n63; and secrets of nature, 97n13; and Wilkins, 248; and philosophical language, 260-62. See also Paracelsus
Adamicism: and science, 12; in 17c poetics, 18-19; and Foucault, 22; in early 19c, 32, 36; in 17c, 59-63

African languages, 99n39
Agrippa, Cornelius, 267n19
Alchemy: Leibniz on, 97n13
Alembert, Jean le Rond d': and Du Marsais, 103, 112, 171; and Condillac, 210
Algebra: and philosophical language, 43; and signs, 63
Allegory, and protestantism, 59
Alsted, J. H., 105
American languages, 93, 98n27, 99n39
Anabaptists, at Oxford, 254
Andreae, Johann Valentin, 10
Angels, and poetry, 62
Animals, why speechless, 215
Anthropology: and language study, 15, 343, 345-46; Wilhelm von Humboldt on, 347-48
Antiquity, authority of, 242
Anti-Sage. See Victorian Sage
Arabic language: close to primitive language, 65
Arabic numerals: and philosophical language, 43
Arbitrariness of linguistic sign: Madvig on, 14, 299-300; Bréal on, 17; denied by Trench and Victorian Sage, 39, 41; Locke on, 54, 63-64, 87-88, 284; Leibniz on, 64-66; and sufficient reason, 88, 90-91; in Condillac and followers, 291; in Saussure, 295, 363; reasserted in late 19c, 317

Arbitrary signs: animals do not have, 170; Locke and Condillac on, 170; and reflection, 188

Arens, Hans: on German and French language study, 6, 149-50, 176, 217,218-19, 314

Ariadne thread, and languages in Leibniz, 94-95

Aristotle, 149, 278

Aristotelians, at Oxford, 255

Arminians, 257

Arnauld, Antoine, 104, 167

Asian languages, 93

Asiatic Researches, 304

Association of ideas: in Locke, 29, 114, 130, 173, 284; and connection of ideas in Condillac, 29, 155, 221n2, 284; and enthusiasm, 75n28; and poetry in Condillac and Wordsworth, 377-78

Astrology, 247

Augustinianism, and linguistic thought, 104

Auteuil, Society of, 348

Automata, 249, 251-52

Aveyron, Wild Boy of, 280, 352n18

Babel: repairing the ruins of, 10, 13, 260; and Royal Society, 228; confusion at, 248, 281-82

Bacon, Francis: and Royal Society, Sprat on, 12, 227-28, 313; and Copernicus, 12, 270n41; and Mersenne, 12-13; vs. Mersenne, Wilkins, and Locke, 22; in Foucault, 22; on languages having been made by ordinary people, 78n43; on grammar, 105; Coleridge on, 126; on signs, 179; and William Gilbert, 246; and Wilkins, 251; on language and philosophy, 260; and scientific method in 19c, 314, 317; mentioned, 138, 307. *See also* Mill, J. S.

Bain, Alexander, and Taine, 309, 365

Bainbridge, John, 247

Balzac, Honoré de: on Cuvier, 34; *Louis Lambert* and *La Peau de Chagrin*, 38-41; on mysticism, 38-39; on Sage, 38-41; on science and language, 40

Barrow, Isaac, 258

Basque language, 15, 338

Bate, John, 269n33, 269n37

Bathurst, Ralph, 225, 255

Baxter, Richard, 257, 259, 272n60

Bayle, Pierre, on enthusiasm, 52

Beausobre, Louis Isaac de, on language change, 184-85

Beauzée, Nicolas, 112

Beck, Hanno, 349

Becker, K. F. 298

Bédier, Joseph, 392

Benfey, Theodor: on history of language study, 5, 149, 313; on Maupertuis, 207n113

Bentham, Jeremy, 37. *See also* Mill, J. S.

Berkeley, George: and Locke, Hazlitt on, 127; and Condillac, 153; and Maupertuis, 181-82; mentioned, 8, 148

Berkeley, George, Baron Berkeley (1601-1658), and Wilkins, 245

Berkeley, George, first Earl of Berkeley (1628-1698), and Wilkins, 258, 264, 273n69

Berlin Academy: opens debate on origin of language, 146-47; and Frederick the Great, 176-77; and Maupertuis, 177; its statutes and organization, 177-78; first prize-topic on language, 189; report on Herder's essay, 196-97; its history, 206n103

Bernard, Claude: on physiology and anatomy, 14, 318; on method and discovery in science, 20, 214-217; on aim of science, 41; and Comte, 309; on intellectual history, 311

Bernardin de Saint-Pierre, Jacques-Henri, 340, 348

Bernegger, Matthias, 246

Bernhardi, A. F., 350n4

Besnier, Pierre, S. J.: on Adam as etymologist, 59; on languages, 81n69, 81n74

Bettini, Mario, 268n30

Bible, and science, 242

Bibliander, Theodor, 47

Bill of Comprehension, 259

Binarism, in Bréal, 17, 390

Birch, Thomas: on Boyle, 53; on Sprat's *History*, 230-31

Bishop of Llandaff, 379

Bisterfeld, Johann Heinrich, 10

Blackwell, Thomas, 148

Blair, Hugh, 379

Blake, William, 38

Bloomfield, Leonard: and history of linguistics, 101, 294, 312; and origin of language, 290

Boehme, Jacob: and enthusiasm, 52; and Adamic language, 59, 60, 65, 87, 97*n*13, 260, 282; popular in England, 60; on language of nature and baroque poetry, 73*n*14; and origin of language, 84; and etymology, 92; and German mystics, 97*n*13; and John Webster, 248, 251; and Wilkins, 256; Romantic interest in, 317; mentioned, 278

Boindin, Nicolas, and Maupertuis, 182

Bonald, Louis de, 163

Book of Nature, 43

Book of Scriptures, 43

Bopp, Franz: in Foucault, 22; and Bréal, 291, 303, 384, 385; and 19c language study, 294; and Saussure, 387; and F. Schlegel, 394*n*12. *See also* Madvig

Bopp-Schleicher tradition, 6, 13, 16

Borges, Jorge Luis, 275*n*81

Borst, Arno, 314

Boswell, Sir William: his learned contacts, 253, 270*n*44; life of, 270*n*43

Boyle, Robert: on aim of science, 41; and sacred languages, 43; opinions of, 53; and Locke, 55, 56, 62, 77*n*39-41, 283; on words and things, 56-57; on essences, 56; and Adamic language, 61-62; and Hebrew, 62; on poetry, 62; on nature and Scriptures, 62; on study of languages, 70*n*61; on David, 79*n*61; on signs, 179; invited to Oxford by Wilkins, 255; mentioned, 8, 12, 232, 264, 294

Brahe, Tycho, 294

Brandes, Georg, 33, 365*n*1; 369*n*22

Bréal, Michel, 303-08 *passim*; and Saussure, 6, 17, 20, 21, 359, 387, 391-92; and Taine, 6, 385, 387, 391-92; critic of Bopp-Schleicher tradition, 8, 13-14, 296, 305, 310, 384; and mentalism, 13, 16; on organicism and language study, 13, 295-96; and uniformitarianism, 14, 298, 307, 327*n*36; his 'sémantique,' 15-16, 297; on Renan, 16, 308, 321*n*6; and Gaston Paris, 21, 392, 304-05; rejects philosophical language, 27; as Anti-Sage, 41; and origin of language, 290, 308; and Bopp, 291, 303, 384, 385; on language change, 293, 383-86; on 18c language study, 296; Meillet on, 296, 311; on Jespersen, 296-98; and Whitney, 297, 303, 310, 326*n*32; and Wilhelm von Humboldt, 297, 349;

and Max Müller, 303; on universal grammar, 305, 307, 310, 386, 388; on form and meaning, 306; on mind and syntax, 306, 388-90; and linguistic relativism, 306-307; and 18c thought, 307; and Rousseau, 308; and educational reform, 310; on nature of language, 310; his importance, 311; and Claude Bernard, 317-18; on chauvinism, 325*n*30, 385, 394*n*2; on Condillac and *idéologues*, 349; on Schleicher, 382-83, 388; on language and mind, 382-84; and *langue, parole*, 383; on 19c language study, 384; on history and language, 384, 386-87; on F. Schlegel, 385; on mysticism in language study, 385-86; on form and function, 386; on Greek and Indian linguistics, 386; on comparative grammar, 386; and *signifiant*, *signifié*, 387; on philosophical language, 388; on structure, 388; and syntagmatics, 389-90; and binarism, 390; and *valeur*, 390-91; on etymology, 390; his critique of linguistic literature, 391; his basic orientation, 392; and Hermann Paul, 396*n*25; uses architectural metaphor, 397*n*31. *See also* Renaud

Briggs, Henry, 247, 270*n*44

British Association for the Advancement of Science, 290

Brooke, Christopher, 271*n*49

Brosses, Charles de, 9, 148, 308

Brougham, Henry, on Locke, 122

Brouncker, William, 232

Brown, John, 148

Brown, Thomas: on Locke, 123; on Locke and Condillac, 144*n*35

Brucker, Johann Jakob, on Locke, 141*n*15

Buckingham, second duke. *See* Villiers, George

Budgell, Eustace, on Boyle, 53

Buffon, Georges-Louis Leclerc, 285, 383

Buhle, Johann Gottlieb, on Locke, 141*n*15

Burnet, Gilbert: on Sprat, 236; on Wilkins, 265; on Latitudinarians, 272*n*60

Burnett, James. *See* Monboddo

Burnett, Thomas, 49, 50, 52, 74*n*26

Bysshe, Edward, 273*n*67

Cabalism: and linguistic thought, 10, 282-83; and Adamic language, 60

Cabanis, Georges, 129, 348

Calvin, John, and Wilkins on reading of the Bible, 266n12

Cambridge Platonists, 257, 272n60

Cambridge University: Locke's standing at, 123-24; philosophy at, 131-32; Trinity College, 133; Locke and Cousin required reading at, 144n38; and Wilkins, 257-58

Campanella, Tommaso, and Wilkins, 246, 267n28

Carlyle, Thomas: as Victorian Sage, 37; and Locke, 121, 129; on Cabanis, 129; on German philosophy, 129

Carpenter, Nathaniel, 247

Cartesian linguistics, 101-19 passim; and history of linguistics, 4, 11; and Locke, Condillac, 170-76

Cassini, Gian Domenico, on Oldenburg and Royal Society, 235

Cassirer, Ernst: on language study, 149; on 'reflection' in Herder, 341

Catherine the Great, 93

Caus, Salomon de, 269n33

Chambers, Robert, 35

Charles I, 257, 270n40

Charles II: and philosophical language, 263; mentioned, 233, 239, 259

Charles Louis, Elector Palatine, 245, 249, 267n25, 267n27

Charleton, Walter, 245

Chauvinism: Bréal on, 325n30; in language study, 385, 394n2

Cheat of words, 24, 43

Children found in the wild, 280-81

Chillingworth, William: and Wilkins, 266n12; and Sylvester, 267n24; and latitudinarianism, 272n60

Chinese language and writing: and philosophical language, 43, 90; Leibniz on, 99n39; F. Schlegel and Jespersen on, 298

Chomsky, Noam: and history of linguistics, 101-02; and Du Marsais, 102-03, 106, 167; and Locke, 106-07, 114-116, 172; on Herder, 112; on innateness, 115, 173-74; on universal grammar, 165; and romantic linguistic thought, 170. See also Cartesian linguistics

Christmann, H. H., 370n30

Church Fathers, 278

Ciampini, Giovanni Giusto, 85

Cicero, cited by Locke, 45

Citation, reliability of, 21

Clarendon, first earl of. See Hyde, Edward

Clarke, Edward, 53

Clauberg, Johann: on etymology, 66-67; and Locke, 67; on mental words, 67-68; Leibniz's opinion of, 98n32

Clavius, Christoph, 266n12

Coleridge, S. T.: as Victorian Sage, 38; on Stillingfleet, 125; on Locke and Leibniz, 125, 205n98; on Locke and Newton, 125-26; on Hobbes, Hume, 126; on ethics, 126; on Locke and innateness, 126, 135; on Locke and Descartes, 126, 283-84; on Bacon, 126; on Hartley, 126; J. S. Mill on, 136-37; and Chomsky, 170

Collège de France, 15, 37, 384, 385

Collins, Anthony: and Locke's Essay, 55, 123, 174

Comenius, Jon Amos: and enthusiasm, 52; and Adamic language, 59; on grammar, 105, 106; and Royal Society, 231; mentioned, 10, 275n81

Communication: Locke on, 54; and language, 63

Comparative anatomy: and language study, 33-36; and physiology, Claude Bernard on, 318; and Taine's method, 361-63

Comparative anthropology: in Locke and Condillac, 161; in 18c, 179; and Maupertuis, 183. See also Anthropology

Comparative philology: and philosophy of language, 5; and Victorian Sage, 7, 37-38; as model humanistic discipline, 32; and 18c thought, 32-33, 289-90; in 19c and study of language, 280, 281; Madvig on, 300; Bréal on, 305. See also Linguistics, history of

Comte, Auguste, and Taine, 361

Conceptualization: and terminology, 20; and citation, 21

Condillac, Étienne Bonnot, Abbé de: position in history, 9; his speechless statue, 11, 153-55, 211-16, 377; and Taine, 15, 309, 359, 363-64, 381, 392; and Wordsworth, 17-18, 374-80; on subjectivity of language, 27, 31, 344; on knowledge as function of language, 28-31; on human nature, 28-29; in 19c opinion, 29, 211, 216-17; on genius of languages, 30, 195-96, 307, 376; and Volksgeist, 30-31, 195-96, and linguistic relativism, 30-31; and progress doctrine, 31, 163; and Whewell, 35, 134; and Locke, 49, 107, 148, 163; and Chomsky, 107; on origin of language, 107-10, 163-65, 285-89; on gestures and language, 108-09, 151-52; and history of thought, 109; and Renan, 110, 308; and universal grammar, 111-12, 166, 169; and Du Marsais, 112, 167, 203n73, 212; and Herder, 117n9, 150, 151-52, 195-98, 219, 335, 350n7, 374; Hazlitt on, 127; J. S. Mill on, 137; and Warburton, 148; in Arens's anthology, 149, 176, 217, 219, 314; his *Essai* in history, 149-55; and Rousseau, 152-53, 308; and Diderot, 153-54, 211; and Berkeley, 153; not a materialist, 153, 215-16, 351n13; remains true to argument of *Essai*, 154-55; on man, statue, and animals, 155, 214-15; on connection and association of ideas, 155, 221n2, 378; on signs and language, 157; on simultaneity, successivity, and linearity of discourse, 157-58; on origin and basic principles, 158; and linguistic state of nature, 161; on genetic method and Adam, 162; on reason uniquely human, 163-64, 215; on gestures as natural signs, 163-64; on thinking and origin of language, 166; on primacy of poetic language, 166; on first language and passions, 166; on words and ideas, 166; publication of during Directory, 166, 216; on signs, 170, 223n18, 287-88; on creativity and language, 171, 377; on reflection and arbitrary signs, 188; and Sulzer, 193; member of Berlin Academy, 206n105; and *Encyclopédie*, 210; his influence, 210; on language and nature of man, 211-16; on self-preservation, 211-12, 215; on pleasure and pain, 212; on activity of mind, 212; on instinct, 213-15; on reason and reflection, 215; why misinterpreted, 216-19; chronology of his writings, 217-18; in Germany, 219; popularity in 18c, 221n1; on being plagiarized, 223n15; and Monboddo, 279; and Bréal, 296, 305, 308, 393; and Cournot, 309; and Wilhelm von Humboldt, 340, 341-42, 344, 346; at Auteuil, 348; on *valeur*, 370n29; and romantic aesthetics, 373-74,

377-78; on poetry and prose, 377-78; on meter in poetry, 378-79; on music and poetry, 379-80; mentioned, 69, 105, 128, 280, 365. *See also* Brown, Thomas; Rogers, Henry; Roy, Georges le
Condorcet, Antoine-Nicolas de, 137, 308
Condorcet's widow. *See* Grouchy
Conjectural history, 28, 109-10, 158-59, 160-61, 279
Connection of ideas: different from association of ideas, 29; in Condillac, 108; and reason and reflection, 155; governed by reason, 284. *See also* Association of ideas
Continuity, law of, in Leibniz, 88, 92, 93
Cooper, Anthony Ashley, third Earl of Shaftesbury, 148
Copernicanism, 12, 246-47
Copernicus, Nicholas, 12, 244, 246, 270n41, 294
Coptic language, as philosophical language, Leibniz on, 90
Core vocabulary. *See* Languages
Coseriu, Eugenio, 349, 370n30
Cournot, Antoine-Augustin: on 18c linguistic thought, 309; and Taine, 360
Courtney, W. L., on Locke, 139-40
Cousin, Victor: philosophy of, 31; on 18c thought, 33, 217, 381; on Locke, 124, 130; on sensualism, 130; on enthusiasm as voice of reason, 130; critique of, 130, 131, 137, 139; and Whewell, 145n48; reaction against, 309; and Cournot, 360; Anatole France on, 361; and Taine, 361, 369n29; mentioned, 11
Couturat, Louis, 42
Cowley, Abraham, 226
Creativity: in language, 29, 377; Condillac on, 289
Creuzer, Georg Friedrich, 303, 385
Cromwell, Oliver, 226, 239, 256
Cromwell, Richard, 257
Cryptography, 247-48
Cudworth, Ralph, 272n60, 273n67
Culler, Jonathan, on historicity in Saussure, 395n17
Curtius, William, 72n11
Cuvier, Georges: and comparative anatomy, 33-34; and saltationism, 34; Balzac on, 34; on metaphor in science, 37; and Taine, 360-62; and Bréal, 383; mentioned, 390

Dalgarno, George: on onomatopeia, 80n65; and Leibniz, 81n65; and Wilkins, 274n81

Dangeau, Louis de Courcillon de, l'Abbé de, and Du Marsais, 113, 168

Darmesteter, Arsène, 324n25

Darmesteter, James: on Renan, 21; and social action, 322n13

Darwin, Charles: and Max Müller, 32, 36; and Flourens, 37; and language study, 290; and 19c science, 314, 318; and Malthus, 328n42; on language acquisition, 360; and Taine, 360

Darwin, Erasmus, 124, 125

Darwinism: and Schleicher, 294-95, 320n3; in linguistics, 304; in 20c, 318

David, Boyle on, 79n61

Deaf-mutes: Diderot on, 111, 157; and language study, 281

Declaration of Breda, 259

Dee, John, 270n43

Degérando, Marie Joseph: on Du Marsais and Locke, 114; on anthropology and language, 345-46; and Wilhelm von Humboldt, 348; on Condillac, 351n13

Deism, and Wilkins, 240

Delambre, Jean-Baptiste-Joseph, 338

Delehaye, Hippolyte, 24

Descartes, René: and Leibniz, 9; on the vernacular, 44; and Boyle, 53; and Locke, 53, 67, 120, 160; and John Webster, 60; and method, 106; in 18c linguistic thought, 107; cited by Chomsky, 115; and Locke, Coleridge on, 126; and innateness, 173-74; and Royal Society, 228, 313; in 19c, 363; and romantic thought, 380. See also Universal grammar

Destutt de Tracy, Antoine-Louis-Claude: and Condillac, 21, 363; on subjectivity of language, 27, 344-45, 375; and Stendhal, 38, 364; on Port-Royal grammar, 166; on philosophy of signs, 216-17; and Wilhelm von Humboldt, 335, 344-45, 348, 352n18; on rectification, 345, 369n29, 376; on language as social institution, 350, 365; on language as system, 369n29; on valeur, 369n29

Deutsche Bewegung. See German movement

Diachrony, 17, 58, 299, 362-63, 383, 387, 390. See also Simultaneity, Synchrony

Dialects, Leibniz's interest in, 93; and language study, 99n38

Diderichsen, Paul, 6, 328n44

Diderot, Denis: and Condillac, 9, 110, 153-54, 200n18, 200n20, 210, 211, 218, 285, 308, 374; and origin of language, 111, 148; on linguistic entries in Encyclopédie, 112; and Du Marsais, 112, 167; and Locke, 128, 129; on simultaneity in thought, 157; on inversion, 166-67; on language change, 184

Diede, Charlotte, 340

Digby, Kenelm, and John Webster, 60

Directory, and publication of Condillac, Du Marsais, 166, 216

Discovery, in history of science and linguistics, 314-15

Dod, Jane, 244

Dod, John, 244

Double conformity: in Locke, 24-25, 76n37, 346-47, 357; in Saussure, 24-25, 357; in Wilhelm von Humboldt, 24-25, 346-47, 357; in Condillac, 346-47; in Taine, 357; and poetic diction, 374-75

Douchet, Jacques-Philippe-Augustin, 112

Drabitius, Nicolas: and enthusiasm, 52; Locke on, 75n28

Drebbel, Cornelis, 269n36

Dublin, and study of Locke, 138, 139

Duclos, Charles Pinot, edits Port-Royal grammar, 169, 184

Du Marsais, César Chesneau: is anti-Cartesian, 102-03, 168; and Locke, 102, 113, 168-69; and Sanctius, 105; on reason and memory, 106; rejects innate ideas, 106, 113-14, 168-69, 284; contributor to Encyclopédie, 112, 167; admired by contemporaries, 112, 167; his early career, 112-13; and Jesuits, 113; and grammatical tradition, 113; during Directory, 166, 216; on origin of language and universal grammar, 167; his early work ignored, 167; his definition of mind, 203n60; mentioned, 9

Durkheim, Émile: on Taine, 9, 361, 392; on Montesquieu and sociology, 308-09; and Taine, 362, 364; and Saussure, 365

Dury, John, 252

Eccard, Johann Georg, 47, 86-87
Eckhart. *See* Eccard
Eclectic philosophy in France, 360. *See also* Cousin
École normale, 33
Egger, Émile, suggests translation of Bopp, 324*n*26
Eighteenth-century thought: revived in late 19c, 6, 11, 13, 308-12, 363-64; in early 19c, 7, 31; and Romanticism, 15, 17-18, 343, 380
Elizabeth, Queen of Bohemia, 252
Ellipsis, and Bréal, 388
Emerson, Ralph Waldo: on fossil poetry, 33; as Sage, 38
Empiricism: and rationalism, 9, 11, 283; and Locke, 138-39, 172-73; emergence of term, 139, 142*n*23, 143*n*30; Wilhelm von Humboldt on, 351*n*13
Encyclopédie: Turgot on etymology in, 6, 49; and language study, 9; and Locke, 49; and Condillac, 110, 210, 285, 374; and origin of language, 148; and Sulzer, 193; and Herder, 342
Encyclopédie méthodique: reprints Locke and Condillac, 221*n*1; Adam Smith's essay in, 353*n*29
Enfield, William: translates Brucker, 141*n*15; on poetry, 379
Engel, Johann Jakob, 340
Enlightenment. *See* Eighteenth-century thought
Enthusiasm: and Locke, 52, 130; and Bayle, 52; and association of ideas, 75*n*28; and Cousin, 130
Enthusiasts: named by Leibniz, 52, 97*n*13; Bayle on, 52; Sprat on, 235
Epicureans, 278
Epistemology: and language in 17c, 9, 251; and Adamic language, 9, 25-26, 282-83, 316-17; and science in Locke, 9, 57-58; and origin of language, 165-66, 179-82; and Royal Society, 283; and linguistic relativism, 346
Erastians, 126
Essences: and words, 87; known only to God, 260
Essentialism: and Mersenne, 12-13; and Adamic language, 25-27, 282-83, 316-17; in early 19c, 34-35; and Locke, 54, 56-57;

and Leibniz, 54-55; and Boyle, 56-57; and Adam, 59; in John Webster, 60-61
Ethics, Coleridge on, 126
Etymological metaphysics, 30
Etymology: Turgot on, 6, 49; and materialism, 7; in 17c, 10, 91; meanings of the term, 20; and Sage, 40-41; and Leibniz, 47-48, 58, 116; Leibniz on method in, 66, 91-95; Clauberg on, 66-67; Locke on, 67, 107; as experimental metaphysics, 69; and nature of language, 84; and history, 85-86; Leibniz's interest in, 85-87; Leibniz on history of, 86-87, 96*n*11; and philosophy in Leibniz, 87-91; uncertainty of, 91; and comparative method, 91-92; and things, 92; and Boehme, 92; and law of continuity, 92-95; Henry Jacob on, 98*n*32; as aid to memory, 184; and progress, 194; and Adamic language, 260; and Babel, 282; Bréal on, 298, 390
Eve, naming of, 79*n*60
Evelyn, John, 232, 235, 255, 273*n*69
Experience, as philosophical term, 138
Expression, in poetic theory, 372, 374
Eyben, Huldreich von, 85

Fairfax, Thomas, 254
Faust, 40
Fell, John, 271*n*56
Ferne, Henry, 257
Fèvre de Saumur, Tannegui le, 113, 168
Fichte, Johann Gottlieb, 75*n*27
Fiennes, William, first viscount Saye and Seale, 245
Filmer, Sir Robert, 79*n*63
Fixity of species: and Cuvier, 34, and Whewell, 35; and Sedgwick, 133
Flemish language, in Garden of Eden, 91
Flourens, Pierre, 37
Fludd, Robert, 60, 248, 251, 260, 278, 282, 283
Formey, Samuel: on Maupertuis, 178; secretary of Berlin Academy, 189; on origin of language, 191-92; on state of nature, 192; and Sulzer, 193
Foucault, Michel, 22-23
Fowler, Edward, 272*n*60
Fox Bourne, H. R., 124, 139
France, Anatole: on Bréal, 14; on Cousin and Taine, 361

Franck, Sebastian, 10, 87, 97n13, 97n14
Franklin, Benjamin, 348
Fraser, A. C.: and Locke's *Essay*, 103, 125, 160; and Chomsky, 114, 172; and Peirce, 120, 139
Frederic Henry, Prince of Orange, 253
Frederick the Great, and Berlin Academy, 176-77
French, Peter, 272n57
French Revolution and 19c, 15, 32-33, 343, 363
Fromondus, Libertus, 247
Fuller, Thomas, 273n62

Gabelentz, Georg von, 370n30
Galenists, 255
Galilei, Galileo: and Wilkins, 241-42, 244, 246, 247, 268n32; and uniformitarian view of the universe, 316
Garat, Joseph-Dominique, 348
Garden of Eden, languages in, 91
Gassendi, Pierre: and Locke, 120, 128, 129; and Locke, Coleridge on, 126; and English science, 228, 234, 313; and Wilkins, 268n30
Geijer, Erik Gustaf, 38
Genesis, 281
Genetic method: and nature vs. art, 158; as 18c mode of thought, 158-63; and Herder, 158-59; and philosophical inquiry, 160; and Locke, 160-61; and history, 161; in 19c, 162; and Adam, 162; and progress, 163
Genius of language: Condillac on, 30, 195-96, 307, 376; and anthropology, 345-47; and Voltaire, 347
Geoffroy Saint-Hilaire, Étienne, 338, 360, 362-63
German language: and truth, 46-47; and primitive language, 65; and Hebrew, 91
German movement in language study, 14, 218, 337, 347
German scholarship, and historiography of linguistics, 151
Germanic languages, and Leibniz, 58-59, 65
Germany, and enthusiasm for philosophy, 125
Gestures: and origin of language, 28-29, 108-09, 151-52; as language of action, 109, 148, 288; as language of nature, 163; as natural signs, 166; Diderot on, 166-67

Gift of Tongues, 59
Gilbert, William, 244, 246, 247, 251
Gilson, Étienne, on medieval grammar, 104, 106
Ginguené, Pierre-Louis, 348
Gipper, Helmut, 339-40
Girard, Gabriel, 353n29
Glossocomus, 250, 269n33
Goddard, Jonathan, 255
Godwin, Francis, 246, 253
Godwin, William, 136
Görres, Joseph, 303, 385
Goethe, Johann Wolfgang von, 27, 301
Gomperz, Heinrich, 365
Gothicism in 17c Sweden, 96n4
Grammaire générale. See Universal grammar
Grammar: medieval, 104, 106; use of term 'general grammar,' 105
Greaves, John, 249
Greek studies, in France in early 19c, 32-33
Grégoire, Henri, 347
Gresham College, 247, 258
Grew, Nehemiah, 259
Grimm, Jacob, 5, 38, 301, 386
Grotius, Hugo, 266n12, 272n60
Grouchy, Marie-Louise-Sophie de, and Wilhelm von Humboldt, 348, 353n29
Gubernatis, Angelo de, 321n6
Guichart, Étienne, on etymology, 98n29
Guidobaldo del Monte, 249, 250
Grundtvig, N. F. S., 38

Haak, Theodore: and Mersenne, 231, 234, 253; and early London meetings, 231, 234, 245; at Oxford, 247; and Leibniz, 263; his acquaintance, 270n44; and Wilkins, 273n67; mentioned, 10
Hackman, F. A., 74n26
Hague, The, and French-English contacts, 252-53
Hale, Matthew, 273n70
Hallam, Henry, on Locke, 124
Hamann, Johann Georg: and Michaëlis, 208n134; and Wilhelm von Humboldt, 337; and Herder, 337, 342; mentioned, 197
Hamilton, Sir William: on Locke's language, 123; and Cousin on Locke, 131; on innate ideas, 143n29; on Locke and French philosophy, 144n37
Hare, Julius Charles, 38

Harmony: and innate ideas, 58; of microcosm and macrocosm, 59; Leibniz on, 68; of languages, 85, 93; and Locke, 139

Harris, James, 9, 148, 350n6

Hartley, David: Stewart on, 124; Coleridge on, 126; and Locke, Hazlitt on, 127; and Locke, Stewart on, 129; and Wordsworth, 378; Abrams on, 380; mentioned, 138

Hartlib, Samuel, 252, 268n29, 271n45

Havet, Louis: and Saussure, 360; on 'sémantique,' 397n32

Haym, Rudolf, on Wilhelm von Humboldt, 337-39

Hayne, Thomas, 98n32

Hazlitt, William: as Anti-Sage, 38; on Locke, 123, 126-27; on Condillac, 127; on source of ideas, 127

Hebrew language: studied by scientists, 62; as primal language, Leibniz on, 65, 87; Locke on, 80n63; and German, 91; and Adamic language, 260; as primal language, 280

Hegel, Georg Wilhelm Friedrich, 136

Heine, Heinrich: on Cousin, 31; as Anti-Sage, 38

Helvétius, Claude-Adrien, 129

Helvétius, Mme, 348

Helwig, Christoph: and general grammar, 105; and Leibniz, 117n5

Henry, Victor: on Jespersen, 298; and Whitney, 324n25

Herbert, Edward, first baron Herbert of Cherbury: and Locke, 114, 172, 174-75; and Chomsky, 114; and Descartes, 172; and Boswell, 270n43

Herder, Johann Gottfried: context of prize-essay, 10; and Wilhelm von Humboldt, 14, 220, 335-36, 337, 339-43; on subjectivity of language, 27, 344; and Monboddo, 49, 341; on Locke and Leibniz, 49; and Leibniz, 95; on origin of language as conjectural history, 109; and Chomsky, 112, 170; dependence on Condillac, 117n9, 151; in Strasbourg, 147, 197; and Condillac, 150, 158, 195-98, 218-20, 286, 328n41, 341, 350n7, 374; and Condillac contrasted, 151-52; knowledge of Condillac's *Essai*, 152; on genetic method, 158-59; and Rousseau, 159, 197; and Kant, 159; and art vs. nature, 159; on religion and genetic method, 162; and

Tristram Shandy, 163; and Condillac on primacy of poetic language, 166; and Süssmilch, 187, 198, 208n126; and *Volksgeist*, 195; reputation of, 195, 198-99; Academy reports on prize-essay, 196-97, 341-42; and Diderot, 197; and Bréal, 303; and Hebrew, 327n40; and Hamann, 337, 342; and beginnings of philosophy of language, 339; and Condillac on reflection, 341; his library, 342; reads *Encyclopédie*, 342; on music and poetry, 379-80; mentioned, 9

Hero of Alexandria, 269n33

Herodotus, 280

Herzen, Alexander, as Anti-Sage, 38

Hezenthaler, Magnus, 72n11

Hieroglyphics, and philosophical language, 43

History: contrasted with science, 54; and languages, Leibniz on, 85, 86, 92-93; Leibniz on causes in, 92; Taine's concept of, 361-62; and language study, 384, 386-87, 395n17

History of the Royal Society: organization of, 227-30; its aim, 227. *See also* Sprat, Wilkins

History of science: heroic theory in, 24, 311; and positivism, 312; and professional ideology, 313; internal, 318. *See also* Linguistics, history of

History of thought: and study of language, 29; and etymology, 194; and language, Monboddo on, 279

Hjelmslev, Louis, 328n44, 364

Hobbes, Thomas: Leibniz on, 63; and Locke, 120, 127; Coleridge on, 126; Whewell on, 134; and Bacon, 233; on words as counters, 307; Abrams on, 380; mentioned, 149

Holloway, John, on Victorian Sage, 37

Hooke, Robert: and sacred languages, 43; on Wilkins, 256; and Wilkins, 259, 264, 273n69; and philosophical language, 263

Horace, 45

Horne Tooke, John: in history of linguistics, 5; and utilitarians, 7; and Locke, 8, 76n35, 125; Stewart on, 124, 128

Hoskins, John, 273n67

Hovelacque, A.: and *Revue de linguistique*, 22; and organicism, 321n5

Hugo, Hermannus, 268n29

Humboldt, Alexander von, 336, 349

Humboldt, Wilhelm von: and *idéologues*, 14-15, 335, 337, 344-45, 348, 364; and Herder, 14, 220, 335-36, 337, 339-43; on subjectivity of language, 27, 343-44; and linguistic relativism, 27, 335, 345-47; and Chomsky, 170; and Hamann, 220, 337; reads Condillac, 220, 342; and linguistic anthropology, 220, 347-49; disagrees with Herder, 223n30; in Paris, 289; and language study in German universities, 293; and Jespersen, 296, 349-50; and Renan, Bréal on, 308; and Madvig, 323n20; on culture and language, 336; inception of his linguistic interests, 336, 337-39; and French thought, 336-37, 343; and Wolf, 337; and Kant, 337; his Paris diaries, 337; the study of, 337-39; Kaehler on, 339; on Herder, 340; and Condillac, 340, 341-42, 344, 346; on reflection and language, 342; on sociability of man, 343-44; and Destutt de Tracy, 344-45, 352n18; on language and education, 345; on rectification, 345, 376; and Bréal, 349-50; and Saussure, 370n30; and romantic thought, 372
Hume, David: in Germany, 125; Coleridge on, 126; and Locke, Hazlitt on, 127; on uniformity of human nature, 159; and empiricism, 173; mentioned, 9
Hunter, John, 318
Hutcheson, Francis, 148, 159
Huygens, Christiaan: on Boyle, 53; and Locke, 55; and Royal Society, 232, 233; and philosophical language, 263
Huygens, Constantijn, and Boswell, 253
Hyde, Edward, first earl of Clarendon, 259
Hydraulics, 269n33

Ideas: and words, Locke and Boyle on, 56-57; words as signs of, 63-64. *See also* Association of ideas, Condillac, Connection of ideas
Idéologues: linguistic thought of, 14-15, 17-18, 289, 344-46; and Wilhelm von Humboldt, 14-15, 335, 337, 344-45, 348; and perfectibility, 31; and Bréal, 291, 296, 305, 349, 393; and Condillac, 291, 296, 363, 393; and Taine, 291, 381, 393; and Kantian idealism, F. Schlegel on, 351n13; and English thought, 379. *See also* Napoleon

Ideology, in history of science, 313
Imitation, doctrine of, in 18c thought and Wordsworth, 372, 374, 375, 379
Indebtedness, evidence for, 20-21
Indo-European philology. *See* Comparative philology
Induction, J. S. Mill on, 136
Innate ideas: John Webster and Locke on, 61; rejected by Du Marsais, 106, 113-14, 168-69, 212, 284; and repression, 116, 175-76; and Locke, Stewart on, 128; and Locke, Sedgwick on, 132-33; and Locke, Rogers on, 137; in Locke and Descartes, 143n29; rejected by Condillac, 212
Innateness: and Adamic language, 9, 25-26; rejected by Locke, 27; Leibniz on, 58; in John Webster and Locke, 60-61; and language of nature, 64; and language in Locke, 80n64, 283; Locke on, 108, 115, 174-75; and Descartes, 115; in Leibniz and Locke, 143n34; Chomsky on, 173
Instinct, Condillac on, 213-15
Institut national: reorganized by Napoleon, 31; and *idéologues*, 348
Institutionalization, of academic subjects, 313
Intellectual history, and language study, 3, 11, 14, 15
Interjections, and origin of language, 88
Intranslatability among languages: Locke on, 54, 376; Taine on, 356
Inversion: in grammar, 111; and origin of language, Diderot on, 166-67
Itard, Jean, 280

Jacob, Henry, on etymology, 98n32
James II, 236
Jameson, Fredric, 366n9
Jansenists, and Locke, 104
Jacquemont, Frédéric-François, 348
Jespersen, Otto: and Wilhelm von Humboldt, 14, 349; and Bréal, 14, 296-98; critique of Schleicher, 296-97; on Madvig, 298, 301; and Henry, 298
Jesuits, 266n12
Jews, expulsion from Spain, 281
Johnson, Samuel, on Monboddo, 279
Jones, R. F., 273n60, 275n81
Jones, Sir William: and F. Schlegel, 304, 394n11; and history of linguistics, 314-16; and comparative anatomy, 318;

Hjelmslev on, 328n44; access to his writings in Europe, 328n44

Journal asiatique, 21

Journals, and intellectual history, 21

Kaehler, Siegfried A., on Wilhelm von Humboldt, 339

Kant, Immanuel: Neo-Kantianism, 11; J. S. Mill on, 136; and Locke, 138, 144n43; and Herder, 159, 197; and philosophy of language, 278; and Wilhelm von Humboldt, 337, 338, 351n13; and French thought, F. Schlegel on, 351n13

Kelley, Edward, 270n43

Kepler, Johannes, 12, 244, 246, 247, 294

Kierkegaard, Søren, as Anti-Sage, 38

King, Peter, on Locke, 122, 130

Kircher, Athanasius, 268n30

Knowledge: and arbitrary signs, 29; Locke on, 54

Koerner, Christian Gottfried, 336

Koerner, E. F. K., 320

Komensky. *See* Comenius

Kortholt, Sebastian, 86

Koyré, Alexandre, 8, 312

Krinitz, Elise. *See* Selden, Camille

Kristeller, Paul Oskar, 8

Kruszewski, Nikolai, 365

Kuhlmann, Quininus, 52

Kuhn, Adalbert, 385

Kuhn, Thomas, 8

Kynaston, Sir Francis, 268n29

La Croze, Maturin Veyssière, 90

La Harpe, Jean-François de, 350n13

Lakoff, Robin, 104

Lalande, Joseph-Jérôme-Lefrançais de, 338

Lamarck, Jean-Baptiste de, 363

La Mettrie, Julien Offroy de, 206n105

Lammers, Wilhelm, 341

Lamy, Bernard: in English, 112, 169; and Du Marsais, 113, 168

Lancelot, Claude, 45, 104, 167

Language: and epistemology, 9, 251, 279, 283; and science in 17c, 9, 32, 43, 56-58, 60-61, 251, 283; as social institution, 14, 17, 20, 27, 30, 350, 365, 375; as system, Madvig on, 14, 299-300; subjectivity of, 27, 31, 343-46, 375; of action, 28-29, 109, 148, 288; and creativity, 29, 165, 171, 377; and nature, 42; as tool of

knowledge, 58, 69; of nature, and Locke, 63-64; and sociability, 63, 241, 343-46; and memory, 63; of nature and innateness, 64; Leibniz on change in, 65; as mirror of mind, 69, 85; of nature, and Boehme, 73n14, 87, 97n13, 248, 251, 282; and innateness, 80n64; and knowledge of mind in Leibniz, 94; teaching of, 113, 168; and Condillac's statue, 154-55; and signs advance reflection, 164; reality structured by, 179; and reason, Süssmilch on, 187; and progress, Herder on, 196; and knowledge in Condillac, 215; as system of signs, Cournot on, 309; and educability of man, 345; and anthropology, 347-48; acquisition of, Taine and Darwin on, 360; and poetic theory, 373-381; and mind, Bréal on, 383-84; change in, Bréal on, 383-86. *See also* Adamic language, Arbitrariness of linguistic sign, Etymology, Genius of language, Gestures, Languages, Linearity of speech, Linguistic relativism, Origin of language, Philosophical language, Philosophy of language

Language study: history of before 1800, 5; and literary theory, 17-18; and science, 35; empiricist and rationalist, 101-02; in 19c Germany, 293; academic institutionalization of, 293-94; and organicism, 294-95; in 1890s, 295-99; and sociology, 296, 302; social and semantic orientation in, 305

Languages: made by ordinary people, 57, 78n43; Leibniz on primitive and natural, 65; Leibniz on single origin of, 65; Leibniz and variety of, 84; and prehistory, 85; harmony of, 85; Indo-European, Leibniz on, 85; and Hebrew, 87; Leibniz on natural origin of, 88; in Garden of Eden, 91; and history in Leibniz, 92-93; Ariadne thread in, 94; core vocabulary of, 94; comparison of, 97n18; and history of thought, 179-80; Maupertuis on diversity of, 185-86; single origin of, 281; comparative vs. historical study of, 384. *See also* African, American, Chinese, German, Germanic, Hebrew, Latin, Slavic

Langue, 17, 361-62, 383, 389-90

Lansberge, Philip van, 246-47

Laromiguière, Pierre, 348

Latin, and romance languages, 383, 392

Latitudinarianism, 240, 257, 272n60
Lavoisier, Antoine-Laurent, 313
Law, Edmund, 124
Law of nature, and Locke, 115, 128
Leibniz: and Port-Royal grammar, 4, 117n5; and combinatorial characteristics, 42, 63; and philosophical language, 45; interest in vernacular, 46; and Nizolius, 46; on philosophical style, 46; on etymology, 47-48, 58, 66, 84, 116; on origin of proper names, 48; critique of Locke, 48-52; Locke's opinion of, 49-51; reviewed in *Göttingische Anzeigen*, 49; and Lady Masham, 50; and priority controversy, 51; on enthusiasm in Locke, 52; on Boyle, 53; and essentialism, 54-55; on natural origin of words, 58, 65; and innateness, 58; and pre-established harmony, 58-59; and Adamic language, 59, 63; on two functions of language, 63; and Hobbes, 63, 81n68; on arbitrariness, 64-65, 88, 90-91; on Germanic languages, 65; on Adamic language, 65-66, 91, 97n13; on language change, 65; and Schottel, 66; and harmony, 68; on mental words, 68-69; and Sparwenfeld, 73n17, 81n66, 92, 96n7; on loanwords, 75n27; and Descartes, 76n32; and Dalgarno, 81n65; and Wallis, 81n65; on dictionary of roots, 85; on migration and languages, 85; on Indo-European languages, 85; interest in etymology, 85-87; on history of etymological study, 86-87, 96n11; on Hebrew, 87; on etymology and philosophy, 87-91; on etymology and sufficient reason, 88; on etymology and law of continuity, 88, 92, 93; on origin of language, 88-90; on particles and interjections, 88; and Mosaic chronology, 89; on onomatopeia, 89, 92, 97n17; on Boehme, 89; on climate and nations, 90, 98n27; on single origin of humanity, 90; on Chinese, 90, 99n39; on etymological comparison, 91-92; on method in etymology, 91-94; on historical linguistic evidence, 92-93; on causes in history, 92; on Lord's Prayer and languages, 93-94; on Slavic and German, 93; on Asian and American languages, 93, 99n39; on language and mind, 94; on universal order and etymology, 94; influence on ety-mological study, 94; and Herder, 95; on harmony of languages, 95n3; on mystics, enthusiasts, and alchemists, 97n13; on comparison of languages, 97n18; on Clauberg and Descartes, 98n32; on mapping of languages, 99n39; and Helwig, 117n5; on Locke's reflection, 175; and Berlin Academy, 177; and Wilkins's philosophical language, 263; on Edward Kelley, 270n43; mentioned, 136, 149, 279, 280, 307. *See also* Coleridge, Mackintosh, Stewart

Lessing, Gotthold Ephraim, 374
Lewes, G. H.: on Locke, 121, 131; on Cousin, 131, 144n44
Liaison des idées. See Connection of ideas
Liebig, Justus, 20
Light of nature, 158, 202n40
Limborch, Philip van, 50
Linearity of speech: and Bréal, 17; in Condillac, 30, 157-58, 291, 342; Diderot and Rousseau on, 157; in universal grammar, 158; and progress, 164; Cournot on, 309; and Wilhelm von Humboldt, 342; and Saussure, 363
Linguistic relativism: in French thought, 15, 376; and Wilhelm von Humboldt, 15, 27, 335, 345-47, 376; in Locke, 27, 376; in Condillac, 30-31, 376; Maupertuis on, 181, 185-86; Michaëlis on, 189-90; Madvig on, 301; in Bréal, 306-07; and epistemology, 346; and *Volksgeist*, 347
Linguistic sign: double nature of, 15; Destutt de Tracy on, 344-45; and Saussure, 357, 359; Bréal on adequacy of, 391. *See also* Arbitrariness of linguistic sign, Signs
Linguistic Society of Paris. *See* Société de linguistique de Paris
Linguistics, history of, how understood, 4; and comparative philology, 4; and history of science, 8, 312-14; and Bloomfield, 101; and Chomsky, 101-02; and history of ideas, 102; reflections on, 312-320; internal and external, 319
Linnaeus, Carl von, 194, 294, 383
Littré, Émile, 41
Lloyd, William, 255, 264
Loanwords, Leibniz on, 75n27
Locke, John: and Port-Royal, 4, 11, 45, 104, 175, 283; on state of nature, 10, 140n7,

160-61; reputation in 19c, 11, 120-21, 124, 290, 295; rejects philosophical language, 13, 27, 76n11, 276n91; on cheat of words, 24, 70n2; and epistemology of science, 24, 57-58; on double conformity, 24-25, 76n37, 346-47, 357, 375; and Saussure, 24-25, 317; and Wilhelm von Humboldt, 25, 346, 357; and Adamic language, 25, 61-62; on Adam, 26, 91, 162, 202n52; and linguistic relativism, 27, 376; on subjectivity of language, 27, 346, 352n16; and semiotics, 27-28; on language as function, 28; on association of ideas, 29, 52, 114, 130, 173, 284; and sacred languages, 43; on knowledge and words, 44-45; his reading, 45; and travel literature, 45, 161; and Condillac, 49, 107, 120, 148, 163; and *philosophes*, 49; Herder on, 49; on Leibniz, 49-51; on language of *Essay*, 50; on enthusiasm, 52, 130; on background of *Essay*, 53-54; on natural philosophy, 53; and Descartes, 53, 67, 120; on intranslatability, 54, 346; on mixed modes and relations, 54; on arbitrariness, 54, 87-88, 317; knot-and-bundle metaphor in, 54; and essentialism, 54, 283; and Royal Society, 55; on limited aim of *Essay*, 55; on abuse of language, 55; on words and things, 56-57; on languages having been made by ordinary people, 57; and Hebrew, 62, 80n63; and Leibniz, 63, 120, 139; on two functions of language, 63; on language of nature, 63-64; and Clauberg, 67; in France, 67-68; on etymology of mental words, 67-69; on language as tool, 69; on obscurity of words, 71n7; on species, 71n7; and Drabitius, 75n28; on conduct, 76n39; and Filmer, 79n63; and onomatopoeia, 82n76; and Cartesian linguistics, 102, 107, 172-75; and Du Marsais, 102, 113, 168-69; reflection and sensation in, 107; on progress of mind, 107, 160; grammars in his library, 113, 204n78; on language teaching, 113; Chomsky's view of, 114-16; on law of nature, 115; *Essay* in 19c, 121-22; Carlyle on, 121; at Oxford and Cambridge, 123-24; in Germany, 125; "Of Power," 133, 134; *Essay*'s Book III admired, 141n17; and Kant, 144n43; on uniformity of human nature, 159; *Essay* in 18c, 160; and genetic method, 160-61; on words and origin of ideas, 160; and rationalism, 160; and Herbert of Cherbury, 174-75; and toleration, 175; on signs and reality, 179; and Mersenne, Wilkins on language, 251; and social nature of language, 302, 365; mentioned, 278, 279, 307. *See also* Boyle; Brougham; Brown, Thomas; Brucker; Buhle; Coleridge; Courtney; Dublin; Fox Bourne; Fraser, A. C.; Gassendi; Hamilton; Hazlitt; Hobbes; Horne Tooke; Huygens, Christiaan; Innate ideas; Innateness; Jansenists; Lewes; Mackintosh; Maistre; Mansel; Mill, J. S.; Newton; Nicole; Perizonius; Reid; Richelet; Rogers; Sanctius; Scioppius; Scottish universities; Sedgwick; Stephen, James Fitzjames; Stephen, Leslie; Stewart; Sydenham; Tagart; Tennemann; Vaughan; Veitch; Webb; Webster; Whewell

Lord's Prayer, as linguistic evidence, 93-94

Louis Lambert. *See* Balzac

Louis XIV, 234

Lowth, Robert, 148

Lowther, Anthony, 273n67

Ludolf, Hiob, 85, 86, 91, 93, 95

Lull, Ramón, 260, 275n86

Luther, Martin: and Gift of Tongues, 59; on origin of proper names, 73n16

Lyell, Sir Charles, 290, 322n15

Macaulay, Thomas B., 142n17

Mackintosh, Sir James: on Locke and innateness, 143n34, 205n93, 205n98; and French thought, 380

Madvig, Johann Nicolai: and 19c philology, 14, 298, 299-300; on linguistic sign, 14, 299-300; Jespersen on, 298; on organicism, 298, 300; and Bréal, 298, 306, 307, 310, 326n32; on language as system, 299; and Whitney, 301-02, 310; and linguistic relativism, 301; and Wilhelm von Humboldt, 323n20; mentioned, 38, 314

Magendie, François, 314

Maistre, Joseph de: as Sage, 38; and Locke, 121, 145n48, 163; and Whewell, 140n3, 145n48

Mallet, John, 70n3

Malthus, Thomas R., and Charles Darwin, 328*n*42
Mansel, H. L., on Locke, 145*n*54
Marsais. *See* Du Marsais
Martensen, H. L., 38
Masham, Damaris, Lady Masham, 50
Masson, David, on Locke, 139
Maupertuis, Pierre-Louis Moreau de: in Berlin, 10, 148, 176; on origin of language, 110; on simultaneity in thought, 157; on signs and origin of ideas, 164-65; and German metaphysics, 176; and Berlin Academy, 177; and Voltaire, 177; his character, 178; and Condillac, 178, 181, 185; on language and signs, 178-84; on Lapp language, 180; on knowledge and language, 180-81; on memory and language, 180-81; on substance and mode, 181; and linguistic relativism, 181, 185-86; and Berkeley, 181-82; and Boindin, 182; and comparative anthropology, 183; on parts of speech, 185; on diversity of languages, 185-86; on philosophical language, 186; proposes prize-topic, 189, 346; and 19c, 207*n*113; mentioned, 165, 193, 210, 308
Mauss, Marcel, 322*n*13
Mechanics, Wilkins on, 248-51
Mede, Joseph, 272*n*60
Meier, Gerhard: and Leibniz, 73*n*17, 86, 91, 98*n*32; and Saxon glossary, 98*n*31
Meillet, Antoine: on language acquisition, 4; on Bréal, 16, 296, 393; on Saussure, 16, 299, 311, 322*n*13, 359-60, 393; on sociology and language, 322*n*13; mentioned, 295
Memory: and language, 63; and reason, 106; and signs, 170, 286; and philosophical language, 262; as repository, 275*n*84
Ménage, Gilles, 54
Mendelssohn, Moses, 197
Mentalism in linguistics, 13, 16
Mephistopheles, in Goethe, Balzac, 40
Merian, J. B., 190, 197
Mersenne, Marin: and Wilkins, 12, 244, 248, 249-51; rejects essentialism and Adamicism, 12-13, 283; on method, 117*n*6; and Royal Society, 231, 234, 252, 313; and Locke, 251, 353*n*25; and Haak, 253; and Adamic language, 260; and philo-
sophical language, 262; and Copernicus, 266*n*12; on antiquity, 266*n*14; on nature of mathematics, 270*n*39; on language and knowledge, 271*n*46; and uniformitarianism, 316; on arbitrariness, 317; mentioned, 278, 294
Merton, Robert K.: on evidence of citation, 21; on multiples, 302, 316
Meter in poetry, Wordsworth and Condillac on, 378-79
Method: 17c hopes for, 117*n*6; Bernard on, 317
Michaëlis, Johann David: his prize-essay, 10, 189-91; rejects philosophical language, 27, 190; and linguistic relativism, 189-90, 346; and Herder's prize-topic, 190, 194-95; on language and man, 191; and Hamann, 208*n*134; mentioned, 148, 219
Microcosm-Macrocosm doctrine, 10, 59
Milieu, in Taine, 362
Mill, James: and Horne Tooke, 7; and etymology, 82*n*75
Mill, John Stuart: and Sage, 37; and Locke, 120, 122, 124, 133; on Whewell and Sedgwick, 135-36; on Bacon and Locke, 136; on Godwin, Bentham, and utilitarian ethics, 136; on Germanized philosophy, 136; on Bentham and Coleridge, 136-37; on Condillac, 137; and Taine, 309, 365; on Comte, 361
Mind, 22, 368*n*18
Minguet, Charles, on Alexander von Humboldt, 349
Molyneux, William, 45, 50, 51, 70*n*2
Moment, in Taine, 362
Monboddo, Lord: on language and history of thought, 29-30, 164; in German, 49; on origin of language, 148; and Condillac, 210; Dr. Johnson on, 279; and orangoutang, 285; and Herder, 341; mentioned, 9, 280
Monck, William H. S.: on Locke, 139; on Cousin, 144*n*38
Monconys, Balthasar de, 237
Montesquieu, Charles de Secondat, Durkheim on, 308-09
Montmor Academy, and Royal Society, 234
Moray, Sir Robert, 232, 258
More, Henry, 272*n*60, 273*n*67
Morell, J. D., on Locke, 144*n*45

Moulin, Lewis du, 275n90
Müller, Max: and Charles Darwin, Whitney,
    32; on nature of language, 35-37; and
    organicism, 36; as Sage, 38; and uniform-
    itarianism, 298, 326n34; and Bréal, 303,
    385; mentioned, 11, 30
Music, and poetry, 379-80
Mysticism: in linguistic thought, 10, 385-86;
    and Adamic language, 60; and natural
    philosophy, 61; Leibniz on, 97n13; in
    linguistics, Bréal on, 303, 395n12

Napoleon: and idéologues, 31, 33, 289,
    351n13; favors age of Louis XIV, 32;
    and 18c thought, 381
Natural philosophy: Boyle, Locke on, 53;
    and poetry, 62
Natural theology: and Sedgwick, 132; and
    Wilkins, 240, 264-65
Naturalism, and romantic thought, 382-83
Naturphilosophie, and language study, 293
Natursprache. See Language, of nature
Neile, William, 255
Neogrammarians, 17, 386
Neoplatonism, 282
Newton, Isaac: and sacred languages, 43;
    and Leibniz, 51; and Locke, 55; and He-
    brew, 62; Coleridge on, 125; and 18c
    thought, 148; and Wilkins, 269n37; men-
    tioned, 294
Nicole, Pierre, and Locke, 104, 175
Nietzsche, Friedrich: as Anti-Sage, 38; and
    Taine, 360; and Revue philosophique,
    368n18
Nizolius, Marius, 46
Nomenclature: language as, 24-26, 346, 357,
    388; and science in Balzac, 40
Noreen, Adolf, 5, 20
Nugent, Thomas, 148, 222n2

Oegger, Guillaume, and Emerson, Balzac, 38
Oldenburg, Henry: on study of nature, 57;
    and Leibniz, 74n26; and Sprat's History,
    230, 232; in Paris, 234; on Wilkins's gar-
    dens, 255; on Wilkins, 258
Onomatopeia: Dalgarno on, 80n65; and
    Locke, 82n76; and Leibniz, 89, 92, 97n17
Orang-outang, and speech, 285
Organicism in linguistics: and Bréal, 13, 16,
    295-96, 382-83, 392-93; in Max Müller

and Schleicher, 36; Madvig on, 298, 300;
    and Schleicher, 294-95, 382; and Hove-
    lacque, 321n5
Origin of language: in German 18c thought,
    10; and Boehme, 84; and particles, inter-
    jections, 88; Leibniz on, 88-90; Condillac
    on, 107-10, 286-88; and thought, 108-09;
    and gestures and reflection, 108-09, 151-
    52; and state of nature, 109-10, 161;
    Maupertuis on, 110; and progress, 110,
    163; and universal grammar, 111, 147,
    165-70; understanding of term, 147;
    question of in 18c, 147-48; and linearity
    of speech, 157-58; as conjectural history,
    163; and epistemology, 163, 164-65,
    179-82; Monboddo on rationale for, 164;
    and reason, 164; and rationalism, 165-66;
    Süssmilch on, 187-88; Formey on, 191-
    92; Sulzer on, 193-94; Herder on, 195-
    99; Venturi on study of, 199; and Bréal,
    298, 308; in Condillac, Herder, and
    Hamann, 351n10
Origins. See Genetic method
Oxford. Locke's standing at, 123-24; in
    1640s, 254-55; and Wilkins, 254-57. See
    also Wadham College
Oxford English Dictionary: and 18c thought,
    7; and Balzac, 41

Paley, William, 124, 126, 132
Pappus of Alexandria, 250, 269n33
Paracelsus, Theophrastus Philippus Aureolus
    Bombastus von Hohenheim, and Adamic
    language, 59, 87
Paris, and language study around 1800, 338
Paris, Gaston: and Bréal, 21, 304-05, 386,
    392; and Saussure, 21, 392, 394n4; and
    Schleicher, 304-05; mentioned, 311
Parker, Samuel, 255
Parole, 17, 361-62, 383, 390
Particles. See Origin of language
Parts of speech: formation of, 167; Mauper-
    tuis on, 185; Sulzer on, 194
Pascal, Blaise, and linguistic thought, 104
Passivity of mind, in 18c thought and Ro-
    manticism, 372
Pasteur, Louis, 310
Patrick, Simon, 240, 264, 272n60
Paul, Hermann, 396n25
Peace of Westphalia, 245

Peau de Chagrin. See Balzac
Pedagogy, and language study, 166
Pedersen, Holger, 5, 20
Peirce, C. S.: on Locke, 120; and A. C. Fraser, 120, 139
Pell, John: and sacred languages, 43; and Wilkins, 247; and cryptography, 268*n*29; and Haak, 270*n*44
Pénisson, Pierre, 209*n*150
Pepys, Samuel: and Sprat's *History*, 230; and Wilkins, 241, 259-60
Perfectibility of man, 31
Perizonius, Jacob, and Locke, 113
Persian language, and German, 91
Petty, Sir William, 254, 259, 273*n*69
Philology. *See* Comparative philology
Philosophes, 49, 69
Philosophical language: rejected by Locke, 13, 27; rejected by Bréal and Saussure, 27, 388; rejected by Michaëlis, 27, 190; and Leibniz, 45; Locke on, 72*n*11, 276*n*91; Maupertuis on, 186; and Adamic language, 260-61; and Wilkins, 260-64; and universal language, 261; and memory, 262; and John Ray, 263-64. *See also* Chinese, Coptic
Philosophical style: Leibniz on, 46
Philosophy: and language, Locke on 55-56; in Wilkins, 260-61
Philosophy of language: and comparative philology, 5; and etymology, 84; in 18c France and Germany, 218-19; in 18c, revival of, 308-12
Phonetic change, Bréal on study of, 384, 385, 387
Physiology, and linguistics, 318
Pindar, 336
Plato, 60, 125, 149, 278
Poetics: and linguistic thought, 17, 372-381; in 17c Germany, 73*n*14; and expression, 372, 374
Poetry: and science, 62; and angels, 62; and prose, Wordsworth and Condillac on, 377-78; and association of ideas, 378; and music, 379-80
Poniatowa, Christine, 52
Pope, Alexander, 373
Pope, Walter, 244, 255
Port-Royal: and 18c thought, 107; editions of, 112. *See also* Leibniz, Locke

Positivism: and intellectual history, 218; Comtian, 309-10; and history of science, 312; in history of linguistics, 319
Pott, A. F., 339
Power, Henry, 273*n*67
Prémontval, André-Pierre le Guay de, 189-90
Priestley, Joseph, 124, 126, 148, 203*n*54, 379
Primitive language, Leibniz on, 59
Privacy of language. *See* Language, subjectivity of
Progress: and Condillac, 31; concept of in 18c thought and in social sciences, 110, 279; of mind and language, signs, 109, 163; Maistre and Bonald on, 163; of mind and linearity of speech, 164; and language, Herder on, 196; in history of science, 312-13
Proper names: Leibniz on, 48; Luther on, 73*n*16; Schottel on, 73*n*16
Prose: and poetry, Condillac and Wordsworth on, 377-78; and connection of ideas, 378
Prose style, and Wilkins, 266*n*11
Pross, Wolfgang, 209*n*150
Protestantism, and language study, 59, 87
Psammeticus, 280

Quintilian, 307

Race, Taine's concept of, 362
Racism and language study: in 19c, 295, 307; Bréal on, 321*n*7, 385, 388, 394*n*2
Ramé, Pierre de la, 243
Ramus. *See* Ramé
Rask, Rasmus: and Romanticism, 6; and Turgot, 6; mentioned, 5
Raspe, Rudolf Erich, 49
Rationalism: and empiricism, 9, 11, 283; and Locke, 160, 173; and origin of language, 165-66; and innateness in Descartes and Locke, 173-75; in Bréal, 296; in Madvig, 301
Ratke, Wolfgang, and Helwig, 105
Raumer, Rudolf von, 5, 313
Ravetz, Jerome K., on science in 19c, 318
Ray, John: collects words, 73*n*17; and Wilkins's philosophical language, 263-64; and Wilkins, 273*n*67
Réalisme, in late 19c French thought, 392
Reason: and connection of ideas, 29, 155,

284; relieves memory, 106; in Locke and Condillac, 108; as precondition for language, 164; unique to man, 215. *See also* Reflection

Rectification: and language, 18, 375-77; in Destutt de Tracy, 345, 369*n*29, 376; in Wilhelm von Humboldt, 345, 376; in Taine, 369*n*29

Reflection: and reason in origin of language, 29, 109, 195, 287; in Locke, 107, 128-29, 134, 155; and reason in Condillac, 155, 163-64, 215, 223*n*18, 287, 342; advanced by signs and language, 164, 223*n*18; and arbitrary signs, 188; in Herder, 220, 350*n*7; and language in Wilhelm von Humboldt, 341-42; and language in Condillac, 350*n*7

Reid, Thomas, and Locke, 123

Religion: and genetic method, 162-63; and science, 240; and language study, 290

Renan, Ernest: and Bréal, 16, 308, 321*n*6; on 18c thought, 110, 150, 218; on genetic method in 18c, 162; on origin of language, 308; on Cousin, 309. *See also* Darmesteter, James

Renaud, Paul, and Bréal, 321*n*6

Renaudot, Théophraste: and Mersenne, 252, 266*n*11; on nature of language, 266*n*11; and Herder's prize-topic, 316, 353*n*25

Representation, in Foucault, 22

Resemblance, in Foucault, 22

Revue de linguistique, and Bréal, 22, 295

Revue de métaphysique et morale, 21

Revue des deux mondes, 21

Revue philosophique, 21, 360. *See also* Nietzsche, Ribot

Ribot, Théodule: and *Revue philosophique*, Taine, 360, 368*n*18-19; on French philosophy, 368*n*19; mentioned, 364

Richardson, Charles, 7

Richelet, César-Pierre, and Locke, 76*n*36

Robinson, Henry Crabb, on German and English philosophy, 125

Roe, Thomas, 252

Roederer, Pierre-Louis, 348

Rogers, Henry: on Locke in 19c, 121; on Locke and French philosophy, 137-38; on Locke and Stillingfleet, 138

Rohault, Jacques, on words, 78*n*44

Romanticism: and Realism, 10; thought, 15, 17-18, 343, 380; and linguistic

thought, 293, 335, 372-73; and philology, 317; language and local color in, 378; and organic metaphor, 382; and *réalisme*, 392

Rooke, Lawrence, 254

Rosicrucianism: and science, 12, 252-53, 271*n*48; and John Webster, 60, 256; and Wilkins, 256

Ross, Alexander, 247

Rousseau, Jean-Jacques: and Condillac, 9, 148, 149, 152-53, 155-57, 210, 285; on origin of language, 109, 155-57; on society and language, 156; on gestures and language, 156-57; and Saussure, 157; on linearity of speech, 157; on state of nature, 161; on art vs. nature, 161; on religion and genetic method, 162; Bréal on, 308; mentioned, 350

Routine, in language learning, Locke and Du Marsais on, 168

Roy, Georges le: on Condillac, 153-54

Royal Society: and Rosicrucianism, 12-13; and prose style, 44, 241; motto of, 45, 244; and Locke, 55; early history of, 228, 231; and Descartes, 228; and Babel, 228; charters of, 228, 229; and religion, 228, 229; Sprat's apology for, 229-30; and French science, 231, 234; and Mersenne, 231, 234, 252, 313; and Oxford, 254-55; and philosophical language, 262-63; mentioned, 9. *See also* Sorbière, Sprat, Wilkins

Royer-Collard, Pierre-Paul, 369*n*29

Rudbeck, Olof, and Gothicism, 96*n*4

Russell, Bertrand, 42

Rydqvist, Johann Erik, 38

Sacred languages, studied by 17c scientists, 43

Sacy, Silvestre de, 338, 364

Sage. *See* Victorian Sage

Sainte-Beuve, Charles-Augustin, 38, 104

Salmon, Vivian, 104, 105

Salmony, H. A., 151-52, 195, 196

Saltationism, 34

Sanctius, Franciscus: and Cartesian linguistics, 104-05; on method, 106; and Locke, Du Marsais, 113, 168

Sanskrit, in Dubuc, 10, study of, 301

Sarmatia, 85

Sarton, George, 312, 313

Sartre, Jean-Paul, and Taine, 365n1

Saussure, Ferdinand de: and 19c language study, 6, 13; and Bréal, 6, 17, 20, 21, 303-08, 359, 387, 391-92; and Taine, 15, 21, 387; Meillet on, 16, 299, 311, 322n13, 359-60; his terminological compulsion, 20; and *sémiologie*, 20, 391; and Gaston Paris, 21, 392, 394n4; on linguistic sign, 24-25, 357-59; and philosophical language, 27, 388; and Condillac, Rousseau, 157; on Schleicher, 295; and universal grammar, 307, 386; and Whitney, 310-311; and neogrammarians, 311; and Locke, 317, 375; on *valeur*, 357; his sheet-of-paper metaphor, 357; in Paris, 359-60; and German scholarship, 359, 364, 393; and Durkheim, 365; and Wilhelm von Humboldt, 370n30; on history of linguistics, 395n15; historicity in, 395n17; on uniformitarianism, 396n30

Scaliger, Julius Caesar, 113, 165

Schelling, Friedrich Wilhelm: and Kant, 125; and English philosophy, 125; mentioned, 136

Scherer, Wilhelm, 328n42

Schiller, Friedrich, 301, 336, 340, 350n6

Schlegel, A. W.: and linguistic typology, 349; and Mme de Staël, 381; mentioned, 385

Schlegel, Friedrich: and Chomsky, 170; and Madvig, 298, 300; Bréal on, 303-04, 385; and Renan, 308; and Jones, 315, 394n11; on *idéologues* and Kantian idealism, 351n13; and racism, 388

Schleicher, August: and Bréal, 13-14, 291, 296, 382-83, 384, 388; and organicism, 36, 294-95, 382; Whitney on, 294; and Darwinism, 294-95, 320n3; Saussure on, 295, 387; reaction against, 303-05; mentioned, 6, 8

Schlesier, Gustav, on Wilhelm von Humboldt in Paris, 338-39

Schottel, Justus Georg: on German, 47; and Leibniz, 66; on proper names, 73n16

Schulenburg, Sigrid von der, on Leibniz, 73n17

Schwenkfeld, Kaspar, 87, 97n13

Science: and language study, 9; as nomenclature, 40; and language in 17c, 43; contrasted with history, 54; and Adamic language, 282-83; heroic theory of, 311; as

description and classification, 314; sociology of, 329n45

Scioppius, Gasparus, and Locke, 113, 168

Scottish universities, Locke and Newton in, 142n19

Scythia, 85

Sedgwick, Adam: as Sage, 38; and Locke, 124, 131-33, 135-36; and Whewell, 131-32; and natural religion, 132; J. S. Mill on, 135-36

Selden, Camille, 365n2

Selden, John, 270n44

Selenus, Gustavus, 268n29

Semantics: and comparative philology, 305; Bréal's concept of, 384-85; as *linguistique générale* in Bréal, 391

Sémantique: Bréal's coinage of term, 321n6; and Louis Havet, 397n32

Semasiology, and Bréal's *sémantique*, 385, 393, 396n29

Sémiologie, in Saussure, 20, 391

Semiotics: and Locke, 27-28; and Wilkins, 247-48

Sensualism, and Cousin, 130

Serendipity, 19-20

Shaftesbury. *See* Cooper

Sieyès, Emmanuel-Joseph, 348

Signifiant, 27, 357, 358, 387

Signifié, 27, 357, 358, 387

Signs: in algebra, 63; Condillac on kinds of, 108-09, 170, 287-88; and memory, 170; Maupertuis on, 178-84; and reality, 179; and ideas, 193; and knowledge, 213-14; interaction with reflection, Condillac on, 223n18; imperfection of, 345, 352n19; Taine and Saussure on, 357-59. *See also* Arbitrariness of linguistic sign, Arbitrary signs, Linguistic sign

Simultaneity and successivity: in Diderot and Maupertuis, 157; in Condillac, 157-58; in Taine, 362-63, 387; in Saussure, 362, 387; in Bréal, 387, 390. *See also* Diachrony, Synchrony

Skytte, Bengt, 95n3

Slavery, in antiquity, Madvig on, 301

Slavic languages, 93

Smith, Adam: on origin of language, 148, 279; and linguistic typology, 349; in France, 353n29; and *valeur*, 370n29; mentioned, 9

Smyth, George, 273n67

Sociability and language: in Condillac, 29; in Locke and Leibniz, 63; Wilkins on, 241; Wilhelm von Humboldt on, 343

Social institution, language as: in Bréal, 14, 17; in Saussure, 17, 365; in Locke, 20, 27, 63; in Condillac, 20, 30; in Wilhelm von Humboldt, 343; in Destutt de Tracy, 350, 365, 375

Société de linguistique de Paris, 15, 295

Socinianism, and Adamic language, 80n63

Sociology: and linguistics, 296, 302, 322n13, 325n31; and history of science and linguistics, 313-14; of science, 329n45. *See also* Durkheim

Sorbière, Samuel: and Sprat's *History*, 232-35; in England, 233; and Hobbes, 233-34; on the Royal Society, 233-35, 237

Soundlaws, exceptionlessness of, 17

South, Robert, on Adam, 59

Space travel, Wilkins on, 246

Sparwenfeld, Johan Gabriel: and Leibniz, 73n17, 81n66, 92, 96n7; and Besnier, 82n69

Species and words, Locke on, 54, 71n7, 77n41

Spinoza, Baruch: and Locke, Coleridge on, 126; mentioned, 136

Spiritualism, in Cousin, 31, 361

Sprachgesellschaften, in 17c Germany, 19

Spranger, Eduard, on Kant and Wilhelm von Humboldt, 350n13

Sprat, Thomas: his *History* as ideology, 12, 313; and Wilkins, 225, 228, 255, 273n67; education of, 225; and Cowley, 226; and Oliver Cromwell, 226; composition of *History*, 226-35; on enthusiasts, 227, 230, 235; on Charles I, 227; on Bacon and Royal Society, 227-28; on early history of Royal Society, 228; reliability of *History*, 230, 235; and Sorbière, 233-34; on French Academy, 234; and church politics, 235; on Rye House Plot, 235; victim of blackmail, 236; his character, 236; sources for, 236-38; mentioned, 8. *See also* Royal Society, Sorbière, Stubbe, Swift, Wilkins

Staël, Mme de: and Wilhelm von Humboldt, 336, 348; and Wordsworth, 381; and A. W. Schlegel, 381

Starobinski, Jean, on Rousseau and Saussure, 157, 219

State of nature: in Locke, 10, 140n7, 160-61; and origin of language, 109-10; and conjectural history, 109, 161; and Condillac, 161

Statue in Condillac: and speech, 11, 153-55, 211-16, 377; why speechless, 214; and animals, 214-15

Steffens, Henrik, 38

Steinthal, Heymann, 149, 339

Stendhal: as Anti-Sage, 38; and Destutt de Tracy and Taine, 364

Stephen, James Fitzjames, on Locke, 140n9

Stephen, Leslie: on Locke, 124; on 18c thought, 139

Stewart, Dugald: on conjectural history, 28, 279; on etymological metaphysics, 30; and Locke, 120, 123, 124; on Locke as rationalist, 127-28, 205n93; on Leibniz and Locke, 128; on law of nature in Locke, 128; on Locke and French philosophy, 128; on innate ideas, 128; on reflection in Locke, 128-29; on Hartley and Locke, 129; and Rogers, Tagart, 138; mentioned, 9

Stiernhielm, Georg: on harmony of languages, 95n3; and Gothicism, 96n4

Stillingfleet, Edward: and Locke, Coleridge on, 125; and Locke, Rogers on, 138; and latitudinarianism, 240; and Wilkins, 264

Stoics, 278

Structure: in Bréal, 17, 388, 391; in Madvig, 299; Taine on, 361-62, 364-65; Destutt de Tracy on, 369n29

Stubbe, Henry, on Sprat's *History*, 227

Study of language: and intellectual history, 3, 11, 14, 15; and history of thought, 29; and religion, 290; and history of science, 291-92

Sub-audition, and Bréal, 305, 388

Subjectivity of language: Destutt de Tracy on, 27, 344-45, 375; and Locke, 27, 346, 352n16, 375; Condillac on, 27, 31, 344, 375; Turgot on, 27, 344, 375; in Wilhelm von Humboldt, 344, 375; in Herder, 344, 375; in romantic aesthetics, 375

Substitution: Taine on, 357

Successivity. *See* Diachrony, Simultaneity, Synchrony

Süssmilch, Johann Peter: on origin of language, 187-88; on design in language, 187; on language and reason, 187; and

Rousseau, Condillac, 188; and Sulzer, 193; papers read in Berlin Academy, 207n121; as demographer, 208n126

Sulzer, Johann Georg: on reason and origin of language, 193-94; on parts of speech, 194

Sweden, as first home of humanity, 96n4

Swedenborg, Emanuel, 38

Swedish language, in Garden of Eden, 91

Swift, Jonathan, and Sprat, 236

Sydenham, Thomas, and Locke, 55

Sylvester, Edward, 244, 267n24

Synchrony: in Bréal and Saussure, 17; and diachrony in Saussure, 299; in Taine and Saussure, 362-63; in Bréal, 383, 387, 390

Syntagmatics, 17, 389-90

Syntax: Madvig and Bréal on, 301, 304; Bréal on, 306, 385, 388-90

System, Taine on, 361-62. See also Structure

Taine, Hippolyte: and Bréal, 6, 385, 387, 391-92; as rationalist empiricist, Durkheim on, 9, 361; and Saussure, 15, 21, 387; contribution to linguistic thought, 20; on esprit classique, 23; and Foucault, 23; and Cousin, 31, 309; at École normale, 33; and Condillac, 33, 309, 363-64; as Anti-Sage, 38; and 18c thought, 291, 360, 381; on metaphor, 309; on signs, 309, 357-59, 387; on intranslatability, 356; on valeur, 356-57; on substitution, 357; sheet-of-paper metaphor in, 358; reputation among contemporaries, 360; and Cournot, 360; on language acquisition, 360; his method, 360-63; his achievement, 360-61; Anatole France on, 361; on system and structure, 361-62; concept of history, 361-62; on race, milieu, moment, 362; on simultaneity, successivity, 362-63; and Stendhal, 364; and Destutt de Tracy, 369n29; on rectification, 369n29; mentioned, 13

Tannery, Paul, 312, 313

Tarde, Gabriel, 327n38

Tauler, Johann, 97n13

Tennemann, Wilhelm Gottlieb, on Locke, 141n15

Tentzel, Wilhelm Ernst, 92

Terminology, and conceptualization, 20

Thomas Aquinas, 278

Thomsen, Vilhelm, 5

Thoynard, Nicolas, 76n36

Thurot, Charles, on Madvig, 299, 323n23

Thurot, François: and Harris, 350n6; and Condillac, 351n13

Tieck, Ludwig, 375

Tiedemann, Dietrich, 149

Tillotson, John: and latitudinarianism, 240; and Wilkins, 256-57, 264, 265n1, 265n7

Tombes, John, 245

Tooke. See Horne Tooke

Toussaint, François-Vincent, on language and culture, 192

Translation. See Intranslatability

Travel literature: and Locke, 45; and experimental knowledge of human nature, 161

Tremblay, Jean Frain du, 347

Trench, Richard Chenevix: on fossil ethics and fossil history, 33; and etymology, 38; as Sage, 38; on words as living powers, 39

Trinity College, Cambridge, and turn against Locke, 35, 133, 142n20

Trithemius, Johannes, 268n29

Turgot, A.-R.-J.: on etymology, 6, 49, 69, 184, 314; and Condillac, 9, 148, 210; on subjectivity of language, 27, 344; on origin of language and universal grammar, 111, 167; and valeur, 370n29; mentioned, 285

Typology in linguistics, 349

Tyson, Edward, on orang-outang, 285

Uniformitarianism: in Condillac, 29; in Bréal, 14, 298, 307, 327n36; and Lyell, 290; and Max Müller, 290, 326n34; and Madvig, 299-300, 307; in science and language study, 316-17; and F. Schlegel, Bréal on, 385; in human sciences, 392

Uniformity of human nature: in 18c thought, 159-60; and language, 165; and experience, 179

Universal grammar: and Descartes, 101-17; and invention of parts of speech, 111; and origin of language, 111-12, 165-70; revival of after Condillac, 111-12, 169; in early 18c, 112; and Leibniz, 117n5; and linearity of speech, 158; and Bréal, 305, 307, 386, 388; Saussure on, 386

Universal language, and philosophical language, 261

Ussher, James, 273n70

Utilitarians: and Horne Tooke, 7; and Sage, 38; and ethics, Sedgwick on, 132; and ethics, Whewell on, 135

Valéry, Paul, review of Bréal, 391
Valesius, Franciscus, 266n12
Valeur: and Bréal, 17, 307-08, 390-91; Taine on, 356-57; Saussure on, 357; Destutt de Tracy on, 369n29; in Turgot, Adam Smith, Condillac, 370n29
Vandeul, Marie, and Wilhelm von Humboldt, 348
Vaughan, Robert: on Locke in 19c, 122; on Cousin, Hamilton, 131; on Locke and Cousin, 144n37
Vendryes, Jules: on Bréal and Saussure, 16; on Bréal, 393
Venturi, Franco, on origin of language in 18c thought, 110, 199
Verburg, P. A., 149
Verelius, Olof, and Gothicism, 96n4
Vernacular language: and Descartes, 44, 46; and Leibniz, 46; Wilkins's use of, 243
Victorian ideology, 283, 290
Victorian Sage: and comparative philology, 7, 37-38; John Holloway on, 37; style of, 37; and etymology, 38, 41; and Balzac, 38-41; and arbitrariness, 39, 41
Villers, Charles de, 351n13
Villiers, George: and Sprat, 226; and Wilkins, 226, 259
Vinson, Jules, and *Revue de linguistique*, 22
Volksgeist: and Condillac, 30-31; in Condillac and Herder, 195-96; and linguistic relativism, 347
Volney, Constantin, Comte de, 308, 348
Voltaire, François-Marie Arouet: on Locke, 49; on Leibniz and Locke, 125; on Newton and Locke, 126; on philosophy of Newton, 148; and Maupertuis, 177; on genius of language, 347
Vossius, Isaac, 168

Wachter, Johann Georg, 48
Wadham College, 231, 245, 249
Wallis, John: and Leibniz, 81n65; and early Royal Society, 231, 252, 253, 255
Warburton, William: Webb on, 139; and Condillac, 148
Ward, Seth: and Wilkins, 229, 273n60, at Wadham College, 254; and John Webster,

256; on philosophical language, 262, 275n86
Webb, Thomas E.: on Kant and Locke, 138; on Locke's intellectualism, 138-39; on friends-enemies theme in philosophy, 139
Weber, Max, 33
Webster, John: and Boehme, 60; and essentialism, 60-61; and Rosicrucians, 60, 273n60; on English universities, 60-61, 248, 256; and Locke on innate notions, 61, 251; and Adamic language, 61, 262; and Wilkins, 79n59, 248, 256; on Eve's name, 79n60; and Ward, 256
Wedgwood, Josiah, 125
Weigel, Valentin, 10, 87, 97n13-14
Weil, Henri, 327n39
Westminster Assembly, 231, 245, 267n27
Whewell, William: and fixity of types, 35; and Locke, 35, 121, 124, 133-35; as Sage, 38; and Sedgwick, 131-32; on Hobbes and Locke, 134; on Locke and utilitarian ethics, 134; on Condillac, 134; J. S. Mill on, 135-36; and Maistre, 140n3, 145n48; and Cousin, 145n48
Whichcote, Benjamin, 272n60, 274n71
Whitney, William Dwight: and Madvig, 14, 301-02, 310-11; and Max Müller, 32, 290; on language study in Germany, 293; on Schleicher, 294, 302-03, 304; and Bréal, 298, 310-11, 326n32; and Saussure, 310-11, 393; on Hovelacque, 321n5
Wilkins, John: and Copernicanism, 12, 244, 246-47; his *Essay*, 13, 241, 260-64; and Leibniz, 72n11, 263; and Sprat's *History*, 229, 232, 244, 259; at Wadham College, 231, 245, 254; and Oliver Cromwell, 239, 256, 257; basic outlook, 239-244; and latitudinarianism, 240, 257, 260, 272n60; on harmony of science and religion, 240; on reason and human nature, 240-41; on language and social nature of man, 241; on biblical authority, 241-42; on authority of antiquity, 242; on authority of books, 242-43; on dignity of mechanical arts, 242-43; and use of vernacular, 243; as scientific educator, 243-44; visits to the Continent, 244, 245; early career, 244-54; and William Fiennes, 245; and Charles Louis, 245, 249, 267n25, 267n27; publications in 1640s, 245-52, on space travel, 246; and Aristotelianism, 246,

251; on semiotics, 247-48; and universal language, 248; on mechanics, 248-51; and Guidobaldo del Monte, 249, 250; and Bacon, 251; and Locke, Mersenne on language, 251; at Oxford, 254-57; and Cambridge Platonists, 257, 272n60; and Richard Cromwell, 257; at Cambridge, 257-58; and formation of Royal Society, 258; as bishop of Chester, 258, 259; last years, 258-65; and Baxter, 259, 272n60; and nonconformists, 259; and church governance, 259-60; and philosophical language, 260-64; and Willoughby, 263; influence of, 264; death of, 264-65, 276n94; on moderation, 265n8; on prose style, 266n11; and Westminster Assembly, 267n27; and Hale, 273n70. *See also* Adam; Adamic language; Berkeley, George, (1601-1658); Berkeley, George, (1628-1698); Boyle; Burnet; Campanella; Chillingworth; Dalgarno; Galileo; Gassendi; Haak; Hooke; Mersenne; Natural theology; Oxford; Ray; Tillotson; Villiers; Ward; Webster; Wood
Williams, John, 270n44
Willis, John, on memory, 275n84
Willis, Thomas, 255

Willoughby, Francis, 263, 273n67
Windischmann, Karl Joseph, 303, 385
Wolf, F. A., and Wilhelm von Humboldt, 336, 337, 345
Wood, Anthony à, on Wilkins, 244, 265
Words: as living powers, 39, and things, 42, 56-57, 92, 98n32; natural origin of, 58; as arbitrary signs, 63-64; Leibniz on origin of, 65; mental, origin of in Locke, 67-69, 300; obscurity of, 71n7; as abbreviation, 108
Wordsworth, William: his poetics and 18c thought, 17-18, 372-81; and subjectivity of language, 27, 375; on sincerity and affectation, 373; on epitaphs, 373, 376, 378; and Condillac, 374-80; on society and language, 376; and linguistic relativism, 376; on poetry and prose, 377; on poetry and association of ideas, 377; on poetic meter, 378-79
Worthington, John, 272n60
Wrangham, Francis, 374
Wren, Christopher, 225, 255
Wright, Edward, 266n12
Wynne, John, 71n5

Zanchi, Girolami, 266n12, 273n60
Zimmer, Karl E., 104

K